D0894683
00037 6301

ALLIES AT WAR

The Franklin and Eleanor Roosevelt Institute Series
on Diplomatic and Economic History

General Editors: Arthur M. Schlesinger, Jr., William J. vanden Heuvel, and Douglas Brinkley

1. FDR AND HIS CONTEMPORARIES:
   Foreign Perceptions of an American President
   Edited by Cornelis A. van Minnen and John F. Sears

2. NATO: THE CREATION OF THE ATLANTIC ALLIANCE AND THE INTEGRATION OF EUROPE
   Edited by Francis H. Heller and John R. Gillingham

3. AMERICA UNBOUND:
   World War II and the Making of a Superpower
   Edited by Warren F. Kimball

4. THE ORIGINS OF U.S. NUCLEAR STRATEGY, 1945-53
   Samuel R. Williamson, Jr. and Steven L. Rearden

5. AMERICAN DIPLOMATS IN THE NETHERLANDS, 1815-50
   Cornelis A. van Minnen

6. EISENHOWER, KENNEDY AND THE UNITED STATES OF EUROPE
   Pascaline Winand

7. ALLIES AT WAR:
   The Soviet, American, and British Experience, 1939-1945
   Edited by David Reynolds, Warren F. Kimball and A.O. Chubarian

8. THE ATLANTIC CHARTER
   Edited by Douglas Brinkley and David Facey-Crowther

ALLIES AT WAR

The Soviet, American, and British Experience, 1939-1945

Edited by David Reynolds, Warren F. Kimball, and A. O. Chubarian

St. Martin's Press
New York

First published in the United States of America 1994

ISBN 0-312-10259-3

Library of Congress Cataloging-in-Publication Data

Allies at war : the Soviet, American, and British experience, 1939-1945 / edited by David Reynolds, Warren F. Kimball, and A.O. Chubarian.
p. cm. — (The Franklin and Eleanor Roosevelt Institute series on diplomatic and economic history ; 7)
Includes bibliographical references.
ISBN 0-312-10259-3
1. World War, 1939-1945—United States. 2. World War, 1939-1945—Great Britain. 3. World War, 1939-1945—Soviet Union. I. Reynolds, David, 1952- . II. Kimball, Warren F. III. Chubar'ian, Aleksandr Oganovich. IV. Series.
D743.A58 1993 93-22957
940.53'32—dc20 CIP

Interior design by Digital Type & Design

Printed in the United States of America

Table of Contents

Preface vi

Introduction
David Reynolds xi

PART I—STRATEGY

1. Great Britain: The Indirect Strategy
Alex Danchev 1
2. The Soviet Union: The Direct Strategy
Oleg A. Rzheshevsky 27
3. The United States: The Global Strategy
Mark A. Stoler 55
4. Coalition: Structure, Strategy, and Statecraft
Theodore A. Wilson, et al. 79

PART II—ECONOMY

5. Great Britain: Cyclops
Richard J. Overy 113
6. The Soviet Union: Phoenix
Lydia V. Pozdeeva 145
7. The United States: Leviathan
Theodore A. Wilson 173
8. Co-operation: Trade, Aid, and Technology
Richard J. Overy, et al. 201

PART III—HOME FRONT

9. Great Britain: The People's War?
Jose Harris 233
10. The Soviet Union: The Great Patriotic War?
Mikhail N. Narinsky 261
11. The United States: The Good War?
Charles C. Alexander 285
12. Mutual Perceptions: Images, Ideals, and Illusions
Mikhail N. Narinsky, Lydia V. Pozdeeva, et al.. 307

PART IV—FOREIGN POLICY

13. Great Britain: Imperial Diplomacy
David Reynolds 333
14. The Soviet Union: Territorial Diplomacy
Lydia V. Pozdeeva 355
15. The United States: Democratic Diplomacy
Lloyd C. Gardner and *Warren F. Kimball* 387
16. Legacies: Allies, Enemies, and Posterity
David Reynolds, et al. 417

Notes on the Contributors 441

Index 445

PREFACE

The initiative for this project came from Russia. In 1989, Alexander Chubarian, director of the Institute of World History of the Academy of Sciences in Moscow, and his colleague Oleg Rzheshevsky proposed a joint history of the Big Three wartime allies. They initiated discussions with Warren F. Kimball and David Reynolds, both known in Moscow from recent scholarly contacts during the *glas'nost* era. Together they defined the project as an examination of the strategies, economies, home fronts, and foreign policies of each state, both separately and as members of the coalition. Each editor selected teams of historians from his country to write essays. The Russian authors were all senior scholars from the Institute of World History. The American and British contributors were teacher-scholars from various universities. The work advanced through three crucial working conferences—at Rutgers University in New Jersey (October 1990), Christ's College, Cambridge University (July 1991), and at Yalta in the Crimea (April 1992). Drafts were exchanged in advance, these were criticized at the meetings, and then revised for further discussion. The resulting book is published in both English and Russian. The Russian authors submitted texts in English which were then edited by David Reynolds and Warren Kimball, with assistance from Charles Alexander and Mark Stoler. While the greatest care has been taken over translation, note that in the case of divergence between the two editions, the definitive version of each essay is that written in the author's native language.

The project is noteworthy in two fundamental ways. First, it transcends the conventional subcultures of academic history. In the last 50 years our profession has become increasingly specialized. Economic history has developed an arcane language characterized by theory, equations, and statistics, which makes it incomprehensible to the uninitiated. Social history, neglected for years except as the anecdotage of high society, has tended to overcompensate by brusque dismissal of all other forms of history. In reaction to such scholarly imperialism, the military and diplomatic historians—cultivators of more traditional fields of scholarship—have recently felt spurned and isolated. This book, however, brings economic, social, military, and diplomatic history back together, where they belong.

The other singularity is, of course, that this is the work of historians from three different countries. Given the vast bulk of archives for twentieth-century history, scholars cannot hope to master even their own national sources for the war. The Public Record Office in London, for instance, calculates that the British government documents for the conflict occupy nearly seven miles of shelving. In the United States, the official history of just the army in World War II runs to 80 volumes. Thus international partnership is essential. Western historians have already learned to cooperate, but only the era of *glas'nost* made possible constructive engagement with Russian scholars. Moreover, the latter are now beginning to gain access to their own archives, and Russian essays in this volume represent the first fruits of what eventually should prove a cornucopia of new learning.

For all involved in this project, the experience was itself deeply enriching. Our conference format taught us to empathize with the original Big Three. We appreciated the effect of wearying travel, time changes, and dietary differences on one's ability to perform intelligently. We grasped the importance of agenda, minute-taking, and the timing of interventions in shaping international decisions. And, traveling along bumpy roads through the rugged Crimea, the Americans and British, thousands of miles from home, understood with new sharpness just how much these decisions must have mattered to Roosevelt and Churchill for them to travel that great distance and undergo such hardships in order to reach a meeting of minds with Joseph Stalin.

There were moments, indeed, when our deliberations seemed almost to mirror those of our famous forebears. At times each national delegation played absolutely to stereotype—British reserve, American brashness, Russian impenetrability. The toasts at our conference dinners were as profuse and prolix as in Moscow or Tehran in 1943. The planning and logistics of our 1992 Yalta meeting caused almost as many headaches as the original gathering in 1945. Communication was a particular problem. As in wartime, keeping in touch with Moscow was a nightmare—not solved for us until the installation there of a fax machine and the successful retraining of after-hours cleaning personnel who had previously insisted on unplugging all appliances at night. Even then, such were the problems of time and technological incompatibility that Russo-American messages were often relayed via Britain—allowing the British to reassume the role they sought during the Second World War as "honest broker" between the Big Two. Throughout, English was our working language, reflecting both the chauvinism of the English-speakers and the excellent command of that language among the Russian scholars. But, like Churchill and

Roosevelt, the British and Americans were not able to agree on some form of "Basic English" to harmonize the idiosyncracies of their common language. With the indulgence of the copy editors, the essayists have therefore retained their own national orthography. "Honour" is "honorable," regardless of the spelling.

Of course, as ever, history did not repeat itself exactly. The wartime alliance, for all its achievements, was deeply flawed. Mutual trust was lacking, and relations, even between the Americans and British, deteriorated precipitously with military victory. Our own meetings had their share of tensions and arguments, but the overwhelming experience was one of genuine scholarly exchange that came to transcend national barriers. Disagreements were sometimes sharper *within* national groups than *between* them. As the leader of the U.S. team observed on one frustrating occasion—referring back to General John R. Deane, head of the wartime U.S. Military Mission in Moscow and a vocal critic of the Russians—"I can't understand General Deane. I have no difficulty doing business with the *Russians*. It's the *Americans* I can't negotiate with." Whatever the brief frustrations, affectionate respect and mutual education were the abiding legacies of the project for all the participants.

The result is, however, in no sense a "common view." While agreeing on a joint agenda, individual contributors were free to decide the appropriate emphases, reflecting the debates and evidence within their own countries. Each chapter is the work of one scholar, but it has then been filtered through the collective wisdom of the group, particularly the specialists in that area. This filtering process was particularly true of each part's final chapter, in which the collaborative experience is analyzed, but even then the perspective of the original draft remains dominant. Nor are the essays in any sense definitive. The Russians, in particular, are embarking on methods of historical scholarship that differ fundamentally with previous practices, and this process will take many years to develop. Because new evidence is only gradually becoming available in Russia, some of their essays concentrate on providing the factual information on which later reevaluations can be based. What these chapters offer is an overview of the current state of scholarship for different aspects of the wartime alliance. Above all, they are a contribution to a long-delayed project—that of understanding the Second World War as a truly international experience.

Acknowledgments are one of the nicer tasks, not just because saying thank-you is pleasant but because writing them signals the end of the project. The editors and authors gratefully acknowledge the support of Rutgers University, the State University of New Jersey; Christ's College,

Cambridge; and the Institute of World History of the Russian Academy of Sciences, Moscow—each of which provided a venue and generous support for an authors' conference. We particularly acknowledge the important role played by Academician G. N. Sevost'ianov of the Russian Academy of Sciences in fostering a dialogue between Soviet and American historians of the Second World War even before the arrival of *glas'nost*. Crown copyright documents in the British Public Record Office are quoted by permission of the Controller of H.M. Stationery Office.

The individual American authors acknowledge the support of the following: at Rutgers University—the Research Council, Dean of the Faculty of Arts and Science at Rutgers/Newark David Hosford, then Academic Vice-President of Rutgers University T. Alexander Pond, and—with a smile and thank you—Tishawn Brown and LaChone McKenzie of the Rutgers/Newark History Department for their help; at the University of Vermont—the College of Arts and Sciences (Faculty Development Awards), Department of History; at Ohio University—the College of Arts and Sciences; at the University of Kansas—the Social and Economic History Seminar and the Hall Center for the Humanities. Limited funding for meetings of the authors came from IREX, with monies provided by the Andrew W. Mellon Foundation, The National Endowment for the Humanities, and the U.S. Department of State.

On behalf of the British team, David Reynolds wishes to acknowledge generous support from the Economic and Social Research Council of the U.K. (which funded the visit to Russia/Crimea and much of the Cambridge Conference) and the British Council (which financed travel to the Rutgers Conference). For additional support of the Cambridge Conference, thanks are due to the Research Fund Managers of Christ's College, the Master and Fellows of Churchill College, the British Academy, and the Centre of International Studies at Cambridge (Richard Langhorne, director). The smooth running of the Cambridge Conference was greatly assisted by Mrs. Frances Barker, Mrs. Susan Clements, Dr. Richard Aldous, Dr. Simon Ball, and Dr. Philip Hemming. Frances Barker and Dr. Andrew Cliff helped reduce the frustrations of international computer incompatibility. David Reynolds is also grateful to the Leverhulme Foundation for a research fellowship that enabled him to devote uninterrupted time to final editing.

The Russian editor and authors acknowledge, with pleasure, the help of the Russian Fund of Advanced Studies, the willingness of the head of the Department of History, Russian Academy of Sciences (RAS), I. D. Kovalchenko, to make available the time and support necessary for research and writing. The Russian authors also acknowledge support from the following: I. V. Lebedev, chief of the Historical Documentary Department of the Foreign Affairs Ministry, and K. M. Anderson, director of the Russian Center for the Conservation and Study of Documents on Contemporary History, for access to unpublished documents on the war years; in Russia—the Institute of Scientific Information on the Humanities (RAS), the State Lenin Library, and the State Public Library for History, all of which provided useful periodicals, literature, and other materials on World War II; in England—the staffs of the Public Record Office, Kew, the Churchill Archives Centre, Cambridge, and the Mass Observation Archives (Dorothy Sheridan, director) at Sussex University Library for making it possible to study unpublished World War II materials. Special thanks to O. Sviridenko, director of the Hotel Artist in Yalta, Crimea, for providing so generous a reception to the American, British, and Russian historians who met there; and to M. V. Kouzmina for her invaluable help with typing and organization.

Chapters 4, 8, 12, 16, and the Introduction were drafted by the cited authors, but with considerable input from the other contributors: hence the "et al."

We add the *de rigueur* caveat for all those receiving government funds, regardless of how indirectly: in all cases, the views expressed are, of course, those of the authors, not the fundors.

David Reynolds
CAMBRIDGE, ENGLAND

Warren F. Kimball
SOMERSET, NEW JERSEY, U.S.A.

A. O. Chubarian
MOSCOW, RUSSIA

INTRODUCTION

David Reynolds, et al.

Victory is an egotistical experience—for states as well as individuals. The years 1941-45 saw the United States, Great Britain, and the Soviet Union joined in an unprecedented coalition to defeat the Axis powers—Germany, Italy, and Japan. After victory, however, each of the Big Three celebrated its achievements and mourned its losses in splendid isolation, with little sense of what its partners had experienced. For all three states the war assumed a central place in the mythology of national uniqueness—the Battle of Britain, the American production miracle, the Soviet Union's Great Patriotic War. Moreover, World War was quickly eclipsed by Cold War. Even before Hitler's funeral pyre had been extinguished in the ruins of Berlin, the Allied partnership was crumbling in suspicion and rivalry. Accounts of the war were written with one eye on the Cold War—the past became ammunition for the present.

This combination of patriotic myth and political ideology has militated against a full and dispassionate account of the war-time coalition. The West downplayed, even to the point of ignoring, the Soviet Union's struggle against Hitler. The battles of Guadalcanal and El Alamein received more attention in America and Britain respectively than the simultaneous epic of Stalingrad (now Volgograd) even though the latter was both bloodier and far more significant. In the USSR, histories of the conflict often belittled the military endeavours of the United States and Great Britain, made little reference to the role of their economic and technical aid in the Soviet war effort, and failed to take seriously the major war both were waging against Japan. Each country extolled the sacrifices of its own civilian population, but said little of substance about life on the home fronts of its allies.

The passage of time has, however, made possible a fuller and more balanced account. That is partly because the main protagonists of these war-time events have passed from the scene. Writing has moved beyond the simple imperatives of praise, blame, and self-justification. It is also because the American and British archives are now largely open, making possible documentary validation for the claims and counter-claims of memoir and biography. Above all, the end of the Cold War has defused the war's ideological charge, made possible new scholarly contacts, and begun to open up Russian archives for the first time. At last it is becoming possible to analyse and compare the war experience of all three Allies. This book is the first effort to do so in a systematic and scholarly way.

Four main areas are examined: strategy (Part I), economy (Part II), the home front (Part III), and foreign policy (Part IV). The first three chapters of each part are essentially national in form, looking first at Great Britain, then the Soviet Union, and finally the United States (a sequence paralleling the chronology of their involvement in the war against Germany). Blending original research with synthesis of recent scholarship, they provide overviews of the national story in the four areas. These chapters serve to confirm the diversity of the American, British, and Soviet war experiences—a diversity that reflected their contrasting forms of government, their very different social and economic structures, and the varying degree to which they directly experienced Nazi aggression.

Yet a purely national approach is not sufficient. As the last chapter of each part demonstrates, the war experience of the three countries can and should be examined in interconnection. This became, however imperfectly, a military coalition (chapter 4), sustained by economic co-operation (chapter 8), that exhibited a sense of shared purpose and mutual interest at the popular level (chapter 12). Moreover, the coalition's successes and failures in concerting foreign policy left legacies that not merely influenced the Cold War but also endured into our contemporary world (chapter 16). This book is therefore a pioneering attempt to see the war-time alliance as both national and international history.

This introduction does not purport to summarize each chapter. It does, however, offer an overview of the main themes of these essays, by outlining, first, some of the diversities in the war experience of the three states and then some elements of unity. These themes of diversity and unity are developed further in the final essay, which rounds off not only the foreign policy section but also the whole book.

To begin with the basics: The United States and the Soviet Union were vast continent-wide states, whereas Great Britain was a small island off the continent of Europe. In 1940 "the United Kingdom of Great Britain and Northern Ireland" covered 92,000 square miles and contained some 48 million people. By contrast, the 48 states of the United States had a population of 132 million inhabiting nearly 3 million square miles. The Union of Soviet Socialist Republics, with its 15 members, was even larger—nearly 200 million people spread across over 8.6 million square miles. Thus, the Soviet Union was nearly one hundred times larger than the United Kingdom, while even the vast 48 United States amounted to only one-third of the area of the USSR and barely two-thirds of its population. Size was reflected in extremes of climate and life-style in both giants, from the bitter cold of Murmansk and Minnesota to the deserts of Tashkent and New Mexico. This fundamental difference between two great continental states and one small island was partially blurred, however, by the existence of the British Empire. An historical ragbag of possessions, accumulated through trade and conquest over several centuries and bound with varying degrees of tenuousness to London, it still covered about quarter of the world's population and land area in the 1930s. The heart of the empire was India—massive both in manpower and resources—but the so-called white Dominions of Canada, Australia, New Zealand, and South Africa included substantial numbers of recent British settlers who felt strong ties to the mother country. In every aspect of its war effort—strategy, economy, and diplomacy—Britain behaved imperially—of necessity, because it was the empire that made Britain great. Nevertheless, its greatness was less substantial and secure than that of the two future superpowers, whose power base lay within their own continents and not across the oceans. In their own ways, of course, the other two were also empires. The Soviet state was a continuance of the old Russian empire of the Romanov dynasty, which had nearly broken apart in civil war after the Bolshevik Revolution of 1917, only to be consolidated by Lenin and Stalin until its eventual demise in 1991. Even the United States had imperial aspects, being the creation of European colonialism and then American expansion at the expense of the native population, while the economy of the South depended until well into the twentieth century on labour relations that were a legacy of the Atlantic slave trade. Moreover, Hawaii, various Caribbean territories, and the Philippines were among the reminders of America's own brief flurry of colonialism at the end of the nineteenth century. But, considered both as a source of power and an issue of morality, Britain's empire was distinctive and, in both of these senses, it was to be a particular casualty of the war.

As polities, the Big Three also had little in common. The most glaring contrast was between the communist dictatorship of the USSR and the capitalist democracy of the United States. Under Stalin, the Bolshevik party bureaucracy had consolidated its control of all aspects of life, with monstrous purges of party leaders, recalcitrant peasants, and independent-minded soldiers. Economy and society were closely directed by a horde of party functionaries, all under the ultimate control of that master of bureaucracy, Stalin himself. In an apt phrase, biographer Dmitrii Volkogonov calls the system "absolute bureaucracy"—a grotesque mixture of Louis XIV and Franz Kafka.[1] The reiterated justification for this endless terror was the need to transform a backward agrarian society into a modern industrial power before the forces of capitalism and, later, fascism strangled the revolution. In the end, however, the terror became simply an expression of Stalin's all-consuming struggle to stay on top.

In the United States, by contrast, power emanated from the bottom up—in theory and, to a large extent, still in practice. The economy was organized around the myriad activities of individual entrepreneurs, big or small, with little official regulation; the principle of government was one man, one vote (since the 1830s—although the inclusion of women and non-whites came much later); and the federal government in Washington was still relatively limited in its powers over both the states and their component cities, towns, and counties (despite the New Deal's centripetal tendencies). Democracy in Abraham Lincoln's myth-making definition ("government of the people, by the people, for the people") may have been an ideal—but it remained a potent one. What the word really connoted was populist localism, a rooted conviction that the people who lived on the spot were those best qualified to run their affairs. This was the heart of Americanism—"Live Free or Die," as the state motto of New Hampshire puts it, traditionally one of the most fiercely independent of American states.

Britain lay somewhere in the middle of this political spectrum. Its own traditions of liberalism in political and economic life had been a fundamental influence on its American colonies. Since the seventeenth century its Parliament had consolidated the rights of the legislature over the executive until the monarch was reduced to head of state rather than head of government. Yet Britain was not a democracy in the American sense. In size, it was little bigger than a largish U.S. state, such as Idaho or Utah, and was consequently far more centralized than the United States, with London at the heart of political, economic, and social life. Its deeper tradition of governmental paternalism was apparent in a welfare state founded in the 1900s—more than a quarter-century before Roosevelt's New Deal. A democratic franchise was a far more recent innovation than in the United States and the elective principle, which pervaded American government at all levels, was overshadowed in Britain by the practice of appointed offices and the powers of a career civil service. Moreover, although the monarchy and aristocracy were emasculated in power, they remained centres of wealth and status. The country was in fact permeated by a deep and nuanced sense of social place—the British obsession with "class." This helps to explain their debate, explored in chapter 9, about whether the war produced a more united and egalitarian Britain.

Yet to talk of "the war" may imply another spurious unity, as chapters 1 to 3 demonstrate. For one thing, there is the matter of timing. Britain declared war on Germany on 3 September 1939, after Hitler had invaded Poland. Prime Minister Neville Chamberlain's policy of appeasement had proved ineffectual, and, rather than allow Germany to dominate the Continent, the British had guaranteed Poland and other Eastern European states in the spring. At this stage the United States was neutral, though sympathetic to Britain and France, while the Soviet Union had signed the Non-Aggression Pact with Hitler. Unable to forge an alliance with the suspicious British, Stalin bought off Hitler for the moment, even supplying Germany with substantial economic aid in 1940-41. The fall of France in June 1940 transformed the international situation, leaving Britain alone against possible German invasion and struggling to retain Egypt and its Middle Eastern colonies against Italian and, later, German forces. Moreover, with France eliminated, Hitler was able to turn east with apparent impunity against his real enemy and his surprise attack on 22 June 1941 (operation BARBAROSSA) forced the Soviet Union into the war. Although the United States had been drawn into greater material support of Britain after France fell, including Lend-Lease of supplies and increased naval patrolling across the Atlantic, what forced it into war was Japan's attack on the fleet at Pearl Harbor on 7 December 1941. This was the upshot of a deepening crisis in the Pacific, in which U.S. efforts to contain Japan ultimately proved counter-productive. After Hitler declared war on the United States, Congress responded on 10 December.

Thus, Britain's war began in 1939, Russia's and America's in 1941. Furthermore, each country's focus was different. By 1942 Britain was at war with Germany, Italy, and Japan, but, in practice, it cut its losses in the Far East and concentrated, first, on the defence of the British Isles against Germany and then on securing North Africa and the Mediterranean to shore up its imperial communications and threaten the weakest member of the Axis, Italy. For the Soviet Union, Germany was always the real enemy. Indeed until well into 1943, a Soviet victory was far from certain. In these circumstances, Stalin maintained the neutrality pact with Japan and did not enter the Asian war until after Germany had been defeated. To many Americans, by contrast, Japan was the true enemy. The humiliations of Pearl Harbor and Bataan had to be avenged. Although the army and army air forces, with Roosevelt's firm support, managed to maintain the Germany First principle, the extent of Japan's victories by the spring of 1942 (threatening Australia and India) and the demands of the U.S. navy ensured a massive effort to hold the line against the Japanese. The year 1942 ended with more American combat forces in the Pacific than in the Atlantic theatre.[2]

Focusing on different enemies at different times, the three countries also had quite distinctive experiences of war on the home front (chapters 9-11). No war is "good" but America's war was about as good as one could get. The continental United States was neither invaded nor occupied and only a few random Japanese bombs and shells disturbed the North American continent. Only some of its territories—the Philippine Islands, Hawaii, and Alaska's Aleutian Islands—experienced the devastation of war. Although every death is an absolute to the bereaved, casualties were tiny relative to the total population (0.25 per cent). Britain's suffering was greater. The sustained German Blitz of 1940-41 and the renewed V-bomb attacks of 1944 killed 60,000 and caused extensive physical destruction, particularly in London. Around 4 million people were moved out of the cities by government evacuation schemes and an estimated 2 million more left voluntarily in 1939, anticipating an air-borne holocaust when war began. Although traditional claims for the war as a stimulus of radical change in Britain are contested in chapter 9, there is little doubt that 1940 was a traumatically unifying experience and it boosted Britain's image abroad as well as at home. "Why," wrote American journalist "Scotty" Reston, then a correspondent in London, "it has even got so now that total strangers speak to each other on the streets, a completely un-English thing to do."[3]

Yet Britain's sufferings were nothing next to those of the Soviet people. For more than two years the war ebbed and flowed across Eurasia, leaving millions the victims of occupation, imprisonment, and Nazi extermination squads. Perhaps one-seventh of the pre-war Soviet population lost their lives and Soviet agriculture, in particular, took years to recover. This destruction was partly the consequence of Hitler's genocidal policies, partly the result of the simple fact that for three years the Red Army was fighting the bulk of German forces because the British and Americans were engaged in their own wars elsewhere. Between June 1941 and June 1944—from Hitler's attack on Russia to the Anglo-American invasion of France—some 93 per cent of total German army battle casualties were inflicted by the Soviet forces.[4]

Thus the Soviet home front was a battlefront. This basic contrast with the other two allies is also fundamental if we want to understand the Soviet war economy. It was not simply a matter of converting industrial production to the needs of war-time. As chapter 6 makes clear, it meant physically moving much of Soviet industry as well. Stalin had not anticipated having to fight a defensive war deep in the heartland of industrial Russia. To maintain its productive capacity as the Nazis thrust deep into Soviet territory in 1941, the Soviet leadership had to arrange the massive evacuation and relocation of Soviet industry east of the Urals, which involved herculean efforts on the part of the population and amazed both Allied and Axis observers. By 1944 the gross industrial product exceeded pre-war levels. Yet, as chapter 6 also suggests, the Soviet victory was not simply due to superior resources and manpower—to a phoenix risen from the ashes of disaster in 1941. Technologically, the USSR was able to match Germany in key weaponry, such as the T-34 tank or the fearsome "Katyusha" rocket launchers. The poignant and still unresolved question is how far Stalin's brutal industrial revolution, for all its appalling cost in the late 1920s and early 1930s, had created the basis for victory in 1941-43. Certainly the triumph of a communist state over a "capitalist" aggressor explains much of the international prestige of the Soviet Union and its ideology after 1945.

The American war economy (chapter 7) was, even more obviously, the success of the war. The production boom from 1940 (first for Britain and France, then for U.S. needs) did what the New Deal had failed to do, pulling the country out of the long depression of the 1930s. Uniquely among all the belligerent states, the U.S. war economy produced not merely guns but butter on an unprecedented scale. Close examination shows mismanagement and uncertainty aplenty, yet enterprises of mythic proportions—such as those of the giant Willow Run bomber plant and Henry J. Kaiser's Liberty Ships—testify to the scale of American mass production for war. This massive output could have been devoted to a separate and largely self-contained American war effort in the Pacific, and this was always an intense political pressure on President Roosevelt. Yet the pressures were resisted. America's productive surplus was diverted in significant amounts to its Allies abroad. As chapter 8 makes clear, this was one of the most fateful policies of the war. American industry became not just the arsenal of America but also, in Roosevelt's prophetic words of 1940, "the arsenal of democracy." By 1944, the United States was producing about 60 per cent of the Allies' total output of combat munitions.[5]

Again, the British economic experience lies somewhere in the middle (chapter 5). Britain's earlier entry into war and its centralized administrative system meant that as early as 1942 the government had established comprehensive control over the economy, which it enforced with reasonable equity and efficiency. Unlike America, the country was wrenched out of peace-time by the disasters of 1940, which necessitated concentration on munitions production to ensure survival, but the trauma was not nearly as great as that faced by the Russians in 1941. Reliant on the empire, Britain was obliged to husband its resources and guard its sea-lanes in a way unknown to America, let alone the Soviet Union, and the consolidation of the sterling area and the system of Imperial Preference in trade created serious diplomatic friction with the United States. Yet, ultimately, the facts of Britain's size and insular position proved decisive limitations. Its own resources and those of the truncated empire were insufficient and the country's all-out war effort depended on American credit to cover over half the yawning payments deficit. Thus, British power was exposed as great but limited—it was a one-eyed giant in contrast to the American leviathan.

The Allies fought very different wars—and, but for Hitler, their three leaders would have virtually nothing in common. Josef Vissarionovich Dzugashvili (1879-1953) was a genuine proletarian. Son of a Georgian cobbler and former serf, he studied for five years in an Orthodox seminary before converting to Marxism and then spent nearly two decades as a revolutionary organizer, in and out of Tsarist prisons. By 1914 he had assumed the pseudonym Stalin—"man of steel." He played a limited role in the Bolshevik Revolution, but subsequently exploited his position as General Secretary of the party, ostensibly an administrative office, into an unrivalled source of patronage and power after Lenin's death in 1924. Although never feeling secure, as his brutal and paranoid purges testify, he was effectively the absolute ruler of his country for a quarter-century. In the purge of 1937-38 alone, some 8 million people were imprisoned, of whom 1 million were executed and 2 million died in camps. The mastermind of that purge, the malicious and brutal dwarf Nikolai Yezhov was himself purged, terrorized, and broken by Stalin. For a while in 1939 he still retained the token position of Commissar of Water Transport but rarely attended meetings. When he did so he never intervened but spent his time making paper birds or planes, launching them into the air and then scrabbling under chairs to retrieve them. When the NKVD finally came to arrest him, he stood up, placed his gun on the table, and declared: "How long have I been waiting for this!"[6] Such was Stalin's terror—as much psychological as physical.

Franklin Delano Roosevelt (1882-1945), in a totally different fashion, was also a supreme manipulator of politics and bureaucracy. His background was patrician—scion of a landowning family in the Hudson Valley north of New York, fifth cousin to President Theodore Roosevelt, and

Woodrow Wilson's assistant secretary of the navy (1913-21). FDR was an adored and adoring only son, but his character was hardened by a seven-year battle against polio from 1921. Thereafter he plunged back into Democratic party politics, making his name as governor of the state of New York (1929-33) before being elected to the presidency on an unprecedented four occasions. But it should never be forgotten that throughout his White House years (March 1933 to April 1945) he was a semi-invalid, unable to walk unaided and often in serious pain. Neither of his war-time protagonists had to overcome such obstacles.

By nature secretive, by preference a procrastinator, by illness forced back on his inner resources—Roosevelt developed these characteristics masterfully as political tools. "You won't talk frankly even with people who are loyal to you," complained Interior Secretary Harold Ickes. "You keep your cards close up against your belly. You never put them on the table."[7] Few indeed were taken into his confidence. During the war Harry Hopkins was the prime exception, and even his influence waned after his illness in early 1944. Telling one person one thing, another something different; dividing up authority so no one could dominate an area of policy; moving only when he was sure of a consensus among Congress and opinion leaders—these were his techniques for retaining power in his own hands. It was a messy system, productive of mistakes and dependent on his personal powers, which were on the wane in the last year of war. Yet it kept Roosevelt in general control of the most unruly political system of all the great powers for a remarkable 12 years.

Winston Leonard Spencer Churchill (1874-1965) shared with Stalin a passion for detail, ever challenging his officials on the minutiae of diplomacy and strategy. Like Roosevelt he was the product of an essentially patrician background—son of a prominent Cabinet minister, cousin of the Duke of Marlborough—and he lived in sybaritic style on money made largely from writing. But Churchill lacked the practised skills of Stalin and Roosevelt in manipulating bureaucracies. He was in fact a political loner, by instinct and habit, who changed political parties twice. After serving as Tory Chancellor of the Exchequer in 1924-29, he then spent a decade in the political "wilderness," not merely because of his frequent criticism of government policy towards Nazi Germany but also because of his quixotic support of King Edward VIII during the abdication crisis of 1936 and his general reputation as a poor team player, notorious for erratic brilliance. In the words of one Tory politician of the 1920s, he was the sort of man ideally suited to moving a mountain, but not one to be consulted afterwards "if I wanted to know where to put it."[8] Consequently, in the 1930s Churchill had only a small personal following: Most of the Tory opposition to Prime Minister Neville Chamberlain coalesced around Anthony Eden. Only the advent of war and the failure of Chamberlain's government in the war's prosecution gave Churchill his chance. He became prime minister in May 1940, and Britain's crisis of 1940-42 was ideally suited to his pugnacity, determination, and energy. Even so, he ran a highly personal war, relying on a small staff of loyalists, and he concentrated on foreign and military policies, leaving the economy and domestic politics to others. For this he paid the price in the election of 1945.

What Churchill and Roosevelt shared was rhetorical power. Churchill's was the eloquence of the nineteenth century, steeped in the speeches of Pitt and Gladstone, which seemed outdated in the 1930s but struck the right note at home and abroad in the dark days of the war. Then, to quote the American radio commentator Edward R. Murrow, he "mobilized the English language and sent it into battle."[9] Roosevelt's hall-mark, by contrast, was studied intimacy. A master of the radio "fireside chat," broadcast into the homes of ordinary Americans, he used commonplace but vivid phrases to move his hearers (Lend-Lease was likened to lending your neighbour a hose to put out a fire that threatened you both). Both leaders employed their verbal skills as instruments of diplomacy. Churchill pressed his case by relentless torrents of carefully directed words, both written and spoken, to drown the opposition. FDR—affable, conversational, deliberately imprecise—gradually enmeshed his interlocutors in a web of implicit agreements. (The first time his army chief of staff, General George C. Marshall, dared visit the president's home at Hyde Park, N.Y., was for FDR's funeral because, he said, "I found informal conversation with the president would get you into trouble. He would talk over something informally at the dinner table and you had trouble disagreeing without creating embarrassment."[10])

On the face of it, Stalin was less suited to international diplomacy. Although a man of great presence, he lacked the fluency of a Roosevelt or a Churchill. Nor did he have their urbane background, the product of frequent foreign travel and deep interest in history and geography. Indeed Stalin had advanced his early career by representing himself as a man of the people, unlike his "cosmopolitan" party colleagues, and he did not cross the borders of the Soviet Union once in the two decades between the world wars. Yet the Russian leader proved himself a skillful diplomatist. Sparing of words yet quick in debate, blessed with a formidable memory, he drew the more voluble Roosevelt and Churchill into commitments and concessions. And, for a man known to his fellow revolutionaries as rough and coarse—Lenin's famous adjective *grubost'*—it was a remarkable triumph of public relations to become the "Uncle Joe" of the West, puffing his pipe and grinning at the camera.[11]

How did the three compare as military leaders? Stalin shared Churchill's hands-on approach—ever involved in strategy and operations—whereas Roosevelt left the details much more to his Joint Chiefs, though, as the decision to invade North Africa in 1942 demonstrates, he would exert his authority as commander in chief to override them where he believed it politically necessary. Of the two more "interventionist" statesmen, Stalin's approach, by instinct and necessity, was the more direct (chapter 2). Unlike Roosevelt, who had to struggle with the conflicting strategic and political demands of war against two enemies—Germany and Japan (chapter 3)—for Stalin the enemy was Germany, first in defence and then, from 1943, in attack. Operationally, his approach was equally direct, with prodigal use of manpower in frontal assaults on the enemy, particularly until Stalingrad. Thus, as a military leader, "the first year and more of the war was a time of education for him, at terrible cost to the Red Army and the Soviet people."[12] Churchill, by contrast, favoured an "indirect" approach, saving British lives by chipping away at Hitler's Fortress Europe and hoping against hope that airpower would deliver all but the *coup de grace*. As argued in chapter 1, this approach had more to commend it as a contribution to Allied victory than some accounts have suggested. Moreover, as chapters 1 and 2 show, the contrast between the strategies of Churchill and Stalin was more than personal. It reflected fundamental differences between a state with enormous manpower under autocratic control, and a small country with a vocal public and grim memories of the carnage of 1914-18.

In their attitudes to the war effort, each leader was deeply nationalistic. Churchill's patriotism was the most public and passionate (chapter 13). "I have not become the King's First Minister in order to preside over the liquidation of the British Empire," he declared in November 1942.[13] Roosevelt's nationalism had greater ideological content. This "persistent evangel of Americanism"[14] sought to spread the values of American economic and political liberalism, and the United States' extensive power by 1944 gave him the leverage to do so (chapter 15). Stalin, for his part, was as much a nationalist as an ideologue. Marxism-Leninism remained the ideological lens through which he viewed the world, but his war-time focus was on specific territorial gains (chapter 14). He wanted to regain the historic borders of the Romanov empire and to guarantee security against Germany, its allies, and for himself.

Distinctive states, contrasting societies, unique leaders, separate wars: So far this overview seems to confirm the conventional Cold War image of the war-time partnership between America, Britain, and Russia as "a shotgun marriage forced upon them by World War II."[15] Yet there was unity underlying the diversity.

Chapter 4 makes clear that a genuine coalition did emerge. It was closer on the Anglo-American side of the triangle, where cultural and linguistic ties facilitated communication (though not always consensus). It was much slower to develop with regard to the Soviet Union, and mutual suspicion remained strong. But this was partly because, until June 1944, the British and Americans were only tangentially engaged in the struggle against Germany. The last year of the war, by contrast, saw growing strategic and even operational co-operation—something approaching a working military alliance. This period, often treated merely as a preamble to the Cold War, is given particular attention.

New research also makes clear the extent of their economic co-operation (chapters 6 and 8). Again, the Anglo-American axis has long been recognized—American Lend-Lease and, in return, British Mutual Aid. What now becomes clear is the utility of Western aid to the Soviet Union, not so much in the defensive phase of the war (1941-43) when the Russians repulsed Germany almost single-handedly, but in the offensives of the last two years when the Red Army drove vigorously towards Berlin. Even in 1941-42, however, Allied aid was a valuable morale-booster for an otherwise isolated Soviet population for whom victory seemed by no means certain.

Chapter 12 explores the assumptions and perceptions that each populace had of the others. The Blitz encouraged a new image of British heroism in America, though doubts about the vigour of Britain's war effort never died away. British fascination with American popular culture, mediated through music and the cinema before the war, was given life by the visitation of several million American GIs. In both countries, there was profound popular admiration for the heroism of the Soviet people, even encouraging extravagant illusions in America about the convergence of the two cultures. Perhaps the most bizarre example was *Life* magazine's assertion in March 1943 that the Russians were "one hell of a people . . . [who] to a remarkable degree . . . look like Americans, dress like Americans and think like Americans," and that the NKVD was "a national police force similar to the FBI."[16] As for the Russians, they warmed more to the Americans than the British, but both countries were now promoted and praised in the Soviet media. American goods were tangible and welcome tokens of co-operation but, as many Russian jokes made clear, opening a can of U.S. tinned meat was no substitute for the opening of the Second Front.

In its military, economic, and cultural facets, the partnership remained flawed, and it fractured dramatically after victory was won. Yet its true significance can only be measured against historical realities rather than abstract ideals of international co-operation. Specifically (chapter 16), this was a much closer partnership than that of the German-Japanese axis, who fought totally separate wars with virtually no contact. The succession of war-time conferences, involving the Big Three leaders and their aides, had no counterparts on the enemy side. Of course, while winning a war, the United States, Great Britain, and the Soviet Union failed to concert a peace and the Cold War was, in part, the consequence of that failure (chapters 13-15). Nevertheless, in this post-Cold War world, we can now take a broader view of the legacies of the war-time Alliance, and discern positive achievements that have lasted to the present day. Among these, institutions such as the United Nations Organization and the International Monetary Fund stand out. In origins, the Alliance may have been a shot-gun marriage. But, like many such relationships—it worked. Fifty years on, its achievements as well as its failings deserve reassessment.

NOTES

1. Dmitrii Volkogonov, *Stalin: Triumph and Tragedy* (London, 1991), 557.

2. Richard M. Leighton and Robert W. Coakley, *Global Logistics and Strategy, 1940-1943* (Washington, 1955), 662.

3. *New York Times*, 21 September 1940, 2. On bombing see Basil Collier, *The Defence of the United Kingdom* (London, 1957), 528, and on evacuation see Richard M. Titmuss, *Problems of Social Policy* (London, 1950), 355-56.

4. Jonathan R. Adelman, *Prelude to the Cold War: The Tsarist, Soviet, and U.S. Armies in the Two World Wars* (Boulder, Colo., 1988), 128. For total Soviet losses see chapter 16, note 36.

5. Alan S. Milward, *War, Economy and Society, 1939-1945* (Berkeley, 1979), 70.

6. Alan Bullock, *Hitler and Stalin: Parallel Lives* (London, 1991), 558-60.

7. Robert Dallek, *Franklin D. Roosevelt and American Foreign Policy, 1932-1945* (New York, 1979), vii.

8. J. C. C. Davidson (1926) in Martin Gilbert, *Winston S. Churchill, 1922-39* (London, 1976), 173.

9. Edward Bliss, ed., *In Search of Light: The Broadcasts of Edward R. Murrow* (London, 1968), 237.

10. Forrest C. Pogue, *George C. Marshall*, vol. 1: *Education of a General* (London, 1964), 341.

11. For the creation of that avuncular image in the United States, see Charles C. Alexander, "'Uncle Joe': Images of Stalin at the Apex of the Grand Alliance," in N. N. Bolkhovitinov, ed., *Annual Studies of America: 1989* (Moscow, 1990), 30-42 (in Russian).

12. Robert H. McNeal, *Stalin: Man and Ruler* (London, 1988), 242.

13. Martin Gilbert, *Winston S. Churchill: Road to Victory, 1941-1945* (London, 1986), 254.

14. Warren F. Kimball, *The Juggler: Franklin Roosevelt as Wartime Statesman* (Princeton, 1991), chapter 9.

15. Walter LaFeber, *America, Russia, and the Cold War, 1945-1980* (4th ed., New York, 1980), 7.

16. John Lewis Gaddis, *The United States and the Origins of the Cold War, 1941-1947* (New York, 1972), 38.

PART I ■ STRATEGY

1

GREAT BRITAIN: THE INDIRECT STRATEGY

Alex Danchev

"How are we to win the war?" Prime Minister Winston Churchill posed the question rhetorically for the Defence Committee of his War Cabinet in October 1940.[1] After the Blitzkrieg, Germany was the master of Europe. The German army could move with impunity where it pleased—excepting only the island kingdom itself. Hitler had conceded the Battle of Britain, apparently, but nothing else. The five pitiless months since Churchill's sudden-death succession to the premiership in May 1940 seemed to show that Britain could at least remain in being, impoverished but imperishable, a scrawny chicken with its neck stubbornly unwrung. The British might be able to "continue the war indefinitely," as Churchill maintained, but a starveling army and a turbid economy meant that in 1940 they could do little more. Churchill hoped that peak production could be reached in the third rather than the fourth year of war: in 1941 rather than in 1942. This would depend on help from the United States, as yet imponderable. Then, and only then, "we should be able to deliver very heavy overseas attacks," the prime minister averred optimistically. Meanwhile it was a question of attrition—the "wearing out" of the first war translated into the "wearing down" of the second—and blood, toil, tears, and sweat.[2]

The salient point to emerge from this early and inconclusive disquisition on strategy was that Britain thought and fought for a long time. After the fall of France in June 1940 she had no option. To misappropriate Braudel, the *longue durée* was central to the British experience and, just as important, the British perception of the Second World War.[3]

How are we to think of this long, long war? Our conception of it is framed in the terminology we choose. Here the Western world is prisoner of Winston Churchill's sublime phrasemaking. The Battle of France, the Battle of Britain, the Battle of the Atlantic: These dramatic tropes are all Churchillian inventions or appropriations; not battles at all, but more or less protracted campaigns.[4] The Grand Alliance itself was in a sense the product of his heroic imagination.[5] Above all, Churchill was the great propagandist of a "special relationship" between "the English-speaking peoples" and mythologist of his own carefully cultivated Former Naval Person relationship with President Roosevelt, the enigmatic arbiter of Anglo-American strategy.[6] Rhetorically, it was his finest hour.

> You ask, what is our policy? I can say: It is to wage war by sea, land, and air, with all our might and all the strength that God can give us; to wage war against a monstrous tyranny, never surpassed in the dark, lamentable catalogue of human crime. That is our policy. You ask, what is our aim? I can answer in one word: It is victory, victory at all costs, victory in spite of all terror, victory, however long and hard the road may be; for without victory there is no survival.[7]

Churchillian rhetoric and victorious retrospect tend to obscure the profoundly defensive construction of British strategic thinking at this time. "Everything in war is very simple," said Clausewitz, "but the simplest thing is difficult."[8] Until the TORCH landings in North Africa in November 1942, perhaps even until the successful outcome of the see-saw Atlantic campaign in May 1943, British strategy was very simple indeed. It was *not to lose the war*. "Victory" was indefinitely postponed. Churchill spoke the truth when he told the Soviet ambassador in July 1940 that his general strategy at present was "to last out the next three months," a philosophy pithily expressed in his private dictum "we must just KBO"—Keep Buggering On.[9] The immediate and overwhelming strategic priority was national self-preservation. In realistic terms this meant securing the home islands, maintaining a presence in the Mediterranean and some kind of position in the Middle East, and salvaging whatever was possible in South East Asia. In the Far East, Britain's role was first ignominious and then inconspicuous. Burma apart, the war in the West was where she cast her lot. There was a need to raise not only armies but also morale. Influencing public opinion, in Britain and in the United States, was a critical function of Churchill's speeches. "He mobilized the English language and sent it into battle." The implacable Stalin had somehow to be placated, with hard-won supplies and future undertakings, but the keeper of the key to the American strategic arsenal had to be wooed. If the United States could be induced to enter the war "up to the neck and in to the death," as Churchill wrote, eventual victory was assured.[10] He could see no other way.

When Churchill and Roosevelt first met as co-belligerents, at the ARCADIA conference in Washington in December 1941, the United States had been at war for exactly two weeks. Britain had been at war for over two years and in mortal danger of invasion for several months in the second half of 1940; she had fought on, if not exactly alone, then shorn of major allies for a full year until the fateful operation BARBAROSSA, the German invasion of the Soviet Union in June 1941. The strategic consequences of this formative experience, and the festering consciousness of the Anglo-American disparity, were enormous. Some were attitudinal, some organizational. Some were more positive than others. One was primal. In every theatre in which the two armies had encountered each other, the British had been beaten by the Germans. British forces had been unable to retain even a toehold on the European mainland. They had been summarily expelled from Dunkirk in May 1940, Narvik in June 1940, and Greece in April 1941, not to mention Crete in June 1941 and the sacrificial raid on Dieppe in August 1942. The skillfully handled withdrawal to Dunkirk and the astonishing success of the evacuation provided a reprieve and a rallying cry, but in the nature of the case that could scarcely mask the sour aftertaste of swift and comprehensive defeat. Nor was this a passing phase. As late as June 1942, with the benefit of two years' experience of desert warfare and with copious current intelligence now on stream, the talismanic stronghold of Tobruk in North Africa capitulated in a day, disgorging a garrison of some 35,000 men and supplies essential to Rommel's continued operations. If the surrender of Singapore to the Japanese in February 1942 was proverbially the worst disaster for British arms, the loss of Tobruk seemed very nearly as bad. Churchill was again in Washington to bargain over Anglo-American strategy. The news was conveyed to him at the White House in the middle of a meeting with the president. "Grimacing, Mr. Churchill must taste the gall of his situation," wrote James Gould Cozzens astutely. "Fine phrases and selected words might show it almost a virtue that, far call'd our navies melt away; that on dune and headland sinks the fire; but those circumstances also kept him from the leading position." For once bereft of fine phrases, Churchill himself allowed the wound to show. "It was a bitter moment. Defeat is one thing; disgrace is another."[11]

It should be no surprise that there were deep reservations in the British high command about the capacity of their own soldiers pitted against the Germans, and in particular about the quality of British military leadership. The evidence is fragmentary and necessarily anecdotal, but it is mounting. The lurid nightmares of "Channel tides running red with Allied blood" of which Churchill unburdened himself to Eisenhower as OVERLORD loomed ever nearer;[12] the inadmissible doubts about cross-Channel operations which the chief of the imperial general staff, General Sir Alan Brooke, confided periodically to his apologetic diary;[13] the reluctance of generals as temperamentally diverse as Auchinleck and Montgomery to commence operations without the greatest possible concentration of firepower and air support—until everything was properly tee-ed up, as Monty would say—these were differing manifestations of the same gnawing uncertainty. It was not only the searing memory of Passchendaele and the Somme that preyed on the British minds in 1942-44. It was also the immediate experience of Narvik and Dunkirk and the Western Desert. Not until the end of 1942 was it possible convincingly to refute Neville Chamberlain's laconic aside to Anthony Eden, then secretary of state for war, in the dark days of 1940—"I'm sorry, Anthony, that all your generals seem to be such bad generals."[14] An appreciation prepared by the Chiefs of Staff in October 1942 declared frankly: "The Russian army is, today, the only force capable of defeating the German army or, indeed, of containing it." On his copy, Churchill scribbled "I hope Stalin will not see this," but he did not dispute the premiss.[15] His own reaction to Montgomery's much-acclaimed triumph over Rommel at El Alamein in November 1942 is equally instructive. Churchill was transported. In the unmistakable cadence of his finest oratory he exulted to a rapt audience at the Mansion House in London: "We have a new experience. We have victory . . . Rommel's army has been defeated. It has been routed. It has been very largely destroyed as a fighting force." Not only a *British* victory, then, but a British *army* victory, over a German-led opponent. A few days later, once he had made quite sure, the bells were rung in national celebration. It was a heady moment. "A victory at last," wrote the king in his diary. "How good it is for the nerves."[16] It was also the last major victory in the West that British or Commonwealth forces were to win on their own account in the Second World War. Future occasions would be irretrievably Anglo-American.

The second attitudinal consequence of what one might call the "old" war of 1939-41 was in some sense the antithesis of that canker of the heart concerning fighting capability. It was a deep-seated feeling that, after all, the British knew best. The feeling was less pronounced with respect to the quasi-autonomous Soviet war, about which the British knew remarkably little, than to the developing Anglo-American war, about which they had decided preferences and advanced expectations. It was all too easy to receive the impression that they also knew best with regard to the

Americans themselves, who found that "a certain condescension in foreigners" was rife among the British officers with whom they had to deal.[17] The attitude found typical expression in the negotiation of Allied strategy. One of the most striking themes in Brooke's diary—a theme barely moderated in his post-war reflections—is the strategic imbecility of Americans in general and the U.S. army chief of staff in particular. "I liked what I saw of Marshall," Brooke recorded on first acquaintance in April 1942, "a pleasant and easy man to get on with, rather over-filled with his own importance." A few days later: "He is, I should think, a good general at raising armies and providing the necessary link between the military and political worlds, but his strategical ability does not impress me at all." Marshall's cross-Channel offensive plan "does not go beyond just landing on the far coast. Whether we are to play *baccarat* or *chemin de fer* at Le Touquet . . . is not stipulated." The plan was nothing more than "castles in the air." Looking back on May 1943, in a passage excised from the published edition, Brooke lamented how "Marshall was quite incapable of grasping the objects of our [British] strategy"; that is, "how we were preparing for a re-entry into France through our actions in the Mediterranean." Why could the American not see what for Brooke himself "stood out clearer and clearer every day"? As late as August 1943, "I entirely failed to get Marshall to realize the relation between cross-Channel and Italian operations and the repercussions which the one exercises on the other. It is quite impossible to argue with him as he does not begin to understand a strategic problem." For Brooke, Marshall was ever the strategic idealist. He did not—could not—know, as Brooke knew. Marshall eventually graduated to being "a big man and a very great gentleman," but as a strategist he was not to be taken seriously.[18]

There were honourable exceptions to this unfortunate tendency on the British side "to regard Americans *de haut en bas*," in Christopher Thorne's apt phrase, though fewer perhaps in the army than in the other services.[19] The outstanding one was Field Marshal Sir John Dill, friend and confessor to Brooke and Marshall both, from December 1941 until his death in November 1944. From his vantage point in the British Joint Staff Mission in Washington, Dill was well placed to appreciate how the British attitude compounded the fundamental difficulty of coalition warfare—the efficient reconciliation of competitive national strategies. In October 1942, Brooke complained to Dill: "We are all in favour of give and take but cannot help feeling it is we who are doing all the giving and our friends who are doing all the taking." This was not merely the habitual exasperation of the Chief of the Imperial General Staff (CIGS); it was an axiom of British strategic thought. Dill recognized that still in the middle period of the war there were equal and opposite American insecurities. His reply was just, though unexpected. "We have in fact imposed our strategy on them and they are very conscious of it."[20]

Echoing Dill, the years 1942-43 have been called "the period of British strategic hegemony."[21] If this were so, the phenomenon may be attributed in part to the organizational consequences of the old war. The terrifying combination of Hitler and Churchill, the one as threat, the other as goad, meant that the British were organized and mobilized for global war sooner and better than their principal Allies, or for that matter their principal antagonists. This applied to every aspect of the war effort. We now know, for example, of Churchill's "extreme priority" order of October 1941 to meet the needs of the denizens of Huts 6 and 8, Bletchley Park; that is, the cryptanalysts who broke the crucial German ENIGMA codes to yield unprecedented riches in signals intelligence—"the Ultra secret."[22] Most fundamentally, the problematic issue of how best to integrate "the frocks" and "the hats"—the politicians and the generals—in the overall direction of the war was successfully resolved in a relationship that stamped its authority on strategic decision-making in both London and Washington: the self-governing adversarial partnership between Winston Churchill, as prime minister and minister of defence, and the tri-service Chiefs of Staff (COS) committee.

Formally, the ultimate responsibility for the conduct of the war rested with the War Cabinet—"the only ones who had the right to have their heads cut off on Tower Hill if we did not win"—but during the period 1940-41 their authority over strategy was progressively and voluntarily ceded to the distinctive combination of the old war man and his professional advisers. Strategy was argued out in the Staff Conference, the quintessentially Churchillian device for war management. The Cabinet became "the last court of appeal," in the words of the official historian. Their position was expressed with characteristic pugnacity by Ernest Bevin, then minister of labour:

> He knew nothing about war himself, he declared, and doubted if the opinion of the other members of the Cabinet was worth having either. They had put him in [he told Churchill] to win the war. If they lost confidence in him, they would put him out. But as long as he had their confidence he should get on with it and not come asking the Cabinet for its opinion on matters which they knew nothing about and which were too serious to be settled by amateur strategists.[23]

With the comfort of hindsight, and bolstered by the bulldog Bevin, it is easy to underestimate just how much of a gamble this development appeared at the time. The new Prime Minister's manners and methods were profoundly disturbing. His war direction was supremely personal. His inquisitorial approach meant that the success of the experiment depended as much on the character as on the competence of his collocutors. His hours were exhausting, his temperament maddening, his invective wounding, his demands outrageous. This was precisely what was needed. Yet for Churchill to have had his untrammelled way, as Dill put it, would have been a strategic disaster. It was vital that he should be corralled and harnessed to Chiefs of Staff who were congenial, certainly, but also fearlessly critical. Not the least part of his uneven genius was to sense that requirement and act upon it.[24]

The COS committee, formalized in 1924 with an individual and collective responsibility to advise on defence policy as a whole, had never before worked with a prime minister and minister of defence, still less a Churchill, in war. The committee Churchill inherited in May 1940 was wholly inadequate to the task. Almost immediately the incumbent CIGS, General Sir Edmund Ironside, bowed to his own supersession by Dill, who was in his turn "retired" in December 1941 to Washington in favour of Brooke, a spectacularly good choice who lasted out the war. In October 1940 the long-serving chief of the air staff (CAS) Air Chief Marshal Sir Cyril Newall, was allowed to withdraw into decent obscurity, to be replaced by Air Chief Marshal Sir Charles Portal, arguably the most complete of the war-time Chiefs of Staff and the prime minister's eventual favourite. Portal too lasted out the war, in itself a considerable feat. The chief of the naval staff (CNS) from June 1939 until his death in October 1943 was Churchill's "true comrade," Admiral Sir Dudley Pound, who was succeeded by Admiral Sir Andrew Cunningham, a magnificent fighting admiral in the Nelsonian tradition, steadfastly immune to Churchill's witchery, but by his own account no dialectician. Pound's professional relationship with the Former Naval Person has been the subject of a protracted dispute between the two foremost naval historians of the modern era, Arthur Marder and Stephen Roskill. Marder argued that Pound "feared neither God, man, nor Winston Churchill"; Roskill that "Churchill had a ready, indeed too ready, mouthpiece in the compliant Pound." He remains something of a puzzle, about whom two things are certain. Like Portal, but unlike Dill or Brooke or Cunningham, he was congenial to Churchill. The two men used to meet in the early hours of the morning for an insomniac whisky in the Admiralty Map Room. A more propitious circumstance for nurturing a relationship with Churchill can scarcely be imagined. Secondly, compliant or not, Pound confined himself strictly to naval matters. In conference it often took the trigger words *battleship* or *sea* to rouse him from the notorious "sleepiness" that once provoked Brooke to liken him to a dormouse. Neither Pound nor Cunningham was in the habit of contesting Churchill in the realm of grand strategy. The three who did were Dill, Brooke, and, to a lesser extent, Portal.

Dill's 18-month contest with Churchill was a losing one, not because Dill was ineffectual as is commonly supposed, but because the prevailing circumstances gave him no prospect of short-run success. Quite apart from the dire external situation, the prime minister himself was not yet accustomed to the trammelling of professional advice. Dill's caution was like medicine: The PM knew he had to take it, but he found the taste revolting. Churchill was an incurably impatient strategist. "He was not a *calm* thinker, whose attention was naturally directed to grand strategy, a student of campaigns in their academic aspect, a Liddell Hart or a Clausewitz," wrote Ian Jacob, an admiring but exceptionally acute observer:

> He was a man who required to push away at some concrete project, not a cold, aloof strategist. He had studied battles, and by instinct tended to think of life as a series of conflicts with barriers to be overcome, opposition to be borne down. He hated those periods which are inevitable in a war when operations have come to a conclusion, and there must be a pause for planning and preparation, for regrouping and reorganisation. His mind chafed, and he turned always to any project however minor, or however irrelevant to the main theme, in the hope that it would fill the gap. His frequent efforts to get the Chiefs of Staff and the planning staffs to work out an operation in Norway sprang not so much from a desire to free that country or to close German access to the oceans, but from his wish to have something happen before the next major operation was due to start. One of his favourite phrases was that the enemy must be made "to bleed and burn," everywhere and all the time. . . .[25]

This congenital urge of Churchill's to do *something,* linked with a strong political imperative to be seen to act, and act successfully, would have tremendous repercussions on the course of Anglo-American strategy in 1942. In 1940-41, however, to do *anything* was as difficult as Clausewitz had suggested. To do what Churchill wanted was exceedingly perilous, and it was Dill who shouldered the chief burden of telling him so. Without the palliative of victories in the field—General O'Connor's startling success against the Italians in North Africa in December 1940 was quickly if undeservedly written down—this relationship was unsustainable.[26] Thus Dill gave place to Brooke, only to rise again across the Atlantic. In the confines of the Cabinet War Rooms he was never comfortable with Churchill's unrestrained behaviour or disputatious nature, but during his tenure as CIGS Dill did more than anyone else to establish the ground rules for a constructive adversarial partnership with the prime minister. His translation to Washington was entirely fortuitous. Before Pearl Harbor, Churchill had intended that he should become governor of Bombay, "a position of great honour, followed by a bodyguard with lances"—in fact a sinecure. Against all expectation, Dill's presence in the U.S. capital, and his singular rapport with Marshall, ensured that the doubtful experiment of a Combined Chiefs of Staff (CCS) committee began to work immediately and successfully on the adversarial model developed in London, now broadened to allow the Anglo-American CCS to engage both prime minister and president. The CCS themselves and the fretwork of Anglo-American committees established under them were serviced in exemplary fashion by a secretariat drawn from and patterned on the secretariat of the War Cabinet, organized initially by the charismatic Brigadier Vivian Dykes, who built a similar rapport with his influential opposite number Brigadier General Walter Bedell Smith.[27] This characteristic mode of "combined" strategic decision-making was a direct product of the British experience of 1940-41. Its importance to the Alliance can hardly be overstated. The manner in which strategy was determined crucially influenced the direction and timing of the outcome, particularly in the period of flux from 1942 to 1944. In a certain sense the process of disputation in committee, regulated informally by close personal understanding, represented the fundamental British contribution to Western war strategy.[28]

If Dill was necessary but not sufficient to make the adversarial enterprise work, Brooke, it is tempting to say, was more than enough. The new CIGS was a forbidding presence. The overpowering impact he made on others, "his quite remarkable and palpable extension of personality . . . that curious electric awareness felt down to the tips of one's fingers of a given presence imparting a sense of stimulation . . . the consoling thought that someone of the sort was at the top," has been brilliantly caught by the novelist Anthony Powell.[29] Brooke wore a cowl of impregnable self-mastery over seething emotions, the state of which his colleagues were blissfully unaware at the time. His vitriolic and often over-wrought war-time diaries, published in the late 1950s, came as a complete revelation.[30] Dykes's nickname for him was an appropriate one: Colonel Shrapnel. Where Churchill had an iron whim, Brooke had an iron will. In debate his characteristic rejoinder was a bleak negative—"I flatly disagree"—accompanied by the snapping of a pencil. He was a formidable advocate, the natural spokesman for the British in international strategic negotiation. He was an expert chairman of the COS committee. He was, in short, a worthy adversary for Churchill on one side and Marshall on the other. At the same time he was prey to doubt, instinctively conservative with regard to men and issues—it is clear the he always had the gravest suspicions about the Combined Chiefs of Staff organization in Washington—and cautious in the extreme in his strategic thinking. Brooke had what his biographer appropriately calls a "dissective" mind. He was a man for exact calculation, precise information, exhaustive appreciation. For sheer technical competence he was unsurpassed. In terms of grand strategy, he was careful, logical, and distinctly unimaginative.[31]

How did these men propose to win the war? Dostoyevsky said that nothing is harder than an idea or easier than cutting off heads. British (and American) ideas on strategy were in distressingly short supply. Churchill's fertile imagination notwithstanding, the possible permutations seemed to be remarkably few. To meet the president's absolute requirement for a major Anglo-American operation in the European Theatre in 1942, for example, the invasion of North West Africa (TORCH) was eventually selected almost by default. The *only* alternatives seriously suggested were a lodgement in North West France (SLEDGEHAMMER) or an operation of indeterminate character in Northern Norway (JUPITER). The first of these, canvassed by the U.S. army high command, was admittedly precarious and pitifully small scale (perhaps six divisions at a time when there were some 27 German divisions in the West, to say nothing of approximately 180 engaged by the Soviets in the East).[32] SLEDGEHAMMER was vetoed by the British Chiefs of Staff, who would have had to provide the majority of the troops. The second alternative was a cherished project of the prime minister's. "Our whole power to help Russia in any effectual manner this year," he wrote in early July 1942, "depends upon our driving the enemy aircraft from the northern airfields of Norway"—strategic dogma of breathtaking unreality. JUPITER was an idea, but a poor one. Fortunately, it was never taken seriously by the chiefs of staff of either nation. "We'd better put an advert in the papers," Churchill joked thinly a few days later.[33]

To disparage the prime minister's strategic thinking is all too easy. It was a favourite sport at the time. British staff officers would go through his appreciations "paragraph by paragraph scoring as in boxing rounds (WSC v. Hard Facts). He won heavily on points but was nearly KO about the 12th round." And yet, as if in defiance of professional pettifogging, "Churchill sometimes saw visions, and sometimes they came true."[34] The most controversial of these visions took the form of a reptile. It was a vision borne of some desperation. It came to him during his first, marathon meeting with Stalin in Moscow in August 1942.[35] Churchill had taken upon himself the unenviable task of explaining to "Uncle Joe" that there would not, after all, be a Second Front of the kind that he had been led to expect: large-scale Anglo-American landings in France in 1942. Churchill was acutely aware of the need at once to mollify and impress his host; aware, also, of a troubling lack of clarity. The stupendous battles on the eastern front did not linger in his mind's eye like those of other far-away places. "Remember that on my breast there are the medals of the Dardanelles, Antwerp, Dakar, and Greece," he once exclaimed to Anthony Eden. These were all amphibious operations (and all failures): it was the sea, the sea that captured his imagination. For Churchill, Moscow was no farther away, but infinitely more remote. The road to Orel was a road he never travelled. Stalin, angry and unpredictable, was "the ogre in his den."[36] Given the circumstances, the atmosphere of the meeting was strongly oppressive. After much heavy-handed banter and largely negative discussion, Churchill decided that the moment had arrived to divulge to Stalin the Anglo-American decision for TORCH. He gave an outline of the plan. He spoke of the "true" Second Front. He expatiated on the many virtues of the operation. "If we could end the year in possession of North Africa," he argued finally, "we could threaten the belly of Hitler's Europe." Then, in a spontaneous gesture of mute eloquence, he drew a picture of a crocodile. He explained that "it was our intention to attack the soft belly of the crocodile as we attacked its hard snout." There could be no more expressive demonstration of the lure of an idea.

The following month, in a letter to Roosevelt, Churchill speculated on the possibility of "attacking the under-belly of the Axis" through Sardinia, Sicily, or the Italian mainland, once North Africa was in Allied hands. In October, ever hopeful, he added to this list the French Riviera, "or perhaps even, with Turkish aid, the Balkans." In November he again urged the president to consider how best to use bases on the North African shore "to strike at the under-belly of the Axis in effective strength and in the shortest time."[37] In late 1942, therefore, the idea was still in the process of gestation. It would be further articulated in the course of 1943, reprised with variations in 1944, and continually reinterpreted ever since. Its graphic qualities soon outstripped its strategic significance. In truth, the strategy of the soft under-belly was a nullity. As Michael Howard has pointed out, it played no part in the decision for TORCH in 1942; that decision had already been taken on other grounds. Churchill's explanation of it was inspired but essentially misleading.[38]

Nor was it the vision of a soft under-belly that lured the British, and so the Americans, "down the Mediterranean garden path" in 1943.[39] At the

Casablanca conference in January 1943 it was decided that the strategic exploitation of the TORCH landings should be followed by an invasion of Sicily (HUSKY). However, the clearance of the North African shore was completed only in May, just as the next Allied conference convened in Washington. Finding themselves in something of a quandary, the CCS invited General Eisenhower to suggest where they might go after Sicily. No resolution could be achieved before HUSKY was mounted in July 1943. Not until a week after that operation commenced did Eisenhower opt definitely for an invasion of mainland Italy. Not until Sicily was safe one month later did he decide how it was to be done. In September 1943 the U.S. Fifth Army landed innocently at Salerno, south of Naples (AVALANCHE). A few days earlier the British Eighth Army crossed the Straits of Messina into Calabria (BAYTOWN) and began its buglike crawl up the Italian leg.[40] The Quebec conference in August had stipulated that the primary objectives of this campaign should be the elimination of Italy from the war and the establishment of air bases in the Rome area. The question of exploitation further north had been left deliberately open. In the event Italy surrendered, somewhat confusedly, on the very day of BAYTOWN and immediately in advance of AVALANCHE. The Italian campaign nonetheless continued its incremental progress. At the Tehran conference in November the Americans eventually conceded that the Pisa-Rimini line, far to the north of Rome, should be the new objective. Self-evidently, this sequence of events is quite incompatible with the methodical unfolding of a strategic vision. It is instead a rudimentary tale of opportunism and improvisation. There was no certainty that the prime under-belly of Italy would ever be reached; no clear conviction about how far or how fast to crawl. So often, strategic thinking coheres only in retrospect. Michael Howard has observed: "The development of British—and Allied—strategy was a piecemeal affair, in which the military leaders had often simply to do what they could, where they could, with the forces which they had to hand."[41]

It remains extraordinarily difficult to evaluate the Anglo-American campaign in Italy from 1943 to 1945. Even among those who sponsored it most ardently at the time—the British—there is still no agreement on the most basic questions. Did the campaign achieve its aims? How, if at all, did it contribute to the Allied victory in the West, or for that matter in the East? The issue is further complicated by a second layer of questions which superimposed themselves on the campaign whilst it was still in progress, and which continue to generate controversy to this day. Those who take a benign view of the campaign tend naturally to ask whether it could have achieved more than it did; their assumption is positive. Those who take a malign view, on the other hand, tend to ask whether it should have been undertaken in the first place; their assumption is negative. The campaign which was actually fought, therefore, has become something of a strategical football, kicked this way and that, according to the predisposition (and often the nationality) of the players.

The Italian campaign was considered to be the strategy "best calculated to eliminate Italy from the war and to contain the maximum number of German forces," as prescribed by the Combined Chiefs of Staff. In the event the first of these aims was achieved almost before the campaign began, with the Italian surrender. The second aim was at once prosaic and open-ended. It provided little more than a frame of reference. The "containment" of German forces may be more accurately described as *tying down* of German forces. This constitutes the main test of success. The Italian campaign was not, of itself, decisive. Apart perhaps from a brief flutter in the heart of Field Marshal Sir Harold Alexander in late 1944, no one thought it could be. On some measures it was not even very important. The absolute numbers of combat divisions engaged, for example, were a tiny fraction of those engaged on the eastern front. Nevertheless, throughout 1944 between 19 and 23 German combat divisions (some 15 percent of the total) were tied down in Italy. They were therefore lost to other theatres, particularly to Normandy in June and July 1944, when even a small mobile strategic reserve could have complicated the Allied breakout enormously. There were seven good panzer and panzer grenadier divisions in Italy in late June 1944. Had they been deployed in timely and aggressive fashion in France it is entirely possible that the war would have been prolonged by several months. Moreover the Italian campaign (and the Mediterranean as a whole) did not tie down only land forces. In 1943, fully one-third of all *Luftwaffe* losses were sustained in the Mediterranean theatre. If tying down was the first priority of the Italian campaign, attrition was the second.

As is well known, however, containment and attrition can be mutual. In this instance the war of attrition clearly favoured the Allies. By May 1945 the Italian campaign had cost the Germans 536,000 casualties to the Allies' 312,000. The war of containment is harder to assess, but there is no doubt that Alexander's total manpower substantially exceeded his German opposite number Kesselring's—according to one estimate, by a factor of three. And it was less costly for the Germans to supply their forces (direct from Germany) than it was for the Allies to supply theirs (through the Mediterranean). Who, then, was being tied down? Was

Alexander containing Kesselring, or Kesselring containing Alexander? Progressively, the strategic initiative in the Second World War passed to the Allies. But did they have any realistic alternative? Until 1944, the British answer was a resolute no.

Churchill did have an earlier and grander strategic vision, classically enunciated in December 1941 and encapsulated in one Winstonian phrase: closing the ring. Over a prodigious five-day period on board the HMS *Duke of York,* bound for Washington in the wake of Pearl Harbor, the prime minister dictated a majestic four-part conspectus of "the war policy of 1942 and 1943" as he hoped and expected it would develop in every theatre. In order of composition, part one dealt with what he called the Atlantic front; part two with the Pacific front; part three with 1943; part four with the Pacific once more.[42] Taken together, these papers constitute one of the seminal strategic documents of the war. Addressed to the COS but composed for the president, for himself, and perhaps subconsciously for posterity, they were a purposeful blend of rally and entreaty, program and prognostication.[43] The first paper focused on operation GYMNAST (later TORCH) in French North Africa, then conceived as an Anglo-American occupation by invitation. The strategic goals of this operation were clearly stated in the paper's conclusion. "The war in the West in 1942 comprises, as its main offensive effort, the occupation and control by Great Britain and the United States of the whole of the North and West African possessions of France, and the further control by Britain of the whole North African shore from Tunis to Egypt, thus giving, if the naval situation allows, free passage through the Mediterranean to the Levant and the Suez Canal"—in spite of the delays, a remarkably accurate forecast.[44]

The third and most important paper, on 1943, continued this train of thought. It posited a situation in which "Turkey, though not necessarily at war, would be definitely incorporated in the American-British-Russian front" and "the Russian position would be strongly established." In this situation, "it might be that a footing would already have been established in Sicily and Italy, with reactions inside Italy which might be highly favourable." Churchill then considered the necessities of the case. "All this would fall short of bringing the war to an end. The war cannot be ended by driving Japan back to her own bounds and defeating her overseas forces. The war can only be ended through the defeat in Europe of the German armies"—a formulation that recalled Douglas Haig's often-quoted pronouncement on an earlier war: "We cannot hope to win until we have defeated the German Army."[45] In December 1941, however, Churchill clung to the vestiges of an alternative road to victory, internal collapse in Germany "produced by the unfavourable course of the war, economic privations, and the Allied bombing offensive." It may be that the British high command never completely lost hope of that outcome, but Churchill himself was neither temperamentally nor intellectually prepared to rely upon it. The strategic consequences were spelled out in his paper.

> We have, therefore, to prepare for the liberation of the captive countries of Western and Southern Europe by the landing at suitable points, successively or simultaneously, of British and American armies strong enough to enable the conquered populations to revolt. By themselves they will never be able to revolt owing to the ruthless counter-measures that will be employed: but if adequate and suitably equipped forces were landed in several of the following countries, namely, Norway, Denmark, Holland, Belgium, the French Channel coasts and the French Atlantic coasts, as well as Italy and possibly the Balkans, the German garrisons would prove insufficient to cope both with the strength of the liberating forces and the fury of the revolting peoples.

More specifically, Churchill envisaged an Anglo-American "liberating offensive" of some 40 divisions, "of which Great British would try to produce nearly half," during the summer of 1943. The essential prerequisites of such an operation were "command of the sea"—that is to say, victory in the Battle of the Atlantic—and air superiority, both of which were nothing more than pipe dreams at the time he was writing. Withal, the prime minister was optimistic. "If we set these tasks before us now, . . . we might hope, even if no German collapse occurs beforehand, to win the war at the end of 1943 or 1944."[46]

Churchill's first paper had contained a glancing reference to "the ring that is closing" around the Germans. In conference with the Chiefs of Staff he summarized his famous conception of a three-phase war:

1. Closing the ring.
2. Liberating the populations.
3. Final assault on the German citadel.[47]

At the same time an appreciation prepared for the Chiefs of Staff by their directors of plans spoke of "a gradual tightening of the ring around Axis-controlled Europe."[48] Accordingly the British position paper for the ARCADIA conference identified as one of the essential features of Allied grand strategy "closing and tightening the ring round Germany," a ring defined by the Chiefs of Staff as a line running (clockwise) from the Soviet port of Archangel to the Black Sea, south through Anatolia, west along the northern shore of the Mediterranean, and thence round the western seaboard of the European mainland—more succinctly described by Arthur Bryant, with a degree of geographical license, as "a ring of salt water and desert."[49] The declared object was to strengthen this ring and close the gaps in it, "by sustaining the Russian front, by arming and supporting Turkey, by increasing our strength in the Middle East, and by gaining possession of the whole North African coast." The argument pursued here was of fundamental importance, for it was this paper—the British paper—that was the template for the agreement reached at ARCADIA and embodied in what the British designated *WW1*—"American and British Strategy," a document referred to as "The Bible" in subsequent Anglo-American controversy.[50]

Following British strategic orthodoxy, *WW1* dismissed the possibility of any large-scale Anglo-American operations on the European mainland in 1942. In 1943, on the other hand, it acknowledged in guarded terms that "the way may be clear for a return to the Continent, across the Mediterranean, from Turkey into the Balkans, or by landings in Western Europe." The ordering of the alternatives was Churchill's, though his fanciful suggestion of several *simultaneous* operations had not survived professional scrutiny.[51] Meanwhile, the inexorable process of attrition had to be continued, if not intensified. "Wearing out" the enemy in this war was meant to be accomplished, not by encounter battles on a static front, but by proxy: by the celebrated trio of bombing, blockade, and subversion. Given the predicament in which the British found themselves in 1940-41, a tendency to place excessive faith in each of these strategic expedients was readily understandable. It was, perhaps, consoling to forget that they were expedients. In the case of strategic bombing, faith assumed fanatic proportions. For those charged with carrying out the mission, it may be that such fervour was a kind of psychological necessity, as Joseph Heller has suggested.[52] We now know that the fanatics were tragically misled. As was cruelly demonstrated during the winter of 1943-44, the combined bombing offensive did not and could not wear out the city of Berlin, let alone the Third Reich.[53]

In total, *WW1* was a surprisingly faithful reproduction of Churchill's view of the way the war should be prosecuted. His three-phase strategic conception—and the hopes and fears which lay behind it—may be said to reject Clausewitz and embrace Fabius. In the Second Punic War of 219-202 B.C. the Roman statesman Quintus Fabius Maximus, surnamed Cunctator ("The Delayer"), foiled the brilliant Carthaginian general Hannibal by a strategy of "masterly inactivity": that is, the prudent and deliberate avoidance of any large-scale direct engagements except in circumstances of his own choosing. Fabius held that "long taking of counsel" was essential before the Romans could hope to realize their aims. He was naturally accused of being dilatory—one of many modern parallels—though it is salutary to recall that the premature abandonment of this strategy led to disaster for the Romans at the great battle of Cannae (216 B.C.). "Fabian tactics" have been well summarized as follows, in terms richly evocative of British strategic preferences in the Second World War:

> . . . never to accept battle when the enemy offered it, never to offer it on equal terms, never to attack him in his camp; but to destroy his army in detail as time and opportunity offered, to defend vigorously all the places that had remained loyal to Rome, to try to recover by force or fraud the places that had fallen into Hannibal's hands, profiting by Rome's numerical superiority, and Hannibal's inability to keep the two theatres of war . . . both under his own eye.[54]

From December 1941 the arch-exponent of this strategy was the CIGS, General Brooke. His version of masterly inactivity was "never leaving anything to chance."[55] It is often forgotten that he would have preferred *not* to do TORCH—bracketed ignominiously with North Norway in his diary as "not possible"—nor indeed any other Anglo-American amphibious operation in 1942. In this, unexpectedly, he was at one with the U.S. Joint Chiefs of Staff.[56] He would rather have continued the concentration of forces in the U.K. (BOLERO) with the questionable promise of a cross-Channel operation in 1943 (ROUNDUP), perhaps in May. If ROUNDUP had to be postponed, so much the better: for Brooke, the elimination of Italy was at once more enticing and more realistic. He did favour the early clearance of the North African shore, but preferred the nourishment of a British offensive westward from Libya as a means to that end. His fundamental concern was shipping. Reflecting after the war on his diary entries for December 1942, he penned some characteristic guidance for Arthur Bryant:

> I was quite clear in my own mind that the moment for the opening of a Western Front had not yet come and would not present itself during 1943. I felt that we must stick to my original policy for the conduct of the war, from which I had never departed, namely, to begin the conquest of North Africa, so as to reopen the Mediterranean, restore a million tons of shipping by avoiding the Cape route; then eliminate Italy, bring in Turkey, threaten southern Europe, and then liberate France. This plan, of course, depended on Russia holding on. Although in the early stages of the war I had the most serious doubts whether she would do so, by the end of 1942 I did not think such an eventuality [a Soviet collapse] likely.[57]

Brooke was by nature categorical, but the extreme clarity of vision touted here was exaggerated in hindsight—only to be further embellished by

Bryant himself in *The Turn of the Tide.* Nevertheless, the emphasis of Brooke's strategic shopping list is revealing. There was so much to do, so far to go, before the culminating point. ". . . *And then* liberate France." But when?

There is no question that "Brooke feared above all things a premature and unsuccessful return to the mainland of Europe."[58] Was he right to argue for a delayed Second Front? Was he completely averse to crossing the Channel?

A bona fide Second Front has always focused on one scenario only: a large-scale cross-Channel assault; the establishment of a beachhead in North Western France; a concerted breakout; and a drive eastward towards Paris and ultimately Berlin. With the comfort of hindsight we know that this scenario describes operation OVERLORD. That operation called for landing five infantry divisions, three airborne divisions, and three armoured brigades on D-Day, 6 June 1944—the maximum possible given the capacity of the available assault landing craft. These eight divisions would be built up to 24 by the end of the first month, and 30-plus by the end of the second. This was the biggest operation of its kind in the history of warfare; but it was not a wide margin of superiority. Within immediate range of the D-Day beaches were six German infantry divisions and one panzer division. Within 200 miles were a further 17 infantry and two panzer divisions. Other things being equal, the Germans could have been expected to concentrate superior forces in the area of the beachhead at any time during the first week of the operation. In fact, by 1944 other things were not equal. To mention only the most crucial, the Allies enjoyed the priceless advantage of complete air superiority. "If you see fighter aircraft over you," said Eisenhower in his D-Day briefing, "they will be ours." No such assurance could have been given in 1942 or 1943.

This, then, was the scale of the problem. In December 1942 there were 36 German combat divisions in the West; in June 1943, there were 42. Operation SLEDGEHAMMER, planned for November 1942 but mercifully never mounted, envisaged a maximum of six British and American divisions. Operation ROUNDUP, canvassed for May 1943, envisaged 48. In numerical terms alone these forces were totally inadequate to the task—even supposing there had been sufficient assault shipping to lift them, or merchant shipping to supply them, or aircraft to cover them, or signals intelligence to guide them, which in each case there was not.

No one now argues seriously for a Second Front in 1942. However, it is sometimes suggested that it would have been possible to husband resources for an OVERLORD in 1943: Second Front soon, one might say.

This wholly unrealistic conception was rejected at the time and has not gained in credibility since. It fails to comprehend two kinds of difficulty. First, there was the operational difficulty of mounting a full-scale, opposed, Allied assault landing, for the first time, with unbloodied troops—and then achieving a breakout—against a formidable enemy as yet undepleted. Secondly, at a different level, there was the political difficulty of doing nothing of consequence for 18 months whilst the Soviet Union was continuously engaged in a merciless battle of attrition of epic scale, uncertain outcome, and unimaginable cost. Strategic bombing was neither an acceptable nor an effectual Second Front. Hoarding for 1943 was a political impossibility. The imperative to do *something* in 1942 was too great—something conspicuous, something graspable, something successful, and something that could be sold to Stalin and to American and British electorates as a worthwhile operation of war. Hence TORCH. Without the TORCH landings and the ensuing North African campaign, the encounter in Normandy would have taken on a quite different character. The British Eighth Army was made by fighting its way from Alamein to Mareth. American troops were entirely without combat experience in 1942; the salutary battle of Kasserine taught lessons which were learned with great rapidity, but Kasserine was not until mid-February 1943. North Africa was finally cleared only in May 1943. Pursuit and exploitation were not Anglo-American strong points. For a bona fide Second Front, the conclusion is as plain as could be. The British were right: It was not only wise but essential to wait.

What were the British and American forces to do in the interim? Brooke argued publicly that Fabian tactics in the Mediterranean were not merely complementary but indispensable to a successful cross-Channel attack: Without closing and tightening the ring to its utmost, the final assault would certainly founder. In private he often argued the same—but he also suffered relapses. Late in 1942 he came to realize that a ROUNDUP on the scale projected simply would not be practicable before 1944.[59] The relief he experienced was only temporary. During the following year he was regularly tormented by dispersionist demons. In October 1943 at a Chiefs of Staff meeting, for example, "we received a note from the PM wishing to swing the strategy back to the Mediterranean at the expense of the Channel. I am in many ways entirely with him, but God knows where this may lead us as regards clashes with the Americans." A few days later: "Our build-up in Italy is much slower than that of the Germans and far slower than I expected. We shall have to have an almighty row with the Americans who have put us in this position with their insistence to abandon the Mediterranean operations for the very problematical cross-Channel operations. We are now beginning to see the full beauty of the Marshall strategy! It is quite heart-breaking when we see what we might have done this year if our strategy had not been distorted by the Americans." The following month: "When I look at the Mediterranean I realize only too well how far I have failed. If only I had had sufficient force of character to swing those American Chiefs of Staff and make them see daylight, how different the war might be. We should have had the whole Balkans ablaze by now, and the war might have been finished in 1943." By November 1943, it seems, the garden path led straight to a ripe Mediterranean orchard: "Our next step should be to shake the fruit trees and gather the apples."[60]

There were other moments like these, not all of them emotional outbursts. They were surely significant, but their significance requires careful interpretation.[61] They do not appear to mean that Brooke refused a cross-Channel operation, absolutely. They *do* appear to mean that he had a visceral objection to it. He was too sound a strategist not to recognize that amphibious landings in North West Europe might ultimately be necessary and even desirable. At the same time he was content to postpone the day almost indefinitely—"till the Greek kalends," as Michael Howard has said—in the fraying hope that a favourable decision could be achieved without it. To employ out-moded American terminology, he longed for a mop-up but acquiesced in a power-play.[62] That startling piece of wishful thinking, "the war might have been finished in 1943," was really a private lamentation. It was written as the tripartite Tehran conference impended and Brooke began to sense that hopes were dupes. For Brooke Cunctator, "the dangers of spelling the word *Overlord* with the letters *Tyrant*" were always especially acute.[63] In terms of casualties, this Fabianism certainly paid off. The British lost some 485,000 in the Second World War, historically a high figure, but by the standards of this gargantuan war proportionately and comparatively very light.

From a British perspective, full American belligerency marks the great fault line of the Second World War. Pearl Harbor ushered in a new era. The turning points of the old war were June 1940, October 1940, and June 1941. In June 1940 the sceptred isle was suddenly bereft. In October 1940 the danger of imminent invasion was known to have passed. In June 1941 an eastern front was involuntarily established. The old war was literally a struggle for survival. "Led . . . by a master of rhetoric, Britain . . . became the victim of her own rhetoric. She fondly imagined she had won the war. She had not. America and Russia had won the war.

Britain had in her finest hour not lost it."[64] After Dunkirk, all was strangely anticlimactic. The poets had gone, J. B. Priestley said, and the politicians had come back.

The new war emerged as a different kind of national struggle. The turning points were November 1942, May 1943, and November 1943. In November 1942 the North African landings—the biggest yet—met with overwhelming tactical success. Montgomery of Alamein began the triumphal passage through the European theatre of operations that concluded so sweetly as *victor ludorum* on Lüneburg Heath in May 1945, a passage of enormous psychological significance for the British. Less auspiciously, the King's First Minister declared himself the president's lieutenant in the combined undertaking that was TORCH. Jubilant, he also declared: "We mean to hold our own."[65] In this he was sadly deceived. In May 1943 came the long-awaited sequel to these events, the final clearance of North Africa. More importantly there was at last a decisive and favourable outcome to the epic Battle of the Atlantic. In November 1943 at the Tehran conference table a poor little English donkey, squeezed uncomfortably between a great Russian bear on one side and a great American buffalo on the other, was compelled to submit to an overriding commitment and a set date for the tyrant OVERLORD.[66] The prime minister protested with some asperity that "he could not in any circumstances agree to sacrifice the activities of the armies in the Mediterranean, which included 20 British and British-controlled divisions, merely in order to keep the exact date of May 1 for OVERLORD." He was effectively ignored.[67] Late in the new war, Churchill could still secure concessions—in this instance a postponement of one month—but he could no longer sway campaigns. Fine phrases were no substitute for armoured divisions. In one sense, however, rhetoric won out. The Italian campaign was made to yield. Ironically for Churchill and happily for us, the beneficiary of that painful process was "the final assault on the German citadel."

Notes

1. DO(40)39, 31 October 1940, CAB 69/8, Public Record Office [PRO], London. Cf. Martin Gilbert, *Winston S. Churchill: Finest Hour* (London, 1983), 879-81.

2. "Wearing down" or "attrition" was explicitly advocated in position papers for the Washington and Casablanca conferences, printed in J. M. A. Gwyer and Michael Howard, *Grand Strategy*, vols. 3 and 4, (London, 1964 and 1972), 345-48 and 602-7 respectively.

3. On the fall of France as "fulcrum" see David Reynolds, "1940," *International Affairs* 66 (1990), 325-50.

4. For the Battle of France (General Weygand's term) and the Battle of Britain see Churchill in the House of Commons, 18 June 1940, printed in Robert Rhodes James, ed., *Churchill Speaks* (London, 1981), 714-20; quoted extensively in Gilbert, *Finest Hour*, 570-71. The Battle of the Atlantic is the title of Churchill's directive of 6 March 1941, printed in Winston S. Churchill, *The Second World War* (6 vols.; London, 1948-54), 3, 107-9.

5. *The Grand Alliance* is the title of Churchill, 3.

6. The *locus classicus* for the "special relationship" is Churchill's speech at Fulton, Missouri, on 5 March 1946, in *Churchill Speaks*, 876-84. The Churchill-Roosevelt relationship is laid bare in Warren F. Kimball, ed., *Churchill & Roosevelt: The Complete Correspondence* (3 vols.; Princeton, 1984).

7. Churchill in the House of Commons, 13 May 1940, in *Churchill Speaks*, 703-5. For an interesting comment on his own rhetoric see Churchill, 2, 199.

8. Michael Howard and Peter Paret, eds., *On War* (Princeton, 1976), 119.

9. Ivan Maisky, *Memoirs of a Soviet Ambassador* (London, 1967), 100; Peck to Seal, 11 December 1941, quoted in Gilbert, *Finest Hour*, 1273.

10. Edward R. Murrow, quoted in David Cannadine, ed., *Blood, Toil, Tears and Sweat* (London, 1989), 11; Churchill 3, 539.

11. James Gould Cozzens, *Guard of Honour* (London, 1949), 394; Churchill, 4, 344. Cozzens borrowed from Kipling's resonant poem marking Queen Victoria's Jubilee in 1897, "Recessional."

12. Eisenhower to Ismay, 3 December 1960, Eisenhower Presidential Papers, Eisenhower Library [DDEL], Abilene, Kans.

13. Brooke diary, 19 and 26 October 1943, 1 November 1943, 5 June 1944, quoted in Arthur Bryant, *Triumph in the West* (London, 1959) [Bryant, 2], 55, 56, 59, 205-6.

14. Lord Avon, *The Eden Memoirs*, vol. 2 (London, 1965), 129.

15. COS(42)345(0)(Final), "American-British Strategy," 30 October 1942, PREM 3/499/6, PRO.

16. Churchill at the Mansion House, 10 November 1942, in *Churchill Speaks*, 198-203; George VI diary, 4 November 1942, quoted in Martin Gilbert, *Second World War* (London, 1990), 375.

17. The phrase is James Russell Lowell's: "On a Certain Condescension in Foreigners" (1869), reprinted in Henry Steele Commager, ed., *Britain Through American Eyes* (London, 1974), 426-43.

18. Brooke diary, 9 and 15 April 1942, 18 May 1943, 15 August 1943, quoted in Arthur Bryant, *The Turn of the Tide* (London: Collins, 1957) [Bryant, I], 354, 358, 619-20, 706; "Notes for my Memoirs," Alanbrooke Papers, 3A/VIII/693, Liddell Hart Centre for Military Archives, King's College London [KCL].

19. Christopher Thorne, *Allies of a Kind* (London, 1978), 97.

20. Brooke to Dill, and Dill to Brooke, 2 and 4 October 1942, WO193/334, PRO. On Dill in Washington see Alex Danchev, *Very Special Relationship* (London, 1986).

21. Trumbull Higgins, "The Anglo-American Historians' War in the Mediterranean," *Military Affairs* 34 (1970), 86.

22. The order and the extraordinary appeal which prompted it are printed in F. H. Hinsley *et al., British Intelligence in the Second World War* (4 vols.; London, 1979-90), 2, 655-57.

23. Churchill, 2, 12; John Ehrman, *Grand Strategy,* vol. 6 (London, 1956), 324; Alan Bullock, *Ernest Bevin* vol. 2 (London, 1967), 108.

24. Dill to Brooke, 26 Aug. 1943, Alanbrooke Papers, 7/2/3, KCL. For a fully documented exploration of these themes see Alex Danchev, "The Central Direction of War, 1940-1941," in John Sweetman, ed., *Sword and Mace* (London, 1986), 57-58; and "Dilly-Dally, or Having the Last Word," *Journal of Contemporary History* 22 (1987), 21-44.

25. Jacob to Marder, n.d. [1966], Roskill Papers, 7/219, Churchill College, Cambridge. Other interesting analyses include Ronald Lewin, *Churchill as Warlord* (London, 1973), and Basil Liddell Hart, "The Military Strategist," in *Churchill: Four Faces and the Man* (London, 1969), 155-202.

26. Tinged with racism, the usual Anglo-Saxon assumptions about the Italians need some re-examination. See Lucio Ceva, "The North African Campaign," *Journal of Strategic Studies* 13 (1990), 84-104; James J. Sadkovich, "Understanding Defeat," *Journal of Contemporary History* 24 (1989), 27-61.

27. Dykes's diary of this period is printed in Alex Danchev, ed., *Establishing the Anglo-American Alliance* (London, 1990).

28. See Alex Danchev, "Being Friends: the Combined Chiefs of Staff and the Making of Allied Strategy in the Second World War," in Lawrence Freedman, *et al.*, eds., *War, Strategy and International Politics* (Oxford, 1992).

29. Anthony Powell, *The Military Philosophers* (London, 1968), 53-54, 183. On the Anglo-American consequences see Danchev, *Special Relationship,* 38-47, 122-24.

30. Bryant 1 and 2. See also Bryant's epilogue to David Fraser, *Alanbrooke* (London, 1982), 540-63.

31. *Ibid.*, especially the judicious summation on 525-39. For other assessments see Basil Liddell Hart, "Western War Strategy," *RUSI Journal* CV (1960), 52-61; and Brian Bond, "Alanbrooke and Britain's Mediterranean Strategy," in Freedman, *International Politics*.

32. The exact figures tend to vary in the literature. I have relied on the calculations in the hefty statistical appendix to John Ellis, *Brute Force* (London, 1990). See the instructive tables 35 and 36. SLEDGEHAMMER was not expected to dislodge the Germans in France but to divert some German forces from the Russian front where Axis forces threatened to break through.

33. Churchill minute, 5 July 1942, quoted in Gilbert, *Winston S. Churchill: Road to Victory, 1941-1945* (London: 1986), 143; *Diaries of Sir Alexander Cadogan*, David Dilks, ed. (New York, 1972), 8 July 1942, 461.

34. Dykes diary, 11 January 1942, printed in Danchev, *Establishing the Alliance*, 88; Fraser, *Alanbrooke*, 534.

35. The British record is in PREM 3/76A/12, circulated as WP(42)373, 23 August 1942, CAB 66/28, PRO; paraphrased in Churchill, 4, 430-35; extensively quoted in Gilbert, *Road to Victory*, 174-82. Churchill and Roosevelt habitually referred to "Uncle Joe" (or "UJ") in their more uninhibited exchanges.

36. Churchill to Eden, 5 July 1941, quoted in John Keegan, *The Second World War* (London: 1990), 312; Gilbert, *Road to Victory*, 173.

37. Churchill to Roosevelt, 22 September and 18 November 1942, in Kimball, *Churchill & Roosevelt*, 1, 602-4; 2, 10-15; WP(42)483, "Policy for the Conduct of the War," 24 Oct. 1942, CAB 66/30, PRO.

38. Michael Howard, *The Mediterranean Strategy in the Second World War* (London, 1968), 34. See also "The Mediterranean in British Strategy in the Second World War" (1969), reprinted in Howard, *Studies in War and Peace* (London, 1970), 122-40.

39. Dill to Wavell, 25 November 1942, Wavell papers, privately held.

40. "Why should we crawl up the leg like a harvest bug, from the ankle upwards? Let us rather strike at the knee." Churchill minute, 13 July 1943, quoted in Gilbert, *Road to Victory*, 442.

41. Howard, *Mediterranean Strategy*, 2.

42. Kimball, *Churchill & Roosevelt*, 1, 294-308. The COS response, "Note on the sequence of events in the offensive against Germany" (20 December), and the PM's spirited rejoinder (21 December) are in PREM 3/499/2, PRO. See also Gilbert, *Road to Victory*, 9-13, 20-22.

43. See Churchill, 3, 572-74. On Churchill's writing "for the book" see Philip Mason, *A Shaft of Sunlight* (London, 1978), 171.

44. "The Atlantic Front," para. 12, in Kimball, *Churchill & Roosevelt,* 1, 298.

45. Haig diary, 28 March 1915, quoted in John Terraine, *Douglas Haig* (London, 1963), 67, 135, 482. For a commentary on the interpretation of this pronouncement see Alex Danchev, "Haig Revisited," *RUSI Journal* 135 (1990), 71-74.

46. "1943," paras. 1-3, 5, 7, 9, in Kimball, *Churchill & Roosevelt,* 1, 301-4.

47. "The Atlantic Front," para. 4 in Kimball, *Churchill & Roosevelt,* 1, 295; CR 8, Record of a Meeting of the Chiefs of Staff, 18 December 1941, PREM 3/458/2, PRO. "Closing the Ring" is also the title of Churchill, 5, covering the period June 1943-June 1944.

48. Quoted in *Grand Strategy,* 3, 343. Apparently drafted by Brigadier Dykes and Captain Charles Lambe RN. See Dykes diary, 16 and 19 December 1941, printed in Danchev, *Establishing the Alliance,* 74-75.

49. Bryant, 1, 28.

50. The two papers are printed in *Grand Strategy,* 3, 345-48 and 669-72; a textual comparison is made on 358. See paras. 12 and 13 respectively. The American designation for *WW1* was ABC-4/CS1. "The Bible" was Dill's expression: JSM 342, Dill to COS, 8 August 1942, CAB 105/39; Dill to Marshall, 8 August 1942, AIR 8/1075, PRO.

51. Churchill to COS, 21 December 1941, PREM 3/499/2, PRO; "1943," para. 3; British paper, para. 16; *WW1,* para. 17.

52. Joseph Heller, *Catch-22* (London, 1964).

53. See the unusually forthright official history, Sir Charles Webster and Noble Frankland, *The Strategic Air Offensive against Germany* (4 vols. London, 1961). See also the scrupulous re-examinations in Ellis, 165-226; and Martin Middlebrook, *The Berlin Raids* (London, 1990).

54. "Hannibal", *Encyclopaedia Britannica* (London, 1950 ed.), 11, 155. See, in general, Nigel Bagnell, *The Punic Wars* (London, 1990).

55. Lord Brookeborough (his nephew), quoted in Fraser, *Alanbrooke,* 538.

56. Brooke diary, 20 June 1942, quoted in Bryant, 1, 403; Dykes diary, 20 June 1942, printed in Danchev, *Establishing the Alliance,* 158-59. See also Fraser, *Alanbrooke,* 257-60.

57. Alanbrooke notes, quoted in Bryant, 1, 530. Cf. the diary, 30 November, 11 December 1942, *ibid.,* 528-29, 534-35.

58. Fraser, *Alanbrooke,* 268.

59. Brooke to Dill (unsent draft), 16 December 1942, WO 193/146, PRO.

60. Brooke diary, 19 and 25 October, 1 November 1943, quoted in Bryant, 2, 55, 56, 59; notes, 3A/X/828, Alanbrooke Papers, KCL.

61. Bryant tries strenuously to defend Brooke, 1, 361, 429, 537-38, 551, 636. Fraser, *Alanbrooke,* is more dispassionate, if a shade ambiguous, 240-70, especially 258.

62. Howard, *Mediterranean Strategy,* 54. The terminology is Kent Roberts Greenfield's. See Richard M. Leighton, "OVERLORD Revisited," *American Historical Review* LXVIII (1963), 919-37.

63. Brooke diary, 24 November 1943, quoted in Bryant, 2, 82. OVERLORD succeeded ROUNDUP as the codeword for the invasion of North West Europe.

64. Noel Annan, *Our Age* (London, 1990), 358.

65. Churchill at the Mansion House, 10 November 1942, printed in *Churchill Speaks,* 809-11.

66. The parable of the donkey exists in several versions. The original appears to have been related by Churchill to Lady Asquith. See her interview with Kenneth Harris in *The Listener,* 17 August 1967.

67. Churchill at 1st plenary meeting, 28 November 1943, CAB 99/25, PRO.

■ ■ ■

2

The Soviet Union: The Direct Strategy

Oleg A. Rzheshevsky

Soviet strategy during World War II cannot be analyzed in chronological or topical isolation. Strategy is often determined long before the actual outbreak of hostilities and heavily influenced by a host of nonmilitary as well as military factors, most notably politics, the general alignment of forces, the internal situation within a nation, and international affairs in general. The development of Soviet strategy was influenced first and foremost by international events during the 1930s, most importantly the coming to power of the Nazis in Germany, their desire to gain "living space" at the expense of the Soviet Union, and their rapprochement for this purpose with militarist Japan. These events brought the European and Asian borders of the USSR under unprecedented threat. Strengthening the nation's defenses and preparing both the country and its armed forces for a direct struggle on the Eurasian continent thus became the main task of Soviet strategy during the 1930s. Simultaneously, however, Soviet policy also attempted to avoid war, to find allies, and to divide its enemies.

These efforts were largely unsuccessful. Internationally the antagonism between the social and state systems of the western democracies on the one hand and communist Russia on the other prevented the emergence of an effective coalition during the 1930s capable of preventing war or containing the Axis threat. Inside the USSR, groundless mass purges and other lawless actions on the part of Stalin simultaneously weakened the energetic efforts to strengthen the country's defenses. Consequently a still-unprepared Soviet Union had to face a massive invasion in June of 1941 from a Germany tremendously strengthened by its previous conquests.

In this regard the Soviet wartime experience differed dramatically from the American and British experiences, and Soviet strategic options were much more limited than those available to its allies. Indeed, the only viable strategy after the German invasion was one of direct, desperate, and costly defense, followed by an equally direct and costly series of counter-offensives. Acceptance and implementation of such a strategy was unavoidable. Whether it had to involve such enormous casualties, however, is questionable.

Throughout the 1930s, Soviet policy had aimed at avoiding war by setting up a collective security system against German and Japanese aggression based on regional defense agreements, as illustrated by the Soviet-French and the Soviet-Czechoslovak treaties of mutual assistance signed during this time period and energetic Soviet actions in the League of Nations. Yet it is also clear that the Soviet government did not take advantage of every opportunity to promote collective action. For example, the initiative of French Premier Leon Blum, who had planned to visit the Soviet Union for talks with Stalin, was not realized in 1936. Nevertheless, overall Soviet policy continued to promote the concept of collective action until the 1938 Czechoslovak crisis and Munich conference, when France's failure to fulfill its commitment to protect the Czechoslovak state forced the USSR to drastically revise its policies. The Soviet-British-French talks of March-August 1939 marked the last effort at collective security, and their failure led to the Soviet-German Non-Aggression Pact of 1939.

The failure of the 1939 Soviet-British-French talks in Moscow flowed from many factors. These include not only the Western democracies' prior appeasement policy and perceived desire to shift the German military threat from their own countries to the Soviet Union, but also Stalin's repressions within the USSR and British-French fears of any leftist alternative that might arise in their countries as had happened in Spain. These fears were heightened by the Soviet leaders' double-dealing policies, as the Comintern remained oriented toward world revolution while the Soviet government promoted collective security. Clearly, the Western leaders were constantly apprehensive of a possible Soviet-German rapprochement.

Mutual distrust played a major role in the failure to come to any military agreement that could have aided the Czechs in 1938—or the Poles in 1939. A brief account of the Moscow talks prepared by the Soviet delegation on 26 August 1939, after they had failed and the Soviet-German Non-Aggression Pact had been signed, noted in this regard that

> the passage of the Soviet armed forces through the territory of Poland and Rumania [in case of German aggression] is a military axiom. And if the French and British sides have made a big deal of this issue, calling for a protracted study, there is every ground to question their desire for effective military cooperation with the

> USSR. That is why the responsibility for the disruption of the talks rests entirely with the French and British side.[1]

So an anti-Hitler coalition was not formed in 1939 and, consequently, all attempts to prevent World War II proved futile.

In signing the Non-Aggression Pact of 23 August 1939, the Soviet government took into consideration the consequences of Poland's inevitable defeat by Germany and deemed it necessary, in the national interests of the state, to extend its western borders and thus prevent the *Wehrmacht*'s deployment in close proximity to the country's vital centers. This objective was guaranteed, according to calculations in the Kremlin, by the "the spheres of influence" division of Eastern Europe stipulated in the additional secret protocol to the pact (its contents and the very fact of its signing were acknowledged in the Soviet Union only in 1990).

After Germany had overrun Poland and World War II had broken out, the Soviet Union, taking advantage of its agreement with Germany, moved its troops into Poland's eastern regions as well as Lithuania, Latvia, Estonia, Bessarabia, and Northern Bukovina, thus incorporating these territories into the USSR (except for North Bukovina, they had belonged to Russia up to 1918), with the support of certain elements of the local population.[2] The desire to fortify the Soviet northwestern border and provide guarantees for the defense of Leningrad and Murmansk led to the severe "winter war" against Finland (December 1939-March 1940), and Soviet exclusion from the League of Nations.

Discussion about who profited most from the German-Soviet agreements is highly hypothetical. By June 1941, Germany had managed to create optimal conditions for its attack against the USSR. Yet the USSR had gained almost a two-year respite to expand its frontiers and fortify its defenses, and had signed a treaty of neutrality with Japan that would prove vitally important in the initial and most difficult period of the Great Patriotic War. When that war broke out, priority in Japan's military designs was given to a southward thrust, which would eventually culminate in the seizure of the Pacific possessions of the United States and other Western countries. Units of Soviet Far Eastern forces could thus be sent to the Soviet-German front from the first days of the war.

Stalin's propagandistic praises of "the German army's victories" in Poland and abusive attacks against Britain (which, after France's defeat, held out against German aggression single-handedly for over a year) are now condemned. However, in spite of such statements and mutual assurances of friendship, Soviet-German relations at that time were marked by steadily growing and insoluble tensions. These were rooted in Hitler's continued preoccupation with and preparations for an attack against the USSR.

Conquest of the USSR had always been Hitler's primary objective, although Germany's 1939 Polish campaign and, later, those in Northern and Western Europe, temporarily shifted German attention to other areas. But even then Hitler never renounced the idea of war against the USSR. Plans for such a war were stepped up after the defeat of France, since the Nazi leaders then believed they had consolidated their rear and were in possession of sufficient resources to launch such a campaign. On 18 December 1940, Hitler signed Directive No. 21, code-named BARBAROSSA, which set out the general concept of warfare against the USSR.

The Blitzkrieg, or lightning war, theory formed the strategic core of the BARBAROSSA plan: the Soviet Union was to be crushed by a sudden blow in a matter of five months at most, even before the end of the campaign against Britain. Leningrad, Moscow, the Central Industrial Region, and the Donets Coal Basin were regarded as the main strategic objectives.

Germany would not be alone in her attack on the USSR. The 1940 German-Italian-Japanese tripartite pact, an aggressive military coalition signed by their satellites as well as the three powers, would be invoked against the USSR in 1941. Although Japan did not attack the USSR, Italy, Rumania, Finland, and Hungary did. Furthermore, the governments of Bulgaria and the "independent" Slovak and Croatian states, as well as those of Vichy France, Spain, Portugal, and Turkey, cooperated with Nazi Germany. Hitler also made effective use of the economic and manpower resources of the 12 European countries he had by then occupied. Moreover, the economic assets of neutral countries such as Sweden and Switzerland, which were in many respects subordinated to his interests, were also available to Germany.

The Nazi leaders were so confident of success in their BARBAROSSA plan that approximately in the spring of 1941 they started working out the details of additional designs for world domination. As they rode in their special staff trains they drew up diagrams for the direction of future strikes that circled the globe. Hitler's instructions were described in a 17 February 1941 entry to the service diary of the *Wehrmacht* Supreme Command (OKW). Proceeding from these instructions, the OKW Staff started drawing up plans for future *Wehrmacht* operations in the late autumn of 1941 and the winter of 1941-1942. These plans were set out in the draft Directive No. 32, dated 11 June 1941, which dealt with preparations for the period after the realization of BARBAROSSA and was sent to the commands of the ground forces (OKH), air forces (OKL), and the navy (OKM).[3] Even in the autumn of 1941 they planned to conquer Afghanistan, Iran, Iraq, Egypt, the Suez Canal area, and later India, where the German troops were to join forces with the Japanese army. The Nazi leadership planned, by making use of Spain and Portugal, to seize Gibraltar, cut off Great Britain from its raw material sources, and besiege the British Isles. Building on Directive No. 32, as this and other documents testify, the Nazis intended, after the defeat of the USSR and settlement of "the British problem," to invade the American continent jointly with Japan.

The lightning victory over the USSR, the aggressors believed, would pave the way to world domination. They did not have serious doubts about the successful outcome of their *Blitzkrieg.* As Nazi General G. Blumentritt wrote prior to a meeting of the Supreme Command of the German ground forces scheduled for 9 May 1941:

> The history of all wars waged with the participation of Russians shows that the Russian soldier is staunch, undemanding, can stand bad weather and fears neither blood nor losses. That's why all battles—from those fought by Friedrich the Great to World War I—were extremely bloody. In spite of those traits of the troops, the Russian Empire had never won victories. At present we have great numerical superiority. . . . Our troops have far superior combat experience than the Russians. . . . We shall have to fight fierce battles for 8-14 days and after this we won't have to wait long for successes.[4]

The German attack on the Soviet Union was not totally unexpected, and did not find the USSR totally unprepared. With the mounting threat of war, the country, army, and people as a whole had persistently been making preparations for defense. The rapid industrial development of the national economy served as a basis for priority development of the nation's military potential. The material requirements of the army and the navy were met not only by defense enterprises but also by many civilian industries, which had been steadily involved in military production ever since the 1930s. At the same time, additional defense enterprises were also being set up in the country's eastern regions to duplicate those situated in the west of the country.

The most formidable problem the USSR faced at this time was overcoming the significant gap between its industry and Germany's, which was superior both qualitatively and quantitatively. Two key areas of qualitative difference were machine tools and effective utilization of raw materials. Quantitatively, Germany, together with the countries it occupied, produced twice as much steel, cast iron, cement, and energy as the USSR.

The Soviet leadership concentrated its prewar efforts on promotion of military production. Slowly but steadily the USSR overcame the quantitative gap and in late 1940–early 1941 even outstripped Germany in the output of such major weapons as aircraft, tanks, guns, and mortars. In some types of military hardware, such as rockets, artillery, and tanks, it went ahead of the enemy qualitatively and retained this advantage throughout the war. Overall, however, the USSR failed to close the gap in scientific and technological development, despite the efforts and achievements of Soviet scientists and designers. Consequently many Soviet armaments were inferior to the German ones in terms of tactical and technical properties. This was especially true in regard to military aircraft. The gap was also great in firearms, especially submachine guns, in antiaircraft guns, and most of all in radio communications. The impact of this qualitative gap was also felt in the Soviet Navy.

The size of the Red Army and the Navy was considerably increased between 1939 and 1941, from 1.9 million to 4.9 million. However, this rapid growth was not matched by a sufficient increase in the production of arms, ammunition, means of communication, and motor transport. This was particularly true in regard to tank units and antiaircraft defenses. Thus, on the eve of war, the newly created Soviet tank and mechanized units lacked 12,500 medium and heavy tanks, 43,000 tractors, and 300,000 motor vehicles needed to reach full strength.[5] Consequently the combat capacity of the mechanized corps of the western military districts, which were the first to bear the brunt of the enemy's main blow, was very low.

The Soviet Union was also weakened by the failure of the political and military leadership to draw up a realistic war plan before June of 1941. Was it necessary to strike a preemptive blow at the enemy? If not, where and what would be the defense lines, and how should the troops act in case of a sudden attack and major enemy offensive? These cardinal problems of grand strategy, on which an effective rebuff to an attacker and the destinies of millions of Soviet people hinged, had not been adequately addressed or solved. The concept of a possible retreat beyond the weakened fortification lines on the old western frontier, and the issue of the subsequent defense line, were as yet in the initial stages of elaboration. And it took quite a long time to draw appropriate conclusions from the results of the 1939-40 war against Finland, which had laid bare Soviet strategic and political miscalculations as well as major shortcomings in combat training and logistical support.

Soviet leaders thought they would have extensive time to solve these problems because they expected the war in the West to be protracted. The defeat of the Anglo-French armies in the course of a 44-day campaign in the summer of 1940 came as a complete surprise in strategic terms, tipping the balance of forces significantly in favor of the Germans. There was no time to be lost in the country's defense preparations. The military events in the West, particularly the mass-scale engagement of tanks and air forces in combat operations, called for a radical review of many ironclad strategic and tactical principles, as well as extensive efforts to provide a larger supply of new combat hardware and means of transportation. It also called for psychological preparation of officers and men for war under far more difficult conditions than had occurred in Mongolia and Finland.[6]

Lacking the necessary time and resources, and burdened by numerous miscalculations, the country's political leadership did not cope adequately with any of the outstanding problems. Indeed, throughout the spring of 1941, increasing signs of disarray as well as concern had been evident in the actions of Stalin and his entourage. In May 1941, for example, the General Staff drew up a draft plan for dealing a preemptive blow against the German forces then concentrating on the Soviet border, to be followed by the overrunning of Poland and Eastern Prussia.[7] On 21 June, however, one day before the outbreak of war, the Political Bureau of the Soviet Communist Party Central Committee (CPSU CC) adopted a different plan for the deployment of the second echelon of troops largely in the Dnieper area. This decision reflected growing doubts as to the Soviet troops' ability to deal a successful blow against the aggressor and transfer operations to enemy territory in line with existing Soviet military doctrine. New, alternative strategies were thus only beginning to take shape shortly before the zero hour.

Numerous additional factors further complicated the task of strengthening the country's defenses. Germany had started orienting its economy to the output of the latest combat material well in advance of the Soviet Union. It had also captured the armaments of over 200 divisions of the armies of the European countries it had conquered. In France alone this included 4,930 tanks and armored personnel carriers, 3,000 aircraft, and sufficient motor transport to supply 92 German divisions. The *Wehrmacht* also had two years' experience in war to draw upon, and its professional training was superior to that of the Red Army. Equally important, groundless accusations and purges of the leading cadres of the Soviet armed forces, as well as leaders of the economy and military industry, had considerably undermined efforts to strengthen the country's defenses and led to havoc in the sphere of personnel—especially in the top echelons of military leadership. Furthermore, gross miscalculations occurred in the operative deployment of the first strategic echelon of troops as to the timing of a possible German attack and the probable direction of the main blow.

"It is now an open secret," Admiral of the Fleet of the Soviet Union Nikolai Kuznetsov pointed out in his recently divulged reminiscences, "that when analyzing the first days and hours of the war, we can see that, apart from errors on the part of the head of government, gross mistakes were also made by us, the military."[8] Overestimation of the potential of the Soviet troops and underestimation of that of the enemy in particular had far-reaching negative consequences. On 28 December 1940, General of the Army Dmitrii Pavlov, the commander of the Western Special Military District whose troops would receive the *Wehrmacht*'s main blow, had observed that a Soviet tank corps would be able to cope with the task of smashing one-to-two tank or four-to-five German infantry divisions. On 13 January 1941, General of the Army Kirill Meretskov, head of the General Staff, made the following statement at a meeting in the Kremlin with the top commanding and political officers of the armed forces:

> In drawing up the (Ustav) Manual, we proceeded from the idea that our division is far stronger than that of the Nazi army and that in the hand-to-hand fighting it would certainly smash the German division. And in defense operations our division would rebuff an attack by two-to-three enemy divisions. On the offensive, one and a half Soviet divisions would break the defenses of an enemy division.[9]

In this context, delays occurred in deploying and bringing to combat readiness the troops needed to cover any retreat. Combined with the subsequent forced shift to an unprepared defensive strategy and the crushing effect of the sudden mighty blow by the *Wehrmacht,* this naturally put the army in the field in a critical situation.

Such difficulties notwithstanding, the morale of the public and the army was on the whole very high. Most of the Soviet people and the servicemen of the armed forces were proud of their country, being largely unaware of the groundless repressions and concentration camps. They remained loyal to the party and firmly believed in the inevitable defeat of the enemy "by a mighty blow with little blood." Prewar propaganda and most works in literature and the arts had emphasized the high potential of the people and army—a potential based on patriotism, friendship among the various Soviet nationalities, and conviction of the superiority of socialism as an economic and political system. Strict state, ideological, and military discipline contributed to this.

Although all realized that a military conflict was inevitable, the timing of the attack came as a surprise to most of the army and public. The troops of western military districts had not been brought into combat readiness in hopes that Germany would continue to observe the Non-Aggression Pact—hopes based on the misconception that it would be impossible for Germany to fight on two fronts. The Soviet political leadership's consequent calculations that the USSR would not be involved in war until 1942 proved incorrect. So did its belief that a German attack could be postponed by diplomatic actions and denials, such as the January 10 protocol which transferred territory to the USSR in the Suvalki region for $7 million in gold, the well-known 14 June TASS statement that war rumors were groundless, and the 21 June Soviet agreement to supply Germany with grain via Rumania. Inadequate intelligence assessments were also an important factor, as they failed to see through the Nazi disinformation campaign designed to insure strategic surprise.

However, it is also obvious that on the eve of the war the alignment of forces in the world gave grounds for real prospects of alliance between the USSR, Great Britain, and the United States in their fight against the aggressive bloc. Intensive British-Soviet and Soviet-American talks had been taking place since 1939, and although only limited progress had been reached by June of 1941, they contributed to the eventual realization of those prospects after the German attack.[10]

In the early hours of Sunday, 22 June 1941, Nazi Germany and its Allies dealt a blow of massive force against the Soviet Union. The Germans had 190 divisions, some 3,000 tanks, over 43,000 guns and mortars, about 5,000 warplanes and up to 200 warships. In the enemy's first echelon 103 divisions were engaged. Thus began the struggle that would go on for 1,418 days and nights, not counting the military operations against Japan in August-September 1945.

Nazi Germany's war against the USSR was of a special nature. The Nazis strove not only to capture Soviet territory but also to destroy the Soviet social system and to exterminate whole nationalities that were proclaimed "subhuman." British historian Alan Bullock has written that even taking into account the fact that in any war of this scale cruelties were inevitable on both sides, the scale of inhuman actions by the German side was enormous—the direct consequence of Hitler's racist convictions:

> In Hitler's view, Germans were not only superior to the peoples of Eastern Europe, but the gap which separated them from Slavs, even more widely from Jews, was based not on cultural differences, the product of different historical experiences, but upon inherited biological differences. They were creatures of a different kind, not members of the human race at all—'subhuman' in the case of the Slavs; in the case of the Jews, parasites who preyed upon and destroyed human beings.[11]

The Soviet Union was to be divided and eliminated, with four German provinces (*Reichkommissariate*) to be set up in its place. Moscow, Leningrad, Kiev, and a number of other cities were to be razed to the ground, and large portions of the population exterminated. Racial goals, hatred of the Soviet Socialist system, and the predatory designs of the Nazi aggressors were thus reflected in policy as well as the strategy and methods of warfare.

The BARBAROSSA plan provided for sudden, mighty blows by large tank and mechanized units, supported by the air forces. The aim was to separate, encircle, and exterminate the main forces of the Red Army deployed in the western part of the USSR, and subsequently to advance into the country's central regions so as to occupy Soviet territory up to the Archangelsk-Kuibishev-Astrakhan line.

Three army groups were assigned different components of this task. The Northern group, commanded by Field Marshal General W. Leeb, incorporated the Sixteenth and Eighteenth field armies and the Fourth Tank Group, a total of 29 divisions deployed in Eastern Prussia and supported by the 1st air fleet. Its goal was to crush Soviet troops in the Baltic area and capture Baltic seaports, including Leningrad and Krondtstadt, thus cutting the Soviet Navy from its ground bases. The Center group, commanded by Field Marshal General F. Bock and concentrated in the direction of Moscow, included the 4th and 9th field armies and the 2nd and 3rd tank groups, a total of 50 divisions and two brigades supported by the 2nd air fleet. Its goal was to break the Soviet front facing it, encircle and exterminate Red Army troops in Byelorussia, and continue its offensive on Moscow. The Southern group was deployed in the direction of Kiev under the command of Field Marshal General G. Rundstedt. It included the 6th, 11th, and 17th German field armies, the 3rd and 4th Rumanian field armies, the 1st tank group and a Hungarian corps, for a total of 57 divisions and 13 brigades supported by German and Rumanian air forces. Its task was to eliminate the Soviet troops in the area of the right bank of the Dnieper in the Ukraine, advance to the Dnieper, and develop further its eastward offensive.

In addition to these three army groups, the German, Norwegian, and two Finnish armies were deployed in Norway and Finland—a total of 21 divisions and three brigades—supported by the Fifth German Air Fleet and the Finnish air forces. The Germans' goal was to capture Murmansk and Polyarny, while the Finnish troops were to act jointly with the North group of armies in capturing Leningrad.

Opposing these forces in the western border military districts were 170 Soviet divisions (103 rifle, 40 tank, 20 motorized, and 7 cavalry) and two brigades, a total of 2,680,000 officers and men, 37,500 guns and mortars (without 50mm guns), 1,475 tanks of new designs (KV and T-34) and 1,540 warplanes of new designs. The Red Army possessed overall superiority in the number of tanks and warplanes. Command organization was transformed from military districts on 22-25 June 1941, into the following fronts: the northern, commanded by Colonel General M. Popov; the northwestern, commanded by Colonel General F. Kuznetsov; the western, commanded by General of the Army D. Pavlov; the southwestern, commanded by Colonel-General M. Kirponos; and the southern, commanded by General of the Army I. Tyulenev. Soviet maritime borders were covered by the Northern Fleet under Rear Admiral A. Golovko, the Baltic Fleet commanded by Vice-Admiral V. Tributs, and the Black Sea Fleet under Vice-Admiral F. Oktyabrsky.

On 22 June Soviet border guards and the advance units of the covering troops, as well as the antiaircraft defense units of the army and the navy, bore the brunt of the enemy's first blows. Many border units were completely destroyed. Military operations on the Soviet-Finnish border were launched on 29 June and on the Soviet-Rumanian border on 1 July 1941. Many units of the Soviet air forces were either eliminated or knocked out of action at their airfields, which made it possible for the Germans to dominate the air. Troops sent to cover withdrawals sustained great losses. Counterattacks by the Soviet troops in the Shauliai and Grodno directions were unsuccessful. A counterblow by the units of the southwestern front and a major tank battle did prevent the Germans from breaking through to Kiev on the southern front. On the whole, however, despite stubborn resistance, the covering forces proved unable to stop the German offensive in the border area in all three directions. Furthermore, prewar assessments had incorrectly regarded a southwestern thrust (south of Polesye, in Byelorussia) as the most dangerous. Actually, the enemy aimed the main blow at Smolensk and Moscow, which made it possible for Nazi troops to surround the Soviet troops, deployed in the area of Lvov and Bielostok, in deep pincers.

As a result of their victories in these border battles, German troops rapidly advanced some 400-450 kilometers in the northwestern direction, 450-600 kilometers in the western direction, and 300-350 kilometers in the southwestern direction. In the process they captured Latvia, Lithuania, part of Estonia and the Ukraine, almost the whole of Byelorussia and Moldavia, and the western portions of the Russian Federation. By August they were at the far approaches to Leningrad and were threatening to seize Smolensk and Kiev. The Soviet Union was in mortal danger.

From a strategic viewpoint, the situation was similar to what had happened in Western Europe in 1940, although in that case events had taken an irreversible turn. It was also similar to the rapid Japanese advance that would come later, in late 1941-early 1942, in the Pacific.

Every effort was made to rebuff the invaders. The Directive of the USSR Council of People's Commissars and the CPSU CC, dated 29 June 1941, outlined a program of emergency measures. "All for the front, all for the victory" was its main idea, later expressed in Stalin's broadcast address of 3 July 1941. Stalin sought to rally confidence by stating his conviction that the Soviet peoples' just struggle for the freedom of their Motherland would be crowned by the defeat of the aggressor and would "merge with the movement of the peoples of Europe and America for their independence and democratic freedom."[12]

On 23 June, the Staff of the Chief Command (after 10 July, Staff of the High Command and after 8 August, Staff of the Supreme Command, which will be hereafter referred to as the Supreme Command) was set up as the supreme body for strategic guidance of the armed forces. On 23 June, the State Defense Committee (SDC) was formed, which became the supreme body of state power. Stalin was first appointed chairman of the SDC and later, on 8 August, supreme commander of the Soviet armed forces.

Meanwhile, the Red Army was retreating. On 10 July, the Battle of Leningrad broke out, which drew considerable Nazi forces and the Finnish army. In the Battle of Smolensk (10 July-10 September 1941), which was fought on a front 60 kilometers deep and 250 wide, the enemy offensive was checked, though only for a short period. The forces of the southwestern and southern fronts, after fierce fighting, left first Kiev and Odessa and later the western areas of the Donets Coal Basin. The enemy invaded the Crimea and approached close to Sevastopol, and in November captured Rostov-on-Don.

The Soviet Union sustained vast losses in these operations. In the first months of hostilities Soviet casualties totaled about 1 million, of which 700,000 were taken prisoner. In September, 650,000 more were taken prisoner in the course of battles on the left bank of the Dnieper, in the Ukraine. And that was not all. In the period from June to December 1941 3,138,000 officers and men of the Red Army and Navy were either dead, captured, or missing. Also 1,336,000 were wounded, shell-shocked, or fell ill. Over 6 million units of firearms, 20,000 tanks and assault weapons, 100,000 guns and mortars, and 10,000 warplanes were destroyed. By December 1941 the *Wehrmacht* had occupied over 1.5 million square kilometers of Soviet territory with a prewar population of 74.5 million.[13]

The Supreme Command, the commands of the fronts, military leaders, and commanding officers of various ranks all underwent on-the-job training in waging warfare under the most difficult conditions. As would be expected they made the almost inevitable mistakes. Yet their staunch defense of Brest, Liepae, Tallin, Mogilev, Leningrad, Kiev, Odessa, Sevastopol, and Smolensk, among many others, all contributed to thwarting Hitler's plans for quick victory. In early October, however, the Nazis broke through the front in the main, Moscow direction: Five Soviet armies were encircled in the area of Vyazma. On 20 October, a state of siege was proclaimed in Moscow and the neighboring districts. The situation reached its most critical point after the enemy had forced the Moscow-Volga Canal and broken through to Khimki, now a Moscow city region.

However, in those fierce battles the strength and heroism of the general public, both at the front and in the rear, proved of increasing importance. Thousands upon thousands joined the ranks of the large-scale partisan movement and underground resistance struggle organized in the regions occupied by the enemy. In 1941, 41 partisan detachments and 377 subversive groups operated in the Moscow Region alone. Furthermore, with every passing month the Soviet troops' resistance grew more and more stubborn, and their skill in defensive operations steadily improved. This prevented the enemy from carrying through its rapid offensive according to its strategic plans. Whereas in the first three weeks of hostilities the Nazi troops had advanced on average 20-30 kilometers daily, from mid-July to 7 August all the Germans could manage was to advance some 3.5-8.5 kilometers daily. In the period from 8 August to mid-September this progress became even slower. During the offensive against Moscow in October-November they advanced at a rate of 2.5-3 kilometers daily. By September, German forces had been stopped near Leningrad, and in November their southern advance was stopped at Rostov-on-Don. On 29 November that city was temporarily liberated by the Red Army. Then in early December the Germans cut short their offensive on Moscow.

The Soviet armed forces inflicted vast losses on the enemy in the course of these defensive operations. The *Wehrmacht*'s ground forces alone suffered 750,000 killed, wounded, and missing. In the period from 22 June to 10 November the *Luftwaffe* lost 5,180 warplanes. Thus, the German plan of concluding the Soviet campaign before wintertime was thwarted.

In early December the Red Army launched a strategic counteroffensive near Moscow, signaling the first major defeat for the *Wehrmacht*. The effect went far beyond the Soviet borders, helping to convince both the Americans and the British that effective support to the USSR would not be wasted. "I want to tell you once more," U.S. president Franklin D. Roosevelt informed Stalin on 16 December, "about the genuine enthusiasm throughout the United States for the success of your armies in the defense of your great nation."[14]

The Battle of Moscow was fought for about seven months, from 30 September 1941 to 20 April 1942, and constituted the largest battle of World War II: It included over 3 million soldiers and civilians, up to 3,000 tanks, over 2,000 warplanes, and over 2,200 guns and mortars. On 5 December 1941, when the Soviet counteroffensive was launched, the *Wehrmacht* had before Moscow 40 percent more guns and 60 percent more tanks at its disposal than the Red Army, although the latter had 60 percent more aircraft.

The Soviet Supreme Command and the General Staff had concentrated reserves in strict secrecy and organized concerted action. A devastating blow was dealt to the Nazi Center group of armies in the course of the counteroffensive near Moscow, where 38 Nazi divisions were defeated. German tank units, which were designed to play the main part in the war, sustained especially great losses. By late March 1942, the Germans had only 140 combat worthy tanks remaining in the 16 tank divisions deployed on the eastern front, and the casualties sustained by their Center group of armies totalled 796,000.[15]

As for the air war, in October-November 1941, only about 100 German bombers out of the more than 4,000 that took part in air raids on Moscow managed to break through to the city. Nevertheless strategic domination of the air on the eastern front remained in German hands.

In assessing the ensuing strategic situation, the Soviet Supreme Command decided in early January 1942 to launch a general and direct counteroffensive all along the front rather than continue to focus on one area. Near Leningrad the thrust was to be in the western and southwestern directions, with the goal of breaking the German siege of the city. Simultaneously, Soviet forces on the western and southwestern fronts were set the task of encircling and crushing the center group of German armies in front of Moscow, and with launching an offensive near Tikhvin and Rostov-on-Don. That was easier said than done, however, for this strategy was not supported by the necessary forces, in particular by motorized units. Consequently, these operations achieved only limited success and resulted in major Soviet losses.

The greatest advances occurred in the center. Troops of the western front under the command of General of the Army Georgi Zhukov, the Kalinin front under Colonel General Ivan Konev, and the Bryansk front under Colonel General Ykov Cherevichenko drove the enemy 350 kilometers away from Moscow, liberated the Moscow Region and a number of others, and eliminated the danger of encirclement and the capture of Tula south of Moscow. By late April 1942, the losses of the *Wehrmacht*'s ground forces at the Soviet-German front in killed, wounded, and missing totaled over 1.5 million servicemen. The Germans also lost 4,000 assault weapons and about 7,000 aircraft before the end of 1942, which exceeded by 400 percent their total losses in Poland, Northwestern and Western Europe, and the Balkans. Consequently the Nazi command had to dispatch to the East 30 more divisions to reinforce its groupings.

From the first days of the war—in the border battles of the tragic summer of 1941, in the Battle of Moscow, and along the thousand-kilometer Soviet-German front that stretched from the Baltic to the Black Sea—Soviet armed forces had been locked in a life-and-death struggle against Germany and its allies for the freedom not only of their country but also of the entire world. Roosevelt clearly recognized this fact, as well as the subsequent need for Anglo-American military support. "Your people and mine demand the establishment of a front to draw off pressure on the Russians," he wrote Churchill on 3 April 1942, "and these peoples are wise enough to see that the Russians are today killing more Germans and destroying more equipment than you and I put together. Even if full success is not attained, the *big* objective will be."[16]

The failure and defeat of the German *Blitzkrieg* in the Battle of Moscow was a turning point in the course of war. However, the strategic initiative had been snatched from the *Wehrmacht* only temporarily. In the summer of 1942, having concentrated over 90 divisions on the southern front, the Germans launched another strategic offensive with the aim of capturing the areas of the Caucasus, the Don, the Kuban, and the lower Volga reaches. The goals of this offensive were to ensure supplies of oil and food, crush the resisting Red Army troops, and thereby pave the way for dealing a final blow in the Moscow direction.

Three factors contributed to the *Wehrmacht*'s initial success. First, the Supreme Command in general and Stalin in particular miscalculated the main thrust of the *Wehrmacht*'s offensive, seeing Moscow as once again the immediate objective, and underestimated the enemy's striking capacity. Secondly, the Soviet Union had been further weakened by setbacks in the operations carried out in the Crimea and in the area of Kharkov in May 1942, and by the fall of Sevastopol on 4 July after eight months of desperate defense. Thirdly, the absence of an Anglo-American Second Front in Europe, despite Roosevelt's 3 April comments as to its importance, allowed the *Wehrmacht* to concentrate, almost exclusively, on the Soviet front once again.

In mid-July the *Wehrmacht*'s strike forces broke through to the Don's large curve and its lower reaches. As a result the great Battle of Stalingrad (17 June 1942-2 February 1943) and the Battle of the Caucasus (25 July 1942-9 October 1943) were launched simultaneously.

The Battle of Stalingrad, which involved on both sides over 2 million servicemen by mid-November 1942, was fought on a vast area of 100,000 square kilometers for 200 days. The Germans began their offensive with the Sixth Field and units of the Fourth Tank Armies, assisted by Rumanian, Hungarian, and Italian troops, and soon approached the Stalingrad suburbs. In the Battle of the Caucasus the Nazi troops also attained major success at first. The joint forces of the Soviet North Caucasian front commanded by Marshal of the Soviet Union Mikhail Budenny and the Transcaucasian front commanded by General of the Army Ivan Tyulenev were far inferior to the group of German armies commanded by Field Marshal Wilhelm List in manpower and military hardware, especially in tanks (the Germans had 80 percent more tanks and 70 percent more aircraft). As a result Soviet troops had to retreat to the main Caucasian Range spurs, but there in fierce battles they managed to stop the enemy's advance before the end of 1942. They were supported from the sea by the Black Sea Fleet and the Azov and Caspian Military flotillas.

During the period of the Red Army's retreat in the summer of 1942, the Soviet Union's southern and Far Eastern borders were under increasing threat. Turkey was engaged in preparations for war against the USSR. In talks with German ambassador von Papen in the summer of 1942, the Turkish government demanded a share in the occupation of Soviet territory containing Turkish-speaking populations, with buffer states to be set up there later.

A similar threat came from Japanese Premier Hideki Tojo in August 1942 when he informed the German embassy in Tokyo about a proposed sudden attack on Vladivostok by Japanese troops and a diversionary operation to be launched in the Blagoveshchensk area with the aim of expanding the Japanese "sphere of influence" up to Lake Baikal.[17] Although neither Turkey nor Japan did enter the war, the threats influenced Soviet strategy by requiring the disposition of forces on the southern and Far Eastern borders of the country.

On 28 July 1942 Stalin signed Order of the Day No. 227—described as the "not a step back" order, which was exactly its meaning. The first order of this kind, Order No. 270, had been signed on 16 August 1941, during the Red Army's retreat. Its goal had been to end displays of cowardice and cases of desertion. Protective detachments were to be placed "right in the rear of unstable divisions, to shoot dead on the spot panic mongers and cowards. . . ." Both orders are often regarded as inhuman and even criminal. At the time, however, those repressive measures were designed to put an end to retreat, which on many occasions took on the appearance of blind panic and could have brought about disastrous consequences.[18]

The assault on Stalingrad turned into a giant slaughter, and it was far from clear that the Soviet troops would be able to hold the city. By mid-November casualties at Stalingrad were in excess of 300,000. Marshal of the Soviet Union Alexander Vasilevsky, who was responsible for coordination of the fronts' operations and stayed in Stalingrad, later told this author about the most memorable days of that battle:

> On the first day, August 23, 1942, the entire city was in flames after the fierce bombing raids by the enemy. On a certain stretch, enemy units broke through to the Volga bank. It was difficult to keep calm in that situation. All of us realized that the fall of Stalingrad would be fraught with mortal danger to the country. All our reserves were sent to the city's northern suburb. A message was addressed to the population. That was the day of greatest tension. Another memorable day was November 23, 1942, three months after the Nazis had broken through to the Volga. On that day the units of the Stalingrad and the Southwestern fronts joined their forces at Sovetsky hamlet, thus closing the pincers and encircling the 330,000 strong enemy grouping.[19]

It should be emphasized that by this time the greatest enemy forces of the war were concentrated along the Soviet-German front: 226 divisions (over 6.2 million officers and men), about 52,000 guns and mortars, over 5,000 tanks and assault weapons, and 3,500 warplanes.

The Soviet counteroffensive at Stalingrad was launched on 19 November. The troops of the southwestern front under Lieutenant General Nikolai Vatutin, the Stalingrad front under Colonel General Andrei Yeremenko, and the Don front under Lieutenant General Konstantin Rokossovsky, surrounded the German Sixth Army in Stalingrad via a pincer movement and rebuffed an attempt by the German Don group of armies, under Commander Field Marshal General Erich Manstein, to break the Soviet encirclement and save the Nazi troops caught in the Stalingrad "kettle." What remained of the Sixth Army (91,000 men and officers), with its commander, Field Marshal General Friedrich von Paulus, were captured by 2 February 1943. The overall losses of the Red Army (killed, wounded, and missing) exceeded 1.1 million, while those of the Germans and their allies approximated 800,000. That costly victory by the Red Army was a major factor behind changes in the military-political situation on the international scene in favor of the coalition against Hitler and gave a mighty impetus to the development of resistance movements in Europe and Asia against the invaders. "Politically," wrote John Erickson, a prominent British historian, "Stalingrad was a victory full of long-term potency, a slow-burning fuse which worked its way through the subsequent history of the war both on the Eastern front and at large."[20]

At that time the Battle of Caucasus was also in its final stages. An offensive was launched there in January 1943 by the forces of the southern front commanded by Colonel General Andrei Yeremenko and the North Caucasian front commanded by Lieutenant General Ivan Maslennikov, as well as the Black Sea group of troops of the Transcaucasian front commanded by Lieutenant General Ivan Petrov and supported by the forces of the Eighth, Fourth, and Fifth Air Armies and the Black Sea Fleet. Having liberated the Northern Caucasus, the Soviet troops approached the Taman Peninsula in early May 1943. However, they met with stubborn German resistance on the "blue line" that ran from the Azov Sea to Novorossiisk, and took up defensive positions.

In the north, the siege of Leningrad had been partially broken during January of 1943 on a narrow strip along the southern bank of Lake Ladoga. Meanwhile, in the center, successful operations made it possible to launch an offensive later in the Kharkov and Kursk directions. After the Soviet air forces had won battles in the Kuban area in April-June 1943, their strategic domination in the air over the whole Soviet-German front was ensured. Combined with Stalingrad and the Caucasus, these early 1943 victories allowed Soviet forces to assume the strategic offensive in the second half of 1943.

Since March 1943, the Supreme Command had been elaborating a plan for this strategic offensive, which aimed at crushing the main forces of the South and North groups of German armies and breaking of their defenses on the front from Smolensk to the Black Sea. The Soviet troops were supposed to be the first to go on the offensive. However, in mid-April intelligence revealed that the *Wehrmacht* command was planning to launch an offensive at Kursk. The Soviet Supreme Command decided to bleed the German forces white by large-scale defensive operations before going on the counteroffensive. With strategic initiative to rely upon, the stronger side would thus intentionally open hostilities with defensive operations, not an offensive. Further developments proved that this idea was correct, although very risky.

It should be pointed out that in spite of the intelligence information, the Soviet side was far from convinced that the Germans would be the first to launch an offensive. General G. Antipenko, commander of the rear of the central front, later described in this way the situation that prevailed at the front's command post: "The rear was oriented on defensive, not offensive, version. So frankly speaking, I was extremely anxious while waiting for the German offensive to be launched. The silence seemed to last for eternity."[21]

To carry out its offensive at Kursk, code-named CITADEL, the Germans concentrated major forces under the command of their most experienced military leaders: 50 divisions, including 16 tank and motorized divisions of the Center group of armies commanded by Field Marshal General E. Manstein and the Southern group of armies commanded by Field Marshal G. Kluge. Their strike groups included a total of over 900,000 officers and men, about 10,000 guns and mortars, up to 2,700 tanks and assault weapons, and over 2,000 warplanes. Special importance in the German plans was attached to massive use of the latest combat matériel—Tiger and Panther tanks, Ferdinand assault weapons, and warplanes of the latest designs (Fokke/Wolfe-190 fighters and Heinkel bombers).

The Nazi offensive against the northern and southern lines of the Kursk bulge on 5 July 1943, was met by staunch Soviet defensive operations. The attack from the north was stopped four days later, although the Germans had by then managed to drive a wedge in the Soviet defense lines 10 to 20 kilometers deep, while the attack from the south had advanced 35 kilometers. On 12 July, having inflicted considerable losses on the enemy, Soviet troops began their counteroffensive. On that day the greatest head-on tank battle in the history of war was fought in the area of Prokhorovka railway station, involving up to 1,200 tanks and self-propelled guns on both sides. In developing their offensive, the Soviet ground forces, supported by massive strikes from the air by the Second and Seventeenth Air Armies and long-range aviation, drove 140-150 kilometers westward by 23 August and liberated Orel, Belgorod, and Kharkov.

The *Wehrmacht*'s losses in the Battle of Kursk were enormous: 30 picked divisions, including 7 tank divisions; more than 500,000 officers and men; 1,500 tanks; over 3,700 warplanes; and 3,000 guns. Thus, the balance of forces on the front had been sharply tipped in favor of the Red Army. This paved the way for its ensuing general strategic offensive, which was launched in the summer of 1943 near Kursk and Orel. That offensive went on relentlessly until the spring of 1944, when the German invaders were completely driven out of Southern Russia.[22]

The victories in the Battle of Kursk, and later in the Battle of Dnieper, marked the final stages in the radical change in the course of the war which occurred globally in 1943. The Anglo-American defeat of the Italian-German troops in North Africa by May 1943, their ensuing invasion of Sicily and Italy, and the stabilization of the situation in the Atlantic and the Pacific as well as in Southeast Asia, testified to the fact that a turning point was taking shape in the course of World War II.

The *Wehrmacht*'s offensive strategy thus proved a complete failure. In the autumn of 1943, Soviet troops continued their advance on the Taman Peninsula, which was completely liberated on 9 October. By early 1944, the Red Army faced the strategic task of completely driving the Nazi invaders from Soviet soil and then dealing them mortal blows in Eastern Europe and Germany.

The result was a series of major Soviet offensives and victories in the spring and summer of 1944. First, a large-scale offensive along the 1,300- to 1,400-kilometer front line in the Ukraine in December 1943-April 1944 resulted in the defeat of the opposing enemy grouping, and the advance of the Red Army to the Soviet State frontier in the Carpathian foothills and into Rumanian territory. Then in the summer of 1944, the Battle of Leningrad was finally won.

The struggle for Leningrad, running from 10 July 1941 to 9 August 1944, was the most protracted campaign of the war and claimed the greatest number of casualties: some 800,000 civilians died of starvation or were killed as a result of bombing raids and shelling in the course of the 900-day-long siege of the city. In developing their 1944 offensive, the forces of the Leningrad front under General of the Army Leonid Govorov, the Volkhov front under General of the Army Kirill Meretskov, and the 2nd Baltic front under General of the Army Markian Popov, supported by the navy and partisan detachments, lifted the siege of the city, liberated almost all of the Leningrad Region and part of the Kalinin Region, and came to the approaches of the Latvian border.

The 1944 offensive gradually assumed new strategic objectives as the Red Army crossed the Soviet western frontier on 27 March 1944 and entered the territory of the East European countries. By that time operations by the Red Army were being coordinated with actions by the Western Allies, who were making preparations for opening the Second Front in Europe.

Soviet offensives were also timed to support the establishment of that Second Front. Blows dealt by the Red Army in the course of the winter-spring campaign of 1944 forced the German Command to redeploy

40 new divisions to the East. At the time of the Allied landing in Normandy on 6 June 1944, about two-thirds of the most combat worthy *Wehrmacht* divisions were concentrated in the East and unavailable to counter the Anglo-American forces. Then on 10 June, the Red Army launched the offensive it had promised the Anglo-Americans against the Nazi troops in the north. That was quickly followed by the Byelorussian offensive on 23 June, the most extensive offensive of the war, beginning on a stretch of over 300 kilometers of the front line—an offensive that eventually extended along 1,000 kilometers in its final stage. Over 4 million troops, about 62,000 guns and mortars, over 7,500 tanks and self-propelled mounts, and over 7,100 warplanes took part in this campaign on both sides. By the end of August, Soviet troops had almost completely crushed the Center group of armies, including the additional forces sent from Germany, Norway, and Italy. As a result the Red Army liberated Byelorussia and part of Lithuania and Latvia, entered the territory of Poland, and approached the borders of Eastern Prussia, having forced the rivers Narev and Vistula. The Lvov-Sandomierz, the Yassy-Kishinev, and the Baltic operations, as well as shuttle bombing raids by the U.S. warplanes on Nazi positions in the summer of 1944 (with Ukrainian airfields used as landing sites), were new events important to the successes of the Allied forces at Normandy and during their subsequent operations in France and the low countries, as well as to the Soviet-German front itself. By this time the Soviet offensive extended from the Baltic to the Carpathians. In the autumn of 1944 the enemy was almost completely driven from Soviet territory and Soviet troops entered Bulgaria, Yugoslavia, Czechoslovakia, Hungary, and Norway.

The efficiency of these coordinated blows at Germany, which found itself squeezed in between two fronts, was further increased in the winter of 1944-1945. As a result of the German counteroffensive in the Ardennes, the Allied troops were in a difficult position. The Red Army, at the request of Churchill to Stalin, began a new offensive along the entire front prior to its scheduled date.[23] This helped to thwart the *Wehrmacht*'s Ardennes offensive and ushered in the final stage of the war against Germany and its allies in Europe.

By mid-April 1945, the main Nazi groupings had been defeated at the Soviet-German front, and almost the whole of Poland, Hungary, western Czechoslovakia, and Austria with its capital Vienna had been liberated. Now the final and decisive battle was to be fought—the Battle of Berlin.

At that time the Nazi Reich was completely isolated from the rest of the world. The only way out of this quandary, the Nazis believed, was to sign a separate peace treaty with the United States and Great Britain. Proceeding from the argument that "it would be better to turn over Berlin to the Anglo-Saxons than let the Russians capture it," they decided to maintain defensive operations on the eastern front at any cost and do their best to destroy the anti-Hitler coalition. The Nazis' wishful hopes for a split among the Allies were heightened by the news of Franklin Roosevelt's untimely death on 12 April—but to no avail.

The issue of Berlin had another important dimension. On 1 April 1945, Marshal Zhukov (commander of the 1st Byelorussian front) and Marshal Konev (commander of the 1st Ukrainian front) had been summoned to Moscow, where Stalin asked them the following question: "Now, who will take Berlin, we or the Allies?"[24] On the same day Churchill sent a message to Roosevelt that included an expression of concern about the same issue:

> The Russian armies will, no doubt, overrun all Austria and enter Vienna. If they also take Berlin, will not their impression be that they have been the overwhelming contributor to our common victory be unduly imprinted in their minds and may this not lead them into a mood which may raise grave and formidable difficulties in the future? I therefore consider that from political standpoint we should march as far East into Germany as possible and should Berlin be in our grasp, we should certainly take it. This also appears sound on military grounds.[25]

Once again, concern was clearly being expressed for the political considerations on which strategic decisions hinged.

The German command concentrated a million-strong army, 10,400 guns and mortars, 1,500 tanks and assault weapons, and 3,300 warplanes in the Berlin area. Those forces were incorporated in the Vistula group of armies under Colonel General G. Heinrichi and the Center group under Field Marshal General F. Schoerner. On the Soviet side, troops of three fronts were involved in the Battle of Berlin: the 1st Byelorussian, the 1st Ukrainian, and the 2nd Byelorussian commanded by Marshal of the Soviet Union Rokossovsky, as well as four air armies, part of the Baltic Fleet forces, long-range aviation and antiaircraft defense forces, and the Dnieper Military Flotilla. Also participating in the operation were the First and Second Armies of the Polish Forces under generals Z. Berling and K. Swierczewski. On 25 April, the troops of the above-mentioned Soviet fronts joined forces in the area of Potsdam and encircled a 300,000-strong German grouping, which held fortified positions in Berlin. At the same time Soviet troops advanced to the Elbe, and on 25 April, the troops of Soviet Fifth Guards Army under the command of General A. Zhadov met with the First U.S. Army of General C. Hodges. What remained of the Nazi armies were separated and isolated.

In the small hours of 1 May, the Soviet Banner of Victory was hoisted over the Reichstag. On 2 May, the German garrison in Berlin capitulated. On 9 May, Soviet troops liberated the Czech capital of Prague (an uprising against the Nazi invaders had taken place there shortly before). Thus the war came to a close in Europe.

Late in the evening of 8 May, representatives of the Allied Supreme Commands, Soviet marshals whose troops had assaulted Berlin, and journalists gathered in the assembly hall of the Karlshorst military engineering academy, decorated for the occasion with the state flags of the USSR, the United States, Great Britain, and France. Seated at the table were Marshal of the Soviet Union and Deputy Supreme Commander-in-Chief of the Soviet Armed Forces Georgi Zhukov, Air Chief Marshal of the British RAF and Deputy Supreme Commander-in-Chief of the Allied Expeditionary Forces Sir Arthur Tedder, and Supreme Commander of the French Army General J. M. G. de Lattre de Tassigny. Representatives of the German Supreme Command were led into the hall. Point 1 of the Act of Military Surrender ran as follows: "We, the undersigned, acting on behalf of the German Supreme Command, accept an unconditional surrender of all our ground, naval, and air forces, as well as all forces that are now under the German Command, to the Supreme Command of the Red Army and at the same time to the Supreme Command of the Allied Expeditionary force."[26] The criminal Nazi regime had finally toppled.

On 8 August 1945, the USSR joined the hostilities against Japan, thus fulfilling the commitments made by Stalin in 1943 to enter that war after termination of the fight against Germany. The leaflet-address issued by the political administration of the 1st Far Eastern front illustrates how the move was explained to the common soldiers of the Red Army:

> Comrade Soldiers! Servicemen of the Land of Soviets! You have entered Manchurian territory with a great and noble goal of crushing the Japanese aggressors' forces and stamping out the second hotbed of the world war in order to bring closer the date of restoring peace throughout the world and ensure the security of our Far Eastern borders. You have come here also to assist the Chinese people in liberating their country from Japanese slavery. Be equal to the great liberation mission you've been entrusted with by your country and keep unblemished the honor of Soviet soldiers![27]

On 14 August, the Japanese Kwantung Army was defeated by the joint blows of the forces of the Zabaikalsky front commanded by Marshal of the Soviet Union Rodion Malinovsky, the 1st Far Eastern front commanded by Marshal of the Soviet Union Kirill Meretskov, the 2nd Far Eastern front commanded by General of the Army Maxim Purkayev, and the Mongolian People's Revolutionary Army commanded by Marshal of the Mongolian People's Republic Horlogin Choibalsan, in cooperation with the Pacific Fleet commanded by Admiral Ivan Yumashev and the Amur Military Flotilla. By advancing 600-800 kilometers, the Red Army liberated Northern China, North Korea, and also Southern Sakhalin and the Kuriles. This campaign was conducted under the general military guidance of the Chief Command of the Soviet Troops in the Far East and Marshal of the Soviet Union Alexander Vasilevsky.

In the West these events were for a long time virtually unknown. In the first fundamental study of them in the West, Colonel D. Glantz of the U.S. Command and General Staff College remarked: "Our neglect of Soviet operations in World War II, in general—and in Manchuria, in particular—testifies not only to our apathy toward history and the past in general, but also to our particular blindness to the Soviet experience. That blindness, born of the biases we bring to the study of World War II, is a dangerous phenomenon. How can we learn if we refuse to see the lessons of the our past for our future?"[28]

The atomic bombs dropped by U.S. bombers on Hiroshima and Nagasaki on 6 and 9 August were, of course, pivotal in the Japanese decision to surrender. Indeed, as the heaviest burden in the war against Germany had been borne by the Soviet Union, so the heaviest burden in defeating Japan had been carried by the United States, with Great Britain making a major contribution in both conflicts. Yet the 1945 offensive launched by the Red Army was another important factor that forced the Japanese government to admit the country's final defeat. On 2 September 1945, an Instrument of Surrender of Japan was signed on board the American battleship *Missouri,* thus bringing to an end World War II.

The war, especially in its initial stage, brought to light serious miscalculations by the Soviet military and political leadership and revealed its insufficient competence in military strategy and operative skill as well as in control of forces. At the same time, the Soviet armed forces eventually proved their superiority over the military skill of the *Wehrmacht,* which was then the most powerful military machine in the world with the best professional training to its credit.

The staunchness of Soviet soldiers and the mass-scale partisan movement that operated in the enemy's rear were widely recognized at the time. The names of outstanding Soviet generals such as Georgi Zhukov, Alexander Vasilevsky, and Konstantin Rokossovsky, among others, were quite famous. American General Douglas MacArthur, who was commander of the U.S. forces in the Far East, in 1942 highly praised the military operations conducted by the Soviet Armed Forces. He noted that in his life he had taken part in several wars, observed some others, and had thoroughly studied the campaigns fought by outstanding military leaders of the past. Never, however, had he witnessed such effective resistance offered to such a powerful enemy, resistance followed by a counteroffensive that drove the enemy back to its own territory. The scale and brilliance of effort, he said, made it the greatest military achievement in all history.[29]

The Soviet Supreme Command learned much the hard way in the first two years of hostilities. After the turning point in the course of the war, the Supreme Command acted with increasing confidence. In 1943-44 major offensive operations were conducted successively at various sections of the Soviet-German front, and in 1945 it became possible to launch strategic offensive operations simultaneously along the entire front line. This called for concerted action by the fronts and armies and a thorough organization of their material and technical supplies. That was especially important, for the size and the rate of the offensive operations were constantly growing. In the winter of 1941-1942, offensive operations were conducted in an area of 70-100 kilometers, whereas a year later, at Stalingrad, the respective figure was 140-160 kilometers. In the course of the Vistula-Oder Operation in 1945, offensive operations at the front were conducted in an area of up to 500 kilometers. Accumulated experience and greater military skill contributed to a considerable extent to the success of these military operations, carried out jointly by the ground, naval, and air forces.[30]

Fierce battles were being fought at the Soviet-German front until the last hour of hostilities, with rapid changes in the situation, which, naturally, called for rapid optimal decision making by the Soviet Command. Historians have yet to give an all-around assessment of the actions by the Soviet Command and headquarters, with due account of casualties not only on the Axis side but also among the Soviet troops, including the closing stage of the war. It is yet to be explained, for instance, whether it was appropriate to deal head-on blows on strongly fortified lines which resulted in great casualties among the Soviet troops, as was the case in the course of the offensive at the 1st Byelorussian front, at the Zeelow Heights in April 1945, and in the course of the Berlin Operation when 70-90 tanks, 90-210 guns and mortars, and 25-40 warplanes were destroyed every day. Soviet casualties in killed and wounded totalled 350,000 in that operation (of that number 101,961 were killed).

Studies of the Second World War, including studies of strategy, are now (in 1993) in progress in Russia, making use of numerous documents that were heretofore strictly classified. Many aspects of the war should be reviewed. A number of the former assessments have not stood the test of time and are being re-examined. There is no doubt that as a result of these new studies the tragedy suffered by the various national groups within the former Soviet Union as well as their exploits will assume a new dimension.

According to the latest estimate (study is still in progress) the overall losses of the Red Army and other units at the front were 11.4 million killed, mortally wounded, missing, or taken as prisoners of war (4 million were POWs). Those of the German army and its allies on the eastern front totaled 8.6 million, including 3.7 million POWs.[31] Such was the enormous price of the direct confrontation of the main forces of both countries on the battlefield. For the Red Army it could and should have been lower.

NOTES

1. Foreign Policy Archive of the Russian Federation (FPA RF). Fund 06, schedule 18, file 27/5, p. 75.

2. For more detailed information see *Documents on Relations of the USSR with Latvia, Lithuania and Estonia, August 1939-August 1940* (Moscow, 1990) [in Russian].

3. *Hitlers Weisungen für die Kriegfuhrung, 1939-1945* (Frankfurt a/M, 1962), 129-33.

4. Klaus Reinhardt, *Die Wende vor Moskau: Das Scheitern der Strategie Hitlers in Moskau Winter 1941/1942* (Stuttgart, 1972), 21.

5. Dmitrii Volkogonov. *I. V. Stalin: Political Imige,* book 2, part 1 (Moscow, 1989), 75 (in Russian).

6. In July-September 1939 severe fighting took place between joint Soviet-Mongolian and Japanese forces in the Khalkhin-Gol (Nomonhan) River region of Mongolia. The Japanese ground force (75,000 troops) and its air support were defeated.

7. Russian General Staff Archive (RGSA). Schedule 16, file 2951, p. 1115.

8. *Pravda,* 20 July 1991, "Kuznetsov's Reminiscences" [in Russian].

9. Yurii Peretscnev, "On Some Problems of the Preparation of the Country and Armed Forces to Repel the Fascist Aggression," in *Military-Historical Journal,* 4 (1988), 46 (in Russian).

10. Soviet ambassador K. Umansky and U.S. under-secretary of state Sumner Welles held more than 30 meetings in Washington during 1940-41. Although the results were limited and disappointing overall, they did include the opening of a U.S. consulate in Vladivostok and extension of the U.S.-Soviet trade agreement, which enabled the United States to become the USSR's second most important trading partner after Germany. The U.S. record of these meetings can be found in U.S. Department of State, *Foreign Relations of the United States* (Washington, D.C., 1958), *1940,* 3, 244-441, and *1941,* 1, 667-768. Recently released Soviet documents provide evidence that these meetings may have been more fruitful, at least from the Soviet point of view, than previously recognized; see Archives of the President of the Russian Federation. Fund 3, schedule 66, file 279, pp. 35-37, 146-156; Foreign Policy Archives of the Russian Federation (FPA RF), Fund 059, schedule 1, file 345/2361, pp. 86, 87, 215-25, 328-40 (Welles-Umansky talks).

11. Alan Bullock, *Hitler and Stalin: Parallel Lives* (London, 1991), 821.

12. Joseph Stalin. *On the Great Patriotic War* (Moscow, 1947), 16 (in Russian).

13. *History of the Second World War* vol. 5 (Moscow, 1974), 129 (in Russian).

14. *Correspondence Between the Chairman of the Council of Ministers of the USSR and the Presidents of the USA and the Prime Ministers of Great Britain During the Great Patriotic War of 1941-1943* (Moscow, 1957), 2, 18. For a recent evaluation of the impact of the battle of Moscow see *Zwei Wege Nach Moskau: Vom Hitler-Stalin-Pakt bis zum "Unternehmen*

Barbarossa," im Auftrag des Militärgeschichtlichen Forschungsamtes, ed. Bernd Wegner (München & Zürich, 1991).

15. *Die Wende vor Moskau,* 381.

16. Warren F. Kimball, ed., *Churchill & Roosevelt: The Complete Correspondence* (3 vols.; London, 1984), I, 441.

17. *History of the Second World War,* vol. 5 (Moscow, 1975), 103, 105 (in Russian).

18. For the complete text of the orders see: *The Great Patriotic War 1941-1945. Short Historical Guide* (Moscow, 1990), 423, 424, 435, 436 (in Russian).

19. As told to the author by Marshal Vasilevsky.

20. The Stalingrad casualties estimates are from Grigori Krivosheev, ed., *Secrets Are Opened: Losses of the Armed Forces of the USSR in Wars, Combat Actions and Military Conflicts, Statistical Study* (Moscow, 1993), 179, 182. The broad strategic impact of Stalingrad is discussed in John Erickson, *The Road to Berlin* (Boulder, Co., 1983), 43.

21. As told to the author by General Antipenko.

22. The scope of the Soviet victory was quickly apparent to its allies, as indicated in the U.S. Army publication, *The World at War, 1939-1944: A Brief History of World War II* (Washington, D.C., 1945), 244.

23. See *Stalin's Correspondence with Churchill and Attlee, 1941-1945* (New York, 1965), pp. 294-95 (docs. 383-85).

24. I. Konev, *Notes of the Commander of the Front* (Moscow, 1991), 373.

25. Kimball, *Churchill & Roosevelt,* 3, 605.

26. *History of the Great Patriotic War of the Soviet Union,* vol. 5 (Moscow, 1963), 351 (in Russian).

27. Russian Ministry of Defence Archives (RMDA). Fund 66, schedule 3191, file 1, p. 44.

28. David Glantz, *August Storm: The Soviet 1945 Strategic Offensive in Manchuria,* Leavenworth Papers No. 7 (February 1983), xv.

29. F. Shuman, *Soviet Politics at Home and Abroad* (New York, 1947), 432, 433.

30. The actions of the Soviet Navy, not discussed here, focused on submarine warfare. Thus, in 1941, the number of destroyed Soviet submarines was equal to that of sunken enemy warships, whereas in 1945 the ratio was 1:30.

31. Krivosheev, ed., *Secrets Are Opened,* 130, 131, 337, 391, 392. After the war, 1.8 million Soviet and 1.9 million German POWs returned home. Of those Soviet missing, 900,000 returned to units at the front. For German estimates see Wolfgang Michalka, ed., *Der Zweite Weltkrieg* (München, 1990), 862.

■ ■ ■

3

THE UNITED STATES: THE GLOBAL STRATEGY

Mark A. Stoler

World War II began with the United States possessing neither the means nor the desire to become a major belligerent. Its army of fewer than 200,000 ranked 18th in the world in size in 1939, while its economy was neither recovered from the Great Depression nor geared to war production. Politically the Neutrality Acts of 1935-37 remained in force, and public opinion polls showed a strong desire to remain aloof from the war.

All of this would change dramatically within the next six years as the United States became a belligerent, undertook one of the largest military mobilizations in history, and played a decisive role in the outcome of the war. By 1945 its armed forces had grown to nearly 12 million men and women whose wartime activities were so extensive that they would eventually require more than 100 volumes of official history to document.[1] An army of 8.2 million was the largest army in U.S. history, an army that had defeated Axis forces in North Africa, Italy, Western Europe, and the Pacific. Of these, 2.3 million, along with 159,000 aircraft, constituted the world's largest and most powerful air force, one which had destroyed Axis cities and now held sole possession of the awesome atomic bomb. A force of 3.4 million (including 484,000 marines) manned the largest and most powerful navy in history, a fleet of 1,200 warships as well as 50,000 supporting and landing craft that had destroyed Axis sea power and conducted a series of decisive amphibious operations across the globe. At home, the fully recovered and converted industrial base had almost doubled its output and was producing more than twice the Axis powers combined, thereby enabling the United States to supply its allies as well as its own forces with an unprecedented quantity of war matériel. By war's end this included 86,000 tanks, 120,000 artillery pieces, 14 million shoulder weapons, 2.4 million trucks and Jeeps, 207,000 aircraft, 82,000 landing craft and ships, and 3,300 merchants ships and tankers.[2]

The effort had been costly. More than 400,000 Americans had died (292,000 in combat), a figure larger than in any other U.S. conflict save the 1861-65 Civil War, and government spending had been greater than in all the preceding years of the republic combined. Yet the United States ended the war with fewer deaths than any other major belligerent, fought no major battles on or even near its own soil, and was the only power to emerge with an economy stronger than when the war had begun. By almost any standard the American military effort had been extraordinarily successful as well as extensive, and had left the United States as the world's dominant power.

Yet that effort came under intense criticism after the war for its supposed waste, high casualties, unnecessary duration, flawed strategy, and political naivete. Most of these criticisms centered on the American high command, especially President Franklin D. Roosevelt and his key military advisers and commanders. To parody Winston Churchill, never had so many accusations been leveled at so few for accomplishing so much.

To assess the validity of these criticisms one must first understand the goals of U.S. military operations in the war, the strategic means used to obtain these goals, and the reasons such means were selected. The basic goal of the U.S. effort was the total military defeat of the Axis powers, which were perceived as posing a mortal threat to the nation's physical security as well as its values and interests. The basic strategic means for obtaining this objective consisted of a massive and unprecedented military mobilization, in war matériel as well as manpower, to enable the United States to send extensive military supplies to its allies while simultaneously creating large air, naval, and ground forces for overseas military action. U.S. strategy had further stipulated that these forces be used in conjunction with those of its allies and concentrated in the Atlantic-European theater so as to defeat Germany first, after which they be redeployed to achieve victory over Japan. In all theaters they were to destroy the enemy capacity as well as will to resist, and to do so in the shortest possible time.

Although enunciated in basic form by military leaders before official U.S. entry into the war, this global strategy evolved over time rather than being fully asserted at any one moment. Furthermore, and contrary to the conclusions expressed by many critics, it resulted from a host of political as well as military factors. The most important of these were the armed services' strategic doctrines and rivalries, America's unique geographical position during the war, domestic politics and public opinion, civil-military relations, inter-Allied relations and the demands of coalition war, and wartime events. These factors also led to some major deviations from and modifications of stated American strategy after the United States became a formal belligerent in late 1941, most notably in terms of the Germany-first approach. Although officially reasserted on numerous occasions from 1942-45, that strategy was fundamentally altered in practice by the U.S. decision after Pearl Harbor to devote substantial resources to the war against Japan.

The roots of U.S. strategy can be traced back to the interwar years when the armed forces developed first a series of contingency "color" plans for war against individual powers and then, in 1938-39 when international events made these plans obsolete, a new series of "RAINBOW" plans to fight Germany, Italy, and Japan simultaneously rather than as individual "colors." Both sets of plans contained key assumptions and conclusions that would underlie U.S. strategy during World War II. Most fundamentally, virtually all of them called for military operations outside the continental United States, thereby illustrating a critical if seldom stated axiom of U.S. military thinking: Due to its unique geographical situation, the United States could and should fight its major battles overseas rather than on home soil. That would require not only transporting troops abroad but also amphibious landings against hostile forces, a complex and highly dangerous type of operation which the marines began to explore during the interwar years and which would become one of the most distinguishing characteristics of the U.S. military effort during the war.

Of equal importance, the earliest scenario to anticipate a multi-front global war against an Asian-European coalition, the ORANGE-RED plan for war against a Japan allied with England, called for a defensive posture in the Pacific so as to be able to concentrate first against the more powerful and dangerous as well as geographically closer European enemy in the Caribbean/Atlantic. Such concentration for defense of America's eastern and southern frontiers, when combined with the desire and ability to avoid battles on home soil, led logically to the idea of eventual offensive operations against the European enemy in the Atlantic theater. Later plans provided for such a possibility in RAINBOW 5, which called for a defensive effort in the Pacific and offensive operations against Germany should the United States find itself allied with Britain and France against the Axis. Within these conclusions lay the origins of America's Germany-first strategy during the war.[3]

For many years, however, political as well as military factors precluded the development of this strategy. RED ORANGE was an unlikely scenario that received little attention, while RAINBOW 5, the last plan in this series to be listed and ordered developed in 1939, implicitly constituted the least likely eventuality military planners thought they would face. Nor could they agree on a proper response to any other scenario. Facing growing Axis aggression worldwide and a gross imbalance between policy objectives and the very limited military means Congress was willing to appropriate, some interwar army planners pronounced the ORANGE plan against Japan unwinnable and urged both a retreat from overseas commitments and a return to their traditional mission of continental defense. Relying upon conceptions of national greatness posited by Alfred Thayer Mahan during the 1890s as well as their traditional overseas mission, navy planners disagreed vehemently and proposed an aggressive strategy and policy in the western Pacific as well as discussions with the British to see if a united front could be formed against Japan.[4]

Compounding this interservice conflict were bureaucratic struggles within the War and Navy departments and the rise of a new doctrine of strategic air power within an army air corps desirous of independent status and mission. Led by the flamboyant Colonel William "Billy" Mitchell, advocates of this new doctrine argued that independent air power organized in fleets of bombers could replace naval as well as ground forces and provide the United States with both effective defense and awesome offensive striking power. Such claims infuriated admirals as well as generals and further intensified the divisions within the interwar armed forces.

President Roosevelt at first did little to settle these disputes. Preoccupied with the Great Depression and his New Deal domestic program, and unwilling to challenge isolationist opinion within Congress, he provided the armed forces with little guidance and support until 1937-38, when the growing world crisis led him to endorse Anglo-American staff conversations, expansion of the navy and air forces, and creation of the RAINBOW plans. Then in 1939 he appointed new army and navy chiefs of staff, General George C. Marshall and Admiral Harold R. Stark, and began to work closely and directly with them on U.S. rearmament. But these limited moves failed to provide sufficient politico-military coordination or resolve the interservice disputes.

Hitler's stunning 1940 victories in Western Europe did. With France beaten and Britain on the verge of defeat, military logic dictated that the United States prepare for unilateral, continental, and hemispheric defense against Germany as outlined in RAINBOWs 1 and 4 and supported by army planners. Fear of Nazi infiltration of Latin America further reinforced this logic. A massive military buildup would be necessary even for such a limited effort, as well as for any possible overseas operations at a later date, and a frightened Congress therefore passed the first peacetime draft in U.S. history and provided funds for an unprecedented expansion of the armed forces. Such expansion would take much time, however, thereby reinforcing the desire to avoid overseas commitments for the time being.

Roosevelt disagreed. Apparently convinced before his military advisers that continued British survival was both possible and vital to U.S. security, he pressed for immediate military aid to Britain, even if it hindered the growth of the armed forces, and forced his reluctant military advisers to agree. During the summer of 1940 the president also replaced his secretaries of war and navy with two members of the opposition Republican party who shared his views, Henry L. Stimson and Frank Knox, and approved the sale of military equipment to England. In September he traded 50 of the U.S. Navy's overage destroyers for 99-year base leases on British islands in the Western hemisphere. Then in December he asked congress to make the United States the "arsenal of democracy" by giving him the power to lend or lease war matériel to any nation whose defense he deemed essential to U.S. security. Simultaneously he ordered the Pacific fleet to remain at Pearl Harbor in Hawaii, where he had first moved it as a temporary measure in the spring of 1940, in hopes it would deter Japan from further aggression.[5]

Fear of the consequences of such global dispersion and overcommitment galvanized Naval Chief Stark in the fall of 1940 into writing a clear statement of U.S. priorities that enunciated for the first time a U.S. global strategy for the war. Stark bluntly stated that Britain now constituted the first line of American defense and should therefore continue to receive material assistance, but that London could not defeat Germany alone and that the United States might eventually enter the war. In examining the strategic alternatives in such a scenario he rejected previous hemispheric and Pacific strategies, as well as the idea of merely sending maximum material assistance to anti-Axis allies, in favor of a fourth option. Labeled Plan "D" (or "Dog" in naval parlance), this alternative proposed an eventual U.S. land offensive in conjunction with Britain against Germany in the Atlantic/European theater, and a consequent defensive secondary effort in the Pacific. For the present, staff conversations with the British were to be initiated immediately and proceed on the basis of these conclusions.[6]

Roosevelt agreed, and while Congress debated Lend-Lease in early 1941 Anglo-American military planners secretly met in Washington to map out combined strategy in the event of U.S. entry into the war. ABC-1, the resulting document, affirmed Germany-first as their global strategy. So did the ensuing revision of RAINBOW 5, which now became the basic U.S. war plan.[7] Of equal importance was Congress's approval of Lend-Lease aid to Britain in March, Roosevelt's extension of such aid to China in May and the Soviet Union later in the year, his expansion of the hemispheric "security zone" in the Atlantic to include occupation of Greenland in April and Iceland in July, and congressional extension of the peacetime draft in August.

By mid-1941, months before official entry into the war, political as well as military factors had thus led the United States to enunciate the essential components of its global wartime strategy: material assistance to any nation fighting the Axis, simultaneous mobilization of large-scale forces for overseas campaigns, concentration of those forces in the Atlantic/ European theater for eventual offensive operations against Germany, and a defensive posture against Japan in the Pacific pending the outcome of the European conflict. In August the U.S. chiefs of staff discussed with their British counterparts possible implementation of this strategy during the first Churchill-Roosevelt summit conference off the coast of Newfoundland. In their September "Victory Program," military planners estimated the manpower and material necessary to implement it successfully.[8]

These preparations constituted an enormous achievement, and a sharp break with tradition. U.S. policy before previous wars had been, in the words of one historian, "first to declare, then to prepare."[9] Now, for the first time in its history, the United States had raised a large armed force via conscription before formal hostilities commenced, adopted an overall strategic plan in conjunction with a potential ally, and estimated its human and economic requirements. Yet U.S. mobilization was far from complete in 1941, and by the standards of the other belligerents it remained woefully unprepared for hostilities. Furthermore, the strategic agreements reached in 1941 masked deep Anglo-American, interservice, and civil-military disagreements that would surface in the ensuing months and years.

From the American perspective, British requests for naval support at Singapore violated the Germany-first strategy and suggested an attempt to manipulate U.S. forces into defending British postwar imperial interests. So did London's emphasis on an "indirect" strategic approach in the European theater centering on naval blockade, air bombardment, and limited operations in North Africa and the Mediterranean. "We cannot afford," U.S. military planners warned in this regard early in 1941, "nor do we need to entrust our national future to British direction. . . . Never absent from British minds are their postwar interests."[10] United States planners also attacked British strategy as a violation of the military principle of concentration of force. Citing the "almost invariable rule" that "only land armies can finally win wars," they responded with a reassertion of the "direct" strategic approach that had been the U.S. army's hallmark since the Civil War by arguing that Germany could be defeated only through an invasion of Europe and confrontation with the *Wehrmacht*. For this purpose army planners proposed the Victory Program creating a 215-division force of 8.75 million men, with a 195-group air force of 2 million, to be used for a massive continental assault by the summer of 1943.[11]

Roosevelt disagreed, for political as well as military reasons. As he told Stimson on 25 September, any proposal "that we must invade and crush Germany" would elicit "a very bad reaction" from a public still desirous of staying out of the war.[12] Furthermore, the president sympathized with Britain's indirect strategic approach and seemed to believe at this time that large-scale air and naval contributions from the United States might be sufficient to defeat Germany.

These problems remained unresolved as the United States entered the war—first via an undeclared naval conflict with German U-boats in the Atlantic; then officially when Japan on 7 December attacked and crippled the U.S. fleet at Pearl Harbor. Ensuing formal declarations of hostilities turned the preexisting wars in Europe and the Far East into a truly global conflict, one the United States would fight in a truly and uniquely global manner.

That became clear just a few weeks after Pearl Harbor at the Anglo-American ARCADIA conference in Washington. Despite the fact that war had formally begun for the United States with a devastating Japanese surprise attack in the Pacific, Roosevelt and his advisers quickly reaffirmed their commitment to the Germany-first strategy, Lend-Lease aid to Allied powers, and a collaborative military effort with England. To promote such an effort they agreed to the formation of the Anglo-American Combined Chiefs of Staff (CCS), unity of command in all theaters, global and theater priorities within the Europe-first approach, and a combined offensive in North Africa for 1942. Equally important was reaffirmation of the precedent Roosevelt and Churchill had established in August of meeting with each other and their military chiefs to determine combined strategy. Never before in the history of warfare had two nations agreed to such a meshing of their military efforts.[13]

These decisions had profound consequences for the U.S. military effort in the war. Unity of command fused not only Anglo-American but also U.S. army and navy forces under a single commander in each theater, thereby forcing a termination, albeit only partial, of the intense interservice rivalry and hostility that had marked U.S. military history. The ARCADIA decisions also resulted in the creation of a new and important U.S. military body, the Joint Chiefs of Staff (JCS). Composed by mid-1942 of Army Chief Marshall, new Navy Chief Admiral Ernest J. King, Army Air Chief General Henry H. Arnold, and Presidential Chief of Staff Admiral William D. Leahy, the JCS were organized so as to allow the U.S. service heads to meet their British counterparts on a parallel and equal basis within the CCS. Throughout the war these four individuals served as the supreme U.S. military command and Roosevelt's most important military advisers. So essential were their services that after the war their organization was perpetuated as the centerpiece of the U.S. military establishment.[14]

Of equal importance to the U.S. war effort were major army and navy reorganizations during March of 1942. In that month Admiral King replaced Stark as chief of naval operations while retaining his former position as commander-in-chief of the U.S. fleet, thereby giving the naval chief full operational control of forces for the first time. Simultaneously General Marshall, who Churchill would later label the "organizer of victory," drastically restructured the army general staff to support a global war effort and continued the process, begun in 1940-41, of massively expanding the army and preparing it for overseas combat. Of critical importance in this process were the organization and training of millions of draftees under General Lesley McNair, and the wholesale replacement of older army commanders with younger ones Marshall believed capable of conducting aggressive, independent, mobile warfare. Many of these new generals had served and trained under Marshall during the interwar years, especially during his 1927-32 tenure as assistant commandant of the army's Infantry School at Fort Benning, Georgia. Their overall wartime performance would be unsurpassed in U.S. military history.[15]

Along with these reorganizations came a clarification of the global responsibilities of the JCS when Roosevelt and Churchill agreed in March that the United States would direct the Pacific and Britain the Middle East and India theaters, while the Atlantic-European theater remained an area of combined and equal responsibility. This decision formalized and reinforced the Joint Chiefs' unilateral direction and control of the war against Japan, even though 12 other allied nations were also involved in that conflict, with the war against Germany remaining under combined direction and control.[16] It also recognized the U.S. obsession with the Pacific conflict. Despite the official recommitment to Germany first, Pearl Harbor and ensuing Japanese conquests led to a major modification of U.S. strategy and a much greater emphasis on the war against Japan than had originally been anticipated as the JCS sent all available reinforcements to the Far East in an effort to stem the Japanese tide.

By March of 1942 it was obvious this effort had not only failed but also further dispersed U.S. forces. Seeking to halt such diffusion, check naval and British plans for additional dispersions in the Pacific and North Africa, and provide the hard-pressed Soviets with the military assistance they had been demanding, Army Operations Division Chief General Dwight D. Eisenhower proposed in that month a strictly defensive effort in all theaters except the Atlantic so as to be able to concentrate U.S. and British forces in the United Kingdom for a cross-Channel invasion of Europe as soon as possible. As approved first by Marshall and then Roosevelt, all available Anglo-American forces were to begin immediate concentration in England (BOLERO) for a 48-division cross-Channel assault in the spring of 1943 (ROUNDUP) or a much smaller landing of 5-10 available divisions in the fall of 1942 if either the Germans were seriously weakened or the critical Soviet front appeared to be in danger of imminent collapse (SLEDGEHAMMER).[17]

London agreed to these proposals in early April. In May Soviet foreign minister Vyacheslav Molotov discussed them with Churchill and Roosevelt, and on 10 June a public communiqué stated that "full understanding" had been reached "with regard to the urgent tasks of creating a Second Front in Europe in 1942."[18] Actually no such understanding had been reached. Britain had agreed to U.S. plans primarily to preclude further Pacific dispersions, and in July rejected SLEDGEHAMMER on the grounds no 1942 landing could maintain itself or divert any German forces from the eastern front. As an alternative London suggested recommitment to the invasion of French North Africa in 1942, in conjunction with a renewed British offensive from Egypt against German-Italian forces in that theater.

The JCS vehemently opposed such a strategic shift, arguing it would provide no aid to the Soviets and would so disperse Allied forces as to postpone cross-Channel operations for at least two years; instead they proposed a threat to abandon the Germany-first strategy in favor of immediate offensive operations against Japan if Britain persisted in its opposition to SLEDGEHAMMER. This proposal echoed the cries for such a shift in strategy that had been emanating from U.S. Pacific commanders, naval planners, a public intent on immediate revenge for Pearl Harbor, and America's frightened Asian and Pacific allies. Roosevelt, however, angrily vetoed it as both militarily unsound and an immoral bluff. Intent upon preserving Germany-first and launching some offensive operation in the European theater in 1942 for the political purpose of mollifying and encouraging both the Soviets and U.S. public opinion, especially in light of his recent discussions with Molotov and the critical situation on the eastern front as well as the upcoming fall congressional elections, the president forced his reluctant Joint Chiefs to accede to operation TORCH for the invasion of North Africa.[19]

On no other issue during the war were Roosevelt and his military advisers so far apart, and on no other occasion did the president so clearly exercise his powers as commander-in-chief. As a result of his insistence Anglo-American forces under Eisenhower's overall command successfully landed in French North Africa on 8 November 1942. They did so too late to influence the congressional elections, however, and advanced too slowly to reach Tunisia before Axis forces retreating from their defeat at El Alamein. The year 1942 thus ended with Roosevelt's congressional majority diminished and Anglo-American forces besieging the reinforced Germans in the French Tunisia.

Despite Roosevelt's strong recommitment to the Germany-first approach with TORCH, most of America's 1942 deployments and battles were against the Japanese. This resulted not only from early efforts to contain Tokyo's advance, but also from a mid-1942 U.S. decision to launch limited counteroffensives in light of both the military situation in the Pacific and the strategic decisions being made for the European theater.

For approximately 100 days after Pearl Harbor, Japan faced little effective opposition and achieved all its objectives in the South Pacific. These included conquest of the Philippines, where General Douglas MacArthur led a continuing but doomed defense on the Bataan peninsula until ordered in February to abandon his post and proceed to Australia to take command of all Allied forces in this theater. On 6 May remaining U.S. forces on the Corregidor fortress in Manila Bay surrendered, thereby completing Japan's conquest of U.S. as well as British and Dutch possessions in the South Pacific. By this time Japanese forces were also invading New Guinea and the Solomon Islands in an effort to isolate Australia. Within the month, however, the U.S. Navy would succeed in checking this advance and irreparably crippling Japan's naval air arm in two critical engagements: the 3-8 May Battle of the Coral Sea, a tactical draw which temporarily halted further Japanese naval advances to the South; and the 4-6 June Battle of Midway, in which Japanese efforts to lure the remnants of the U.S. fleet into a final Mahanist battle of annihilation backfired when U.S. naval aircraft, making good use of cryptographic information from broken Japanese naval codes, surprised and sank four of Tokyo's aircraft carriers.

Both the navy and MacArthur sought to take advantage of these battles via immediate counteroffensive action. They were strongly supported by a public intent upon revenge for Pearl Harbor, and by the Australian, New Zealand, and Chinese governments. With the British withdrawing their support from SLEDGEHAMMER at this time, the JCS felt justified in sanctioning limited counteroffensives in early July. Naval/marine forces consequently retook the island of Guadalcanal in the Solomons on 8 August, while MacArthur's U.S.-Australian forces launched the Papuan campaign one month later along the northeastern coast of New Guinea. Japan responded furiously, and both offensives became long-term campaigns of attrition that ended only in early 1943. The Americans triumphed in both of these campaigns, but each had expanded and required forces far beyond what had originally been anticipated. Even TORCH did not compensate for this Pacific tilt.

The end of 1942 thus found the United States deploying more forces against Japan than Germany.[20] Although their counter-offensives in both the North African and Pacific theaters succeeded and helped to stem the Axis tide of 1942, U.S. forces remained widely dispersed and deployed in violation of its stated strategic priorities.

This situation improved somewhat in 1943 as U.S. forces in the Atlantic/European theater undertook a series of operations in conjunction with the British. These were peripheral, however, with cross-Channel operations postponed for another year. Although the Americans had called for an immediate return to BOLERO-ROUNDUP at the January Casablanca conference, they were outargued by the better-prepared British who insisted that the initiative must be retained in the Mediterranean and Germany severely weakened by additional peripheral operations prior to any cross-Channel attack. "We came, we listened, and we were conquered," was the bitter comment of one U.S. planner.[21] Reinforcing British arguments was the continued German presence in Tunisia and submarine challenge to Allied naval supremacy, the fact that crossing the Channel in 1943 would require halting Pacific as well as Mediterranean operations in progress, and the continued political need for quick offensive successes to mollify the Soviets and public opinion. Consequently the Americans acceded at Casablanca to an indirect strategy for 1943 focusing on defeating the Germans in the Atlantic, the Mediterranean and Tunisia, invading Sicily (HUSKY), and launching a combined strategic bombing campaign against Germany (POINTBLANK).

The most important but least-heralded of these campaigns was the one against German submarines. Effectively using numerous technological improvements, air power, and high-level cryptographic information from broken German military codes as well as the enormous U.S. shipbuilding capacity, Anglo-American forces had by mid-1943 won this crucial "Battle of the Atlantic." Simultaneously the U.S. Eighth Air Force began its strategic bombing campaign against German industrial targets, while U.S. ground forces in North Africa pressed eastward against the Axis armies within Tunisia in conjunction with a British thrust from the South. A February German counterattack at Kasserine Pass bloodied and humiliated the green American troops, but in May 1943 Anglo-American forces under Eisenhower's overall command finally broke through the Axis lines and captured 240,000 prisoners. In July, again under Eisenhower, they successfully invaded Sicily, which precipitated the overthrow of Mussolini, Italian surrender, and a decision to invade the mainland. On 9 September the U.S. Fifth Army under General Mark Clark landed at Salerno (AVALANCHE) and joined British forces that had landed farther south for a combined drive on Rome. Hitler sent reinforcements while rescuing Mussolini, however, and succeeded by October in halting Allied forces substantially south of Rome while inflicting heavy casualties.

The strategic bombing offensive from the United Kingdom met with equally mixed results in 1943 as air requirements for North African/Mediterranean operations delayed concentration in England and the Americans learned what the British already had through bitter experience—that "precision" bombing was not very precise and that unescorted bombers were easy targets for German fighters. The result was a series of disastrous losses in ineffective raids over Germany during the summer and fall. But whereas the British had responded to similar losses by shifting to area bombing at night, the Americans retained daylight raids on specific targets and sought to improve precision and defense via a host of technological and tactical innovations, the addition of large numbers of extended-range fighters, and the activation of the separate Fifteenth Air Force in Italy, which forced the Germans to defend against two separate bomber forces from opposite directions. Not until 1944, however, would these changes produce major results; by that time bomber forces had to be temporarily diverted to isolate the Normandy beachhead.

The 1943 American effort in the Atlantic/European theater remained limited not only because of continued postponement of cross-Channel for these peripheral operations, but also because of continued and expanded operations against Japan. Although the land battles on Pacific islands involved small numbers of combat troops by European standards, their nature and distance from the United States necessitated very large naval and logistical support services. Furthermore, their duration and high percentage of casualties required constant reinforcement at levels and for time periods not originally anticipated. Both the Guadalcanal and New Guinea campaigns had begun as extremely limited operations in the summer of 1942, for example, but then rapidly expanded and continued into 1943.

So did public and naval demands for additional offensive action against Japan. Both tended to view the Pacific campaign in the aftermath of Pearl Harbor as their private war of revenge that deserved greater emphasis. As Stimson informed Churchill in mid-year, "only by an intellectual effort" had the American people "been convinced that Germany was their most dangerous enemy and should be disposed of before Japan; . . . the enemy whom the American people really hated, if they hated anyone, was Japan which had dealt them a foul blow."[22]

Chinese demands for supplies and offensive operations to help reopen the Burma Road led to additional emphasis on the war against Japan. Although China remained a weak priority behind both the European and Pacific theaters, it could not be ignored without risking a collapse or separate peace whose consequences were greatly feared. Despite his military weakness and the lack of major action in his theater, Chiang Kai-shek's continued belligerency tied down more than half of Japan's army divisions and precluded Tokyo from successfully making the war an anticolonial and racial struggle of all Asians against Anglo-Americans. China was also perceived as an excellent base from which eventually to attack Japan by air. Consequently Roosevelt and his advisers agreed on a series of major politico-military gestures throughout 1942 and 1943 to mollify Chiang and build up his forces. In 1942 they sent General Joseph Stilwell, one of Marshall's most highly regarded commanders, to serve as head of the U.S. China-Burma-India Theater, Lend-Lease director, and chief of staff to Chiang, while loans and Lend-Lease supplies were made available to the Chinese leader. All of this proved to be a consistent drain on U.S. resources, as did the creation in 1943 of the new and connected Southeast Asia Command under the British and promises to launch coordinated attacks on Burma.[23]

Further reinforcing the deployment of additional forces against Japan was the U.S. decision to maintain two separate Pacific campaigns and theaters of operation in which unity of command was not really practiced. The primary reasons were political rather than military once again, and centered on personal and interservice conflicts. Given his rank and status, MacArthur could not be subordinated to any naval commander. Given his egocentric personality and recent Philippine defeat as well as the fact that the Pacific was primarily a naval conflict, however, the navy refused to give him control of its capital ships and strategy. The solution to this impasse was the creation of two separate theaters, the Southwest Pacific Area under MacArthur and the Pacific Ocean Areas under Admiral Chester W. Nimitz. In 1942 the navy took primary responsibility for opening operations at Guadalcanal while MacArthur was placed in charge of later operations, New Guinea, and future offensives against the major Japanese base at Rabaul on New Britain Island (CARTWHEEL), with special naval task forces being temporarily assigned to work with him when necessary. This compromise and its 1943 revision worked well. By the end of 1943 Japanese forces had been encircled in the Solomons by Admiral William F. Halsey's actions at New Georgia and Bougainville as well as Guadalcanal, and isolated at Rabaul by MacArthur's New Guinea/New Britain/Admiralty islands campaign.

Long before that time, however, MacArthur and Nimitz had begun to argue over future operations. Whereas Nimitz favored the old ORANGE concept of a gradual advance from Hawaii westward across the central Pacific islands, MacArthur countered with plans for a campaign from his Australian base and through New Guinea westward and northward designed to culminate in the Philippines, which the navy wished to bypass entirely in favor of Formosa. This MacArthur vehemently opposed on political and personal as well as military grounds: The humiliating Philippine defeat of 1942 had to be avenged to restore both his and U.S. prestige in the Far East. Rather than settle the issue one way or the other, the JCS compromised and postponed by endorsing both sets of plans, something made possible by U.S. successes in the field and their willingness/ability to assign additional forces to these theaters. Of perhaps equal importance was their disillusionment by this time with the performance of Chiang Kai-shek's armies and lack of belief that the China theater either could or would realize its potential in the war against Japan.[24]

Throughout the remainder of 1943 MacArthur's forces fulfilled their responsibilities in this dual strategy by their New Guinea operations and isolation of Rabaul. After completing the Solomons campaign, Nimitz began his central Pacific advance in November with a successful amphibious assault on Tarawa and Makin in the Gilbert Islands. Of equal if not greater importance, U.S. submarine attacks on Japanese shipping crippled Tokyo's ability to exploit the resources of its empire, while U.S. war production began to dwarf that of its Asian enemy.

While militarily and politically successful, the dual offensives in the Pacific, and the production priorities necessary to maintain them, constituted a consistent drain on and dispersion of resources that were supposed to be going to the European theater. The situation in China only compounded this problem. Despite the campaigns in North Africa, Sicily, and Italy, 1943 thus ended with as many American forces deployed against Japan as against Germany, and the Germany-first strategy thus still more hypothetical than real.[25]

From the point of view of U.S. army planners, all the 1943 operations constituted diversions from what should have been the focus of U.S. strategy—a cross-Channel operation and major confrontation with the German armies in northwestern Europe, the one theater where massive U.S. forces could be deployed, aid the Soviets, and force Germany into a two-front war. Throughout 1943 they therefore pressed for a firm limit to Mediterranean operations so that a cross-Channel assault could be launched in 1944. The British insisted that additional Mediterranean operations were first necessary to overextend the Germans so as to ensure cross-Channel success, and that both sets of operations could be undertaken if less emphasis was placed on the secondary and diversionary Pacific theater. The Americans countered that the Mediterranean was as diversionary from decisive operations against Germany as the Pacific, as well as militarily unsound and politically inspired. After days of intense argument at both the May TRIDENT conference in Washington and the August QUADRANT conference in Quebec, the CCS finally agreed to a compromise whereby sufficient forces would be allocated to invade and knock Italy out of the war as well as retain the initiative in the Pacific, yet sufficiently limited to allow for a 29-division cross-Channel attack in May of 1944 (OVERLORD).[26]

Before and during the November Cairo conference (SEXTANT) Churchill sought to modify these decisions and delay OVERLORD in order to launch operations in the Aegean as well as break the Italian stalemate, but at the ensuing Anglo-Soviet-American summit conference in Tehran (EUREKA) Roosevelt and Stalin insisted the cross-Channel attack take place as scheduled and that remaining Mediterranean forces be used for a supporting invasion of southern France (ANVIL). For the first time the British were outvoted and overwhelmed by their more powerful Soviet and U.S. allies, who in effect struck a global strategic bargain at the expense of London's indirect approach. By the terms of that bargain, Roosevelt would deliver the long-promised and delayed Second Front in France during the spring of 1944, while Stalin in return would provide both a simultaneous offensive on the eastern front to support OVERLORD and his own "second front," via entry into the Far Eastern war once Germany had been defeated, to limit U.S. preoccupation with the Pacific. The Germany-first strategy of 1941 would thus, finally, be translated into reality.[27]

This did not mean the termination of operations in the Pacific, or the Mediterranean. British strategy had dominated Anglo-American operations in 1942-43 and neither could nor would be simply discontinued. Rather, European strategy would be a compromise, with Mediterranean operations extending and weakening Germany after as well as before OVERLORD. Furthermore, by 1944 the United States was simply too committed in the Pacific to narrow all its energies into the European theater. Indeed, its global military effort now resembled a giant octopus on the map, with the continental United States as the head and multiple shipping tentacles of men and matériel spreading out across the world's oceans to end in multiple battlefields and Allied ports. By 1944 the nation was sufficiently mobilized and militarily balanced to maintain all these tentacles, undertake continued offensives in the Pacific and the Mediterranean, and launch simultaneously from England the largest amphibious operation in history—provided, of course, that the Grand Alliance maintained itself. Continued Soviet participation in the war always had been and remained essential for the successful implementation of U.S. global strategy. Indeed, army planners concluded in 1943 that, given present trends on the critical eastern front as well as the labor needed for Lend-Lease commitments to the allies and the enormous logistical support required for overseas combat, the United States could and should mobilize no more than 90 divisions for all planned and ongoing offensives.[28]

Throughout the first five months of 1944 massive Anglo-Canadian-American forces gathered in England and on 6 June successfully crossed the Channel under Eisenhower's overall command, with British General Sir Bernard Montgomery in charge of all ground forces. By July the buildup in Normandy had proceeded sufficiently to establish the separate Twelfth U.S. Army Group under General Omar N. Bradley in the western sector, while Montgomery retained command of the British-Canadian Twenty-first Army Group farther east. In late July Bradley's forces broke out of Normandy and swept across southern and central France, liberating Paris on 25 August, while Montgomery broke out farther north.

Anglo-American forces in Italy did not remain inactive during this time. In January, U.S. forces launched a successful amphibious assault behind the German lines at Anzio, just south of Rome, but failed to exploit their surprise and thereby almost lost the beachhead. Continued heavy fighting, high casualties, and stalemate ensued until May, when Allied forces under General Clark succeeded in breaking the German lines, linking up with the beachhead, and capturing Rome on 4 June. They then halted their offensive to prepare for the invasion of southern France that had been approved at Tehran but postponed due to delays in taking Rome, increased OVERLORD demands, and British desire to replace the operation with one aimed at the Ljubljana gap in the Balkans and Vienna. This the Americans flatly rejected as simply another flawed peripheral proposal that could lead to military disaster, dangerous conflict with the Soviets, denial to Eisenhower of a needed port in southern France, and a subsequent unacceptable threat to and lengthening of his campaign. U.S. preponderance in manpower and material by this point forced British acquiescence rather than agreement, with Churchill renaming the operation DRAGOON to reflect his feelings of being dragooned into accepting it. Successfully launched on 15 August, it quickly moved up the Rhone valley to link up with the main Anglo-American forces racing through France. Those forces slowed in September, however, as the Allies outran their supplies and faced stiffening German resistance near the Rhine.[29]

Despite these extraordinary successes, the entire European campaign of 1944 would be marred by a series of debates and confrontations between British and U.S. generals, each of whom claimed he could cross the Rhine and end the war in 1944 if given all available resources. Montgomery's failure to do so at Arnhem in September ended Eisenhower's willingness to attempt such gambles in the future and reinforced his predilection to pursue a more conservative "broad-front" approach as a politico-military compromise, the howls of his subordinates notwithstanding. Then in December the Germans launched a surprise counterattack in the Ardennes that, although a failure, stretched U.S. forces to their limit and made clear the Rhine would not be crossed until 1945.

A similar pattern of extraordinary military success combined with command/strategic disputes and stiffening enemy opposition that would delay final victory occurred in the war against Japan during 1944. In February Kwajalein in the Marshall Islands fell to Nimitz's forces while MacArthur continued to "leapfrog" along the northern coast of New Guinea and nearby islands, thereby isolating the major Japanese bases of Rabaul and Truk and setting the stage for further advances in the dual Pacific offensive. During the summer Nimitz's forces conquered Saipan, Tinian, and Guam in the Marianas and virtually annihilated the remnants of the Japanese naval air forces in the Battle of the Philippine Sea. In October of 1944 the Joint Chiefs finally decided to bypass Formosa in favor of the

Philippines. Consequently MacArthur's forces landed at Leyte Gulf later that month. An effort by the Japanese surface fleet to challenge the landings resulted in the largest battle in naval history and the final one of the Pacific War, as the Japanese fleet was destroyed. By this time, however, Japan had begun to use new suicidal tactics, most notably *kamikaze* air attacks against U.S. ships. While these did not lead to U.S. defeats, they clearly increased the length of battles and number of U.S. casualties, thereby helping to push the war's end into 1945 and setting the stage for the bloody battles on the islands of Iwo Jima and Okinawa.

Military failure and political turmoil in China during 1944 similarly played a role in delaying final victory. During that year an air offensive strongly supported by both U.S. Air General Claire Chennault and Chiang but opposed by Stilwell precipitated a major Japanese ground offensive that overran the air bases and created a major diplomatic as well as military crisis. Although Chiang succeeded by November in forcing the recall of Stilwell (who by this time had lost all faith in Chiang and wished to explore working with the Chinese Communists), the 1944 failures in China led the JCS to place much less emphasis on this theater and more on both the Pacific and obtaining quick Soviet entry into the war, something they were able to accomplish at the February 1945 Yalta summit conference via Stalin's pledge to declare war on Japan two-to-three months after German defeat.[30]

Despite the stiffening Axis resistance, victory came swiftly in each theater during 1945. In March, U.S. forces captured an intact bridge over the Rhine River at Remagen. Seizing the opportunity, Eisenhower altered previous plans which had emphasized an offensive by Montgomery in the North and instead allowed U.S. forces farther south to take the initiative. When Montgomery did cross the Rhine two weeks later, Anglo-American forces succeeded in surrounding 350,000 German troops in the Ruhr while spearheads raced through central Germany. After another heated Anglo-American debate, Eisenhower then emphasized a limited U.S. movement southeastward to the Elbe River rather than a British-directed move against Berlin, thereby leaving conquest of the German capital to the Red Army. His reasoning included political as well as military factors: The city was no longer militarily significant or worth U.S. casualties, especially in light of the fact that the United States had already obtained an occupation zone at Yalta, and he needed to preclude a potentially catastrophic collision with the advancing Red Army as well as a feared retreat by Hitler into the Bavarian Alps. United States forces linked up with the Soviets at Torgau on the Elbe on 25 April. Germany surrendered two weeks later.[31]

The end in the Pacific was almost as swift. While MacArthur reconquered the Philippines in a campaign that would eventually involve 250,000 men, Nimitz's forces moved northward within bombing range of the Japanese home islands. In February they suffered their worst casualties of the Pacific War in taking the island of Iwo Jima as 25,000 entrenched Japanese defenders killed 8,000 Americans, wounded 20,000 more, and fought virtually to the last man. The invasion of Okinawa in June of 1945 produced even higher casualty figures, as over 100,000 Japanese troops and hundreds of *kamikaze* pilots inflicted 12,500 deaths on U.S. forces, sank 21 ships, and damaged 67 others. Yet U.S. forces emerged victorious in both battles, and from March through July simultaneously used their new Pacific island bases to launch massive and unopposed firebombing raids against Japanese cities that killed hundreds of thousands of civilians. On 6 August a special such raid designed primarily to shock the Japanese but also the Soviets in light of growing Allied friction dropped the first atomic bomb on the city of Hiroshima, killing 135,000 people. Two days later the Soviet Union declared war on Japan and on 9 August a second atomic bomb was dropped on Nagasaki. For months Japan's military situation had been hopeless. These August events made clear just how hopeless, and on 14 August Japan accepted U.S. surrender terms.[32]

Despite the successes of the American military effort in achieving victory over the Axis powers, U.S. strategy became the subject of intense criticism and debates in the years after 1945. Many of these simply continued wartime controversies. The Anglo-American debates over European strategy, for example, were replayed after the war by many of the participants in their memoirs and then by their biographers and the historians of each nation.[33] Debate continues to this day as to the wisdom of the "direct" U.S., as opposed to the "indirect" British, approach in Europe, whether the Channel could have been crossed in 1942 or 1943, why it was not crossed until 1944, whether the North African and Italian campaigns were worthwhile, whether the invasion of southern France was necessary, and the wisdom of Eisenhower's broad-front approach and decision to bypass Berlin. Proponents of British strategy argue that the American approach was wasteful and ignored important political objectives, whereas supporters of U.S. strategy maintain the British approach was incapable of achieving victory, threatened the necessary continuation of the alliance, and was geared to English rather than U.S. political objectives.

A similar debate took place after the war regarding operations in the Pacific, with MacArthur arrayed against the navy in a battle for historical distinction and correctness that mirrored the wartime battle for priority and supplies. To his supporters, MacArthur's campaign stood as a model of what could be done with artful use of limited forces, while the navy's central Pacific campaign deserved condemnation for its directness, obviousness, and resulting heavy casualties. Naval supporters countered that Nimitz's campaign was decisive, whereas MacArthur's was unnecessary. The successes of both campaigns, and the fact that the dual offensive consistently confused the Japanese as to the next U.S. move, has somewhat dulled the sharpness of the debate, but many historians still condemn one or both components of the dual offensive as unnecessary and distracting from the war against Germany.[34]

Similar but more intense debate continues to surround the strategic bombing campaigns against Germany and Japan. Defenders point to the diversion and destruction of the German air force and oil industry as well as Japanese surrender, whereas critics note the increasing German war production throughout the conflict, the maintenance of civilian morale despite the bombing, the enormous diversion of U.S. resources to a campaign of marginal significance, the very high casualties suffered by bomber crews over Germany, and the questionable morality of bombing civilians—be it with firebombs or nuclear weapons.[35]

Criticism and debate has also continued over U.S. wartime strategy vis-à-vis China. Sharply negative domestic reaction to the 1949 success of Mao Tse-tung's communist forces in the Chinese Civil War led to savage attacks on U.S. World War II military as well as foreign policy for having "lost" China. With the normalization of Sino-American relations during the 1970s that attack faded and has today been replaced by criticism of U.S. policymakers for refusing to work with Mao during as well as after the war.[36]

The 1950s attack on U.S. China policy was actually part of a broader, Cold War era attack on all of U.S. strategy, policy, and civil-military relations during World War II. In searching for the roots of Soviet-American conflict during World War II and the numerous frustrations and failures the United States faced in the Cold War, many critics blamed Roosevelt, the JCS, and specific theater commanders such as Eisenhower and Stilwell for planning strategy on a "purely military" basis rather than with an eye on blocking Soviet expansion in the postwar world. This violation of Clausewitz's basic dictum that war is a political act, they argued, had extremely negative consequences for the United States in the postwar era.[37]

As this essay has attempted to illustrate, U.S. strategy was seldom if ever determined in a political vacuum and on a "purely military" basis.

Both the president and U.S. military leaders were consistently aware of political factors and included them in military calculations. Indeed, such factors often played a decisive role in the determination of U.S. strategy. Those political factors were quite different *during* World War II, however, than the ones that existed *after* the war's successful termination. Given the ones that did exist during the war, most notably the need to maintain public support, interservice cooperation and the Grand Alliance, U.S. global strategy succeeded remarkably well in obtaining maximum results with minimum loss of life—even if it deviated sharply from what had been planned in 1940-41.

NOTES

1. The largest and most detailed of these is *United States Army in World War II* (79 vols.; Washington, D.C., 1947-85). See also Samuel E. Morison, *History of United States Naval Operations in World War II* (15 vols.; Boston, 1947-62); Wesley F. Craven and James L. Cate, eds., *Army Air Forces in World War II* (7 vols.; Chicago, 1948-58); *History of U.S. Marine Corps Operations in World War II,* (5 vols.; Washington, D.C., 1958-71). Most of the massive documentation on which these works are based is in the U.S. National Archives (Washington).

2. Allan R. Millett and Peter Maslowski, *For the Common Defense: A Military History of the United States of America* (New York, 1984), 408-12; "The United States Armed Forces in the Second World War," in *Military Effectiveness,* Allan R. Millett and Williamson Murray, eds. (3 vols., Boston, 1988), 3, 47-52.

3. Louis Morton, "War Plan 'Orange': The Evolution of a Strategy," *World Politics,* 11 (January, 1950), 221-250; "Germany First; The Basic Concept of Allied Strategy in World War II," in *Command Decisions,* Kent R. Greenfield, ed. (Washington, D.C., 1960), 11-25; *The War in the Pacific: Strategy and Command, The First Two Years,* 21-44, 67-72, in *U.S. Army in World War II.* The most recent study is Edward S. Miller, *War Plan ORANGE* (Annapolis, 1991).

4. See note 3; JB 305 with JPC Development File, Serial 573, RG 225, NA; Fred Greene, "The Military View of American National Policy, 1904-1940," *American Historical Review,* 66 (January 1961), 366-76; Russell F. Weigley, "The Role of the War Department and the Army" and Waldo H. Heinrichs, Jr., "The Role of the United States Navy," in *Pearl Harbor as History: Japanese-American Relations, 1931-1941,* Dorothy Borg and Shumpei Okamoto, eds. (New York, 1973), 172-75 and 201-3.

5. William Emerson, "Franklin D. Roosevelt as Commander-in-Chief During World War II," *Military Affairs* 22 (Winter, 1958-59), 183-88; Mark S. Watson, *Chief of Staff: Prewar Plans and Preparations,* 105-18, in *U.S. Army in World War II*; David G. Haglund, "George C. Marshall and the Question of Military Aid to England, May-June, 1940," *Journal of Contemporary History,* 15 (October 1980), 745-60; Lester H. Brune, *The Origins of American National Security Policy: Sea Power, Air Power and Foreign Policy, 1900-1941* (Manhattan, Kans., 1981), 62-63, 106-16; Robert Dallek, *Franklin D. Roosevelt and American Foreign Policy, 1932-1945* (New York, 1979), 212-58; Morton, *Strategy and Command,* 74-80.

6. Morton, "Germany First," 34-38; *Strategy and Command,* 81-83. Mark M. Lowenthal, "The Stark Memorandum and American National Security Process, 1940," in *Changing Interpretations and New Sources in Naval History,* Robert W. Love, Jr., ed. (New York, 1980), 352-361; "Roosevelt and the Coming of the War: the Search for United States Policy, 1937-1942," in *The Second World War: Essays in Military and Political History,* Walter Laqueur, ed. (London, 1982), 60-62; *Leadership and Indecision: American War Planning and Policy Process, 1937-1942* (New York, 1988), 386-475.

7. Morton, *Strategy and Command,* 84-91; Maurice Matloff and Edwin M. Snell, *Strategic Planning for Coalition Warfare, 1941-1942,* 32-48, in *U.S. Army in World War II.*

8. JB 355, Serial 707, RG 225, NA; Robert Sherwood, *Roosevelt and Hopkins: An Intimate History,* rev. ed. (New York, 1950), 410-18; Watson, *Chief of Staff,* 331-66; Craven and Cate, *Army Air Forces in World War II,* 1, 131-32, 146-47.

9. Maurice Matloff, "Allied Strategy in Europe, 1939-1945," in *Makers of Modern Strategy: From Machiavelli to the Nuclear Age,* Peter Paret, ed. (Princeton, N.J., 1986), 679.

10. Matloff and Snell, *Strategic Planning,* 1941-42, 29-30.

11. Sherwood, *Roosevelt and Hopkins,* 415; Watson, *Chief of Staff,* 331-66; Charles E. Kirkpatrick, *An Unknown Future and a Doubtful Present: Writing the Victory Plan of 1941* (Washington, D.C., 1990), 125-38; Russell F. Weigley, *The American Way of War: A History of United States Military Strategy and Policy* (New York, 1973), 316-17.

12. Henry L. Stimson Diary, 25-26 September 1941, Stimson Papers, Yale University, New Haven, Conn.

13. See ch. 4 and *Foreign Relations of the United States* [*FRUS*] (Washington, D.C. 1862-): *The Conferences at Washington and Casablanca.*

14. Vernon E. Davis, "The History of the Joint Chiefs of Staff During World War II: Organizational Development," 2 vols.; RG 218, NA; Grace P. Hayes, *The History of the Joint Chiefs of Staff in World War II; The War Against Japan* (Annapolis, 1953, 1982).

15. Forrest C. Pogue, *George C. Marshall* (New York, 1966), 1, 248-59; 2, 82-83, 289-98; 3, 585.

16. D. Clayton James, "American and Japanese Strategies in the Pacific War," in *Makers of Modern Strategy,* 722-23.

17. Alfred D. Chandler, Jr., *The Papers of Dwight David Eisenhower: The War Years* (5 vols.; Baltimore, 1970), 1, 149-55, 205-8; Matloff and Snell, *Strategic Planning, 1941-42,* 177-87, 383.

18. *FRUS, 1942,* 3, 594. See also ch. 15.

19. Mark A. Stoler, "The 'Pacific-First' Alternative in American World War II Strategy," *The International History Review,* 2 (July 1980), 432-42; Richard W. Steele, *The First Offensive, 1942: Roosevelt, Marshall and the Making of American Strategy* (Bloomington, 1973).

20. Matloff and Snell, *Strategic Planning, 1941-42,* 389-90.

21. Maurice Matloff, *Strategic Planning for Coalition Warfare, 1943-1944,* 106, in *U.S. Army in World War II.*

22. Henry L. Stimson and McGeorge Bundy, *On Active Service in Peace and War* (New York, 1948), 429-30.

23. Barbara Tuchman, *Stilwell and the American Experience in China, 1911-1945* (New York, 1971), 256-414; Michael Schaller, *The U.S. Crusade in China, 1938-1945* (New York, 1979), 87-145.

24. Hayes, *The Joint Chiefs,* 88-507; D. Clayton James, *The Years of MacArthur,* (3 vols.; Boston, 1975), 2, 157-374.

25. Millett and Maslowski, *For the Common Defense*, 433.

26. *FRUS: Washington and Quebec*; Matloff, *Strategic Planning, 1943-44*, 1-76, 106-84, 211-69; Robert Beitzell, *The Uneasy Alliance: America, Britain, and Russia, 1941-1943* (New York, 1972), 76-123; Mark A. Stoler, *The Politics of the Second Front: American Military Planning and Diplomacy in Coalition Warfare, 1941-1943* (Westport, Conn., 1977), 74-85, 92-116.

27. See sources in note 26 above and *FRUS: Cairo and Tehran.*

28. Maurice Matloff, "The 90-Division Gamble," in *Command Decisions*, 365-81.

29. Martin Blumenson, "General Lucas at Anzio" and Maurice Matloff, "The ANVIL Decision," in *ibid.*, 323-50 and 383-400.

30. Tuchman, *Stilwell*, 455-509; Schaller, *U.S. Crusade*, 147-230; Ronald Spector, *Eagle Against the Sun The American War With Japan* (New York, 1984), 365-81; Hayes, *Joint Chiefs*, 645-52, 668-85.

31. Stephen Ambrose, *Eisenhower and Berlin: The Decision to Halt at the Elbe* (New York, 1967).

32. Spector, *Eagle Against the Sun*, 487-561; Martin Sherwin, *A World Destroyed: The Atomic Bomb and the Grand Alliance* (New York, 1975).

33. Trumbull Higgins, "The Anglo-American Historians' War in the Mediterranean, 1942-1945," *Military Affairs* 34 (October 1970), 84-88.

34. See Spector, *Eagle Against the Sun*, vs. Peter Calvocoressi, Guy Wint, and John Pritchard, *Total War: The Causes and Courses of the Second World War* (2 vols.; New York, 1989), 2, 1073-87.

35. See Craven and Cate, *Army Air Forces*, 2, 3; David MacIsaac, *Strategic Bombing in World War II: The Story of the United States Strategic Bombing Survey* (New York, 1976); Ronald Schaffer, *Wings of Judgment: American Bombing in World War II* (New York, 1985); Michael S. Sherry, *The Rise of American Airpower: The Creation of Armageddon* (New Haven, Conn., 1987), 116-300.

36. Compare, for example, Anthony Kubek, *How the Far East Was Lost: American Policy and the Creation of Communist China, 1941-1949* (Chicago, 1963), with Schaller, *U.S. Crusade in China.*

37. Hanson W. Baldwin, *Great Mistakes of the War* (New York, 1949); Samuel P. Huntington, *The Soldier and the State: The Theory and Politics of Civil-Military Relationships* (New York, 1957), 315-44.

Coalition: Structure, Strategy, and Statecraft

Theodore A. Wilson, et al.

A British World War II poster portrayed a jutjawed Winston Churchill, with a line of Matilda tanks in the background, a flight of Spitfires overhead, and the hazy outline of naval guns on the horizon, proclaiming: "Let Us Go Forward Together." Often taken as invocation of the British people's problematic unity, this Churchillian sentiment also signified the ideal of Allied solidarity in the epochal struggle with the Axis. The reality behind the World War II coalition of the British Empire, the United States, and the Soviet Union was rather less stirring. It was compounded—in unequal parts among the three principals—of highflown rhetoric, promises either insincere or impossible to honor, and often parsimonious provision of information and matériel; yet, by dint of tremendous national sacrifices and a grudging but ultimately remarkable coordination of military effort, this unlikely triumvirate crushed its chief adversary, Nazi Germany, and, in bitterly contested sideshows, the other members of the Axis.

The Allied coalition was called into being by shortsighted actions of its adversaries, existed for essentially negative purposes, and functioned by putting the best face on necessity. At the same time, these pressures produced an array of institutional arrangements to sustain and facilitate communication between the three allies. Indeed, it appeared that embryonic multinational organizations such as Allied Forces Headquarters (AFHQ) in North Africa, the Munitions Assignment Board, and the Combined Intelligence Committee would metamorphose into fully integrated agencies imbued with a supranational outlook. Of course, habits of cooperation and the advent of an "alliance mentality" did not infect and affect all coalition members with equal potency. Coordination between Britain and the United States was far more wide-ranging and intense than between these two nations and the USSR.

The misapprehensions of the period when the three nations were going their separate ways—distrustful, even actively hostile to their future partners—served as an enormous drag on effective cooperation. The history of the Allied coalition is a story of disjunctive actions and unforeseen outcomes. The situation each partner confronted when it came into the coalition shaped the contribution, in relative terms, each made to, first, survival and, then, ultimate victory. By circumstance but also by design, an asymmetrical linkage was inherent in the administrative structure created to further inter-Allied relationships, the strategic debates within the coalition's councils, and the statecraft, the overt and secret stratagems employed by the partners in this "grand" alliance. To think of the British-Soviet-American wartime relationship as an alliance of equals is without point until the floodtide of victory began to crest in spring 1944. Thereafter, until war's end, a sort of symmetry and the substance of cooperation did prevail. Nothing comparable bound together the three allies during the USSR's momentary participation in war against Japan.

The period from the outbreak of war to the entry of the USSR and the United States was one of great shocks, ironic reversals of fortune, and unexpected realignments. These tumultuous two years pose, in retrospect, the intriguing question: "What if" the anti-Axis coalition had been created prior to the outbreak of war in Europe? How different might have been the development of the Allied combination and of its overall program for waging war?[1] Issues of timing were pivotal. Had World War II begun with a general declaration of hostilities between the Axis and those nations that ultimately comprised the Allied coalition, a practical division of effort might have taken place: Russia providing the bulk of military forces; Britain contributing naval and air support, shipbuilding and repair facilities, munitions, and a significant accretion of ground strength; and the United States equipping and supplying its allies, sending to the war fronts primarily air and naval elements while only in the Pacific committing any large body of troops. As it happened, the origins of the Allied coalition were messy and long drawn-out, and assumptions later shown to be irrelevant or mistaken exerted lasting influence.

Even had the coalition that won the war existed at its commencement, it is unlikely that the antagonisms of the previous two decades could have been overcome. Neither Britain nor the United States was prepared to create a military colossus, the Red Army, without substantial countervailing power; and Stalin was hardly willing to rely totally for vital logistical support upon the Western democracies. Geographical and political necessities dictated that any pooling of resources and coordination of strategy be limited, episodic, and conditional upon national perceptions of comparative advantage.

In 1940, having led the failed effort to control German ambitions, Britain found itself alone and committed to military challenges for which its leaders possessed small enthusiasm and less capacity. Rather than husband its dwindling resources by waging a limited war likely to result in a negotiated peace with Nazi Germany *or* spending those same resources profligately to hold on until the United States came in, Churchill bet on the American card. That blunt sentiment was what remained when one stripped away the rhetoric expressed in Churchill's renowned "New World . . . steps forth to the rescue and liberation of the Old" speech of 4 June 1940.[2] A year later, Churchill added the USSR to the list of rescuers, though his true feelings were conveyed in that aside on hearing of the German attack: "If Hitler invaded Hell he would at least make a favorable reference to the Devil."[3]

During the 18 months between Dunkirk and Pearl Harbor, Britain mortgaged its future as a world power, entered into an informal alliance with the United States, and found its survival assured by Russia's unaccountable fortitude. Churchill's overriding goal was American belligerency as Britain's loyal ally. He believed he and FDR had established a unique personal relationship; in an important sense, the Anglo-American aspect of the Allied coalition was an effort to give institutional form to the personal linkage between the two leaders.

Both Churchill and Roosevelt found personal diplomacy congenial. Many critical decisions derived from communications between FDR and the Former Naval Person, the title Churchill adopted after becoming prime minister.[4] After Churchill became prime minister in May 1940, their exchanges became an indispensable channel between the two governments. However, their dialogue stayed within exact if unspecified boundaries and the rate of flow depended upon political circumstances. Though Churchill tended to wax eloquent about a "special relationship," the Churchill-Roosevelt connection was never as close as Churchill claimed, and President Roosevelt was not the thoroughgoing Anglophile Churchill made him out to be.[5] While neither man established with Premier Joseph Stalin the casual comradery that entered into their relationship, after 1943 the triangular connection between the three leaders achieved relative equilibrium. Most historians judge the Roosevelt-Churchill attachment to have reached its zenith at Casablanca; indeed, it is arguable that the relationship peaked at their first meeting in August 1941, before America's entry into the war introduced other elements into the equation.[6]

A second source of the organizational structures that defined Anglo-American cooperation were the dealings between British and Americans during 1940-41 to facilitate American initiatives to aid Britain. Here too may be found the origins of those contrasting views of "cooperation" that were to characterize the coalition. President Roosevelt's magical expedient of "Lend-Lease" underwrote Allied purchases of weapons and other war material and services. But the Lend-Lease Act did not repair the damage sustained when Britain was fighting alone. The British long had espoused "pooling," which in theory put the total resources of each nation into a common reservoir, as the most efficient mechanism for prosecution of the war.[7] In fact, Americans proved reluctant to give up any significant control over the components of military policy-making—whether weapons design, force structure, logistical and strategic priorities, or command relationships.

Though there had been ongoing discussions between naval representatives and episodic communications about the desirability of more general sharing of technology, the origins of Anglo-American coordination are to be found in those hectic weeks following the fall of France.[8] The British Purchasing Commission took charge of all orders for munitions and other supplies throughout North America, and, as well, London fired off requests for information about American manufacturing processes, technical specifications of U.S. weapons, and, on one occasion, a blanket order for U.S. Army drill manuals. Over the next year, large numbers of British officials, concerned with procurement, intelligence, and "publicity" in its overt and covert forms set up shop in Washington and New York. Working behind the scenes, they faced the challenge of forging bonds to sustain wartime cooperation with officials of a nation still comfortably at peace.[9]

The British government also began to press for secret staff talks, looking toward coordination of strategy and some sort of inter-Allied administrative apparatus should the United States enter the war. These maneuvers led directly to dispatch of the Emmons-Strong Mission to Britain in August 1940 and the parallel assignment of Rear Admiral Robert L. Ghormley as "Special Naval Observer" attached to the U.S. embassy in London.[10] Indirectly, they triggered that reassessment of U.S. strategy leading from Chief of Naval Operations Harold R. Stark's "Plan 'Dog'" memorandum to the secret ABC-1 staff talks of spring 1941, and RAINBOW 5—blueprints that called for a defensive posture toward Japan and concentration first of forces in the Atlantic/European theater to achieve the decisive defeat of Germany.[11]

The ABC-1 agreement became the fundamental statement governing Anglo-American strategy. It did not, however, resolve basic difference in aims and assumptions. The British approach called for U.S. primacy in war finance and production, U.S. naval participation, and an indirect strategy, based on bombing, blockade, and limited military operations in North Africa and the Mediterranean, to "close the ring" around Nazi Germany.[12] British strategy reflected its historic commitment to an indirect approach to war, limited manpower and resources, need to defend a sprawling empire, and desire to avoid the catastrophes visited by the trench warfare of World War I. All of these factors were personified in the individual who was to defend British strategy throughout the war, Prime Minister Winston S. Churchill.[13]

Virtually every British proposal and strategic concept met with American opposition during 1941 and for at least the next two years. An ardent Mahanist and recent convert to strategic air power, Roosevelt himself found appealing a strategy of indirection and limited war.[14] However, his military advisers resisted, terming Britain's indirect approach militarily unsound (flouting the basic principle that wars are won by destroying the enemy's armed forces) and politically motivated. Undergirding their opposition was the U.S. military tradition that emphasized overwhelming advantages in manpower and material, a direct approach, and campaigns of annihilation rather than attrition. Also important was an intense suspicion of British motives.[15]

British determination to overcome American parochialism formed a basic element in the effort to formulate a "Coordinated Balance Sheet"—ascertaining current and potential American munitions production and establishing priorities for its allocation—that surfaced in spring, 1941. Outcomes of the British pressure were the self-protective attempts at inter-service cooperation that resulted in creation of the U.S. Joint Chiefs of Staff *and* the principal continuing expression for British-American wartime coordination, the Combined Chiefs of Staff (CCS) organization.[16]

The parameters of what the CCS would become were revealed by the course of the ABC-1 discussions. U.S. participants, in contrast with "the more coherently organized" British delegation, always met separately in preparatory sessions and spoke as representatives of their own service.[17] The U.S. delegates consistently espoused the view that no overall Anglo-American command was needed. Cooperation and limited coordination was appropriate, but the idea of "single centralized control" was unacceptable.[18]

In contrast, the British, "imbued with the principles of their well-developed and integrated Chiefs of Staff Committee and War Cabinet organization," advocated "the most direct relation possible at all levels . . . of the United States and the United Kingdom." Their proposed administrative setup had each ally set up a political-military mission, with full authority to speak for its government, in the other's capital. The British also envisaged some sort of "Supreme War Council" charged with political and military direction of the Allied war effort.[19] These proposals reflected profound misconceptions of the American governmental structure. Perhaps wishful thinking about American flexibility in a wartime emergency was a factor, In any event, they were left out of the final ABC-1 report.[20]

Although reference to a "Supreme War Council" was retained, nothing was said about machinery to ensure continuing collaboration. Clearly, memories of Pershing's experience in World War I and American institutional chauvinism were at work.[21] Nonetheless, ABC-1 confirmed the principle that the two nations would engage in coalition warfare under a "jointly agreed" grand strategy. As the implications spread among U.S. military leaders, they gradually accepted British terminology (i.e., "combined" and "joint") and, to a degree, British staff procedures. Debate continued throughout the war about how much if any national autonomy was to be sacrificed in the interest of furthering coalition objectives.

The ABC-1 discussions brought into sharp relief the lack of coordination between the U.S. services. There ensued a discreetly waged but bitter struggle to devise an effective mechanism for army (and, after June 1941, army air forces)-navy cooperation.[22] The bureaucratic modus vivendi hammered out eventually held sway for the entire war. It featured direct access by representatives of the British Military Mission (designated on 9 July 1941 as the British Joint Staff Mission BJSM to the U.S. Chief of Naval Operations and the U.S. Army Chief of Staff. The process also provided for periodic meetings of the Chiefs of the British Military Mission with the U.S. Chief of Naval Operations and Army Chief of Staff (also, subsequently, the Chief of Staff of the Army Air Forces, General Henry H. Arnold).[23] These arrangements were given additional weight at the Atlantic conference in August 1941, which first brought together the military and naval leadership of the two nations. Although sharp differences arose over strategic priorities, the U.S. and British Chiefs were given an opportunity to become acquainted with and judge their counterparts.[24]

Moves by the British government to reorganize and strengthen its representation in Washington were paralleled by U.S. military representatives (officially designated "Special Observers") in Britain. Although the army and navy heads of mission were separate and had little to do with the American "expediter" of Lend-Lease in London or with the U.S. embassy, the intent was clearly that the U.S. Special Observer Group perform the functions of the BJSM and that it eventually serve as the nucleus of a U.S. theater headquarters.[25]

When Nazi aggression brought the Soviet Union into the war, an elaborate network of personal and organizational communication linked British and American officials. Nothing comparable was to characterize the Anglo-Soviet-American connection. No one thought about the effect of BARBAROSSA on coalition arrangements, for pessimistic initial assessments about Soviet chances against the German juggernaut prevented both London and Washington from regarding the USSR as a full partner in the anti-Axis coalition.[26] Prime Minister Churchill quickly approved the appointment of a Military Mission to the Soviet Union, and the forward elements, including the Head of Mission, Lieutenant General N. Mason-Macfarlane, former military attaché in Berlin, reached Moscow on 27 June. The British Military Mission under Macfarlane made little progress toward either of its primary aims: to offer the Soviets insights gained from fighting the Germans, and to obtain intelligence about the eastern front. The BMM was largely excluded from political matters and evaluation of Soviet aid requests.[27]

In early July, the USSR dispatched a formal mission, headed by General F. I. Golikov, with Admiral Nikolai Kharlamov as chief deputy. Soon after arrival, Golikov was recalled to Moscow to be debriefed before journeying to the United States with a list of Soviet requests for weapons and vital materials.[28] Pressed by the White House, the War Department General Staff sought to cooperate with the Soviet representatives, even scheduling special demonstrations of new weapons. But given widespread belief that the Red Army would collapse in months if not weeks, the War Department showed little interest in anything more ambitious, preferring to rely for information upon the U.S. military attaché in Moscow and British intelligence sources.

The Roosevelt administration decided at the outset that the Soviet Union was to be a special case.[29] In late July, presidential intimate Harry Hopkins flew to the USSR for consultations with Premier Stalin, and Hopkins' optimistic report caused FDR and Churchill to approve a three-power supply conference in Moscow. In early August a meeting of Soviet, British, and American officials considered a proposal by Soviet ambassador Constantine Umansky to have a "Tripartite Committee" tackle the coordination and allocation of the three nations' military production. However, Britain, represented by Jean Monnet, deputy head of the British Purchasing Mission, blocked "concrete negotiations" and ensured that any tripartite agency would be only a consultative body.[30] The Beaverbrook-Harriman Mission of October 1941 confirmed the policy of treating the Soviets as an object of joint regard rather than as a partner to be dealt with on the basis of equality.

Efforts to expand the connections between Moscow and Washington met a similar fate. The tragic death of Lieutenant Colonel Townsend Griffiss, sent to the USSR in November 1941 to negotiate routes for delivery of U.S. aircraft to the Soviet Union, appeared to typify the difficulties of dealing with an ally so distant geographically and in other ways.[31] A long-delayed, ultimately miscarried attempt to install a U.S. Military Mission served to reinforce War Department suspicions about the insularity of their Soviet "ally."

These circumstances resulted in yet another asymmetrical linkage. Unlike its coalition partners, the United States never dispatched a formal military mission to Great Britain and only in autumn 1943 was a U.S. Military Mission accredited to Moscow.[32] As the war widened, British and American officials acknowledged that efforts to implement their distinctive versions of the "military mission as control mechanism" were being frustrated. Only the USSR conducted coalition business primarily through its military missions (complemented by purchasing agencies in both London and Washington) for the duration of the war.

While Pearl Harbor gave formal status to the anti-Axis coalition and to many of the institutional links already in place, its immediate aftermath witnessed an unexpected reconfiguration of Anglo-American strategic and logistical coordination. Logic suggested a move to confirm and extend existing arrangements for the use of military missions as the principal medium of British-U.S. communication and, as well, what coordination was to be effected between Washington, London, and Moscow. However, Churchill, anxious that the United States not abandon its commitment to Europe (and Britain) in the wake of Japan's surprise attack, pressed for an immediate meeting of himself, President Roosevelt, and the British and U.S. Chiefs of Staff.

At the ARCADIA conference in Washington momentous decisions regarding grand strategy were taken. Europe first was affirmed. ARCADIA also witnessed a battle over "the military direction of the war," a global arrangement to correspond to the regional unified commands provided for under ABC-1. For a time there occurred a reversal of roles—with President Roosevelt taking a strong stand in behalf of the proposed supreme military authority, the Combined Chiefs of Staff (CCS).[33] When apprised of the plan to have representatives of the British Chiefs of Staff in Washington and their American opposite numbers in London, FDR was decidedly unenthusiastic. Apparently responding to press clamor and to State Department planners who pushed for a World War I-style Supreme War Council, the president proposed to locate a "Combined Chiefs of Staff" organization in Washington and to have theater commanders route all queries to Washington for transmission to "national" groups: the BCOS, JCS, and general staffs of other allies.[34] The Supreme War Council would include the U.S., British Empire, Russia (taking part only in discussions relating to the conduct of the war against Germany because of its neutrality agreement with Japan), China, and possibly the Netherlands.[35]

The British balked at this hastily conceived scheme. One reason was chauvinism, for "requiring theater commanders to report only to Washington meant that on a daily basis the war would be run there." Also at issue was the emerging "special relationship" between Great Britain and the United States. Churchill acceded only after having persuaded the president that the difficulties of controlling affairs "to the interest of the United States" within an inter-Allied council including, at the very least, British, American, Soviet, and Chinese representatives and possibly the Netherlands and various of the Dominions might prove insurmountable. Clearly, the British desired to ensure Anglo-American control over the war effort. Such an approach, they argued, accurately reflected existing circumstances: the fact that the U.S. and U.K. were the only major powers engaged in hostilities with the entire Axis combine, their freedom of action and geopolitical situation contrasted with the "geographically isolated" USSR and China, and the pivotal role of the United States in supplying war material. FDR conceded the point on 31 December, the day before proclamation of the United Nations Declaration. Thus, whether or not Stalin desired a seat on the CCS, he was not consulted.[36]

A further decision affecting structure was the short-lived experiment with unity of command in the Southwest Pacific, the so-called "ABDA Command." Again, the British first opposed the concept and gave way when the depth of American commitment was made clear and when overall command of Allied forces was given to General Sir Archibald Wavell. Unfortunately, command relationships remained imprecise, the principal U.S. military leader in the area, General Douglas MacArthur, acted as if Wavell did not exist and dealt exclusively with Washington (behavior that MacArthur was to maintain with regard to the CCS), and Japanese victories soon submerged the ABDA.

Its legacy was a division of the world by the Combined Chiefs of Staff into several spheres of operation, subsequently termed "theaters" by

Marshall. Since the Pacific theaters were "predominantly American," the CCS ruled that the chain of command should go via the U.S. Chiefs of Staff. Similarly, forces in Southeast Asia and the Middle East were "so predominantly British" that reporting to the Combined Chiefs should go through the British Chiefs of Staff. Thus, "only in the European theater did the senior officer report directly to the Combined Chiefs of Staff."[37] That commonsense principle was applied almost without exception for the duration of the war.

This changed environment soon had effect on the American military representation in London. Though intended to be the nucleus of an American Expeditionary Force headquarters in Britain, there remained essentially General James Chaney and a dozen "observers" or so officers saddled with murky instructions and dependent upon the British for basic needs including secure communication facilities. Looking to creation of a unified headquarters, Marshall asked General Dwight D. Eisenhower of the War Department's Operations and Plans Division to draft the directive to govern the future European Theater of Operations. A few weeks later, in June 1942, Eisenhower replaced Chaney and was designated as "Commanding General, U.S. Army European Theater of Operations."[38] The scheme of organization he had set down was with only modest modifications to govern Allied command relationships in the North African, Mediterranean, and European theaters.

Alfred D. Chandler later observed: "Of all the field commanders—Allied or Axis—Eisenhower had the most complex unified and allied command. . . . During the early part of the war Eisenhower's command was the only one that was allied as well as unified. . . . To be called on to combine units of the army and navy was challenge enough for any military commander. . . . To blend three disparate elements of more than one nation into a single operating unit was, indeed, a formidable task demanding innovation and imagination." Opposition to the idea of a "unified" command proved a serious obstacle, for the British had always embraced the management of campaigns by an interservice committee. American commitment to the concept was theoretical and only applied at this juncture to a "task force," a unified command created to achieve a specific objective.[39] Such questions as to whom did an individual seconded to a multinational command owe primary allegiance had to be confronted.

The cooperative spirit manifested in AFHQ (Eisenhower's headquarters in North Africa) and to a lesser degree in MTO and SHAEF stand as testimony to the strength of coalition loyalties. No doubt had any of the early plans (such as the Petsamo scheme or dispatch of Allied troops to the

Caucasus) materialized, placing British or American forces under Soviet operational authority, these issues would have posed significant challenges for all three coalition partners; as it happened, combined command was to be solely an Anglo-American problem until quite late in the war.

While ARCADIA affirmed Anglo-American dominance across the spectrum of coalition relationships, it also made Washington the headquarters for almost every aspect of the conduct of the war and Franklin D. Roosevelt de facto the first among equals. Power was flowing westward across the Atlantic. The political and bureaucratic dynamics of each nation affected cooperation at the three-power level, but from spring 1942 onward even these battles were fought largely on America's turf and reflected Washington's internal rivalries and organizational priorities.

Accepting this reality, Britain continued to expand its representation in the United States. At its peak the British Army Staff establishment was more than 400 officers and 500 other ranks, and the total number who served exceeded 1,500 at 45 locations across North America. The British Army Staff's genesis was those independent military missions sent out to the United States in 1940 and 1941. First had been the "Dewar Tank Mission" (representing both the War Office and Ministry of Supply) in July 1940 followed in August 1940 by the "Pakenham Walsh Mission" to discuss the re-equipping of the British Army after Dunkirk. In January 1941 the War Office organized these two groups into "200 Military Mission," charged with advising the British Purchasing Commission and maintaining contact with the War Department "on the user aspect of U.S. equipment required by British forces." In July 1941 two further missions "No. 29 MM" (intelligence under LTG Sir Colville Wemyss) and "No. 208 MM" (Directorate Quarter Master General, North America, under Brig. H. R. Kerr) arrived. Soon after the three MMs were amalgamated as the British Army Staff (Washington), with an establishment of some 40 officers under Wemyss. Over the next nine months "the functions of the British Army Staff expanded to cover practically all spheres of liaison between the War Office and the U.S. War Department," and by June 1942, when LTG G. N. Macready took command, the strength of the BAS had risen to some 150 officers. Its main functions were to provide British military representation on the CCS and various Combined Committees and Sub-Committees; second, to act as the liaison channel between the War Office and War Department on military organization, training, and research and development; third, provide operational support to the British Supply Mission in connection with procurement of military equipment and to obtain assignments through the CMAB and Canadian

Munitions Assignment Committee; fourth, to arrange for shipping and maintenance of U.S. and Canadian equipment in use by British Forces in the field. At first the BAS was organized as a "normal military headquarters," but by late 1942 "much overlapping" between the British Supply Mission and BAS in spheres of procurement, assignment, and processing of equipment led to the branches of the two organizations responsible for handling similar types of equipment being merged under a single military head.[40]

The British grappled with recurrent organizational problems, for the lines of authority between the Joint Staff Mission and its major elements were redefined as personnel and missions changed. There was also the eternal problem of coordination. For example, on 28 December 1942, the JSM begged the War Cabinet: "We note that you are communicating with Eisenhower direct on matters which may have repercussions this side." Since Dill had been pressing the War Department "to ensure repetition to you of their unilateral signals on policy matters, request you reciprocate by repeating your signals to us."[41] Of course, American and Russian emissaries were also frustrated by tangled lines of communication.

The Russian war effort before Stalingrad was so focused upon survival that little concern could be expended on any but short-term needs. Soviet attention to coalition politics understandably began with the supply protocols. In early 1942 a Soviet Purchasing Commission was organized in Washington. This agency was responsible for communication with the various arms of the U.S. government involved with Lend-Lease, for oversight of the supply contracts and shipment of cargoes from the United States to the USSR. Issues arising from the British military supply program were dealt with by the Soviet Navy Mission and the Soviet Trade Mission in London. By mid-1942 Soviet inspectors were on hand at factories, shipyards, and ports throughout North America and in Britain.

In effect, military collaboration with the Soviet Union in early 1942 consisted of procurement and delivery of Lend-Lease, episodic communication of intelligence data, and a Churchill-Roosevelt-Stalin correspondence featuring repeated, increasingly acrimonious Soviet demands for a Second Front. Almost two years would pass before the three Allies worked out a coordinated strategy. The highly successful Axis offensives of spring-summer 1942 first caused the strategic pot to boil over. Attacking southeast, German forces quickly reached Stalingrad on the Boga River and threatened the vital Caucasus oil fields. Simultaneously, German and Italian forces in Libya blunted a British offensive and launched a counterattack that led to the surrender of Tobruk and brought the Afrika Korps within striking distance of the Suez Canal. Ranging into the western Atlantic and Caribbean, German submarines were wreaking havoc upon Allied shipping, thereby threatening the Anglo-Soviet-American supply routes that were the Alliance's lifeline. Throughout the Pacific and Southeast Asia, Japanese forces were smashing Western-led garrisons and organizing an empire. With the Soviet Union and China on the brink of collapse and with India, Australia and New Zealand, and Hawaii seemingly within Japan's grasp, a German-Japanese linkup in Iran or India was a distinct possibility.

The American response to this crisis was a proposal to halt the panicky dispatch of forces to the Pacific and to reconcentrate against Germany in accordance with ABC-1. U.S. strategists emphatically rejected Britain's indirect approach and focus on the Mediterranean. Instead, they urged an immediate buildup of Anglo-American forces in the United Kingdom (BOLERO) for cross-Channel operations, thereby confronting Hitler with a two-front war and relieving the hard-pressed Red Army. Two operations were proposed: a 48-division cross-Channel assault (ROUNDUP) in spring 1943; second, should the Soviets face imminent defeat, a much smaller assault using all available troops in fall 1942 (SLEDGEHAMMER) to divert German forces and to establish a beachhead for 1943.[42]

An apparent agreement on strategy was hammered out in high level meetings between the U.S. and British military chiefs and discussions among coalition political leaders. President Roosevelt approved the U.S. scenario in late March 1942 and Prime Minister Churchill and the British Chiefs of Staff signed on shortly thereafter. In May Soviet foreign minister Vyacheslav Molotov journeyed to London and Washington to consult about proposed operations.[43] On 29 May FDR instructed the Soviet envoy to tell Stalin "that we expect the formation of a second front this year," and a joint communiqué proclaimed that "full understanding" had been reached "with regard to the urgent tasks of creating a Second Front in Europe in 1942."[44] In fact, no such "understanding" existed and national apprehensions continued to prevail. The British had agreed to the U.S. scheme to reverse the American obsession with the Pacific War and to bind Washington to a Europe-first strategy via BOLERO. London was unalterably opposed to SLEDGEHAMMER (and, the preponderance of evidence suggests, to ROUNDUP), for any cross-Channel attack would be mounted principally by British and Commonwealth troops and would be a highly dubious proposition without control of the air and the Channel approaches and lacking overwhelming superiority in ground forces. Nor would such an operation divert even one German soldier from the eastern front. On 10 June, just as the communiqué was being released in Washington, Churchill informed Molotov privately that he could "give no promise" of a Second Front in 1942.[45]

Facing phalanxes of Nazi armies, the Soviets needed immediate help. It is no wonder that the apparent British-American stance of delaying their leap across the English Channel until conditions were perfect caused the Soviet leadership to question whether their allies desired to achieve victory with little spillage of blood except by the Red Army. FDR, too, urgently desired immediate military action in Europe, though his motives reflected short-term political calculation and long-term diplomatic aims rather than the desperation endemic in Moscow. The American public was clamoring for counteroffensives in the war with Japan, and Roosevelt risked losing support for the Europe-first strategy (and the congressional elections in November, 1942) without some sort of bold stroke against Nazi Germany. As well, he had used the promise of a Second Front in 1942 to obtain Moscow's agreement not to press for a treaty on postwar territorial arrangements.

When the British refused to undertake SLEDGEHAMMER, Roosevelt intervened decisively. Ruling out both the policy of inaction (BOLERO-ROUNDUP) and the Pacific-first scenario pushed by Marshall and Admiral Ernest J. King, the president opted to return to GYMNAST (now christened TORCH), the 1941 plan to invade North Africa.[46]

A notable manifestation of personal communication took Churchill to Moscow in August to explain these Anglo-American strategic decisions. Justifying focus on the Mediterranean via the analogy of first thrusting at a crocodile's "soft under-belly," Churchill promised an alternately enraged and bemused Stalin that the Western allies would attack the Nazi reptilian's snout by crossing the channel in force in 1943.[47]

Allied paralysis about strategic priorities fortunately was overcome by hard-won victories by Soviet, British, and American forces. In May and June 1942 the U.S. Navy in the Battles of the Coral Sea and Midway halted Japan's advance in the Southwest and Central Pacific and dealt a crippling blow to its carrier-based air power. U.S. and Australian forces then seized the strategic initiative by counterattacking in the Solomon Islands and New Guinea. In the Middle East, British forces won a critical victory over Rommel's Afrika Korps at El Alamein and pushed the Germans all the way back to Tunisia. On 8 November, TORCH dumped a combined amphibious force on the shores of Morocco and Algeria, opening the way for the clearing of North Africa. Two weeks later, having survived numerous hammer blows from *Wehrmacht* spearheads pushing to the Volga

River and south into the Caucasus to seize Stavropol and the Maikop oil fields, the Red Army launched a tremendous counteroffensive. Its Stalingrad front and elements of the Don front and southwest front trapped the German Sixth Army in Stalingrad and won the most decisive military victory of the entire war. With only remnants of his command still resisting, Field Marshal Friedrich von Paulus surrendered on 31 January 1943.

These Allied triumphs staved off defeat but did not by themselves assure final victory. The Axis at year's end controlled all of Europe and western Russia, Tunisia, coastal China, Southeast Asia, and the vast reaches of the western Pacific. German U-boats threatened Allied supply routes and during fall 1942 halted temporarily sailings on the Arctic convoy route to the USSR. The vaunted air campaign against Axis industrial and population centers was having little apparent effect. With the possible exception of TORCH, the 1942 successes represented isolated national victories rather than the precisely coordinated, combined operations that—all presumed—would be required to crush still-powerful adversaries. As well, the exertions necessitated to win these struggles had depleted Allied reserves and dispersed their forces. As some had warned, 1942 had brought commitment of British and U.S. forces to two secondary theaters, thus ruling out taking full advantage of the great Soviet victory at Stalingrad. Concentrating sufficient forces for a cross-Channel invasion in 1943 would be exceedingly difficult even without additional diversions, and the absence of any strategic consensus suggested that further "alarums and excursions" would arise.

By late fall 1942 the system of communication and deliberation by which coalition relations were implemented for the rest of the war was in place. Over the next year, while coalition leaders journeyed from North Africa to Moscow to Washington to Quebec and thence to Tehran, additional functions continued to be added at subordinate levels. What evolved was a jury-rigged setup, one featuring notable gaps in inter-Allied communications linkages and carelessly soldered connections that tended to short out when high-voltage messages sizzled between London, Moscow, and Washington. Cases in point would be the misunderstandings and failures of communication at SYMBOL, the January 1943 meeting of Roosevelt and Churchill, over postponement of a Second Front, the question of who had promised how much shipping to alleviate Britain's imports crisis, and the vituperative exchanges over landing craft allocations.[40] SYMBOL revealed the limits of existing arrangements for trilateral cooperation and—even at the bilateral level—the narrowly circumscribed appreciation Americans and British had of the other's needs.

Both the strengths and limits of these arrangements were to be found in the Casablanca debates between FDR, Churchill, and their advisers. In Warren Kimball's apt imagery, Stalin was the "ghost in the attic" at Casablanca, the sought-after guest who had declined to attend the party. Whether his presence would have produced an ironclad commitment to invade northwest Europe instead of Sicily in 1943 remains an intriguing possibility. The British, however, were present in force, and, determined to limit ground operations to the Mediterranean, they overwhelmed an ill-prepared, poorly-supported American delegation. "We came, we listened, and we were conquered," acknowledged a U.S. participant.[49] When the dust settled, the CCS had assigned first priority to defeating the German U-boat menace and ensuring that supplies reached the USSR. Second came clearance of Axis forces from North Africa, the invasion of Sicily (HUSKY), and the combined bombing campaign (POINTBLANK) against Germany. A modified BOLERO and organization of a combined planning staff for a 1943 cross-Channel attack were approved; but Marshall stated flatly that HUSKY made any such operation "difficult if not impossible." The conferees agreed to tell Premier Stalin that Russia's allies would cross the Channel "as soon as practicable." The Kremlin correctly termed this meaningless, and a crisis loomed.[50]

At TRIDENT, the meeting of Anglo-American leaders in May 1943 the CCS acknowledged manpower and logistical bottlenecks (especially shipping) ruled out an assault on northwest Europe in 1943. The cumulative effects of dispersal of effort and miscalculations about the war to be fought had negated the two allies' lists of extravagant operations. Not even this shock produced a unified strategy. The British Chiefs of Staff pressed for expanded operations in the Mediterranean and against any significant increase in allocation of troops and material to the Pacific. Predictably, the U.S. Chiefs took the opposite position. Days of intense discussions resulted in a compromise—sufficient forces to knock Italy out of the war, to maintain the initiative in the Pacific, and also enough for a 29-division thrust across the English Channel in spring 1944.[51]

Success on the battlefield seemed inversely correlated to the spirit of cooperation. In the aftermath of Stalingrad, Ambassador Maxim Litvinov, apostle of Soviet rapprochement with the West, was recalled. During the same period, British policies on sharing of intelligence stiffened. The celebrated tantrum of Ambassador William H. Standley—who in an impromptu press conference on 8 March 1943 accused the Kremlin of deliberately withholding the extent of U.S. Lend-Lease aid—proved a temporary disruption of Soviet-American harmony. The failure of the

Western Allies to deliver on their promise of a Second Front produced a rift in the coalition. Stalin bitterly protested in June 1943 to FDR and Churchill about the grave effects of their broken promises upon the "subsequent course of the war" and about not being consulted beforehand. Rumors of a separate peace began to circulate.[52]

That the Western members of the Allied coalition were able to wage war without, as Marshall repeatedly observed, a "coherent strategic plan for defeating the Axis," had only been possible because they had engaged in defensive operations and because of the unexpected survival of the USSR. The significance of the Soviet contribution, documented by ULTRA, increasingly influenced the course of U.S. and British planning and allocation of precious resources. During the summer of 1943 Kent Roberts Greenfield noted, following a discussion with Army Ground Forces Chief of Staff General James Christiansen: "I remarked that it had seemed . . . when it was decided to freeze the Army at 7,700,000, with 3,200,000 and the cream of quality allocated to the Air Forces, a fateful decision had been made, on the assumption that an air war plus the Russians could produce a decisive victory, and that this was to stake the future of the nation on a gamble. General C[hristiansen] said that he felt that this was exactly true."[53] On 8 November 1943 General John R. Deane had cabled from Moscow: "Belief current here that cross-Channel operations involve same problems as river crossing. Soviets actually believe Channel no more difficult than Dnieper."[54] Failure to grasp the other's difficulties cut both ways.

Awareness of their dependence on the Red Army and, also perhaps, growing political and strategic maturity brought about a determined effort to reach closure on a mutually agreed strategy. At the Quebec conference (code-named QUADRANT) in August, the CCS and their political chiefs assigned highest priority for 1944 to the cross-Channel assault. Reassured, Stalin agreed to host an October meeting of Big Three foreign ministers in Moscow and to attend a tripartite summit conference at Tehran in November.

Summer and fall of 1943 witnessed victory in the U-boat war, the invasion of the Italian mainland and Italy's surrender in September, and the Red Army's checkmating of the *Wehrmacht* via Operation CITADEL, the enormous armored engagement in the Kursk salient. By year's end a major counteroffensive had expelled the Germans from huge sections of Soviet territory. Tehran made clear how the linkages between the three partners were being deformed by battlefield successes and the multiplying Soviet and American military strength. When, at Cairo, the British proposed to delay transfer of combat troops and landing craft from the

Mediterranean and to push back the date of OVERLORD, FDR refused to discuss the matter without Stalin being present.[55]

At Tehran, for the first time, the Soviets played a direct role in the determination of overall strategy. Insisting that the OVERLORD timetable be honored, Stalin spoke against giving priority to the Mediterranean and urged that Anglo-American forces in Italy support OVERLORD by invading southern France (ANVIL) as the CCS planners had earlier proposed. Simultaneously, Stalin promised, Soviet forces would launch a major offensive, making impossible German withdrawals from the East. He reiterated the pledge made at the Moscow Conference of Foreign Ministers to enter the war against Japan after Germany's defeat.[56] Churchill protested but, outgunned, was outvoted by FDR and Stalin.

Although Britain's strategy of indirection had been repudiated at the highest levels, it continued in effect, given the impossibility of withdrawing Allied contingents from myriad points on the periphery of the Axis empire. Whether this interminable dispute over strategy hindered ultimate victory remains a matter of intense controversy.[57]

Lack of empathy and, indeed, of basic information characterized Anglo-Soviet-American relations. Recognition of the problem in the aftermath of Tehran (and of the requirement for planning and discussions at lower levels) caused all three nations to enlarge their military missions. In one sense the most important "military mission" (and symbol of inter-Allied cooperation) was OVERLORD's commander. That post was filled after Tehran by designation of General Dwight D. Eisenhower as Supreme Allied Commander of the Allied Expeditionary Force. Relying on military missions led to major and minor problems. For example, lack of a formal means of integrating Soviet requirements into the deliberations of the Combined Shipping Board exerted baneful effects throughout the war.[58] The military missions did serve as go-betweens for assorted exchanges of technical data and intelligence. Between August and December 1943 Soviet officers made 52 visits—most outside London—to British offices, training stations, and bases. They inspected a torpedo factory, witnessed a degaussing demonstration, and observed a heavy bomber raid depart RAF Oakington.[59] This openness typified British and U.S. behavior toward their guests.

Modest progress occurred with regard to sharing of information on such subjects as the enemy order of battle. Considerable Anglo-Soviet and Soviet-American sharing took place with regard to deciphered Axis intelligence and weapons technology, although it paled by comparison with Anglo-American collaboration in the intelligence realm. Roosevelt and

Churchill adamantly rejected the idea of making known to the Russians either the fact of research on an atomic bomb or technical information about its development. Ironically, Soviet wartime espionage rendered this ban mostly ineffective.[60]

Willingness to divulge knowledge about one's own forces, their disposition, weaponry, and casualties depended on circumstance and national sensibilities. All through 1942 and much of 1943 American and British representatives complained bitterly about the refusal of Soviet authorities to provide complete, up-to-date briefings and access to the battlefronts. In the rapidly improving situation after Stalingrad, the Russians became more cooperative. A visit by LTG Gifford Martel to the southwest front in May 1943 and an extended tour by his successor testified to the new openness.[61]

Instances of attempting to withhold information in order to extract concessions did persist. Though the British were typically less forthcoming, U.S. and British military missions provided a wide range of information to each other and to their Russian partner.[62] Here again, openness tilted in favor of the Anglo-American relationship. A wartime study concluded: "By 1944 British officers were established on the staffs of all important U.S Development and Training Establishments, British students attended a number of U.S. schools, and an unrestricted flow of information in both directions was achieved."[63] A parallel effort to obtain information about Soviet military technology was negotiation of "An Agreement on the Exchange of Technical Information" and arrangements for a British mission headed by Sir Henry Tizard to go to Moscow in February 1943. Postponed because of Tizard's illness, War Cabinet misgivings led to putting off the mission indefinitely. This may well have been the zenith of Soviet-Western cooperation in non-political spheres.

The period from spring 1944 to war's end embraced both the full flowering of coalition hybrids planted in the gloom of 1941-42 and their shriveling in the cold gusts generated by resurgent chauvinism. During the months before D-Day, Allied military collaboration proceeded on multiple levels. From bases in Britain, Anglo-American air flotillas escalated their attacks on Germany (POINTBLANK). The United States initiated a "shuttle bombing" campaign (FRANTIC) between Italian and Soviet bases. Controversy dogged both programs. British and American strategists debated POINTBLANK's targeting and tactics. The potential benefits of bombing Axis targets from the USSR had been bruited since early in the war, and American and Soviet officials finally worked out arrangements for three bases (Poltova, Mirgorod, Piryatin) in early 1944. One scholar has claimed that the operation had political aims.[64] In any case, FRANTIC produced disappointing results and major frustrations. Language and cultural difficulties, differing methods of operations and the oppressive atmosphere encountered by the American crews, and logistical problems posed by the enormous distances made FRANTIC a case study of the challenges of combined operations.[65]

As planning proceeded for operation OVERLORD, an awkward debate ensued within the CCS concerning how much and when information about the plan should be given the Soviets. To answer Russian claims that the Allies had stockpiled enormous forces in Britain, Anthony Eden proposed that Ambassador Maisky be told how many divisions were presently in the United Kingdom. The COS reluctantly agreed, acknowledging that "the one decision in which the Russians took an absorbing interest was Overlord."[66] In late October the U.S. Military Mission in Moscow began to provide daily briefings about OVERLORD. The British COS objected that OVERLORD "was a Combined British-U.S. responsibility and, as a matter of principle, any information given to the Russians concerning it should come from the Combined Chiefs of Staff." Eventually, a compromise—to supply information "on the broadest lines"—was reached.[67]

Allied coordination proved among the most striking features of the cross-Channel assault on 6 June 1944. The list of successes started with the creation of a integrated multinational staff at SHAEF-London. Before, during, and subsequent to the Normandy invasion, clashes of prima donnas, xenophobic outbursts, and strong disagreements over operational matters tested the Anglo-American link; but, tempered by friendship and mutual respect at lower levels of SHAEF, Eisenhower's leadership was never seriously challenged.[68] As casualties mounted and the expectations of an immediate German collapse were dashed, popular support for the coalition remained unshaken.

Though OVERLORD was delayed to increase the weight of the invasion force, the situation on the Soviet-German front certainly influenced the Anglo-American timetable. On the third anniversary of BARBAROSSA, the Red Army began its promised major offensive in Byelorussia. Operation BAGRATION threw 118 infantry divisions, supported by tanks and massed artillery, against a *Wehrmacht* already battered by relentless Soviet assaults in the north. In less than two weeks, Army Group Center had been reduced to a scattered remnant of eight divisions, and the Red Army had reconquered Byelorussia and opened a gaping 250-mile hole in German defenses. The road was open to Poland and beyond. BAGRATION ensured there would be no transfer of forces from the East to stiffen resistance to the Anglo-American forces pushing out of Normandy. By destroying the

German defensive system in this pivotal area, BAGRATION arguably was the most spectacular military triumph of the entire war.[69]

Consultation among the Allies, with several significant exceptions, continued to improve. Admiral Kharlamov toured Normandy in July 1944. Once OVERLORD was concluded, concerted action between Soviet, British, and American leaders at the operational level broadened into arrangements approximating full-fledged cooperation. By September 1944 the Allies were poised for the final descent upon Germany itself. The Nazi war machine's unexpected resilience and logistical difficulties (primarily the penchant of mechanized/motorized forces to outrun their fuel and ammunition supplies) slowed the Allied drive. Soviet forces had halted at the Vistula (watching the Warsaw Uprising flare and sputter out), and the fulcrum of struggle in the East shifted south, as the Red Army mounted a powerful drive into the Balkans and Hungary. British and American armies were checked west of the Rhine River. In Italy some 26 German divisions still opposed the Allied armies and difficult terrain had negated the substantial superiority of the Fifteenth Army Group. In mid-December came the stunning German counterattack in the Ardennes, as Hitler expended his last reserves in a suicidal attempt to split apart the Grand Alliance.

The Battle of the Bulge affirmed how strong were the links between the Allies. Shrugging off the recriminations following operation MARKET GARDEN (Montgomery's scheme to breach the Rhine barrier) in September, Eisenhower placed U.S. forces north of the German breakthrough under Montgomery's command. Aided by improving weather for Anglo-American tactical air forces and the opening (Stalin's response to an impassioned plea from Churchill) of a gigantic Soviet offensive all along the central sector of the eastern front, the British from the north and Patton's Third Army from the south eliminated the Ardennes salient. Ignoring the clamor to permit Montgomery to dash for Berlin, Eisenhower returned to the strategy of a broad-front advance in early March. This decision reflected a desire to ensure adequate separation between British, U.S., and Soviet units.

The Red Army's General Headquarters and the People's Commissariat for the Defense of the USSR worked to coordinate military operations on the eastern front with the advancing forces of the Western Allies. The primary medium of communication continued to be the U.S. and British Military Missions. Another area of cooperation was the combined discussion of "strategic disinformation" during the last stages of the war. Especially important were the "bomb line" discussions to ensure that

Allied strategic air forces flying missions in the Balkans and elsewhere in Eastern Europe not inadvertently attack advance columns of the Red Army. These efforts gained urgency when U.S. P-38 Lightnings in November 1944 strafed a Soviet infantry unit, killing a lieutenant general and five other soldiers.[70] On 6 February 1945 an agreement between the headquarters of the Soviet, British, and U.S. Army Air Forces established a line of demarcation for air raids. This agreement also stipulated an exchange of information about present and projected operations of the three air forces. A month later came a formal agreement on joint air operations to cover advancing Allied ground forces.

As the end neared, interaction at the operational level became extensive. From the west, elements of British and Canadian forces under Field Marshal Bernard Montgomery and of the U.S. First and Third Armies were approaching their designated "stop" lines. On the Soviet side, the drive into Germany was done by the First Byelorussian, First Ukrainian, Second Byelorussian, and Third and Fourth Ukrainian fronts. There occurred a series of personal meetings and radio communications between operational commanders. The coming linkup led to bilateral exchanges between SHAEF Commander Eisenhower and Montgomery with their Soviet counterpart, Marshal Georgi K. Zhukov. These communications (which triggered a bureaucratic firestorm in Washington because of the CCS's claim to sole authority in any negotiations between the Allies) dealt with boundaries, signals protocols, and arrangements for artillery and air attacks. Crude but functional signs and identification signals were agreed to between Soviet, U.S., and British forces.[71] These ad hoc arrangements sufficed until the historic linkup of American and Soviet forces at Torgau on the Elbe River. Germany's surrender on 7 May 1945 at Rheims was made jointly to representatives of the coalition.

Growing political tensions during the concluding months of the war have obscured the very real manifestations of allied cooperation at the operational and strategic levels. At the Yalta conference in February 1945 the Allies agreed to continue coordination of air and ground operations, to effect a zonal occupation of Germany that approximated the projected final positions of individual armies, and to implement a three-power occupation of Germany and of Berlin. Too, the Soviet reaffirmation at Yalta of their pledge to enter the war against Japan and to engage the substantial Japanese forces still in China reassured American military leaders then calculating the costs of operation DOWNFALL, the invasion of the Japanese home islands. Of course, Hiroshima made irrelevant the projected Soviet role in reducing American casualties and speeding the Pacific War to a victorious close.[72]

In hindsight, any assessment of relative contributions to victory is problematic. U.S. and British aid to the USSR, despite the complications that attended settling priorities, quarrels over specifications, and the delivery problem, proved an important adjunct to the Soviet war effort. Conversely, the achievement of Soviet forces in pinning down and then destroying the greater part of the German military juggernaut was pivotal to assuring the strategic freedom of choice of the Western Allies. But ascertaining *how* crucial was each partner's contribution and *how much* the journey to ultimate triumph was thereby shortened leads again into the nebulous dimension of "what if." Nonetheless, certain aspects deserve mention.

The contribution of operational and strategic intelligence (exemplified by ULTRA but also comprising U.S. decrypting of Japanese codes—MAGIC, espionage, photo reconnaissance, and document analysis) is widely acknowledged even if impossible to demonstrate. British and American cooperation in the intelligence realm stands as a remarkable manifestation of inter-Allied unity. The super secret ULTRA—shared liberally with the United States and on an episodic basis with the USSR—was the principal component.[73] It undergirded the triumphal effort to overcome the U-boat threat, which some historians claim saved Britain and shortened the war by two years. It assured Britain's retention of Egypt and thereby made possible the conquest of North Africa and reopening of the Mediterranean in 1943 rather than 1944. In combination with MAGIC from Japan's ambassador in Berlin, Admiral Oshima Hiroshi, ULTRA revealed the state of German defenses and the Nazi leadership's views during the run-up to OVERLORD.[74]

ULTRA's ambiguous role in eastern front operations is well documented. F. H. Hinsley has observed that British intelligence, mostly derived from decrypted *Luftwaffe* traffic, permitted Whitehall "to follow the day-to-day fighting on the eastern front in considerable detail." While caution about not disclosing the fact of the ULTRA secret and frustrations about Soviet refusal to provide systematic, comprehensive information about Red Army and German dispositions limited the amount of high-level intelligence passed to the Russians, the British did provide timely warning of German capabilities in a number of instances until early summer 1942. Thereafter, with the exception of operational intelligence during one critical stage of the battle of Stalingrad and regular assessments about Berlin's "main intentions," the dispatch of high-level intelligence ceased, a victim of British demands for a quid pro quo and Soviet stonewalling. Nor did Moscow share high-level information obtained from the Richard Sorge ring in Tokyo or the *Rote Kapelle* network. Recent assertions to the contrary regarding an independent Soviet capability to read ENIGMA, ULTRA ensured that Soviet forces could be disposed at critical junctures to deflect German attacks. That did not mean Western intelligence would be trusted or wisely used by Stalin.[75]

Often forgotten is the hidden face of intelligence: strategic and operational deception. The ability to conceal one's own order of battle and intentions and the parallel aim of deception, as Michael Howard has written, "to affect the actions of the adversary" are vital in modern warfare. World War II featured numerous successful Allied deception operations, ranging from the German acceptance of British notional armored divisions in the Western Desert to the imaginative use of double agents (conspicuously, of course, the "Double Cross System" employing turned German agents to feed disinformation to Berlin), and the operations—FORTITUDE and BODYGUARD—to confuse the German High Command about Allied intention to launch a cross-Channel attack, the makeup of invasion forces (inventing a U.S. First Army Group under Patton), and the site and timing of the assault.[76] The Soviets, who perceived deception and disinformation (*maskirovka*) as a basic principle, employed it at Stalingrad and prior to BAGRATION and succeeded in misleading Berlin about the Red Army's real and potential strength.[77] These accomplishments benefitted the Allied cause indirectly. The one unarguable achievement was the fact that no strategic commitment or operational timetable chiefly affecting another ally was betrayed—inadvertently or by design—by any member of the coalition.

The impact of the Anglo-American bombing offensive upon the eastern front is controversial. For many years, exaggerated claims as to the efficacy of air power led Soviet and some Western historians to deny *any* contribution of the Allied air forces to winning the war. Today, again in large measure thanks to the magisterial study of intelligence by F. H. Hinsley, it is clear that, however wasteful and ill coordinated may have been the combined bomber offensive, it caused Hitler to move large numbers of aircraft from the eastern front and give priority to production of fighter interceptors over the fighter-bombers, tanks, and towed artillery in such short supply on the eastern front. British intelligence attributed the *Luftwaffe*'s decline in Russia "mainly to the over riding claims of the defence of the Reich and of the fighting in other western theaters. . . . Fighters withdrawn from the eastern front in the autumn of 1943 to bolster the defence of the Reich were never replaced."[78] When added to the human and industrial replacement costs from Allied bombing, the shift of German resources from the battlefronts was substantial. Air power zealots perhaps would perceive as unworthy the essentially negative conclusion that all those B-17s and Lancasters served chiefly to reduce the *Luftwaffe*'s fighter formations; but Soviet troops crossing the Vistula and American, British, and Canadian forces wading ashore in Normandy were grateful for the diversion.[79]

It is striking that Cold War-generated pressures to rewrite the historical record quickly blotted out these instances of mutual assistance. Shortly after VE-Day, Eisenhower spoke with his aide, Captain Harry C. Butcher, about the likelihood of continued cooperation with the USSR. He commented that Anglo-American-Soviet relations were "at the same stage of arms-length dealing that marked the early Anglo-American contacts in 1940." However, just as British and Americans had become "allies in spirit as well as on paper" a determined effort to maintain and strengthen contacts with the Russians, relying on "blunt and forthright" communication, would produce similar results.[80] That was not to be.

Writing about the Napoleonic Era but also, perhaps, with an eye toward the demise of the World War II coalition, Henry A. Kissinger once observed:

> As long as the enemy is more powerful than any single member of the coalition, the need for unity outweighs all considerations of individual gain. Then the powers of repose can insist on the definition of war aims which, in all conditions, represent limitations. But when the enemy has been so weakened that each ally has the power to achieve its ends alone, a coalition is at the mercy of its most determined member.[81]

The Allied coalition's first two years reflected frank communication and the creation of mechanisms for coordination between London and Washington but, as well, limited military collaboration, sharp and seemingly interminable disagreements over strategy, assorted military debacles, and the near collapse of the Allied coalition. The year 1943 brought a floodtide of victories in widely dispersed theaters and the eventual settlement of a global (though hardly unitary) strategy, but also featured continuing misperceptions and paranoia. The final year of the war, characterized by the assured ability of each partner to follow its own course, did witness the crumbling among the coalition's leaders of political and psychological bonds held in place by the cement of necessity. Those months from spring 1944 to war's end also, however, beheld the flexing of structural and emotional connections between inter-Allied staff, the soldiers, sailors, and civilian populations of the coalition. The Axis "have always planned on a split of the Allies," General Marshall observed after Yalta. "They never for one moment calculated that the Allies could continue to conduct combined operations with complete understanding and good faith."[82] Comprising nations with conflicting ideologies and starkly differing cultural outlooks, the survival of the Grand Alliance was remarkable.

What stands out today is how little systematic communication over these matters took place between Washington, London, and Moscow. This is made especially acute by comparing the paucity of structural links between the Western allies and the Soviet Union with the proliferation of such connections between British and Americans. Moscow's exclusion from the Combined Chiefs of Staff and the "protocol" approach to assignment of war material led to the Soviets asking for the stars and the West promising the moon, a certain guarantee of mutual frustration. Equally unsystematic for rather different reasons were arrangements for sharing of intelligence broadly construed. In addition to the sketchy procedures for exchange of battlefield intelligence, agreements were signed to facilitate the transfer of information about technological innovations deemed relevant to the coalition war effort. Those arrangements were among the first victims of the growing tension between Russia and its western partners as victory neared. Nor was the Anglo-American record in these matters substantially more encouraging.

Compared with the historical record, the Allied coalition of World War II stands as an impressive achievement. Whatever the motives of the partners, their behavior embodied substantial coordination and instances of generous support. Only if compared against the archetype of unity and if cardinal emphasis is accorded the haste with which the connections linking the British, Russian, and American peoples were ripped asunder at war's end does the performance of this coalition rate as less than remarkable. The current situation, when the elaborate postwar system of compacts on both sides have crumbled and even such an abiding symbol of alliance as NATO appears headed for the rubbish heap of history, dramatizes how difficult is the process of creating and sustaining a political/military coalition. Memories of a common endeavor may yet prove the most powerful bond forged during World War II.

NOTES

1. For a comprehensive examination of European diplomacy prior to the outbreak of the war, see Donald C. Watt, *How the War Came: The Immediate Origins of the Second World War, 1938-1939* (New York, 1989).

2. Winston S. Churchill, *History of the Second World War* (6 vols.; Boston, 1948-53), III, p. 118.

3. Quoted in Martin Gilbert, *Winston S. Churchill: Finest Hour, 1939-1941* (Boston, 1983), 1118-19, 1121.

4. See the exchanges in Warren F. Kimball, ed., *Churchill and Roosevelt: The Complete Correspondence* (3 vols.; Princeton, 1984), I, 24 and *passim.*

5. Kimball, ed., *Churchill & Roosevelt,* I, 3-20. Also see Raymond A. Callahan, *Churchill: Retreat from Empire* (Wilmington, Del., 1984), and David Reynolds, "Roosevelt, Churchill, and the Wartime Anglo-American Alliance, 1939-1945: Towards a New Synthesis," in William Roger Louis and Hedley Bull, eds., *The Special Relationship: Anglo-American Relations Since 1945* (New York, 1986).

6. Theodore A. Wilson, *The First Summit: Roosevelt and Churchill at Placentia Bay, 1941* (rev. ed., Lawrence, Kans., 1991), 225-226; Kimball, *Churchill & Roosevelt,* I, 227-28, and Warren F. Kimball, *The Juggler: Franklin Roosevelt as Wartime Statesman* (Princeton, N.J., 1991), 64-81.

7. H. Duncan Hall, *North American Supply* (London, 1955), 298-333.

8. For prewar naval exchanges, see Tracy B. Kittredge, "United States-British Naval Cooperation, 1939-1947," unpublished monograph (5 parts, Naval Historical Center Archives, Washington, D.C., n.d.), and James R. Leutze, *Bargaining for Supremacy: Anglo-American Naval Relations, 1937-1941* (Chapel Hill, N.C., 1977).

9. For these issues, see Richard M. Leighton and Robert W. Coakley, *Global Logistics and Strategy, 1940-1943* (Washington, 1955), Mark S. Watson, *Chief of Staff: Prewar Plans and Preparations* (Washington, D.C., 1950), W. K. Hancock and M. M. Gowing, *British War Economy* (London, 1949), H. Duncan Hall, *North American Supply* (London, 1955), and Vernon E. Davis, *The History of the Joint Chiefs of Staff in World War II: Organizational Development,* (2 vols.; Washington, D.C., 1972), I.

10. Davis, *History of JCS: Organizational Development,* I, 112-114.

11. Maurice Matloff and Edwin M. Snell, *Strategic Planning for Coalition Warfare, 1941-42* (Washington, D.C., 1953), 32-48.

12. Matloff and Snell, *Strategic Planning for Coalition Warfare, 1941-42,* 21-25, 53-55; Wilson, *The First Summit,* 93-96, 111-34; J. R. M. Butler, ed., *Grand Strategy* (London, 1957), II, 424-27, 547-51.

13. See Michael Howard, *The Mediterranean Strategy in the Second World War* (London, 1968), 1-18; and the chapter, "Great Britain: The Indirect Strategy," in this volume.

14. Wilson, *The First Summit,* 116-18; Michael Sherry, *The Rise of American Air Power: The Creation of Armageddon* (New Haven, Conn., 1987), 97.

15. Matloff and Snell, *Strategic Planning for Coalition Warfare, 1941-42,* 29-30; Russell F. Weigley, *The American Way of War: A History of United States Military Strategy and Policy* (New York, 1973), especially ch. 14.

16. See Hall, *North American Supply,* and Richard M. Leighton and Robert W. Coakley, *Global Logistics and Strategy, 1940-1943.*

17. Davis, *History of JCS: Organizational Development,* I, 111.

18. Testimony of General Leonard T. Gerow, U.S. Congress, *Pearl Harbor Attack,* Part 3, 991, quoted in Davis, *History of JCS: Organizational Development,* I, 112.

19. USA: Staff Conversations file, WO 191/345, PRO.

20. USA: Staff Conversations file, 10 August 1940, WO 191/345, PRO.

21. Davis, *History of JCS: Organizational Development,* I, 114-20.

22. Mark S. Watson, *Chief of Staff: Prewar Plans and Preparations* (Washington, D.C., 1950), 319. See Davis, *History of JCS: Organizational Development,* I, 56-59, 221-39, for the emergence of the JCS.

23. U.S. Secretary for Collaboration to Secretary, British Military Mission, Subject: "Methods of Collaboration between the United States Army and Navy and the British Military Mission in Washington," 3 June 1941, WPD 4402-29, RG 165, NARA; see also Davis, *History of the JCS: Organizational Development,* I, 126-28.

24. The Atlantic Conference both proclaimed the existence of an anti-Axis combination and signaled its limits. The fullest treatment of the Atlantic Conference is Wilson, *The First Summit.*

25. Chief of Staff to Chaney, Subject: "Letter of Instructions," 26 April 1941, WPD 4402-89, RG 165, NA; during summer and fall 1941, Chaney and Ghormley met regularly with the British Chiefs of Staff and served as the conduit for communications between Marshall, Stark, and Arnold and the British War Office. The British at first viewed SPOB as equivalent to a U.S. military mission but soon grasped its limitations; Annex to Note by Joint Planning Staff, "Establishment of Missions in Washington and London," J.P. (41) 425, 2 June 41. The Americas: U.S.A.-Intercommunication, 17 December 1940-7 November 1943, and Note on C.O.S. (41) 470, 2 August 1941, WO 193/317, PRO.

26. On 19 June 1941, the Joint Planning Staff reviewed the benefits and defects of sending a military mission to the USSR following the expected German attack. The JPS concluded that prolonged Russian resistance would make necessary a British presence in Moscow. Should the Russians collapse, that mission could operate "in such parts which remain free from German occupation." See the documentation in "Russia: British Liaison Mission, 1941-1945," WO 193/645, PRO.

27. See Mason-Macfarlane's communications with the War Office for the problems

encountered, LTG Mason-Macfarlane, Personal Correspondence with CIGS, 24 June 1941-23 April 1942, WO 216/124. Also consult Joan Beaumont, *Comrades in Arms: British Aid to Russia, 1941-1945* (London, 1980), and Gabriel Gorodetsky, *Stafford Cripps' Mission to Moscow, 1940-1942* (Cambridge, 1984).

28. N. Kharlamov, *Difficult Mission: War Memoirs of a Soviet Admiral in Great Britain during the Second World War* (Moscow, 1983), 32-34, 43-44.

29. George Herring, *Aid to Russia, 1941-1945: Strategy, Diplomacy, the Origins of the Cold War* (New York, 1973), 13-17; Theodore A. Wilson, "In Aid of America's Interests: The Provision of Lend-Lease to the Soviet Union, 1941-1942," in G. N. Sevost'ianov and W. F. Kimball, eds., *Soviet-U.S. Relations, 1933-1942* (Moscow, 1989), 126-27, 132; Leighton and Coakley, *Global Logistics and Strategy, 1940-1943*, 97-104.

30. Edward R. Stettinius, Jr., *Lend-Lease: Weapon for Victory* (New York, 1944), 124-25.

31. Griffiss was in Moscow from mid-November 1941 until mid-February 1942. He made only limited progress in getting an agreement about air routes before being recalled. He was killed when the Liberator bringing him back to Britain was shot down on 15 February 1942 by a Polish Air Force fighter off the south coast near Plymouth. See Townsend Griffiss "201 File," U.S. Air Force Historical Center, Maxwell AFB, Montgomery, Ala.

32. Herring, *Aid to Russia*, 41-42, 103.

33. This debate was complicated by the presence of Field Marshal Sir John Dill, whom Churchill had "exiled" to Washington. See ch. 1 in this volume.

34. Cordell Hull, *Memoirs* (2 vols.; New York, 1948), II, 1116-19; see also the documentation in the papers of Adolph Berle, FDRL, and Davis, *Origin of the Joint and Combined Chiefs of Staff*, I, 35-36.

35. Hull to FDR, 22 December 1941, ABCD folder, PSF "Safe Files," Box 1, FDRL. A parallel WPD study recommended that a Supreme War Council be "composed of the Head of the Government of each of the Allied Powers or his representative," with an executive secretariat made up of two members from the army, navy, air force, and "production management" of each nation, WPD, "Notes on Agenda proposed in British Message of 18 December 1941," ARCADIA Files, WPD 4402-136, RG 165, NA.

36. "CCS" folder, PSF "Safe Files," Box 10, FDRL.

37. Alfred D. Chandler, Jr., ed., *The Papers of Dwight D. Eisenhower: The War Years* (5 vols.; Baltimore, Md., 1970), I, xx.

38. For the evolution of ETO and the authority of its commander, see Chandler, ed., *The Papers of Dwight D. Eisenhower: The War Years*, I, 331-35. Chaney's desire to work closely with the British and conviction that the Army Air Forces commander should head a combined force clashed with General Arnold's advocacy of a separate headquarters for the AAF, Interview Transcripts, 34, 64, Box 6, Charles L. Bolte Papers, MHI.

39. Chandler, ed., *The Papers of Dwight D. Eisenhower: War Years*, I, xx-xxi.

40. G. N. Macready, "Report on work of British Joint Staff Mission to North America, 1940-1945," 17 January 1946, WO 32/12178, PRO.

41. JSM (Dill) to War Office, 22 December 1942, WO 106/3318. The offending document was C.C.S. (42), 100th meeting, item 2.

42. Maurice Matloff and Edwin W. Snell, *Strategic Planning for Coalition Warfare, 1941-1942* (Washington, 1953), 174-86; see also Michael Howard, *Grand Strategy*, IV (London, 1972), 225-85.

43. See Kimball, ed., *Churchill & Roosevelt*, I, 437-66; Ministry of Foreign Affairs of the USSR, *Correspondence Between the Chairman of the Council of Ministers of the U.S.S.R. and the Presidents of the U.S.A. and the Prime Ministers of Great Britain During the Great Patriotic War of 1941-1945* (2 vols.; Moscow, 1957), II, 22-25.

44. U.S. Department of State, *Foreign Relations of the United States* (Washington, 1862-), *1942*, III, 577, 594.

45. J. M. A. Gwyer, *Grand Strategy* (London, 1964), III, 596-97, 682-83.

46. See Mark A. Stoler, *George C. Marshall: Soldier-Statesman of the American Century* (Boston, 1989), 98-102.

47. Winston S. Churchill, *The Second World War* (6 vols.; Boston, 1948-1953), IV, 472-502.

48. These issues are dealt with in Mark A. Stoler, *The Politics of the Second Front: Military Planning and Diplomacy in Coalition Warfare, 1941-1943* (Westport, Conn., 1977); Kimball, *The Juggler*; Leighton and Coakley, *Global Logistics and Strategy, 1940-1943*, 661-686; Richard M. Leighton, "U.S. Merchant Shipping and the British Import Crisis," in Kent R. Greenfield, ed., *Command Decisions* (Washington, 1960); and Robert P. Browder and Thomas G. Smith, *Independent: A Biography of Lewis W. Douglas* (New York, 1986).

49. Maurice Matloff, *Strategic Planning for Coalition Warfare, 1943-1944* (Washington, 1959), 106.

50. U.S. Department of State, *Foreign Relations of the United States: The Conferences at Washington, 1941-42, and Casablanca, 1943* (Washington, 1968), 627-37, 760-61, 791-98, 803-7.

51. Matloff, *Strategic Planning for Coalition Warfare, 1943-44*, 126-45; *FRUS: Washington and Quebec*, 364-71.

52. *Stalin's Correspondence*, I, 131-41, II, 70-76; also see Vojtech Mastny, *Russia's Road to the Cold War: Diplomacy, Warfare, and the Politics of Communism, 1941-1945* (New York, 1979), 73-85.

53. Interview with BG James G. Christiansen, 12 May 1944, Box 19, RG 319, Records of the General Staff: OCMH Files, NA.

54. Moscow to AGWAR, for Colonel Nelson from General John R. Deane, 8 November 1943, Folder: "Mil. Trng. ASF-1: Radiograms," Box 19, Arthur Trudeau Papers, MHI.

55. Matloff, *Strategic Planning for Coalition Warfare, 1943-1944,* 244-69, 347-60; Department of State, *Foreign Relations of the United States: The Conferences at Cairo and Tehran, 1943* (Washington, 1961), 487-508.

56. *Ibid.*, 489, 499-500.

57. See, for example, Kent Roberts Greenfield, *American Strategy in World War II: A Reconsideration* (Baltimore, 1963), Walter S. Dunn, *Second Front Now* (Tuscaloosa, Ala., 1980), John Grigg, *1943: The Victory that Never Was* (New York, 1980), and Trumbull Higgins, "The Anglo-American Historians' War in the Mediterranean, 1942-1945," *Military Affairs*, 34 (October, 1970).

58. Memorandum for the head of Army Section, 30 Military Mission, (August 1943), WO 202/911. The Soviet viewpoint—describing the inefficiency and bureaucratic snarls their representatives encountered and concluding that Western poor performance cloaked Machiavellian motives—is found, for example, in N. Kharlamov, *Difficult Mission,* 110-115.

59. "List of visits made by Soviet Military Mission members," Status of Items shipped to Russia, etc., WO 202/911. See also the files (WO 202/914) of the Russian Liaison Group, chronicled in a monograph of October 1945.

60. See Bradley F. Smith, "Sharing Ultra in World War II," *International Journal of Intelligence and Counterintelligence* 2 (Spring 1988), and his "Soviet-American Intelligence and Technical Cooperation in World War II," unpublished paper delivered at Fourth Soviet-American Colloquium on World War II, Rutgers University, October 1990; F. H. Hinsley, *et al., British Intelligence in the Second World War: Its Influence on Strategy and Operations* (4 vols.; London, 1979–90), II, 41-66; and Martin Sherwin, *A World Destroyed: The Atomic Bomb and the Grand Alliance* (New York, 1975).

61. "Report of Visit by LTG Martel to Russian South West Front, 11-19 May 1943," British Military Mission in Russia files, WO 232/4, PRO.

62. See, for example, the file of information about British casualties broken down by theater and by type provided to the Soviet government in May 1943, "British Casualties: Information Provided to the Russian General Staff," 12 May 1943, WO 202/912.

63. "Report on Work of British Joint Staff Mission to North America, 1940-1945" (January 1946), WO 32/12178, PRO.

64. Sherry, *Rise of American Air Power,* 265.

65. Richard C. Lukas, *Eagles East: The Army Air Forces and the Soviet Union, 1941-1945* (Tallahassee, Fla., 1970), 192-201.

66. "Information for the Russians and Moscow Conf-Oct. 43" Box 0301/1, WO 106/4161; Kerr to F.O., 22 October 1943, *ibid.*

67. After fighting a rearguard action, British chiefs agreed to periodic disclosure of the details of the buildup for OVERLORD. Indeed, C.C.S. 4261, 6 December 1943, authorized "deception experts" to proceed to Moscow to coordinate plans with the Soviet General Staff, J.S.M. Washington (Dill) to W.C.O, London (COS), 29 October 1943, 79/misc/1368 (14540) WO 32.

68. Among studies detailing these issues are Stephen E. Ambrose, *Eisenhower* (New York, 1983), Nigel Hamilton, *Monty: Master of the Battlefield, 1942-1944* (London, 1983), Omar Bradley, *A General's Life* (New York, 1983), Richard Lamb, *Montgomery in Europe, 1943-1945: Success or Failure?* (London, 1983), and Carlo D'Este, *Decision in Normandy* (London, 1983).

69. John Erickson, *The Road to Berlin* (Boulder, Colo., 1983), 224-30.

70. Lukas, *Eagles East,* 183-84.

71. See David Eisenhower, *Eisenhower At War, 1943-1945* (New York, 1986), 754-59.

72. See Louis Morton, "Soviet Intervention in the War with Japan," *Foreign Affairs* 40 (July 1962), 653-62, and Barton J. Bernstein, "Writing, Righting, and Wronging the Historical Record: President Truman's Letter on his Atomic Bomb Decision," *Diplomatic History* 16, 1 (Winter 1992), 163-73; recent debates about Soviet participation in the Pacific War are ably presented in Leon Sigal, *Fighting to a Finish: The Politics of War Termination in the United States and Japan, 1945* (Ithaca, N.Y., 1988).

73. See, for example, Bradley Smith, *The Ultra-Magic Deals: And the Most Secret Special Relationship, 1940-1946* (Novato, Calif., 1992).

74. F. H. Hinsley, "British Intelligence in the Second World War," in Christopher Andrew and Jeremy Noakes, eds., *Intelligence and International Relations, 1900-1945* (Exeter Studies in History Number 15, Exeter, 1987), 209-18; Hinsley, *British Intelligence,* III, 2, 41-102; for Oshima and MAGIC, see Carl Boyd, "Significance of MAGIC and the Japanese Ambassador to Berlin: (V) News of Hitler's Defense Preparations for Allied Invasion of Western Europe," *Intelligence and National Security* 4, 3 (July 1989), 461-79.

75. Hinsley, *British Intelligence,* III, Part 1, 19-20; also II, 60-62. For recent assessments of ULTRA's role, see the studies by Geoffrey Smith already cited, Geoff Jukes, "The Soviets and Ultra," *Intelligence and National Security* 2 (April 1988); P. S. Milner-Barry, "The Soviets and Ultra: A Comment on Jukes' Hypothesis," *Intelligence and National Security* 2 (April 1988); and Timothy Mulligan, "Spies, Ciphers and Zitadelle: Intelligence and the Battle of Kursk," *Journal of Contemporary History,* 22 (1987), and Christopher Andrew and Oleg Gordievsky, *KGB: The Inside Story of Its Foreign Operations from Lenin to Gorbachev* (New York, 1990).

76. Michael Howard, *British Intelligence in the Second World War: Strategic Deception* 5 (New York, 1990), ix, *passim.*

77. See David M. Glantz, *Soviet Military Deception in the Second World War* (London, 1989), and his *The Role of Intelligence in Soviet Military Strategy in World War II* (Novato, Calif., 1990).

78. Hinsley, *British Intelligence,* III, Part 1, 21.

79. See R. J. Overy, *The Air War, 1939-1945* (New York, 1980), 132-62; Sherry, *The Rise of American Air Power,* 152-66; and Charles Messenger, *"Bomber" Harris and the Strategic Bombing Offensive,* 1939-1945 (New York, 1984).

80. Harry C. Butcher, *My Three Years With Eisenhower* (New York, 1946), 855.

81. Henry A. Kissinger, *A World Restored* (new edition; New York, 1964), 109.

82. Mark A. Stoler, *George C. Marshall: Soldier-Statesman of the American Century* (Boston, 1989), 127.

PART II ■ ECONOMY

GREAT BRITAIN: CYCLOPS

Richard J. Overy

During the years between the two world wars Britain remained one of the largest and most prosperous of the industrial economies. Given Britain's relative decline since 1945, it is important to recall that on the eve of war she was still a key part of the international economy, investing and trading abroad on a scale unmatched by any other European state. In terms of manufacturing Britain was second only to the United States. The living standards of her people were among the highest in the world. British prosperity depended a good deal on trade, much of it with the captive markets of the British Empire. It also rested on Britain's tradition as the centre of worldwide capitalism, providing the finance, shipping, and services to keep much of the world economy going. When war came in 1939 the British economy was widely regarded as a great source of strength for the Allied cause.

Yet during the inter-war years the British economy was subject to all kinds of difficulties, many of them generated by the effects of the war fought between 1914 and 1918. British trade, hit by growing competition abroad, never recovered the heady levels of 1913. In the aftermath of the Great Slump, during which world trade had been halved, Britain finally abandoned its defence of laissez-faire and adopted tariff protection. For much of the inter-war period Britain remained over-committed to old-fashioned industries—coal, shipbuilding, cotton—and was slow to adapt to the new industries. The result was high unemployment for much of the period, and a serious regional imbalance in economic growth. Britain's capitalists responded to these market forces very slowly and unevenly. Increasingly the government was compelled to extend regulation and controls in order to maintain economic growth and technical modernization.

State intervention produced by the late 1930s a kind of "managed economy," a capitalist system whose effective functioning depended on state guidance and high levels of state spending.

Nothing stimulated government intervention more than the deteriorating international circumstances of the 1930s. By 1934 the British began to think seriously about the problems of rearming for another war. Their thinking was coloured by the experience of 1914–1918. The government started from the assumption that any future great war would require full-scale mobilization of the economic resources of the nation. British leaders regarded economic strength and staying-power as important as military strength; indeed the military effort was seen to depend very heavily on the ability to maintain a stable and productive economy.[1]

These two things—preparing for large-scale mobilization of the economy, and maintaining economic stability—lay at the core of Britain's war preparations before 1939. British and French strategic planning in 1939 was predicated on the belief that Western financial and industrial strength would help to wear Germany down in a war of attrition. During the period of rearmament the government concentrated on building up industrial capacity, retraining labour, stockpiling scarce resources, and encouraging the production of strategically important materials and equipment. From 1937 onwards government orders for goods and services began to distort the pattern of trade and investment. Rearmament raised employment levels and encouraged fresh investment. Though businessmen sometimes resented the increase in state interference brought about by war preparation, there was a general acceptance by British capitalism that Britain's security required co-operation with government in building up Britain's armed strength.

By 1939 war preparation dominated the British economy. It was calculated that the soldier of 1939 needed three times the level of economic back-up enjoyed by his counterpart in 1914.[2] The financing of rearmament was higher than at any time in Britain's peace-time history. Indeed the scale of Britain's commitments for defence at home and abroad were so great that serious economic strains became evident even before the outbreak of war. Large-scale war preparations exposed a number of obvious vulnerabilities which had to be overcome before Britain's economic strength could be exercised effectively. In the first place the expansion of military production underlined Britain's very high degree of dependence on outside sources of supply. During the 1930s over half of British food supplies came from overseas. Almost all the basic strategic materials (oil, aluminum, tin, rubber, manganese, etc.) had to be imported. The maintenance of secure shipping links with the outside world remained a top priority throughout the war. Britain might have survived a blockade for some months, but there was no doubt that without reasonable access to world markets a total war economy could not be sustained. British leaders knew that their nation's economic effort could not rely on domestic resources; even before the outbreak of war the flow of essential goods from the Empire and the United States was used to supplement domestic supplies. Throughout the war the British economy was sustained by the rest of the free world. The question of how to buy and ship these supplies remained a critical one for the British war effort.

The second issue was money. By the late spring of 1939 the Chancellor of the Exchequer warned the government that they could not continue the current level of military expenditure without risking financial collapse. During 1939 Britain ran a high balance-of-trade deficit and a substantial deficit on the domestic budget. Yet the government remained committed to maintaining financial stability: "The maintenance of our financial and economic front is as essential to our war effort as . . . the prosecution of our military activities" wrote the chancellor in 1941.[3] At all costs the government wished to avoid the high inflation of the previous war, which brought the threat of social unrest and raised the cost of the war unnecessarily. The problem was solved by careful financial planning and an exceptional degree of state control over the capital market and home demand. But here, too, Britain needed the generosity of her allies, who provided goods for nothing when Britain could no longer pay, or were willing to extend credit until Britain was in a better condition to pay.

The final issue was the production of weapons. By 1939 there was increasing competition between the claims of the military and the claims of civilians on the economy. The government wanted arms, but it also wanted a reasonably contented population and an acquiescent business community. Willy-nilly the state had to assume responsibility for converting civilian economic resources to war use, and for rationing the use of resources between the different claimants. Britain did have the advantage of a very large manufacturing base and a small farm sector. No structural shift was required to produce the capacity to manufacture weapons. Yet there was little alternative to the strategy of converting civilian production to military. Munitions could not be bought abroad in large quantities; there were only limited unemployed resources to use by 1939. The state came to control the physical production of goods to ensure on the one hand the reasonably efficient supply of good quality weapons, and on the other the maintenance of acceptable civilian living standards. State officials, working closely with the business community, gradually transformed British industry into one large government contractor working, in Churchill's words, "under complete authority of Government."[4] This did not make Britain into a collectivist economy, but it did require a high degree of consensus between government, business, and labour in order to achieve the economic goals of the regime.

These three issues—maintaining overseas supply, paying for the war effort, and controlling the production of goods—depended on political factors as much as economic. They could be mastered only by careful planning and administrative capability, and this in turn rested on the willingness of the political leadership to extend its influence into the economic market-place. The success of the war economy depended on the willingness of businessmen and labour to accept the sacrifices this entailed and to renounce freedom of manoeuvre. The history of Britain's economy in wartime is a reflection of the deep-seated conviction of her population that political and military survival was well worth the temporary loss of economic freedom.

The commitment to large-scale economic mobilization meant that there was little alternative to the state assuming very general responsibilities for running the economy. This had happened in the First World War, though only after a long period of muddle and uncertainty. By the late 1930s government intervention in the economy was more substantial and wide-ranging than it had been in 1914 (government expenditure was roughly double pre-war levels) and the transition to state control or regulation was technically more straightforward and politically less resistible. An apparatus for control was already in place before the outbreak of war. In the early stages of the war this apparatus revealed its limitations and was modified and extended; as the war went on the structure was revised in ways that brought almost all aspects of economic life under state control. By 1944 the British economy was as close to a command economy as it has ever been.

The initial instruments of control grew out of the parliamentary system itself. Ultimate responsibility for decisions affecting the economy always lay with the prime minister and Cabinet. But most of the routine work and much of the executive responsibility lay with the individual departments of state or with special Cabinet committees. Where a particular need was felt, new ministries were created (the Ministry for Co-ordination of Defence in 1936, the Ministry of Supply in 1939, the Ministry of Aircraft Production in 1940, etc.), but for much of the war the traditional ministries (Treasury, Board of Trade, Labour) dealt with day-to-day issues.

Their work was supplemented by the special committees set up to deal with economic questions. Most were ad hoc committees, established to deal with particular issues such as those for investment and savings, for foreign exchange, and for exports set up in 1939.

The committee system had deep roots in British constitutional practice. It was a flexible instrument, designed to fill gaps and trouble-shoot, able to gather information, discuss priorities, and offer advice and recommendations to Cabinet. Though it had the disadvantages that quick, decisive action could not usually be taken, it had the great advantage that issues were scrutinized fully and reasonably. The British system, in contrast to the dictator states, retained an open structure of criticism and review—what Churchill called "honest differences of opinion"[5]—which produced decisions that were judicious rather than intuitive, considered rather than impulsive. Nor did the British structure exclude urgent action when necessary. Committees could be established, meet, and report in two weeks.

The main problem facing the war-time administration was effective co-ordination of effort. As the degree of economic mobilization increased and the army of bureaucrats directing it grew, so it became imperative to link the different parts of the economic machine together, to prevent overlapping jurisdiction, or competition for resources or lack of priority. In the wake of Chamberlain's resignation in May 1940, Churchill insisted on a streamlining of the whole structure of committees and delegated powers. Five main co-ordinating committees were established—for Production, Economic Policy, Food Policy, Home Policy, and Civil Defence. All final decisions on policy were the preserve of the War Cabinet.[6] Churchill also encouraged a general rationalization of administrative procedures and a modification of bureaucratic protocol. Some ministers—notably Lord Woolton at the Ministry of Food—were able to achieve this, but partly because they were outsiders. Woolton came from industry, Lord Beaverbrook, minister of aircraft production, from the press, Hugh Dalton, minister of economic warfare, from academic life.

Yet on the whole the system in 1940 was not a great improvement on the more improvised structure it replaced. Under mounting criticism in the press and Parliament over the lack of clear planning and priority in the economy Churchill overhauled the system again early in 1941. Now he reduced to three the number of committees with responsibility for the economy. The first was the Lord President's Committee, which was charged with overseeing the home economy and general economic strategy; the second was a Production Executive, placed under the vigorous Minister of Labour, Ernest Bevin; the third was an Import Executive, designed to deal with the problems of paying for imports and shipping them back to Britain. The main ministers involved in economic policy met on the Production Executive where they were to reach consolidated agreement on issues that could not be resolved by one department alone. At the same time the Executive set up regional Production Executive Boards to co-ordinate action at the local level, a notorious weakness in the old structure. But the real strength of the two main committees derived from the quality of their chairmen as much as the inherent rationality of the structure. Sir John Anderson as Lord President of the Council and Ernest Bevin as chairman of the Production Executive were well suited to the task of knocking ministerial heads together and insisting on action. Bevin was an ideal choice because as minister of labour and national service he sat on the War Cabinet as well, and was responsible for the one resource, manpower, of which the British economy was genuinely short. This meant, in effect, that the rest of the economy could not move at a pace faster than labor supply, and made Bevin the key ministerial figure in economic planning.

The one drawback of the new system was the difficulty in demarcating responsibility between the Production Executive and the military supply departments. Too often detailed decisions on armaments were demanded of the Executive which might have been taken further down the organizational chain. The Production Executive found it difficult to take initiatives and instead reacted to issues raised by other ministries. During 1941 its meetings became less and less regular.[7] Most key decisions were taken in Churchill's Defence Committee or Anderson's Lord President's Committee. Early in 1942 Churchill decided to replace the Production Executive with a Ministry of Production to co-ordinate the programs and production of the armed forces. The new ministry was set up first under Lord Beaverbrook, then Oliver Lyttelton, who had distinguished himself at the Board of Trade during the early part of the war. Churchill was anxious to have a single voice to speak for British production on the Combined Boards then being set up with the United States, and the minister of production filled this role neatly. In practice many of the decisions about war production were still taken at Cabinet level, so that Lyttelton's role became that of supervisor and co-ordinator of war production.

By 1942 the governmental structure had become much more centralized. This was inevitable. In war time, decisions had to be taken and executive action authorized in a way which would not give rise to confusion or argument. Since only the War Cabinet could do this, it was natural that the administrative system would come to rely on central authority. At the same time controls at local level became more extensive and the army of officials more conspicuous. Government white-collar employment rose from 1.38 million in 1939 to 1.9 million in 1944.[8] The reorganization in 1942 was designed to strengthen the hand of local officials, through Regional Production Boards and Ministry of Labour controllers, so that the flow of directives from the centre could be used effectively where it mattered, on the ground.

The organization of the war economy proved sufficiently flexible and coherent to avoid any serious limitations on war production. It had the advantage that it could call on the help of experts who shared common goals and common outlook with their civil servant colleagues. Academic economists, social scientists, and statisticians were drafted to help with organizing information and outlining economic strategy; industrialists were seconded to work in government because of their technical and organizational skills.

This was not always a smooth development. There was a residue of deep distrust of state power in a country with a powerful laissez-faire tradition. There was considerable public skepticism about the competence of state officials and widespread hostility to "red tape" and creeping bureaucratization. Nevertheless there was little alternative to state control and as the war went on public unease gave way to a growing confidence in the ability of the state to cope with economic issues. In early 1944 the American ambassador John G. Winant wrote to Cordell Hull in Washington about the manifest success of Britain's war-time economic administration:[9]

> A most important factor in Britain, which does not have equal force for all countries, is that the wartime methods and controls have been operated with impressive efficiency in the civilian sector of the war economy as well as in production for the armed forces, with the result that on the whole distrust of the ability of government in economic matters has diminished. . . .

The civilian war effort was run by an administrative elite that proved reasonably homogeneous and co-operative. Above all, the great accretion in state power did not produce incompetent dictatorship on the one hand, nor stifling political conflict on the other. It is difficult to imagine that a voluntary system could have been more successful. It was the nature of the conflict that demanded the growth in state power; it was the nature of the British political system that kept such power within acceptable bounds.

Britain based its economic war effort on the assumption that supplies from abroad would continue to be available. Food and raw materials were essential to maintain domestic living standards and to sustain levels of weapons production. Some effort was made before 1939 to stockpile scarce resources, but the government recognized that this could never satisfy demand. British naval power and Britain's wide-flung commercial network were regarded as central weapons in her economic armoury. Together they would guarantee the flow of supplies. Little effort was made to adopt the strategy of autarky, or import-substitution, favoured in Germany and Japan.

The heavy dependence on overseas supply after 1939 was regarded not as a military problem but as an economic one. Not only did rearmament and war production push up the demand for imports, but they also reduced the capacity available from British factories to produce the exports to pay for them. It was clearly impossible to satisfy military demands and export demands at the same time. Yet without exports Britain was exposed to a sharp deterioration in the balance of payments and a substantial increase in overseas debts. After 1939 the major problem for the British war economy was to find a way to pay for essential imports without having to export in return.

At first the government hoped to achieve this aim by the simple expedient of cutting all inessential imports and promoting British exports. Export industries were given preferential allocations of scarce materials, and were encouraged to push up prices to take advantage of world shortages. During the first half of 1940 British firms took up export orders that German firms could no longer fulfill because of the blockade. But a number of factors undermined this aim. The pound weakened as the war position of the Allies grew worse. World prices for raw materials and food rose steadily in response to the war emergency. This produced a sharp increase in the cost of British imports and nullified any gains from higher export prices. In 1940 the balance-of-trade deficit was double the level of 1939. The entry of Italy into the war in June and the defeat of France cut off other areas of supply and trade, while war with Japan in December 1941 cut Britain off from her East Asian supplies and sent world prices up even higher. The sheer scale of the military production programs which were regarded as essential for Britain's strategic plans, made it impossible to keep up levels of exports. By 1941 exports were less than two-thirds of the level in 1938, by 1943 only one-third. Imports were running at three times the level of exports. By 1941 the gold and foreign currency available to pay for imports was almost gone and Britain faced the gloomy prospect of international bankruptcy or a collapse of the war economy.

The government resorted to a number of expedients to cope with the crisis. Ways were found to restrict imports to only the most essential.

Import licenses were issued for the import of raw materials, and all inessential trade was suspended. Between 1940 and 1944 the volume of imported materials declined from 22 million tons to just under 12 million. To reduce reliance on overseas supplies of food every effort was made to grow what was needed on British soil. A great deal of new land was brought into cultivation; parks and gardens were dug up to provide vegetables. Food consumption was rationed and luxury foodstuffs disappeared from the shops. In 1939 Britain imported 29 million tons of food; in 1944 only 10 million. For vital materials that could only be found abroad, the government assumed complete control, buying and distributing the goods. In the case of aluminium, Britain undertook extensive investment in Canada to guarantee a sufficient supply to maintain aircraft production. When Japan captured British sources of rubber supply in the Far East, the government poured money into developing rubber production elsewhere. All these initiatives guaranteed the continued flow of vital supplies while reducing the overall level of imports substantially. In case the worst happened, large stockpiles of food and materials were built up in Britain, equivalent to about nine months' supply.[10]

Nonetheless it proved impossible to avoid the disaster. By the end of 1940 Britain had almost exhausted her ability to pay in dollars for the resources she needed from the Americas. Payments in the sterling area could only be maintained by freezing the sterling balances built up by Empire suppliers in London. By the end of the war British debts to the sterling area totaled £3,355 million. Canada provided generous gifts and loans, which totaled almost $3,500 million over the course of war.[11] The Belgian government-in-exile lent Britain $300 million of gold. Britain had substantial overseas assets, estimated at £4,000 million. Half of these were sold off to fund the trade deficit. But despite all these stop-gaps the point arrived in December 1940 when Britain could no longer pay for the goods contracted from the United States. On 7 December Churchill warned Roosevelt that "the moment approaches when we shall no longer be able to pay cash for shipping and other supplies," and he threw the British war effort on the mercy of the United States.[12]

No doubt, as the American government suspected, there was something in this appeal beyond economics. Churchill wanted Roosevelt to give a larger and less equivocal commitment to the Allied cause. But there was no disguising the fact that Britain on her own would not be able to defeat Germany. "There is one way, and one way only," William Layton, editor of the *Economist,* told a meeting of American industrialists in October, "in which the three to one ratio of Germany's steel output can be overwhelmed and that is by the 50 or 60 million ingot tons a year of the United States."[13] Nor was there any disguising the fact of Britain's imminent bankruptcy. Roosevelt, though skeptical of British claims that there was no more cash in the till, was sufficiently persuaded. Late in December he pledged that the United States would become the "arsenal of democracy," providing the goods with which the British Empire would continue the fight. In January 1941 he introduced a bill to Congress authorizing what became known as Lend-Lease, the grant of materials and equipment to the enemies of Nazism on extended loan. While the bill went through Congress, the Reconstruction Finance Corporation lent Britain an emergency $425 million to pay for outstanding contracts and avoid the embarrassment of default. On 11 March the bill became law and the British war effort was salvaged. "Without this aid," Churchill privately minuted, "the defeat of Hitlerism could not be hoped for."[14]

The scheme took time to develop. Most of the weapons and equipment purchased before Pearl Harbor were still bought for cash. Only 100 out of 2,400 aircraft sent in 1941 came under Lend-Lease. In the same year 60% of the raw materials imported from the U.S.A. were paid for in cash. Though there was no firm agreement on repayment, the Americans wanted a quid pro quo, and got it in the form of a loosely worded promise from Britain to reduce tariffs and promote liberal trade after the war.[15] But once American munitions and material output began to expand rapidly from the middle of 1941 the proportion made available to Britain and the Empire rose prodigiously. By 1943-44 about 25 per cent of all military equipment came from the United States. In 1942-44 almost all raw material exports to Britain came under Lend-Lease. Throughout the war the U.S.A. made available to Britain $21,000 million of aid—$14,000 million in military supplies, and $7,000 million in raw materials and petroleum. The total net deficit with the dollar area reached $25,000 million during the war, the equivalent of a whole year's British GNP.[16]

There can be little doubt that the decision in the United States to provide unconditional aid to Britain was a critical turning point in the war. In retrospect it could be argued that such a decision was hardly surprising. Roosevelt was demonstrably on Britain's side and had found ways since 1939 to provide her with purchased supplies. But the decision could not be taken for granted at the time. Roosevelt was still faced with widespread isolationist opinion—even those who favoured aid to the Allies remembered the unpaid war debts of the First World War. The decision was a triumph for Roosevelt's view that Britain's fight against the forces of darkness was America's too. It was an act of political goodwill for which the

British had agitated for six months. But for all the "unsordidness" of the act, Britain paid a price. Her cash purchases in America had provided much of the initial investment for America's own rearmament and saved the American taxpayer. The collapse of British trade contributed to the rise of America's phenomenal export record during the war. Finally Britain's war effort was no longer under her own control. The economic dependence on America shifted the balance between the two states. In the middle of 1941 they began to plan war production and raw material output together, and in 1942 set up Combined Boards to oversee war output. From then on any crisis in Britain's own supply position became, in effect, an issue of American foreign policy.[17]

There were plenty of such crises. American aid did not automatically end Britain's economic problems. Far from it, for the United States always insisted that Britain should meet as many of her own economic requirements as possible. The crisis in shipping was the clearest example. In 1941 and again in late 1942 early 1943 the British economy faced its severest tests as German submarine warfare began to bite. For Britain the maintenance of sea transport was essential. Without it the population could not be adequately fed and the production of armaments, particularly aircraft, which was dependent on overseas supplies of aluminum, would be dramatically cut. Churchill wrote to Roosevelt in December 1940 that "It is in shipping and in the power to transport across the oceans . . . that in 1941 the crunch of the whole war will be found."[18] During 1940, Britain lost one million tons of shipping. From an original plan to import 42 million tons of supplies in 1941, the figure was revised down by April 1941 to only 28 million because of shortages of shipping. By the spring of 1941 it was clear that without additional shipping space either food or munitions supply would have to reduced to dangerous levels.

For Churchill there was no real choice. He insisted that food must take priority: "Nothing must interfere with the supplies necessary to maintain the stamina and the resolution of the people of this country."[19] A new Ministry of War Transport was set up to rationalize shipping space. The convoy system was tightened up. A Shipping Mission was dispatched to Washington under Sir Arthur Salter to persuade the United States to yield up 2 million tons of cargo space and embark on an 8 million ton shipping program for 1942. Roosevelt accepted the latter, since the United States also needed merchant shipping in great quantity, and with more misgivings offered the 2 million tons as well, some of it from idle U.S. shipping, some from requisitioned Axis shipping in American and Latin American ports.[20] The result was that during 1941 the total merchant tonnage available under the British flag or chartered to Britain remained more or less constant at 21 million tons and the import volume actually exceeded expectations. But during 1942 the situation worsened. Britain lost 3,963 merchant ships and added only 2,600. Import volumes dropped to only 22 million tons and vital domestic food and materials stocks were consumed. In late 1942 and again in the spring of 1943 British missions crossed the Atlantic to beg for help. Each time an American promise was forthcoming; in 1943 the offer of 7 million tons of cargo capacity to bring total imports up to 26 million tons was the lifeline that allowed Britain's production programs to continue in full.[21]

In the end the shipping crisis was solved by naval and air action against the submarine threat in 1943. In the sea battle one-third of Britain's merchant seamen lost their lives and 13 million tons of shipping under the British flag was sunk. At least 5.5 million tons was made good from British shipyards, itself a very considerable economic effort. The survival of adequate economic links with the outside world was a vital key to Britain's survival in the war. If it looks from hindsight a relatively smooth process of control and organization, planning and allocation, this was far from the case. The British faced a constant set of shifting problems in finding sources of raw materials, shipping them to Britain, and financing overseas purchases. This meant a great deal of diplomatic effort and ingenuity in arguing for credit or special privileges; a great deal of organizational and commercial skill in hunting down and securing supplies; and ultimately dependence on the goodwill of British creditors and allies alike.

The British knew when they entered the war against Germany that it was likely to be long and certain to be costly. The question of how to pay for the war effort became, in Keynes's words, "the central problem of the home economic front."[22] From the outset the government decided to cut back sharply on civilian consumption and to divert resources to the needs of war. Such a strategy was fraught with all kinds of difficulties. The civilian population had to be persuaded that economic sacrifices—tax increases, rationings, and the like—were justified and supportable. Some way had to be found to avoid inflation as civilians and military chased a shrinking quantity of goods. The government wanted to avoid anything that sapped home morale or produced unequal sacrifices or might prompt social unrest. The trick was to find sufficient domestic funds for the war while maintaining stable prices and a reasonably contented work force.

In the early stages of the war the government hoped to achieve this aim simply by raising taxes. The Treasury drew up a "War Plan" in August 1939 which recommended increases in taxation for consumers, an Excess

Profits Tax for industry, and state controls over investment and savings.[23] The tax on industry, which met with much hostility from business, was introduced partly to avoid press accusations of war-profiteering and to win trade union support. The government was sensitive to the kind of problems that had emerged in the Great War, and was keen to demonstrate its conspicuous commitment to greater equality of sacrifice. In 1938 there were 19,000 taxpayers with net incomes above £4,000; by 1942 there were only 1,250.[24] All these measures served to raise government revenue in 1940 by over 40 per cent. But the costs of the war escalated much faster than had been anticipated. The Chiefs of Staff on the eve of the Battle of France recommended that "financial considerations should not be allowed to stand in the way" of providing all the forces needed to defeat Germany.[25] In 1940 government expenditure reached £3,970 million, but revenues brought in only £1,495 million. This "budget gap," the difference between income and expenditure, had to be bridged if Britain were to maintain a large-scale war effort.

Most of the gap was made good by increasing the state debt. But loans on this scale could be secured only if the population saved more and consumed less. How this could be done without compulsion, which was rejected on political grounds, was a delicate issue. People would only save more if they had less to buy in the shops, and they would only loan their savings to the government if they were reasonably sure that their investment was safe or would be used sensibly. The government solved the first issue by limiting the supply of consumer goods to encourage people to put their surplus income in savings. A vigorous propaganda campaign was operated to encourage the patriotic saver. Once the money was in the banks the government encouraged them to take up government loans. In this way the ordinary saver would rest content that there was money put away for the end of the war, without realizing that his money was being used, like tax revenue, to pay for the war. So successful was this strategy that the budget gap was made good throughout the war, without the need to resort to more draconian measures of financial coercion.[26]

Increased saving and taxation did not altogether solve the problem of inflationary pressures. The price of goods in short supply rose rapidly during 1939 and 1940. The overall price level rose 12 per cent in the first three months of the war. By the end of 1940 the cost of living was a third higher than the year before.[27] This rise created growing pressure to increase wages. Earnings began to rise rapidly in the key armaments sectors. By July 1940 earnings in the metal and engineering industries were 42 per cent higher than in 1938, in industry as a whole 30 per cent higher.[28] The government was reluctant to introduce a comprehensive prices and incomes policy because it was felt that wage controls would alienate labour. As Keynes put it, inflation had to be tackled "in a way which satisfies the popular sense of social justice."[29]

The control of wages and prices was approached not by direct legal restrictions but through a number of indirect instruments, developed through co-operation with businessmen and workers. In August 1940 the Cabinet decided on a policy of food subsidy for essential foodstuffs to keep prices stable. Controls over foodstuffs became a central instrument of price control for the rest of the war.[30] For the budget of 1941 the government made price stability a major aim. Rents and fuel prices were pegged. Most major foods were subsidized and efforts made, through the concentration of production and rationalization, to keep down the cost of non-rationed consumer goods. To keep down wage demands the government set up machinery for arbitration and got the Trade Unions to agree to abide by its decisions. Government contracts were scrutinized more carefully to eliminate excessive labour costs. Finally the movement of labour between regions and industries was closely monitored to prevent local labour shortages pushing up wages. The result was that hourly wage-rates lagged behind the rise in the cost of living by 1941. Labour unrest was averted only by higher earnings which came from longer hours, bonuses and overtime payments. Ultimately wage controls depended on the goodwill of the labor force and the Trade Union movement which accepted the government's aim "to reduce wage claims to a minimum,"[31] as long as the government was seen to be acting responsibly over prices and living standards. Without this co-operation legal compulsion might well have been necessary (it was strongly supported by some of the Cabinet later in the war when inflationary pressures re-appeared) and with it all the social tensions and political confrontation that the government was anxious to avoid.[32]

The budget of 1941 proved to be the turning point. Acting on the advice of academic economists, the Treasury agreed to raise direct taxation in order to reduce surplus purchasing power to achieve price stability, and to increase total revenue sources substantially. Revenue in 1942 was almost double revenue in 1940; prices did stabilize for the remainder of the war; wage restraint was practiced under Bevin's watchful eye; and saving reached levels adequate to fund the government's growing deficit. Close controls over consumption and the capital markets prevented excess purchasing power from creating serious levels of inflation, while the government's commitment to equality of sacrifice avoided the black marketing and social resentments of 1914-18.

The problem of restricting consumption proved more tractable than had been thought. The public showed itself willing to accept sacrifices as long as they were explained clearly, shared equally, or reasonably so, and a satisfactory minimum living standard maintained. Stockpiling of foodstuffs and controls on imports ensured that the shops were supplied with sufficient quantities of essential goods, so that rationing was only necessary for a narrow range of products in the early years of war.[33] Not until 1942 did British rationing begin to resemble the comprehensive system introduced in Germany in September 1939. The war-time decline in expenditure on consumption (about 20 per cent at constant prices) took consumers back to where they had been in the late 1920s, but did so in such a way that consumption was spread much more evenly across the population, without the extremes of unemployment and poverty seen in the pre-war years. In the early years of war the fall was relatively modest—about 10 per cent—and cuts in consumption only began to bite in the course of 1941.[34] The goods most restricted were furnishings, clothing, and household goods. Consumption of major foodstuffs was maintained well but supplies of imported foods (fruit, sugar, meat) fell, while basic foods (potatoes, bread, cheese, margarine, milk) went up over the war period. But at no point in the war did a serious crisis occur in provisioning the home population. By 1944 civilian consumption began to increase again.

A concerted strategy on savings and consumption avoided the problems of the First World War. The strategy evolved piecemeal as the war intensified and the diversion of resources became more urgent. Wage and price policy came to assume a greater significance when inflationary pressures emerged and the purchasing power gap widened. But the macro-economic policies worked well enough to curb inflation, provide revenue and loans, and avoid necessity for legal compulsion. The success of this strategy determined the extent to which the government could organize and convert domestic industry for war production.

The provision of strategic imports and the finance to pay for the war effort created the framework within which the conversion of Britain's industrial economy to war production could take place. The only limit set on this conversion was the provision of what was perceived as a necessary minimum of consumer goods and exports. "The life of the community must continue," wrote the chairman of the Manpower Committee late in 1941, in response to further demands for munitions labour. Essential supplies and services could not be cut further "without making it difficult to maintain the spirits of the people."[35] Nonetheless, as the scale of warfare increased the proportion of Britain's productive effort devoted to war supplies steadily increased. By 1943, one official later wrote, the Ministry of Production "concentrated on getting the last gram of production of the most essential supplies."[36] In 1944 only 2 per cent of the work force was engaged on work for exports; 33 per cent of the work force produced munitions and 22 per cent was in the fighting services. This was as close to "total war" as the British war effort got.

There were two complementary stages in the mobilization of the industrial economy. The first was planning what was to be produced. The second was getting industry to produce it on time, in sufficient quantities, and with the efficient use of resources. Neither stage worked perfectly; the war produced a long learning curve for planners and producers alike. The government would always have liked more and cheaper; the producers were seldom entirely happy with the planners. Planning was the most difficult side of the equation. The criterion for planning in Britain was not "what can industry produce," but "what do the services need to secure the grand strategic claim?" These requirements were never constant, and as the war went on there developed a growing gulf between what the armed forces thought was necessary and what British industry could actually provide. The gap had to be made good from American sources.

British planning in any formal sense was in its infancy when the war began. Academics and industrialists were drafted into government service to provide planning and statistical expertise. Over the first year of war the picture of what the forces needed to defeat Hitler, and what industry could realistically supply, gradually took shape. The service programs were synchronized to replace a system where each service scrambled for its own share of the industrial spoils. Manpower emerged as the main resource in short supply and by 1941 manpower budgeting became the main instrument in allocating factory capacity and meeting future programs. By this stage of the war forward planning reached a degree of sophistication and statistical comprehensiveness to allow for the exchange of resources between programs with much less disruption to production than was the case earlier in the war; but from its very nature war-time production planning was never entirely free of problems of duplication or misdirection.[37]

Planning the military programs required the planned allocation of raw materials and production equipment and the allotment of factory space and labour. Productive capacity for war industry was developed from 1936 onwards. Government investment programs, including the "Shadow Factory" scheme for aircraft production and the large-scale expansion of the chemical and munitions industries, laid the foundation. Some of the new industrial plant was run directly by government, but most of it was operated by existing firms using government money and under state supervision. Capital expenditure by Imperial Chemical Industries (ICI) totalled £78 million during the period of rearmament and war, but £58 million was invested on behalf of the state. ICI acted as an agent for government and established "agency" plants, run by the parent firm but paid for with public money.[38] This system was widely used. By 1942 the government had authorized 170 agency factories in the aircraft, chemicals, and explosive industries. New government factories were set up for the large scale manufacture of munitions. By December 1939, ten new Royal Ordinance Factories were already in operation, employing 54,000 workers. By March 1942 there were 40 factories, with a work force of 311,000. The Royal Dockyards were also expanded, but so large were demands for new ships, naval and merchant, that the government was forced to use commercial producers as agents or buy out private dockyards for government use. By 1944 employment in the Royal Dockyards was 37,000; in the commercial yards it was 233,000.[39]

These new capital programs had the advantage that they could produce factories built on a large scale and using the most up-to-date equipment. The government recruited firms in the growth areas of British business—motor vehicles, chemicals, electrical goods—where modern factory practice and large production units were becoming the norm, and where managerial and technical expertise existed for the operation of large and complex production units. In the aircraft industry over 80 per cent of the work force worked in factories employing more than 1,000 workers.[40] The Royal Ordnance Factories were built to take full advantage of economies of scale, so much so that from 1942 munitions production was run down because more had been produced than the army could hope to use. Over the whole war the government invested $1,000 million in industry, about half for extensions to existing private firms, one quarter for agency factories and the rest for state-run enterprises. Private share issues fell to an average of only $14 million in the war years. During the war years the capital market was dominated by the state. Investment and profit levels were fixed by government officials. Free market capitalism was effectively suspended in favor of state-sponsored investment and production.[41]

Extensive though the new investment programs were, they could never hope to meet all the demands of war-time production. Some of this extra capacity had to be funded by converting existing civilian firms to war work. Plans along these lines existed before the war. The motor vehicle industry and the locomotive industry were earmarked for tank and military vehicle production. By 1943 motor firms produced 20 per cent of all tanks, railway shops some 47 per cent. The conversion of other firms to war was carried out slowly during 1940 and 1941. Firms were faced, as one Treasury official put it, "with a choice of specialization for export, adaptation of plant for munitions, or extinction."[42] During 1940 a great number of inessential firms found themselves starved of raw materials and labour as the Raw Material Controllers allocated scarce resources to arms producers, and workers moved away to where wages were higher. Faced with this choice a great many businesses sought out government work in order to keep going.

In September 1940 the Board of Trade set up a monthly census of 24 industries to help with the task of searching out spare factory space and labour and identifying inessential production for closure. The major producers and agency factories used the smaller and medium firms as subcontractors for equipment and components. In 1943 the production of Lancaster bombers was contracted out to 135 firms spread across the country.[43] As a result of this process 50 per cent of the industrial work force was engaged on government orders by the summer of 1941.

The government had at its disposal a number of instruments to ensure that civilian production was restricted and war production expanded. Firms which needed machine-tools had to apply to the Controller of Machine Tools to get them. Most were earmarked for war production; less essential firms had to accept the deterioration of their plant and longer operating times for their machinery. The Controllers of Raw Materials not only undertook to purchase materials abroad and to control stocks, but had the final say in their allocation. Priority was given to military programs, export industries, and essential civilian supplies, in that order. In 1940 out of the 10 million tons of steel, 64 per cent went to war essential production; in 1943 the figure was 89 per cent. By 1943 99 per cent of aluminium supplies went to the armed forces; and so on. Small businesses producing luxuries and inessential civilian goods were starved of materials and forced to close down.

The third physical resource was manpower. In the early stages of the war Britain still had substantial levels of unemployment. There were one million unemployed in the summer of 1940, and 200,000 a year later. But these resources proved insufficient to meet even the initial demands for labour. Shortages of skilled workers began to appear in the metal and engineering trades early in 1940. No clear system of priority had been established at the start of the war, and the armed forces recruited essential skilled workers. Some firms poached labour by offering higher wages or better conditions; others hung on to more labour than they needed in case the war ended quickly and civilian production started again. The hostility of the labour movement to Chamberlain made it difficult to reach agreement with the unions on improving the labour market, but when Churchill replaced him in May 1940 a more co-operative relationship was established. His appointment of Ernest Bevin, leader of the Transport and General Workers Union, as minister of labour and national service inaugurated a period of close collaboration between government and labour that lasted for the duration of the war. Though labour disputes did not disappear, the trade unions promised to accept wage restraint and state control of the labour market in the common cause against fascism.

Bevin was hostile to the idea of simple labour conscription as an answer to manpower shortages because he thought it would produce "serious labour opposition."[44] But he accepted that labour had to reallocate somehow to war industry and the armed forces. In effect this involved labour conscription in all but name. Regulations were drawn up that established the right to allocate labour where it was needed and gave Bevin, as he admitted, a degree of power "which had no precedent in the country." In fact his new powers were used sparingly; firms usually co-operated in releasing or redirecting labour, and the unions seldom objected. In the first year of operation less than 1,000 cases of formal direction were recorded. Bevin's new powers were still insufficient, however, to meet all the demands made on the labour force. In the summer of 1940 Bevin recruited officials with a technical or engineering background to go from factory to factory to inspect the way labour was utilized or improvements in labour efficiency. Unions and employers were also compelled to accept the employment of women in skilled trades, while the government sponsored large-scale retraining programs to increase the number of skilled and semi-skilled workers. By the end of the war 420,000 had acquired some additional training to make them more suitable for war work.

All of these policies were designed to speed up the transfer of labour to where it was needed most and to encourage its efficient utilization. But in November 1940 a manpower investigation under Sir William Beveridge showed that over the following year the services would need another 1.7 million men and the war industries 1.5 million more workers. The process of conversion and transfer was slower than expected. There were widespread complaints in the press about wasted effort and idle workers. The government responded by strengthening Bevin's position in allocating and recruiting essential labour and by introducing a policy of "concentration" in industry designed to weed out all inessential and inefficient firms and concentrate both war and civilian production in the most efficient.

The Concentration of Production program was announced in March 1941 and gave the government sweeping powers to close down firms and reallocate resources. The scheme was applied to 29 industries and involved 28 per cent of the industrial work force. From each industry a number of nucleus firms were chosen which continued production while the remaining firms either acted as sub-contractors for the nucleus firm or were closed down or converted to other war work. By 1943, 257,000 workers and 70 million square feet of floor space had been freed for the war effort. The aim was to ensure that the nucleus firms would work at full capacity, and that economies of scale and concentration on the most efficient units would keep prices down and maximize productive performance.[45]

The scheme operated with new powers for the Ministry of Labour. The Essential Work Order allowed Bevin's ministry to protect workers from call-up and to give priority to war industry. By the end of 1941, 30,000 firms and 6 million workers were protected. Bevin also introduced a Register for Employment, which made it possible to keep track of all workers and to allocate them more rationally.[46] The long-term result was the gradual decline in the number of skilled male workers and their replacement with female and young labour with a lower skill level. This was not always a straightforward process, since skilled workers were anxious to retain their privileges, work customs, and their high earnings. In some industries union opposition to the "dilution" of the work force meant the survival of unnecessarily high levels of skilled men. In shipbuilding, for example, only 7 per cent of the work force was made up of "dilutees" in 1943.[47] But in industries where women could be employed in large numbers, such as aircraft production or radio equipment, the ratios were much higher. Female employment in the motor vehicle and aircraft industries reached 36 per cent by 1943. Over the whole course of the war the female work force expanded from 5 million to 7 million, providing almost half of the labour required to make up for the loss of men to the armed forces.

From 1941 onwards shortages of manpower and the pursuit of greater efficiency were the central issues of industrial mobilization. As the supply of new labour and factory space slowed down, more effort was devoted to getting as much as possible out of existing resources. Some improvements in efficiency came of their own accord, with greater economies of scale, the concentration of production in the best firms, and the use of more advanced factory methods. There was a very wide difference in performance between the best and worst firms in an industry, and government inspectors were installed to educate the poorer firms so that overall levels of productivity could be raised. The level of efficiency was never ideal, partly because changes to the program or modification of design interrupted plans for mass production, partly from the resistance of managers and workers to abrupt changes in work practices.[48] But by the middle of the war only the most obdurate or artful firm could hide its incompetence from the authorities. Most major firms were more efficient users of labour and resources at the end of the war than they had been at the beginning. Long production runs and the adoption of mass production techniques, together with the more rational distribution of labour and materials, were bound to improve productive performance. At English Electric the production of Halifax bombers showed a typical improvement. In April 1942 the firm required 487 workers for every aircraft delivered; by April 1943 the figure was down to 220.[49]

British factory practice never approached the efficiency levels achieved in the United States, but it was close to German levels, and in some cases exceeded them. The German aircraft industry used twice the aluminum and labour to produce fewer aircraft than Britain between 1939 and 1943. Though German steel production was almost three times greater than British, the output of most major classes of weapon in Britain exceeded German production for most of the war.[50] The record of British war production is set out in the following table:

TABLE 5.1

THE OUTPUT OF WEAPONS IN BRITAIN 1939-44

(October-December 1939=100)

	1939	1940	1941	1942	1943	1944
Naval ships	100	569	1,160	1,550	2,690	2,300
Guns, small arms	100	177	321	677	752	428
Shells	100	197	506	963	719	538
Small arms ammo.	100	316	827	2,662	4,478	4,606
Armoured vehicles	100	265	892	1,699	1,671	n.a.
Wheeled vehicles	100	303	305	345	336	312
Aircraft	100	189	269	298	330	333

The results of the large-scale conversion of industry to war production were not uniformly successful. Aircraft production faced periods of crisis—the struggle for greater fighter production in 1940, or greater bomber output in 1941 and 1942. Tank production languished for much of the war, so that British forces came to rely much more on American supplies. By 1944 the sheer scale of American production allowed Britain to reduce levels of war output and begin the slow re-conversion to civilian goods. Britain's overall production achievement continues to excite controversy.

It is now evident that Britain mobilized its economy to a lesser extent than either the Soviet Union or Germany, where the desperate conditions imposed by invasion and defeat led to much higher levels of sacrifice.[51] Yet given the weaknesses and character of the British economy—its high dependence on overseas supply, the large number of small-scale and conservative businesses, the existence of a large skilled work force jealous of its skills—it could be argued that British productive performance was close to a realistic optimum. There is no doubt that more could have been produced, but this would have compromised the government's commitment to maintaining living standards, a co-operative work force, and the allegiance of the business community. As long as this commitment remained a central feature of British politics higher levels of sacrifice would have been difficult to impose. The "command economy" worked in the end because government used its new powers, in Bevin's words, "with caution in their exercise."[52]

Throughout the war the economic effort relied on a careful balance of the interests of the state on the one side and employers and labour on the other. State power was, according to Bevin, unworkable in circumstances "which would not receive the support of public opinion." Its unscrupulous use "might well have impaired public morale and led to widespread disturbance."[53] Politicians and bureaucrats were united in a desire to keep the work force reasonably satisfied and to prevent the war from becoming an avenue to social revolution. They were equally wary of penalizing or inhibiting businessmen, whose goodwill was just as essential. "To make it impossible that any profits should be made out of war conditions is not a practicable aim," according to one Treasury official, "in a country which sets store by the stability of existing institutions (including the normal structure of trade) . . . . "[54] The system remained a capitalist one despite the intrusive spread of state power.

It was never likely that British capitalism would subvert the war effort. Yet from the onset of rearmament businessmen were anxious lest military production should mean more state power and interference, and they never shed this distrust throughout the war. Business leaders wanted to take as much responsibility as the government would permit in running the industrial defence effort. Up to 1939 they were involved in policy discussions, and local trade associations were the vehicle for much of the routine work of war preparation. An advisory council composed largely of business gave expert opinion to Chamberlain's government. During the war the government was careful to temper its more severe restrictions, the Excess Profits Tax for example, with a number of concessions. Industrial profits rose almost two-fold over the war period, but taxation reduced the increase to an average of 14 per cent. Yet firms were able to extend their physical assets at government expense; they were granted generous depreciation allowance and were able to build up substantial reserves.[55] Efforts were made to ensure that firms closed down during the war would not be disadvantaged when peace-time trading conditions were restored. In the cotton industry firms remaining in operation were compelled to pay a levy of one-penny a spindle to cover compensation payments to the firms closed down. Businessmen were closely involved in the day-to-day running of the apparatus of war-time control, and in the formulation of post-war policy on demobilization and reconstruction.

During the war businessmen were brought fully into the organization of the war economy at national and local level. Though Churchill was wary of bringing businessmen into politics ("whenever men trained in business had come into Government it had been disastrous"[56]), there was no question that they were indispensable in helping to run and organize the various new ministries and committees. The Steel Controller, for example, was Sir Andrew Duncan, chairman of the British Iron and Steel Federation. ICI at the height of the war had two directors and five chairmen of committees seconded to run government factories.[57] There was extensive interchange of personnel and close co-operation between officials and businessmen at every level. Engineers and technologists and company scientists found themselves part of the exchange too. An evident strength of the British war economy was the ability of these different groups to work together with an acceptable level of friction. Unlike Germany, where the military enjoyed extensive responsibilities at the expense of civilians, British technical experts were recruited into a largely civilian establishment and were allowed related freedom to develop weapons, advise on production, and organize resources.

With labour the problem was perceived to be more delicate. The governing elite remembered the industrial conflicts of the First World War and its aftermath, and were fearful of the growth of left-wing radicalism in the 1930s. Chamberlain found it difficult to overcome his hostility to the Trade Unions and organized labour, and relations with labour in the early months of war were poor. But with Bevin's appointment in May 1940 the situation changed. The Trades Union Congress (TUC) was brought into full consultation with government; Labour party politicians held major ministerial office. The Ministry of Labour pursued policies to ensure that "the general body of the workers shall be contented."[58] In July 1940 the National Arbitration Tribunal was set up to adjudicate in industrial disputes.

Between 1940 and 1942 the tribunal settled 358 out of 999 industrial stoppages. The rest were settled without need to resort to arbitration.[59] Bevin also insisted that if the work force were expected to work long hours, restrain wage claims and co-operate with the state, it should only be in return for improved conditions and increased responsibility. "Measures of compulsion would have been accompanied," he told the second meeting of the Production Executive, "by measures for the protection of labour."[60] These concessions took the form of better amenities at work; there were 2,000 works canteens in 1939, 18,000 by 1944.[61] Transport and creche facilities were provided for female labour. Trade Unions were recognized in a great many more plants, including the motorcar industry which had been notoriously anti-union before the war. To win greater co-operation Joint Production Councils were established in 1941 on which representatives of labour met with employers and managers to discuss production questions. Though the councils were less effective than the propaganda made out—they met infrequently and had no real power—they were widely regarded as a significant step forward in granting a greater say to labour.[62]

It would be wrong to pretend that labour unrest melted away with Bevin. The war-time strike record was very different from the Great War, but labour disputes were regular occurrences, particularly in the coal industry. Between 1915 and 1918, 4.2 million working days were lost per year; the average for 1940-45 was 1.8 million.[63] Strikes during the Second World War usually lasted less than one week and involved small numbers of workers. In the worst year, 1940, 821,000 workers were involved and 3.7 million working hours lost. Bevin was supplied with a regular weekly bulletin of trade disputes throughout the war. The records show that post strikes were over wage rates, piece-rates and demarcation or dilution. There were tensions over the introduction of female labour and a great many strikes by apprentices protesting their low wages. Some strikes were trivial—complaints at "the dictatorial attitude of a forewoman" or "objection to working with Irishmen"—but the great bulk reflected genuine fears on the part of the work force that dilution and war work would undermine inherited customs and acquired skills or produce unfair wage differentials.[64] The Trade Unions' promise that wage restraint and arbitration would be respected, in fact, worked well.

Strikes were difficult to mount without prior union approval. Absenteeism, undiscipline, and high labour turnover were more frequent barometers of labour dissatisfaction. Widespread resentment could be aroused by indications that the war was in any sense a "class war": the entry of the Soviet Union produced, according to opinion surveys, a renewed enthusiasm for the war, and the worst period of trade disputes coincided with growing public frustration at the failure to mount a Second Front to help Russia in late 1943 or early 1944.[65] Labour was also very hostile to what it saw as inefficiency and self-interest on the part of employers. In 1942 the Amalgamated Engineering Union drew up a long report on war production in which it accused those in authority of dragging their feet over full-scale war: "The challenge to those in authority—managers and ministers alike—to eliminate the inefficiencies and self-interest hamstringing a total war effort in this country cannot be ignored." The union claimed that work people had done all that was demanded of them. The report continued:

> There is little sense that a similar sense of urgency has swept over managements in this period and there are well-sustained complaints of firms still carrying out peace time work, allocating unduly high proportions of both floor space and skilled labour to non-essential products . . . of managements both planning and producing with an eye to post-war competition, and a rigid interpretation of "managerial functions" which rejects workers' co-operation in solving production problems as something akin to desecration.[66]

Labour hostility was based on a distrust of managerial competence and integrity, not upon any fundamental rejection of the war effort or of the part labour was to play in it. Conditions and wages generally improved, for on questions of living conditions and earnings the government remained committed to keeping up home morale, and made timely concessions when necessary. Over the course of the war earnings far outstripped the rise in the cost of living. The performance of wages and prices is set out in Table 5.2:

TABLE 5.2

WAGES, PRICES, AND CONSUMPTION 1939-1945

	Weekly Earnings	Wage Rates	Cost of Living	Per Capita Consumption	Real Personal Consumption
1939	n.a.	100	100	97.2	100
1940	130	113-14	121	89.7	90
1941	142	122	128	87.1	83
1942	160	131-2	129	86.6	82
1943	176	136-7	129	85.5	79
1944	181.5	143-4	130	88.2	83
1945	180.5	150-1	133.5	n.a.	86

(column 1 1938=100, columns 2/3 September 1939=100, column 4 1938=100 [constant prices], column 5 1939=100)

Improved working conditions and union representation added to the general strengthening of labour's position. The promise of better post-war conditions, increased welfare, and full employment had the same effect. Though Churchill privately deplored what he called "harping and insatiable left-wing propaganda,"[67] social concessions had the effect of sealing the compact between ruling class and labour for the duration of the war. Bevin was more clear-sighted about the significance of the changing climate of opinion: "Individualism is bound to give place to social action, competition and scramble to order. There is no other way a nation can save itself . . . . Thus will we defeat Hitler."[68]

The economic war effort was never a straightforward story of smooth transition from peace to total war. The transition was slow, piecemeal, and punctuated by periodic crises that threatened to undo the work in hand. In truth the British had exaggerated the strength of their economy before 1939. They found themselves pursuing a degree of economic mobilization which their resources simply could not meet without crisis. In late 1940 Britain faced external bankruptcy, domestic inflation, and severe manpower shortages. The promise of American aid was the vital turning point for Britain; the 1941 budget mastered the inflationary threat; the concentration of production and labour conscription solved the manpower crisis. Then in 1941 the shipping crisis became, in Churchill's words, "at once the stranglehold and sole foundation of our war strategy."[69] For two years the supply of vital materials to be fabricated in Britain hung in the balance until the submarine threat receded in 1943. A third critical point came late in 1942 when Britain was close to the peak of war-time economic mobilization. The Lyttelton Mission, which arrived in Washington in October of that year, came to persuade the American leadership to give Britain more supplies to equip the troops needed for D-Day, and, more important, to ship 7 million tons of additional imports to Britain in American ships. Without these supplies, Churchill warned Roosevelt, Britain would have no choice but "to reduce our general contribution to the overseas war effort."[70]

All the crises were surmounted, but Britain's survival as an effective economic partner came to depend on American and Empire assistance. Britain became a forward manufacturing base for the Western war effort. Such an outcome played, in a sense, to Britain's strength: her established links with the world economy and her high proportion of manufacturing. Britain, unlike Germany, was never in a position to develop autarky, or to exploit captured areas. As long as the links overseas were maintained, Britain's domestic war effort involved the rational organization of resources to secure large war supplies and a reasonable standard of civilian life. The domestic administration of the economy was a problem-solving structure, regulating production through controls over physical resources and extensive state planning. The ultimate success of this war effort in giving British forces the flexibility and strength to survive on three fronts may indeed have pandered, as historian Correlli Barnett has since claimed,[71] to a collective illusion of greatness, but it is undeniably a part of the explanation for the ultimate victory of the Allied powers.

The war economy was successful in its own terms. British forces were supplied with the weapons they needed in sufficient quantities to keep Britain in the war and to equip half the forces fighting the Axis outside Russia by 1944. The home economy was kept stable enough to avoid the damaging social confrontations of the Great War and to maintain a satisfactory level of home morale. A third priority, to prevent the war from destroying British economic prospects in peace-time, produced more mixed results. Churchill's appeal to Roosevelt in 1940 not to let Britain "stand stripped to the bone" after victory was won avoided British bankruptcy, but it did not prevent the collapse of many export markets nor the sale of half Britain's overseas assets nor a total balance-of-payments deficit of £10,000 million.[72] Britain never recovered the prominent role it had played in the world economy before 1939. Economic power passed inexorably to the United States. At home the government faced a massive cumulative debt totalling £16,000 million in 1945. The disruptions of the war made it necessary for the government to maintain close watch over the economy for a further five years. Though the British economy returned to its capitalist complexion, it was a very different system from 1939. The state assumed a much wider range of responsibilities, and, as result of war-time achievements, enjoyed broad public approval in doing so. The war accelerated the trend towards both the "mixed economy" and the welfare state.

On the credit side Britain did end the war with a range of modern industries—electronics, radio, aviation, pharmaceuticals—which could be switched easily to civilian work, and a work force and managerial class used to working with large factories and modern technology. The British economy was more modern by the end of the war than it had been in 1939; the work force enjoyed better conditions; more women remained in employment; and American managerial practice and technology were more widely adopted. And for the foreseeable future many one-time competitors abroad lay in ruins. For a decade or more after 1945 market conditions were generally favourable to the rapid recovery and growth of the British economy. The fact that in the long run Britain failed to exploit all these circumstances to her full advantage must be explained by factors outside the impact of war.

Notes

1. On British rearmament see R. Shay, *British Rearmament in the Thirties* (Princeton, 1977); G. Peden, *British Rearmament and the Treasury 1932-1939* (Edinburgh, 1979); N. Gibbs, *Grand Strategy, Vol I: Rearmament Policy* (London, 1976).

2. Public Record Office, Kew, (PRO), T 161/1069, Treasury to Washington Embassy on conversion to war, 9 February 1942, 2.

3. PRO, LAB 10/161, Memorandum by the Chancellor of the Exchequer, Sir Kingsley Wood, "The Wages Situation and Inflation," 4 December 1941.

4. PRO, T161/1069, Treasury to Embassy, 4.

5. House of Commons Debates, 361, cols. 769-70, 22 January 1941.

6. J. D. Scott, R. Hughes, *The Administration of War Production* (London, 1955), pp. 49-78; D. N. Chester. "The Central Machinery of Economic Policy" in Chester (ed.) *The Lessons of the British War Economy* (Cambridge, 1951), 7-8.

7. PRO, CAB 92/54, Production Executive, minutes of meetings 1941-42.

8. H. M. Parker, *Manpower* (London, 1957), 481-2.

9. U.S. Department of State, *Foreign Relations of the United States* [*FRUS*] (Washington, 1862-), 1944, 2: 12, Winant to Hull, 23 February 1944.

10. C. B. A. Behrens, *Merchant Shipping and the Demands of War* (London, 1955), 325. The stock position during the war developed as follows (in millions of tons):

	Food (other than farm stocks)	Imported Raw Materials	Total
1941	5.36	11.57	16.93
1942	6.07	10.63	16.70
1943	6.45	10.07	16.52
1944	7.10	10.30	17.40

11. S. Pollard, *The Development of the British Economy 1914-1967* (London, 1969), 333-35; W. F. Kimball, "'Beggar My Neighbor': America and the British Interim Finance Crisis 1940-1941," *Journal of Economic History* 29 (1969), 758-72.

12. W. F. Kimball, ed., *Churchill & Roosevelt: The Complete Correspondence* (3 vols.; London, 1984), I: 108, Churchill to Roosevelt, 7 December 1940.

13. Speech by Sir William Layton to the Associated Industries of Massachusetts, 17 October 1940 in *The American Speeches of Lord Lothian July 1939 to December 1940* (Oxford, 1941), 128.

14. Kimball, *Churchill & Roosevelt*, I, 139, Churchill Memorandum, 1 March 1941.

15. W. Hancock, M. Gowing, *The British War Economy* (London, 1949), 239-44; D. Reynolds, *The Creation of the Anglo-American Alliance 1937-1941* (London, 1981), 155-67; Joel Hurstfield, *The Control of Raw Materials* (London, 1953), 464.

16. R. S. Sayers, *Financial Policy 1939–1945* (London, 1956), Appendix 3, 551. At the end of the war it was agreed that Britain should repay only $650 million.

17. R. Clarke, *Anglo-American Economic Collaboration in War and Peace 1942-1949*, ed. A. Cairncross (Oxford, 1982), 3-9, 13-17.

18. A. Salter, *Slave of the Lamp: a public servant's notebook* (London, 1967), 151-2. In Salter's view "the issue of the whole war depended upon the maintenance of adequate sea transport. . . ."

19. Behrens, *Merchant Shipping*, 198.

20. Salter, *Slave of the Lamp*, 152-66. In fact the United States gave Britain 1 million tons during 1941, but extensive chartering filled the gap. Foreign chartered tonnage increased from 2 million tons in June 1940 to 4 million tons in September 1941.

21. Behrens, *Merchant Shipping*, 263, 363-65.

22. *Keynes Collected Writings*, XXII, 42, "Paying for the War," *The Times*, 14/15 November 1939.

23. PRO, T 161/1069, Treasury minute for Sir Horace Wilson and the Chancellor of the Exchequer, 7 June 1939, "Treasury War Plan."

24. "National Finances in 1944," *The Banker*, 74 (1945), 66.

25. W. F. Kimball, *The Most Unsordid Act: Lend-Lease 1939-1941* (Baltimore, 1969), 39.

26. PRO, T 160/1289, Draft report, committee on control of savings and investment, August 1939, which recommended the strategy. By August 1945 government paper and cash accounted for 83 per cent of the deposits of the London clearing banks. Banks became principally agents for government finance.

27. PRO, BT 64/210, Board of Trade note on price control for Sir Alan Barlow, 17 November 1942, 1-2. The price rise by the same point in the First World War was calculated at 85 per cent.

28. PRO, LAB 10/161, War Cabinet, Lord President's Committee: Memorandum by the Minister of Labour, "The wages situation and inflation," 8 December 1941, Table III. By July 1941 weekly earnings had risen by an average of 42.3 per cent, in engineering by 49.3 per cent.

29. *Keynes Collected Writings*, XXII, 223. "Notes on the Budget II," 28 September 1940. On Keynes role in policy making see T. Wilson, "Policy in War and Peace: the Recommendations of J. M. Keynes," in A. P. Thirwall, ed., *Keynes as a Policy Adviser* (London, 1982), 41-45.

30. PRO, BT 64/210, Ministry of Food, "Outline of the History and Methods of Price Control under the Ministry of Food," 16 April 1943.

31. PRO, LAB 10/161, Memorandum by the Minister of Labour, "Wages Policy," 17 December 1941, 1-8.

32. PRO, LAB 10/161, Memorandum of the Chancellor of the Exchequer, "The Wages situation and Inflation," 4 December 1941.

33. Earl of Woolton, *The Memoirs of the Rt. Hon. the Earl of Woolton* (London, 1959), 191-230. As Minister of Food, Woolton insisted on rationing only those goods whose supply could be guaranteed to meet the ration.

34. PRO, BT 64/210, Board of Trade Journal, 2 December 1944, 435-37. By the end of the war most inessential production was only a fraction of pre-war levels. The following table gives the indices of major consumption items other than food:

Personal Expenditure of Consumer Goods 1938-1943
(at constant prices)

	Clothing	Boots & Shoes	Furniture Furnishings	Private Cars Bicycles	Fuel & Light
1938	100	100	100	100	100
1939	99	104	91	82	99
1940	82	93	84	24	93
1941	59	79	52	16	97
1942	58	77	35	10	98
1943	55	73	33	11	93

35. PRO, CAB 92/103, War Cabinet, Man Power Priority Sub-Committee, draft report "Survey of Man Power," 10 October 1941, 3.

36. Clarke, *Economic Collaboration,* 19.

37. Very little modern research has been done on planning British war production. The best accounts can be found in E. Devons, *Planning in Practice: Essays in Aircraft Planning in Wartime* (Cambridge, 1950); M. M. Postan, D. Hay, J. D. Scott, *Design and Development of Weapons* (London, 1964). More recently A. Cairncross, *Planning in Wartime* (London, 1991).

38. W. J. Reader, *ICI: a History. Volume II 1926-1952* (Oxford, 1975), 256-57, 263-66.

39. W. Hornby, *Factories and Plant* (London, 1958), 69, 90; M. M. Postan, *British War Production* (London, 1952), 23-26, 58-65.

40. Hornby, *Factories,* 338. See also C. M. Kohan, *Works and Buildings* (London, 1952), ch. xiv.

41. T. Barna, "Profits During the War," *The Banker, 74* (1945), 68-72.

42. PRO, T 161/1069, Treasury telegram to Washington Embassy, 8 February 1942, 2.

43. PRO, AVIA 10/269, Ministry of Aircraft Production, Chief Executive.

44. PRO, LAB 8/106, "Labor Supply Policy since May 1940," Draft Memorandum by Minister of Labour for War Cabinet, 17 July 1941, 1.

45. PRO, BT 64/829, Board of Trade minute, "Contraction of Production", 11 Mar. 1941; Statement by the President of the Board of Trade on the scheme see G. Worswick,

"Concentration—Success or Failure?" in Oxford University Institute of Statistics, *Studies in War Economics* (Oxford, 1947), 346-55; G. C. Allen, "The concentration of production policy," in Chester, *Lessons*, 166-77.

46. A. Bullock, *The Life and Times of Ernest Bevin: Vol II. Minister of Labor 1940-1945* (London, 1967), 55.

47. *Ibid.*, 62-63. On problems of dilution see PRO LAB 8/340.

48. R. Croucher, *Engineering at War 1939-1945* (London, 1982), 121-22.

49. PRO, AVIA 10/289, memorandum by Prof. Jewkes, "The supply of labor and the future of the aircraft industry program," 19 May 1943, 4.

50. On German productive performance see R. J. Overy, "Mobilization for Total War in Germany 1939-1941," *English Historical Review* 103 (1988), 630-38.

51. M. Harrison, "Resource Mobilization for World War II: the U.S.A., U.K., U.S.S.R. and Germany, 1938-1945," *Economic History Review* 41 (1988), 171-92; R. J. Overy, "'Blitzkriegswirtschaft?' Finanzpolitik, Lebensstandard und Arbeitseinsatz in Deutschland 1939-1942," *Vierteljahrshefte für Zeitgeschichte*, 3 (1988), 379-435.

52. PRO, LAB 8/106, Minister of Labour, "Labour Supply Policy since May 1940," 17 July 1941, 3.

53. *Ibid.*, 3.

54. PRO, BT 64/210, Note by G. Peakes for Sir. A. Barlow on price control, 17 November 1942, 1.

55. For details see W. Ashworth, *Contracts and Finance* (London, 1953), 197-227; J. Steindl, "Economic Incentive and Efficiency in War Industry," in Oxford Institute of Statistics, *War Economics*, 375-81.

56. Woolton, *Memoirs*, 176-77.

57. Reader, *ICI*, 252-53.

58. PRO, LAB 10/161, Minute by E. W. Leggett, "The wages situation and inflation: a note on the Chancellor's memorandum," 19 January 1942, 2.

59. PRO, LAB 10/434, Ministry of Labor, "Industrial Relations in Great Britain 1939-1942: History and Policy," 17. During the period ending July 1942, 2,000 workers were prosecuted under the new legislation and 21 stoppages out of 2,500 declared illegal (pp. 19-20).

60. PRO, CAB 92/54, Minutes of the Second Meeting of the Production Executive, 8 January 1941, 4.

61. PRO, BT 64/210, Board of Trade Journal, 2 December 1944, 437.

62. Croucher, *Engineers at War*, 373-75.

63. Bullock, *Ernest Bevin,* II, 63.

64. PRO, LAB 10/132, Trade Stoppages: weekly returns of the Ministry of Labour, 1940-1944, especially reports for 28 October 1942 and 26 January 1944.

65. Croucher, *Engineers at War,* 119-22, 374-75. On absenteeism see Inman, *Labor,* 271-87.

66. PRO, LAB 8/480, Amalgamated Engineering Union, "Final Report and Statistical Findings of Production Committee Enquiry, April 1942," 4, 13.

67. Letter from Churchill to Kingsley-Wood, 19 February 1941, reproduced in Sayers, *Financial Policy,* Appendix iv, 557.

68. Bullock, *Ernest Bevin,* II, 41.

69. Behrens, *Merchant Shipping,* 263.

70. Kimball, *Churchill & Roosevelt,* I, 650, Churchill to Roosevelt, 31 October 1942.

71. C. Barnett, *The Audit of War: the illusion and reality of Britain as a Great Nation* (London, 1986).

72. Kimball, *Churchill & Roosevelt,* I, 108, Churchill to Roosevelt, 7 December 1941.

■ ■ ■

6

THE SOVIET UNION: PHOENIX

Lydia V. Pozdeeva

On 22 June 1941, Nazi Germany had attacked a country that had progressed far in its economic development but was not prepared for war.

During the two prewar five-year plans, the USSR had built large-scale industry and mechanized its agriculture. The third five-year plan (1938-42), approved by the 18th Party Congress in March 1939, had given priority to the growth of heavy industry, particularly defense related, in face of increased military threat. Judging by the production levels of primary industrial products, the USSR had taken its place among the most developed nations. In 1940, the country was producing 29.9 million tons of iron ore, roughly twice the output of Nazi Germany. The country was also producing the same amount of steel and cast iron as Germany and had surpassed Germany in oil production. However, in 1940 the Reich took over and exploited the economic resources of practically all Europe. For that reason its capacity to produce metal, coal, and electro-energy was more than double that of the Soviet Union. On the other hand, the Soviet economy was not as dependent as Germany on the import of primary types of strategic raw materials. It also had a more productive and stable oil base. Soviet oil industry was located in regions far from the center of European Russia such as the Ural-Volga Region ("the Second Baku"), Kazakhstan, and Sakhalin.[1] These geo-economic advantages were crucial in the years that followed.

The hardening of totalitarianism over the previous decade had complex consequences for the Soviet national economy. The country still experienced the effect of economic losses and social stresses from the time of industrialization, collectivization of agriculture, and the purges of the early

1930s. In spite of generally good production rates, certain fields of industrial production lagged behind, for example the machine-tool industry and transport engineering. The development of the fuel and raw materials base in ferrous metallurgy was in serious trouble. During the third five-year plan there was in fact a substantial *decrease* in iron and steel capacities.

Since the time of the Civil War (1918-21), Soviet defense industry had been at the center of official attention, and it had been developed according to ideological tenets about the impending armed confrontation with imperialist forces. By June 1941 the material-technological base for Soviet defense capabilities was in shape. However, the country was still not completely prepared for the struggle against aggression. Not long before the war, a group of Soviet industrial designers, headed by M. I. Koshkin, A. A. Morozov, and N. A. Kucherenko, had designed a medium-size tank, designated the T-34. At the same time, the heavy tank, KV-1, had taken shape in the Zh. Kotin design bureau. Basically, these tanks were superior to those of Nazi Germany, but only 1,861 of them were built before the war.[2] New types of airplanes were also designed: fighter planes such as the YAK-1, LAGG-3, MIG-3, the dive bombers PE-2 and IL-2, and armored low-flying attack aircraft. All of these could compete with the powerful, organized, and technically well-equipped *Luftwaffe*. However, such aircraft made up only a small part of the actual Soviet arsenal at the time. Thus, important new military designs were at prototype rather than production stage. It appears, according to B. L. Vannikov (People's Commissar for Ammunition in 1942-45), that the industry that produced artillery and small arms was probably best prepared at the beginning of the war; it operated with the largest reserves required for product manufacture.[3]

Through the fault of Josef Stalin and his aides, the process of rearmament exhibited tremendous errors, miscalculations, and belated judgements. For example, at the beginning of the war, Marshal G. I. Kulik and the Main Artillery Board did not assess properly such powerful missile equipment as the BM-13 rocket launchers. The BM-13, which later earned world fame under the nickname "Katyusha," was not ordered into mass production until the Defense Committee's decree of 21 June 1941.[4] Economic planning also reflected the rigidities of Soviet military doctrine. Stalin and his closest aides stubbornly maintained that the Red Army would immediately succeed in pushing the enemy back into his own territory, thus attaining speedy and easy victory. For that reason, possible burdens on the economy from a defensive war in the hinterland of the Soviet Union were underestimated. British economic historian Mark Harrison has rightly emphasized the exceptional complacency on the part of the Soviet Union in its evaluation of the economic scope of the future conflict.[5]

Other reasons for the inadequate readiness of Soviet military-industrial potential included lack of experience in weapons development and in organizing their mass production, miscalculations in reorganizing the armed forces, the shortage of motor transport and technical expertise, and sheer incompetence by the leadership.[6] In general, the needs of the country remained unanswered. Agricultural problems were not being solved. The demands of the military were not being met. Despite the fact that, in the words of Marshal G. K. Zhukov, "the heart of heavy industry, of the defense industry was beating faster,"[7] the toughest times lay ahead.

The coming of war had found the Soviet national economy in a state of wide-ranging reorganization. Numerous resources were being developed, particularly in the East. An American historian, John E. Jessup, suggested: "There is little question that the Soviet Union had made preparations for a rapid and all-embracing mobilization of industry in the event of war."[8] The potential for industrial and military mobilization could be viewed as high. Regardless of the fact that the Soviet Union was producing less strategic materials than Germany, it was still able to supply substantial military needs. Among the advantages of Soviet economy were huge territory, possession of all basic types of natural resources, and relative self-sufficiency from foreign trade (as opposed to Germany, Japan, and Great Britain).[9]

But Nazi Germany wanted to destroy the Soviet Union in a speedy campaign in order to prevent the country from mobilizing all its resources. Would the USSR be able to restructure its national economy and supply its troops in a very short period of time? The fate of the Soviet people and the outcome of its struggle with fully mobilized enemy troops depended on this. For this reason, the extreme measures taken by the USSR in the first weeks after the Nazi attack played such an important role in the future struggle.

According to the decree of Sovnarkom (the Council of People's Commissars—CPC), adopted on 23 June 1941, the ammunition manufacture mobilization plan was put in action. This was followed by decrees about wartime development of tank and aviation industries, evacuation of industrial plants from areas close to the front lines, as well as evacuation of government personnel and civilians. On 24 June, the Evacuation Council was set up. On 29 June 1941 CPC, together with the Central Committee of All-Union Communist Party (CC AUCP), signed a directive ordering all Party and Soviet organizations in the front-line regions to mobilize the entire nation for the total defeat of the enemy and for any possible measures to undermine the enemy's plans to seize the industrial and agricultural resources.

The State Defense Committee (SDC), created on 30 June 1941 and headed by Stalin, concentrated full power over the economy in its hands. The president of SDC or its members took, among other things, direct responsibility for production of munitions, food, and oil, as well as for stores, railways, and so on. Everything depended in practice upon the will of a single person—Stalin; decisions were taken without following democratic rules, often by fiat.

It would be wrong, nevertheless, to assess the meaning of SDC only from this one point of view. Tens, even hundreds, of people participated in its work; thousands and millions took part in the realization of its orders. SDC promulgated 9,971 decrees and decisions in the period ending 3 September 1945, and nearly two-thirds of them were connected, one way or another, with economic and war production questions.[10]

Severe losses suffered by the Soviet Army in the first stages of the war called for drastic measures. On 4 July 1941, the SDC had outlined the strategy of concentrating all economic efforts in the country's rear, where a new military-industrial complex was being built in the east. A special committee was set up under N. A. Voznesensky[11] and instructed to work out a blueprint which was approved on 16 August 1941. Its full title was the "Military-Economic Plan for the fourth quarter of 1941 and for 1942 of the Volga, Ural, Western Siberia, Kazakhstan and Central Asian regions." This plan projected the speediest manufacture of arms and ammunition for the army, the navy, and the air force, as well as increasing industrial and agricultural production.

Economic restructuring began in the summer of 1941 and was carried out in exceptionally difficult conditions. It was not only the Red Army that had sustained the enemy blows. Tremendous burdens had been laid upon the shoulders of the civilian population as well. The enemy had taken over cities and villages, plants and factories, equipment and crops, bringing everywhere death and destruction. Civilians from the occupied territories had been forcibly taken to Germany. Economic losses were incalculable.[12]

The wartime economic program was long-term. Aimed at achieving economic superiority over Germany, it outlined the following measures: reallocation and mobilization of all material, financial, and labor resources to provide for wartime needs; accelerated development of war industry and war construction; achievement of arms superiority—in quantity and in quality—over the enemy; mobilization of agricultural resources and collective farm labor in order to satisfy the needs of both the front lines and the rear; organization of transportation, paying particular attention to the movement of military loads and the construction of new roads in both the European and Asian regions of the country; and restructuring of the government apparatus.

The funds allocated for military needs by the government had been substantially increased. (Compared with the first half of 1941, spending for the second half of the year was 20.6 billion rubles greater.[13]) State loans, along with taxes, collections, and voluntary donations by the population, became the source of financing. Creating the Defense Fund was an important start.

Workers, farmers, and the intelligentsia understood in the main the importance of voluntary labor to save their homeland. The slogan "Everything for the front, everything for victory!" had been endorsed by the entire population. The Soviet labor force played a colossal role in the organization of the military economy and in the failure of German *Blitzkrieg*. The tough government and party policies for mobilization of labor together with the activity and mass initiative of the population would basically satisfy the industrial needs for qualified personnel, particularly in defense, by the summer of 1942.

The greatest role in the mobilization of available material resources was played by the acceleration of war industry and of military-construction work, as well as the conversion of civil industries. From the very beginning, all heavy industry plants and the overwhelming majority of light industry plants were used to manufacture cannons, tanks, and ammunition.

Practically the entire Soviet stock of capital equipment began working for the needs of the front. In many cases plants began the conversion to military production without any directives from above, strictly on personal initiative. Moscow itself was turned into a powerful arsenal for the Red Army. Military equipment was sent to all the front lines, north and south. Mass production of the Shpagin machine gun, for instance, was organized in plants that had previously produced automobiles, typewriters, machine tools, and even sporting goods. The pattern was repeated elsewhere. The trolleybus garage in the Leningrad district of Moscow began manufacturing hand grenades, confectionery factories produced food concentrates, small dry goods factories turned out antitank grenades and explosives.[14] Likewise in besieged Leningrad. There, 116 factories and plants manufactured missiles and mines, 15 plants produced mortars. Not a single light industry remained idle. "Red Bavaria," a brewery, manufactured missiles and firebombs, a perfume factory made mines, and grenades now issued from a prewar musical-instrument factory. Even during the first terrible winter of the blockade Leningrad had sent to the front lines 95,000 cases of missiles and mines, 380,000 grenades, and 435,000 detonators. The workers toiled in unheated buildings, lived on meager rations, and endured constant enemy bombardment.[15]

One of the genuine heroic epics of World War Two was the relocation of front-line industrial centers to the rear. All party decisions regarding evacuation and civilian relocation emphasized one point, namely, not allowing the enemy to seize the country's national wealth or to destroy industrial plants located in the European region of the country. Evacuation took place mainly in the months of July, August, and October 1941. The rapid advance of the German armies meant that it had to be completed in a very short time, working under constant fire.

The relocation process was directed by the Council of Evacuation (from July 1941 headed by the trade union leader, N. M. Shvernik; the former president of this body, transport commissar and Stalin's deputy L. M. Kaganovich, having failed to organize the work) and by the representatives of the Council on the spot. In July, aviation, arms, and ammunition plants as well as the factory shops of Leningrad, the Khar'kov tractor plants, and other installations were all transported into the rear.[16]

Over 100 aviation plants, with all their equipment and raw materials, were moving to the Volga, Ural, Central Asia, and Far East regions. A. I. Shakhurin, the People's Commissar of the aviation industry, comments that evacuation of even one aviation or engine plant meant the dismantling and loading of 3,000 to 5,000 units of equipment and transportation of up to 50,000 workers with their families. "In essence, evacuation of a single plant was equivalent to the evacuation of the population of a small town. Almost the entire aviation industry was on wheels and on the move."[17] Other military industries were in similar situation. According to D. F. Ustinov, by the end of 1941, 80 percent of all military industrial plants had been evacuated. Many plants were transported to similar plants and then merged.[18]

It would not, in fact, be an exaggeration to say that the entire country was on the move. Evacuation of the western border regions of Ukraine and Byelorussia was carried out under life-threatening conditions. Not only industrial plants, but grain and cattle were evacuated as well. Losses from constant bombing were unavoidable. In Leningrad, the evacuation of defense plants began at the end of July. The blockade, which gripped the city on 8 September, temporarily slowed down this process. But on 4 October SDC ordered immediate evacuation from Leningrad of machines and equipment, skilled workers, engineers, and technicians of the Kirov and Izhor plants, and of plant N174, which specialized in production of the KV and T-50 tanks.[19] From the beginning of 1942 the "Road of Life," laid across frozen Lake Ladoga, allowed partial retreat to the mainland.

In Moscow, evacuation activities peaked in the fall of 1941. The *Wehrmacht*'s operation TYPHOON, which began on 30 September, had moved up practically all roads toward Moscow. Fierce battles were being fought on all the approaches to the capital. Enemy front-line tank divisions had advanced farther and farther and yet no one in Moscow had made any moves. It was only when the situation had become highly critical that the SDC took the decision (15 October) entitled somberly "On evacuation of Moscow—the capital of the USSR." In view of the unfavorable situation, the SDC ordered evacuation the same day of the supreme governmental and military bodies. In case of enemy troops reaching the gates of Moscow, the SDC entrusted the NKVD to blow up the enterprises, storehouses, and institutions that could not be evacuated, as well as the entire electrical equipment of the subway system (with the exception of water lines and the sewerage system).[20] People's commissars summoned to the Kremlin on the morning of 15 October were ordered to leave immediately for their scheduled destinations and to supervise the relocation of plants managed by them. The People's Commissariat of Defense was evacuated to Perm' (though most of its staff returned in February of 1942).[21]

Evacuation denied essential industry to the Nazis, but only successful relocation could ensure its utility for the Soviet war effort. People were transported predominantly by rail, although some equipment, together with workers and their families, were loaded into steamboats and barges. Over the first six months of the war, 1,523 industrial plants and 30-40 percent of workers, engineers, and technicians were evacuated by rail into the rear regions. These were joined by scientific establishments and dozens of universities and research institutes. Overall, 10 million people were resettled. It is fair to say that the world had never before seen organized relocation on such a grand scale. Practically entire industries, together with millions of workers, were moved east thanks to herculean efforts by Soviet transport workers.[22]

Many in the West, familiar with the weaknesses of Soviet transport system, were astounded. Air Marshal Sir John Babington, head of the British Military Mission's air section in the USSR, noted in 1943: "It had always been generally assumed—and with good reasons—that nearly all forms of Russian transport were both inadequate and inefficient. That assumption has not been generally modified. Nevertheless," continued Babington, "not only had the Soviets extricated a substantial part of their forces from

Western Russia, Poland, and the Baltic States; they had simultaneously succeeded in removing to the neighborhood of Urals the bulk of their industrial plants and machinery as well as the civilian personnel for its operation." What he called this "double and unparalleled achievement," had been carried out using means which, judged by ordinary Western standards, would seem to have been totally inadequate. Babington viewed it as of the utmost importance for the future of the war.[23]

Relocation of the means of production was obviously not by itself the panacea for all existing problems. It was necessary to unload the trains, reassemble the equipment, get plants into operation, and make up for interruptions in the production process —all in record time. The "miracle" of speedy relocation and renewed operation would not have been possible without the truly unprecedented heroism of the evacuees and the populace of the eastern regions who worked around the clock in freezing temperatures, often in the open air.

The last two months of 1941, called by A. I. Shakhurin the months of the "battles on the construction sites of the East," were the most difficult and critical time for the Soviet national economy. Due to the incomplete process of evacuation and relocation, industrial productivity had decreased substantially. Between June and November 1941, gross production was more than halved. Production of rolled ferrous metals had declined threefold from June to December. In some vital areas the collapse was even more spectacular: ball bearing production, for instance, was down to 5 percent of what it had been in the first half of the year. The shortage of fuel, specifically coal, was felt by all. In November and December of 1941, not a ton of coal was received from the Donets and Moscow region coal basins. For this reason the greatest difficulties were faced by the war plants. War production was at its minimum in November 1941. Aircraft production had gone down in the fourth quarter, December being the most critical month.[24]

In spite of all the difficulties, losses, and miscalculations, however, 1941 had shown that Soviet Union was able to set up war plants and supply its troops with modern equipment—in short that, even *in extremis,* it was still able to rely on its national economy. Both the Allies and the enemy were surprised by certain new Soviet munitions, for instance rocket launchers. The famous "Katyushas," which were first used by Captain I. A. Flyorov in the battle outside Orsha on 14 July 1941, horrified the Germans. The exceptional simplicity of this design by Shpagin facilitated mass production and the delivery of weapons to the troops within the first few months following the start of the war. The Soviet T-34 tank was also starting to make an impact. On encountering the Fourth German Panzer Division at the beginning of October outside the city of Orel, it had demonstrated its superiority over the enemy in firepower, armor, and maneuverability.[25]

The Soviet counteroffensive in the winter of 1941-42 and the defeat of the German army outside Moscow stimulated the economy, although in February 1942 certain important indicators (steel and cast iron smelting, coal mining, and oil production) were at their lowest for all the war years,[26] and statistics for the first half of 1942 were generally worse even than the second half of 1941—coal production, for instance, being only 35.7 million tons as against 59.5 million.[27]

The fall in industrial production had nevertheless been halted by the end of March 1942 and during the spring military production began to rise. It was due to the fact that the construction of war plants was in the main completed, the activity of its technological services was organized, and the plants now worked utilizing almost all of the equipment available to them.[28] By summer, the overwhelming majority of relocated plants were producing to their full capacity. The Soviet war industry, as the British ambassador in the USSR, Archibald Clark Kerr, reported on 23 June 1942 to the Foreign Office, "has made practically a complete recovery after the events of last year."[29]

Many in the West held the efforts of the Soviet people and the speed of their work in high regard. Yet they also noted the long-term, negative consequences of the evacuation for the country's economy. It was concentrated in the distant regions with severe climates. The increase of production was stimulated only in the war sector, while industrial production and production of food had decreased. The need for rapid production had created a situation in which military equipment was at times of low quality. The arrival of evacuated plants imposed additional strain on the established enterprises of the interior.[30]

By the middle of 1942, party and government organs had completed the restructuring of the economy to suit military needs. The proportion of national wealth used in war production amounted to 55 percent, while military products made up 63.9 percent of overall industrial output.[31] In the Urals, Siberia, Volga Region, Kazakhstan, and Central Asia, military-industrial potential had been strengthened. By the summer of 1942 over 1,200 industrial plants out of 1,523 evacuated in 1941 had been rebuilt and set in operation. The struggle for survival on the industrial front had been won. Although Moscow and the surrounding industrial regions did not lose their economic importance, the east became the main arsenal for the Soviet armed forces. By June 1942 it supplied the troops with three-quarters of all war production, as well as providing increased agricultural production.

The last stages of economic restructuring coincided with fierce battles on the approaches to Stalingrad and the Northern Caucasus. These southern regions had posed particular difficulties for industry and agriculture. Even by the end of 1942 the metal shortage (especially nonferrous metals) could not be overcome. The same held true for coal and electrical energy. Transportation was overloaded, and the army did not have sufficient trucks. The oil industry likewise encountered problems. Dismantling equipment at Kuban' and in Azerbaijan, the evacuation to the eastern regions in 1941 led to a slump in oil production. By midsummer 1942, practically all the oil refineries evacuated to the Ural, Volga Region, and Kazakhstan had been reassembled. But, because of the threat to the Northern Caucasus and the beginning of the German offensive against Stalingrad, protective measures were taken to deny the enemy the use of the Kuban'/Caucasus oil fields. These included sabotage of oil wells and the transfer to the east of some 600 railroad cars of oil industry equipment.

Following the German occupation of the Northern Caucasus and their breakthrough to the Volga River, Second Baku became the main supply base for the front. As the slogan for oil workers in the east put it: "What did you do today to help Stalingrad?" That motto served to inspire the workers, and they increased production dramatically. Tens of thousands of railroad tankers were needed to deliver fuel to the front lines around Stalingrad.[32]

The summer and fall of 1942 had found the southern regions engulfed in war. Nevertheless, the army's ammunition supply did not diminish. In the second half of that year, the aviation industry supplied nearly 1,000 planes per month *more* than the year before, and the flow continued to increase.[33] Table 6.1 illustrates the dynamics of munitions production.[34]

TABLE 6.1

SELECTED STATISTICS OF MUNITIONS OUTPUT, 1941-42

	July/December 1941	January/June 1942	July/December1942
Planes	8,200	8,300	13,400
Tanks	4,800	11,200	13,300
Mortars (82-100mm)	19,100	55,400	70,100

Until September 1942, the Stalingrad tractor plant had been the main works producing T-34 tanks, accounting for about 40 percent of the entire supply. The plant had exceeded its July 1942 plan, though working under the constant threat of advancing German tank divisions. Tank assembly and repair continued at the STP for 42 days under bombing and mortar fire. On 18 October, the plant was finally occupied but by then the equipment, together with the workers, had been evacuated to Siberia.[35]

Despite all the hardships, workers, engineers, and technicians were able to stop the fall in industrial output; a growth of war production began.

Soviet science also played an important role in the development of the war economy. Scholars used all their talent in the struggle with fascism. The research institutions in industry and the Academy of Sciences were reorganized to satisfy the needs of the front. Leading Academicians such as I. P. Bardin and P. L. Kapitsa devoted time and energy to the war effort. Scientists and engineers created new types of weapons; they did much to accelerate the introduction of new techniques into production (to date, the rate of proving and assimilating new methods of production that was reached before and during the war has not been surpassed).[36] Academician Peter Kapitsa, who was also a fellow of the Royal Society, Britain's premier scientific body, told English readers in his article "Science for Red Army" about the fruitful work of Soviet mathematicians, geologists, chemists, and other specialists: "To-day the danger to freedom and the desire to save the country inspire Soviet scientists to concentrate all their efforts on the solution of problems raised by war."[37] Radio electronics, optics, radar, and other technological and scientific fields developed quickly. New missiles were designed. A group of scientists, headed by Academicians S. P. Korolev and V. P. Glushko, were working with theory and practice of rockets and rocket engines. Automatic electrical welding with flux was mastered under the leadership of E. O. Paton, a Ukrainian Academician. This technique was very important in the production of tanks, air bombs, and artillery.

The beginning of war with Nazi Germany stopped research in the field of nuclear physics. It was resumed after intelligence gave reason to suppose that work on the A-bomb was going in the West. A young, gifted physicist, I. V. Kourchatov, was made the head of the Soviet Atomic Project in the fall of 1942. Construction of the Laboratory N2 of the Academy of Sciences (later the world-famous Kourchatov Institute of Atomic Energy) began in Moscow. When President Harry Truman mentioned at the Potsdam conference that the Americans were in possession of a bomb of unusual strength it came as no surprise to Stalin. In any case, by that time a cyclotron was already working in the Kourchatov Laboratory, plutonium—the first in Europe—had been obtained, and construction of an experimental graphite-uranium pile was nearing its end. The first test of an A-bomb in the USSR took place on 29 August 1949, but the secrets of its creation only became known some 40 years later.[38]

At the end of December 1942 Nikolai Voznesensky reported on the state of Soviet economy to the SDC. He said that, in military production, the Soviet Union was superior to Germany and her allies in every respect.[39] Nevertheless, the time to rejoice was still far off. After substantial losses in the Volga Region, the German government had immediately accelerated production in order to make up for its losses. As a result, the Soviet Union had to mobilize all of its reserves and to utilize every branch of the economy in order to retain military superiority over the enemy.

The year 1943 was later characterized by Voznesensky as the turning point in the history of Soviet war economics. This was the year in which the tide turned on the battlefronts and productivity markedly increased.[40] From the the second quarter, industrial production resumed its steady rise, having declined in the first quarter of the year by comparison with October-December 1942. Development in branches of heavy industry maintained its speedy pace. This was especially true for machine building and metal working, both vital to the growth of the war economy. Other significant indicators are shown in Table 6.2.[41]

TABLE 6.2

SELECTED PRODUCTION STATISTICS, 1943-45

	1943	1944	1945
Electrical energy (billion kw/hours)	32.3	39.2	43.3
Steel (million tons)	8.5	10.9	12.3
Çoal (million tons)	93.1	121.5	149.3

In 1944, the machine building, metal working, chemical, and nonferrous metallurgy industries provided the country with more than before the war. For the first time, the gross industrial product index had exceeded the prewar standards. It even became possible to expand the production of goods for civilian consumption. New attention had been turned to the areas damaged by the war.

After the Stalingrad and Kursk victories economic reconstruction began in the liberated areas. The Reconstruction Program was included in state military-economic plans in 1944 and 1945. This program had to consider the substantial loss of national wealth at the hands of the occupiers. Part of the population of the occupied territories had been either wiped out or transported into slave labor camps. After the occupation, 13 percent of industrial plants had remained in the regions of RSFSR. In the Ukraine that figure was 19 percent and in Byelorussia 15 percent.[42] In 1944, following the liberation of Soviet territories, the rebuilding of industrial plants had begun. By the end of 1945, thousands of industrial plants had been fully or partially set into operation. The population of the liberated territories did everything to contribute to the country's rebuilding efforts.

In 1945, development and reconstruction of all branches of the economy continued. In the first half of that year, although military production was maintained, manufacture of tractors and other agricultural machinery had started to increase. Certain measures were taken to increase the production of consumer goods. Over 500 plants were switched over to serve consumer needs. In the second quarter of 1945, consumer goods accounted for 45.7 percent of entire production and in the third quarter, nearly 60 percent.[43] The rebuilding of the peacetime economy had begun.

Although industrial and agricultural development was basically sufficient to satisfy the military-economical needs of the country (see Table 6.3), there were real problem areas.

TABLE 6.3

BASIC INDICATORS OF SOVIET ECONOMIC DEVELOPMENT

(1940 = 100)[44]

	1941	1942	1943	1944	1945
National Income	92	66	74	88	83
Productive fixed assets (excluding livestock)	72	68	76	84	88
Industrial Output	98	77	90	103	91
Engineering Products	111	119	142	158	129
Gross Agricultural Output	62	38	37	54	60
Capital Investment	84	52	57	79	92
Freight Traffic	92	53	61	71	76
Average Annual number of workers/office employees	88	59	62	76	87
State and Cooperative Retail Turnover	84	34	32	37	43

Regardless of the stabilization in the growth rate in the spring of 1943, many branches of Soviet industry could not achieve the prewar levels, even by the end of the war. Lagging behind wartime needs were the aluminum and copper industries. There were also shortages of lead and zinc, and oil production had decreased.

Agriculture suffered from the war more than any other sector of the economy. The already modest wealth of the villages had been mercilessly looted by the enemy. In order to supply the needs of the Red Army, it was necessary to give up a large quantity of automobiles, tractors, and horses. Moreover, the war had also taken a large percentage of the able-bodied population from the villages. Millions of men left to go into the army, war plants, or construction. Women, teenagers, and old men basically comprised the rural work force, women having to assume the decisive roles in agricultural production.

Working and living conditions were extremely difficult for these farmers. There was little equipment, even of outdated varieties. Ploughing was done with the aid of cows. Although, in the last years of the war, the farmers received somewhat more supplies, there were still tractor shortages, particularly in the liberated territories. For example, in 1944, in the Kursk Region, up to 140,000 cows were used during the springtime sowing. The same situation was recorded in Smolensk and other regions.[45]

Kolkhozes (collective farms) were the primary suppliers of the agricultural products. Its members, while living on miserly rations,[46] were each doing the work for two or three people. The minimum number of workdays was increased as were all the methods of control and regulation of the farmers. However, what should be emphasized is that farmers as well as the nation's labor was inspired by the general patriotism and by the more specific and even more intense desire to evict the enemy from their land. For all the harshness of the Stalinist era, strictly totalitarian means would never have been sufficient in such a struggle.

Agriculture was able to overcome the difficulties of the first war years (1943 being the most acute) and to increase the output of grains, meat, milk, and other products in 1944 and 1945. The gross grain yield, for instance, fell from 95.6 million tons in 1940 to 55.9 million in 1941 and to a nadir of 29.7 million in 1942, from which it did not begin to recover until 1944. The yield for 1945 was only 47.3 million tons.[47] In spite of the temporary loss of the agriculturally richest regions, decreased manpower and other unfavorable factors, farmers' efforts together with strict state control helped satisfy the basic needs of the front and rear under conditions of an overstrained economy and minimal food rations. The Soviet Army and, to a lesser degree, its population were supplied mainly by the Soviet food industry.

Yet, as the grain figures indicate, at the end of war the country was barely approaching prewar levels of agricultural production. The measures taken to rebuild the economy could not fully compensate for the destroyed agrarian sector, even though the rebuilding of collective farms in the Ukraine, Byelorussia, and other regions was conducted as speedily as possible. Principal causes were the decrease in agricultural investment and the loss of machinery. By May 1945, tractors only amounted to three-quarters of the prewar stock, and trucks only one-third. All this left its mark on the Soviet postwar economy.

What of munitions production itself, to which all else had been sacrificed? In spite of the fact that Soviet economic development did not generally advance beyond the indicators of 1940, it still allowed for the accelerated rearming of the Red Army and its supply with the newest military equipment. The turning point in industry began in the second half of 1942 and was secured in 1943. In comparison with 1940, military production had increased more than twofold. By July 1943, particularly after the great battle around Kursk, Soviet superiority over the German armies in the basic types of war equipment had increased. Though Germany was extracting three times more steel and almost five times more coal than the Soviet Union (including imports and materials from the occupied territories), the Soviet Union, during the war, had produced almost double the armaments and military equipment. [48] The following data show the contributions of war industries to the country's victory (see Table 6.4).

TABLE 6.4

PRODUCTION OF KEY MILITARY EQUIPMENT BY THE USSR

(in thousands)[49]

	July/December				Jan/August	
	1941	1942	1943	1944	1945	Total
Rifles and Carbines	1,567.1	4,049.0	3,436.2	2,450.0	637.0	12,139.3
Submachine Guns	89.7	1,506.4	2,023.6	1,970.8	583.4	6,173.9
Machine Guns	106.2	356.1	458.5	439.1	156.0	1,515.9
Mortars	42.3	230.0	69.4	7.1	3.0	351.08
Tanks and Self-propelled Guns	4.8	24.4	24.1	29.0	20.5	102.8
Fighter Planes	8.2	21.7	29.9	33.2	19.1	112.1
Warships (single units)	35	15	14	4	2	70

In four years of war the army, according to Marshal G. Zhukov, had received at least 100 million tons of military equipment. Sometimes during the periods of great strategic operations, nearly 100 trains loaded with troops, equipment, and different kind of stores were going daily to the main fronts.[50]

The decrease in production of weapons and mortars in the last years of the war was the result of the increased production of higher caliber artillery. Even in 1942, production in gun plants had increased sufficiently, and there was no need for additional increases in the years to come. The technology and quality of manufactured artillery systems and mortars was continuously improved. In 1943 alone, 21 different designs of artillery equipment were made.[51]

During these years, the Soviet Union had retained superiority over the enemy in armored weapons. Toward the end of 1943 German armies had to revert to defensive strategies. It was then that they began using heavy antitank and antiaircraft artillery. In the Soviet armed forces, the popular, average-size T-34 tank was equipped with a more powerful weapon, namely the 85mm cannon.[52] Large-scale production of self-propelled guns of different calibers was expanded.

To take one final example of the defense industry: The superiority of the Soviet air force had been evident during the defeat of Germany at Stalingrad. In 1943 most Soviet planes were superior as measured by their tactical indicators. New models continuously entered mass production. Leading aircraft designers dedicated themselves to the design and perfection of Soviet aircraft. For instance, 40,000 low-flying attack aircraft designed by S. V. Iliushin and 37,000 fighters designed by A. S. Yakovlev were produced. New aircraft at the end of war made up 96.2 percent of all fighter planes (compared to 46.4 percent in 1942). In bombers, on 1 January 1942, 81.9 percent were "old" machines but the proportion had fallen to 14.5 percent by 1945. In other words, according to A. I. Shakhurin, during the war the Soviet Union not only "supplied its technical needs, but completely rearmed its air force with new equipment."[53]

Harry Hopkins, who visited Moscow in May 1945, said to Stalin: "We never really thought that our aid through Lend-Lease was the main factor in Soviet victory over Germany in the Eastern Front."[54] The Soviet economy was, in the words of American historian William McNeill, "surprisingly independent" in comparison with that of Great Britain or even of the United States.[55] Soviet soldiers had defeated the German armies predominantly by Soviet weapons. What, then, was the role played by Allied supplies of arms, military equipment, and food in the Soviet war economy?

Four percent is the official Soviet figure for the proportion of Western supplies in the total volume of Soviet-made production in 1941-45.[56] This, however, gives only a general idea of the economic aspect of the Allies' relationship. If one looks only at the quantitative indicators, the insignificance of military-economic cooperation between Western countries and the USSR in 1941-42, becomes apparent. The report of the People's Commissariat of Foreign Trade on Britain's fulfillment of its obligations under the first Protocol for October-December 1941 stated that only 487 tanks out of the 1,000 promised were supplied to the Soviet Union. The United States was even further behind schedule. During the whole period of the First Protocol (October 1941 through June 1942) it supplied 267 bombers (instead of 900 promised), 278 fighters (instead of 900), 363 medium-size tanks (instead of 1,125), 420 light tanks (instead of 1,250,) and 16,500 trucks (against 85,000).[57] Similarly the obligations under the Second Protocol, for the year from 1 July 1942, were not fulfilled completely.

Unfulfilled commitments were the result of a number of factors. Among these were losses of shipments in the course of transporting them across the ocean, due to the activities of enemy submarines. There was also unwillingness of some elements within the Allied military bureaucracies to supply weapons and materials to other countries. Nor should one forget the feelings of hostility and mistrust toward the Soviet Union on the part of certain American and British policymakers.

Whatever the reasons, the blunt fact is that the Lend-Lease Act made no substantial contribution to the victories of the Soviet armed forces at Moscow or Stalingrad. As American historian George Herring acknowledges, before the summer of 1943 weapon, tank, and aircraft supplies were small in proportion to the numbers manufactured in the Soviet Union and they did not satisfy the needs of the front. Most of the supplies were light and medium tanks.[58]

That said, it should, however, be borne in mind that weapons and raw materials, though small in amount, arrived by the dangerous northern route in late summer and early fall 1941. The first British convoy appeared in Archangel on 31 August, bringing 16 fighters, 10,000 tons of rubber, and other materials. (Under the code name of the first convoy—DERVISH—jubilee celebrations were held on 31 August 1991, with participation by veterans of the three wartime Allies and other countries.) Fifty-one transports, nine of them Soviet, arrived in the USSR in August-September 1941 as part of seven Allied convoys.[59]

Thus, symbolism mattered as well as substance. The Moscow conference of representatives of the three Allies, the signing of the First Protocol on supplies, the inclusion of the Soviet Union into the Lend-Lease Act on 7 November 1941, and extending a one billion dollar loan to the USSR—all these took place at the most critical time for the Soviet Union. The fate of Moscow was being decided. Leningrad was being gripped vicelike by the blockade. The situation on other fronts was increasingly desperate. Decisions made together with the American and the British governments were therefore of great psychological importance for the Red Army and the whole nation. Support for the Soviet people by the populace of these two countries and actions, such as Lord Beaverbrook's initiative known as "Tank Week" or the collections of funds for "Aid for Russia," did much to boost the morale of the Soviet peoples.

From the economic point of view, the war equipment received in the first two years of war was also a help for the country. The main supply routes then lay across the Pacific Ocean and Northern Russia. After the Moscow conference much attention was devoted to collaboration with Britain in developing the southern supply route. The SDC directive on transport questions concerning Iran (13 October 1941) ordered the

Soviet Railway Commission and the diplomatic representatives of the USSR in Tehran "to give help to all the actions of the English which are intended to increase in a short time the traffic capacity of the Trans-Iranian railway up to the point of full employment of the single-track."[60] The first goods via Iran arrived in the Soviet Union in November 1941. One more decision (taken on 26 March 1942) shows us how carefully the SDC planned the distribution of armaments, war equipment, and materials brought by the "12th Caravan." The planes received were sent directly to the front while Valentines, Matildas, and other tanks were used for the formation and replenishment of Tank Brigades. In 1942, 10–12 ships arrived monthly in the Persian Gulf with supplies for the USSR.[61]

These 1941-42 supplies compensated for shortages or for the total lack of certain products and raw materials necessary for Soviet war production. American shipments of steel, aluminum, copper, telephone cables, leather, shoes for the army, as well as supplies (mainly military) from Great Britain and Canada, aided the Soviet Union during this critical period of the war.[62]

By analyzing Stalin's requests for aid one may see what the needs of Soviet economy were and how the Soviet government tried to satisfy them through Western supplies. While hosting Winston Churchill in the Kremlin in August 1942 Stalin expressed his dissatisfaction with the fact that the promises regarding the shipment of supplies to the Soviet Union were not being totally fulfilled. Stalin asked for aluminum as well as up to 25,000 trucks: "Send us trucks instead of tanks," he said bluntly. New requests for supplying the Red Army with trucks and transport planes were addressed to Anthony Eden in London by Ambassador Maisky.[63] Special Soviet needs in planes and trucks had also been stressed by Stalin in his correspondence with Roosevelt. On 7 October 1942, for instance, he wrote that the worsening of the situation in the south, especially around Stalingrad, was due to the lack of fighters.[64] Next day SDC obliged Mikojan to surrender during October to the Car and Motor Vehicle Board of the Red Army 1,700 imported trucks (among them 1,000 trucks newly arrived with the 18th Caravan), as well as trucks which came through Iran and Vladivostok.[65]

Despite their limitations, then, the supplies to the Soviet Union and the Soviet aid to the West, agreed under the terms of the First and Second Protocols, had created a basis for practical development of military-economic and political cooperation among the three countries. Beginning with the Second Protocol, the terms of the agreements had been agreed through diplomatic negotiations, and, despite the evident difficulties of such a process, they marked a new era in the relationship between the Soviet

Union and the leading capitalist nations. This was intrinsically different from the aloof and suspicious relationship that existed during 1939-41.

The largest portion of supplies under the Lend-Lease Act was shipped during 1943-44. In other words, it arrived during the turning point in the war and the beginning of the offensive strategy of the Soviet armed forces.

During the time of the First and Second Protocols American and British shipments were approximately equal. In 1941, Britain even fulfilled a part of American obligations, sending to Russia planes built in the United States under cash contracts. Later on, however, American aid exceeded that of Britain.[66]

Over the last years of the war, the content of the shipments also underwent significant changes. The Soviet Union no longer needed as many arms, since it was producing sufficient quantities itself. There was a greater need for industrial and medical equipment, transport, and food. The shipments from the West covered certain shortages of equipment (in particular, metal cutting), metal and cable products, and chemicals. The shipments of food and clothing provided great help in supplying the needs of the army and the civilian population. Under the Third Protocol, food supplies made up about one-third of all the shipments. The provision of automobiles, locomotives, tractors and ships had also been extremely valuable. American supplies facilitated the process of restoring the Soviet transport system, as well as organizing and waging major offensive operations that ranged many miles in depth.[67]

Aviation Lend-Lease was particularly important, supplying the USSR with 256 planes of all types in 1941; 1,485 in 1942; 5,320 in 1943; 5,007 in 1944; and 2,058 in 1945. Fighters amounted to 76 percent of all aircraft sent, with 3,594 of them delivered in 1944. Aviation Lend-Lease added significantly to the total aircraft available to the USSR, equalling 20 percent of the bombers and up to 23 percent of the fighters produced by Soviet factories.[68]

According to Soviet sources, the total sum of goods supplied by the United States to the USSR in the period up to 1 June 1945 amounted to $8.86 billion.[69] The American figures for the period ending August 1945 value U.S. aid at $10.67 billion or 24 percent of total aid under Lend-Lease (see Table 6.5).[70]

Nor should the other Allies be forgotten. In the period from the summer of 1941 to September 1945, Great Britain provided the Soviet Union with munitions and war matériel totalling £318 million, or about $1.7 billion—15 percent of Britain's total aid to all nations during the war.[71]

TABLE 6.5

GRAND TOTAL OF SOVIET IMPORTS AND AID FROM THE UNITED STATES IN 1943-44
(millions of U.S. dollars)[72]

	1943	1944
1. Lend-Lease imports	2,501.2	3,702.2
(subtotals): military supplies	(1,264.1)	(1,657.7)
industrial equipment	(261.4)	(572.7)
food	(503.1)	(687.6)
2. Commercial imports (through Amtorg)	9.6	3.3
Total	**2,510.8**	**3,705.5**

Beginning with the Third Lend-Lease Protocol of 1943, Canada became a direct supplier of aid to the USSR. Canadian shipments included weapons, industrial equipment, nonferrous metals, steel, rolled metal, chemicals, and food supplies. Aid from Canada to the USSR over the period 1943-46 amounted to C$ 167 million, or 6.7 percent of total Canadian Mutual Aid.[73]

All shipments under Lend-Lease to the USSR for the period 22 June 1941 through 20 September 1945, according to American data, amounted to 17.5 million long tons (one long ton = 1.016 metric tons). Nearly half came via the Soviet Far East; most of the remainder came in equal proportions through the Persian Gulf and Northern Russia.[74] All these routes opened up an enormous flow of Lend-Lease, especially in 1943-45. The port of Vladivostok was reconstructed and new ports were built in Petropavlovsk-Kamchatiski (across the Bering Sea from Alaska) and other cities to enable the American Liberty Ships to offload their cargoes.[75]

During the Cold War years Soviet authors usually misrepresented or downplayed the obvious facts about American and British supplies to the USSR. But in 1942-45 the role of Allied goods was stressed in many official statements and in the Soviet press and newsreels. On 11 June 1944 the People's Commissariat of Foreign Trade published all data on shipments received in the period from June 1941 through April 1944 from the United States, Great Britain, and Canada. The Soviet government stated that these shipments "aided in the struggle of the Red Army to liberate its homeland from Fascist occupiers and in bringing closer the Allied victory over Nazi Germany and its satellites."[76]

The economic aid from the West could not, however, compensate for the absence of the Second Front until mid-1944. United States General James H. Burns, while visiting Moscow, told the press in April 1943 that he thought it natural "that people here consider it far more important to remove thirty to forty German divisions from the Soviet-German front than to obtain tanks and planes."[77] Lend-Lease had not predetermined the outcome of the war on that front; the contribution of the Soviet Union to the war could not be compared with dollars and tons of American aid, wrote Edward Stettinius. The USSR paid a heavy price for its victory.[78] The economic losses of the Soviet Union were greater than those of any other Allied nation. The damage done to the Soviet economy and to individuals (just as a result of direct destruction and looting) amounted to 679 million rubles.

The help rendered by the USSR under Reverse Lend-Lease cannot be dismissed. Its sum was indeed small—$2.139 million by April 1945. But, as President Harry Truman acknowledged, the Soviet Union had but limited possibilities to help. Still, American ships were repaired and provisioned in Soviet ports. Reverse Lend-Lease also included facilities in Soviet territory for American planes and their personnel. The USSR also supplied strategic materials important for U.S. production, particularly chromium, manganese, platinum, and tin.[79]

Nor should the political significance of the mutual aid program be minimized. Lend-Lease offered a new form of collaboration that was tested for the first time during the war, as contemporaries recognized. The scheme that brought supplies to the Soviet Union through the Persian Gulf, for example, was seen by Soviet and American organizers as a successful experiment in international cooperation. Though it was not a military operation, it could not be reduced to merely a "trade deal." Officers and men attached to the American Persian Gulf forces were decorated with Soviet orders and medals.[80]

Bearing in mind both the substantive and symbolic importance of Lend-Lease to the Soviet Union, we can better understand why its abrupt termination in May 1945 was regarded in Moscow as such a serious blow to relations between the two countries.

In summary, then, the Soviet Union was better endowed with territory and resources than Great Britain or even the United States. But, no less than its two future allies, it was ill prepared for war when it broke out. Promising new prototypes were not in production, the economy had been disrupted by the upheavals of Stalinization, and, above all, few anticipated the likelihood of a long defensive war. The critical period for the Soviet economy was, therefore, the second half of 1941. It was then that almost all Soviet industrial plants were converted to war production. Even more important, those months saw the breakneck evacuation of factories to locations east of the Urals to escape the rapidly expanding German occupation. The short-term consequences of this disruption were severe—in November 1941 production was at its nadir—but by summer 1942 the relocated industries were working close to full capacity, and by 1944 the gross industrial product exceeded prewar levels. It was even possible, with victory in sight, to address some consumer needs and begin the colossal task of postwar reconstruction.

The price for this prodigious war effort was high. Agriculture, in particular, was decimated, and the shortages of workers, equipment, and investment meant that prewar crop output had not been regained even in 1945. But the other side of the coin was a twofold increase in military production between 1940 and 1943, when roughly two-thirds of industrial output was for military needs. Overall, the USSR produced almost twice as much military hardware as Nazi Germany, despite the latter's vastly enhanced resources after 1940. This remarkable effort astonished not only Hitler but also the Western allies. Few had expected so much from Soviet industry and workers, and their feats have only slowly been appreciated in the West. On the other hand, the recent end of the Cold War has enabled Russian scholars to acknowledge more openly the useful role played by Western economic aid—as a morale-building promise of things to come in the dark days of 1941-42, and as a valuable material supplement to Soviet production in 1943-45. Even the remarkably self-sufficient Soviet war effort can only be properly understood in the context of the alliance as a whole.

NOTES

1. A. L. Narochnitski, ed., *The USSR and Its Struggle against Fascist Aggression, 1933-1945* (Moscow, 1986), 243-44; A. D. Budkov and L. A. Budkov, *Soviet Oil Industry during the Great Patriotic War* (Moscow, 1985), 40 (both in Russian).

2. G. K. Zhukov, *Memories and Thoughts* (3 vols.; Moscow, 1990), 1, 308-9; D. F. Ustinov, *In the Name of Victory: Notes of the People's Commissar of Arms* (Moscow, 1988), 122-23 (both in Russian).

3. B. L. Vannikov, "From the Notes of the People's Commissar of Ammunition, *Modern and Contemporary History* 1 (1988), 90-91 (in Russian).

4. Zhukov, *Memories and Thoughts,* 1, 310; Ustinov, *In the Name of Victory,* 123.

5. M. Harrison, *Soviet Planning in Peace and War 1938-1945* (Cambridge, 1985), 61.

6. See: "Round Table: War, People, Victory," *Izvestia,* 8 May 1990, (in Russian).

7. Zhukov, *Memories and Thoughts,* 1, 303.

8. A. R. Millett and W. Murray, eds., *Military Effectiveness* (3 vols.; Boston, 1988) 3, 267.

9. A. S. Milward, *War, Economy and Society, 1939-1945* (Berkeley, 1977), 46.

10. N. Ja. Komarov, *The State Defense Council Orders, Documents, Memories, Commentaries* (Moscow, 1990), 6-7, 10, 426 (in Russian).

11. N. A. Voznesensky—President of Gosplan (1938-March 1941), First Deputy of the President of the CPC from March 1941. He was arrested in connection with the "Leningrad affair" in the autumn of 1949 and shot a year later.

12. For full data see G. S. Kravchenko, *The Soviet Economy during the Great Patriotic War (1941-1945),* (Moscow, 1970), 123-24 (in Russian).

13. G. A. Kumanev, ed., *The Soviet Home Front in the Period of the Great Patriotic War* (Moscow, 1988), 89.

14. Zhukov, *Memories and Thoughts* 2: 222; Ustinov, *In the Name of Victory,* 177.

15. *The Forge of Victory: the Heroism of the Home Front during the Great Patriotic War. Essays and Memoirs* (Moscow, 1985), 77-78, 86-87 (in Russian).

16. *The Echelons are Heading East: From the History of Relocation of the Productive Forces of the USSR in 1941-1942* (Moscow, 1966), 6; A. I. Mikojan, "In the first months of the Great Patriotic War," *Modern and Contemporary History* 6 (1985), 103-4 (in Russian).

17. A. I. Shakhurin, *The Wings of Victory* (Moscow, 1990), 149 (in Russian).

18. Ustinov, *In the Name of Victory,* 150-51.

19. The Russian Center for the Conservation and Study of Documents on Contemporary History (*RCCSDCH*). Fond 644, schedule 1, file 111, p. 169 (in Russian).

20. *RCKSDCH,* F. 644, sch. 1, file 12, p. 155.

21. Shakhurin, *Wings of Victory,* 151; Ustinov, *In the Name of Victory,* 150.

22. *The Forge of Victory,* 13, 172; G. A. Kumanev, *The War and Railroad Transportation of USSR 1941-1945* (Moscow, 1988) (in Russian).

23. Public Record Office (PRO), Kew, England. FO 371/32960, Memo by Air Marshal Sir John Babington "The Riddle of Soviet Military Successes," 12 August 1943.

24. N. Voznesensky, *The War Economy of the USSR in the Period of Patriotic War* (Moscow, 1948), 42-43; Ustinov, *In the Name of Victory,* 151-52; Shakhurin, *Wings,* 158, 179. The planned quota for December 1941 was fulfilled only partially: planes, 38.8 percent; aviation motors, 23.6 percent. See *The History of the Great Patriotic War of the Soviet Union 1941-1945* (6 vols.; Moscow, 1960-64), 2, 160 (in Russian).

25. Vannikov, "Notes," 100, 113.

26. Kravchenko, *Soviet Economy,* 130, 139.

27. *The History of the Second World War 1941-1945* (12 vols.; Moscow, 1973-82), 4, 157 (in Russian).

28. Shakhurin, *Wings,* 179, 201.

29. PRO, FO 371/32909.

30. *From "Barbarossa" to "Terminal": the View from the West* (Moscow, 1988), 459 (in Russian); John Barber and Mark Harrison, *The Soviet Home Front, 1941-1945: A Social and Economic History of the USSR in World War II* (London, 1991), 131-32; Susan J. Linz, ed., *The Impact of World War II on the Soviet Union* (New York, 1985), 17.

31. Narochnitski, ed., *USSR,* 259.

32. Budkov and Budkov, *Soviet Oil Industry,* 69, 93-100.

33. Shakhurin, *Wings,* 207.

34. Estimated data from *The History of the Second World War, 1939-1945,* 4, 158; 5, 48.

35. *The Forge of Victory,* 126-27, 142-43.

36. E. I. Grakova, *Scientists for the Front, 1941-1945* (Moscow, 1989), 219 (in Russian).

37. *Soviet War News,* 3 March 1942.

38. I. N. Golovin, *I. V. Kurchatov* (Moscow, 1978); A. I. Ioirish, I. D. Morochov, S. K. Ivanov, *The A-Bomb* (Moscow, 1980); "Those Who Had Awakened the Geni," *Moscow News,* 41 (1989); *Izvestia,* 8 December 1992 (in Russian).

39. Ustinov, *In the Name of Victory,* 197-98.

40. Voznesensky, *War Economy of the USSR,* 29, 133-34.

41. Voznesensky, *War Economy of the USSR,* 142-43, 155.

42. Voznesensky, *War Economy of the USSR,* 55-57.

43. Ja. E. Chadajev, *The Economy of the USSR during the Great Patriotic War (1941-1945)* (Moscow, 1985), 214 (in Russian). The ratio between military and civilian production in total production was: 1942—63.9 and 36.1; 1943—58.3 and 41.7; 1944—51.3 and 48.7; 1945—40.1 and 59.9; *The History of the Great Patriotic War,* 5, 419.

44. *National Economy of the USSR over 70 Years* (Moscow, 1987), 43 (in Russian).

45. Chadajev, *Economy,* 328, 333; Ju. V. Arutjunjan, *Soviet Farmers during the Great Patriotic War* (Moscow, 1970), 74-75, 98 (in Russian).

46. In 1943 a farmer (*kolchoznik*) received per head about 200 grams of grain and 100 grams of potatoes per day; Chadajev, *Economy,* 326.

47. *The Second World War. Results and Lessons* (Moscow, 1985), 222.

48. *National Economy of the USSR over 70 Years,* 44.

49. *The Second World War: Results and Lessons,* 229.

50. G. K. Zhukov, "The Exploits of the Home Front in the Great Patriotic War," *Modern and Contemporary History* 5 (1987), 107 (in Russian).

51. Vannikov, "Notes," 91; Grakova, *Scientists,* 219.

52. Ustinov, *In the Name of Victory,* 246-49.

53. Shakhurin, *Wings,* 279, 287-88.

54. Robert E. Sherwood. *Roosevelt and Hopkins: An Intimate History* (New York, 1950).

55. W. H. McNeill, *American, Britain and Russia: Their Co-Operation and Conflict 1941-1946* (New York, 1953), 122.

56. Voznesensky, *War Economy,* 74.

57. *The History of the Foreign Policy of the USSR, 1917-1945* (2 vols.; Moscow, 1986), 1, 439 (in Russian).

58. George C. Herring, *Aid to Russia 1941-1946: Strategy, Diplomacy, the Origins of the Cold War* (New York, 1973), 75.

59. *War Diary of the Navy, 1941 1943* (Moscow, 1983), 41-42 (in Russian). According to British data, 8 convoys including 64 ships were dispatched in 1941 to Russia by the Northern route. For the whole period of war 40 convoys (811 ships) were sent: B. B. Schofield, *The Russian Convoys* (London, 1969), 212. See also Hubert Van Tuyll,

Feeding the Bear: American Aid to the Soviet Union, 1941-1945. (New York, 1989), 26-27. For Soviet data see N. G. Kouznetsov, *On the Eve* (Moscow, 1991), 498 (in Russian).

60. *RCCSDCH,* f. 644, sch. 1, file 12, p. 129.

61. *RCCSDCH,* f. 644, sch. 1, file 25, p. 106; A. V. Basov & G. I. Goutenmacher, "The Persian Corridor," *Military History Journal* I (1991), 29 (in Russian).

62. Herring, *Aid to Russia,* 75; Harrison, *Soviet Planning,* 245, 262.

63. *Soviet-British Relations during the Great Patriotic War 1941-1945. Documents and Materials* (2 vols.; Moscow, 1983), 1, 272-73 (in Russian); Martin Gilbert, *Road to Victory, 1941-1945* (London, 1986) 201; PRO. FO 954/25, Anthony Eden to A. Clark Kerr, 7 September 1942.

64. *Soviet-American Relations during the Great Patriotic War 1941-1945. Documents and Materials* (2 vols.; Moscow, 1984) 1, 235, 231, 249-50.

65. *RCCSDCH,* f. 644, sch. 1, file 62, p. 1.

66. W. K. Hancock and M. M. Gowing. *British War Economy* (London, 1949), 365; H. D. Hall, *North American Supply* (London, 1955), 332; Van Tuyll, *Feeding the Bear,* 23.

67. *The History of the Great Patriotic War 1941-1945,* 6, 62; Herring, *Aid to Russia,* 117; John Erickson, *The Road to Berlin: Continuing the History of Stalin's War with Germany* (Boulder, Colo., 1985), 405; Van Tuyll, *Feeding the Bear,* 67.

68. I. P. Lebedev, "Aviation Lend-Lease," *Military Historical Journal* 2 (1991), 27-29, and "Lend-Lease Revisited," *USA: Economics, Politics, Ideology,* I (1990), 71-75. Major General of Aviation Lebedev was a member of the Soviet Purchasing Committee in the United States and was responsible for the delivery of A-20 "Boston" bombers.

69. The Foreign Policy Archives of the Russian Federation (FPA RF), f. 129, sch. 29, box 172, file 48, p. 19.

70. W. K. Hancock and M. M. Gowing, *British War Economy,* 375.

71. Great Britain, Treasury, *Mututal Aid, Third Report.* Cmd. 6931 (London, 1946), 2, 7.

72. FPA RF, f. 129, sch. 29, box 172, file 48, p. 21.

73. S. W. Dziuban, *Military Relations between the United States and Canada, 1939-1945* (Washington, 1959), 295. See also L. V. Pozdeeva, *Canada in the Second World War* (Moscow, 1986), 244-52 (in Russian).

74. Vail T. H. Motter, *The Persian Corridor and Aid to Russia* (Washington, 1952), 481-82 (estimated data).

75. A. Paperno, "Lend-Lease: Fifty-Fifty," *Nachalo,* 24 (1992); Paperno, "Lend-Lease in the Pacific: Dangerous Adventures of `touschonka' tin," *The Moscow Komsomoletz,* 3 June 1992 (both in Russian).

76. *The Foreign Policy of the Soviet Union during the Patriotic War. Documents and Materials* (3 vols.; Moscow, 1946-47) 2, 142 (in Russian). As the celebrations in Archangel in August 1991 indicate, the Soviet public continues to value the heroism of Allied soldiers and sailors, many of whom gave their lives bringing these shipments through dangerous war zones.

77. *RCCSDCH,* 22 April 1943, f. 495, sch. 73, file 173, p. 40.

78. Edward Stettinius, *Lend-Lease: Weapon for Victory* (New York, 1944), 228-29.

79. *Foreign Trade* 9 (1945), 41; Van Tuyll, *Feeding the Bear.*

80. L. I Zorin, *Special Task* (Moscow, 1987), 105, 168-69 (in Russian); Basov & Goutenmacher, 32.

■ ■ ■

7

The United States: Leviathan

Theodore A. Wilson

At its peak in 1943 the United States was outproducing the Axis and generating 60 percent of total Allied war supplies. Truly a Leviathan in size, the U.S. wartime economy seemed like Job's unknowable creature, of whom the testament observed: "Upon earth there is not his like, who is made without fear." The American economy appeared as something beyond human ken, thrashing wildly and with ever increasing power. But was this remarkable animal also Thomas Hobbes's *Leviathan* (1651), a state that embodied perpetual sovereign power? Over the past 50 years an astonishing accretion of mythmaking has occurred about the American economy in World War II. Finding the truth may be as impossible as knowing what Job discovered when invited by God to "lay thine hand upon him."[1]

That the U.S. wartime experience was dominated by political exigencies appears undeniable. During 1938-45, the Roosevelt administration zigzagged between the poles of equity and efficiency, of maximizing output and minimizing inequalities of wealth and power, of the political stances embodied in the slogans of "Dr. New Deal" and "Dr. Win the War." Those metronomic lurches cloaked an all-embracing commitment to economic growth/productivity as the solution to the dilemmas and divisions besetting American society.[2] Whether one's allegiance was to conflict or consensus, to a "broker state" (with the national administration playing off competing interests) or to a "corporatist" model grounded in the claim that continued growth would provide larger and larger slices of the economic pie for all guests at America's banquet table, that rhetorical expression, "arsenal of democracy," offered a commanding if reductionist vision of the American role in World War II.[3]

As a result, America's wartime experience differed in basic ways from that of its principal allies. Only Americans could describe World War II as a "good war," bringing an improved standard of living and requiring few real sacrifices by the great majority. Even the tide of state intervention in the economy proved moderate and temporary. It was not that Americans cared less about smashing the Axis, but except for those months of self-doubt and military disaster in winter-spring 1942 the threat remained an abstraction. Lack of urgency fed an astonishing naivete about the enemy's capabilities and the comparative contributions of the chief players in the Allied coalition. At the heart of this perspective resided the conviction that the American economy was a slumbering giant, a leviathan that, once awakened, would generate the material components of victory.

When Nazi Germany attacked Poland, the U.S. economy was still trapped in the coils of depression. Of its 131 million citizens, millions had not enjoyed a regular paycheck for nine years. The average wage of those in work was some 20 percent below predepression days. A White House conference on children gave one estimate of the damage: 8,000,000 American children were growing up in families on relief, and 22,000,000 —nearly two-thirds of all Americans under 16—were living in inadequate housing, not getting a satisfactory education, and going to bed hungry. Though U.S. national income in 1938 was almost double that of Germany, Japan, and Italy combined, two years later it was still only a miserly 9 percent above 1929. The unemployment rate dropped slightly in 1940 (to 15 percent) from 17 percent or 9.5 million workers in 1939. Expenditures for national defense, while climbing, amounted to $1.24 billion, only 1.4 percent of GNP. Private domestic investment hovered nearly one-fifth below 1929 levels, and the gross value of industrial plant and equipment was below that of *1926*. Farm income and industrial production were only slightly above 1929. But 1940 also affirmed that military orders would soon transform the American economic landscape.

Between 1 June and 31 December 1940 some $10.5 billion in contracts were awarded. America was able to respond quickly to demands for foodstuffs and raw materials. Huge stocks of grains and cotton were on hand, and improved practices (hybrid seeds, pesticides, widespread use of farm machinery) ensured a rapid expansion of agricultural production. The situation was more problematic with regard to armaments production. Persistent industrial unemployment and migration from depressed rural areas to northern cities ensured an ample supply of labor. Further, this work force was better educated and possessed a wider range of skills than its World War I counterpart. However, the U.S. armaments industry was small, factories and equipment such as machine tools and heavy presses that might be converted to munitions production were aging if not obsolete, and business refused to commit to expansion and retooling unless the government provided ironclad guarantees.

Unwilling to risk further delays to rearmament, the Roosevelt administration capitulated to business's demands. Tax concessions were offered. An important step was acceptance of the cost-plus-fixed-fee contract as the norm. Assuring manufacturers that outlays would be recovered plus a reasonable profit meant rapid production of articles for which no cost of production data existed. The downside was a lack of control, overrun costs, and the squandering of scarce resources.

Complaints about favoritism toward big business came into focus with the establishment in March 1941 of the Senate Special Committee to Investigate the National Defense Program. This tribunal (popularly known as the Truman Committee) was the result of Senator Harry S. Truman's shock at the "waste, favoritism, and lack of direction" he discovered during an inspection tour of military installations. Truman also became convinced that the federal bureaucracy was cutting special deals with big corporations in a few heavily industrialized areas. In addition, "the little manufacturer, the little contractor, and the little machine shop have been left entirely out in the cold." The War Department did tend to favor the top tier of corporations, because of mutual familiarity and a sense of confidence that the "big boys" would deliver the goods. Three huge corporations garnered 17.4 percent of all defense contracts awarded before Pearl Harbor, and 100 companies were doing 82.6 percent of all war-related production as of January 1942. That these companies were primarily located in the industrialized states stretching from Massachusetts to Indiana was explained by early emphasis on expanded production of steel-related goods. Subsequently, priority on camp construction, aircraft factories, and shipyards produced a shift to the South, Southwest, and Pacific Coast.[4]

By executive order on 7 January 1941 the "Office of Production Management" (OPM) assumed responsibilities over production, raw materials, and manpower. This was supposed to ensure a "close, high level relationship" between agencies concerned with "civilian" matters and those handling military procurement, but OPM had no authority to decide major policy questions. Those still had to be taken to the president. By late summer 1941 a stalemate loomed. Prices were rising and shortages were beginning to appear. Facing redoubled pressures upon raw materials, plant capacity, and manpower, OPM was reluctant to give priorities to military orders without some understanding of how the production of x-amount of helmets or y-number of 37-mm. antitank guns related to the overall strategic picture. The army stonewalled such requests, asserting its prerogatives but, in reality, fearing to reveal how little coordination existed between strategic planning and procurement. In this environment, conflicts arose between the various interest groups (especially the business community and organized labor) about the rewards of recovery. "Everyone was clamoring for the Government to knock heads together; i.e., other people's heads," wryly noted the Bureau of the Budget.[5]

At this point, the United States found itself propelled into war. Much changed after Pearl Harbor but much did not. Important steps had been taken to resolve problems regarding military procurement and the division of armaments between the United States and its informal allies. But the legacies of quasi war and the sheer complexity of the American economy led to snarls. The struggle over priorities was first perceived in terms of "allocations." Who got to apportion the scanty stocks of weapons already produced? Who got to determine the blend of war goods to be manufactured for the next quarter and the quarters after that? By late 1941, most experts agreed that sufficient capacity for basic materials (steel being the gauge) existed and the stock of factories, tools, and work force were adequate to meet military requirements without imposing undue sacrifices on the civilian sector.[6] Others doubted that sufficient plant capacity and reserves of basic materials and manpower existed to satisfy *all* claimants and objectives for America's production. Their views earned attention with the appearance of spot shortages and supply bottlenecks in critical sectors such as steel.

The cry arose for a rigid ranking of production goals effected and enforced by a tough-minded individual or organization. A debate over mechanisms of control occupied most of the next two years. The success of the solutions depended on the sector—most so with regard to war finance and wage/price controls and energy supplies, somewhat less so in terms of agricultural and industrial production, least effective as concerned manpower and transportation. Efforts to ensure an equitable distribution of economic resources—commodities and return on capital/labor—were so episodic and uncoordinated that they must be considered dependent variables.

A number of agencies were created or given expanded roles in the aftermath of Pearl Harbor. The Office of Price Administration, ably led by Leon Henderson, slowly expanded its powers over price and wage controls. The War Manpower Commission was organized in April 1942 and given oversight but not total authority. Manpower was a minefield for unwary administrators throughout the war. When the Supply Priorities and Allocations Board disintegrated beneath him, Vice President Wallace shifted to coordination of strategic raw materials purchases as chair of the Board of Economic Warfare. Its efforts to fulfill this function led to bureaucratic conflicts with conservatives in Congress and their allies in the executive branch who feared that Wallace intended to create a blueprint for a global New Deal. In marked contrast with the government-business rapprochement elsewhere, BEW became a haven for wartime New Dealers. A number of peacetime agencies (Treasury, the RFC, and, belatedly, Agriculture) played important roles as did various regulatory bodies.[7]

First among equals in the wartime administrative hierarchy was the War Production Board, which replaced SPAB in January 1942. With Donald Nelson of Sears Roebuck as its head, the WPB was charged with "general responsibility" over the economy, and it might have become the superagency so often advocated had Nelson not proved a hesitant czar. Harshly criticized by War Department officials for passive leadership, Nelson made several errors, most crucial that of declining control over manpower. Over time a "rough division of labor" did develop. Manpower was everybody's and no one's responsibility. The Army Service Forces, aggressively led by General Brehon B. Somervell, claimed authority to allocate all manufactured items. The WPB was left to supervise the distribution of basic raw materials and semifinished products.[8]

Even that task seemed insurmountable. Shortages of all sorts retarded munitions production. Copper, tin, aluminum, and, of course, rubber were cases in point. Eventually, in November 1942 the WPB inaugurated a workable system of controls over raw materials, the Controlled Materials Plan. The scheme called for periodic submissions of their needs to the WPB from procurement agencies such as the War Department, the Maritime Commission, Office of Lend-Lease Administration, and Office of Civilian Supplies. The WPB then assigned to each claimant a percentage of available stocks of steel, copper, and other scarce items. Each agency in turn apportioned its allocation among its prime contractors. Setting up the system required another six months (by which time American production had passed its zenith), and the Controlled Materials Plan did not confront the issue of equity among claimants.

For the remainder of the war, indeed, debate focused on the relative balance between military and civilian needs. The Truman Committee zeroed in on cost overruns in camp construction and challenged such costly ventures as the Canol Project, a $134 million pipeline from the

Arctic Circle across Alaska.[9] As food and other items disappeared from stores, many questioned the huge stockpiles of tires, canned meat, and numerous other commodities. The Pentagon's stated policy of acquiring 200 percent of projected requirements provoked widespread irritation. Certainly, General Brehon B. Somervell and his subordinates in the sprawling military procurement empire spawned by the war held to the view that military needs should always take preeminence.

Indeed, military leaders castigated civilian failure to tighten their belts. Somervell drafted a note to Nelson in May 1942 to urge that the pulp and paper industry be made to toe the line. "Our newspapers throughout the United States use a considerable amount of paper . . . and could be greatly reduced in size. . . . The Sunday editions in particular contain very little news, but utilize a great many pages . . . in portraying feature articles, advertisements, miscellaneous columns such as 'Advice to the Lovelorn,' etc." He urged that this material be excised, noting that London dailies had been reduced to two singlefold sheets. The savings in scarce materials and manpower could then be diverted to urgent needs.[10] That letter reflected the opinion of many about the "softness" manifested at home. Much was made of the need for sacrifice, reflecting concern that once the shocks of spring 1942 wore off Americans would assume victory was assured and revert to peacetime ways.

The Roosevelt administration approached financing the war and imposing controls over wages, profits, and prices as aspects of the challenge to sustain public confidence in the American economy. At the same time, FDR's advisers were acutely aware of the need to assure each important constituent group—labor, the business community, farmers, housewives, draftees, retired people—that it was bearing no more than its fair share of the war's burdens and reaping its fair share (or a little more) of the benefits. Though the imposition of controls and the government's preemptive claim upon resources restricted choices, the marketplace remained (or was perceived to be) dominant in almost all areas of economic activity of concern to the average citizen. Nowhere was the abstract concept of a command economy more broadly assumed, and in no case was the door to absolute coercion slammed so quickly and with such force.[11]

First to receive systematic attention was the inflation threat. Spiraling prices could cause panic buying, gnaw into the fragile popular consensus, and endanger full mobilization. Prewar attempts to obtain voluntary conservation of scarce or militarily critical items (such as the fall 1941 crusade of the garment industry to save silk by raising hemlines by three inches) proved laughable. Before Pearl Harbor, measures to put a lid on food prices were blocked by the farm lobby, and the prices of durable goods such as automobiles and refrigerators, boosted by rising demand and scarce raw materials, shot up. In late 1941 the consumer price index exceeded 1929 levels.

In January 1942 OPA gained the authority to dictate maximum prices except for foodstuffs. It shortly issued a comprehensive register, the General Maximum Price Regulation (popularly known as "General Max"), but the failure to include wages or food prices frustrated OPA. Consumer prices jumped almost 5 percent in 1941 and shot up another 10 percent in 1942. Not until early 1943 did the government get the inflation threat under control.

Rationing worked reasonably well, though it was not nearly as severe as experienced by allies or enemies.[12] Rationing of rubber (militarily vital), gasoline (to conserve rubber), coffee, sugar, meat, dairy products, and some other items was imposed as one or another wartime agency deemed necessary. OPA erected a system of 6,000 local rationing boards, mostly volunteers who also served as whistleblowers about violations of pricing regulations. The volume of goods available to consumers remained essentially constant, and Americans as a people ate better and lived better despite wartime restrictions. The books of ration stamps bearing the OPA logo symbolized the war's "sacrifices," a reminder each time someone went to the corner grocery for a quart of milk.[13] This dimension of the wartime economy was complicated by disputes over gasoline ration cards and the recourse of many to the gray market (bartering of proscribed items) and black market (sale of rationed goods at inflated prices). People swapped stamps, slipped money to shopkeepers for extra meat (purchased from ranchers and local slaughterhouses not covered by the government's inspection system), and bartered rationed goods for gas and tires. By one estimate, between 25 and 50 percent of business transactions were being conducted on the black market at war's end.[14] Enforcing effective price/wage controls proved difficult all through 1942. Farmers wanted to harvest the rewards of high food prices after two decades of privation. Faced with rising living costs and tales of huge corporate profits, labor resisted wage controls. And business was operating on a "gouge now" principle, believing that prohibitive taxes and wage increases were just around the corner.

That the period 1943-45 saw only a modest increase in consumer prices resulted from two significant initiatives. First, OPA decided to give local rationing boards a mandate to report violations of consumer prices. Enforcement had been shown to be OPA's greatest problem. Insights from the operation of the Canadian Price Control Law and studies of housewives' performance in monitoring prices in 1,000 U.S. cities convinced the OPA that community-based enforcement was feasible.[15] Second was the administration's success in hammering out an administrative modus vivendi. After months of flouted presidential proclamations, the White House took a hard line, insisting that cabinet heads along with OPA and the Bureau of the Budget devise a workable prices/wages program to go to Congress. FDR's convening of an ad hoc "war cabinet" led to the Office of Economic Stabilization with full authority to set price and wage levels.[16]

Even so, effective controls over wages were not achieved until mid-1943. During summer 1942 labor shortages and industry and regional wage competition threatened to disrupt war production. The War Labor Board then announced that the so-called Little Steel formula, which provided for wage increases up to 15 percent to adjust for inflation, would apply generally. This slowed the push for wage increases, though some union leaders—notably John L. Lewis of the United Mine Workers—challenged the policy. Not until the president again intervened, issuing a "hold-the-line" order on wages and prices, was the situation stabilized. Wages increased somewhat more than prices, but overall the record was impressive.

Finance in a politically hypersensitive environment is both straightforward and extremely delicate. Harold G. Vatter states the problem succinctly:

> In a war economy, total money income, representing potential total demand, greatly exceeds the aggregate volume of civilian products. . . . This excess . . . is a dangerous potential inflationary gap. . . . The harsh facts are that no more civilian products can be gotten than the physical volume produced, plus inventory drawdowns, if any. . . . To face these facts squarely, it would be eminently sensible for the government to tax away, or in some other manner sequester, all the excess money income. But people have always been reluctant to accept such an honest confrontation with sacrifices imposed by war; . . . governmental agencies therefore typically resort, through various policy manipulations, to a variety of piecemeal devices.[17]

The gross federal debt stood at $48.2 billion in 1939 with outlays ahead of receipts from all sources for that year of $2.9 billion. Even before Pearl Harbor it was obvious that America's full-scale participation in a war would require massive borrowing, though the extent was beyond anyone's ken. The federal government's total war-related expenditures between 1941 and 1945 totaled $317 billion.

TABLE 7.1

FEDERAL GOVERNMENT FINANCES, 1939-45

	Receipts	Expenditures	Surplus/Deficit	Total Gross Federal Debt
1939	6.6	9.4	-2.9	48.2
1940	6.9	9.6	-2.7	50.7
1941	9.2	14.0	-4.8	57.5
1942	15.1	34.5	-19.4	79.2
1943	25.1	78.9	-53.8	142.6
1944	47.8	94.0	-46.1	204.1
1945	50.2	95.2	-45.0	260.1

Source: *Historical Statistics of the United States: Colonial Times to 1970* (2 vols., Washington, D.C., 1975), Series Y339-42.

Theoretically, taxation could underwrite all war costs. GNP more than doubled from 1940 to 1945 ($100 billion to $212 billion in current prices) and the four principal categories of taxation (individual income, corporate income, employment, and alcohol/tobacco) plus other government revenue collections never climbed above 24.2 percent of national income in any one year.[18] However, the Treasury feared a draconian approach would stifle private investment and produce nationwide popular resentment. Economists influenced by Keynesian precepts opposed significant tax increases until full employment was attained. According to one estimate, the Treasury generated about 45 percent (variously estimated from $133 to $147 billion) of war expenditures from taxes, with the rest—following the longtime pattern of democratic states—from borrowing. The World War II yield from taxation was much higher than in the Civil War or World War I (though much lower than that of Canada and Great Britain), and some 39 million Americans paid income taxes who had never done so, largely because of the introduction of payroll withholding in 1943. The effects of wartime taxation were revolutionary.

Taxes also proved useful in the battle against price inflation by siphoning money out of the economy. The relative mix of corporate and individual income taxes shifted dramatically. Surtaxes on corporate profits and a sharp climb in the excess profits tax rate produced a jump in corporate tax collections of some $2 billion in 1941, $4.7 billion in 1942, then over $9 billion in 1943, and $16 billion in 1945. Taxes on individual incomes—only $1.4 billion in 1941—more than doubled in both 1942 and 1943 and totaled $19 billion in 1945. Since 80 percent of personal income was claimed by low- and middle-income groups, the almost universal involvement of the American people in the "getting" of war finance is not in doubt.

The record with regard to borrowing is less clear. Of the some $170 billion borrowed by the federal government—well over half the total U.S. war expenditure—was obtained by sale of short-term government securities. Stated differently, only 18 percent of the war debt was in the form of savings bonds by 1946. The Treasury's determination to maintain low interest rates combined with pegging of securities prices and their exemption from reserve quotas to make bonds and other instruments the equivalent of "interest-bearing cash." Their accumulation by banks pushed up the government's bank deposits from less than $1 billion in 1941 to nearly $25 billion in 1945. Had not price controls worked so well, this pool of liquid capital might have fueled tremendous inflation and fatally weakened the impulse to save. Indeed, the total supply of money increased by 150 percent during the war.

A remarkable expansion of individual savings occurred—up 2,000 percent to nearly $50 billion by one estimate. But it appears this was as much a result of the government's restricting war workers' options (clamping down on cheap credit by raising minimum down payments and discouraging commercial loans to consumers, and, of course, rationing goods) as it was a manifestation of patriotism. There were seven War Loans and one Victory Loan, featuring entertainers and war heroes urging Americans of all ages to buy 25-cent war savings stamps and $20 bonds. Every bond drive was oversubscribed, but not one met its quota of individual contributions. Though Treasury officials resorted to such stunts as auctioning items of intimate apparel contributed by Hollywood starlets, most bonds were purchased by corporate investors, banks, and insurance companies. The prevailing opinion is that fiscal policies proved successful though less aggressive than should have been the case. When rationing stopped and wage and price controls were removed, inflationary tendencies in the wartime economy were powerfully strengthened.

Devising policies for the efficient and equitable use of manpower proved the most glaring failure of American wartime mobilization. Under Secretary of War Robert P. Patterson was to admit that "all through the war we had to do our best . . . with various makeshifts. . . . Our serious shortcoming, I submit, was our failure to achieve genuine mobilization of manpower."[19] In large part, this resulted from a widely held conviction that more than enough manpower was available. The Selective Service Act of 1940 conferred authority to conscript males for military service and also to defer those in vital occupations. Only in late 1941, however, did the huge expansion of production fueled by Lend-Lease and the Army's Victory Program raise concern about allocating manpower. How to do so became ensnarled in awkward philosophical issues (the historic American commitment in theory to universal male military obligation and its aversion in practice to comprehensive national service), thorny social questions involving the utilization of blacks and women, and the partisan and bureaucratic political imperatives that flowed from labor shortages. From a total population of slightly over 130 million, 66 million Americans were in uniform or holding civilian jobs during the peak year of 1944. The armed forces increased from some 1.5 million in 1941 to 11.4 million at war's end.

The record of the military services at making the most efficient use of these millions of men and women (and the hundreds of thousands of civilian employees) was justifiably criticized. More successful was deployment of the more than 50 million Americans who served on the home front. Their contribution was as vital as that of the individual soldier or sailor. Some argued more so since production of war matériel was America's special endowment to the Allied coalition.

In 1940 the civilian labor force stood at 47.5 million employed and another 8.1 presently unemployed workers. That slack was taken up by 1942 and from then until VE-Day the U.S. economy wrestled with full employment. With hundreds of thousands of young men each month being called into military service, a manpower crisis was inevitable unless the linkage of manpower and production goals was acknowledged. That linkage was rejected by the War Production Board in early 1942, and the opportunity was never to come again. The government sought to put in place adequate mechanisms to deal with occupational deferments, wage differentials, labor standards, racial discrimination, and other problems. These alleviated some bottlenecks, but intra-agency rivalries and the government's unwillingness to confront the issue of national service (no strikes, no changing jobs without approval) meant that competition became the norm, as skilled workers responded to the lure of higher wages or greener pastures. Numerous wildcat strikes were one consequence. During the three year period, 1942-44, over 11,000 strikes, costing uncounted hours of work, took place. Even greater losses to the economy resulted from job changes and inefficient work assignments.

TABLE 7.2

THE LABOR FORCE DURING WORLD WAR II

				Employed		Unemployed	
	Total	**Armed**	**Civilian**	**Farm**	**NonFarm**	**% of Total**	**% of NonFarm**
1940	56,180	540	55,640	9,450	37,980	14.6	21.3
1941	57,530	1,620	55,910	9,100	41,250	9.9	14.4
1942	60,380	3,970	56,410	9,250	44,500	4.7	6.8
1943	64,560	9,020	55,540	9,080	45,390	1.9	2.7
1944	66,040	11,410	54,630	8,950	45,010	1.2	1.7
1945	65,290	11,430	53,860	8,580	44,240	1.9	2.7

Source: Historical Statistics, Series D1-10

For some, the manpower dilemma represented a choice between voluntarism and compulsion. On one side were the "tender-minded," men such as Nelson, McNutt, and Wallace, convinced that the American people were prepared to give their utmost and that patriotic rhetoric would suffice to create an aroused citizenry. On the other side stood the "tough minded," Spartans such as Patterson and Somervell, convinced that compulsion and sacrifice were essential and, indeed, beneficial. Generally, the advocates of persuasion and a passive approach triumphed. Whether a policy of national service would have proved more effective in the America of 1941-45 is uncertain.[20]

A few at the time and subsequently argued that the problem was one of effective administration at the highest level. Discussions among FDR's advisers of a "war cabinet" in late 1942 acknowledged the White House's crippling obsession with political rather than economic concerns. Isador Lubin pointed out to Harry Hopkins that solving this challenge did not require special machinery. He cited the inflation issue. Hopkins had convened affected cabinet officers, got a statement of the problem, and proposed solutions, then briefed President Roosevelt "in a way that saved hours of his time and helped effectively to meet the problem." The outcome was an executive order. "There are few better practical illustrations of effective operation in our recent government experience than the handling of the inflationary problem. Just the reverse was true in the case of manpower," Lubin noted. That problem had been known for many months. But the agencies involved (Army, Navy, Maritime Commission, WPB, Agriculture, WMC, Selective Service, Labor) had all gone their own way. "The result is that all sorts of confusing statements about manpower have been made by different agencies." Lubin suggested that institutionalizing the inflation experience "would be a sort of experimental war cabinet." Unfortunately, perhaps, for the U.S. war effort Hopkins' poor health and his absence from the president's inner circle ensured that the idea of a war cabinet was stillborn.[21]

The importance of bureaucratic advocacy and coercive authority was amply confirmed by the performance of the energy sector. Before Pearl Harbor, the structure to oversee energy output (solid fuels, primarily coal, and petroleum products) and allocation for transportation, for industrial and agricultural uses, and to consumers, "consisted of a hodgepodge of separate agencies created under executive . . . authority, each vested with limited mandates."[22] Secretary of Interior Harold L. Ickes worked unstintingly to maximize energy production and to gain effective power over vital coal and oil supplies. Ickes never attained the status of "energy czar" and throughout the war he encountered both frontal assaults and bureaucratic back-stabbing from rivals inside the administration and from industry adversaries.

Nevertheless, the jerry-built empire Ickes controlled ensured that no factory shut down and no freight train laden with war matériel was shunted to a siding because of lack of coal, that adequate supplies of oil and such critical petroleum products as aviation gasoline were on hand to meet any contingency, and that Americans were not compelled to make undue sacrifices to conserve energy. A tough survivor of New Deal battles, Ickes knew how to deal with the president's administrative style. As well, he did not carry the trust-busting ideology of other New Dealers into the war. The Solid Fuels Administration for War (SFAW) and the Petroleum Administration for War (PAW) accepted the industry's operational structures and worked closely with the most powerful coal and petroleum companies. The long-term results included higher prices, increased concentration, and depletion of reserves; however, wartime demands were met.

By mid-1943 petroleum output had rebounded from the depression trough of 2.1 to 3.7 million barrels per day, and it rose to 4.6 by war's end. Daily production of fuel oil increased by one-third between 1940 and 1945, and construction of the "Big Inch" and "Little Inch" pipelines ended the distribution crisis. A huge expansion of aviation fuels refineries by PAW led to a leap in production of 100-octane gasoline of 600 percent (to 487,000 barrels daily) between 1942 and 1945. Restriction of civilian consumption reduced production of motor fuels by about 20 percent below prewar, but large reserves were available when family automobiles rolled out of garages and onto the highways in 1945.

The wartime solid fuels record was unspectacular in comparison but still impressive. Despite severe strikes in the anthracite coalfields, a decline of some 75,000 miners in this most labor-intensive of U.S. industries, relatively flat productivity in deep mines, and growing demand because of the government's oil-to-coal conversion program, total production jumped from 395 million tons in 1938 to 681 million tons in 1944. Environmentally ruinous strip-mining was a factor, but higher production came from a stable workforce.

Bitter disputes between the administration, United Mine Workers leader John L. Lewis, and mine owners led to federal seizure of the coal mines in late 1943. This instance of coercion proved self-defeating. As one historian has noted: "Federal responses to strikes, shortages of mine labor, and pricing policies attested to the limits imposed upon government power even during a war. Workers would not be shuffled around like so many robots to suit the needs of the war machine."[23] Only unremitting pressure by Ickes to obtain a longer work week (from 35 to 48 hours) in return for wage and price increases resolved the conflict. The government's steadfast support for collective bargaining contrasted sharply with its scruples against employing POWs and winking at the rebuff by union locals of blacks seeking work in the mines.

Loss of some 10 million able-bodied potential workers to the armed forces was made good by the entry into the labor force in unexpected numbers of women, blacks, the elderly and those not yet out of school, and many physically disqualified for military service. The number of female workers increased from 13.8 million in 1940 to 18.4 million in 1944, with many married women taking first jobs and significant numbers entering factory work.[24] Black workers encountered fierce resistance from employers, unions, and coworkers, and only grudging support from the Roosevelt administration. The war witnessed a movement of black workers into industries heretofore off limits, although their skills were tragically underused.[25]

The total civilian work force grew only slightly (reaching 56.4 million in the peak year of 1942), but the performance of this mixed crew of women, minorities, weary veterans, and novices was remarkable. Manufacturing workers, up in numbers approximately 60 percent, doubled industrial output during those same years. Managerial efficiency and improved training, massive reliance on overtime and multiple shifts, technological innovations and extensive introduction of laborsaving equipment and production techniques resulted in an increase in labor productivity of more than 25 percent. This achievement was widely heralded as proof of the innate superiority of the American "system" of state-underwritten capitalism. The determinants of size, resources sufficiency, and labor scarcity long had pushed the American economy toward mechanized mass production and high output per work hour. World War II demanded precisely those capabilities.

Testing FDR's boast about the United States as the arsenal of democracy was, it would seem, a matter of toting up the production totals and comparing them to prewar levels and to the projected goals set by the president. On this basis, the drum roll of America's wartime output is deafening: a 17 percent increase in agricultural production (50 percent more than in 1917-18 with nine-tenths of the workforce); doubling the production of nonferrous metals; total output of manufactured goods more than doubled, with an astonishing 300 percent increase in production of machine tools, and a 600 percent increase of heavy transport items;

and substantial rises in nondurables such as textiles and alcoholic beverages. The conversion of these percentile figures into actual numbers of weapons and other war necessities is still more remarkable: 300,000 aircraft; 315,000 artillery pieces, 86,000 tanks, warships totalling 8.5 million tons; and 51 million tons of merchant shipping. In January 1942 the president set yearly production goals—20,000 antiaircraft guns, 45,000 tanks, and 60,000 planes—inconceivable only a few months earlier. Most were achieved before year's end. These targets were met by a labor force that grew only 12 percent and with, arguably, an improvement in the standard of living of nearly all Americans.

The challenge to agriculture was to change the behavior of farmers and bureaucrats. Sufficient arable land existed to satisfy any conceivable requirement for foodstuffs and staples. The necessary expertise existed among farmers, Department of Agriculture scientists and economists, and the vast legion of land grant college faculty and county extension agents to exploit the revolutionary troika of mechanization, hybridization, and chemical agents. Limitations on potential production derived from inefficient land use, hidden agricultural unemployment, and the injurious effects of inadequate capital investment. Primarily, however, the need was to shift attitudes from an emphasis on restriction to full-scale expansion of production. American farmers were leery of risking any repetition of the boom and bust cycle experienced during 1917-21.[26]

Both farmers and the federal government moved cautiously, eager to sustain improvement of agricultural prices. Land under the plow stood at 86 million acres in 1940. That figure edged up to 87 million acres in 1942 and to 94 million in 1944. Memories of World War I caused wheat acreage to increase by only 7 million acres between 1940 and 1944, even though prices of wheat and corn nearly doubled. Even so, in 1940 total farm output swelled to 110 percent of 1933 levels and agriculture experienced steady increases through the entire war. Increases came chiefly in livestock (with large grain surpluses and a 22 percent shift to pasture, production of meat increased some 50 percent) and oil-bearing crops such as soybeans, cottonseed, and peanuts to substitute for vegetable oils cut off by Japan's conquests. Agriculture's performance was even more special when set against a sharp decline in the workforce. From 1940 to 1945 over 5 million people left farms for industrial employment or the armed forces. Many were unemployed rural poor from the drought-racked Great Plains and tenant farmers and sharecroppers from the Southeast; nevertheless, potential or actual labor shortages in some regions led to the exemption of many young farmers from the draft, the recruiting of adolescents and women, the "bracero" program utilizing migrant workers, and assignment of soldiers and German and Italian POWs to help with harvests. Farms grew in size and the number of owner-operators increased by over 250,000. While hours of work rose substantially, the single most important compensating factor (along with the spread of fertilizer) was continuing mechanization. Except for a shortfall resulting from demands on steel in 1943, numbers of tractors and other farm machines grew steadily during the war. A critical factor was a succession of remarkable growing seasons. Approximately one-half of total agricultural growth resulted from improved yields. Despite a declining farm population, productivity increases ensured that one farmer—hypothetically—was feeding 14.6 persons in 1945 instead of the 10.7 fed in 1940.[27]

The policies that supported this record did not emerge without difficulties. Efforts to continue production of farm machinery encountered opposition from the WPB and its Office of Civilian Supply and only appeals by the Department of Agriculture, the WPB's Farm Machinery and Equipment Branch, and an intervention by the Truman Committee got these priorities restored. By and large, the federal government's efforts to administer agriculture were largely useless and may have retarded production. Once given assurances about postwar price supports, the farmer responded to the dictates of the market.

Something similar may represent the only useful generalization about the experience of U.S. industry in World War II. The chronicle of industrial mobilization contains numerous examples of waste of time and resources, inefficient use of labor and raw materials, and inequitable treatment of certain sectors and certain regions. The Bureau of the Budget's history of wartime mobilization concluded:

> After a tragically slow start, many a plant was changed over to war production when its normal product was more needed than its new product. Locomotive plants went into tank production when locomotives were more necessary—but the Tank Division did not know this. Truck plants began to produce airplanes, a change that caused shortages of trucks later on. . . . The scramble for a production we could not attain brought us waste instead. . . . We built many new factories which we could not use and did not need. Many of these factories we could not supply with labor or with raw materials or, if we had, we would not have been able to fly the planes or shoot the ammunition that would have come out of them.[28]

Whether the stops and starts and the jurisdictional tangles could have been avoided continues to be debated.

Tapping the nation's entrepreneurial talents produced numerous examples of the American genius for mass production. Henry Ford constructed at Willow Run outside Detroit a gigantic factory for the production of heavy bombers. Though Ford's promise of 1,000 planes a week proved wildly exaggerated, Willow Run did turn out one B-24 bomber every 63 minutes, for a total of 8,685. In a nearby cornfield Chrysler erected in late 1941 an armored vehicle arsenal that soon was churning out 100 medium tanks per week. The miracle of miracles occurred on the West Coast. Though substantial expansion of shipyard capacity had occurred before Pearl Harbor, catastrophic losses to U-boat depredations and the demands from the war's global dimensions lent new urgency to emergency construction of merchant ships. Flamboyant magnate Henry J. Kaiser proposed to mass-produce ships by merging a simple boxlike design with welding of subsections and reliance on prefabrication. By 1943 the production time for such a Liberty Ship had dropped from 30 to 7 weeks. America's shipyards ultimately launched more than 5,000 cargo vessels.

The most remarkable of the technological miracles, the top secret Manhattan Project, created from the musings of emigré physicists an entirely new industry. Begun in 1941, gigantic plants at Oak Ridge, Tennessee, Hanford, Washington, and elsewhere siphoned off mountains of concrete and steel and thousands of engineers and scientists to manufacture the deadly ingredients of the first-generation atomic bombs. Oak Ridge alone swallowed up a significant percentage of the daily generating capacity of the Tennessee Valley Authority. In this instance, too, the priority assigned the atomic bomb cut through the thickest red tape. On occasion, troop trains were stopped to permit cargoes bearing the stamp Manhattan Project to roll through.[29]

Certain industries proved as reluctant as farmers to accept the draft into war production. By insisting that stocks of freight and tank cars were adequate to any need, the railroads jeopardized the war effort and stimulated the growth of such alternate transportation forms as the East Coast oil pipeline and the trucking industry.

Though business invested over $11 billion (more than spent on capital improvements during the decade of the 1930s), the federal government committed nearly $18 billion to munitions facilities. Public funding was especially vital to the development of new industries or opening of those dominated by oligopolistic interests. One such initiative enlarged the pool of enterprises engaged in the production of aluminum. Federally funded synthetic rubber plants were producing nearly all of current inventories by 1944. Government investment was crucial for the development of the electronics industry, plastics, pharmaceuticals, and—most famously—atomic energy. The war stimulated technological innovation of various kinds. Although the miracles of production derived primarily from exploitation of existing industrial technology, the foundations of the post-war technological revolution and of a "military-industrial-educational" complex that was to carry it forward were laid during World War II. Creation of the National Defense Research Council signified the government's support of scientific research, and between 1940 and 1947 the number of privately funded research laboratories nearly doubled.[30]

The massive infusion of capital in an 18-month period generated colossal strains. One casualty of wartime expansion was small business. Despite efforts by the Truman Committee and a congressionally mandated small business contracts program, federal agencies persisted in the view that larger concerns were more capable of fulfilling contracts on time and on budget.[31] This conviction may well have been correct, though it allowed existing facilities and equipment to stand idle. The wide dispersion of essential machine tools and the practice of subcontracting in some industries ensured that small business received a share of war orders. Nevertheless, unable to decipher the mysteries of government bidding, denied raw materials, and suffering losses of workers to high-paying war contractors, 324,000 smaller firms (10 percent of the total as of 1945) closed their doors during the war years. Their problem was not profitability, for overall business profit margins (after tax) averaged 2.8 percent of total assets for 1941-45 compared with 2.2 percent for 1940. Hardest hit were small construction and service firms and retail stores, the "Mom and Pop" operations typical of the American scene until World War II.

An inevitable result of the frantic pace and reliance on large enterprise was the "boom town" phenomenon that afflicted many regions of the country. Successive waves of government contracts left in their wake communities pleased about that new powder plant or helmet factory but swamped by an influx of war workers (or weekend visitors from nearby military camps) and struggling to provide basic services for just-arrived residents.

Evansville, Indiana, a medium-size Ohio River city with many smaller firms and large refrigerator, automobile, and furniture factories, was one such community. The early months of the war had been a disaster for Evansville.[32] Its three largest industries shut down and many other companies closed or cut back because of a lack of war orders and raw material and labor shortages. Between July 1941 and January 1942 over 4,000 jobs were lost. Finally, the Indiana congressional delegation won major contracts for landing craft, shell cases, and assembly of P-47 fighters. That meant huge outlays for plant conversion and construction, and, given its priority claim on steel and other materials, Evansville's economy boomed. Attracted by high wages, workers flooded into Evansville from rural Illinois, Kentucky, and Tennessee. All available housing soon was taken, and clumps of plywood shacks and tiny metal house trailers sprang up in muddy fields surrounding the factories. Utilities and medical services, schools, and recreational facilities were overwhelmed, and crime, prostitution, and racial tensions escalated.

Evansville's contributions to the war effort may also be taken as typical. On 23 December 1944 a small crowd of local citizens joined 19,000 thousand shipyard workers in watching Landing Ship Tank (LST) 826 roll in the muddy waters of the Ohio River as the cradle that had lowered the seagoing vessel was pulled away. Landing Ship Tank 826 was the 100th LST completed in 1944 at the Evansville Shipyard, a gigantic facility which just 30 months earlier had been the site of a municipal dump. To prevent overcrowding of coastal shipyards, the U.S. Navy decided to build landing craft on inland waterways. The first Evansville-built LST was launched on 31 October 1942 and the facility, soon christened "World's Champion LST Builders," set production records of all sorts. In April-May 1944, to offset losses from the invasion of Italy and those anticipated to occur on D-Day, the U.S. government frantically called for stepped-up production. The Evansville Shipyard completed 20 LSTs in that 60-day period and 100 vessels during all of 1944. By war's end, LSTs constructed in Evansville were delivering cargo to ports in northwest Europe, moving men and supplies to occupied Japan, and serving as floating generating stations everywhere from the Aleutians to the Adriatic.

Boom towns and new towns sprung up across the nation. Their locations were dictated by logistical or security considerations (siting a Boeing aircraft factory on the Kansas prairies and a secret atomic research center in the boondocks of New Mexico), by availability of labor, and other factors. Wartime decentralization possessed a skewed logic. Among its results were the rise of the "Sun Belt," vastly improved national communication and transportation systems, and the weakening of regionalism. Not all communities experienced Evansville's problems, but all were transformed.

Overall population growth continued to be moderate, though a jump in the marriage rate portended America's coming baby boom. However, remarkable internal shifts occurred. Millions departed rural areas for cities. While stable or declining populations typified most regions, the South Atlantic and Pacific Coast states experienced significant increases. As a center for aircraft production and shipbuilding, California was the big winner, undergoing a 37 percent jump in population from 1940 to 1945. In retrospect, it has become clear that the government's helter-skelter approach to mobilization shaped American society, its economic and racial problems, and its politics for the next 50 years.

A further caveat to any chronicle of the "miracles" of production relates to magnitude and timing. The "high level of U.S. output even in a peacetime global context" cannot be overlooked, one historian noted.[33] The notable increment—22 percent—in the industrial production index during 1942 was significantly smaller than the percentage increase from 1940 to 1941. Also, the 50 percent increase racked up in the immediate post-World War I years, 1921-1923, compares well with the record of 1940-42. By mid-1943 the U.S. economy was moving toward contraction, a circumstance dictated by the Allied victories on far-flung battlefields well before the arrival of "made in America" B-24s, Sherman tanks, and Studebaker trucks. Of course, agricultural output was neither so variable nor so responsive to external circumstances, and the importance of American food and fiber to allies and former enemies would continue after war's end.

During the last half of 1943 and most of 1944, the compromises that had been formulated over the first year of war held firm. Some top level officials departed and new agencies appeared, but the rationale for change almost always was political. Dissatisfaction with the performance of Nelson and WPB and congressional pressure for a "food czar" led to creation of yet another layer of administration, the Office of War Mobilization. However, little was changed thereby.

Looking toward postwar issues renewed concern about concentration of wealth and monopolistic practices. There was a revival of challenges to "cartels" by liberals in the Department of Justice. Vice President Wallace assaulted "economic imperialists" and triggered a violent counterattack by conservatives in Congress and their allies within the Roosevelt administration.[34] The president himself seemed ambivalent. In December 1943 FDR proclaimed that "Dr. New Deal" had been replaced for the duration by "Dr. Win the War," a move widely hailed by conservatives. But liberals never lost faith that the president intended to revive and extend the New Deal once the war was won. In a ringing State of the Union address to Congress on 11 January 1944, President Roosevelt proclaimed an "Economic Bill of Rights" for the American people. FDR's powerfully worded statement attacked the enemies of democratic liberalism at home and championed postwar economic security and expanding prosperity for all Americans. These were central tenets in the agenda of the Democratic party's left wing.

The Red Army's victory at Stalingrad and the remorseless offensive of summer-fall 1943 that followed turned the tide of war. Although the military progress of the Allies boded well for the priorities—national planning and full employment—advocated by Wallace and other liberals, economic policies followed a different course. Confident of inevitable victory and smugly convinced that the daily expanding production of America's farms and factories had made victory possible, many Americans preferred to look to their own comfort rather than to the needs of a war-devastated world.

The American experience of World War II is unique because the United States did not suffer invasion, significant physical destruction, or even, as a nation, substantial deprivation. The war brought the anguish of loss of loved ones to many American families and, indirectly, to other millions of friends and relatives. The children of wartime, unable to grasp a father's absence and a mother's despair, and those forced to relocate by necessity or by the lure of high-paying jobs found little then or later "good" about World War II. Nevertheless, for the legions of Americans who had stark memories of the depression and feared its return after war's end, wartime America is usually recalled with good feelings. The nature of America's mobilization left intact prewar social and political patterns of behavior and strengthened the power of large corporations.

Symptomatic of the receding wave of federal economic activism was the fate of full-employment policy, one of the hallmarks of wartime economic liberalism.[35] In August 1944 a group of economists in the Federal Reserve, the Bureau of the Budget, and OPA tackled an "American White Paper" on full-employment policies. They hoped the study would provoke a full-blown congressional debate reaffirming the ideas contained in the president's Economic Bill of Rights of January 1944. Also important was concern about a possible postwar relapse into depression. Some saw this initiative as the U.S. equivalent of Britain's "Beveridge Plan." One proposed that the president's message should include a six-point program: (1) commitment to a full-employment policy; (2) measures against a threatening slump; (3) underwriting national minima for social service, education, health, etc.; (4) maintenance of the purchasing power of the dollar (anti-inflation policies); (5) "revitalizing" small and new business, etc.; (6) a detailed study of the "needs for developing a full-employment program" in the circumstances to follow World War II. Subsequent discussion with agency heads made clear that full-employment policy was being embraced as a political slogan in the same category as "two chickens in every pot" and "read my lips."[36]

The next months demonstrated that the administration was traveling in a different direction. FDR focused on diplomacy, contenting himself with vague proclamations about "60 million jobs" as a postwar goal. After his reelection, the issue was buried. The policies advocated by the Committee for Economic Development, an influential group of corporate leaders whom wartime service in Washington had taught that government-business cooperation was desirable if properly managed, held sway. Such stopgaps as the GI Bill, offering benefits to veterans in large part to postpone their descent on the job market, were pushed. Political compromise ultimately yielded the Unemployment Act of 1946, hardly what the full-employment crusaders had envisioned.

The "war is over" mentality swelled to a crescendo in late fall 1944. Frustrations about wartime restrictions were growing and political battlelines were being redefined. Newspapers carried stories about the gouging of the U.S. government by steamship lines for cargoes delivered to war zones. Norden Inc. was indicted by a federal grand jury, charged with intentionally blocking production of the top-secret bombsight to maintain the company's monopoly. Many thousands of workers, expecting an early end of the war, were moving from industries vital to the war effort to seek permanent jobs. Demands for higher wages and improved conditions escalated, leading to conflicts such as the walkout of 1,400 workers at a New Jersey factory that stopped production of ball turrets for B-29 bombers. "Just as soon as the news of our victories comes, everybody wants to put on his coat and stop working. The curious characteristic of our noble people in the U.S. is that they have no more notion that they are in a war or the sacrifices which are involved or needed—just so many children," Secretary of War Stimson complained to General Marshall.[37]

Americans had caught a serious case of war-weariness. Impatient about victory's tardy arrival, they clamored for a return to peacetime pursuits. One signal was the announcement that the West Coast was no longer considered a war zone; thus, Japanese-Americans were free to return to the homes from which they had been dragged three years earlier. In early December 1944 OPA removed most cuts of meat from rationing and reduced the number of coupons needed for a wide range of food items and sundries. The public demanded even more. This attitude posed a serious problem for the production effort. America's military manpower was stretched to its limit, with all but one division deployed and pressure for individual replacements increasing astronomically. The army had exceeded its authorized strength of 7.7 million men, drawing workers from war industries. The numbers of physically qualified males at home available for induction were inadequate to keep up with casualty rates.

The German offensive in the Ardennes, the so-called Battle of the Bulge, shattered illusions. For the first time, a call-up of fathers with children was authorized. To emphasize the seriousness of the crisis, the Director of War Mobilization and Reconversion, on 23 December announced the closing of all horse racing tracks. The proclaimed purpose was to conserve fuel and other critical materials. Next day, Christmas Eve, while Americans were plucking holiday turkeys and preparing standing rib roasts and hams, OPA announced the reinstatement of rationing of all beef products. It had belatedly discovered the war in Europe was not to end by Christmas 1944.

Ironies abound when considering the American economy's performance during the final months of World War II. A panicked response to the Ardennes offensive and to fierce Japanese resistance led to a miniboom in procurement of everything from ammunition and boots to aircraft carriers. Miscalculations about the military timetable, inventories of raw materials and manufactured goods, and pent-up consumer demand nearly wrecked the federal government's elaborate plans for "reconversion," the transition from wartime to peacetime production. Controls were removed rapidly in response to congressional and popular clamor. No serious challenge to prosperity and full employment arose as some had feared, but regional dislocations weakened economic performance and the rate of inflation shot up to levels not seen since 1919-20. Labor conflicts swept the country and a conservative backlash in 1946 appeared to place in jeopardy the New Deal's gains.

That the months following war's end proved painful for the U.S. economy should not obscure the very real achievements registered during World War II. America met its wartime production goals. By most accounts, the American people enjoyed unparalleled prosperity, and this wealth was shared by a higher percentage of the population. The power of the American economy stood unrivalled in a world shattered by war. Over the course of the war, civilian per capita consumption of dairy products (butter excepted), meat, poultry, vegetables, legumes, and grains grew by leaps and bounds. Consumer outlays for food jumped from $14 billion to $24 billion, making a mockery of the wartime conservation campaigns. Certain cuts of meat, canned goods, and cheese had become scarce by early 1943, but that was the result of voracious demand rather than any long-term deficiency.

The outbreaks of gluttony were but one manifestation of improved living standards. Average weekly earnings, benefitting from heavy overtime, increased by 70 percent. There is also evidence that a permanent if modest redistribution of income had taken place. As of 1941 the lowest fifth of American heads of households received 13.6 percent and the highest fifth

48.8 percent of total income. Three years later, those percentages stood at 15.8 and 45.8 respectively. This onetime shift, which went against historical trends, put more money in the pocketbooks of the poorest groups in American society.[38]

Precisely how this was accomplished still is an open question. It is clear that "purely" economic and strategic aims were intermixed with and often made subordinate to partisan and palace politics. How much matériel and that most precious commodity, time, was wasted cannot be ascertained with any certainty. Estimates range from $30-50 billion in supplies thrown away or misassigned to the war's lasting six to nine months longer than necessary. How many lives that cost is yet more hypothetical. A recent analysis asserts that historians and economists have been "misled by inappropriate and inaccurate statistical constructs," and that "wartime prosperity" is a misnomer, given a decline in real private investment, substantial actual inflation, and hidden unemployment. The war's principal achievement was, in fact, psychological. With work for everyone who wanted it and "employment" in the armed forces for many who did not, the war "broke the back of the pessimistic expectations almost everyone had come to hold during the seemingly endless depression." Renewed confidence rather than pent-up demand fueled America's postwar economic growth.[39]

Despite advice from economic historians that nations should mobilize for war using a rational correlation of strategic aims and the economy's potential for waging war[40]—not strategy and grand logistics but short-term responses to political and military exigency drove the U.S. economy in World War II. It is often said that myths are but unexamined truths. Certainly, the history of American wartime mobilization is replete with stories, assertions permitted to acquire the status of myth. One of the most lasting has been the myth of American power as like that of Leviathan—inexhaustible and as inexplicable as the wellsprings of democracy itself.

NOTES

1. Modern-day definitions of "Leviathan" include: 1. A monstrous sea creature mentioned in the Old Testament [Job 41:1]; 2. Any very large animal; 3. Anything unusually large for its kind. See William Morris, ed., *The American Heritage Dictionary of the English Language* (Boston, 1969), 752.

2. Charles S. Maier has termed this the "supposedly apolitical politics of productivity" in "The Politics of Productivity: Foundations of American International Economic Policy after World War II," *International Organization* 31 (Autumn 1977), 607-33.

3. Alan S. Milward, *War, Economy and Society* (London, 1977), ix. Also see William E. Leuchtenburg, "The New Deal and the Analogue of War," in John Braeman, et al., eds., *Change and Continuity in Twentieth Century America* (Columbus, Ohio, 1964), and Robert Cuff, "American Mobilization for War 1917-1945: Political Culture vs Bureaucratic Administration," in N. F. Dreisziger, ed., *Mobilization for Total War: The Canadian, American, and British Experience* (Waterloo, Ontario, 1981).

4. Since 90 percent of American companies employed less than 300 workers and generated 60 percent of total production, the dispersal effect via subcontracts was tremendous. In fact, Truman's hometown of Kansas City did extremely well in the defense contract sweepstakes; Theodore A. Wilson, "The Truman Committee, 1941," in Arthur M. Schlesinger, Jr., and Roger Bruns, eds., *Congress Investigates, 1792-1974* (New York, 1975), 327-49.

5. Bureau of the Budget, *The United States at War,* 28. Generally see Charles E. Kirkpatrick, *An Unknown Future and a Doubtful Present: Writing the Victory Plan of 1941* (Washington, D.C., 1991).

6. Jean Monnet, *Memoires* (Paris, 1976), 149-159.

7. For wartime administration, see the Bureau of the Budget's *The United States at War,* and Richard Polenberg, *War and Society: The United States, 1941-1945* (Philadelphia, 1972).

8. Vatter, *The U.S. Economy in World War II,* 721.

9. H. T. Ueda, *et al., The Canol Pipeline Project* (Washington, D.C., 1977); Wilson, "The Truman Committee," 347-48.

10. Brehon B. Somervell to Donald M. Nelson [draft not sent], 13 May 1942, Box 62, RG 160, National Archives [NA], Washington, D.C.

11. Robert Higgs has asserted that Washington did impose a "command economy" in 1942; "Wartime Prosperity? A Reassessment of the U.S. Economy in the 1940s," *Journal of Economic History* (December 1991), 15.

12. Harvey Mansfield, et al., *A Short History of the OPA* (Washington, D.C., 1947), and "The OPA Under Review," Report No. 18-A (March 1947), Industrial College of the Armed Forces, N-8467-7, Combined Armed Research Library, Ft. Leavenworth, Kans.

13. See John M. Blum, *V Was For Victory: Politics and American Culture During World War II* (New York, 1976), and Mark H. Leff, "The Politics of Sacrifice on the American Home Front in World War II," *Journal of American History* 77, no. 4 (March 1991), 1296-1318.

14. Geoffrey Perrett, *Days of Sadness, Years of Triumph: The American People, 1939-1945* (New York, 1974), 303.

15. See Vatter, *The U.S. Economy in World War II*, 92-95.

16. See Seymour E. Harris, *Price and Related Controls in the United States* (New York, 1945), Paul Evans, "The Effects of General Price Controls in the United States during World War II," *Journal of Political Economy* 90 (October 1982), 944-66, and Geoffrey Mills and Hugh Rockoff, "Compliance with Price Controls in the United States and Great Britain during World War II," *Journal of Economic History* 47 (March 1987), 197-213.

17. Vatter, *U.S. Economy in World War II*, 102.

18. *Historical Statistics*, pt. 2, 1107; *Economic Report of the President* (February 1984), 242.

19. Robert P. Patterson to Harold Stein, 28 December 1949, Patterson Papers, Library of Congress (LC); see also James S. Nanney and Terrence J. Gough, *Manpower Mobilization for World War II* (Washington, D.C., 1982).

20. Keith E. Eiler, "Robert P. Patterson and U.S. Mobilization in World War II," lecture at U.S. Army Command and General Staff College, 30 April 1984 (in possession of author).

21. Isador Lubin to Harry L. Hopkins, 6 November 1941, Box 37, Lubin Papers, Franklin D. Roosevelt Library (Hyde Park, N.Y.); William M. Tuttle, Jr., "The Birth of an Industry: The Synthetic Rubber 'Mess' in World War II," *Technology and Culture* 22, no. 1 (January 1981), 35-67.

22. John G. Clark, *Energy and the Federal Government: Fossil Fuel Policies, 1900-1946* (Urbana, Il. 1987), 300-301.

23. Clark, *Energy and the Federal Government*, 347, 362.

24. Karen Anderson, *Wartime Women: Sex Roles, Family Relations and the Status of Women During World War II* (Westport, Conn., 1981), and Mary M. Schweitzer, "World War II and Female Labor Force Participation Rates," *Journal of Economic History* 41 (March 1980), 89-95.

25. See James A. Neuchterlein, "The Politics of Civil Rights: The FEPC, 1941-1946," *Prologue* 10 (Fall 1978); Norval D. Glenn, "Changes in the American Occupational Structure and Occupational Gains of Negroes During the 1940s," *Social Forces* 41 (December 1962); and John Modell, et al., "World War II in the Lives of Black Americans: Some Findings and an Interpretation," *Journal of American History* 76, no. 3 (December 1989).

26. Peter Fearon, *War, Prosperity, and Depression: The U.S. Economy, 1917-1945* (Lawrence, Kans., 1987), 266-68.

27. Walter W. Wilcox, *The Farmer in the Second World War* (Ames, Iowa, 1947), 56.

28. Bureau of the Budget, *The United States at War,* 113-14.

29. The mass production accomplishments are chronicled in Perret, *Days of Sadness, Years of Triumph,* 174-177, and Bureau of the Budget, *The United States at War,* passim. For the genesis of atomic weapons, see Richard Rhodes, *The Making of the Atomic Bomb* (New York, 1986).

30. James Phinney Baxter, III, *Scientists Against Time* (Boston, 1946), and Kent C. Redmond, "World War II—A Watershed in the Role of the National Government in the Advancement of Science and Technology," in Charles Angoff, ed., *The Humanities in an Age of Science* (Philadelphia, 1968).

31. Vatter, *U.S. Economy at War,* 60.

32. Lyman Hill, "Impact of War on an Economic Area: A Case Study," in G. A. Steiner, ed., *Economic Problems of War* (New York, 1942), 1-19.

33. Vatter, *The U.S. Economy at War,* 15.

34. A succinct description of the BEW-RFC conflict is in John M. Blum, ed., *The Price of Vision: The Diary of Henry A. Wallace* (Boston, 1972), 26-29.

35. See S. K. Bailey, *Congress Makes a Law: The Story Behind the Unemployment Act of 1946* (New York, 1950), and Alonzo Hamby, *Beyond the New Deal: Harry S. Truman and American Liberalism* (New York, 1973).

36. Draft memorandum, "Policies for Postwar Full Employment," Harold D. Smith [by Gerhard Colm] to FDR, 6 October 1944, "Employment Act Symposium" folder, Gerhard Colm Papers, Harry S Truman Library [HSTL] (Independence, Mo.); J. Weldon Jones to Director, Bureau of Budget, 10 October 1944, PPF 41, FDRL.

37. Henry L. Stimson to George C. Marshall, 6 December 1944, Chief of Staff folder, Secretary's "Safe" File, RG 196, NA.

38. *Historical Statistics* (G-319, 320, 323), Part 1, 301, summarized in Vatter, *U.S. Economy in World War II,* 142-43.

39. Eiler, "Robert P. Patterson and U.S. Mobilization in World War II," 19-20; Robert Higgs, "Wartime Prosperity? A Reassessment of the U.S. Economy in the 1940s"; Higgs, *Crisis and Leviathan: Critical Episodes in the Growth of American Government* (New York, 1987).

40. The arguments in Milward, *War, Economy and Society, 1939-1945,* 1-3, 19-23, suggest that, in the U.S. strategic calculus, inconvenience rather than sacrifice was the preferred policy.

8

Co-operation: Trade, Aid, and Technology

Richard J. Overy, et al.

During the Second World War the Allied powers achieved an unprecedented degree of economic and technical collaboration. The war of 1914-18 saw limited assistance in the supply of weapons and money, but never as generously or systematically applied as the economic aid programs between 1941 and 1945. Even more remarkable was the fact that much of this transfer of resources was made without thought of repayment, as a charge upon the donor state and its population. It was done because the sharing of resources in the common cause against the Axis states made sound strategic sense. Economic co-operation was one of the key elements in the ultimate victory of the Allies, and was perceived to be so at the time. None of the Allies was entirely self-sufficient economically, not even the United States, whose vast economic resources were placed at the disposal of all those states fighting Germany, Italy, and Japan. Without economic co-operation both Britain and the Soviet Union would have been compelled to run a smaller war effort and run a much higher risk of defeat.

The circumstances of the war made economic aid a vital consideration. Britain depended for her economic survival on importing large quantities of food, raw materials, machinery, and all of her oil. The German submarine campaign from 1941 threatened to sever the life-line of overseas supply; the Japanese assault on South-East Asia cut Britain off from a large part of her supplies of tin and rubber. Economic assistance, in the form of shipping and supplies, had to be found in the United States. For the Soviet Union the economic problem was a direct consequence of the German invasion in 1941, which secured the food and industrial areas of western Russia and the Ukraine for the German war effort. Although the Soviet

Union succeeded in building up alternative sources of supply in the areas beyond the Ural Mountains, the early losses could only be made good with American and British aid. Moreover, these losses were Axis gains. The economic balance tilted towards Germany and Japan as military victory brought them control over European and East Asian resources. The United States was cut off from important areas of the world market and was forced to rely more on her own or British Empire resources.

The nature of the military technology also necessitated co-operation. Warfare after 1939 was "industrialized warfare," requiring the supply of vast industrial resources to produce in mass the aircraft, trucks, tanks, radios, and ships needed to defeat the Axis. As weapons became more sophisticated during the war, so a higher level of scientific and technical collaboration was called for as well. All the Allied leaders recognized the economic foundation of modern warfare. "The war would be won," Stalin told the Harriman Mission in September 1941, "by industrial production."[1] This economic conception of warfare was shared by Churchill and Roosevelt. Economic collaboration, whether in the prosecution of economic warfare, or the provision of material aid, or the exchange of technical information, was seen by the Allied powers as the precondition for effective strategic and military co-operation.

Nevertheless, Allied economic co-operation should not be taken for granted. The aid programs took time to develop and were always the subject of tough bargaining and political argument. The high point of collaboration was not reached until 1943-44 and came to an abrupt halt in 1945. During the 1930s and the early years of war economic relations between the future Allies were affected by the prevailing mood of protectionism and self-interest which had done so much to blight the political relations between states. During the period of world recession and limited recovery in the 1930s, economic co-operation and trade between states reached a low point. In the United States the Johnson Act (1934) prohibited virtually all overseas investment in Europe, while the high Hawley-Smoot Tariff of 1930 kept out Europe's exports. Britain fell back more on economic dependence on the Empire, based around the protectionist bloc created by the Ottawa Agreement in 1932. Although Roosevelt's secretary of state, Cordell Hull, urged a return to a more open and co-operative world economic system, little progress was made in reducing the economic barriers between states. The onset of rearmament and the scramble for control of economic resources in case of war only hardened attitudes and encouraged the siege-economy mentality.

Political questions also coloured relations between the Soviet Union and the western economies before 1941. The Western states distrusted and disliked communism, which they perceived as a threat to the capitalist order. This fear was increased after the slump of 1929-32 which showed the vulnerability of capitalism. American aid for Soviet industrial modernization was significant in the 1920s, but declined sharply in the 1930s. Western states traded with the Soviet Union out of expediency, to keep up domestic employment and output levels. They extended credit grudgingly and placed restrictions on trade. After the Nazi-Soviet Pact in 1939 relations worsened. Britain placed an embargo on machinery exports, and the American-Russian Chamber of Commerce, which helped to arrange trade deals, was disbanded.[2] In December 1939, following the Soviet-Finnish war, the American government also imposed embargoes on goods for the Soviet Union. Britain and France drew up joint plans to attack the Soviet oil fields in the Caucasus region to deny these resources to Germany.[3] The Western states increasingly saw the Soviet Union as a potential enemy, supplying goods to Nazi Germany. Soviet leaders remained deeply distrustful of the West and its capitalist ambitions. It was reported to London in November 1939 that Stalin's "desire was to improve trade with England; but he was very suspicious of [British] policy."[4] Right up to the German invasion in June 1941 Stalin seems to have believed that the West was chiefly interested in finding a way to bring down Soviet communism rather than defeat Hitler.

If relations with the Soviet Union remained soured by political conflict, the coming confrontation with Hitler's Germany helped to improve economic relations between Britain and the United States. The breakthrough came in the aftermath of the 1938 Munich conference. The British and French governments began to increase levels of military preparedness in order to be able to confront Hitler more effectively in 1939. Since their own industry could not provide what was wanted quickly enough, both states sought to place military orders in the United States.[5] The arms embargo provisions of the Neutrality Acts were repealed in November. Apart from strategic interests, Roosevelt could see that European orders would help American economic recovery; "economically the United States will fare well whether Europe goes to war or not."[6] Production for Britain and France was also seen by America's military leaders as a way to get outside credits to pay for the expansion of the American armaments industry. Despite congressional resistance, Roosevelt was able to offer Britain and France not only raw materials and machinery but also aircraft, aero-engines, and other military equipment.[7] The only conditions were that after November 1939 both states paid in cash and shipped the resources themselves. For the next year both Britain and France maintained purchasing missions in the United States, arranging contracts and the shipping of supplies.

The situation changed considerably when France was defeated in June 1940 and Britain was expelled from the Continent. The United States was suddenly faced with the prospect of a German-dominated Europe and the defeat of European democracy. Economic assistance to Britain was no longer a way of solving domestic issues, but became essential to America's own security. On 10 June Roosevelt pledged the United States to supply the Allies with material resources for the fight against Germany.[8]

By this stage of the war Britain recognized that it would be forced to rely more and more on American resources to avoid defeat. By the end of 1940 Britain placed orders in the United States for $4,500 million of military and industrial equipment.[9] It was Churchill's view that "second only to winning the war, the most important thing was for the British Empire to reach a satisfactory economic accord with the United States."[10] The main difficulty confronting Britain was how to pay for American supplies. By the end of 1940 Britain had placed contracts to a value greater than her dollar assets. This meant that unless some other arrangement for payment could be reached with the United States, Britain would no longer be able to buy any supplies in 1941.[11]

The solution to the British payments problem laid the foundation for economic co-operation for the rest of the war. The choice facing the American government was clear: either ways would be found to lend or give economic supplies to Britain, or Britain would have to fight with only her own resources and face the prospect of defeat or a humiliating peace treaty. But there were also domestic factors to consider before increasing American aid. A widespread belief existed that Britain could actually pay more than she claimed, and was trying to trick the United States into carrying the cost of her war effort. Though the evidence makes it clear that Roosevelt wanted to go further in extending aid to Britain, he was unable to do anything until the British position was manifestly untenable.

That turning point came late in 1940. On 7 December Churchill sent a long memorandum to Roosevelt outlining the British prospects for 1941.[12] In it he made clear that Britain needed American assistance in shipping and finance to be able to continue the war, and he appealed to America's own strategic self-interest as a ground for giving the resources rather than selling them.

Roosevelt favoured some kind of "leasing arrangements" through which the United States gave Britain goods that were "loanable, returnable, and insurable."[13] With Churchill's appeal on his desk Roosevelt was determined "to get rid of the silly, foolish dollar sign" in economic relations between the two states. On 29 December he declared in a national broadcast that the United States was to become "the arsenal of democracy", providing weapons and resources for all those states resisting aggression. On 2 January 1941 he ordered the Treasury Department to draft a bill authorizing the president to "sell, transfer, exchange, lease or lend" supplies to states engaged in conflicts that affected American security. By making it clear that Britain's fight was also America's, Roosevelt hoped to silence all those critics who saw economic co-operation as a financial and diplomatic liability.[14]

The Lend-Lease Bill, which became law in March 1941, was without question one of the turning points of the war. Behind Roosevelt's homely appeals to American citizens to bail out Britain's war effort lay a great deal of hard political bargaining. When the bill was presented to Congress in January it aroused a storm of political protest.[15] The successful passage of the bill depended on the growing evidence that Britain could not pay, and on Roosevelt's personal success in persuading Congress that by giving other states the weapons to fight with, the United States might be able to avoid war altogether. If Lend-Lease was, as Churchill claimed, an unsordid act, it was always presented to the American public as a product of American self-interest.

Churchill was delighted with the news of Lend-Lease—"this is tantamount to a declaration of war by the United States," he told his private secretary in January.[16] But Lend-Lease was never intended to be a one-way arrangement. Roosevelt talked loosely about finding some form of compensation when the conflict was over; Secretary of State Hull saw it as an opportunity to tie Britain, and other beneficiaries of the program, to a reform of the international economy after the war in favor of more liberal trading relations.[17] The British finally accepted this quid pro quo with ill grace (see below). There was less argument over the question of giving economic aid to the United States. During the war Britain provided mutual assistance under the Reciprocal Aid Agreements signed in September 1942. In the end, Britain provided the United States with over 30 per cent of its supplies for D-Day, and by the end of the war had devoted almost as large a proportion of national income to mutual aid as the United States.[18]

Lend-Lease was administered at first by an ad hoc committee run by Roosevelt's personal adviser, Harry Hopkins. Supplies for Britain were negotiated with permanent missions stationed in Washington, but in all other respects the program was run as an American rather than an Allied enterprise. On 28 October 1941 Roosevelt created the Office of Lend-Lease Administration under the businessman, Edward Stettinius. In September 1943 this office was wound up and a Foreign Economic Administration set up under Leo Crowley which combined responsibility for Lend-Lease, economic warfare, and foreign relief programs. By this stage of the war Lend-Lease was supplied to 35 countries and consumed 17 per cent of all American war expenditures.

The great bulk of supplies under Lend-Lease went to Britain and, from the autumn of 1941, to the USSR as well. The German attack in June 1941 raised the delicate issue of Western aid for the Soviet war effort. Like the earlier decision to aid Britain, assistance to the Soviet Union provoked intense political and military argument in Washington and London. Churchill's immediate reaction was to offer the Soviet Union any kind of possible help regardless of the nature of the Stalinist regime: "We should forget about Soviet systems or the Comintern and extend our hand to fellow human beings in distress." Roosevelt, too, at a news conference a few days after the onset of BARBAROSSA announced that "we are going to give all the aid we possibly can to Russia." But in practice there remained a large gap between the rhetoric and the reality. Not for another year did significant supplies begin to reach the Soviet Union.[19]

There were a number of obstacles to overcome before significant aid could be given to the Soviet Union. The mere fact of German aggression did not end the strong anti-communism of many Western politicians. Lend-Lease to Britain was justified by general notions about protecting the fragile plant of democracy. It was difficult for the American government to argue the same case for the USSR. State Department official Breckinridge Long noted in his diary in July that "the great majority of our people have learned that communism is something to be suppressed and the enemy of our law and order. They do not understand how we can align ourselves even a little with it."[20] More difficult was the fact that for the first weeks of the German campaign both the British and American military chiefs predicted that the Soviet Union would shortly be defeated. Under these circumstances there were strong arguments for keeping supplies in the West, for the long-term conflict. In the United States rearmament was still in its early stages; it had proved difficult enough to persuade the American services to give up goods for Britain. Help for the Soviet Union was generally regarded as low priority and strategically undesirable, leading to what General Arnold, head of the army air forces, called "piecemeal reinforcement."[21] Finally there was simply the issue of logistics. Shipping was already a crisis area for Britain. Aid for the Soviet Union required the diversion of scarce shipping resources on difficult routes.

All of these factors help to explain the slow development of the aid program for the USSR. But there were also strong arguments in favour of pursuing a policy of Soviet aid. It was feared that without economic support the Soviet Union might well be defeated, or might seek a separate agreement with Hitler. Roosevelt and Churchill were both of the view that it did not matter who was using the weapons as long as they were killing Germans. Roosevelt also saw the prospect that Soviet forces could, with effective reinforcement, defeat the German armies without the need to create a large American land force. His confidant, Averell Harriman, later recalled that "the overriding motivation of President Roosevelt in giving every bit of help that was possible was that he wanted to keep the Russians in the war."[22] Roosevelt's determination to provide aid to the USSR "as long as she is fighting the Axis effectively" cleared the way in the end for substantial Lend-Lease appropriations.[23]

In the early stages after BARBAROSSA improvisation remained the order of the day. Britain and the United States removed embargoes on Soviet supplies and speeded up supplies already in the pipeline. The Soviet authorities were keen from the outset to receive economic assistance. On 26 June the Soviet ambassador in Washington, Konstantin Umansky, made a formal request for aid; three days later the American embassy in Moscow sent a long list of Soviet requests presented by Foreign Minister Molotov. These requests included not only a wide range of modern armaments but also whole factories for the production of aviation fuel, light alloys, tyres, and so on.[24] Not until August did Roosevelt reach a decision, and then only in the light of Hopkins' conviction, formed during a visit to the USSR in July, that the Soviet Union would survive the initial German onslaught. On 2 August Roosevelt announced that although the Soviet Union would not qualify for Lend-Lease the United States had decided "to give all economic assistance practicable." Two weeks later Andrei Gromyko, a Soviet embassy official, delivered a 29-page list detailing all Soviet requirements.[25]

American and British authorities were reluctant to supply weapons and equipment until it was clear that the Soviet Union could make use of them effectively. The two Western states sent a special mission to Moscow under Lord Beaverbrook for the British and Averell Harriman for the Americans. Stalin repeated the Soviet requests, but expressed his suspicion that the West wanted "to see the Soviet Union defeated."[26] After three days of hard bargaining a protocol was finally agreed listing what Britain and the United States would make available for a 12-month period. The distrust between the three states was temporarily set aside.

When the list of supplies was agreed upon Litvinov, the former foreign minister who was acting as interpreter, leapt up and called out: "Now we shall win the war!"[27]

The protocol agreed upon at the Moscow talks laid the basis for the supply of Western goods for the Soviet war effort. Unlike the offer of aid to Britain earlier in the year, the Soviet Union was to be supplied unconditionally. There was no request to reveal its foreign exchange and gold holdings; nor could the genuineness of Soviet requests for equipment, particularly factories and plants, be effectively assessed. Both Britain and the United States recognized, however, that if they wanted the Soviet Union to stay in the fight against Hitler it would be politically inexpedient to place any political or technical barriers in the way of deliveries. This was almost certainly the right decision, since assistance for the Soviet Union, even if it was slow in maturing, helped to heal the rift between the two sides created by a deep mutual distrust. The promise of economic co-operation came at an opportune psychological moment for the Soviet Union, as the German assault on Moscow began. A month after the Moscow meetings Roosevelt pledged $1 billion in aid, and on 7 November at last agreed on supplying the Soviet Union under the Lend-Lease agreements.[28] The Soviet struggle was certainly not for democracy in any American sense, but Roosevelt was able to persuade Congress that aid to the USSR was "vital to the defense of the United States." By this stage public opinion in the United States had swung round in favour of Soviet aid, as it had in Britain. An opinion poll in America taken in October showed 73 per cent in favour of working with the USSR in defeating Germany.[29]

The aid programs for the USSR were operated differently from Anglo-American mutual aid. In Britain supplies were controlled by the Allied Supplies Executive set up in October 1941.[30] In the United States supplies were based on an annual protocol agreed after negotiations each year between the two sides. The protocol gave a maximum of what the United States could supply, not what the Soviet Union requested, and the agreement did not guarantee that the supplies would be forthcoming. Once shipped to the Soviet Union Western interest in how the goods were assembled and deployed had to be abandoned. Soviet authorities regarded the goods as theirs and rejected most British and American offers of technical assistance or inquiries about their tactical or economic use.

In the Soviet case, as in the British, Lend-Lease supply took a considerable time to come on stream. Most of the British supplies before Pearl Harbor were still paid for in cash. Only 100 out of 2,400 American aircraft sent to Britain in 1941 came under Lend-Lease. During the bitter battles on the eastern front in 1941 the Soviet Union received only 140 aircraft from America and 180 tanks. British supplies were held up because of the military crisis in North Africa; only with reluctance did British military leaders agree to the transfer of aircraft and other matériel to the Soviet front.[31] Lend-Lease began to arrive in strategically significant quantities for both Britain and the USSR during 1943 and 1944. The bulk of supplies from the United States came in the form of finished weapons, trucks, and military equipment, but there were also substantial shipments of food, raw materials and industrial equipment. The figures for the total of Lend-Lease supplies and the different categories of product are set out in Table 8.1.

The contribution of Lend-Lease to the British war effort was larger than that to the Soviet Union. Detailed discussion may be found in chapters 5 and 6 but the general picture is summarized here. In 1941 Lend-Lease provided 2.4 per cent of the total munitions supplied to British Commonwealth forces. In 1943, the figure was 24 per cent and in 1944 27 per cent. Almost one-fifth of all the weapons used by Britain during the war came under Lend-Lease. In the Soviet Union the munitions contribution was more modest, although (see chapter 6) "aviation Lend-Lease" was particularly significant, supplying one-fifth of total Soviet war-time fighters, for instance.[32] In the supply of food and industrial requirements, however, Lend-Lease proved much more important to the Soviet effort. By 1943-44 industrial goods made up 40 per cent of supplies, and included 2.8 million tons of steel, 2.6 million tons of petrochemicals, and 15 million pairs of boots. The United States also supplied the USSR with 4,478 million tons of food under Lend-Lease.[33] The machinery and factory equipment helped the Soviet Union to produce its own weapons and materials, rather than have to rely on irregular seaborne supply. The food sent under Lend-Lease helped to compensate for the loss of three-fifths of the Soviet area under cultivation and two-thirds of the grain supply and also allowed the Soviet authorities to draft more unskilled farm labor into the forces and the arms factories. Nevertheless by 1944, some 40 per cent of supplies sent via the Far Eastern route were kept in stockpiles in Siberia to be used against Japan at a later date.[34] This suggests that the Soviet authorities relied much less on Lend-Lease by this stage of the war.

Very little came back to the Western allies materially from the Soviet Union. Mutual aid was never a requirement under the agreements made with Soviet leaders. American officials calculated at the end of the war that Soviet "reverse Lend-Lease" totalled only \$2 million.[35] But in the British case it was always expected in Washington and London that when

TABLE 8.1

LEND-LEASE SUPPLIES TO BRITAIN AND THE USSR

A. To the British Commonwealth

	1941	1942	1943	1944	1945	
Total (m $)	1,082	4,757	9,031	10,706	4,347	**30,073**
In %						
Aircraft	2.0	17.0	18.8	23.6	27.7	21.0
Shipping	14.1	8.5	17.9	9.3	9.2	12.0
Guns & Ammo	7.8	15.4	12.1	9.0	7.8	10.8
Vehicles	6.7	9.5	17.0	14.6	9.4	13.5
Other Munitions	1.1	2.3	4.5	11.0	10.2	7.1
Total Munitions	31.7	53.6	70.3	67.5	64.3	64.4
Food	29.7	14.3	9.5	11.7	12.7	12.2
Agricultural Goods	8.0	3.2	2.4	2.4	3.7	2.9
Metal	9.3	6.4	4.9	3.5	5.4	4.8
Machinery	2.4	4.2	3.4	2.7	2.6	3.1
Manufactures	1.5	2.7	1.1	1.8	2.4	1.8
Services	17.9	15.5	8.4	10.6	9.0	10.8

B. To the Soviet Union

	1941	1942	1943	1944	1945	
Total (m $)	**20**	**1,376**	**2,436**	**4,074**	**2,764**	**10,670**
In %						
Aircraft	-	22.4	17.4	16.3	12.7	
Guns & Ammo	-	15.8	12.8	5.6	2.6	
Tanks	-	13.1	2.6	4.9	4.0	
Other Vehicles	-	11.0	14.1	14.7	19.3	
Shipping	-	0.8	3.2	2.5	2.1	
Total Military	20	63.2	49.9	43.8	40.7	
Industrial Goods	80	23.1	29.6	39.3	39.5	
Agricultural Goods	-	13.7	20.5	16.9	19.8	

Sources: H. Duncan Hall, *North American Supply* (London, 1955), 430; M. Harrison, *Soviet Planning in War and Peace, 1938-1945* (Cambridge, 1985), 258-59.

and where possible some degree of reciprocal assistance would be given, particularly in the supply of American forces stationed in Britain or the British Empire. Oil was a particularly important item in mutual aid. The United States supplied $2.1 million of oil to Britain, most of it shipped from the eastern seaboard ports. In return Britain supplied $1.8 million of oil, most of it from Middle East oil fields, for American forces in the Mediterranean theatre. The details of British Empire reciprocal aid to the United States are set out in Table 8.2:

TABLE 8.2

BRITISH COMMONWEALTH RECIPROCAL AID TO THE UNITED STATES 1941-45 (m $)

From United Kingdom	
ships and construction	910
military stores	2,014
petroleum	1,187
services	1,195
other goods	361
Total	5,667
From Australia	1,041
From New Zealand	248
From South Africa	1
From India	610
Overall Total	**7,567**

Source: H. Duncan Hall, *North American Supply* (London, 1955), 432.

Until 1943 the United States continued to pay dollars for food and raw materials supplied from the British Empire, but from November of that year Britain agreed to supply commodities produced in the Empire (tea, sisal, palm oil, cocoa, etc.) as direct aid. By April 1945, $164 million worth of goods had been supplied under the new arrangement. Over the whole war the United States devoted 4 per cent of its domestic output to Lend-Lease to Britain, while reciprocal aid consumed 3 per cent of British output.[36]

The global figures on Lend-Lease and mutual aid disguise the different phases through which the Lend-Lease programs passed and the wider political and economic issues to which they gave rise. The first issue that affected both Soviet and British recipients was the significant time lag between the promise of aid and the actual supply of strategically useful material. This situation owed something to the problems faced by American industry as it was converted gradually to war production at very short notice. The investment programs initiated in 1940 and 1941 from their very nature only bore fruit between 18 months to two years later. But there were also military considerations. As the United States edged nearer to belligerency in 1941, the military leadership urged that American forces should be given priority. Each major shipment in the early stages of Lend-Lease had to be argued out with the military. The American services were also keen to introduce more modern weapon types in 1941 and 1942. This led to the slowdown of production of obsolescent types, which had been in many cases destined for the British. It was natural for the hard-pressed American military to send the older equipment overseas as long as they could and to keep the more technically advanced weapons for American forces. Because of this some of the early Lend-Lease supplies were of limited usefulness against superior German equipment.[37] This was even more the case with British equipment, which Soviet military authorities regarded, rightly or wrongly, as technically inferior to American and German weapons.

Yet, of all the issues slowing up the initiation of large-scale aid, none was more important than the shipping question. During 1941 it proved difficult to supply even Britain's minimum requirements. With the Soviet Union there were no entirely reliable routes for supply by sea. Overland supply through Iran was only possible later in the war when adequate rail links were established. The bulk of supplies had to be convoyed in difficult seas against the threat of German submarine and air attack. After December 1941 the United States had also to bear the bulk of the shipping in the Pacific Ocean. In October 1941 the Soviet authorities asked for regular monthly shipping of 440,000 tons for supplies via Archangel and Vladivostok, of which they agreed to supply 90,000 tons.[38] The rest had to be found from Anglo-American sources and this proved to be an almost continuous bottle-neck in supplying the USSR in 1941 and 1942. Not until the defeat of the German submarine in 1943 and the massive American merchant shipping program in the same year did it become possible to match promises and deliveries. But by then most supplies came via the safer Far Eastern route, or overland on the new rail lines built by American engineers in Iran.[39]

The Soviet Union interpreted these delays in political terms. American diplomats warned Washington that Soviet authorities remained skeptical about Western goodwill. As a result Roosevelt made strenuous efforts to get the American political and military establishment to accept the essential character of aid for the Soviet Union and to give it sufficient priority. But there was little that could be done about the squeeze on shipping produced by the submarine campaign in 1942, when more tonnage was lost than could be replaced from Allied shipyards. By the autumn of that year a serious shipping crisis slowed up the flow of materials and weapons from the West, and brought to a temporary halt the northern supply route to Archangel. The Soviet trade commissar warned that the "shortage of munitions is having a disastrous effect on the strategic plans of the Red Army," and accused the Americans of short-sightedness in not recognizing that "American interests are being defended on the Russian front."[40] In the end Stalin made a personal appeal to Roosevelt to give priority to Soviet supplies. Again Roosevelt's personal intervention brought an improvement in the rate of provision. The monthly average of supplies from January 1942 to October 1942, when Stalin sent his appeal, was valued at $99 million; for the following six months the average was $193 million. By the summer of 1943 the shipping crisis was over, and the flow of supplies to the USSR increased to an average of almost $300 million a month until the defeat of Germany.

There were issues over priorities and supply between the United States and Britain too, but they were exacerbated by the questions of economic policy between the two states. American policymakers, particularly in the State and Treasury departments, remained suspicious of British commercial policy and practices. They did not want Lend-Lease to be taken for granted, nor did they want Britain to use Lend-Lease as a cushion for her own commercial survival at the expense of American exporters. During the summer of 1941 rumours began to circulate in the United States that Britain was using Lend-Lease goods to produce her own exports to other countries, and that high profits were being made in Britain by unscrupulous middlemen trading in American goods.[41] The American authorities insisted at the end of July 1941 that the British government give a formal guarantee that Lend-Lease goods would only be used for Britain's own war effort. The British protested innocence but gave the guarantee none the less. On 10 September a White Paper was published in London in which Britain undertook to restrict her exports substantially for all those products which contained Lend-Lease supplies, or goods similar to Lend-Lease supplies but bought on the open market, or goods made of materials considered in short supply in the United States.[42] In effect the British produced a self-denying ordinance that reduced their trade throughout the war and left markets open to American penetration. During the war British exports fell to half the pre-war level, while American exports were three times larger.

The British could afford to make this concession because Lend-Lease removed the need to export in order to earn the food and materials needed for the war effort. Reliance on American supplies allowed British manufacturing industry to concentrate on war production rather than producing for export or domestic consumption. What the British government was less disposed to accept was that Lend-Lease should be used as an instrument to compel them to agree to a post-war economic order on American terms. But the American authorities were keen not only to restrict British war-time exports but also to get a commitment from Britain that she would work with America after the war to restore an open world market and liberal trade policies. This aim was incorporated into the draft Master Lend-Lease agreement presented to the British in the summer 1941. The economist John Maynard Keynes was sent from London to negotiate the terms. The stumbling block was Article VII of the agreement, which called for the commitment to free trade. Keynes warned his hosts that this was "contemplating the impossible," and indicated that the British did not want to rule out a return to controlled, protectionist blocks after the war.[43] The American negotiators rejected this view out of hand. It was Dean Acheson's view that "an effort of the magnitude of the Lend-Lease program on our part imposed upon the British the obligation of continuing goodwill in working out plans for the future. . . . "[44]

For the next six months the British government dragged its heels. The imperialists in Cabinet, and Churchill too, refused to give way on the right to retain Imperial Preference, the core of the British protectionist system. The British feared that this would mean the collapse of the Empire, and a dominant America. Only when Roosevelt insisted in February 1942 that the British sign the Lend-Lease Agreement or risk harmful consequences was their hand forced. The British could not afford to lose American supplies, and agreed to sign. The Master Agreement was provisionally signed on 23 February, but the exact interpretation of Article VII was left for discussion at some unspecified date later in the war.[45] The British saw all this as tantamount to economic blackmail, but there were explanations for the American attitude. American officials and politicians shared the suspicion that the British were canny operators in the sphere of international commerce. A Senate report in 1943 highlighted the supposed contrast between the British ("smart, hard-headed but patriotic") and American officials ("naive and inexperienced").[46] Second, the American administration and public wanted no repeat of the First World War and the unpaid war debts. They wanted a clear commitment that the war would end this time on American terms. Finally, one must never forget that Lend-Lease, if not a totally unsordid act, was certainly unprecedented in U.S. history. Roosevelt always had to struggle to maintain support in Congress for the programs, as the rapid termination of Lend-Lease in 1945 shows. British war-time concessions made his task easier.

Yet in the end the political and economic arguments did not seriously affect the flow of goods worldwide. Lend-Lease remained what Senator Vandenberg called it, "the king pin in the chain of international co-operation for victory."[47] Without it the British and Soviet war efforts would have been much reduced, and Britain's ability to sustain fighting much beyond 1941 seriously at issue. Against that overriding reality, the friction and suspicion among the Allies were always secondary.

Combined production proved a key to the success of the coalition. With America's entry into the war there were strong arguments for pooling the resources and production of the Allied states. In this way wasteful duplication of effort might be avoided and a more rational use made of scarce material and human resources. Combined production also matched other efforts to achieve combined strategic and planning organizations. But in practice, although America proved more than willing to share her output with the Allies, the national economies could only be integrated to a limited extent. Although a structure was set up to administer combined planning and output, a genuine pooling of productive efforts was never achieved. There was a great deal of co-ordinated planning, but no systematic combination of production.

The idea of combining production had its roots in the discussions during 1941 about future requirements for American and British forces to defeat Hitler. The head of the British Supply Council in Washington (an umbrella organization for all the purchasing missions in the United States) recognized that Britain's strategy in 1942 was going to be conditioned by what both states could produce. He began to draw up a balance sheet of existing stocks and future output plans to gain a clearer picture. Henry Stimson, the newly appointed Secretary of War in Washington, became a great enthusiast for planning in 1941 as a means to get Congress to vote larger credits for rearmament. By early September a Consolidated Statement (the so-called Stimson Balance Sheet) of actual and potential production of weapons by Britain, Canada, and the United States was finally drawn up.[48] The figures revealed a worrying deficiency: Anglo-American production would barely cover Britain's military requirements for future strategy. There would be little left over for the USSR or for the equipment of American armies and air forces. The problem for British planners and their American allies was to persuade the Roosevelt administration that plans for large-scale war production should be put into operation before America was even at war.

During September 1941 joint negotiations between the two sides were initiated to draft a "Victory Program." This proved to be a critical step along the road to greater economic co-operation, for it finally confirmed American commitment to the idea of a common production effort. It was also a critical step for the war as a whole, for American authorities came to recognize during the joint discussions that only American production on the largest scale could supply all the weapons needed for the defeat of the Axis states. Supplies for Britain and the USSR were built into the program planning. By the time America came into the war in December 1941 much of the preliminary spade-work of economic planning was already done. On 6 January Roosevelt announced to Congress a huge industrial program.[49]

With American entry into the war it proved possible to set up a formal machinery for economic collaboration. There were advantages in doing so for both sides. First, it matched the efforts to set up a joint structure for strategic and military planning. Both sides recognized how close were the links between military strategy and the supply of weapons. Second, it permitted the Americans to see clearly what level of sacrifice the two sides were making for the war effort, so that, as Roosevelt later said, "no nation will grow rich from the war effort of its allies."[50] The United States wanted parity of sacrifice, even though the absolute volume of weapons produced by the United States would vastly exceed that of any Allied state. Finally, both sides had something the other wanted. America provided Britain with the weapons that could not be produced by her own industry; the British Empire had supplies of raw materials which were needed for the American war effort.

It was in the sphere of raw materials that the first steps were taken. In mid-December Roosevelt initiated an inter-Allied conference "to explore at once how the raw materials of the world can best be brought to bear in the defeat of Hitler."[51] By January it was agreed that a number of combined boards should be established to deal not only with materials, but with the problem of shipping them as well. On 26 January 1941, the Combined Raw Materials Board and the Combined Shipping Adjustment Board were set up, staffed by representatives from both sides who were closely linked with the supply and shipping organizations of their respective governments. The British had been keen to create a general board to discuss production and allocation of weapons as well. American officials were more reluctant to accept this, partly because of issues over jurisdiction and sovereignty and partly because they could see little reason why Britain should be given a half-share in deciding the allocation of what was primarily American production. A Combined Production and Resources

Board was finally set up on 9 June 1942 with instructions to produce "a single integrated program, adjusted to the strategic requirements of the war,"[52] but the question of how much authority the board really had, both in relation to the other combined board, and in the relation to the domestic civilian offices, was never properly resolved. This was also true of the Combined Food Board, set up on the same day, which grew out of the work of the Anglo-American Food Committee set up in May 1941 to decide on the allocation and production of American food supplies.[53]

These boards were established as a response to the widespread feeling in both Washington and London that the Allies now had a "joint pool" of material resources on which to draw. But in practice the work of the Combined Boards proved to be much more modest than was hoped. They were never given executive authority or operational rights. Final decisions were always taken by the supply, production, and shipping authorities within each country. The chief task of the boards was to provide accurate and regular information on the production plans and needs of the two countries, to isolate areas of difficulty and to advise on solutions, and to produce ad hoc agreements on particular issues which could not be resolved through other agencies. The value of collaboration lay principally in the public evidence of joint effort, which acted as a permanent reminder that neither side operated in isolation.

There were obvious reasons for the limitations in economic collaboration. Neither state wished to lose ultimate sovereignty over decision-making about their own economic resources. A report to the American Joint Chiefs of Staff in 1943 made clear that "the control of production facilities within each country remains in the hands of that country, as does the power to determine what and how much those facilities shall produce. . . ."[54] In practice much of the economic co-operation between the Allies was conducted through the Lend-Lease organization which largely by-passed the Combined Boards, while questions concerning the allocation of munitions were handled through the machinery for military collaboration. A great deal of economic collaboration was also undertaken through direct negotiation between national agencies which had the authority to take decisions. In the sphere of raw materials the British Ministry of Economic Warfare and the American Board of Economic Warfare reached their own agreements on the question of procuring and shipping scarce materials. In food supply the American authorities largely ignored the Food Board and continued to negotiate directly with British authorities.

The development of a "common pool" was also inhibited by the unequal character of the relationship between the two sides. Britain was always much more dependent on the United States, and this placed Britain in the role of suppliant rather than supplier. The United States made little use of British war production and once the raw material shortages were overcome, during 1942, the flow of equipment, food, and commodities was very one-way. That the British were allowed to participate as much as they did in economic questions owed a great deal to the experience British officials had gained in the first two years of war, which was shared willingly with their American counterparts. On the more important questions the British were forced to go through direct political channels to get decisions favourable to British interests. The American military took the view that the equipment of their own forces took priority. The British were compelled to make out a case of strategic necessity for any additional supplies, and this left British military strategy hostage to American goodwill. Underlying these tensions were the consequences of global war. Planners in 1941 had not anticipated a major conflict in the Pacific. The Japanese victories of early 1942 therefore upset all previous calculations, logistic as well as strategic, and at the end of 1942 the United States had more troops in combat against Japan than against the European Axis. The logistic implications of the Pacific War left British concerns, particularly in the Mediterranean, low on the list.[55]

These problems of co-operation were at their most acute during 1942. During the summer months the American army cut back on the promised allocations of munitions for Britain. The issue was regarded in London as so critical that the minister of production, Oliver Lyttleton, was sent to Washington to negotiate directly with the American government. During the visit in October an agreement was worked out the so-called Weeks-Somervell Agreement that the United States would supply 25 per cent fewer munitions than Britain had requested, but would guarantee to supply the 75 per cent under any circumstances. Further agreements were reached on the distribution of aircraft production, and on the critical issue of shipping.[56] Twice—in 1941 and the autumn of 1942—Churchill appealed directly to Roosevelt to supply more shipping tonnage for the Atlantic routes. On both occasions concessions were made to the British emergency, but throughout the war Britain remained dependent on American shipping output and the willingness of American politicians to supply British needs. In other areas, the supply of transport aircraft and of tanks, the British recognized the savings to be made by concentrating their production in the United States, but here too the British remained at a disadvantage in making claims on American production.

If production was never genuinely combined, there nevertheless existed a good deal of close economic collaboration between Britain and the

United States over production goals, the allocation of production priorities, and the work of procuring and shipping supplies. The Soviet request to be included in a three-way commission on economic supplies in 1941 was turned down by the West and was not revived.[57] Instead, issues of supply to the USSR were resolved through negotiations at the highest political level. Soviet requirements were built into the programs and plans of the Western states from 1941 onwards. In this case too, "combined production" amounted in effect to discussions about the distribution of the American product. In this sense the critical factor in the Allied economic effort was not just Lend-Lease, but the continued perception by Americans of their role as the Allied arsenal and the willingness of American statesmen to permit Britain to share in its planning and operation. If collaboration had its drawbacks, it was greatly to be preferred to the economic isolation of the Axis states.

Economic co-operation produced willy-nilly a considerable degree of technological and scientific collaboration during the war. This was particularly the case with the supply of machine-tools and equipment to the Soviet Union, which contributed to raising the technical thresholds of the Soviet war effort. But there did not develop during the war any formal agreement on the exchange of technical and scientific information, and very little active scientific collaboration occurred outside the joint contributions to the development of atomic weapons.

Instead, the British and Americans recognized from at least as early as 1940 that each had technical and scientific research and developments useful to the other and that there were no very strong arguments for not revealing them. If there was a remarkable degree of frankness between the two sides, it was a reflection both of a growing sense of partnership and a recognition that each had something the other wanted. Indeed the emphasis on the development of military technology in Britain since at least 1936 meant that in some important respects Britain enjoyed a lead over American science that could only quickly be bridged by British willingness to supply material to the United States. In June 1940 the British released the Rolls-Royce Merlin engine for production in America. In September the British scientist Henry Tizard was sent as the head of a scientific mission to supply American researchers with secret details of British radar, anti-aircraft, and anti-submarine devices, and the cavity magnetron valve which was used in the development of ten-centimeter radar. As a result of the mission's work, Britain was supplied in return with the Sperry bombsight and details of American radar development.[58]

From 1940 until the end of the war there remained very close collaboration and exchange of information between the two states. A Central

Scientific Office was set up in both London and Washington to co-ordinate technical collaboration. The only exception to the rule was the development of the nuclear program, which was fraught with argument and distrust. The decision to try to develop an atomic bomb was taken first in Britain, where a committee was set up in April 1940, the MAUD committee, to oversee the research. In July 1941 the committee reported that a bomb was practicable. At almost the same time American scientists invited the British team to co-operate in uranium research. In October Roosevelt suggested to Churchill that the two states co-ordinate their atomic research. The British demurred on the grounds that the secrets might be let out in America, and continued to research on their own. By the summer of 1942 the situation was reversed. American research had overtaken British, and the sheer cost and effort of constructing a production plant forced the British to seek American help. This time the Americans refused, conscious that the British might use the atomic secret to develop post-war commercial uses at America's expense. Only when Churchill gave a firm guarantee in the 1943 Quebec agreements that Britain would not do so were British scientists brought into the research, though not into the construction of the actual plants involved. Both sides had the post-war situation in mind. Britain was increasingly worried that she might be isolated after the war as the only major power without nuclear weapons, and Americans were anxious about what would happen to their plans for a new world order if other states had the bomb. Stalin was not told about the new weapon until July 1945, following the first successful test, but it came as no surprise (chapter 6). The Soviet atomic project under Igor Kourchatov had been progressing since late 1942 and Truman's demarche only served to accelerate work.[59]

The level of technical and scientific collaboration with the Soviet Union was much lower (see also chapter 4). This was to some extent a product of political distrust and commercial anxiety. When the Soviet Union requested economic aid after June 1941, it was accompanied by specific demands for secret military-technical information and access for Soviet engineers to American military plants. The American authorities refused general access, but did permit the release of material necessary to make effective use of aid supplies.[60] The American military were worried lest secrets fall into the hands of a third party. Later in the war there developed a strong political lobby against giving further industrial aid to the Soviet Union in case it was used to turn out cheap Soviet goods on the world market.[61] In the end none of these pressures prevented the supply of advanced military equipment and machine tools, though what was sent was carefully monitored. Efforts to send American technical teams to help in the installation and operation of the equipment were generally frustrated. Soviet officials regarded this as a breach of trust and lack of confidence in Soviet technical capacity, but the failure to allow American engineers equal access to Soviet industry did as much as anything to sour relations between the two sides.

The transfer of technical information from the USSR was also very limited. In discussions between the two sides on the mutual exchange of information on synthetic rubber production the Soviet authorities obstructed the promised supply of Soviet technical assistance.[62] The problems of regulating the supply of technology between the three Allies prompted the British in late 1943 to call for tripartite agreement on the release of technical information and military secrets. Neither the American nor Soviet authorities were keen to reach a specific agreement and the proposal lapsed.[63] On the American side the supply of technical and scientific information was monitored on a day-to-day basis. The government released material "intended to assist the Soviets to kill Germans," but beyond that disclosures were "limited."[64] How significant the technical aid to the Soviet Union was during the war can only be guessed at. Though there was information showing that industrial equipment was poorly utilized and operated, it tended to be supplied by American informants already hostile to a generous aid program. The fact of Soviet economic resilience during the war says something of the use to which American technology was put. It is none the less difficult not to argue that a more open or regulated system of technical and scientific exchange between all three states might well have produced a more effective technical war effort. When British and American technologists put their heads together, as they did in 1943 when there developed an urgent need to increase fighter aircraft range for the bombing offensive, the result was a more rapid and purposive program of development.

Post-war economic co-operation had, from the beginning of the war, been seen by American leaders as a stepping-stone to a new world economic order. The Lend-Lease agreements themselves contained a loosely worded commitment to more liberal trading policies once the war was over. Roosevelt saw Lend-Lease as an instrument destined "to play a dominant part in weaving the pattern of the post-war policies of the United Nations."[65] There was a widespread feeling in Washington that economic rivalry and protectionism had played a major part in de-stabilizing world affairs in the 1930s. "Nations which act as enemies in the market place cannot long be friends at the council table," William Clayton, assistant secretary of state, told a meeting of Detroit businessmen in May 1945. "Most wars originate in economic causes."[66]

During the course of the war it also became clear to American leaders that the United States would have to take the initiative in planning the new economic order. "We are more convinced than ever," reported Stettinius in April 1944 after a visit to London, "that the United States must play an aggressive role in the creation of the international machinery necessary to ensure world security and economic stability."[67] The immediate result was the meeting at Bretton Woods in July 1944 at which preliminary agreement was reached on the establishment of an International Monetary Fund to stabilize world finances and a Bank of Reconstruction (later the World Bank) which would help war-ravaged countries cope with the costs of the transition from war to peace. Both the British and Americans were keen that the Soviet Union be included in the building of the new economic order, building on the foundation of war-time collaboration. Yet despite the formal commitment to stabilize the post-war economy, the approach of peace produced growing strains in the economic relations between the Allies.

There were two issues chiefly responsible for this state of affairs: the plans for post-war reconstruction and the unravelling of Lend-Lease. These were closely related, because the closer Allied victory came, the more obvious it was that Lend-Lease supplies would serve not only the military effort but the transition to peace as well. Yet the program had always stretched domestic political tolerance, even as a war-time necessity, and American opinion was understandably hostile to the idea that the U.S. taxpayer should continue to subsidize potential commercial competitors in peace-time. During 1944 the American government began negotiations with both London and Moscow on reducing the level of Lend-Lease supplies and rescheduling some of the orders as reconstruction goods, to be paid for under new loan agreements. The flow of Lend-Lease goods with an obvious post-war application was deliberately slowed down.[68]

Lend-Lease raised other problems as well. No formal agreement existed on how much, if any, the Allied governments would repay or give back of the goods supplied under the scheme. The British government regarded the goods, in effect, as a gift. When Stettinius visited London in April 1944 Churchill told him bluntly: "We aren't going to repay the Lend-Lease debts."[69] Roosevelt in general agreed with this interpretation, but he needed some kind of concession from Britain to satisfy domestic opinion, particularly as Britain's dollar assets began to grow rapidly during 1943 and 1944 thanks to the large American presence in Britain prior to D-Day.

There was no agreement either on what would happen to Lend-Lease once Germany had been defeated, for the United States carried the bulk of the war effort in the Far East. During 1944 the American authorities tried to insist on a new schedule for the what they called "Stage II," which would both reflect the balance of fighting in the Asian theater and reduce the chances that Lend-Lease goods would really be applied to reconstruction projects.[70]

The British Government agreed to all these changes with great reluctance. The British economy faced severe difficulties in the post-war world. The dollar balances were tiny by comparison with the estimated $15 billion of additional debts that Britain owed by the end of hostilities. By the autumn of 1944 the British government had succeeded in convincing Roosevelt that Britain's economic prospects were grim, but this situation was used by America to insist that Britain accept the aim of liberalizing world trade. In return Britain was promised continued aid after the defeat of Germany, when the restrictions on British exports would also be lifted, but funding would be at a much-reduced level. Anything else required by Britain for her post-war reconstruction was to be paid for under the terms of a loan to be negotiated between London and Washington.[71]

It proved much more difficult to reach firm agreement with the Soviet Union because the United States was not in a position to exert leverage so easily. From the Soviet viewpoint continued American aid was not only desirable, but was regarded as essential. Ambassador Harriman reported back to Washington in November 1943 that the "question of reconstruction is considered by the Soviet Government as, next to the war, the most important political as well as economic problem."[72] There was plenty of evidence that the Soviet government was keen to continue economic co-operation with America after the war, as well as Britain. Yet in practice little was achieved. British negotiations during 1944 broke down on Soviet rejection of the credit terms for supplying industrial equipment and materials for the reconstruction period.[73] With the United States no agreement could be reached on Stage II supplies, nor on new terms for the supply of goods with a post-war civilian application. The Soviet request for a credit of $1 billion in February 1944, and Molotov's later request in January 1945 for a reconstruction loan of $6.6 billion, were unfulfilled, partly because of the failure to get Soviet agreement on rescheduling Lend-Lease supplies, partly because of the Soviet refusal to supply detailed information about what the goods were to be used for and why they were needed.[74] It is easy to blame the breakdown of economic relations with the Soviet Union on the deteriorating political relations produced by arguments over Eastern Europe. Yet the failure to secure further economic co-operation predated the crisis in political relations; indeed some case can be made for arguing that the deterioration in economic relations was responsible for sharpening political conflicts.

There was initially no shortage of goodwill on both sides. As late as January 1945, Stettinius, by then secretary of state, discussed with Treasury Secretary Morgenthau American economic plans to "reassure the Soviet Government of our determination to co-operate with them. . . ." The same month Molotov made clear how much value the Soviet Union placed on reaching agreements "on a solid economic base."[75] What contributed to the breakdown of economic relations was a mutual misperception. On the American side it was assumed that the Soviet Union was facing severe economic pressures and would need reconstruction credits badly enough to agree to American conditions on reducing or redefining Lend-Lease and placing relations on a commercial footing. American officials found it hard to understand why Soviet negotiators were so unwilling to be open about Soviet requirements or the use to which Lend-Lease goods were being put. They also found it difficult, after what they regarded as a generous strategy of economic aid, to accept the Soviet desire to be treated on equal terms. On the Soviet side it was axiomatic from at least 1943 that the peace would also be difficult for the capitalist states, and their desire for post-war trade would give Soviet authorities a solid bargaining position. Stalin suspected that all American offers were really based on self-interested calculation and that America needed the USSR as much as Soviet reconstruction needed American products.[76]

The breakdown of economic co-operation involved a failure of communication. But as the negotiations dragged on the wider political and military arguments began to blend with the economic differences. By January 1945, American politicians were recommending that credit terms to the USSR be based on Soviet acceptance of a "more tolerant" attitude in Eastern Europe, or genuine adherence to the self-determination clauses of the Atlantic Charter.[77] Popular hostility began to reassert itself in American opinion of the Soviet Union. In Moscow the arguments over Lend-Lease were interpreted as a crude form of economic blackmail to bring pressure on Soviet policy in Eastern Europe or, later in 1945, to get the Soviet Union to join the war against Japan. Some, at least, of these views had substance. What really mattered was that they soured relations between the two allies and hardened attitudes over a whole range of issues.

The final blow for the British came with the sudden collapse of German resistance in May 1945 and the death of Roosevelt a few weeks before.

The new president, Harry Truman, was much influenced by economic nationalists in the State Department. Lend-Lease to the USSR was dramatically cut, and the Stage II supplies to Britain ignored. After vigorous representations from both allies some of the goods in the pipeline were restored. But when Japan was defeated a few months later, Truman ordered the immediate end of Lend-Lease. The decision was not discussed with either ally, though it was not unexpected.[78] Morgenthau, one of the architects of co-operation, condemned the policy of "cutting our allies adrift at a time when they were still maimed and crippled by war." Keynes talked gloomily of Britain's "economic Dunkirk." The Soviet government reacted with shocked dignity, but beneath the surface there was deep bitterness at what was seen as an act of calculated malevolence with little understanding of the bureaucratic and congressional politics that brought it about.[79] American termination of Lend-Lease brought to an end the era of economic collaboration. The reconstruction credit for the USSR collapsed as the political division widened. Britain was compelled to negotiate a large loan in December 1945, and in return gave way in principle on liberalizing trade and dismantling the Empire.

The breakdown of co-operation demonstrated that the war had produced what Adolf Berle of the State Department called "a temporary confluence of interest."[80] All three Allied states shared a common interest in defeating the Axis states. It made strategic sense, whatever the sacrifice involved, to use economic resources to the fullest, wherever they could be employed most effectively. In effect this meant distributing American resources. Only the United States had large, under-utilized economic capacity in 1941. Britain depended heavily on overseas supply, which in war-time she could ill afford; the Soviet Union lost a great deal of its economic potential in the German attack. The United States could have kept the economic surplus for her own war effort. But not only would this have made little strategic sense—for both Britain and the USSR had large forces willing to fight and waiting for equipment—it would also have flown in the face of American public opinion. By 1941 the American public came round to the view that the security both of the United States and of the democratic tradition were mortally threatened by fascism and that aid to Britain and the USSR was essential to defeat that threat.

Economic collaboration was founded on the central issue of expanding and distributing the American productive surplus. This basic fact had a number of implications. It gave American negotiators a strong bargaining position over the terms of economic aid, which was used, at least in the case of Britain, to compel a readjustment of the international economic order in America's favour. This was not done from unscrupulous self-interest alone. After the sequence of depression, protection, and war, American leaders were convinced that a solid peace could only be achieved "if countries work together and prosper together."[81] Victory was perceived as an opportunity to end the drift to economic nationalism apparent in the 1930s. Growing dependence on American economic and military power made it difficult for Britain to resist. The Soviet Union did do so, but only in the end at the cost of any post-war economic collaboration between the two states. In the second place, distributing the American surplus produced all kinds of political friction over issues of military priority, over shipping problems, over the use of Lend-Lease goods, over reconstruction. A higher level of mutual dependence might have reduced these tensions, but there was no alternative to American economic assistance, which was supplied generously enough but inevitably on American terms.

The contribution of economic co-operation to the overall war effort was vital. It enabled the Allies to achieve Roosevelt's stated aim "to outstrip the Axis powers in munitions of war."[82] By 1942 the Allies produced 100,000 aircraft, the Axis states 26,000; the figures for tank production were 58,000 and 11,000. Vast economic superiority gave the Allies greater freedom of manoeuvre, and was compensation for their lack of combat experience and for the sheer military effectiveness of German and Japanese forces. Even with such a large disparity in production it took three years of hard fighting to make the disparity tell. Without the vast resources and industrial capacity of the giant American economy, and the willingness of the American government and people to share this wealth with their fighting partners, there would have been no disparity to speak of. German access to the resources of the "New Order" in Europe, and Japanese seizure of the raw material wealth of East Asia might well have secured victory against Britain and the Soviet Union. American mobilization was essential to the Allied cause.

What was all the more remarkable was the ability of the three Allied economics to co-operate at all. There were strong differences in the ideological outlook of the three states which were reflected in different economic systems. Yet during the war the gap between the centralized, collectivist economy of Stalin's Russia and the free-market, entrepreneurial economies of the West grew narrower. In both Britain and the United States the government intervened in production and regulated economic life to an unprecedented degree. Commercial criteria largely disappeared in favor of the necessity of victory. As a result, government-sponsored aid for the Soviet system, or the transfer of goods between erstwhile trading rivals, generated much less friction than it might have done. The need for greater planning and allocation of resources turned all three Allied states towards the command economy model as long as the war hung in the balance. The failure to sustain co-operation much beyond 1945 reflected the return to pre-war economic practice, the re-establishment of a harsh Stalinism throughout the Soviet Union and its zones of occupation in Eastern Europe, and the return of a freer market for sustaining economic and trade competition in the West. War-time hopes of durable friendship foundered on these basic political differences.

NOTES

1. *Foreign Relations of the United States* (*FRUS*), 1941, 1, 840; Steinhardt to Hull, 3 October 1941, reporting Stalin's speech.

2. J. K. Libbey, "The American-Russian Chamber of Commerce," *Diplomatic History* 9 (1985), 247.

3. C. Richardson, "French Plans for Allied Attacks on the Caucasus Oil fields, January-April 1940," *French Historical Studies* 8 (1973); R. C. Cooke and R. C. Nesbit, *Target: Hitler's Oil. Allied Attacks on German Oil Supplies 1939-1945* (London, 1985), 21-63.

4. F. Leith-Ross, *Money Talks: Fifty Years of International Finance* (London, 1968), 277-78.

5. H. Ickes, *The Secret Diary of Harold L. Ickes* (3 vols.; London, 1955), 2, 469.

6. J. M. Haight, *American Aid to France 1938-1940* (New York, 1970).

7. R. Dallek, *Franklin D. Roosevelt and American Foreign Policy, 1932-1945* (New York, 1979), 200-205.

8. *FRUS,* 1940, 3, 12, Roosevelt speech at University of Virginia, 10 June 1940.

9. D. Waley, "Lend-Lease," in W. McNeill, *America, Britain and Russia: Their Co-operation and Conflict, 1941-1946* (Oxford, 1953), 774.

10. According to Lord Halifax: see Acheson memo, 3 October 1941, *FRUS,* 1941, 3, 38.

11. W. Kimball, "Beggar My Neighbor: America and the British Interim Finance Crisis 1940-1941," *Journal of Economic History* 19 (1969).

12. W. F. Kimball, ed., *Churchill & Roosevelt: The Complete Correspondence* (3 vols.; Princeton, 1984), 1, 102-109, Churchill to Roosevelt, 7 December 1940.

13. Ickes, *Secret Diary,* 2, 40. On the American side of the story see W. F. Kimball, *The Most Unsordid Act: Lend-Lease, 1939-1941* (Baltimore, 1969).

14. D. Reynolds, *The Creation of the Anglo-American Alliance 1937-1941* (London, 1981), 151-60.

15. J. C. Schneider, *Should America Go to War? The Debate over Foreign Policy in Chicago 1939-1941* (Chapel Hill, 1980), 57-83.

16. J. Colville, *The Fringes of Power: Ten Downing Street Diaries, 1939-1955* (London, 1985), 331-32, entry for 11 January 1941.

17. *FRUS,* 1941, 3, 13-15, Draft Proposal for a Temporary Lend-Lease Agreement, 28 July 1941; *The Memoirs of Cordell Hull* (2 vols.; London, 1948), 2, 1151-53.

18. McNeill, *America, Britain and Russia,* 781-83.

19. Colville, *Diaries*, 404-406, entry for 22 June 1941; see also entry for 21 June: "he will go all out to help Russia." R. H. Dawson, *The Decision to Aid Russia, 1941* (Chapel Hill, 1959), 121, and W. F. Kimball, *The Juggler: Franklin Roosevelt as Wartime Statesman* (Princeton, 1991), ch. 2.

20 F. L. Israel, ed., *The War Diary of Breckinridge Long: Reflections from the Years 1939-1944* (Lincoln, Nebr., 1966). See also G. T. Eggleston, *Roosevelt, Churchill and the World War II Opposition: A Revisionist Autobiography* (Old Greenwich, Conn., 1979), 127-28.

21. G. McJimsey, *Harry Hopkins: Ally of the Poor and Defender of Democracy* (Cambridge, Mass., 1987), 152-53.

22. W. A. Harriman and E. Abel, *Special Envoy to Churchill and Stalin 1941-1946* (London, 1976), 74.

23. E. Roosevelt, (ed), *The Roosevelt Letters 1928-1945* (3 vols.; London, 1952), 3, 385, Roosevelt to Stimson, 30 August 1941. See also W. Heinrichs, *Threshold of War: Franklin D. Roosevelt and American Entry into World War II* (Oxford, 1988), 105-106, 173-75 and generally G. C. Herring, *Aid to Russia, 1941-1945: Strategy, Diplomacy, and the Origins of the Cold War* (New York, 1973).

24. *FRUS,* 1941, 1, 769-70 and 771-2, Memorandum of conversation with Soviet Ambassador, 26 June 1941, and Steinhardt to Hull, 29 June 1941.

25. *FRUS,* 1941, 1, 815-16, Welles to Umansky, 2 August 1941; Memorandum by Henderson, Division of European Affairs, 19 August 1941.

26. Harriman, *Special Envoy,* 87-89; Dawson, *Decision,* 249-51.

27. Harriman, *Special Envoy,* 90. On details of the protocol see *FRUS,* 1941, 1, 841, Steinhardt to Hull, enclosing letter from Harriman to Roosevelt, 3 October 1941.

28. *The Public Papers of Franklin D. Roosevelt, 1941* (New York, 1950), 481, Roosevelt to Lend-Lease Administrator Stettinius, 7 November 1941; *FRUS,* 1941, 1, 851, Roosevelt to Stalin, 30 October 1941.

29. R. B. Levering, *American Opinion and the Russian Alliance, 1939-1945* (Chapel Hill, 1976), 61.

30. G. Ross, *The Foreign Office and the Kremlin: British Documents on Anglo-Soviet Relations* (Cambridge, 1984), 14; J. Beaumont, *Comrades in Arms: British Aid to Russia 1941-1945* (London, 1980), 62-63.

31. Beaumont, *Aid to Russia,* 66-67; R. Huhn Jones, *The Roads to Russia: United States Lend-Lease to the Soviet Union* (Norman, Okla., 1969), 50-51, 266-67.

32. See ch. 6. For a detailed discussion of the role of Lend-Lease in the USSR war effort, see H. P. Van Tuyll, *Feeding the Bear: American Aid to the Soviet Union, 1941-1945* (New York, 1989); M. Harrison, *Soviet Planning in Peace and War, 1938-1945* (Cambridge, 1985), 256-66; J. Barber and M. Harrison, *The Soviet Home Front, 1941-1945* (London, 1991), 189-90, 192, 221.

33. Harrison, *Soviet Planning,* 258.

34. Van Tuyll, *Feeding the Bear,* 66.

35. *Ibid.,* 182.

36. Waley "Lend-Lease," 781-82. On oil see D. J. Payton-Smith, *Oil: A Study of War-time Policy and Administration* (London, 1971), 467.

37. On American military attitudes see R. M. Leighton and R. W. Coakley, *Global Logistics and Strategy 1940-1943* (Washington, 1955), 83-96; W. F. Craven and J. L. Cate, *The Army Air Forces in World War II* (Chicago, 1948), 1, 128-34.

38. *FRUS,* 1941, 1, 843, Steinhardt to Hull, 6 October 1941.

39. Details in T. H. Veil Motter, *The Persian Corridor and Aid to Russia* (Washington, D.C., 1957), 23-28. During the war 4.66 million tons came through Iran, 9.24 via the Far Eastern route, and only 4.4 through the northern convoy route.

40. *FRUS,* 1942, 3, 726-27, 731: Faymonville to Stettinius, 3 October 1942, and Faymonville to Hopkins, 9 October 1942.

41. *FRUS,* 1941, 3, 22, Hull to Ambassador Winant, 6 August 1941.

42. A. P. Dobson, *US Wartime Aid to Britain, 1940-1946* (London, 1986), 130-33.

43. *FRUS,* 1941, 2, 10-12, Memorandum of Conversation between Keynes and Acheson, 28 July 1941.

44. *Ibid.,* 12.

45. For the sensitivity of the issue see the messages and drafts in Kimball, ed., *Churchill and Roosevelt,* 1, 344-46, 356-58. See also Kimball, *The Juggler,* ch. 3

46. H. G. Nicholas, ed., *Washington Dispatches 1941-1945: Weekly Political Reports from the British Embassy* (Chicago, 1981), 257-58, Report of 9 October 1943.

47. R. Young. *Congressional Politics in the Second World War* (New York, 1956), 180. Vandenberg was speaking in Congress on 11 March 1943.

48. R. Clark, *Anglo-American Economic Collaboration in War and Peace 1942-1947* (Oxford, 1982), 4-7.

49. H. D. Hall, *North American Supply* (London, 1955) 328-35, 341-42.

50. Waley, "Lend-Lease," 772.

51. S. M. Rosen, *The Combined Boards of the Second World War* (New York, 1951), 11.

52. *Ibid.,* 137.

53. Hall, *North American Supply,* 376-86; Rosen, *Combined Boards,* 193-204. See also E. Roll, *The Combined Food Board: A Study in Wartime International Planning* (Stanford, 1956).

54. R. W. Coakley and R.M. Leighton, *Global Logistics and Strategy 1943-1945* (Washington, 1968), 283.

55. Coakley and Leighton, *Global Logistics*, 628-31 and, generally, ch. 32.

56. Hall, *North American Supply*, 414-15.

57. *FRUS*, 1941, 1, 801, Memorandum of a conversation between Acheson and Umansky, 28 July 1941.

58. Hall, *North American Supply*, 190-91.

59. M. M. Gowing, *Britain and Atomic Energy 1940-1945* (London, 1965); J. Baylis, *Anglo-American Defence Relations 1939-1984* (London, 1984), 4-5, 16-32; A. S. Milward, *War, Economy and Society 1939-1945* (London, 1977), 194-97.

60. B. B. Berle and T. B. Jacobs, eds, *Navigating the Rapids 1918-1971: From the Papers of Adolf A. Berle* (New York, 1973), diary entry, 31 July 1941.

61. T. M. Campbell and G. C. Herring, eds., *The Diaries of Edward R. Stettinius, Jr., 1943-1946* (New York, 1975), 206-7.

62. *FRUS*, 1944, 4, 1104-5, Memorandum on Extent of Dispersal of U.S. Technical Information to Foreign Countries during World War II, 15 Jul 1944, Annex A "Interchange of Technical Information with USSR." See also J. R. Deane, *The Strange Alliance*, (London, 1947), 95-101.

63. *FRUS*, 1943, 3: 792-93, 794-97: Memorandum, State Dept. Division of European Affairs, 8 December 1943; and Memorandum by Division of European Affairs on technical co-operation, 23 December 1943.

64. *FRUS*, 1944, 4, 1101, "Extent of Dispersal of US Technical Information. . . ."

65. *Washington Dispatches*, 47, report of 20 June 1942.

66. R. A. Pollard, "Economic Security and the Origins of the Cold War; Bretton Woods, the Marshall Plan, and American Rearmament, 1944-50," *Diplomatic History*, 9 (1985), 272.

67. *FRUS*, 1944, 3, 1-2, Report to the Secretary of State from Stettinius on his Mission to London, 22 May 1944.

68. Dobson, *Wartime Aid*, 185 ff; on relations with the USSR see *FRUS*, 1944, 4, 1032-1152.

69. *Stettinius Diaries*, 61, entry for 19 April 1944.

70. Hall, *North American Supply*, 441-46.

71. *FRUS*, 1944, 3, 53-56, Memorandum by Secretary of State for President, "Lend-Lease and General Economic Relations with the United Kingdom in 'Phase 2,'" 8 September 1944.

72. *FRUS,* 1943, 3, 788, Harriman to State Dept., 16 November 1943.

73. *Soviet-British Relations in the Period of the Great Patriotic War of 1941-1945* (Moscow, 1983) 2, 94-95.

74. On the loan requests see *FRUS,* 1944, 4: 1041-42, Harriman to Hull, 1 February 1944; *FRUS,* 1945, 5, 942, Harriman to Hull, 4 January 1945.

75. *FRUS,* 1945, 5, 963, Memorandum of Conversation between Morgenthau and Stettinius, 17 January 1945; and 942, Harriman to Hull, 4 January 1945 reporting discussion with Molotov.

76. This view had been suggested to Stalin by Donald Nelson when they met in Moscow in October 1943 (*FRUS,* 1943, 3, 780) and it was certainly one held by Ambassador Harriman as well.

77. *FRUS,* 1945, 5, 945-47, Harriman to Hull, 4 January 1945.

78. G. C. Herring, "Lend-Lease to Russia and the Origins of the Cold War 1944-1945," *Journal of American History* 61 (1969): 93-114; Dobson, *Wartime Aid,* 219-21; Leon Martel, *Lend-Lease, Loans and the Coming of the Cold War: a Study of the Implementation of Foreign Policy* (Boulder, Colo., 1979), 159-60.

79. Martel, *Lend-Lease,* 161.

80. *Berle Papers,* 375.

81. Pollard, "Economic Security," 272.

82. *The Public Papers and Addresses of Franklin Delano Roosevelt, 1941,* Samuel I. Rosenman, ed. (13 vols.; New York, 1938-50), 214, Message to Congress on the Operation of the Lend-Lease Act, 10 June 1941.

PART III ■ HOME FRONT

9

GREAT BRITAIN: THE PEOPLE'S WAR?

Jose Harris

The "home front" in the Second World War has come to occupy a unique position in modern British folklore. The war is widely regarded as perhaps the only period in the whole of British history during which the British people came together as a metaphysical entity—an entity that transcended the divisions of class, sect, self-interest, and libertarian individualism that normally constitute the highly pluralistic and fragmented structure of British society. This transformation is perceived as having occurred on two levels, the practical and the moral. The circumstances of total war forced the British government out of its traditional penchant for market economics and administrative muddling-through, and into adoption of planning, rationing, and economic management. As a consequence, the British people were ultimately subject to a greater degree of state-regulation and compulsory mobilization of physical resources, including both male and female labour, than any other combatant power except the Soviet Union. And, secondly, the sense of desperate unity forged by common danger—particularly during the retreat from Dunkirk and the Battle of Britain—engendered among the population at large a widespread and unprecedented ethic of self-sacrifice, social levelling, and community spirit. The phrase "the Dunkirk spirit" has entered into the English language as a synonym for cheerful communal endeavour against hopeless odds (often used by young people who have only the haziest notions about what Dunkirk actually was). "People were friendlier in those days" is the common refrain of all surveys of public opinion that refer back to the war; a sentiment that becomes ever more marked as British society in the 1980s and 1990s has moved dramatically away from the post-war collectivist consensus into an era of privatization and free competition.

Popular recollection of the war was for a long time reflected in, and perhaps to a certain extent influenced by, contemporary political, journalistic, and autobiographical accounts. Politicians writing both during and after the war continually reaffirmed an image of the war as the cradle of the welfare state, as the launchingpad of Keynesianism, and as an epoch of unprecedented social and moral solidarity. Evacuation, rationing, conscription, and aerial bombardment were credited with bringing people of all classes together and with opening the eyes of the privileged to the condition of the poor. There was much stress upon the link between the confraternity of the common man and the rise of new methods of social organization. "Immediately a nation is involved in a great crisis . . . it is bound to become collectivist," wrote the trade-unionist minister of labour Ernest Bevin. "Individualism is bound to give place to social action; competition and scramble to order, and the rule of law has to be applied in the place of anarchy."[1] A "revolution" had taken place "in the minds of the people," claimed another Labour minister, Emanuel Shinwell; while former Conservative Foreign Secretary Anthony Eden declared that "the old world is dead; none of us can escape from revolutionary changes, even if we would."[2] William Beveridge, author of the famous 1942 Beveridge Plan that was later regarded as the blueprint for the British welfare state, frequently referred to his social security scheme as a "British revolution"; a "revolutionary moment in the world's history is a time for revolutions, not for patching."[3] Popular broadcaster J. B. Priestley constantly dwelt on the theme that the war was "a contest between power and property, on the one hand, and the community and creativeness, on the other . . . a revolution by consent, a revolt against too-long rule by old men whose ideal for their country was a comfortable old age."[4]

Similar views were expressed in the immediately post-war years by the official war histories. The war-time rationing system and food control system was judged by its official historian to have embodied "a revolution in the attitude of the state to the feeding of its citizens"; while the financial historian R. S. Sayers portrayed the switch to a Keynesian-style war-time budgetary program, with its emphasis on compulsory saving and confiscatory taxation of higher incomes, as "the manifestation in the financial sphere of the national change of heart that marked the summer of 1940."[5] Similarly Richard Titmuss's *Problems of Social Policy*—still perhaps the most influential and imaginatively compelling account of the domestic and civilian theatre of war—portrayed the Second World War in general, and Dunkirk and the Blitz in particular, as bringing about a revolution in popular expectations about the role of the state. Government was seen no longer, Titmuss argued, as merely the guarantor of private freedom and the provider of last-resort public assistance to the very poor. "Instead, it was increasingly regarded as a proper function or even obligation of Government to ward off distress and strain among not only the poor but almost all classes of society . . . the mood of the people changed, and in sympathetic response values changed as well." The war had entailed a great and permanent "extension of social discipline"—a discipline that was only tolerable in a democratic society because it was combined with the removal of deep social inequalities. Such a change, Titmuss implied, had brought in its wake not merely administrative and attitudinal change but an intellectual revolution in the fundamental tenets of social and political theory.[6]

In face of the near unanimity of commentators writing during and shortly after the war, it must be a bold historian who attempts to challenge this view of the social history of the Second World War period. And one would be foolhardy as well as bold to ignore popular memory, which must always be a benchmark against which to measure changes in popular sentiment and social structure. If the British people in the 1940s felt themselves to be more equal and more united than ever before, then this in itself is an overwhelmingly significant fact that no amount of analysis of unequal wealth and income distibution can gainsay. Over the past two decades, however, a combination of factors has led to increasing re-assessment and modification of many aspects of the conventional wisdom: the opening up of many of the official and private archives of the war period; the shift of ideological climate in Britain towards a more critical evaluation of collectivism and state control; and the sheer fact of judgmental distance and perspective, as the war recedes inexorably into half-forgotten history. All these factors have led to an opening up of debate and controversy about the social history of the war, and its longer-term implications for the structure and character of British society. These debates centre on many issues that cannot be adequately dealt with in a short article; but the most crucial themes may be summarized as follows:

(a) First, there has been increasing scepticism among historians of both right and left about the supposedly "revolutionary" impact of the war upon British social structure and institutions. It has been suggested that in spite of high war-time taxation, the war made little permanent impact (and indeed surprisingly little short-term impact) upon the distribution of wealth; that the dramatic scientific breakthroughs induced by the war (in electronics, nuclear physics, and biochemistry) were grafted onto an industrial base that remained ramshackle, underfunded, managerially inept, and culturally hostile to innovation and advanced methods of production; that, in spite of the mass mobilization of both men and women, the war reinforced rather than subverted traditional class and gender roles; and that the very fact of ultimate victory in the war helped to arrest rather than accelerate change by buttressing and legitimizing many obsolete and reactionary social, economic, and governmental institutions.[7]

(b) Secondly, there has been much criticism of the "consensual" image of the war. Recent research on the origins of the welfare state and the planning of post-war reconstruction has emphasized not the benevolent unanimity but the many conflicts of principle and policy that prevailed within government and party circles over such issues as provision of a national health service, full employment, universal secondary education, and the nature and extent of "postwar reconstruction."[8] At the level of popular attitudes, historians have pointed to such factors as the very high level of strikes that prevailed in many key industries, particularly in the last three years of the war; to evidence of widespread popular participation in the black market and evasion of government controls; and to the often-expressed resentment of soldiers, and more particularly of soldiers' wives, against the high wages and "cushy numbers" enjoyed by workers in "reserved occupations" (popularly known as "Civvy Street"). There has been questioning too of the mythological and methodological basis of the accumulation of popular memory by which the picture of popular consensus has been built up. Historians have become much more sensitive to the fact that many of the "sources" for the war-time consensus were themselves part of the consensus-creating process. Cinema, radio, war artists, Pathe News, and Picture Post were not passive recording angels but active agencies for promoting a certain frame of citizen mind. Press reporting was inevitably slanted by the fact that expressions of "alarm and despondency" were officially discouraged by a vigorous propaganda campaign; while regulation 39B issued under the Emergency Powers (Defence) Act made it a criminal offence to publish material "likely to be prejudicial to the prosecution of the war or the defence of the realm." And, from a rather different angle, the re-interviewing by Tom Harrisson of people whom he had interviewed for the war-time Mass Observation surveys showed that (not just occasionally but typically) personal memories of war-time episodes differed wildly from on-the-spot impressions of a quarter of a century before.[9]

(c) Thirdly, there has been a widespread reaction, partly ideological, partly based simply on scrutiny of primary sources, against what David Cannadine has called the "welfare state triumphalism" of much British historical writing about the social aftermath of the Second World War.

Historians have begun to question the view that mass participation in the war effort led inevitably to the creation of the post-war welfare state: while some who still share this view have claimed that the war-time enthusiasm for state welfare was to have disastrous long-term consequences for the subsequent growth of British society. This claim has been most forcibly expressed by Correlli Barnett's *The Audit of War* (1986), a book that suggested that the atmosphere of sentimental social solidarity induced by the war had given rise to wholly unrealistic, utopian expectations of the post-war world: expectations that generated programs of job security, deficit financing, universal welfare, and indifference to incentives and overhead costs, which led inexorably to Britain's post-war economic decline. And, less controversially than Barnett, many other historians have analysed the archives of war-time social policy formation and have come to the conclusion that the process was a more complex one than earlier historians had often implied. It now appears that the breach with the past was less abrupt, and that the range of ideologies and interest groups which had a hand in shaping Britain's post-war welfare state system was both broader and less mutually harmonious than was often supposed.[10]

For the rest of this essay I shall outline the main areas of war-time social change, and review the significance of those changes in the light of the controversies outlined above. I shall then try to suggest some possible alternative approaches to the social history of the period and to identify certain themes that have been either ignored or relatively neglected.

Firstly, then, the impact of the war on Britain's traditional social and governing institutions. Did the war period bring fundamental changes in social structure and organization in Britain, or was the semblance of change merely a reflex of the peculiar circumstances of war-time? And, insofar as such changes did occur, were they directly induced by the war, or were they part of a much longer-term process of societal change that was occurring anyway, in which the war was merely a passing phase?

Evidence for far-reaching institutional changes directly linked to the war can be found at many levels—legal, political, social, administrative, and intellectual. The passage of the Emergency Powers Act in August 1939 meant that throughout the war the civil liberties traditionally enjoyed by British citizens were curtailed or in abeyance; and between 1939 and 1945 thousands of aliens (many of them Jewish refugees from Nazism), hundreds of fascists, communists and Trotskyites, and a small handful of industrial militants were detained for shorter or longer periods without trial.[11] Even during the first nine months of war—generally treated by historians as the last ineffective whimper of the regime of

Neville Chamberlain—government commitment to total war policies in the form of conscription, rationing, mass evacuation, requisitioning and excess profits tax came much more swiftly than in 1914. And after the fall of Norway and the invasion of France—events which precipitated the replacement of Chamberlain by Churchill and the entry of Labour into coalition—pressure for new men, new methods, new policies, and new administrative machinery became much more powerful and comprehensive. The traditional arena of high politics was taken over by a nexus of new policy-making institutions: a small co-ordinating War Cabinet, a series of specialist Cabinet committees to supervise key areas of non-military policy, and a cluster of new ministries responsible for supply, information, aircraft production, economic warfare, and reconstruction. From mid-1940 onwards Whitehall was buzzing with business men, academics, and trade unionists, many of them brandishing new brooms with which they aimed to sweep away the last vestiges of orthodox economics and administrative laissez-faire. The appointment of Ernest Bevin as minister of labour and of Kingsley Wood (a leading commercial insurance expert) as Chancellor of the Exchequer, symbolized both a new relationship between government, big business, and labour, and a by-passing and downgrading of conventional party channels. It was Kingsley Wood who imported J. M. Keynes into the Treasury and in 1941 promoted the first "Keynesian" budget—a budget that introduced centralized regulation of national levels of consumption and investment via the mechanisms of low interest rates, high taxation, cost-of-living subsidies for those with low incomes, and compulsory saving for the better-off. Financial controls were paralleled by a massive extension of physical controls over manpower and raw materials, state takeover of many factories and public utilities, and very close state regulation of the management of private industry.[12] As Edward R. Murrow told the people of America in his daily broadcast from London on 22 May 1940, the British government was "taking over control of all persons and all property . . . everything save conscience can now be conscripted in this country."[13]

These changes in governmental structure and economic policy were accompanied by cataclysmic disruption of social life and by an unprecedented degree of state intervention in the provision of social services. At the most basic level the events of total war transformed the physical and material realities of daily life for large numbers of the civilian population, no less dramatically than for those serving in the armed forces. Over the six years of war 62,000 civilians were killed by bombing, and nearly a quarter of a million suffered major or minor injuries. A quarter of a million homes were destroyed and nearly 4 million damaged out of a total housing stock of about 10 million. Two and a quarter million people were made homeless by the worst period of aerial bombardment (August 1940 to June 1941), a fifth of the nation's schools and hospitals were put out of action, and large areas of the business and manufacturing areas of cities and ports were damaged or destroyed.[14]

Such events precipitated a massive pragmatic revolution in British social and public administration. As soon as war broke out in September 1939 the government began to implement pre-war contingency plans to allay popular panic and to protect the health and safety of the civilian population. One and a half million women and children were evacuated from the major cities during the first few months of war, compelling local authorities (reinforced by a wide range of voluntary agencies) to set up reception centres and food and clothing depots and to arrange foster homes in provincial villages and towns. Many trickled back to London and other large cities during the "phoney war" period; but the onset of the *Luftwaffe* bombardment in August 1940 drove many back to the countryside again. Over the whole war period more than 4 million mothers and children were evacuated, some to camps and hostels, a privileged few to North America, the vast majority to the homes of private citizens in the rural counties. From the start of the war all the nation's hospitals—elite voluntary institutions, local authority and Poor Law infirmaries, small cottage hospitals, and thousands of temporary Nissen huts—were requisitioned by a single, national Emergency Medical Service; and many doctors and nurses who had worked in the voluntary sector became aware for the first time of the appalling conditions widely prevailing in many old Poor Law institutions. Moreover, aerial bombardment and medical concentration on acute injury cases soon precipitated an unexpected crisis in the treatment of long-term non-emergency illness. In the summer of 1940 air-raid shelters in big cities were becoming distressingly full of poor, chronically sick, homeless old people who had nowhere else to go—a problem that forced central government for the first time in British history to take direct financial responsibility for civilian medical care and provision of hospital beds.[15]

Similarly, the gradually intensifying economic blockade forced government into the bulk purchase and rationing of nearly all essential materials. Plans for food rationing had been laid as early as 1936, partly to prevent starvation and malnutrition, but partly also (a lesson learnt from the First World War) as a buffer against hoarding, profiteering, and rampant inflation. Petrol was rationed from the start of the war; butter, bacon, sugar, meat, tea, and margarine in 1940; cheese and personal clothing in 1941; soap, sweets, and chocolate in 1942; though throughout the war the government managed to avoid the symbolic blow to civilian morale that would have been dealt by the rationing of bread. "Queueing" for food and retail goods, unknown in peace-time Britain, became a central fact of life. Special rations were allowed to children, nursing mothers, and workers in heavy industry; and food prices were kept down by exchequer subsidies that amounted by 1945 to £200 million per annum (a policy designed not merely to maintain standards of nutrition but to reconcile consumers to high levels and low threshholds of direct personal taxation). Regulated production of rationed "utility" clothing and furniture (the former uniformly hideous, the latter sparsely elegant) gradually replaced production by competitive private enterprise. "National restaurants" were set up in all urban areas to provide cheap, nutritious meals for working people, and from 1941 onwards there was a great expansion of school meals and works canteens. Throughout the country allotments, railway embankments, suburban tennis courts, and the back yards of the poor sprang to life with the growing of vegetables and the keeping of poultry, thereby helping both to maintain standards of nutrition and to fuel the invisible workings of a widespread, localized exchange-and-barter economy. Conscription of men between the ages of 18 and 45 into the armed forces led to the gradual absorption into industry of the residue of the pre-war unemployed, and to massive voluntary recruitment of women (leading in early 1941 to industrial conscription of childless women between the ages of 20 and 30). And in many spheres the powers of local authorities—the traditional backbone of British social welfare administration and parish-pump democracy—were severely curtailed, their functions being taken over by non-elected, Whitehall-appointed regional commissioners with wide emergency and discretionary powers.[16]

All these changes in themselves generated massive upheaval in the lives and assumptions of ordinary people in Britain—accustomed as they were to a somewhat ramshackle free-market economy, to a very parochial and family-centred social structure, and to government by remote control. From the start of the war, however, there were articulate pressure groups in many parts of British society arguing that the experiments of war-time should be seen not merely as transient emergency measures, but as the launching pad for permanent and fundamental structural change. War-time developments in hospital and health care, social and community work, infant feeding, and provision for mothers and children were increasingly viewed as precedents for permanent social reform; and similarly, the government was urged to treat the war economy as a model for economic management in time of peace. As the sacrifices required of the British people intensified it was widely urged that a prospect of radical "social reconstruction" was not merely desirable in itself but an essential means of "giving the British people something worth fighting for" and of sustaining citizen morale. "Reconstruction committees" were set up in all parties, and demands for a "British New Deal" came from across the political spectrum; from liberals like Keynes and Beveridge, from socialists like R. H. Tawney and Evan Durbin, and from Tory social reformers like Hugh Molson and Quintin Hogg.[17] Surveys of public opinion in the early years of war uncovered a widespread swing towards a rather ill-defined popular "collectivism." In spite of the Nazi-Soviet pact there was much interest in and admiration for the planning achievements of Russia; and long before Hitler launched his attack on the Soviet Union there appears to have been a latent popular belief in Britain that the pact was "not to be taken very seriously" and that "Russia is really on our side."[18]

The reformist and state-interventionist mood infected many civil servants, and from 1940 onwards plans were being laid in Whitehall for far-reaching extension of health, education, workmen's compensation, and social insurance services. Public enquiries were commissioned into community control of land values and town and country planning, and a Ministry of Reconstruction was set up under Arthur Greenwood (later succeeded by Sir William Jowitt). Modest plans slowly maturing in the corridors of Whitehall were overtaken, however, in the autumn of 1942 by a dramatic event—in the form of the Beveridge Plan on social security, which catapulted the issue of "post-war reconstruction" into the arena of popular discussion and the mass media. Beveridge's report on Social Insurance and Allied Services called for far-reaching state action to maintain permanent full employment, to set up a national health service, and to secure the British people against poverty by means of family allowances and comprehensive subsistence-level social insurance. The political essence of Beveridge's scheme was that social security should no longer be confined to "the poor" or the "working-class" but should be available to all social groups, without regard to means or social status and without the stigma of dependence; principles that rapidly became the hall-mark of the war-time reconstruction movement. The plan received wide coverage in the press, and was widely portrayed as a sort of social Magna Carta. Early in 1943 widespread popular pressure and a backbench revolt in Parliament forced a somewhat reluctant government to commit itself to eventual implementation of the Beveridge proposals and to detailed post-war planning.[19] This commitment resulted in a long series of White Papers on education, full employment, social insurance, a national health service, family allowances, and care of neglected children.[20] None of these later papers made quite the dramatic impact of Beveridge, but together they rewrote the agenda of public debate in British domestic politics and defined the issues upon which all parties fought the general election of 1945. They formed the basis of the social legislation of 1944-48 that created the British welfare state.

There can be little doubt that these events of war-time affected both the lives of ordinary citizens and the structure and powers of government in many ways. How far did they add up to the kind of underlying "social revolution" that was claimed by many contemporaries? This question may be posed and answered at many levels. At the political and administrative level the war precipitated certain fundamental changes in the relationship of government and society that were to prove irreversible, not merely in the short term but throughout the post-war years. The staff of central government at the end of the war was nearly twice as large as it had been in 1939, local government was never again to recover the degree of autonomy that it had enjoyed in the pre-war era, the annual budget was never to lose its war-time role as the major instrument of macro-economic management, and government policies of all kinds impinged far more directly than in the 1930s on the structure of everyday life. Government after 1945 never recovered from the war-time expectation that it should continually "do something" in all spheres, rather than merely buttressing, subsidizing, and policing autonomous local and private social and economic arrangements. The fact that the 1945 election resulted in the first-ever absolute majority for Labour was in itself indicative, not necessarily of radical social change, but certainly of radical departure from the coalition politics of the 1930s.

On the other hand it has been shown that the war brought little radical change in the actual personnel and composition of government. Labour itself, at least in the House of Commons, was a much more middle-class party than it had been in 1929. The civil service in 1945 was only marginally less dominated by Oxbridge humanities graduates than in the 1930s, and there was no permanent penetration into the upper reaches of public administration of scientists, businessmen, or representatives of the working class.[21] Other traditional governing institutions were in many respects positively strengthened by the war. Parliament, for example, which throughout the 1930s had been attacked from both left and right as hopelessly unsuited to the needs of modern industrial democracy, during the course of the war resumed its ancient role as one of the great representative symbols of liberty and the popular will (a somewhat paradoxical reversal of image, in view of the fact that parliamentary control over government during the war years was weaker than it had been for several centuries).[22] The British monarchy, which had spent much of the 1930s in a state of squalid crisis, operated throughout the war as a potent symbol of national unity, and by 1945 was probably more universally popular than at any previous moment in its history of nearly a thousand years.

Similar double-edged points may be made about many other aspects of social and institutional structure. The war undoubtedly brought some changes in the distribution of income. Average real pre-tax incomes rose slightly over the course of the war, women's wages rose more than men's, unskilled wages rose more than skilled wages, and wages generally rose more than salaries and profits.[23] This pattern was accentuated by the impact of steeply progressive taxation, including a 100 per cent tax on war profits, and many people on professional and rentier incomes were undoubtedly worse off in real terms in 1945 than they had been in 1939. The war virtually eliminated private domestic service, thereby obliterating one of the major traditional frontiers of status and social class. On the other hand the structure of private wealth changed surprisingly little (in the late 1940s 80 per cent of private assets were still held by the richest 10 per cent of the population).[24] And, in spite of the economic gains made by employed women, female earnings in 1945 were still only 55 per cent those of adult males. Moreover, women throughout the work force continued to be largely confined to the most humdrum, repetitive, and menial positions; and there was an almost universal expectation that women who were married would return to husbands, hearth, and home as soon as the war was over.[25] Evacuation and mobilization tore apart many families, sexual mores became marginally more permissive (particularly among younger women), illegitimate births increased by 25 per cent, and the annual rate of divorce rose from one to five per hundred. But despite these difficulties, Mass Observation surveys recorded "the continued and amazing strength of family feelings, loyalties, and economic bonds"; and a recent study of war-time family life concludes that the nuclear family emerged from the Second World War stronger, more tightly knit, and more home-centred than it had ever been before.[26]

Similarly the class structure was dented but by no means dismantled—and may indeed have been strengthened by the ladders of rapid upward mobility that certain sectors of war administration and the war economy gave to ambitious new men. Fashionable educational thought by the end of the war had rejected the notion of an hereditary class hierarchy, but had replaced it by a new one: a meritocracy of precisely measurable intellectual talent. Proposals from progressive Conservatives for the integration of public schools into the state education sector foundered upon a mixture of upper-class defence of privilege and lower-class inverted snobbery. In spite of the equalizing effects of war, access to social services of all kinds remained widely *un*equal—determined not just by class but by region and local tradition. (Scotland, for example, enjoyed a ratio of medical services to population much more favourable than that of Britain as a whole, while that of Wales was much worse.) Moreover, the war-time growth of some social services has to be set against the war-time collapse of others; many schools had to close for long periods, and there was widespread disruption of school health services, maternity clinics, and all forms of non-acute medicine.

Finally, psychological attitudes to social change and to the adoption of new social roles were widely contradictory and ambiguous. The unpublished research of the Nuffield College Social Reconstruction survey in 1942-43 found a widespread popular desire for greater health care, income maintenance, and job security, combined with an almost universal hostility to the prospect of increased official direction of private lives.[27] In spite of the popular euphoria surrounding the Beveridge report, government surveys of popular opinion in the latter years of the war found widespread indifference or hostility to the idea of systematic social reconstruction[28]—a fact that may partly account for the lack of commitment to social reformist issues shown by Churchill and his closest advisers. Moreover, many archival sources suggest that throughout society those most vocally pressing for structural change were often those least willing to contemplate changes that would affect their own interests. Doctors, for example, successfully campaigned for retention of private contracts within a new, centrally funded public health service. Trade unionists demanded permanent state maintenance of full employment together with instant post-war dismantling of controls over deployment of labour, while many employers wanted cheap state loans or interest-free credit but as little as possible of any other form of permanent government control.[29]

What of the evidence for a new national war-time consensus based on a convergence of political beliefs, unity of goals, and a heightened sense of national social solidarity? We know from many sources, from the testimony of right-wing liberals like Lionel Robbins to ex-communists like Stephen Spender, that many intellectuals felt the war suddenly descending upon them like a great moral blanket, smothering and screening out the gigantic battles over principles and ideology that had polarised the intellectual politics of the 1930s.[30] Faced with the menace of Hitler in the Low Countries, in 1939 and 1940 many convinced and card-carrying British communists simply ignored their orders from Moscow and volunteered for military service. The politics of appeasement, which only two years earlier had commanded widespread public support, now became the object of universal revilement. Throughout the war period, from the "phoney war" to VE-Day, from Dunkirk to doodlebugs, surveys of public opinion suggested an extraordinary degree of unanimous and single-minded commitment to unqualified resistance to Hitler. Doubtless, like other aspects of consensual politics, that unanimity was to a certain extent cultivated by the organs of mass opinion. But anyone familiar with the private archives of the period cannot fail to be struck by how unusual it is (in marked contrast to the First World War) to find expressions of the view that the war was not worth fighting or that Britain should seek a negotiated peace.[31] (When there were hints of the latter in elite circles the popular response was one of widespread scorn and indignation.[32])

Unanimity in opposing Hitler was one thing, however; social solidarity and brotherly love towards one's fellow citizens was quite another. After a brief lull in 1939 and early 1940, crimes against property soared throughout the war. Criminologists who had previously ascribed anti-social behaviour to poverty and deprivation now switched their attention to affluence, high wages, and the felonious opportunities offered by the black-out. Indictable offences known to the police rose from 305,114 in 1940 to 478,394 in 1945, while the proportion of the population over 16 found guilty of such offences rose from 150 to 223 per thousand. Female criminal convictions nearly doubled, male juvenile delinquency increased by 60-70 per cent and female juvenile delinquency by 100-120 per cent between 1938 and 1944.[33] Days lost in strikes never reached the astronomical levels of the First World War, but were still high enough to throw some doubt upon the image of national solidarity. The black market still awaits detailed historical investigation; but almost certainly its operations were more extensive than the relatively low levels of prosecution and conviction suggest.[34] And many contemporary records suggest that although large-scale and professional black marketeering was deeply resented, informal disposal of "government surplus" and of goods picked up during air raids was indulged in even by the most respectable citizens—and indeed was cheerfully regarded as part of the "war effort" and the "struggle for national survival."

Historians who have emphasised the theme of social unity have concentrated in particular on four main areas of social life: mass evacuation, military and industrial conscription, the "social reconstruction" movement, and the communal experience of aerial bombardment in the great industrial and commercial cities. So far as I know, no scrutineer of the archives has yet attempted to demythologize the heightened sense of common humanity and melting of class differences that was apparently induced throughout Britain by the Blitz (though even at the time the enforced merging of proletarians and plutocrats was portrayed with barbed irony as well as good humour).[35] In other spheres, however, recent historical writing (including the memoirs of ex-evacuees) has viewed the class unity theme with increasing qualification. It has been suggested that far from generating social sympathy, the evacuation movement served to confirm preconceived rural and middle-class stereotypes about the savage and insanitary habits of the inabitants of city slums. Many rural and suburban households did their best to evade or get rid of evacuees, and where they were unavoidable often treated them with marked lack of sympathy and social imagination. Head lice, insanitary habits, and above all bed-wetting—the latter often induced by the trauma of enforced removal from parents—were widespread flashpoints of recurrent social tension.[36] Domestic servants in particular were haughtily disdainful of the children of the London poor. Ministry of Health officials found that

> it was almost impossible to find billets for an unmarried mother with a new-born baby, and in the opinion of voluntary welfare workers some of these mothers would not have been suitable for billeting. They needed a period of convalescence and training before they were fit to be in charge of a baby.[37]

Similarly, it has been claimed that conscription and war production, far from acting as social levellers, were fraught with continuing conflicts based on skill, status, sector, gender, wages, and social class, a claim for which there is extensive contemporary support in both the published and unpublished records of Mass Observation. "It is unfortunate that so many of the officers have loud, unfriendly, patronizing voices, and speak what they think is King's English with so much affectation and over-emphasis," recorded a woman voluntary worker who was involved in recruiting working-class girls into the ATS. "The officers seem to think that if a girl speaks with a Northern accent she is uneducated, uncouth, insensitive—in short a barbarian, and proceed to treat her as if she were a kitchen-maid being interviewed by an ill-bred duchess."[38] A Mass Observation survey of 1942 (published just before the Beveridge Report with its ecstatic vision of the unity of the British people) found that throughout industry there was widespread resentment of both management and government, widespread absenteeism and work-dissatisfaction, widespread fear of displacement by women and unskilled workers, and widespread anger among managers about the perceived breakdown of industrial discipline that had been brought about by war.

> In some sections of industry the things one group says about another are more belligerent than the things either of them say [*sic*] about the enemy, Germany, Italy, Japan . . . In the conflict between employers and men . . . one looked and listened in vain for any sign of a unity binding all parties in the fight against Germany . . . Both sides claim to be concerned only with improving the situation to increase the strength of the struggle against Fascism, but nevertheless, the real war which is being fought here today is still pre-war, private and economic.[39]

Lack of consensus has also been a central theme of recent writing on the reconstruction movement. Two decades ago historians emphasised the dominant role of a widely diffused, largely non-partisan "progressive ideology" of which Beveridge and Keynes were "the patron saints." By contrast, more recent historians have stressed the extreme reluctance of the coalition government to espouse social reform, the deep divisions within the Conservative party about reformist goals, and the yawning gulf between the cautious pragmatism of Labour ministers and the far more radical and utopian aspirations both of Labour backbenchers and of Labour supporters in the country at large.[40] And, finally, the 1945 election result itself—following upon Labour's withdrawal from government and Churchill's insistence on calling an early poll—may be seen as evidence of both politicians and people turning their backs on the politics of consensus after a prolonged interlude of coalition government that stretched back to 1931.

Thirdly, there is the issue of the impact of war upon the emergence of the "welfare state." It is perhaps important to emphasize that the putative progression from "people's war" to "universal social welfare" was never quite so "triumphalist," even in the writings of the 1940s and 1950s, as Cannadine and others have claimed. On the contrary, even Richard Titmuss, who first spelled out the causal connection between the high moral tone of war-time and the growth of "the caring society," *also* emphasized the crucial role of competing interest groups in social-policy formation, and the continuing prevalence in post-war British society of long-term structural inequalities.[41]

Titmuss did, however, construct a loose chronological model of welfare-state history, followed by many other post-war historians, in which the depressed and deprived society of the 1930s gave way to the universal social security of the 1940s and 1950s—the agent of change being central government intervention, and the catalyst of change being the social and moral revolution of the Second World War. This pattern of interpretation has been questioned and modified over the last two decades on a number of fronts. Although the "pessimist" view of the 1930s still has powerful adherents, many recent studies have questioned the traditional account of the British social services during that decade. It has been shown that public social welfare expenditure during the 1930s in fact grew at a faster rate than in any other peace-time period before the late 1960s; and that far from being a time of stagnation and retrogression the inter-war period was a time of experiment and innovation in many areas of social reform. In many repects British social welfare provision in the 1930s was more extensive than anywhere else in Europe. In particular, the exponential growth rate of health services in the hands of local authorities and approved societies *before* 1939 was considerably higher than under central government *after* the Second World War; and although the war is still seen as a unique catalyst of centralization, this in itself is no longer viewed as a self-evident litmus test of progressive social change.[42]

More specifically, studies of war-time social policy now present a more complex and ambivalent picture than that once fashioned by the official war historians. Archival sources suggest that the range of interests and ideologies involved in reconstruction was much broader than was once supposed. The route from war-time "reconstruction" to post-war welfare state was much less direct and more contested than was often imagined (partly because economic constraints made many war-time plans impracticable, but partly also because much reconstruction thought was premised upon the permanent continuance of many war-time social and industrial controls that rapidly proved unacceptable in time of peace).[43] And, in all quarters, the attachment not to "brave new world" but to old-established methods and principles was much stronger than the post-war reformers cared to admit. Universal family allowances, for example, often portrayed as one of the direct practical outcomes of war-time solidarity, proved on closer inspection to be the fruit of a series of administrative trade-offs in Whitehall: trade-offs inspired partly by militaristic pro-natalism, partly by the need to offset the social impact of high taxation, and partly by a cautious desire to invest the new social insurance system with the old Poor Law safeguard of "less eligibility."[44] And it has been argued recently that the conception of a universal "subsistence minimum" in the Beveridge Plan was much more Spartan and restrictive, much more limited by orthodox budgetary and fiscal constraints than many historians of social policy (including myself) had allowed.[45] Research of this kind has tended to undermine the view that social policy in war-time constituted a fundamental break with tradition, and suggests on the contrary a high degree of gradually evolving continuity. In social policy, no less than in high strategy, war looks increasingly like mere politics by other means!

All these new emphases in historical research suggest, not that the old "home front" thesis is categorically wrong, but that it needs modification and revision. Titmuss himself in his classic history of war-time Britain from time to time expressed misgiving about whether there really was an entity that could be referred to as the "popular conscience" or the "people's mind"; and his descriptions of life under bombardment did continually stress the rich diversity and unpredictability of human reactions to the strains of war. But this aspect of Titmuss's work was much less prominent than the theme of war-time national solidarity. This latter emphasis was a potentially misleading one on several different counts. First, it underestimated the fact that it was precisely the defence of the untidy, atomistic, ramshackle, customary pluralism of British social life that for many people seems to have made the war worth fighting. And, secondly, it underestimated the degree of ambiguity and contradiction in the popular desire for post-war social change. Much has been written about the war's reinforcement of the global trend towards institutional collectivism. By contrast, surprisingly little has been said about the opposite effect: its strengthening and legitimation of a highly privatized and unstructured psychological individualism—an individualism that was explicitly opposed to fascism, but that also presented definite boundaries to collectivization of all kinds. After 1941 the Ministry of Information tactfully fostered a favourable presentation of life in Russia, which harmonized with and reinforced the widespread popular interest in the political and economic system of the Soviet Union. But this interest coexisted with an almost universal mistrust of political authority and officialdom in the context of day-to-day life in Britain. The popular cherishing of privacy was well expressed by the diary of Stephen Spender, spokesman of numerous pre-war leftist causes, who suddenly found himself in the autumn of 1939 at one with Neville Chamberlain.

> The fundamental reason is that I hate the idea of being regimented and losing my personal freedom of action . . . I dread the idea of being ordered about and being made to do what I don't want to do in a cause that I hate. This fear has

> even forced me into a certain isolation, in which I find that the personalities of my fellow beings often impose a certain restraint and unwelcome sense of obligation on me.
>
> There you are, you analyse your hatred of Fascism and it comes to a desire to be left alone.[46]

Numerous humdrum descriptions, including diaries of day-to-day life, in the war-time period suggest that Spender's feelings were shared by the vast majority of the British people in all social settings—at home, at work, in love, and at play.[47] Through the dark days of 1940 many dreamed of escape to "little quiet villages in the country where there are no telephones and where the blackout has always been a normal state of affairs."[48] Later in the war Mass Observation enquiries recorded with some disapproval that visions of the post-war world consisted overwhelmingly not of social reconstruction but of "retreat into private worlds of the imagination" and "a desire for a simple life."[49] Among the recipients of evacuees—even among those of an altruistic and hospitable disposition—several years of compulsory billeting left many with a deeply engrained desire never to have visitors again. Popular humour and popular culture (expressed in songs, cartoons, radio shows, and forces' entertainment) were not collectivist but anarchic, celebrating not the unity of mankind but its absurdity; not the righteousness of the national cause, but the fallibility of all in authority, be they civil or military, British or German, American or Russian.[50] Official exhortations against spreading alarum and despondency were obeyed in public, but treated with widespread private derision. Expressions of a more idealistic or portentous note came mainly from two sources; from the small minority who were ideologically committed to a more thoroughgoing, principled collectivism; and from the immediate experience of those subject to bombing and aerial bombardment.

This latter exception points toward a further weakness of the consensus approach—which is that it lumps together the six years of the war as a uniform chronological period and fails to distinguish adequately between the ebb and flow of popular opinion and behaviour in different contexts and at different times. After the the fall of Dunkirk, and during periods of nightly and sometimes daily bombardment—such as occurred during the late summer of 1940—there is indeed evidence to suggest that fear, excitement, desperation, and the random immediacy of death induced in many people an almost ecstatic sense of transcendence of self and immersion in a mystic whole. "Living became a matter of the next meal, the next drink. The way in which people behaved to each other relaxed strangely.

Barriers of class and circumstance disappeared . . . For a few months we lived in the possibility of a different kind of history."[51] Such attitudes affected not merely private lives but wider social and economic behaviour, as was shown in the upward surge of productivity that occurred in British factories during the summer and autumn of 1940. But at both the personal and the economic level such feelings were for most people fairly transient; and what historians have sometimes overlooked is the much longer and more dreary period of waiting for the opening of a Second Front—a period whose tensions, aimlessness, and low morale were minutely chronicled in diaries, fiction, and private correspondence (that "lightless middle of the tunnel" poignantly captured by Elizabeth Bowen's mid-war masterpiece, *The Heat of the Day*). It was significant that a Mass Observation report in the autumn of 1942 wrote about the "Dunkirk spirit" nostalgically, as though it were an episode in a distant and irrecoverable past.[52]

A third aspect of the social history of the period to which perhaps too little attention has been given is the sheer diversity of the war-time experience of different individuals, localities, organizations, and social groups. Even detailed social histories of the war, such as those by Calder and Marwick, have been mainly concerned with identifying overall trends and the onward march of nation-wide social democracy. But in all periods of modern British history social life has been characterized by microscopic diversity as well as by broader social movements, and the Second World War is no exception. There were many individuals who undoubtedly "had a good war"; many others (quite apart from the dead and injured), who suffered excruciatingly from separation from home and loved ones. For many the war meant years of compulsory employment at work that they hated; whereas for others it brought welcome rescue from futility and boredom (like the mediaeval scholar whose work-in-progress was destroyed in the Blitz: "In a state of indescribable elation, I walked into a pub and ordered a triple whisky and soda. 'Heil Hitler!' I almost shouted aloud, thankful to world's enemy No. 1 for having taken the load off my hands, mind and heart"[53]). For some conscripted women the war brought excitement, romance, travel, career opportunities, and a general enhancement of status; but for many more it meant a daily struggle to cope with work, shopping, transport, housework, queues, child care, and marital deprivation, often with minimal community support.[54] The women who kept diaries for Mass Observation included many who lived in daily fear of the violent death of their loved ones; but they also included some for whom conscription of their husbands meant a blessed release from the brutality of married life.[55] In many parts of the country habits of religious worship and church attendance were dramatically disrupted by war, in some cases permanently; yet the role of the war in accelerating the national slide into secularism must be set against evidence of widespread conversion, "revival," and resort to prayer in certain specific contexts.[56] If there is one common theme that constantly recurs in letters and diaries (and indeed in the poetry and creative writing) of the period, it is not the grandeur of great events but the passionate cherishing of small, private, domestic, idiosyncratic matters—matters that often seemed doubly important because the pressures of war rendered them fleeting and precarious. The very nature of such a unifying common theme merely serves to underline the element of infinite diversity. "There is no one mood," concluded Mass Observation at the end of 1942:

> . . . [T]here is no one all-pervading plan, purpose and drive, *no one mood shared by workers, managers, directors and civil servants*. . . . [A] complete sweep of the prewar pattern might produce a drastic change in people's work rhythms, liquidate the distinction of days, roles and rights . . . . But in war any country depends on the roots of its culture . . . .[57]

The social historian of the Second World War needs therefore to look closely not merely at large-scale, communal, "progressive" forces, but at those miniscule roots of idiosyncratic private culture. The latter were not only a major feature of British social structure in the period, but—no less authentically than the desire for equality and welfare—they embodied a tacit expression of popular war aims. Neglect of such roots has frequently led astray commentators who have viewed the domestic history of the war mainly in terms of utopian promises that were later unfulfilled. However, in stressing the importance of those roots I have no desire to swing the pendulum too far in the other direction. The oral and written evidence of witnesses to the Beveridge Social Insurance committee provides overwhelming evidence that the British public (or at least that sector of it that was organized into pressure groups and voluntary associations) endorsed Beveridge's vision of collective social security.[58] Revisionist accounts of the war that minimize consensus and national solidarity may run the risk of overlooking significant archival "silences"—silences that indicate certain areas of common agreement that were simply too profound and too self-evident to generate explicit comment or debate. And the war undoubtedly generated many long- and short-term processes of social change, including some that I have had no time to examine in detail in this essay.

Key areas of long-term structural change that deserve further attention from historians may be identified and summarized as follows. It seems probable that the sheer material fact of state control on such a massive scale permanently modified the character of British political culture, and played an important part in the long drawn-out transformation of Britain from one of the most localized and voluntaristic countries in Europe into one of the most centralized and bureaucratic. On the other hand the fact that Britain, alone among the European combatants, survived the war without invasion by foreign armies may account for the stubborn persistence of certain traditional habits and values—the peculiar conjunction of libertarian rights with collectivist entitlements—that were such a marked feature of post-war British life. The liquidation of massive foreign assets and the partial shut-down of the City of London as a major international finance centre meant that throughout the war and for some years thereafter financial elites and interest groups played a much more limited role in British politics and society than had been common over the previous half-century (and was to become so again when the post-war epoch came to an end). In spite of the large-scale absorption of women into the work force, it is arguable that the war at least temporarily strengthened rather than weakened traditional perceptions of masculine and feminine gender roles (since the organization of society for war buttresses patriarchy and masculinity far more imperatively than any form of purely economic relationship[59]). Changing class relationships merit further analysis: We have heard a great deal about the impact of slum-dwellers upon the conscience of the middle classes, far less about the impact of those same middle classes upon the political consciousness of the slums.

Another key area of social change lay in British perceptions of and contacts with the outside world. For the first time the British people were exposed to the full blast of North American culture, initially through the suspension in 1942 of the pre-war official quota on foreign films, and later through the physical presence of 2 million American and half a million Canadian troops stationed on British soil. Unsurprisingly, British attitudes to America changed markedly during the course of the war: In October 1940 opinion surveys showed that Americans ranked below Greeks, Poles, and Jews in popular favour; but by March 1942 there was "at the back of many British minds the idea that Americans are a rather eccentric kind of Englishmen."[60] Mass Observation records include many picaresque examples of Anglo-American culture shock—among them an American serviceman who was overheard saying "Oh Yeah!" in a village pub in Norfolk. He was arrested as a German spy. The American military presence introduced many British people to their first encounter with black people, to whom they responded with their usual diversity—ranging from colour-blind hospitable bonhomie, through self-conscious high-minded liberalism, to unabashed racial hostility.[61] The war also brought to Britain a large contingent of European refugees and prisoners of war, of whom nearly a quarter of a million (many of them Polish) were allowed to acquire permanent British citizenship. The impact upon British society and culture of this often highly enterprising and largely Roman Catholic group is beginning to attract historical enquiry.[62] In terms of future cultural change perhaps the single most significant social occurrence of the war was the temporary migration into Britain of several thousand West Indian workers, sailors, and servicemen, many of whom returned after the war as permanent settlers.[63] But there was no inkling in 1945, nor indeed for long afterwards, that Britain was on the brink of a major ethnic revolution.

A final point that should be stressed is that nearly all the structural changes that occurred in Britain during the Second World War were paralleled by comparable changes in all other Western European countries, both Allied and Axis, both combatant and neutral. Such comparisons can be overstressed, and each country has had its own unique institutional, demographic, and cultural history. But no country in Western Europe has escaped the impact of mass social welfare, advanced health care, ethnic migration, consumerism, and fiscal management; and in many cases such trends have been far more extensive than in Britain.[64] The wider history of Europe provides an indispensible back-cloth against which to weigh the extent, meaning, and significance of social trends and developments in Britain between 1939 and 1945.

NOTES

1. Ernest Bevin, *The Job to be Done,* (London, 1942), 10.

2. Quoted in Hamilton Fyfe, *Britain's Wartime Revolution,* (London, 1944), 5.

3. [Sir William Beveridge], *Social Insurance and Allied Services,* Cmd. 6404, 1942, 6.

4. Cited in Edward R. Murrow, *This Is London* (New York, 1941), 136.

5. R. J. Hammond, *Food,* vol. I (London, 1951), 353-59 and vol. II (London 1956), 753-59; R. S. Sayers, "1941—the First Keynesian Budget," in Charles Feinstein, ed., *The Managed Economy* (Oxford, 1983), 108.

6. Richard M. Titmuss, *Problems of Social Policy* (London, 1950), 506-8; and *Essays on the Welfare State* (2d ; London, 1963), 84-85.

7. J. S. Revell, "Income and Wealth 1911-50," paper to the International Economic History Congress, 1970; Correlli Barnett, *The Audit of War* (London, 1986); Penny Summerfield, *Women Workers in the Second World War. Production and Patriarchy in Conflict* (London, 1984); Anthony Howard, "We are the Masters Now," in M. Sissons and P. French, *The Age of Austerity 1945-51* (London, 1964).

8. Harold L. Smith, ed., *War and Social Change. British Society in the Second World War,* (Manchester, 1986); Rodney Lowe, "The Second World War, Consensus, and the Foundations of the Welfare State," *Twentieth Century British History* I (1990), 152-82.

9. J. S. Lawrie, "The Impact of the Second World War on English Cultural Life" (Sydney University Ph.D. thesis, 1988); Philip M. Taylor, ed., *Britain and the Cinema in the Second World War* (London, 1988); Neil Stammers, *Civil Liberties in Britain during the Second World War: A Political Study* (London, 1983); T. Harrisson, *Living Through the Blitz* (London, 1976); Penny Summerfield, "Mass Observation; Social History or Social Movement?" *Journal of Contemporary History* 20 (1985), 3, 439-52.

10. Barnett, *The Audit of War*; Harold Smith, *op. cit.*; Kevin Jeffreys, "British Politics and Social Policy during the Second World War," *Historical Journal* (1987), 30, 123-44; Jeffreys, *The Churchill Coalition and Wartime Politics, 1940-45* (Manchester, 1991).

11. Stammers, *Civil Liberties*: 24-5, 34-62, 66, 69-70, 117-20; Bernard Wasserstein, *Britain and the Jews of Europe* (Oxford, 1979), pp.81-133.

12. Paul Addison, *The Road to 1945* (London, 1975), chs. 2-5; D. N. Chester, *Lessons of the British War Economy* (London, 1951); Margaret Gowing, "The Organisation of Manpower in Britain during the Second World War," *Journal of Contemporary History* (January-April 1972) 1-2, 147-67; Alan S. Milward, *War, Economy and Society 1939-45* (London, 1977), chs. 4, 7, and 8.

13. Edward R. Murrow, *This is London* (New York, 1941), 103-4.

14. Titmuss, *Problems,* 324-31, 462-3, 557-61.

15. Titmuss, *Problems*, 183-202, 442-505.

16. Hammond, *Food*, II, *passim*; H. M. D. Parker, *Manpower. A Study of Wartime Policy and Administration* (London, 1957), 416-23; Titmuss, *Problems*, 17, 199, 275, 315-18; J. M. Lee, *Reviewing the Machinery of Government 1942-1952* (London, 1977), 114-16, 129-136.

17. Jose Harris, *William Beveridge. A Biography* (Oxford 1977), 380-81; J. M. Keynes, *How to Pay for the War* (London 1940); R. H. Tawney, "The Abolition of Economic Controls", *Economic History Review* (1943) XIII, i, 1-30; Stephen Brooke, "Revisionists and Fundamentalists: the Labour Party and Economic Policy during the Second World War," *Historical Journal* 32 (1989), 1, 157-75.

18. Mass Observation archives (Sussex University Library, Sussex, England), Box 4, File A on "Russia," 1939-41.

19. Harris, *William Beveridge*, chs. 16 and 17.

20. *Educational Reconstruction*, Cmd. 6458 (1943); *A National Health Service*, Cmd. 6502 (1944); *Control of Land Use*, Cmd. 6514 (1944); *Employment Policy*, Cmd.6527 (1944); *Social Insurance*, Cmd. 6550-1 (1944); *Report of the Care of Children Committee*, Cmd. 6922 (1946).

21. R. K. Kelsall, *Higher Civil Servants in Great Britain* (London, 1955), 146-60; Roger Eatwell, *The 1945-51 Labour Governments* (London, 1979), 45-48.

22. Lee, *Machinery of Government*, 114, suggests that "suspension of regular elections to both the House of Commons and local authorities for the duration of the war may . . . have surprisingly done something to strengthen loyalties to traditional constitutional practice."

23. A. M. Carr-Saunders, D. Caradog Jones, and C. A. Moser, *A Survey of Social Conditions in England and Wales* (London, 1958), 136-53.

24. *Ibid.*, 173-82.

25. Summerfield, *Women Workers*, 185-91.

26. Sheila Ferguson and Hilde Fitzgerald, *Studies in the Social Services* (London, 1954), 103-9; J. M. Winter, "The Demographic Consequences of the War," in Smith, ed., *War and Social Change*, 176.

27. Jose Harris, "Did British Workers Want the Welfare State? G. D. H. Cole's Survey of 1942," in J. M. Winter, ed., *The Working Class in Modern British History* (Cambridge, 1983), 200-214. (The archives of the Reconstruction Survey are in the library of Nuffield College, Oxford.)

28. Lowe, "The Second World War," 174-80.

29. British Library of Political Science: Beveridge Papers, IXa, 15, Employment investigation, report of a meeting with the TUC, 9 February 1944; Jose Harris, "Some Aspects of Social Policy in Britain during the Second World War," in W. J. Mommsen, ed., *The Emergence of the Welfare State in Britain and Germany* (London and Berlin, 1981), 247-60; Charles Webster, *The Health Services since the War* I (1988), 107-20.

30. Lionel Robbins, *Autobiography of an Economist* (London, 1971); Stephen Spender, "September Journal," in *Journals 1939-83*, John Goldsmith, ed. (London, 1985).

31. A notable exception was the diary of Naomi Mitchison: *Among You Taking Notes: The Wartime Diary of Naomi Mitchison,* Dorothy Sheridan, ed. (London, 1985), 62-63.

32. Murrow, *This is London,* 71, 90, and 163, records the contempt felt for the bevy of literary refugees to Hollywood (Auden, Huxley, Isherwood) and for the circle of fashionable defeatist cosmopolitans believed to surround the American ambassador, Mr. Joseph Kennedy.

33. Hermann Mannheim, *Comparative Criminology* II (London, 1965), 597-98; Mannheim, *Social Aspects of Crime between the Wars* (London, 1940), esp. pp. 105-22; Mannhem, *War and Crime* (London, 1941), 129-44.

34. Edward Smithies, *The Black Economy in England since 1914* (Dublin, 1984), 64-84.

35. As demonstrated by innumerable cartoons of the period. See Andrew Sinclair, *The War Decade: An Anthology of the 1940s* (London, 1989), 21; and Roy Douglas, *The World War 1939-1945: The Cartoonists' Vision* (London, 1990), 264-79.

36. Travis Crosby, *The Impact of Civilian Evacuation in the Second World War* (London, 1986), *passim*; John Macnicol, "The Effect of the Evacuation of Schoolchildren on Official Attitudes to State Intervention," in Smith, *War and Social Change,* 3-31.

37. Ferguson and Fitzgerald, *Social Services,* 104.

38. Dorothy Sheridan, ed., *Wartime Women. A Mass-Observation Anthology* (London, 1990), 151.

39. *People in Production: An Enquiry into British War Production: A Report by Mass Observation* (Harmondsworth, 1942), 24-25.

40. Compare, for example, Addison, *The Road to 1945,* written in 1975, with Stephen Brooke, "Revisionists and Fundamentalists: the Labour party and Economic Policy during the Second World War," *Historical Journal* 32 (1989), 1, 157-75, and Jefferys, *Churchill Coalition,* 221.

41. See, for example, Richard M. Titmuss, *Income Distribution and Social Change* (London, 1962), and Titmuss's contribution to Morris Ginsberg, ed., *Law and Opinion in England in the Twentieth Century* (London 1959).

42. Roger Middleton, "The Treasury and Public Investment: a Perspective on Interwar Economic Management," *Public Administration* 61 (Winter 1983), 4, 352; Noelle Whiteside, "Private Agencies for Public Purposes: Some New Perspectives on Policy-making in Health Insurance between the wars," *Journal of Social Policy* 12 (1983), 2, 165-83.

43. Harris, *Beveridge,* ch. 17; R. P. Chapman, "The Development of Policy on Family Allowances and National Insurance in the United Kingdom 1942-1946," University of London M. Phil. thesis (1990).

44. John Macnicol, *The Movement for Family Allowances 1918-45* (London, 1980), 156, 169, 183-86, 202.

45. John Veit-Wilson, "Muddle or mendacity: The Beveridge Committee and the poverty line," *Journal of Social Policy* (1992), 21, 3.

46. Cited in Sinclair, *War Decade,* 14.

47. J. S. Lawrie, *Impact of the Second World War, passim*; *People in Production,* parts C, D, and E.

48. Murrow, *This is London,* 72-73.

49. Mass Observation archives, FR 1364, "Reconstruction. People's Hopes and Expectations," July 1942. The author of this report remarked that "this is basically self-centred and a move away from responsibilities into an individual and private peace."

50. PRO. INF 1/292, "A Review of Some Conclusions Arising out of a Year of Home Intelligence Reports," by Stephen Taylor, October 1941; *People in Production,* 63-67, and *passim.*

51. Julian Symons, *Notes from Another Country,* cited in Sinclair, *War Decade,* 76.

52. *People in Production,* 54-55.

53. Cited in Sinclair, *War Decade,* 90-93.

54. Summerfield, *Women Workers, passim.*

55. Sheridan, *Wartime Women,* 142-43.

56. Robert Currie, Alan Gilbert, and Lee Horsley, *Churches and Churchgoers. Patterns of Church Growth in the British Isles since 1700* (Oxford, 1977), 27, 30, 35-37, 62, 114-15. Mass Observation recorded a decrease in church-going but a "strengthening" of faith, particularly in 1942 (Mass Observation archive, FR 1200).

57. *People in Production,* 178-79.

58. PRO, CAB 87/76-8, minutes of the Social Insurance Committee, March-August 1942.

59. "Certain things go inevitably with war and are war," commented an anonymous member of the Mass Observation team in April 1940. "The main thing is fighting, winning, killing, and being killed, being masculine and aggressive and abnormally vigorous, violent, and physical" (Mass Observation archive, FR 89).

60. Mass Observation archives, FR 1095, "Opinion on America". See also C. P. Stacey and Barbara M. Wilson, *The Half-Million. The Canadians in Britain, 1939-1946* (Toronto, 1987).

61. Graham Smith, *When Jim Crow Met John Bull: Black American Soldiers in World War II Britain* (London, 1987).

62. Keith Sword, *et al., The Formation of the Polish Community in Great Britain 1939-50* (London, 1989).

63. Peter Fryer, *Staying Power: The History of Black People in Britain* (Atlantic Highlands, N. J. 1984), 330-67.

64. Peter Flora, *State, Economy and Society in Western Europe 1815-1975*, vol. I, *The Growth of Mass Democracies and Welfare States* (Frankfurt, 1983); and Peter Flora, ed., *Growth to Limits: The Western European Welfare States since World War Two*, vols. I, II, and IV, (New York and Berlin, 1987-88)

■ ■ ■

10

THE SOVIET UNION: THE GREAT PATRIOTIC WAR?

Mikhail N. Narinsky

On 22 June 1941, *Pravda* carried an innocuous editorial headlined "Public Solicitude for the School." It was a Sunday, the only day of rest in the national six-day workweek. By the time that issue of *Pravda* reached its readers, war was already raging on the western Soviet borders. Commissar for Foreign Affairs Vyachleslav Molotov declared in a radio address, "Today, at four o'clock in the morning, German troops invaded our country, attacked our border in many localities, and made bombing raids on our cities."[1]

Two days later, two newspapers carried a poem whose opening lines ran:

Arise, o mighty land of ours,
Arise to mortal war
With evil fascism's dark powers,
With the accursed horde!
Let noble fury seethe and rise,
And like a breaker roar—
This war our people proudly fight,
A righteous, holy war!

The poem caught the public spirit and became the most popular verses during the war years. It constituted a clarion call and a solemn oath. The vast land was rising to fight a powerful and perfidious enemy.

What was the Land of Soviets like at the war's outset? In 1941 the USSR was firmly established among the industrial countries, at the cost of colossal efforts and enormous human sacrifices. It had overcome its backwardness (as compared with the Western European nations) in the volume of output in the key industries. In the late 1930s the Soviet Union either outstripped or closely approximated Germany, Great Britain, and France in output of electricity, fuel, cast iron, steel, and cement. Yet other kinds of output—especially of consumer goods—fell considerably below most industrialized countries. The skill and efficiency of the workforce were also considerably lower.

By 1940, at the end of the first decade of the collectivization drive in rural areas, the bulk of agricultural production was done on 4,000 state-run farms and some 237,000 collective farms. Collectivized food output was supplemented by what those farmers managed to grow on their individual land plots.

Collectivization in agriculture, while intended to solve many sociopolitical problems, came about through ruthless methods; life on collective farms, based as it was on forced labor, could hardly yield positive results. The best farmers, real masters of their trade, had been either repressed or eliminated altogether, and farming standards increasingly deteriorated.

The portion of the total population engaged in agriculture shrank from about 80 percent of the gainfully employed in 1928 to 54 percent in 1940. As the process of industrialization went forward and the masses of people for the first time gained access to education, medical care, and cultural opportunities, traditional patriarchal family relations gave way to new life-styles, especially in the towns and cities. Yet wherever people lived, labor was arduous and living conditions were hard.

It seems, though, that overwhelmingly the people of the vast country believed in the advantages of socialism and the wisdom of "the leader of the peoples," and looked confidently to the future. That was true despite an atmosphere of fear created by Stalinist repressions and constant reiteration of the official line that the USSR was a besieged fortress, surrounded by hostile capitalist states intent on destroying the Land of Soviets.

Then came the war!

The consequences of the war for the Soviet peoples were staggeringly severe—far more so than for the peoples of the other major nations allied against Germany. The war brought not only enormous death and destruction but a massive transfer of resources from the civilian to the military sector of the economy. As the British authors John Barber and Mark Harrison have written, "What made the Soviet experience uniquely traumatic was that it had to wage total war largely on its own territory, with all the devastation implied, and with substantially diminished industrial and agricultural capacity, due to enemy occupation of the western part of the country."[2]

On 23 June 1941, a decree of the Supreme Soviet established mobilization of all reservists born between 1905 and 1918. After reporting at recruiting stations, they took leave of their near and dear ones and left for the front. Within a week some 5.3 million people were mobilized.

Although the mobilization seemed to proceed smoothly, at the front the massive blows of the German army and its Italian, Rumanian, and Hungarian allies inflicted terrible losses.[3] In August a new decree extended recruitment to reservists born between 1890 and 1923. Eighteen-year-old lads and 50-year-old *muzhiks* alike went to fight the enemy, and the burden of most industrial and agricultural production had to be shouldered by women, teenagers, and old people. (Skilled workers in the defense industries and other enterprises vital to the functioning of the national infrastructure were exempted from military recruitment.)

On 26 June the Presidium of the Supreme Soviet decreed a longer workday and suspended all vacations. A special wartime national workforce distribution committee proclaimed that those employed in military production and associated industries were officially mobilized for compulsory service at their workplaces and could not leave their jobs. The whole country quickly moved to a wartime footing.

Stalin's radio address of 3 July 1941 urged all Soviet citizens to muster their forces for the struggle. People listened intently to the address, broadcast in public places over loudspeakers. Stalin's voice betrayed his agitation; sometimes he stopped and took a gulp of water. At that hour of supreme danger, the Kremlin dictator found the right words and touched people's hearts: "Comrades, citizens, brothers and sisters! Soldiers of our army and navy! I address you, my friends!" He tried to reassure and inspire them with hope for victory, stressing that the initial setbacks were temporary. "We have innumerable forces," he said. "The enemy is carried away by its success but he will see this fact. Thousands upon thousands of workers, collective farmers, and intellectuals will join their efforts with the Red Army to fight the enemy. Our multimillion-strong masses will rise, too."[4]

Over the following weeks, mass recruitment of volunteers and organization of militia units went forward everywhere in the European part of the USSR. Manual workers provided the majority of volunteers, but large contingents of white-collar workers, intellectuals, and students also enlisted. By autumn 1941, such *opolchentsy* numbered an estimated 4 million. Minimally trained and inadequately equipped, they would fight heroically but often tragically.

It was a harsh time—a time of privation and hunger. Vast food stocks were destroyed by the invading armies; much farmland came under enemy occupation. On 18 July 1941 a government decree introduced food rationing; henceforth rationing cards for basic foodstuffs and consumer goods were required in Moscow, Leningrad, and other major cities. On 1 November, rationing of bread, sugar, meat, fish, fats, macaroni, and other items went into effect in all towns and workers' settlements.

Different rationing cards were issued for workers and such persons as engineers, technicians, teachers, and medical workers; for employees in industrial enterprises; for dependents; and for children up to 12 years of age. Initially the rations were reasonably adequate; daily bread rations were 600-800 grams for industrial workers, 400-500 grams for clerical employees, and 400 grams for dependents and children. Monthly sugar rations were 600-800 grams for workers, 600 grams for employees, 400 grams for dependents, and 400-600 grams for children. Monthly rations for other foods included 1.8 kilograms of meats and fish, 0.4 kilograms of fat, and 1.3 kilograms of coarse grains and macaroni.

Although the above norms were substantially reduced later in the war, overzealous workers sometimes received extra food. At Aviation Plant No. 3, for example, such *Stakhanovites* had special passes to food stores and access to special canteens. That, remembered the chairman of the Trade Union Committee for the plant, "stimulated them for still better work."[5]

Light industry also went on a wartime footing, and in the spring of 1942 rationing of consumer goods went into effect. It became a matter of luck to find some necessary article of clothing or footwear, and prices soared. Black market operations thrived; townspeople bartered clothing and other articles for peasants' bread, milk, and potatoes.

Stalin's government fought the danger of a collapse of morale and authority with tight controls on information and severe repression of any suspected threat to public order. All private radios had to be turned in to local authorities. The only regular source of information about the war was the state-run Sovinformburo. Attempts to prevent bad news from reaching the public had limited effect; reports of military reverses and other troubles spread quickly by word of mouth.

Yet fear reinforced fervent belief, and the Soviet people generally did what they were told. A decree of 13 February 1942 mobilized all able-bodied men between 16 and 55 years of age and women between 16 and 45—anyone not already employed in essential industry or construction. The following September, employees in state enterprises and establishments close to the front who left their jobs without permission legally became deserters, to be apprehended and tried before military tribunals.

Severe punishments threatened those who failed to fulfill work quotas or violated labor discipline in any way. As Alec Nove has written, "One reason why the Russians were able to out-produce the Germans is the single-minded mobilisation of everyone and everything, men, women, children, under conditions of severe discipline for the war effort, and the degree of sacrifices borne by the civilian population. . . ."[6]

With the Germans seizing more and more areas of the European USSR, it was imperative to relocate and reorient war production in the Volga and Urals regions and areas farther east. The policy undertaken by the Central Committee of the Communist Party of the Soviet Union (CPSU CC) and the Soviet government on 27 June 1941 determined that nothing should be left for the enemy: "All assets of any value, all raw material stocks, grain crops, and stocks of foodstuffs, which could not be evacuated, may be used by the enemy, so in order to prevent this, by decision of the fronts' military councils, *they should be immediately destroyed or burnt.*" Accordingly, the Dnieper Hydropower Station was blown up, as well as many coal mines and industrial enterprises.

The policy dictate further stated: "Priority should be given to evacuation of: (1) major industrial values (equipment-essential machine tools and machines) valuable raw material resources and foodstuffs (non-ferrous metals, fuel, and grain), and other things of value and of national importance; (2) skilled workers, engineers, and employees should be evacuated together with their enterprises from the frontline areas, as well as the population and primarily young people eligible for military services, executive Soviet and party functionaries."[7]

Every effort went into evacuating as much as possible. Herds of cattle from collective farms were driven along the roads, while trainloads of workers and industrial equipment headed eastward.

It took two weeks to two months to deliver cargoes to the east by train. People often traveled with equipment and endured shelling and bombing raids along the way. Having their children with them only added to their difficulties. Upon arrival, the evacuees found accommodations in clubs, canteens, and other people's houses.

The equipment was installed in buildings still under construction; machine tools were placed in the shops of light-industry factories or remained out in the open. I. Rostovtsev, who headed the design bureau of the Krasny Proletary machine tool plant, later recalled: "We were taking with us practically all, from clerks to skilled workers. . . . Machine tools were outside near the railway or just thrown on the frozen ground and were soon covered with snow. We pulled them with a steel rope on a steel sheet attached to a tractor which took them to the place of destination, which was from 400 to 1,500 meters away—there were no roads as a rule there."[8]

Between July and November 1941, 1,523 enterprises were evacuated and assembled in the Urals, Siberia, the Volga region, and Kazakhstan. In the first five months of the war about 1.5 million railcars carried equipment from west to east. Mistakes and confusion were frequent; some enterprises even received orders to return to their original locations as they were being installed in the eastern areas!

As early as 27 June, the Political Bureau of the CPSU CC adopted a policy on evacuation from Moscow of holdings of the Soviet Diamond Fund and the Kremlin Armor Chamber. Preparations began for removing Lenin's body from Moscow; in strictest secrecy, it was later taken to Siberia.

From the beginning, a wartime regime prevailed in Moscow. All lights had to be shadowed. On 22 July the *Luftwaffe* began bombing raids on the capital; 122 raids took place over the next four months. Moscovites took turns on night watches in the yards of their apartment houses and workplaces and learned to extinguish incendiary bombs. V. Glushnev, a Moscow chemist, made the following entry in his diary: "In the night of 30 October, I heard a loud cannonade and bomb explosion: a demolition bomb had hit the University, the window frames and roof were torn away from the University's new building and the library. Mikhail Lomonosov's monument was destroyed. The frames and doors of the Manege were also torn off. The windows of the U.S. Embassy and the National Hotel were broken."[9]

One of the most striking aspects of civilian mobilization that summer and autumn of 1941 was the mass utilization of labor conscripts in building defensive fortifications. Hundreds of thousands of inhabitants of cities in danger of being taken by the Germans were ordered to dig trenches, bunkers, and tank traps and erect observations points, pillboxes, and firepoints. In July-August about 1 million Leningraders, at least a third of its working-age population, worked on defense construction, mainly along the Luga line, while some 600,000 Moscovites took part in building fortifications on the approaches to the capital. With the enemy drawing ever closer by late autumn, fortifications were built right in Moscow's streets. Barricades of paving blocks and sandbags stood across streets alongside antitank hedgehogs.

The tension in Moscow reached its climax by 15 October, when setbacks in the area of the Mozhaisk defense line prompted the State Defense Committee to order the immediate evacuation to Kuibyshev of foreign missions, as well as the offices of the People's Defense Commissariat and the People's Commissariat of the Navy. ("Comrade Stalin," the order added, "will be evacuated tomorrow or at a later date depending on the situation.") If enemy troops broke through to the outskirts of Moscow, the People's Commissariat of Internal Affairs (NKVD) was to blow up factories, power plants, ammunition and oil-storage dumps, and anything else of value that could not be moved.[10]

That evening the Party District Committees summoned managers of enterprises still remaining in Moscow and told them to close down operations and be prepared to blow up their most valuable equipment. Workforces had to be discharged and convinced to leave Moscow on foot. Panic-stricken people were already hiding their valuables and making hasty preparations to flee; officials were burning documents; marauding bands started raiding light-industry establishments. M. Danilova, secretary of the Party Committee of the Confectionary Factory Rot Front, recalled that "on October 16, our workers were waiting for their wages, [and] some of them kicked up a row and started pilfering. We had to take our produce away. There were also residents of the nearby districts among the pilferers. Of course, they were after the sweets. Then Rozen [the chief engineer] stepped in—he used a fire-engine water pump against this crowd, and they ran away. Other factories lost more, and we didn't lose much. . . ."[11]

A massive exodus from Moscow began on 16 October. Teachers of Vocational School No. 12 sadly recalled the day: "We distributed some food among our students and at 3:00 P.M. the students, led by the headmaster and other leading officials, left the school on foot. Part of them returned later, for they were not used to walking."[12]

On 17 October, A. Shcherbakov, secretary of the Central Committee and Moscow Party Committee, sought to inspire the city in a radio address, vowing, "We shall fight for Moscow for all we are worth, fiercely to the last drop of our blood. We must thwart Hitler's plans by all means."[13] Two days later, with Moscow officially under a state of siege, law and order had generally returned to the capital. As enterprises continued to be dismantled and put on westbound trains, civilians built more fortifications. Moscow prepared for battle.

In those dramatic days, preparations nonetheless proceeded for the celebration of the twenty-fourth anniversary of the Great October Socialist Revolution. Although German bombing raids never ceased, the Moscow Soviet of Working People's Deputies met underground, in the glittering hall of the Mayakovskaya Metro station, with representatives of the Party and public organizations. Stalin delivered a report attributing the Red Army's defeats to the enemy's sudden and treacherous attack. He cited wholly mythical figures on losses sustained by the enemy. The war, he told the assembled officials, had created a united national effort "which has been put at the service of the army fighting at the front, our Red Army, our Navy."[14]

Detachments of the Red Army paraded in Red Square on the anniversary of the Revolution. The demonstration had been prepared in great secrecy; special measures were taken to reinforce the city's air defenses. A snowstorm was blowing as the parade—led by military school cadets and infantry regiments, followed by cavalry squadrons, submachine gun carts, and more than 200 reserve tanks from General Headquarters—wound its way into Red Square. From the Lenin Mausoleum, Stalin addressed the troops. "We are waging a war of liberation, a just war," he proclaimed. "Let Lenin's victorious banner be a source of inspiration to you!"[15] Not only did the parade boost the army's morale, but the citizenry now knew that Stalin was in Moscow and the city would never surrender.

After the victorious Battle of Moscow, conditions in the capital improved considerably. By the spring of 1942, many of the previously evacuated factories and shops had returned, and Moscow slowly but surely came back to life.

For Leningrad, the USSR's second largest city, it was a different and far more harrowing story. Late in August 1941 the rapidly advancing German forces cut the Moscow-Leningrad railway line and thereby created a grave threat to the onetime capital of Czarist Russia. Stubborn resistance from the city's defenders prevented its capture, but the fighting advanced literally to its suburbs. On 30 August the *Wehrmacht* severed the last railway line connecting Leningrad to the rest of the country; nine days later the last overland road out of the city came under German control. Then the tragedy of the 900-day siege began. German troops were so close that their positions could be seen from Leningrad's rooftops. When the streetcar stopped at the Kirov Plant on the city's southern edge, the conductor would quip, "It's the last station; over there is the front line."

Food stocks in the city for both troops and the civilian population became extremely limited. On 12 September 1941, only a month's supply of bread and meat, 45 days of fats, and sixty days of sugar and confectionery still remained in the city's storehouses. Incendiary bombs had destroyed large food stocks in the nearby Badayev storehouses. That autumn, cargoes reached Leningrad exclusively by transport aircraft.

Bread rations were reduced several times, and there was almost no other food to speak of. On 20 November the daily bread ration for workers was reduced to 250 grams and for all other categories of inhabitants to 125 grams. What bread was available was of poor quality, with additives making up two-thirds of its content. People suffered from scurvy and malnutrition. More than 640,000 Leningraders died from hunger during the long siege; tens of thousands more died during various evacuation efforts.

After mid-November 1941, what was called Narrow Military Motor-Road No. 102, which was 308 kilometers long, connected Leningrad with the mainland. A 30-kilometer segment, extending across frozen Lake Ladoga and consisting of little more than truck ruts with black marking poles stuck in the frozen surface, was its most dangerous part. Besides German bombs and shells, motor-transport drivers had to contend with cracks in the ice and snowstorms. Yet more than 360,000 tons of supplies made it across the lifeline and into the city that unusually severe winter, and some 539,400 people made it out.

Those remaining in the besieged city suffered not only from hunger but from numbing cold. Fuel stocks soon ran out, so that Leningraders had neither electricity, water supply, nor communal services. Small groups of people could be seen making their way to the banks of the Neva River to draw up water. Many died of starvation and cold; those still alive lacked the strength to bury their own dead, let alone strangers. And through it all, German bombs and shells continued to fall. A notice commonly affixed to the walls of buildings read: "Attention! This [north] side of the street is especially dangerous during shelling." In November 1941 German artillery shelled the city at a rate of nine hours per day.

Still the city refused to surrender. Olga Berggolts, a prominent Leningrad poet, gave the New Year's address over Leningrad radio. "Despite our hardships," she said, "let's celebrate New Year's, for we shall do it on the first day of 1942, in Leningrad. Our army and all of us have not surrendered it to the Nazis, have not let them invade it. We've stopped the enemy. We are besieged but neither captured nor enslaved. And this is really very much."[16]

Late in March 1942, at the request of the city authorities, all Leningraders who could still do any work undertook to clean up the city. Emaciated people went into the sunlit streets and squares and, armed with shovels, pickaxes, rakes, and brooms, took away corpses, cut away ice, disposed of sewerage, and dumped snow into the Neva and Leningrad's numerous canals. Those heroic efforts did much to prevent contagion in the city and to keep it alive—to fight on.

A gas pipeline and electric cable, laid across the bottom of Lake Ladoga in the summer and autumn of 1942, improved the Leningraders' circumstances. The siege finally ended in January 1944, and the next month trainloads of food, raw materials, and ammunition started arriving. By that time only about 800,000 people (out of a prewar population of three million) remained in Leningrad. The city's ordeal had become a symbol not only of incredible suffering but also of the astonishing courage and endurance of the Soviet people.

The situation in the European USSR's countryside was also often one of suffering and privation. Collective farmers not only had to provide for themselves but to meet state procurement demands. The burden of farm operations was shouldered by women and elderly people and teenagers of both sexes. Often having little or no farm machinery at their disposal, they cultivated and harvested with ploughs, simple mowers, and scythes. Only 20 percent of the USSR's grain was harvested with tractors and combines.

A. Sheveleva, chairman of a village Soviet in the Vologda Region, recalled a harvesting campaign in the war years: "I asked Pyotr Tarabanov to teach Shura, a twelve-year-old lad, to plough and watch nearby. He refused, saying that he was too old (he was seventy then) and that the horses would not obey the boy."[17] It was such old people and little more than children who fulfilled the responsibilities of that and thousands of other village Soviets.

As the war progressed, the number of compulsory workdays registered to each collective farmer steadily increased; each adult had to be able to show from 80 to 150 *trudodny* (workpoints). Even 12 to 16-year-olds received a quota of 50 *trudodny.* Those who had not fulfilled their quotas were expelled from the collective farm (*kolkhoz*) and lost their private garden plots.

Work on wartime Soviet collective farms was both compulsory and poorly paid, for the workers did not receive wages for workpoints. Instead they got certain quantities of grain and potatoes, depending upon workpoints. What bread was to the urban worker, the potato was to the peasant. Rural people ate potatoes for breakfast, lunch, and dinner—most often boiled, with a salted cucumber or pickled cabbage. And if there were no potatoes—or no bread or milk, either—Soviet peasants resorted to nettles, grass, and acorns.

Moreover, to insure the necessary state procurements, peasants had to sell their own livestock (usually without cash reimbursement). For instance, in Kirghizia in 1940-44, the central authority procured 100-200 percent more cattle over and above the scheduled amounts. As a result, the number of peasant homesteads left without livestock in that traditionally stock-breeding republic increased from 10 percent in 1940 to 35 percent in 1944. While peasants may have accepted the need for sacrifices to feed the nonfarming population (including, of course, their own loved ones at the front), the state's virtual confiscation of their own produce sometimes resulted in angry confrontation, even violent resistance.

The war claimed immense financial outlays. Taxes and loans served as a major source of central-government funding. On 2 July 1941, agricultural and income taxes increased as an emergency measure, and at the beginning of 1942 a special war tax went into effect, to be paid by all Soviet citizens upon reaching age 18, with the exception of servicemen, members of servicemen's families, and pensioners. The severity of the war tax depended on a person's annual income. For instance, workers and employees in the 2,400-ruble bracket paid a war tax of 180 rubles. The war tax, which added 72.1 billion rubles to state revenue, remained in effect until July 1945.

An even greater amount—some 76.1 billion rubles—came from four wartime loans subscribed by workers, clerical employees, and people on collective farms. Although those loans appeared to manifest the Soviet people's patriotic feeling, they were actually compulsory. "All for the front, all for victory!" was the official motto for workers and peasants, scientists and students. Among their other sacrifices, Soviet citizens sent parcels to those serving in the Red Army and donated funds for other military needs. They waited impatiently for the latest news from the front, always hoping for some decisive victory. In Moscow, M. Danilova recorded that "everybody is all the time talking about the war. As soon as you enter the shop they start asking you about the news, about how soon the enemy will be defeated. This is their only hope. Everyone has someone fighting at the front—a son, a father, a brother, a husband. Many of those have already fallen in battle."[18]

Factory, district, city, and regional Party committees played an important part in the war effort, acting as political and often administrative guiding bodies. They were really organs of power and often organizational centers.

During the war years, the CPSU's orientation and activities changed considerably. The Party renounced its historic objective of promoting socialist revolution on a global scale and its overly optimistic concept of an international proletariat. Fascism had demonstrated the powerful appeal of chauvinistic nationalism and racial prejudice. The CPSU now sought to inspire a mighty wave of Soviet patriotism—a readiness to die not for socialism but for one's country. In response, tens of millions of Soviet citizens identified their own destinies with that of the Motherland; to save the Soviet state meant to save one's home, family, and loved ones. Russian historical traditions were invoked to rally the Soviet people for the struggle against the fascist invaders.

Recourse to Russian tradition and history proved a mighty weapon in what quickly came to be called the Great Patriotic War. Stalin well understood the immense potential of nationalistic emotion and readily made political capital from it. It was not accidental that in his Red Square address on 7 November 1941, he recalled Russian patriots and generals such as Alexander Nevsky, Dmitry Donskoy, Kuzma Minin, Dmitry

Pozharsky, Alexander Suvorov, and Mikhail Kutuzov. A broad propaganda campaign intended to popularize the Russian people's glorious past got underway.

According to Robert C. Tucker, the war only accentuated tendencies already at work under Stalin's regime. As Tucker has written, "The war gave a powerful further impetus to the Great Russian nationalism which had become evident in Stalin's personal political make-up by the beginning of the 1920s and a prominent motif in Stalinist thought and politics in the 1930s." The regime's official glorification of pre-Revolutionary military heroes, as well as its establishment of training academies for Soviet officers (named after such heroes), further manifested the nationalistic trend. The coming of war heightened Soviet militarism, which in fact dated from the period of War Communism (1918-22). Finally, Tucker notes, the war "strengthened and further developed the hierarchial structure of Stalinist soviet society as reconstituted during the revolution from above of the 1930s, and augmented the already far-reaching Stalinist hypertrophy of the state machine."[19]

To rally the population, the Soviet leadership sought to make use not only of history but also of religion. Antireligious propaganda stopped; the Union of Militant Atheists and the museums of atheism were closed down. From the beginning of the war, Metropolitan Sergius, head of the Russian Orthodox Church, urged believers to rise to the country's defense. "The fascist crusade has been launched against our country," declared the Metropolitan. "They kill our people, desecrate what is sacred to us, destroy historical monuments, and subject to reprisals the unarmed civil population. . . . The church must obviously once and for all join its destiny with that of its flock in life and death."[20]

The Orthodox Church launched a drive to collect contributions to the Defense Fund, as well as funds to assist the wounded and children and families of Soviet soldiers. By late 1944 the church's donations had reached 150 million rubles. For the first time since 1926, Orthodox bishops were allowed to elect a patriarch (Metropolitan Sergius) and reestablish the Synod. In 1943 the Council for Russian Orthodox Church Affairs came into being to maintain good relations between the church and the Soviet government.

Anti-Nazi propaganda was expertly written and rapidly produced. Newspapers printed the best verses, stories, and plays of the war years—works by such leading journalists as Ilya Ehrenburg and V. Grossman. Early in 1942 *Pravda* carried Konstantin Simonov's poem "Wait for Me," which became a symbol of faith and hope. People learned it by heart, copied it, carried it to the front. *Krasnoarmeiskaya pravda,* a daily newspaper printed at the front, was the first to publish Alexander Tvardovsky's "Vasily Tyorkin," a poem glorifying the toughness and resilience of the Russian soldier. Among other memorable wartime writings were such stories as Alexei Tolstoy's "Russian Character," Mikhail Sholokhov's "The Science of Hatred," Vanda Vasilevskaya's "The Rainbow," and Boris Gorbatov's "The Unvanquished," as well as plays such as Simonov's *Russian People* and Alexander Korneichuk's *The Front.* Such writings hailed the Soviet people's heroism and exhorted them to continue the struggle against the Nazi aggressors.

Despite the hardships of the war years, reading remained a popular activity. Tired and hungry, people nonetheless bought and avidly read the works of Leo Tolstoy, Chekhov, Pushkin, Shakespeare, Dante, Heine. Even in the worst parts of the war, books were still published on music, world theater, cinematography, and painting.

One of the most remarkable creative works of the war period was Dimitri Shostakovich's Seventh Symphony. The symphony was composed in starving and besieged Leningrad and first performed in Moscow on 30 March 1942. Four months later it was performed in Leningrad itself, where the bombing and shelling never stopped. As Shostakovich wrote in his program notes, "They say that when guns speak, Muses are silent. This may well be applied to the guns that by their fire try to suppress life, joy, happiness, and culture. Those are the guns of violence, evil, and the dark forces. We are fighting for the triumph of justice over barbarism."[21]

Although Soviet citizens may have believed they were fighting for freedom, justice, democracy, and humanistic values, in reality they enjoyed none of those in the country they defended. The USSR was a totalitarian society, ruled by a despot. The democratic language of the 1936 Soviet Constitution meant little in practice. All power rested with the CPSU and the state, and the apparatus of repression controlled every aspect of Soviet life. The official propaganda machine portrayed Stalin, standing at the apex of the pyramid of power, as a demigod, endowed with superhuman wisdom.

The British correspondent Alexander Werth, who was in Moscow during the first months following the German invasion, recalled that "whenever in cinemas Stalin appeared in newsreels, there was frantic cheering—which, in the dark, people presumably wouldn't do unless they felt like it. There could be no doubt about Stalin's authority, especially since that July 3 broadcast. He was the *khoziain,* the boss, who it was hoped knew what he was doing."[22] Stalin became the symbol of the nation, as well as of socialism and Soviet might. The slogan "For the Motherland! For Stalin!" conveyed the spiritual atmosphere of the period.

Yet side by side with courage and selfless heroism were to be found denunciations and fear, arbitrariness and repression. Carelessness or some small failure at work carried the danger of official reprisal. The huge Gulag network—53 labor camps, 425 corrective labor colonies, 50 colonies for delinquent youth (as of 1 March 1940)—continued to operate throughout the war. At least 1.5 million people inhabited those places at the start of the war; by 1 January 1945, because of the release of 1,622,098 and the death of 577,789 others, the Gulag population was down to 715,506.[23]

Some sources estimate the number of people serving prison terms at the outbreak of war as high as 2.3 million. Soon afterward the USSR Supreme Soviet decreed the release of convicts whose crimes "were not of great danger to public security." Such people were promptly dispatched to the front; by the end of 1945 about 420,000 ex-convicts had served in the Soviet Armed Forces. Following that initial decree were others releasing "special contingents." All in all, about 1 million convicted criminals went to the front, and many of them served honorably.

Other criminals were assigned to defense construction and work in industry and agriculture. According to the available data, about 40,000 prisoners worked in arms and ammunition manufacture, 20,000 in tank assembly, and 40,000 in coal mining and petroleum production. Convict laborers turned out industrial goods to the value of 3,651 million rubles and farm products to the value of 1,188 million rubles. They performed arduous jobs, working in abominable conditions on semistarvation rations.

That portion of the population remaining in enemy-occupied territory—some 60 million—endured awful hardships. Trying simply to stay alive, they procured what food they could, used any shelter available, worried about their families elsewhere, and snatched at every bit of news about the progress of the war.

An active minority of this captive population took part in the partisan movement. Partisan groups formed in various ways—sometimes under special commissars sent behind enemy lines, sometimes under Red Army officers or even ordinary soldiers cut off from their units, sometimes under local civilian leaders in occupied areas. Ultimately about 1 million people belonged to some 6,000 partisan units.

Partisan activities were most successful in the vast woods and marshes and in mountain regions. Partisans collected intelligence, attacked enemy detachments, and destroyed supplies, communications, and transport. In the summer and fall of 1943, partisan operations against German-held rail lines contributed substantially to the success of the Red Army's offensive.

At the same time, some in the occupied territories collaborated with the Germans. The actions of the Stalin regime in the 1930s—successive purges of suspected dissenters, enforced collectivization of agriculture, persecution of religious groups, and the like—had created much discontent in the population. That discontent was most widespread in the Baltic republics of Lithuania, Latvia, and Estonia, in the western Ukraine, in the North Caucasus, and in the Crimea. The Germans recruited *Wehrmacht* volunteers (*Hilfswillige,* or "little helpers") from local populations and from Soviet prisoners of war. "National legions" were formed from natives of the Baltic republics, Georgia, Armenia, Turkistan, and the Moslem areas of the North Caucasus. Baltic and Galician divisions of the *Waffen SS* and a "Russian Liberation Army," headed by the captured Soviet general A. Vlasov, also came into being. People enlisted in these units for a variety of reasons—some because they were conscious foes of Stalinism, some because they were weak men seeking to survive. Uncertainty surrounds the numbers involved; estimates have ranged from 250,000 to 1 million.

Those who supported the Organization of Ukrainian Nationalists, led by S. Bandera and A. Mel'nyk, wished to collaborate with the German occupiers but only, according to Alexander Dallin, on their own terms. "Although claiming to speak for the Ukrainian people," writes Dallin, "they met initially with little popular support in the Soviet Ukraine. They formed partisan units but refrained from attacking the Germans. Their leaders were put in German jails and concentration camps. Yet when released in 1944, they again rallied to the Nazi side to resume the struggle against Moscow."[24]

On the other side of the front, the Stalin regime ruthlessly uprooted and deported entire populations. The first to go were the Soviet Germans. In August 1941 the Autonomous Soviet Socialist Republic of the Germans of the Volga area ceased to exist; on the trumped-up charge of cooperation with subversive agents and spies, Moscow disbursed its inhabitants to the Novosibirsk and Omsk regions, to Kazakhstan, and to the Altai Territory.

The next wave of mass reprisals against ethnic minorities, in the winter of 1943-44, came after the liberation of Soviet territories. Ethnic groups such as the Karachayevs, Kalmyks, Chechens, Ingushes, Balkars, and Crimean Tatars fell victim to Lavrenti Beria and the NKVD Early in March 1944, Beria sent a message from Grozny in the Northern Caucasus: "State Defense Committee. Comrade Stalin. The Operation involves 19,000 officers and men of the Political People's Commissariat of Internal Affairs, who have arrived from various regions. Most of them took part in the deportation of the Karachayevs and Kalmyks, and will also take part in the future deportation of the Balkars. . . . As a result of three stages of deportation, 650,000 Chechens, Ingushes, Kalmyks, and Karachayevs have been deported to the eastern areas of the U.S.S.R."[25] Some of these people were deported right from the front, where they were honestly fighting for their country. They were relocated in the Kazakh, Uzbek, Tajik, and Kirghiz republics and in Siberia.

Deportation was carried out by brutal methods. H. Arapiyev, head of a department of the North Ossetian Regional Party Committee and an Ingush, recollected: "We were travelling for an unknown destination by rail in cargo cars, without lighting or water. Many people went down with typhus, and they did not receive any medical assistance. We buried our dead near the train in soot-blackened snow during short stopovers at god forsaken sidings (we were forbidden to move farther than five meters from the train—the guards would shoot one dead, if you dared to do so)."[26]

Tens of thousands died during these operations. Those who survived would live for many years as settlers in exile, without the prerogative to move elsewhere and stripped of virtually all their rights under law. More than 3 million Soviet citizens were subject to official reprisals on ethnic grounds.

While trainloads of deportees headed east, other trains carrying people and cargoes moved west, to the front and recently liberated areas. The turning point in the war came in the summer of 1943; after that time the belief in ultimate victory was no longer just a hope but a generally shared expectation.

On 5 August 1943 a salute of 12 salvos from 814 guns was fired in Moscow to celebrate the liberation of Orel and Belgorod. It was the first in a total of 354 such salutes up to the end of the war. The salutes were fired in the evening from antiaircraft guns, accompanied by fireworks of signal flares illuminated by searchlights. Children especially enjoyed the salutes, several of which might take place in one evening.

In July 1944 a seemingly endless column of some 60,000 German prisoners of war tramped through Moscow's streets. Unshaven, shabbily clad, downcast, the captured members of the *Wehrmacht* showed no traces of their former arrogance. Street-washing machines followed the column.

As Victory Day approached, it became increasingly clear what an immense price the Soviet Union had paid. At least 26-27 million people lost their lives in the war (estimates are still rising); much of the countryside was depopulated and the birth rate fell sharply.

In 1941-42, the most able-bodied part of the population went to the front, while increasing numbers of people went to work in the rapidly expanding war industry. By 1943 the number of people working on collective farms had declined by 38 percent (from 1940) to about 47.3 million.

The proportion of women and youths employed throughout the economy rose sharply; whereas 38 percent of the workforce consisted of women in 1940, 57.4 percent of workers were women by 1944.

Academician Evgeni Paton, who worked in the Urals during the war, recalled:

> I shall never forget the way women worked in those years. They came in hundreds to factories, more often than not with their sons, as yet teenagers. Women then performed arduous jobs, stood for hours in long lines for food products, brought up children, acting as both parents in absence of their husbands, never bending under the brunt of misfortunes when they received notifications of death of their husbands, sons, fathers. They were real heroines of the labor front, worthy of admiration.[27]

By war's end, citizens 25 years old or younger accounted for many of those employed in industries, on construction sites, and in transport. More than one-fourth of the workforce consisted of people aged 18-25—some 40-60 percent of those in war industry.

The national system of vocational training—set up prior to the war under the national preparedness program that introduced military discipline into the workplace—became an integral part of the war effort. Under a 1940 law, able-bodied boys and girls 14 years of age were enrolled in vocational training schools for skilled and industrial work. Students in the schools received free board and uniforms.

By 1942, 80 percent of such students worked in war production. Vocational schools increased from 1,500 in 1940 to 2,500 in 1945. Most were located in the eastern regions of Kazakhstan, Uzbekistan, Tataria, and Siberia. About 2.5 million young workers received their training in such schools.

In the face of enormous losses in population, the Soviet government took steps to buttress the institution of the family and promote population renewal. A decree adopted in July 1944, entitled "Measure to Prevent Disorganization of the Family and to Promote Higher Birth Rate," repealed the 1926 law on de facto (common-law) marriages and made divorce more difficult. Now one had to place an announcement in a local newspaper before the divorce petition was heard in court (in two stages), and the court exacted a higher divorce tax than under the earlier law. Under the tougher 1944 regulations, divorces fell to a small fraction of the prewar rate. Abortion, moreover, had long been illegal in the USSR, and no contraceptives were available.

Meanwhile special financial allowances were introduced for the births of the third and subsequent babies (as opposed to an allowance for a seventh baby previously in effect), and subsidies for nurseries and child-care centers were cut in half to encourage mothers to remain at home—and presumably have more babies. The honorary title "Mother-Heroine" was introduced for those who gave birth to ten or more children, as well as the order of Mother's Glory.

A new law required single men and women and families with no more than two children to pay up to six percent of their wages or salaries as taxes. Thus on one hand the state sought to stimulate childbearing; on the other, it robbed unmarried people and small families of part of their earnings.

Besides underpopulation, another grave problem of the postwar years would be the huge number of war invalids. By early 1945 about 1 million such people had returned to work, although obviously many never would. The disabled received modest pensions, often barely enough for survival. Groups of Young Pioneers helped care for war invalids, as well as the families of officers and men at the front.

As the Red Army advanced westward, the Soviet government had to confront the task of rehabilitating the war-ravaged areas. Priority went to restoring the Donets Coal Basin, twice subjected to destruction—first by the retreating Red Army, then by the retreating Germans. All electric power stations, plants, railways, and equipment had been blown up, mines were flooded, and the whole area was in ruins.

At first, work resumed in shallow mines, using picks, spades, barrels, wheelbarrows. After two years of hard restoration labor, repaired equipment was again functioning; 129 main mines plus nearly 900 medium and small mines were in operation; and small electric stations were back in service. Slowly but surely the Donets Basin returned to life.

Other restoration work carried out in the closing stages of the war returned to use much heavy industry in liberated areas. By war's end some 7,500 enterprises and 116,000 kilometers of railway track had been repaired or rebuilt.

Little could be done to restore light industry, whose output had declined drastically in the occupied regions. Production of knitwear, for example, was down by 60 percent, footwear by 40 percent. The workforce in light industry received considerably lower wages and food rations than that in heavy industry. At the close of the war, women made up 80-95 percent of those working in light-industry enterprises.

All basic consumer goods were in short supply during the war; grain-crop failures added to a bad situation. People spent hours on end (sometimes all night) in long lines waiting for their bread rations, which by mid-1943 had been cut by 50 grams for everybody except workers, engineers, and technicians in war industry. Although most people eventually accepted wartime hardships, to lose one's ration card or have it stolen could easily doom to death a person already weakened by months of privation.

G. Semenov, leader of a Young Communist League group, made the following diary entry for 22 November 1943: " . . . bread rations have been cut. We agitators have a lot of work to do these days. People ask me to explain why it has been done. So I explain as best I can: first, it's due to the crop failure, second, no bread has been supplied by the Ukraine, third 700 grams isn't so bad after all. I tell them about the besieged Leningrad and its courageous residents. And the people agree. . . . On some occasions some people complain. I for my part am far from happy to tighten my belt. But what's to be done? It's a life and death struggle. You can't pick and choose."[28] In 1944 the food situation began to improve; rations were increased from time to time.

In April 1942 the Soviet government and the CPSU CC tried to improve the food situation, adopting a measure entitled "On Allocation of Land Plots to Workers and Employees for Vegetable Gardens." Factory, plants, and military units received allotments of land near populated areas and not already under cultivation; and workers and salaried employees could have plots ranging from 650 to 1,000 square meters for vegetable gardens. "The cultivation of vegetable gardens is now a matter of state importance rather than a private affair of individual workers and employees," editorialized *Pravda* a year later.[29]

Part of what was grown on such subsidiary plots went to the national food fund. In November 1943 the Kazakh Party Central Committee reported that "today all our major industrial enterprises have their subsidiary land plots. . . . The share of products supplied by them per worker has considerably increased, especially with regard to vegetables and potatoes."[30] By 1945, 38 percent of all potato production and 59 percent of other vegetables were supplied to workers and salaried employees from subsidiary plots. Indeed, individual vegetable gardens often made the difference between survival and starvation.

Soap, matches, salt, thread, footwear, and ready-made clothing were also scarce. Much of what was available went to factories, vocational schools, hospitals, and nurseries. The situation was especially bad in 1942-43, for by then people's clothing and footwear were wearing out. Workers in the Urals and Volga regions began producing footwear from quilted jackets, sheepskin coats, and coarse cloth. Traders in Moscow sold such homemade footwear as well as old galoshes, which were in especially great demand.

While all of the aforementioned articles were acutely scarce in the devastated areas liberated from Nazi occupation, housing was simply nonexistent for nearly 25 million people. Many lived in dugouts or among ruins. Housing was only a little better in many other places. Workers dwelt in barracks or rented rooms in private homes. More than 20,000 miners in Karaganda, the Urals, and the Kuznetsk Coal Basin slept in hostels on double-decked cots.

Not nearly enough bathhouses and laundries were available. Urban transport functioned inadequately or not at all; many people reached their workplaces on foot.

Life in the countryside was almost as bad, the big difference being that rural dwellers had their own houses—as a rule, quite small ones. No consumer goods were available in village food stores; country people provided for themselves as best they could.

Peasants bore the double burden of laboring on collective farms and working their individual plots. Agriculture regained vitality in liberated territories with great difficulty. Able-bodied workers on collective and state farms decreased by half; weeds grew on formerly cultivated lands; draft animals were in short supply. As areas were liberated, thousands of tractors, combine harvesters, and other pieces of farm machinery arrived; herds of cattle were driven back westward. Yet by 1945 only 72 percent of the arable land in the liberated areas was back in cultivation.

Working people throughout the USSR bent their efforts for the sake of victory. Originally established on a voluntary basis by people moved by patriotic sentiment, the Defense Fund quickly assumed a compulsory character. Yet residents of the most remote areas—Kamchatka, Kolyma, Magadan, the Okhotsk coast—willingly contributed as much as they could to the Defense Fund, including 500 million rubles from the Dalstroy construction association workers, many of whom were convict laborers. The reindeer breeders of Chukotka contributed 12,600 of their animals.

Workers everywhere commonly donated their wages to the Defense Fund, while collective farmers sowed "hectares of defense" over and above what their plans called for. Intellectuals and artists contributed their fees from lectures, concerts, and sales. All in all, more than 17 billion rubles in cash, 131 kilograms of gold, 9,519 kilograms of silver, 13 kilograms of platinum, 1.7 billion rubles worth of jewels, and 500,000 rubles in bank-account transfers were given to the Defense Fund and the Red Army Fund. Citizens purchased an additional 4.5 billion in government bonds.[31]

Despite the terrible sacrifices and hardships they endured, despite the authoritarian and often cruel practices of the Stalin regime and the reality of money grubbing and chiseling by private citizens, the Soviet people as a whole persevered in their hopes for victory and for a better life after the war. Alexander Dovzhenko, a leading Soviet cinema director, caught that spirit in a January 1944 diary entry: "The Russian people must win this war with glory. It is worthy of a better destiny, of the greatest respect. The postwar period will certainly bring it great achievements in the arts and science, and a new Renaissance must set in."[32] Alas, the postwar reality proved something quite different from what Dovzhenko envisioned.

Yet the ghastly ordeal had not been in vain. The Soviet people preserved their country's independence, made the biggest contribution to the final defeat of Nazi Germany and its satellites, and insured the liberation of European peoples from fascist oppression. Early on the morning of 9 May 1945, citizens of the USSR learned that late the previous night, representatives of the German high command had signed an act of unconditional surrender. In his victory address Stalin said: "Our great sacrifices in the name of our Country's freedom and independence, our people's innumerable privations and sufferings in wartime, their ceaseless work in the rear and at the front were put at the altar of the Fatherland, [and] they were crowned with victory over the enemy."[33]

The long-awaited Victory Day had come at last. People in Moscow, Leningrad, and everywhere were frantically jubilant. Total strangers embraced each other and sang and danced in the streets. Officers and enlisted men were joyously tossed into the air and caught by laughing civilians.

A month later Ilya Ehrenburg, who had become the country's foremost unofficial propagandist, wrote that "we knew victory when it marched in our armed units, when it was warming itself at the camp fire next to our soldiers. Now victory is shining among banners held aloft at parades. It will soon come to every home; it will be tangible and warm, so close to us that it will cut off a slice of bread and sip some wine. And then the people will know the taste of victory, the taste of happiness they have suffered for so much."[34]

NOTES

1. *Pravda,* 23 June 1941.

2. John Barber and Mark Harrison, *The Soviet Home Front, 1941-1945: A Social and Economic History of the USSR in World War II* (London and New York, 1991), 78.

3. The Spanish "volunteer" units that fought against Soviet forces did not start arriving until October 1941.

4. J. Stalin, *About the Great Patriotic War of the Soviet Union* (Moscow, 1953), 9, 16 (in Russian).

5. *Department of Manuscripts' Funds, Institute of History of Russia* (Moscow), fund 2, section 5, inventory, 8, carton, 5, leaf 2 (in Russian; hereafter cited as *DOMF*).

6. Quoted in *Stalin* (London, 1990), 17.

7. *Proceedings of the Central Committee, Communist Party of the Soviet Union,* N 6 (Moscow, 1990), 208 (In Russian).

8. *DOMF,* fund 2, section 5, inventory 4, carton 1, leaf 2.

9. Quoted in L. V. Pozdeeva, *The Book Is Fighting: Catalogue of the Exhibition* (Moscow, 1978), 85 (in Russian).

10. *Proceedings of the CPSUCC,* N 12, p. 217.

11. *DOMF,* fund 2, section 5, inventory 4, carton 1, leaf 2.

12. *Ibid.,* fund 2, section 5, inventory 6, carton 1, leaf 1.

13. *The Second World War: A Short History* (Moscow, 1984), 144 (in Russian).

14. Stalin, *About the Great Patriotic War,* 19.

15. *Ibid.,* 40.

16. O. Berggolts, in *Nine Hundred Days* (Leningrad, 1957), 231 (in Russian).

17. *DOMF,* fund 2, section 5, inventory 40, carton 2, leaf 4.

18. *Ibid.,* fund 2, section 5, inventory 4, carton 1, leaf 2.

19. Robert C. Tucker, *Political Culture and Leadership in Soviet Russia: From Lenin to Gorbachev* (Brighton, 1987), 99.

20. Quoted in Pozdeeva, *The Book Is Fighting,* 128-29.

21. Quoted in *ibid.,* 106.

22. Alexander Werth, *Russia at War, 1941-1945* (London, 1964), 184.

23. *Arguments and Facts* (Moscow, 1989), 45 (in Russian).

24. Alexander Dallin, *German Rule in Russia, 1941-1945: A Study of Occupation Policies* (London and New York, 1957), 122.

25. N. F. Bugai, "The Truth about Deportation of Chechen' and Ingushe' Peoples," *Questions of History* 7 (1990), 40 (in Russian).

26. *Ibid.*, 40-41.

27. Quoted in *The Great Patriotic War of the Soviet Union, 1941-1945* (Moscow, 1965), 283 (in Russian).

28. A. V. Mitrofanova, ed., *The Soviet Home Front during the Period of the Radical Turn in the Great Patriotic War, November 1942-1943* (Moscow, 1989), 327 (in Russian).

29. *Pravda,* 10 April 1943.

30. M. Kozybaev, *Kazakhstan: Arsenal of the Front* (Alma-Ata, 1970), 146 (in Russian).

31. *The Great Patriotic War, 1941-1945, Encyclopedia* (Moscow, 1985), 762 (in Russian).

32. *Pravda,* 11 September 1989.

33. Stalin, *About the Great Patriotic War,* 193.

34. I. Ehrenburg, *Chronicle of Courage: Wartime Articles Carried by the Press* (Moscow, 1983), 339 (in Russian)

■ ■ ■

11

The United States: The Good War?

Charles C. Alexander

The news reached us early that Sunday afternoon, 7 December 1941, at a little Protestant church in northeastern Texas where my parents and I were attending a hymn-singing festival ("song convention," in local parlance). The music was interrupted when somebody burst in shouting, "The Japs bombed Pearl Harbor! The Japs bombed Pearl Harbor!" At that, the church quickly emptied; everybody piled into automobiles and started for home.

I was barely six years old (not yet in school), much occupied in playing at war (already possessing a substantial collection of toy pistols and miniature soldiers), and of course little able to comprehend what had actually happened. That evening, in a scene no doubt replicated in millions of homes across the United States, I watched my parents as they listened intently to the radio news broadcasts. I remember asking, "Are they going to come over here to fight?" My father replied, "No, son, you don't have to worry; they'll never fight over here." At least for the time being, that was sufficient reassurance.

For several months after the Pearl Harbor attack, rumors of the presence of a huge Japanese naval force off the Pacific Coast triggered successive panics among Californians. Early on the morning of 8 December, 16-year-old Frank Keegan and five pals drove 20 miles from Santa Rosa to Bodega Bay, where, armed with a .22 rifle and two small shotguns, they prepared to repel what they fully expected to be a Japanese invasion. "We loaded our guns," recalled Keegan 40 years later, "hid behind the dunes, and waited. . . . We peered, we saw nothing. But we knew the Japanese were subtle, deceitful. We waited and waited, until it got dark." Then they piled back into their Ford automobile and headed home, their vigilance unrewarded.[1]

A few days later, a message reporting a flight of planes presumed to be Japanese prompted antiaircraft batteries around Los Angeles to fire thousands of rounds into the empty night sky. (In February 1942 a Japanese submarine *did* surface at dusk and lobbed a few shells at an oil refinery near Santa Barbara, causing slight damage. A similar shelling occurred off Fort Stevens near Astoria, Oregon.)

Meanwhile people on the Atlantic Coast worried that the *Luftwaffe* might launch one-way "suicide" attacks from western Africa (or somewhere), and Americans in the middle-western states read warnings to the effect that Minneapolis could be bombed by German aircraft via the North Pole. On beaches from Texas to New England, large amounts of debris and occasional corpses washed ashore—grim evidence of the frightful toll German submarines took on Allied shipping throughout 1942. Cities on both American coasts kept their streetlights turned off in compliance with blackout regulations; Civil Defense wardens in their white helmets patrolled neighborhoods to make sure everybody's curtains were drawn.

Yet as my father had assured me, "they" never did "fight over here." As compared to what the people of the Soviet Union or even the United Kingdom had to endure, the most obvious contrast in the war experience of Americans was that—besides the two minor shelling episodes in California and Oregon and, later in the war, a number of Japanese-launched, balloon-borne bombs that landed harmlessly in the northwestern part of the country—the U.S. mainland remained physically untouched by enemy action. For Americans, the war became a matter either of leaving home to fight (and, for close to 400,000, meeting death), or staying at home and pursuing one's life essentially out of harm's way.

The war eventually put some 11 million men and 2 million women into the U.S. military services. That enormous manpower dislocation, in combination with a burgeoning war production effort, totally transformed the national employment situation. As late as 1940 the Great Depression was still very much at hand; as many as 9 million people—about 15 percent of the workforce—remained unemployed. By the time Pearl Harbor was attacked, however, the U.S. government was already spending $2 billion per month on rearmament; within another six months, a third of all economic activity was concentrated in war production. By 1945 the federal budget had exceeded $100 billion (versus $9 billion in 1939), while the gross national product (the total annual value of all goods and services) had grown from $91 to $166 billion. In nearly doubling American industrial production, the war effort opened up 17 million new jobs.

Yet for all the emphasis on the production of matériel, supplies, and foodstuffs not only for the U.S.'s armed forces but, in large part, for its allies as well, the American people as a whole experienced little acute privation. In the most devastating war in human history, Americans generally ate better and were better clothed and sheltered than in the prewar decade.

Of course they did have to put up with shortages and inconveniences—lots of them. To cite one less-than-critical situation: after the last cargo of raw silk arrived from Japan in midsummer 1941, the Office of Production Management ordered all silk stocks diverted to military purposes. Subsequently the government also monopolized output of the new synthetic product nylon, so that "for the duration," in the memorable phrase of the war years, American women either managed with cotton stockings or went bare legged. (If sufficiently desperate, they might even paint stocking lines on their legs!)

In a society wedded to personal automobile transport for both essential and recreational purposes, gasoline rationing (imposed mainly to conserve tires after overseas rubber supplies were cut off) compelled people to stay closer to home, form car pools, use mass transport (if available), and sometimes resort to hitchhiking. Rationing and periodic shortages of red meat, sugar, butter, distilled liquor, and cigarettes produced such widespread unhappiness that those items became staples of a flourishing "black market" economy. Given the growing disdain for such consumables in a later, more health-conscious generation, one can hardly view their scarcity as a matter of suffering; but in fact plenty of Americans were willing to satisfy their wants from illegitimate sources, including the precious ration stamps themselves (widely available on the black market in both authentic and counterfeit varieties).

It has become a truism to note that the Roosevelt administration's rearmament program finally ended the Great Depression, whereas its manifold (if little-coordinated) efforts under the domestic New Deal had achieved only modest economic recovery. As farm income reached all-time highs, the New Deal's scheme for achieving agricultural "parity"—a level of buying power for farm producers comparable to that in the general population—became utterly irrelevant. Now the Department of Agriculture and the Office of Price Administration vainly struggled to keep commodities prices from outstripping the parity formula. As a onetime New Deal official and wartime European Red Cross administrator recalled, "Farmers in South Dakota that I administered relief to, and gave 'em bully beef and four dollars a week to feed their families [before the war], when I came home were worth a quarter-million dollars, right? What was true there was true all over America."[2]

While military contracts went preponderantly to the country's biggest corporations, the wartime economy spawned thousands of small businesses—groceries, bars, repair shops, and the like—to service the needs of the newly prosperous population. "It didn't take a genius to make money during the war," according to a man who started a highly successful grocery chain in California. "All you had to do was to open a store and not get dead drunk. You had customers ready and willing and able to buy all you could get. It didn't take any brains or hard work."[3]

Not only were jobs available for virtually everybody, but a severe labor shortage brought into the workforce close to 4 million workers under the age of 18, as well as some 14 million women, many of whom had never sought employment outside their homes. Although they toiled in virtually every area of war production, womens' "delicate hand and eye operations" supposedly made them particularly suitable for handling precision-made parts.[4] In the aircraft industry, women came to make up 65 percent of all workers (versus 1 percent before Pearl Harbor); and the archetypal "Rosie the Riveter," in her coveralls and snugly wound head scarf, became a favorite character in home-front propaganda and an enduring part of American folklore.

Marguerite Kershner, who installed electrical wiring at the Boeing Company's vast bomber factory in Seattle, Washington, and Alice R. Wagner, who worked at the Vega aircraft plant at Burbank, California, typified single women in wartime industry. Before the war both had been employed in low-paying "women's jobs"—Kershner as a sales clerk, movie theater "usherette," and elevator operator, Wagner as a laundry worker. By mid-1942 Kershner was earning 93 cents per hour and working up to 70-hours per week, while Wagner, usually putting in 48 hours per week, received 75 cents per hour. Both expressed general satisfaction with their job situations, even though they were still paid about a third less than comparable male workers and even though, as the popular weekly magazine *Life* described Kershner at the end of the day, "her hands may be bruised, there's grease under her nails, her make-up is smudged and her curls [are] out of place." Wagner liked her work so much that she looked forward to staying on the job for the duration of the war "and maybe after."[5]

Unmarried, earning twice what they had been paid in peacetime, Kershner and Wagner could spend their hard-earned money as they wished—at least in terms of what was available in the domestic consumer economy. Although new automobiles, refrigerators, stoves, washing machines, and other "durable goods" were unavailable on the home front, a population whose collective income reached $150 billion in 1944 spent record amounts eating in restaurants, frequenting theaters and nightclubs, gambling at casinos and horse tracks, and buying such luxury items as jewelry, perfumes, and furs.

Despite gasoline rationing and crowded trains, in the winter months wealthy Americans managed to enjoy casinos, races, and beaches at the Florida resorts. Such wartime hedonism prompted a stream of reproachful press comment about "the smug, serene attitudes assumed by those Americans capable of taking life easy in the midst of a world-gutted conflict," as the biweekly *Look* put it. "If the fighting men of Anzio and Kwajalein could see Miami and Miami Beach now," scolded *Life* early in 1944, "the anger they bear toward their enemies would probably turn against their countrymen."[6]

In general, the times were good for Americans on the home front, so good that many of them would later look back on the war as a profoundly alleviating circumstance—little less than salvation, in some cases. Jean Bartlett, a Berkeley, California, teenager during the war, recalled how everything improved once her father went to work at the Oakland shipyards: "That's where the money started getting good. It made a big difference in our lifestyle. . . . We didn't have to worry about which child will get shoes that month. We could pay the bills. I didn't hear my mother complaining. . . ."[7]

Meanwhile the 25-member Braukmiller family—father, mother, offspring, in-laws, and assorted other relatives—moved from rural Iowa to work in the Kaiser yards at Portland, Oregon, where the famous Liberty merchant ships were built. By the summer of 1943 the combined weekly wages of the 13 working Braukmillers had reached $996, or nearly $52,000 a year.

Yet for wartime breadwinners such as Bartlett's father and the Braukmillers, the workday was usually long and also frequently dangerous; by 1945 about 1 million Americans had suffered serious injuries in war industries, about the same as the number wounded in combat.

Working women with husbands in uniform, besides enduring everything that male workers did on the job, also frequently struggled as the principal support of fatherless families. Twenty-two-year-old Lillis Wells, who operated a drill press at the Bendix/Eclipse Machine Division plant in Elmira, New York, while her husband was in the Army Medical Corps, was a representative working war mother. Six days a week, Wells left her two small children with their grandmother and commuted 20 miles to Elmira, where she worked a 6:30 A.M.-3:00 P.M. shift that was broken only by two five-minute respites and a half-hour lunch period. After work, she cared for her children, a small flock of chickens, and one of the millions of "victory gardens" Americans planted under government encouragement.

Of course many other women remained at home and, if their husbands were in military service, faced responsibilities they would never have thought to assume in peacetime. Thirty-year-old Barbara Holmes Drum, mother of four, was an authentic socialite whose name appeared in the New York City *Social Register*. With her husband serving as an army captain, she took over management of their farm at Far Hills, New Jersey. "All of a sudden," she related in 1943, "I had to find out about a lot of things." She had learned to get along with one remaining servant (of a prewar five), to do her own grocery buying, and even to frequent local auctions in search of secondhand farm equipment with which to cultivate her own vegetable crop.[8]

For wives such as Wells and Drum with husbands away in uniform, a journalist who specialized in "women's subjects" advised putting most of the couple's furniture in storage and moving into a smaller place. Wives should also seek to make new friends, try going to church regularly, perhaps even go back to school. Above all, they should avoid "wolves"—civilian men out to take advantage of their loneliness.[9] (Some of them may have thoughtfully purchased "furlough nightgowns," a successful line of lingerie designed by Evora Bonet Eaton, wife of a naval officer.)

Many military wives sought to follow husbands as they were ordered from place to place. Dellie Hahn, the bride of an air force sergeant, found herself traveling from Florida to Michigan to Texas as her new husband was repeatedly reassigned. "That's how I got to see the misery of the war, not the excitement," she remembered many years later. "Pregnant women who could barely balance in a rocking train, going to see their husbands for the last time before the guys were sent overseas. Women coming back from seeing their husbands, traveling with small children. Trying to feed their kids, diaper their kids. I felt sorriest for them. It suddenly occurred to me that this wasn't half as much fun as I'd been told it was going to be. I just thanked God I had no kids."[10]

If weekly paychecks were bigger, and people could afford to eat better and spend more of their money on personal enjoyment, war workers and their families also commonly had to settle for substandard housing, sometimes at considerable distances from war production centers. Some of the tens of thousands of people who migrated north from West Virginia, Tennessee, and Kentucky to work in the Ford Motor Company's famous Willow Run bomber factory near Detroit moved into what had recently been chicken houses; others were still living in tents when the harsh

Michigan winter set in. The war-bred squalor of Mobile, Alabama, which acquired a large flight-training school and sprawling shipyards, appalled the novelist John Dos Passos. In 1943 Dos Passos observed packed streetcars, lunchrooms, and movie theaters, sidewalks teeming with pedestrians, overflowing garbage cans, crowded trailer parks and barrackslike tenements, men sleeping in eight-hour shifts on "hot beds" in rooming houses.

Yet for the country folk attracted to Mobile by jobs and high wages, acknowledged Dos Passos, "everything's new and wonderful. . . . They can buy radios, they can go to the [motion] pictures, they can go to beer-parlors, bowl, shoot craps, bet on the ponies. . . . Housekeeping in a trailer with electric light and running water is a dazzling luxury to a woman who's lived all her life in a cabin with half-inch chinks between the splintered boards of the floor. . . . At night the streets are bright with electric light. Girls can go to beautyparlors, get their nails maincured, buy ready-made dresses."[11]

Beginning in 1943, everybody's weekly (as well as monthly) paychecks were subject to an unprecedented withholding-tax provision. Enacted by the Congress in lieu of more radical proposals (including one, which President Roosevelt himself briefly considered, to limit personal incomes to $25,000 annually), the federal withholding tax was designed to provide an almost continuous flow of revenue for financing the war. Sharp rises in personal incomes and the extension downward of tax liabilities meant that, for the first time, nearly all U.S. wage- and salary-earners were subject to some form of federal taxation. The federal withholding tax—despite being based on the debatable premise that one need never even see a portion of one's earnings—gained remarkably easy acceptance, and would become a permanent feature of Americans' lives in the postwar years.

Whether attracted by higher wages or motivated by a clear sense of patriotic duty, nearly all Americans found themselves directly involved in the war effort. Besides striving to grow their own vegetables in victory gardens and joining in successive war-bond drives (as well as making weekly or monthly bond purchases through payroll deductions), patriotic citizens saved and salvaged what their government assured them was vital to victory. Cooking fats, electric batteries, and virtually any kind of metal (even tinfoil chewing-gum wrappers) were among the materials dutifully collected and turned in at government offices. "Scrap drives," which commonly involved competition between schools and communities to amass the biggest pile of used (often unusable) metal, became veritable crusades. (One of my wartime memories is of a mountain of scrap metal, perhaps 50 feet high, standing on the school grounds in China, Texas. At its summit was the impossibly rusted shell of a Model T Ford.)

Those who were reluctant to contribute were apt to find themselves under both strong popular pressure and government coercion. Early in 1942, for example, a Valparaiso, Indiana, junk dealer named Frank Schumak, protesting that his scrap-metal pile represented his savings for his old age, would not sell at the Office of War Production's price of $18.75 per ton, whereupon rifle-bearing military police, acting under congressional legislation passed the previous October, seized it all—some 200,000 pounds.

If Schumak and lots of other Americans protested but then finally submitted, some people absolutely refused to join the national consensus forming in the wake of the Pearl Harbor attack. Nearly 43,000 men refused to enter military service and were officially classified as conscientious objectors (COs). Most of them submitted to some form of noncombatant duty (often in highly regimented Civilian Public Service camps), but about six thousand adamant COs—of whom members of the Jehovah's Witnesses religious sect made up the biggest number—were confined in federal prison.

Other dissenters became the object of investigation and prosecution under the Espionage Act, the Alien Registration Act, and other federal statutes. In the fall of 1944, following the death of the presiding judge, the U.S. Justice Department's two-year-old legal proceedings against 26 outspoken pro-fascists ended in a mistrial, and they remained free (if still carefully watched). On the political left, the tiny, Trotskyist Socialist Workers Party (SWP) was kept under close surveillance by the Federal Bureau of Investigation; eventually the Justice Department brought charges against several SWP members for subversive activities, but only one person was convicted and imprisoned.

Although German and Italian resident aliens were watched closely and a few were interned in the early months after Pearl Harbor, citizens of Italian and German ancestry continued to live in a climate of general tolerance. Whereas during the First World War, one in every three persons in the United States had been either an immigrant or an offspring of an immigrant, by the early 1940s two decades of declining immigration—a consequence of restrictive legislation in the twenties and the economic ills of the thirties—had greatly reduced the number of resident aliens. Of the remaining 256,000 German and 599,000 Italian noncitizens, most had children who were citizens. Then, too, the emphasis in the Roosevelt administration's propaganda efforts was not to teach hatred of the German and Italian people as such, but of the Nazi and Fascist regimes they lived under. (The fact that American military leaders bore such names as Eisenhower, Nimitz, Spaatz, and Eichelberger helped to confirm the loyalties of German-Americans in general.)

In the aftermath of Pearl Harbor, by contrast, persons of Japanese ancestry experienced what would come to be regarded as the most massive and egregious violation of civil liberties ever perpetrated by the U.S. government. In the Hawaiian Islands, where they were most numerous (and an indispensable part of the labor force), nearly all such people were able to maintain their residences and, in most instances, their occupations, albeit under strict wartime martial law. On the mainland Pacific Coast, however, the 110,000 resident Japanese and Japanese-American residents—of whom two-thirds were U.S. born and the remainder native Japanese ineligible for citizenship under a 1924 law—quickly came to appear as an intolerable element.

Fears on the part of national, state, and local officials of possible espionage and sabotage activities now combined explosively with long-standing racial prejudices and economic resentments. In February 1942 General John DeWitt, army commander on the Pacific Coast, spoke for white Americans in general when he declared, "A Jap's a Jap. It makes no difference whether he is an American citizen or not. . . . I don't want any of them." The Japanese, announced *Life* magazine, had "a special affinity for naval establishments, docks, power lines, reservoirs and war factories." Furthermore, they lived "in close communities, 100% nonabsorbed into the rest of the population."[12]

In March 1942 a newly formed War Relocation Authority (WRA), acting under President Roosevelt's executive order, undertook physically to isolate all Japanese and Japanese-Americans at places in the interior U.S. By mid-summer they had been resettled in 11 camps east of the Sierra mountain range— desolate sites enclosed by barbed wire, where they lived in flimsy wooden barracks that provided one room per family. Under such harsh circumstances, feelings on the part of the internees, who had lost hundreds of millions of dollars in property values when they were forced to dispose of their holdings on short notice, were understandably bitter.

By 1943 the WRA had instituted a program for certifying camp residents as loyal Americans and releasing them for outside employment, including service in the U.S. armed forces. When more than a quarter of the male Nisei (U.S.-born Japanese) refused to comply with Selective Service regulations, they were transferred to the worst of all internment sites, at Tule Lake in the eastern California desert. Meanwhile Nisei volunteers in the U.S. and Hawaii formed several army units, of which the best-known was the 442nd Regimental Combat Team, whose members won an extraordinary number of medals and citations in the Italian campaign. Early in 1945 the WRA allowed all remaining interns to leave the camps.

Sometimes even those determined to behave as loyal Americans could not gain acceptance from their countrymen. Early in 1944 George Yamamoto, an Issei (Japanese-born) farm laborer who left a camp in California and settled at Rehoboth Beach, Delaware, encountered such hostility from the local people that he had to move to a nearby town in New Jersey, despite his employer's affirmation that he was hard-working and law-abiding. In New Jersey it was the same story, and when last heard from, Yamamoto had again relocated, this time in Bucks County, Pennsylvania.

It is hard to exaggerate the hatred Americans felt—and freely expressed—for the Japanese enemy. Many children growing up in the war years (including the present writer) nurtured an ambition someday to "kill a Jap." A woman who spent much of the war making shells in a munitions plant at Paducah, Kentucky, recalled that "we were just ready to wipe them out. . . . They were yellow little creatures that smiled when they bombed our boys. I remember someone in Paducah got up this idea of burning everything they had that was Japanese. . . . They had this big bonfire and people came and brought what they had that was made in Japan."[13]

Given the circumstances of the Pacific War—a conflict precipitated by an act of supreme treachery (as Americans saw it) and fought with powerful racial feelings (on both sides), against an enemy that fully lived up the image of fanaticism and viciousness portrayed in home-front propaganda—only a far more tolerant and reasonable people would have been willing to leave the Pacific Coast Japanese and Japanese-Americans alone. The relocation and internment policy—subsequently given constitutional sanction by the U.S. Supreme Court in a series of cases—proceeded from the rarely questioned assumption that racial identity was a more powerful behavioral determinant than long-term residence, or even U.S. citizenship.

By far the nation's largest racial minority consisted of black Americans—10-11 per cent of the total 1940 population of about 135 million. The war created a profoundly ambivalent situation for black citizens. Plentiful jobs and better wages brought relatively greater improvement in living standards for blacks than for whites, and after a decade of generally hard times, large-scale migration of blacks out of the Southern states resumed. The black population of California, for example, more than doubled during the war years. Yet long-entrenched discrimination in hiring and pay practices persisted among war contractors and in virtually every sector of the economy, and the Fair Employment Practices Commission—

created by President Roosevelt's executive order in 1941 to ward off a massive "March on Washington" being organized by A. Philip Randolph of the sleeping-car porters' union—proved generally ineffective. At the end of the war, "Jim Crow" (the traditional American term for racial segregation and exclusion) was still a basic feature of U.S. society—whether as official, codified policy in the Southern states or as extralegal, customary practice elsewhere.

Throughout the war, the U.S. military services persisted in maintaining segregated units; and while the air force trained a squadron of black pilots, the navy commissioned a small number black officers, and a few black infantry and armored units saw combat, the majority of black volunteers and draftees ended up assigned to construction, supply, maintenance, and food-service duty.

In a number of places around the country—such as Mobile, Alabama; Alexandria, Louisiana; Hubbard; Ohio; and Camp Shenango, Pennsylvania—friction between black and white workers or between black military personnel and local white residents produced ugly violence, though on a fairly small scale. Three outbreaks in the summer of 1943, however, qualified as major race riots.

One, in Harlem in New York City in August, started with a rumor that a white policemen had killed a black soldier, whereupon rampaging blacks, mostly young males, burned and looted much of Harlem's business district. Six people died before order was restored.

While the Harlem riot found black property owners sometimes arrayed against black looters, civil disturbances two months earlier in Detroit, Michigan, and Beaumont, Texas, amounted to all-out interracial wars. For more than a year Detroit had seethed with racial hostility, as tens of thousands of newly arrived black and white war workers—from all over the U.S. but mostly from the South—poured into the area. In the spring of 1942, at the mayor's request, hundreds of Michigan state troopers were deployed to protect twenty black families when, after much acrimony and delay, they finally moved into a newly built housing project for war workers and their families.

Then, on Sunday evening, 18 June 1943, rumors of interracial rape and murder triggered black destruction of white-owned businesses and retaliatory white shootings and beatings of blacks on streets, aboard trolleys, in theaters, and wherever else they could be found if they ventured outside black residential sections. After several days of carnage and devastation, finally brought to an end when U.S. army detachments occupied the city, 25 blacks and nine whites were dead and at least $2 million in property had been stolen, wrecked, or burned.

A few days later Beaumont, a shipbuilding and oil refining complex near the Gulf Coast, erupted into four days of rioting that mostly featured forays by mobs of gun-toting and club-wielding whites into the city's black districts. After about a dozen deaths, Texas National Guardsmen, ordered in under a martial law order issued by the governor, quelled the disturbance. (Another personal memory: Several years past draft age, with a crippled arm and only three fingers on his right hand, my father joined the Texas National Guard and, as a member of a unit made up of high school boys and middle-aged men, drilled on the China, Texas, school campus in the evenings. Based only 15 miles away, the local Guard unit was mobilized during the Beaumont riot. Early on a Saturday morning, after nearly a week's absence, my father arrived home—sleepless and utterly exhausted, his feet and legs swollen from long stretches of tense sentry duty—and headed straight for his bed.)

A fourth major riot that bloody summer took place in Los Angeles, where tens of thousands of people of Mexican ancestry had moved with their families in search of war-created job opportunities. (Hispanic employment at the Los Angeles shipyards, for example, grew from zero in 1941 to 17,000 by 1944.) At night, bands of wispy-moustached Mexican-American youngsters, called *pachucos,* roamed East Los Angeles wearing their trademark "zoot suits"—long, wide-shouldered jackets, "pegged" pants flared at the knees and tight at the ankles, knee-length watch chains, and low-crowned, wide-brimmed hats. Offensive to local "Anglos" by their appearance, language, and reputation for petty crime, the zoot-suiters finally, in June 1943, became the objects of assaults by mobs of sailors who dragged dozens of them from bars, cafes, and movie theaters, then stripped and beat them. Los Angeles policemen were mostly content to watch, and the riot ended only when navy police herded the sailors back to their quarters.

Harassment and prosecution of political and religious dissidents, forced relocation of persons of Japanese ancestry, racial and ethnic violence at home (as well as sometimes between American servicemen stationed overseas)—all that provided harsh reminders that, despite its rhetoric of democracy and tolerance, the United States remained a country with strong majoritarian notions of what should and would be tolerated, especially under the circumstances of wartime.

Yet the fact remains that the Pearl Harbor attack—by ending the "Great Debate" on the Roosevelt administration's "all-aid-short-of-war" policies in the European and Asian conflicts—inaugurated a 45-month period in which the people of the United States were more nearly unified, more nearly in agreement on a collective purpose, than at any time before or since in their national history. Despite continuing disputes at home over grand military planning (widespread sentiment for an "on-to-Tokyo" strategy versus Roosevelt's commitment to defeating Germany first), the vast majority of Americans accepted the war as something that was not only necessary but just and moral. If the effect of the Great Depression had been to aggravate class and ideological divisions, the war provided a powerful sense of common purpose and direction—a willingness to fight until the nation's enemies were forced to accept "unconditional surrender," the goal Roosevelt and a reluctant Winston Churchill proclaimed at Casablanca.

Among American intellectuals, the war culminated a process of reconciliation with national values and institutions—a process underway at least since the mid-1930s, when the formation of the Popular Front had brought together liberals, non-Marxist radicals, and Communist Party members and fellow travelers in a broad coalition of antifascist "progressives." Although the Nazi-Soviet pact in August 1939 wrecked the original Popular Front, the German invasion of the USSR, five-and-one-half months before the Japanese attacked Pearl Harbor, prompted the revival of the Left coalition. Once the U.S. and the USSR became formal allies in the struggle against Nazi Germany, the neo-Popular Front reached its peak late in 1943, at the time of the Tehran conference.

While wartime public-opinion polls indicated that a substantial majority of citizens remained hostile to the Communist Party and Marxist-Leninist ideology—what they understood as "Communism"—admiration for the USSR's war effort reached remarkable levels. In November 1942, for example, 20,000 people packed Madison Square Garden in New York for a rally staged by the Congress of Soviet-American Friendship, with Vice President Henry A. Wallace as the principal speaker. The war, said Wallace, must achieve "a democracy of the common people," one that combined American political democracy with Soviet economic democracy.[14]

Meanwhile audiences at the concerts of the New York Philharmonic, the Boston and Philadelphia symphonies, and other major ensembles heard a greal deal of work by Russian composers, especially the contemporaries Sergei Prokofiev and Dimitri Shostakovich. Among American composers, Roy Harris and Morton Gould both wrote symphonic works celebrating the Red Army and Soviet people. From Hollywood came a succession of motion pictures glorifying the Soviets in their struggle against the German invaders; in some instances movie studios went so far as to ask the Soviet embassy in Washington to review screenplays and provide technical assistance.

Soviet ambassador Maxim Litvinov and his wife, the British-born Ivy Low, became celebrities who entertained lavishly and were eagerly sought for public appearances. The dignitaries at one of the Litvinovs' receptions at the Soviet embassy (held the night before the big Soviet-American Friendship rally in New York) included, besides Vice President Wallace, five members of Roosevelt's Cabinet, Director Donald Nelson of the Office of War Production, several U.S. senators, and Supreme Court justices Hugo Black and William O. Douglas.

With the Popular Front spirit running high not only in such liberal magazines as the *Nation* and *New Republic* but in much more widely read, once-hostile weeklies and monthlies such as *Time, Life, Newsweek, Saturday Evening Post,* and *Business Week,* the Communist Party of the United States (CPUSA) enjoyed the most favorable circumstances in its history. Reorganized following the Stalin regime's dissolution of the Communist International in the spring of 1943, the CPUSA led impatient demands on the Left for a U.S.-British Second Front in Western Europe, denounced strikes or anything else that might interfere with war production, and zealously supported Roosevelt's leadership—quite a lot more zealously, in fact, than many non-Communist Americans. In 1944 Earl Browder, general secretary of the CPUSA, openly called for Roosevelt's reelection to a fourth term (which FDR won by his smallest margin thus far—fewer than 3.6 million votes).

Beginning in the fall of 1941, the popular image of Stalin—hitherto that of the ruthless dictator of the 1936-38 purges, the cynical partner in the Nazi-Soviet pact, and the aggressive instigator of the Soviet-Finnish war—underwent a striking transformation. In Henry Luce's magazines *Time* and *Life,* in numerous other publications, and not least in Hollywood's *Mission to Moscow* (based on Joseph E. Davies's best-selling memoir of his tour as ambassador to the USSR in 1937-38), Stalin emerged as pipe-smoking "Uncle Joe," the tough but benign leader of a nation united in its determination to expel the German hordes from the sacred soil of Mother Russia. "It is entirely possible," wrote the journalist Kenneth Davis in a fairly typical wartime assessment, "that when the final history of this great world crisis is written, Stalin will stand out as the man who saved the civilized world in spite of itself. . . ."[15]

In embracing Stalin's USSR as one of the "democracies" arrayed against fascist barbarism, Americans also increasingly supported the concept of a United Nations organization that, building on the wartime Grand Alliance, would become the most powerful instrument for peace in the postwar years. In the autumn of 1942, millions of them bought and read *One World,* Wendell Willkie's account of his recent globe-circling air journey as President Roosevelt's personal emissary. The message of the Republican party's 1940 presidential candidate—that Americans had to put aside their insular nationalism and think in terms of global humanity—seemed beyond dispute, as did similar urgings from many other quarters: Henry Luce's influential magazines, spokesmen for the Council on Foreign Relations and the Woodrow Wilson Foundation, the respected journalist Walter Lippmann, the distinguished jurist Jerome Frank, to name a few.

The motion picture *Wilson,* the most expensive ever made when it was released in 1944, was a sprawling, confused, simplistic account of President Woodrow Wilson's futile struggle to gain U.S. membership in the League of Nations following the First World War. Yet it was also a powerful warning that Americans must not again reject what Vice President Wallace termed "a second chance to erect a lasting structure of peace. . . ."[16]

A mixture of grim determination and confident hope, realism and naivete, preponderant attitudes found expression in much of the popular culture of the war years. Although less than half of the motion pictures produced in the U.S. between 1942 and 1945 directly treated the war, the several hundred "war movies" coming out of Hollywood tended to follow a predictable formula, in accordance with the guidelines and directives of the Office of War Information (the foremost war propaganda agency) and in the spirit of neo-Popular Frontism.

The Japanese were always treacherous, the Germans always brutal, the British always laconically brave, and the Soviets always robustly heroic. Except that blacks were rarely depicted, Americans appeared in an assortment of religious, ethnic, and regional guises. The "typical" U.S. combat outfit—whether on land, sea, or in the air—would consist of somebody from Brooklyn (perhaps of Italian ancestry and invariably a devotee of the Brooklyn baseball team), somebody from the rural South, a tough working-class representative (often Eastern European), a scholarly or poetic young man (often Jewish and usually killed early), a grizzled veteran (who sometimes provided the Irish flavor), and assorted other types—American Indian, Mexican-American, perhaps even a Chinese-American.

Suggesting (frequently trumpeting) that the fundamental strength of the American nation was in its motto *e pluribus unum,* such movies had their counterparts in much of the radio drama of the period, especially in the scripts of Norman Corwin, the most admired writer in the history of the medium. Whether in war-inspired movies, radio offerings, popular songs, magazine fiction, or childrens' comic books (which were widely consumed by men in the armed services), the message was essentially the same: Americans, blessed with liberty but forced to defend it, had to join forces with freedom-loving peoples everywhere to smash the fascist enemy and then construct a peace that would last.

Though often more artistically impressive, documentary motion pictures were hardly more sophisticated in their depiction of why and how the war had come about, and what was really at stake in the conflict. Besides being thrilled by the exploits of John Garfield and his fellow B-17 crewmen in *Air Force,* Robert Taylor's last stand in *Bataan,* or John Wayne's bloody revenge-taking in *Back to Bataan,* American movie audiences also gained inspiration from the *Why We Fight* multipart documetary made by the acclaimed Hollywood director Frank Capra, as well as from John Ford's brilliant recapitulation of the battle of Midway and Soviet-produced documentaries such as *Moscow Strikes Back* and *Stalingrad.*

While one might question the overall quality of Hollywood's output during the war years, the fact remains that record numbers of people paid their way into theaters to see the movie industry's offerings. That, of course, was a consequence of both surging wartime prosperity and the difficulty people experienced in traveling much distance from their homes for recreation and entertainment.

The same circumstances account for a boom in spectator sports during years when the caliber of available athletic talent declined steadily. Sooner or later, collegiate athletic teams lost most of their top performers to the armed forces, and had to rely on first and second-year students and a few young men classified as "4-F"—physically unfit for military service. Some of the best football of the war years was played by teams representing such military installations as Great Lakes Naval Training Center near Chicago, Norfolk (Virginia) Naval Base, and the El Toro (California) Marine facility. In 1944-45, teams of the U.S. Military Academy at West Point, New York, dominated the collegiate football scene.

Collegiate basketball suffered from the same talent shortages, with the advantage passing to those teams—such as St. Johns University, DePaul University, and Oklahoma A & M College—that featured at least one player exempted from military service by the official height limitation of 6 feet-6 inches. The war thus speeded the ascendancy of the "big man" in basketball.

Although the War Department closed the tracks in the winter of 1944-45, horse racing generally flourished in wartime, while professional boxing, with heavyweight champion Joe Louis and most other top-quality fighters in uniform, packed arenas for matches between third-rate performers.

Meanwhile professional baseball, still the nation's number-one spectator sport and still widely regarded as the "National Pastime," continued the strong attendance revival that had begun in 1941, even though, within four years, some 60 percent of the prewar players were in military service. Instead of tapping the abundant talent in the Negro professional leagues, "Organized Baseball"—officially recognized, all-white professional leagues—continued to exclude black players. Not until 1946, the first postwar season, would Jackie Robinson finally breach baseball's color barrier. (Like Organized Baseball, the National Professional Football League limped through the war years with overage and 4-F players, and also continued to be a for-whites-only operation.)

If people could not attend a particular sports event in person, more than likely they could hear it described in a radio broadcast; by the early 1940s sports coverage had come to occupy a major portion of radio time, particularly on locally owned stations with limited broadcast ranges. Five afternoons a week the three national radio networks also filled the airwaves with 15-minute serialized dramatic episodes (called "soap operas" because they were commonly sponsored by soap-products advertisers). Then, in the evening hours when the listening audience was biggest, the networks offered the nation a mélange of musical, quiz-game, dramatic, and comedy programs. The war years were the heyday of radio comedy, with the likes of Jack Benny, Bob Hope, Fred Allen, and "Fibber McGee and Molly" cracking jokes destined to be repeated by Americans everywhere.

But radio also brought the experience of war directly into homes, workplaces, and wherever any of the 85 million American-owned radios might be located. Radio affected Americans' lives during World War II as it never had and never would again. "From the pre-Munich days through . . . V-J Day," observed Norman Corwin after the war, "there was the greatest concentration of highly dramatic news in all history, and radio lost little of that drama and less time in transmitting the news to the public."[17]

Intrepid correspondents who took their microphones into perilous circumstances became radio's real-life romantic heroes. Their prototype was the Columbia Broadcasting System's Edward R. Murrow, who transmitted accounts of the 1940 Blitz from London rooftops and also flew with a British bombing crew on a mission over Germany, describing the raid as it happened for listeners in the United States. Eric Sevareid parachuted into the Burma jungle to report on the war there, while Richard C. Hottelet bailed out of a burning U.S. bomber over Germany. (Rescued and flown back to his transmitter in London, Hottelet had his report on the airwaves within a few hours.)

At home, commentators such as H. V. Kaltenborn, Lowell Thomas, Walter Winchell, and Raymond Swing, to name but a few, analyzed, interpreted, and editorialized on the progress the United States and its allies were making—or weren't making—against their enemies. Virtually the entire spectrum of political opinion had at least one spokesman—from the bitterly anti-New Deal, anti-British, and anti-Soviet Upton Close and Fulton Lewis, Jr., to the ardently pro-Roosevelt, pro-Allied Edward R. Murrow and William L. Shirer.

The work of Norman Corwin, who insisted that radio offered the potential to develop a literature of its own, qualitatively equal to stage drama, became virtually synonymous with "serious" dramatic efforts in the new medium. A pronounced liberal and unapologetic patriot, Corwin freely acknowledged seeking "to indoctrinate the people" on why they were at war.[18] A week after Pearl Harbor was bombed, all the networks carried Corwin's celebration of the U.S. Bill of Rights; on four other occasions his lyrical, idealistic renderings received all-networks transmission. In May 1945 his *On a Note of Triumph* commemorated victory in Europe; his "14 August," broadcast within hours of the Japanese surrender, envisioned a world of understanding and cooperation built on the ruins of war.

If the war established radio as the first source of news for most people, daily newspapers remained indispensable for detailed information and perspective. Yet a cursory look at American newspapers for 1942-45 shows that, though full of war news and analysis, they also preserved their essential prewar format. That left plenty of room for sports and fashion news, comic strips, gossip about goings-on in "high society," and of course coverage of scandals, murders, and natural and man-made disasters. Thus in 1942, while the Allies landed in North Africa and the struggle for Stalingrad raged, a fire at a Boston nightclub that killed 491 people dominated the front pages. The next year, as the Soviets took the offensive and the Germans yielded Africa, the murder of Harry Oakes, a wealthy Britisher living in New York, compelled readers' attentions, as did the sexual and legal entanglements of the movie celebrities Charlie Chaplin and Errol Flynn. And in 1944, to judge from newspaper coverage, the controversy over whether the government should ban horse racing might have been as important as the liberation of Paris.

Nor did popular magazines change in basic form and content. *Life,* the most popular of all with an official weekly circulation of about 5 million and a readership (or "viewership") many times greater, was the magazine equivalent of the highly successful "newsreels" shown in movie theaters. Founded in 1936 on the premise that most people preferred pictures to words, *Life* sought not just to illustrate textual material, but to present its picture layouts as virtually self-contained descriptive processes. As Henry

Luce's *Time* covered the news in words with interpretation, Luce's *Life* covered it in pictures with dramatization.

Life (as well as its biweekly rival *Look*) purported to show it all, but in fact picture-magazine editors, like everybody else in the American press, worked under government restrictions on what could be printed or shown. It was a full year after the Pearl Harbor bombing before the Navy Department released photographs and films of the sinking of the battleship *Arizona* and other devastation wrought by the Japanese raiders. Not until early 1943 did *Life* publish photographs of American combat dead; subsequently the Office of War Information was so upset over newsreel and magazine pictures of the Marines' bloody assault on Tarawa atoll that no more American war dead were pictured for public consumption until early 1945.

Although they might complain about wartime censorship, American newspaper and magazine publishers, editors, and reporters, as well as radio reporters and commentators and Hollywood newsreel producers, were generally willing to accept such constraints, in the interest of keeping up the morale of both military and civilian personnel. The adversarial, frequently antagonistic relationship between government officialdom and what would later be generically referred to as "the media" had not yet surfaced as one of the characteristic features of American public life.

Of course newspapers and magazines in the United States relied mainly on advertising revenues to keep going. The advertising industry itself, under the aegis of the newly formed Advertising Council, took advantage as best it could of the circumstances of wartime. Until 1944 business corporations tended to tout the absolute indispensability of their products and services—everything from aircraft, tanks, and field telephones to pasteurized milk, valve switches, and fertilizers—to a successful war effort. Americans were exhorted to live with shortages and sacrifices, and to understand that manufacturers were just as unhappy about the situation as their customers. A 1942 magazine advertisement by the B. F. Goodrich Rubber Company, for example, showed four Americans trying to thumb an automobile ride, because "It's the patriotic gesture now."[19]

The Advertising Council made a major contribution to the war effort by working closely with the Office of Price Administration, Office of War Information, Treasury Department, and other government agencies to convince Americans to shun the black market, save scrap, conserve rubber, donate blood, grow their own vegetables, and do all the other things patrotic citizens ought to be doing. Most of all the council helped the government sell war bonds; by 1944 some 85 million Americans had purchased federal securities.

By the middle of that year, with Allied forces advancing on all fronts and victory virtually assured, the advertising industry had started to show off the promised cornucopia of postwar consumer goods. When Germany was defeated, recalled an executive in one of New York's leading advertising agencies, "a rash of utopian word-pictures of the postwar product-world broke over the nation so fast that the faithful Advertising Council, remembering Japan, sent warnings that the war job was not finished."[20]

Within another three-and-one-half months, the "war job" was finished. In Franklin, Louisiana (where I was staying with my aunt and uncle while my mother underwent surgery in Texas), we finally received authentic news that the Japanese had surrendered—after two false reports. I found a photograph of the Emperor Hirohito in the local newspaper, carefully marked an X over it, and mailed it to my parents. Upon my return home a couple of weeks later, I found that the 200 or so Germans held at a local prisoner of war camp (of some 200,000 in the United States as a whole) were all gone, and the camp was being dismantled.

The "U.S. relaxes," proclaimed *Life* in October 1945. While servicemen were glad to be home, they were "in no hurry to go to work."[21] Nor were recently laid-off war workers in a hurry to take other jobs at lower pay. Millions of women, rapidly displaced by returning servicemen, left the workforce for good and, sooner or later, settled for the domesticity of wifery and motherhood that was idealized in postwar advertising and popular culture.

In truth, many home-front Americans—having enjoyed the best jobs and highest wages of their lives—had not been particularly anxious for the war to end, even though it was risky to express such sentiments openly. If nearly everybody had accumulated savings (more than $100 billion in the population as a whole by 1945), nearly everybody also feared that a major economic slump—maybe even another full-scale depression—was in the offing.

As things turned out, though, the pent-up demand for consumer goods, in combination with the enormous personal savings accumulated during the war, produced unprecedented peacetime prosperity. Ahead was a rapid enlargement of the American middle class and an epochal movement of urban populations into suburban areas. Better diet and various medical advances coming out of the war, especially the development of antibiotics, made for substantial improvements in public health. Meanwhile American higher education, nearly overwhelmed by an influx of veterans guaranteed benefits under wartime legislation (hailed as the "G.I. Bill of Rights"), would be permanently transformed. So, it soon became evident, were

American race relations, as increasing numbers of black people, having either served in the armed forces or benefited from the economic advantages of wartime, demanded the rights of full citizenship.

Among many other consequences of the war-generated prosperity was that the birth rate, rapidly rising since 1941-42 when the marriage rate took a big jump, continued to climb until the late 1950s. A surging postwar divorce rate also dated from the war years; as early as 1944 nearly 18,000 divorces were granted in Los Angeles County, equal to 53 percent of the number of marriage licenses issued in the county that year.

A Long Beach, California, woman thought of the war years as a time when "the patriotism was so thick you could cut it." "While the rest of the world came out bruised and scarred and nearly destroyed," another American remembered, "we came out with the most unbelievable machinery, tools, manpower, money. The war was fun for America. . . . I'm not talking about the poor souls who lost sons and daughters in the war. But for the rest of us, the war was a hell of a good time."[22]

An exaggeration, of course. Among the obvious social costs directly attributable to the war were increased racial and ethnic violence, intolerance of antiwar radicals (of both Left and Right), incarceration of citizens who happened to be of Japanese ancestry, disruption of family life and an unprecedented divorce rate, and a spiraling incidence of youth crime (or "juvenile delinquency," as sociologists, social psychologists, and other supposed experts quickly labeled it). But if not wholly just and moral, the Second World War did give Americans both a revitalized economy and a cause in which the overwhelming majority of them could readily and fervently believe. In various respects it really was "the good war"—or about as close to one as the American people are likely to get.

Notes

1. Studs Terkel, *"The Good War": An Oral History of World War Two* (New York, 1985), 34.

2. *Ibid.*, 575.

3. *Ibid.*, 312-13.

4. *Look* 7 (5 May 1942), 42.

5. *Life* 15 (8 July 1942), 41; *Look* 6 (30 June 1942), 24.

6. *Look* 9 (20 March 1945), 33; *Life* 16 (21 February 1944), 40.

7. Quoted in Terkel, *"The Good War,"* 239.

8. *Look* 7 (15 June 1943), 25.

9. Ethel Gorman, *So Your Husband's Gone to War* (New York, 1942), *passim.*

10. Terkel, *"The Good War,"* 116.

11. John Dos Passos, *State of the Nation* (Boston, 1944), 95.

12. *Life* 12 (16 March 1942), 34; DeWitt quoted in Allan M. Winkler, *Home Front U.S.A.: America during World War II* (Arlington Heights, Ill., 1986), 72.

13. Quoted in Terkel, *"The Good War,"* 107.

14. *Life* 13 (30 November 1942), 138.

15. Kenneth Davis, "Have We Been Wrong about Stalin?" *Current History* l (September 1941), 6-11.

16. Quoted in Robert A. Divine, *Second Chance: The Triumph of Internationalism in America during World War II* (New York, 1967), 48.

17. Norman Corwin, "The Radio," in Jack Goodman, ed., *While You Were Gone: A Report on Wartime Life in the United States* (New York, 1946), 386.

18 Corwin quoted in Milton Allen Kaplan, *Radio and Poetry* (New York, 1949), 11.

19. *Life* 13 (6 July 1948), 1.

20. Raymond Rubicam, "Advertising," in Goodman, ed., *While You Were Gone,* 444.

21. *Life* 19 (15 October 1945), 29.

22. Quoted in Terkel, *"The Good War,"* 234, 575.

■ ■ ■

Mutual Perceptions: Images, Ideals, and Illusions

Mikhail N. Narinsky, Lydia V. Pozdeeva, et al.

World War Two was a very public war. To a greater extent than in any previous conflict in history, the populations of the three Allied countries were aware of the progress of the conflict, abroad as well as at home. Newspapers, newsreels, radio, and movies conveyed the words, sounds, and images of battle. In Great Britain, the United States, and the Soviet Union, the public were informed not merely about their enemies but also about their allies. Manipulating the images portrayed and managing the emotions aroused became a major task for governments in all three countries, not least because, in each case, the wartime alliance entailed substantial shifts in attitude from the 1930s. In this chapter we examine the evolution of public opinion and official propaganda in each country toward their new and often perplexing allies.

Bringing together the member states of the coalition and overcoming negative views and stereotypes was an important task for the intelligentsia. In October 1941, the darkest period of what in the USSR was always called the Great Patriotic War, Soviet scientists and researchers urged their colleagues throughout the world to cooperate in opposing Nazism: "It is the duty of the whole artistic and academic community to join actively in the fight and help foil completely Hitler's design of enslaving the nations one by one. Now the issue of independence, freedom, and the very existence of the people is being decided on the battlefield. This is the issue at stake: Will science triumph over barbarism, will world progress triumph over the Hitler reaction?"[1] That appeal was echoed by Soviet men of letters. In their reply to greetings from the Organization of Young American Writers, participants in the antifascist meeting held in Moscow in October 1941 stated: "In the crucial struggle for the elimination of brutal fascism, we are happy to learn that young U.S. authors are marching shoulder to shoulder with us . . . Let the truthful pen of all honest writers of the world strike at the low and vicious enemy of humanity, freedom, culture and democracy."[2]

Such language may seem stilted today. At the time, the phraseology was typical of public Soviet statements, but the sentiments were definitely not. Calls for communists and capitalists to cooperate sounded very strange to the Soviet public. They had been taught to believe in the future world revolution, were deeply hostile to imperialism, and had lived in an atmosphere of isolation, as if in a siege. In the 1920s and 1930s the "Entente imperialists" were described as the main anti-Soviet force, with Great Britain in the vanguard. Soviet people remembered Lord Curzon's "Ultimatum," the rupture of diplomatic relations with the USSR by Austen Chamberlain and the policy of appeasement climaxing in Munich. "British colonizers" and "British imperialists" were the adopted Soviet propaganda clichés, and negative stereotypes were the rule.

As to the United States, the attitude to it among the Soviet population was less antipathetic. They regarded the United States as a land of magnificent scientific and technological achievements, worthy of respect. At the same time, the Soviet mass media stressed in its propaganda statements that the United States was a country of deep social contrasts and racial contradictions, whereas in external relations the United States was viewed as a potential partner rather than as a hostile force.

After Nazi aggression had been launched against the USSR and the foundation of the anti-Hitler coalition was laid, Soviet leaders and propagandists focused on the new allies. Stalin was the first to do so in his broadcast address on 3 July 1941, when he declared

> Our war for our country's freedom will become part of the European and American people's fight for their independence and democratic freedoms. That will be a united front of the nations for freedom against enslavement by Hitler's Nazi armies. In this context, the historic statement by Great Britain's Prime Minister, Mr. Churchill, about assistance to the Soviet Union and the U.S. Government's declarations of its readiness to render assistance to our country, are quite understandable and meaningful and evoke only gratitude in the hearts of the peoples of the Soviet Union.[3]

The Soviet propaganda machine dutifully fulfilled injunctions by the political leadership and manipulated mass consciousness. All press reports were subjected to strict censorship. No public opinion polls were then held in the USSR, but, judging by recollections of the war that have been preserved, there are no grounds to speak about any significant difference between public opinion and the official stand with respect to the Allies. As a bridge with the prewar era, they often tried to differentiate between the American and British people, on the one hand, and their political leaders and ruling circles, on the other.

Soviet journalists praised highly the typical characteristics of the British and American peoples and their will in the fight against Nazi aggression. Hitler "has underestimated this English people's capacity for resistance," *Pravda* wrote in August 1941, praising "their typical stubbornness and composure."[4] Popular writer and journalist Ilya Ehrenburg pointed out: "People who do not know anything about England often confuse Britons' composure with lack of determination. Actually you can hardly find a nation more stubborn than the British. They lose their temper calmly, become embittered calmly and fight calmly but fiercely."[5]

"The freedom-loving American people has taken the side of the opponents of Nazi barbarians and obscurantists," *Pravda* observed. "The American people are full of hatred of Nazism. This hatred is being manifested ever more actively."[6] Georgy Baidukov, a prominent Soviet pilot who took part in the nonstop USSR-United States flight over the North Pole in 1937, wrote: "It is interesting to note that there are many American customs similar to our Russian ones. Just like Russians, Americans are affable, talkative and sociable."[7]

In wartime Soviet people learned more about British and particularly American culture. In the grim summer of 1942 evenings of English and American films were organized in Moscow. About at the same time the prominent Soviet film director Sergei Eizenstein wrote this: "Mutual interest of American and Soviet film-makers is growing with each passing day. This seems to reflect the sentiments our great peoples experience with respect to each other."[8] American films such as *Mission to Moscow* and *The North Star* (about resistance in a Soviet village to German invaders) were shown in the Soviet Union. In June-July 1942, a course of lectures on art in the United States was delivered in the Moscow State Museum of New Art.

At the same time one should not exaggerate the importance of all this and paint too rosy a picture. In reality, the Soviet population could hardly imagine, on the basis of the available information, what military efforts were being exerted by Great Britain and the United States or the nature of British and American daily life in wartime. Soviet propaganda of the period laid its principal stress on Soviet patriotism and the Soviet people's heroic efforts in their fight against the Nazi invaders.

The allies' assistance to the USSR and supplies under Lend-Lease were not, of course, passed over in silence, although public attention was never directed to the subject. The speeches of Franklin Roosevelt and Winston Churchill, as well as statements by U.S. aid officials, were carried by the Soviet press. However, Soviet readers could hardly judge the amount of aid given by the allies. Soviet newsreels in the summer of 1943 pictured U.S. Lend-Lease aid in a very favorable light, but the Soviet mass media stressed aid in food products, even though supplies of armaments and matériel were of greater value (see chapter 6). In this way the fact of U.S. assistance was admitted, as it were, but certainly belittled. Take, for instance, a typical episode described by Konstantin Simonov in his long story *Days and Nights,* devoted to wartime events. The episode deals with the fierce battles fought at Stalingrad, where battalion commander Saburov and head of staff Maslennikov found themselves at the time.

> Without taking off their trench coats Saburov and Maslennikov sat down at the table facing each other, and Saburov poured vodka into small home-made vessels. They drained them and only then noticed that there was nothing to go with their vodka . . . Having fumbled on the table for some eatables, Saburov reached for an elegant rectangular American can with colourful pictures on its four sides depicting the dishes that could be prepared from its contents. A neat can opener was soldered to the can.[9]

That bright and elegant American can, of course, came in quite useful, although it looked strange and out of place amid the inferno of embattled Stalingrad.

There were elements of watchfulness and distrust among all the members of the coalition. The Second Front was then "Problem Number One." Again the tone on this issue was set by Stalin. In his effort to find some justification for the Soviet troops' major setbacks in 1942, he said this in his report at a meeting held on the occasion of the 25th anniversary of the Great October Revolution: "So, the main reason behind the Germans' tactical success at our front this year is the absence of the Second Front in Europe which enables them to send all their free reserves to our front and ensure great numerical superiority in the southwestern direction."[10]

Ilya Ehrenburg came out energetically for the opening of the Second Front. In September 1942, he insistently pointed out to the British readership: "It's high time, it's high time . . . Fifty divisions on the Atlantic coast would have made a greater contribution to the fight for the Volga and the Caucasus than all the supplies. Of course the supplies are also indispensable, but they can hardly be of equal importance."[11]

In March 1943, Ehrenburg already wrote about the over-long expectations of the Second Front with bitter irony: "A few weeks ago I visited tankmen in a village house. Master-sergeant Vasilchenko, a handsome man with a childlike smile and two decorations on his tunic, was preparing supper. Taking an American can of sausages, he said: 'Let's open the Second Front.' I laughed but Vasilchenko's eyes were sad."[12] That joke must have been very popular among Soviet officers and men at the time. It was also mentioned in Simonov's *Days and Nights*. When battalion commander Saburov was receiving a journalist, who had come from Moscow to the Stalingrad front line, he said: "Have some American canned meat, please. Here we jokingly call it the Second Front."[13]

In view of the Soviet side's exaggerated (even oversensitive) interest in the Second Front issue, one can imagine the effect of the sensational news of the Allied landings in Normandy. A few days after the operation began, all Soviet newspapers frontpaged Stalin's interview, granted to a *Pravda* correspondent in connection with the Allies' landing operation in Northern France. This is part of what Stalin said: "Summing up the results of the seven days of fighting by the Allies' liberation army, after it landed in Northern France, one may say confidently that the massive forcing of the English Channel and landing of the Allied troops in Northern France have been crowned with success. This is no doubt a brilliant victory of our Allies. It should be admitted that this operation is something unprecedented in world history for its grand scale and high skill of implementation." Pointing out that neither "the invincible Napoleon" nor "hysterical Hitler" had been able to cross the English Channel, Stalin stressed: "It is only the British and American troops that have managed to realize this grand plan of forcing the Channel and implementing their massive landing operation. This will go down in history as an achievement of the highest order."[14]

Military experts, news analysts, journalists, and poets also praised the Allies' landing operation, following in the footsteps of the "Great Marshal." Poet Demyan Bedny even wrote a rather poor fable-parable, which included such lines as:

> They've invaded the Nazi's forest,
> And are fighting at its edge,
> And our Allies' artillery
> Is thundering in Normandy . . .[15]

That period in mid-1944 was probably marked by the most favorable attitude to the allies on the part of the Soviet leadership and public. Most of the disputes about the postwar arrangement of the world were yet to arise, and those that were already in progress were conducted behind the closed doors of officialdom.

Positive attitudes toward the United States and Great Britain were to some degree manifested in the attitude toward those countries' leaders, Franklin Roosevelt and Winston Churchill. Soviet newspapers carried pictures of the three leaders during their meetings in Tehran and the Crimea, and also of those of Stalin and Churchill during the British premier's visit to Moscow in October 1944. However, of the two, Roosevelt was viewed more favorably. As *Pravda* writers put it in November 1944 when he was running for reelection: "Roosevelt has been working fruitfully for the United States to take a worthy place in the militant alliance of democratic countries and make a valuable contribution to the struggle against Hitlerite Germany. It should be admitted that he has attained his goal."[16]

Warm respect for Roosevelt was manifested in comments and press reports about his sudden death. Stalin sent a message of condolence to President Truman and Eleanor Roosevelt. The official Soviet statement called him "one of the most outstanding and popular American political leaders in that country's history."[17] Probably no major politician of the capitalist world has ever received such high praise. "We've lost one of the greatest statemen the world has ever known and a great man," stated then Soviet Ambassador to America Andrei Gromyko.[18] "The greatest politician of a world wide caliber . . . an outstanding fighter for the cause of democracy and progress" was the way *Izvestia* described Roosevelt.[19]

On the whole the United States enjoyed greater sympathy and respect than Great Britain in the Soviet Union. The Soviet press quoted with great sympathy the words of Eric Johnston, chairman of the American Chamber of Commerce, after he visited the USSR: "Russians most of all admire the American production genius. Any person who symbolizes this production, no matter what his attitude to the Soviet system may be, is sure to receive a cordial reception."[20] These words harmonized with the following pronouncement by Ambassador Gromyko in Washington: "The science, art and literature of the United States have won recognition and respect in the Soviet Union."[21]

It may be said that, in general, the Soviet people were favorably disposed to the allied nations and armies at the end of the war. However, this attitude was not deep-rooted, for basically a narrow class approach prevailed. Moreover, the victory legitimized anew, as it were, the Stalinist political regime, which, under the smoke screen of praise to the Soviet people, actually gave itself the credit. And Soviet leaders still retained their distrust of the allies. According to journalist Felix Chuyev, this is how Vyacheslav Molotov recollected Victory Day in San Francisco: "They congratulated me on May 8. However they did not celebrate it in a big way. A minute of silence was observed, according to custom. But there was no real feeling in it. . . . Not that it did not concern them, but they were wary and suspicious of us, and we still more so of them. . . ."[22]

Various factors had shaped public attitudes in Britain to the USSR before World War II. Pictures of Stalinist horrors coexisted in people's minds with images of Soviet advocacy of collective security and with recognition of the country's economic and social achievements. The idea of Anglo-Soviet cooperation was quite popular in the British Isles. In April 1939 some 87 percent of Britons assessed favorably the prospects for conclusion of the military treaty by Britain, France, and the USSR.[23]

The signing of the Soviet-German Non-Aggression Pact and the war against Finland bewildered advocates of rapprochement between Britain and the USSR. Nevertheless, the majority still favored normalization of Britain's relations with the USSR as a prospective ally in the struggle against Nazism, so the British were impatiently looking forward to signs of discord between Hitler and Stalin.[24] One of the documents of the private British survey organization Mass Observation observed:

> Public opinion about Russia and the Russians has been exceptionally consistent over the past years, despite direct and indirect propaganda against her, and even through the blackest periods of the Russo-German treaty and the Finnish war. . . . There has been a consistent and deep underlying feeling that Russia represents the interests of the ordinary person . . . , but this feeling is far removed from any real sympathy with, or understanding of, communism as such.[25]

Churchill's broadcast on 22 June 1941 was widely approved in Britain and his pledge of assistance to the USSR was generally "accepted as both a practical and logical move." In the first days of fighting on the Soviet-German front, government intelligence reports suggested, a large section of the British public took a skeptical view of the Soviet military potential and felt that the most that could be hoped for was that Russia would "be able to hold out long enough to give us some real advantage." According to other sources, however, many ordinary Britons from the start had faith in the might of Soviet resistance, believing that Russia was invincible, although they could hardly see any chance of its gaining an easy victory over the Reich. Only 25 percent of those polled in London in the week from 27 June to 4 July 1941 believed that the war in the East would last less than a year. Yet even "in the first few days only 7 percent expected Germany to get the best of it."[26]

The Soviet army's fierce battles against the *Wehrmacht,* Soviet setbacks and losses, and the Soviet people's bearing at the front and in the rear evoked a lively response in the hearts of Britain's population. Since early July their skepticism had been slowly but surely replaced with confidence in the final Soviet victory. In the days of great tension in October 1941, when Hitler's army was at the approaches of Moscow, public opinion polls conducted in Britain did not indicate any expectation of Soviet capitulation. On 15 October, for example, the situation "revealed the depth and intensity of public sympathy for Russia" and "increased admiration for the tremendous efforts of the Soviet troops and civilians."[27] On that day Mass Observation recorded the following fragments of comment about the USSR: "The Russians will certainly go on fighting even if they lose Moscow . . . they won't give in even if Hitler reaches Moscow. They've got a lot of important industries farther east and can quite well carry on the war. They're much better organized than we realize . . . ." In late December 1941, analysis of British reaction to the counteroffensive of Soviet troops near Moscow revealed that: "An increasing number of people considers that Russia has saved this country from being destroyed by the Germans, and there is a very deep sense of gratitude in evidence."[28] By that time Soviet resistance had noticeably boosted Britons' morale and their confidence in victory.

The weekly reports of the people's attitude to the situation at home and abroad, which were sent to the Ministry of Information in London, as well as other data on public opinion in Britain, indicated that the strongest and most durable enthusiasm in Britain was manifested in connection with the exploits performed by the Red Army and the Soviet people. In the second half of 1941 and in 1942, all reports of the Home Intelligence Division of the Ministry stressed the British people's concern over developments at the Soviet front and among civilians.[29]

A broad movement of solidarity with the USSR swept the British Isles, with workers and trade union organizations taking the lead. British scientists actively supported the patriotic efforts of their Soviet counterparts, they highly appreciated the attention paid by the USSR to Britain's prominent scientists. (Even in the summer of 1941 the Soviet Academy of Sciences did not stop its publications in the history of Russian and international science; a collection of Isaac Newton's letters was in progress, timed for the 300th anniversary of his birth.[30]) In January 1944 the British diplomat John Balfour presented to the Academy of Sciences in Moscow a gift of the Royal Society—the first edition of Newton's *Principia* and his original manuscript. Later the Academy was presented with a copy of the letter Newton had sent to Alexander Menchikov—the first Russian member of the Royal Society. When handing this document to the Academician Vladimir Komarov, Sir Henry Dale, President of the Royal Society, asked for it to be seen as a sign of the great admiration felt by the Society for the part played by the Academy of Sciences in the common struggle for victory.[31]

The majority of the British artistic community made a tangible contribution to promoting friendly relations with the Soviet Union: H. G. Wells, J. B. Priestley, James Aldridge, and other prominent authors were among those who expressed admiration for the Soviet people's valiant feats. Tolstoy's *War and Peace* became a best-seller, and translations of war poems by Russian poets, including many Stalin Prize winners, were regularly published in British periodicals such as *Tribune* and *The Spectator*. Alexander Werth's "Russian Commentary"—a series of his Sunday reports on the BBC—had an audience of some 12-13 million in Britain. Members of various political parties contributed to the public funds for assistance to the USSR, as well as such prominent British theatrical personalities as Sybil Thorndyke, Vivien Leigh, Laurence Olivier, and Michael Redgrave. The most important of those funds was headed by Clementine Churchill, wife of the British premier. Olivier's film of Shakespeare's *Henry V* (1944) translated into an Anglo-Saxon idiom many of the images of patriotic national history used in Eisenstein's *Alexander Nevsky* a few years before.[32]

Lectures and talks on the history of Russian literature added to the popularity of the Soviet Union as an ally. In response to the British people's desire to learn more about the life and struggle in the USSR, the left-wing magazines *Tribune, New Statesmen and Nation,* and *Left News* and also the Conservative press carried informative material on this subject. While speaking about Soviet domestic and foreign policy, many left-wing Labour supporters, Liberals, and Communists avoided discussion of negative aspects of life in the Soviet Union.

Concerned about the leftward shift in public opinion, in the autumn of 1941 Churchill instructed the Ministry of Information to oppose the new trend in the country "to forget the dangers of Communism over the resistance of Russia."[33] His concern was not completely justified. According to Mass Observation, the indisputable optimism about the Soviet war effort[34] and admiration for the Soviet fighting spirit were not equivalent to acceptance of the Soviet system in Britain. Communists are "wonderful fighters," an Englishman said soon after the victory at Stalingrad. "They're . . . more capable of taking knocks than any other nation, because they know what they are fighting for." But, he added, "I doubt if the Russian system could work in England." The desire to sacrifice everything in order to help the USSR, which had saved Britain, as well as the movements for the opening of the Second Front did not signify endorsement of communism. "[W]as 'Russian fever' the same as an enthusiasm for Communism? Hardly. There was nothing to show that the public at large desired a radical alteration in the political system."[35]

Mass Observation materials also testify to the obvious fact that the successful defence of Moscow, Leningrad, Stalingrad, and hundreds of other Soviet cities and villages obliged many sectors of British society to review their attitude to the USSR. The stereotyped views of the Soviet Union's weakness and fragmentation were discarded: "Complete national unity" was described as one of the main features of the Soviet authoritarian system (with obvious exaggeration). In a Mass Observation report, prepared in November 1942, Tom Harrisson, its founder and head, quoted a number of typical pronouncements made in Britain about the Soviet system of government, approval of "these good brave Russians" and their indisputable achievements in the social sphere. Such admiration even extended to the Soviet leader himself. "I am so grateful to Stalin," reported one Mass Observation contributor in August 1941. "What a brain to have outwitted Hitler the outwitter." The British, Harrisson wrote on another occasion, no longer believed in anti-Soviet propaganda and had even started exaggerating Russia's potentialities and efficiency.[36] A positive stereotype was now displacing the negative one.

The Soviet army's victories over the *Wehrmacht,* especially near Moscow and on the Volga, in fact projected a somewhat idealized image of the USSR among a large section of the population in the West, arousing their gratitude to the Soviet ally. Reports by the Ministry of Information often mentioned Britons' desire to render "greater assistance" to the USSR and deep sympathy for it, especially among the workers. Russia was regarded as "a genuine country of ordinary people. For some people in Britain Stalingrad seems to be their own native town."[37] On 20 January 1943, George Orwell wrote that so far as Britain was concerned, Soviet Russia was never more popular than at that moment,[38] and one could hardly suspect *him* of sympathizing with the Soviet system. Stalingrad's "public apotheosis" reached its peak on 23 February 1943, during the celebration of Red Army Day. A Gallup poll, conducted in March-April 1943, revealed British awareness of the fact that the Soviet military effort for victory was far superior to that of Britain.

True, certain apprehensions about the USSR's postwar plans were voiced in some circles, for instance, in the Catholic press, in particular in its coverage of revelations about the mass murder of Polish officers by the Soviets in the Katyn forest, near Smolensk.[39] However, as time went on, most of the population of the British Isles as a rule supported the idea of postwar British-American-Soviet cooperation, proclaimed in the 1941-45 Allied treaties and agreements. In April 1944, according to data from the British Institute of Public Opinion, 76 percent of the British population were in favor of the three countries' cooperation in European policy. Only 9 percent said they would prefer the USSR to be engaged in East European affairs after the war, leaving Britain and the United States to concentrate on West European affairs. In October 1944, 90 percent of those polled approved the policy of postwar cooperation.[40]

In the final stage of the war the British public was largely oriented toward promoting friendly relations with the Soviet Union and, in spite of the still existing mistrust, firmly believed in the possibility of such cooperation. Sentiments of goodwill then prevailed among both the British and Soviet people. The last meeting of the Big Three in Potsdam in 1945 did not lead to any open split among the Allies. Isaiah Berlin, the philosopher and wartime British diplomat, recalled later that the general mood in official circles in Washington and London was optimistic but watchful, whereas the broad public and the press were far more optimistic and even enthusiastic.[41]

The average American's understanding of the Soviet State was very vague. William H. Chamberlin, a prominent journalist, pointed out in 1941 that even an educated American was much less informed in Russian history than in the history of Western Europe.[42]

The USSR's entry into World War II reaffirmed Americans' optimistic view of its outcome, while the number of people who thought that the participation of the United States in that war was inevitable was somewhat reduced.[43] Most Americans, however, did not discard their prejudices, suspicion, and even hostility with respect to the USSR, for all these had sunk deep roots due to biased propaganda, the 1939 Nazi-Soviet pact, and other features of the prewar period. However, astonishment, respect, and the pragmatic assessment of the Soviet Union's role in the war against Nazi Germany had eventually gained an upper hand. Along with the increased aggressiveness of the Reich, those factors helped the U.S. president and his supporters to win the battle for public opinion.

By the time of the August 1941 Atlantic conference between Roosevelt and Churchill, Soviet resistance, in spite of all losses and setbacks, was described by most American publications as staunch, firm, and demanding the utmost effort from Nazi Germany. Sharp anti-Soviet attacks by the Hearst press did not much impress American readers. *The Christian Science Monitor* stated with good reason that the American people had given firm support to the government's line of cooperation with the USSR. "The American people . . . recognized that while American democracy and Russian Communism have no common cause, they have today a common enemy."[44]

The policy of giving help to the Soviet Union and the decision to convene a meeting of representatives of the three powers in Moscow were regarded by Americans as necessary moves to uphold the "basic U.S. interest"—the defeat of the Axis powers. A public opinion poll in *Fortune* magazine in October 1941 revealed that 51.4 percent of respondents were for cooperation and assistance to Russia so long as it contributed to the Nazi defeat, and that only 13 percent were against any assistance or even encouragement to the USSR.[45]

A substantial role in the American-Soviet rapprochement was played by contacts between public organizations, scientists, writers, journalists, and members of the artistic community. The American Council on Relations with the USSR, which enlisted such prominent Americans as journalist Corliss Lamont, singer Paul Robeson, painter and sculptor Rockwell Kent, the writer Theodore Dreiser, and the whole League of American Writers, as well as hundreds of other American cultural figures, took part in the movement for assistance to the Soviet Union.[46] Close friendly links between Americans and Soviet scientists and researchers, as well as reports and books by prominent journalists and authors, which helped both peoples to learn more about each other, also contributed to that process.[47]

Information about the USSR carried by *Soviet Russia Today* and other magazines; Henry Cassidy's *Moscow Diary*; Soviet feature and documentary films shown in the United States; performances of compositions by Dimitr Shostakovich, Sergei Prokofiev, and other prominent Soviet composers, all served to reveal the rich spiritual and cultural world of Soviet people to Americans. After Pearl Harbor American enthusiasm about Soviet resistance was even more pronounced. However, in the United States this enthusiasm was never manifested with such force as in Britain and in Nazi-occupied Europe.

America's pluralistic society of course did not take a uniform view of the Soviet Union. Various social groups and political forces opposed cooperation with it. At the same time, in 1942-43 the number of advocates of wartime and postwar cooperation was on the increase in the United States, and the process continued largely because of the greater availability of information of the Soviet Union among people who had only a hazy idea of it before.[48] Academic and military circles in the United States then started an in-depth study of the Soviet Union; extensive Russian and Soviet studies were carried out there after 1945. In late 1942, a crash course in Russian was introduced at Cornell and later in other American universities.[49]

According to the data from a nationwide opinion poll held by *Fortune* in June 1943, 80.7 percent of respondents were in favor of the United States acting as Russia's equal partner in the war, and only 9.4 percent said they were against it. The National Opinion Research Center (NORC) found that the USSR was regarded as the country that was exerting the greatest effort for victory, as compared with Britain, the United States, and China.[50] Almost all U.S. periodicals paid tribute to the valiant Soviet troops.

The Battle of Stalingrad had the widest repercussions. The vast counteroffensive of the Soviet troops launched on 19 November 1942 strengthened the faith of the Americans in a victorious outcome of the war with the Third Reich. Newspapers covering the fight on the Volga River were almost unanimous in believing that it meant an end to the Nazi advance into Russia. The *New York Times* even announced on 24 November: "The siege of Berlin has begun." An equally optimistic tone was taken by six weeklies ranging from *Business Week* (28 November) to the *New Masses* (1 December). Among these the *New Republic* on 20 November went so far as to hail the Russian counterattack as a "turning point" of the war.[51]

Stalingrad strongly influenced various sections of American society. Even die-hard isolationists welcomed the Russian victory. One result of this admiration for the military achievement in the East was seen in the reactions of the moderate American press and radio to controversial issues involving Russia during the year 1942 (Second Front, Lend-Lease, and so on). One British survey of American opinion noted: "Despite inevitable uneasiness over Russia's territorial ambitions in Europe there has been no nationwide campaign to stop Russia now. Indeed there has been more criticism of Britain's imperialistic war aims than of Russia's." By autumn 1943, public showings of the U.S. army film, *The Battle of Russia* (part of Frank Capra's *Why We Fight* series), no longer contained the descriptions of the Soviet Union's move into the Baltic states following the Nazi-Soviet pact found in the original. By the time of the Moscow and Tehran conferences in the autumn of 1943, pro-Soviet sentiments among Americans had reached a peak.[52]

While admiring their Soviet ally, public opinion in the United States (as well as Britain) did not have at its disposal all information about the war in the East and could not fully appreciate the significance of the Soviet-German front. Wartime American perceptions about the fight of the Soviet Union were often imprecise and vague.[53]

Take, for instance, the American image of Stalin. In 1942-43, the U.S. mass media often tended to exaggerate Stalin's virtues. Switching from distrust to friendliness, Henry R. Luce's magazines started singing his praises. *Time* even carried Stalin's picture on its cover on 4 January 1943. It nominated "the man of steel" with his "granite face" as its "Man of the Year" for 1942—"All that Hitler could give, he took—for the second time." The Soviet leader was generally praised by prominent journalists and statesmen, and almost no one doubted the possibility of liberalizing the Stalinist totalitarian regime. According to Wendell Willkie, after Tehran Stalin was regarded as the most powerful statesman in international affairs. However, as frictions and contradictions between the USSR and Western members of the anti-Hitler coalition accumulated, Stalin's image lost its appeal, and his attractive traits were no longer publicized by the press and documentaries as before.[54] This did not, however, affect most Americans' friendly attitude to their Soviet ally. The U.S. public had always been aware of the differences between the two countries, and therefore their intensification did not make Americans renounce the idea of postwar cooperation with the USSR.[55]

In his study of changes in U.S. public opinion, historian Ralph Levering stressed that in the period from spring 1942 to autumn 1943 "those expressing trust in Russia's willingness to cooperate after war [shifted] from a decided minority to a clear majority of all respondents." After March 1945, however, the widespread favorable attitude to the USSR in America was on the ebb. Levering attributed this to the fact that "almost all Americans simply were unprepared for the realities of the rapidly approaching postwar world."[56] Moreover the people of the Allied countries lived in expectation of the future victory while still gripped by mutual suspicions and fears. About one-third of Americans had their doubts about the Soviet Union's intentions in 1944-45.

Nevertheless, the findings of public opinion polls in Western coalition countries allow us to assert that at the end of the war preservation of mutual understanding and cooperation was the dominant desire. According to American Institute on Public Opinion (AIPO) data, on 8 August 1945 54 percent of U.S. respondents tended to believe that the Soviets could be trusted to cooperate after the war, and only 30 percent expressed doubt.[57] The British Embassy in Washington stated in its quarterly report for the period July-September 1945: "Although the extreme Right maintained its usual attacks on Soviet policy and aims in Eastern Europe . . . , the general feeling towards the Soviet Union remained one of qualified optimism. Russophobes who talked of an inevitable war between the United States and the USSR were widely denounced."[58]

The shaping of public opinion in Britain with respect to the United States was facilitated by the fact that both countries had much in common—for example, language, traditions, and an underlying "Anglo-Saxon" culture. Consequently Britons tended to view Americans from a different angle than other foreigners, regarding them as quasi relations. In the 1920s and 1930s, close contacts in the arts, the press, law, economics, and other academic subjects developed more rapidly between the two countries than those on an official level. American mass culture (films and jazz music) had a pronounced impact on British society, particularly among the young.[59] Before the outbreak of the war the threat of Nazi aggression to democracy in both countries and to their national sovereignty brought them closer together.

Nevertheless, in 1939, just as in the post-Versailles period, the Old World evinced great distrust of the New. Britain still resented U.S. isolationism and criticized "Uncle Shylock" for demanding payment of the war debts. Frequent protests by isolationist leaders against Roosevelt's policy of assistance to Britain in 1939-40 only exacerbated anti-American sentiments. A substantial change in the British public mood was not evident until the spring of 1941, after the Lend-Lease Act had been passed. The U.S. Congress had finally made a tangible and public commitment to Britain. In April 1941 Mass Observation registered "a strong majority of favorable opinion from a quarter to nearly two-thirds."[60]

News of the United States' entry into World War II was received with a feeling of great relief on the British Isles. Weekly reviews of public opinion by the Ministry of Information indicated that Britons were looking forward to close military cooperation in the Far East and that they hoped for the rapid elaboration of a joint military strategy by the United States, Britain, its Dominions, and the USSR. On the other hand, some reports noted continued doubts: "While the public are prepared to make any sacrifice necessary to help Russia . . . they have no such disposition toward America. There appears to be a widespread feeling that America is 'too damned wealthy,' that Americans are too mercenary-minded, and that the hardship and suffering of war will 'do them a lot of good.'"[61]

The Pearl Harbor tragedy and American setbacks in the initial months of hostilities in the Pacific were said to have "undermined the [British] efficiency idea" with respect to America. The latter's obvious unpreparedness for the war came as a great shock. Only a tiny proportion of those questioned in the British Isles in early 1942 were satisfied with the U.S. military effort. "Though, it should be stated that satisfaction with our own conduct of the war was at that time also at its lowest ebb," the author of the Mass Observation report admitted.[62]

Later assessments of the U.S. role were more favorable, although many of Washington's political and diplomatic moves met with open disapproval by Europeans. Most Britons were, for instance, astonished at and displeased by Washington's determination to act jointly with Admiral Darlan. It was impermissible, they believed, that a deal with that traitor should threaten the position of the Fighting French.[63]

The absence of a full and continuing interchange at supreme political and military levels ensured that little "hard" information about progress on the various battlefronts reached the soldiers and sailors of the Allied Coalition. All three governments launched "information" campaigns to influence public opinion toward unstinting support for national priorities and policies. So far as is presently known, the British public relations effort in the United States was by far the most ambitious; ironically it appears to have achieved the least success.[64] The British later admitted that public relations "have presented a difficult problem for all the Service Missions throughout the war." While the British Information Services and the Joint Liaison Committee did "much good," British information programs "have not resulted in a proper appreciation of the British war effort in the United States." Examples cited included the notion that the landing at Salerno was purely American, that the proportion of British troops in the Normandy invasion was "almost negligible," and that the entire war against Japan was an American affair.[65] While American efforts to affect Soviet and British perceptions ran the gamut of official propaganda and unofficial publicity, the U.S. government was principally concerned about shaping attitudes at home.[66]

The stationing of U.S. forces on British soil created serious complications for Anglo-American relations. Concern about potential antagonism between British and American forces grew as U.S. troops flooded into the United Kingdom in 1942 under the BOLERO buildup. The American presence generated a wide range of initiatives to ease conflict among American and British Commonwealth forces and between the GIs and their British hosts, ranging from home hospitality to the "Joint Committee on Venereal Disease," set up in 1943 to deal with promiscuous GIs and predatory prostitutes. The extent and duration of such a large American presence in the British Isles inevitably meant problems. They were compounded, however, by the U.S. army's importation of racial segregation and its rigid insistence on enforcing absolute legal authority over American personnel.[67] Discrimination against black GIs disturbed many Britons, unused to nonwhites or to a color bar. On the whole, however, the stay of the U.S. troops in the British Isles (peaking in June 1944 at

1,750,000 officers and men) helped strengthen bonds between the people of the two countries.[68] Anglo-American personal contacts in wartime had important consequences at all levels of society. At the same time, according to one opinion poll conducted in southern England, "people began to realize . . . that the Americans really belong to a different nation, with different standards, customs, manners of approach."[69]

America's image was enhanced in the second half of 1942. This was primarily explained by the recognition of the major U.S. military and economic contribution to the fight against the Axis powers, especially in the Far East, where Britain's position and military influence had been noticeably undermined. Mass Observation reported in January 1943: "General MacArthur's defence of Bataan peninsula, and, later his organization of the defences of Australia, did much to revive confidence in the American war effort, and this confidence has steadily risen during the past eight months until satisfaction now stands at 74 percent, and 80 percent among those most interested in the subject."[70] Positive assessment by the British public of the experience of joint action with the U.S. armed forces was reflected in numerous opinion polls conducted in the British Isles. No matter how different might be the figures or methods of their calculation, the number of respondents and their social status, one tendency was clearly pronounced, that is an increase in 1944-45 in the number of respondents who expressed favorable attitude to Americans.

Britons also expressed great admiration for American statesmen, particularly President Roosevelt, Vice President Henry Wallace, and Navy Secretary Frank Knox.[71] Franklin Roosevelt enjoyed the greatest popularity among the broad mass of the British public; even in prewar years he was regarded as a prominent leader of the opposition to the Axis powers. His popularity ratings had always been higher than those of the American nation as a whole. In 1943 and 1944, 85 and 76 percent of Britain's population, respectively, expressed their favorable attitude toward him. The news of Roosevelt's death in April 1945 was received as a great shock in Britain. For most Britons Harry Truman was an obscure nonentity.[72]

Britain associated its hopes of a stable and lasting peace in the postwar world with the figure of Roosevelt. At first, ideas of Anglo-Saxon solidarity were more popular in the United Kingdom, but later priority was given to plans for broad international cooperation with the participation of both the United States and the USSR. According to an opinion poll taken for *Fortune* magazine in April 1942, 54 percent of respondents wanted to preserve the bilateral mutual assistance obligations in the postwar period, describing the United States as a "favoured nation."[73] To Mass

Observation's question about which form of cooperation was preferable—with the United States or the Soviet Union—most of the British respondents (including 54 percent of men) replied in January 1943 that cooperation with both countries was of vital importance; 17 percent of the men polled preferred cooperation with the United States alone, and 20 percent, with the USSR alone. According to these polls, in the final stage of the war only an insignificant number of respondents expressed concern about America's possible reversion to isolationism and the desire for durable friendly relations with the United States was almost unanimous.[74]

American views of Britain's political system and people tended to change depending on the situation and were rather contradictory. On the one hand, Americans were firm in their belief that the American and British models of democracy were entirely different (which was true) but they tended to idealize their own system and criticized the British ruling elite for its machinations and governmental inability. Manifestations of Anglophobia, quite frequent in 1939-40, were a vestige of America's Colonial past. This was fostered by the idea of New World superiority over European countries and other stereotype isolationist ideas (Anglophobia was a typical, though not the main, feature of American isolationism[75]). On the other hand, British traditions and institutions have always been a subject of close study by Americans. It was not by accident that U.S. press and radio programs supplied much more detailed information on British affairs than their British counterparts did on America.[76]

The American public increasingly regarded Britain as the front line of its defenses. In September 1939, a majority took the side of Britain and France. Later they followed with alarm and sympathy the lonely struggle of the British people against Germany; a shift in the popular attitude was particularly evident after the capitulation of France. In June 1940, 80 percent of those polled were in favor of giving help to Britain; 65 percent believed that American entry into the war was inevitable, although they thought that it should not occur immediately.[77]

The Battle of Britain increased American sympathies for that country, which was holding the Nazis at bay single-handedly (aided by its colonies and the Commonwealth). All opinion polls indicated that about 85-90 percent of the American electorate were in favor of extensive support of England short of war. The American government, by referring to public opinion, time and again exerted decisive influence on the representatives and senators whenever they wavered. It should also be borne in mind that, on instructions from the White House, the Department of State arranged for polls on subjects of interest to itself.[78] Since the summer of

1940, U.S. public opinion had been intensively shaped by William Allen White's Committee to Defend America by Aiding the Allies, the Century Group, and other pro-British organizations.

The Lend-Lease Act and other moves by the Democratic administration in support of Britain (still undertaken within the framework of U.S. neutrality) reflected the sentiments of most ordinary Americans. A number of public opinion polls testify to it. On 6 May 1941 AIPO asked: "Do you think we should continue to help England, even if we run [the] risk [of war]?" To this 76 percent of respondents replied in the affirmative and 21 percent in the negative. On 24 June 1941 the following question was posed: "Do you think President Roosevelt has gone too far in his policies of helping Britain, or not far enough?"—to which only 20 percent said that he had gone too far, whereas 17 percent said "not far enough" and 57 percent that the situation was more or less satisfactory.[79]

After the United States entered the war in December 1941 and became Britain's ally, rapprochement between the two countries became even closer, although the process of consolidating Anglo-American relations was not quite free of the prejudices and intellectual baggage of the past. Public debates on a number of issues, such as the future destiny of British colonies, revived the old negative image of British politicians among the American public. The *Nation* and *Pacific Affairs* magazines and the mass media sharply criticized British leaders for their refusal to grant independence to India, Britain's largest colony. American newspapers, the London *Economist* noted, regard India as "the American cause" and Britain's policy as negation of Roosevelt's "four freedoms."[80]

Most Americans were outspoken in support of eliminating colonialism.[81] When *Life* magazine, on 12 October 1942, carried an "Open Letter" urging Britons to do away with the Empire, Lord Halifax, the British ambassador in Washington, warned his government that there was evidence of a feeling that as an empire

> we owe the USA and the world a justification of ourselves in these respects. Something of this sentiment is undoubtedly almost universal amongst Americans, though it varies in intensity. It is a barrier to mutual confidence and holds plain danger for future Anglo-American collaboration on terms which we would consider acceptable.[82]

Many Americans assessed Britain's contribution to the joint struggle against the Axis powers with a large degree of skepticism, which was hardly justified. Underrated estimates of Britain's military and economic effort were registered in a number of U.S. opinion polls. On 22 June 1943 the AIPO asked its sample which country, in its opinion, had "made the greatest contribution to winning a victory?" Responding, 32 percent named Russia; 4 percent, China; 9 percent, Britain; and 55 percent, the United States. The question posed on 24 August 1943 was this: "From what you have read, in which country do you think the people—not soldiers—are working hardest to win the war, Britain, U.S. or Russia?" In reply, 13 percent said "in Britain"; 26 percent, "in the USA"; 45 percent, "in Russia"; and 16 percent did not reply.[83]

Transatlantic aspersions on Britain's war effort did not, as a rule, affect America's basic orientation toward the Alliance. One illustration is the conclusion of the report "American Attitudes towards the British" prepared in April 1943 by the U.S. Office of War Information and based on a poll of 3,600 Americans. The report stressed the following points as the most typical:

1. Americans' favorable attitude to Britons substantially overweighed their antipathy;
2. although most Americans regarded Britain's war effort as quite insignificant, compared to the contributions made by Russia, China, and the United States, they believed that Britain was doing its level best and that, after victory over Germany, Britain would continue war against Japan;
3. even most of those who were not fond of Britain deemed it necessary to maintain cooperation after the war. "It is of paramount importance," the report asserted, "that nine out of ten Americans are overwhelmingly in favor of continued Anglo-American cooperation after the war."[84]

A Big Two concept was clearly forming in American public opinion by 1945; the power and influence of Britain was viewed as inferior to that of the United States and the Soviet Union. But this did not mean that Americans had written off Britain as a factor in international politics.[85] The end of hostilities in Europe and Asia and the Soviet Union's drifting away from Western countries added new importance to the health of the Anglo-American alliance. This became a subject of lively political and public discussion in the United States, particularly at the time of Churchill's "Iron Curtain" speech at Fulton, Missouri, in March 1946.

Public opinion polls and press reports of course did not register with absolute precision the climate in Britain and America, but they make it possible to determine the main trends and zigzags in the public mood.

According to various sources, most Americans and Britons were favorably disposed toward the other members of the coalition against Hitler. Since the second half of 1941 they had manifested their positive attitude to the their Soviet ally. However, some sections of American and British society still retained their hostility to the USSR and openly expressed disapproval of it. Distrust of the Soviet totalitarian system prevailed among many in the West, although those people were in favor of cooperation with the USSR. This, no doubt, partly accounts for the fact that the Soviet Union's positive image was rather short-lived and that soon after 1945 it was replaced by "the enemy image." Closed Soviet society, the system of supersecrecy, the lack of free speech, and the stringent control over the press and the entire sociopolitical fabric—these were also reasons for the limited opportunities to form more complete and creditable ideas about each other in the countries concerned.

Thus, despite the successful operation of the most powerful and effective military coalition in history, different perceptions—frequently misconceptions—persisted among the peoples of the Grand Alliance. While governments waged war and concerted diplomacy, popular attitudes, prejudices, and stereotypes that both predated the war and were influenced by it combined to shape the way ordinary citizens worked, sacrificed, and struggled for victory. The common struggle against Nazi Germany encouraged all three countries to highlight favorable characteristics of their allies. But these masked, rather than eliminated, older stereotypes, which recovered their potency, especially in East-West relations, once victory had been won.

NOTES

1. *International Working People's Solidarity in the Struggle for Peace and National Liberation against Fascist Aggression, for Complete Elimination of Fascism in Europe and Asia, 1938-1945.* (Moscow, 1962), 361-62 (in Russian).

2. *International Working People's Solidarity,* 357-58 (in Russian).

3. J. Stalin, *About the Great Patriotic War of the Soviet Union* (Moscow, 1949), 16 (in Russian).

4. *Pravda,* 12 August 1941 (in Russian).

5. *Pravda,* 13 June 1942 (in Russian).

6. *Pravda,* 7 August, 12 October 1941 (in Russian).

7. *Pravda,* 20 December 1941 (in Russian).

8. *Literature and Art,* 15 August 1942 (in Russian).

9. Konstantin Simonov, *Days and Nights* (Moscow, 1945), 63 (in Russian).

10. Stalin, *About the Great Patriotic War,* 67 (in Russian).

11. Ilyia Ehrenburg, *Chronicle of Courage: Wartime Articles Carried by the Press* (Moscow, 1983), 164-66 (in Russian).

12. Ehrenburg, *Chronicle of Courage,* 218 (in Russian).

13. Simonov, *Days and Nights,* 93 (in Russian).

14. *Pravda,* 14 June 1944 (in Russian).

15. *Pravda,* 1 July 1944 (in Russian).

16. *Pravda,* 11 November 1944 (in Russian).

17. *Izvestia,* 13 April 1945 (in Russian).

18. *Krasnaya Zvezda,* 14 April 1945 (in Russian).

19. *Izvestia,* 14 April 1945 (in Russian).

20. *Pravda,* 10 December 1944 (in Russian).

21. *Pravda,* 22 October 1944 (in Russian).

22. *One Hundred and Forty Talks with Molotov: From F. Chuyev's Diary* (Moscow, 1991), 65 (in Russian).

23. Robert J. Wybrow, *Britain Speaks Out, 1937-1987. A Social History as Seen through the Gallup Data* (London, 1989), 6.

24. Sussex University Library, Brighton, England: Mass Observation Archive (MO). File Report 849/19 by Tom Harrisson, "Public Opinion about Russia," 27 August 1941.

25. MO File Report 1623, "Some Notes on Feelings about Russia," 10 March 1943.

26. Public Record Office (PRO), INF 1/292. Home Intelligence (HI) Weekly Report No. 39; MO File Report 848/9.

27. PRO, INF 1/292, HI Weekly Report, No. 54.

28. MO, Topic Collections, Political Attitudes and Behaviour, Box 4, 4F.

29. Bradley F. Smith, *The War's Long Shadow: The Second World War and its Aftermath. China, Russia, Britain, America* (New York, 1986), 70.

30. *Izvestia,* 6 August 1941 (in Russian).

31. Foreign Policy Archive of the Russian Federation (FPA RF). Fund 69, schedule 28, box 93, file 93, pp. 5, 10-11 (in Russian).

32. *English Authors about the Land of Soviets* (Lenizdat, 1984), 78; Ivan M. Maisky, *Recollections of a Soviet Ambassador: The War 1939-1943* (Moscow, 1965), 298-99 (both in Russian).

33. Ian McLaine, *Ministry of Morale: Home Front Morale and the Ministry of Information in World War II* (London, 1979), 199.

34. On 22 February 1943, 95 percent of London suburban residents expressed "quite definite optimism" with respect to the war in the USSR, and only 5 percent withheld their opinion (MO, File Report 1623).

35. *Ibid.*; Peter Lewis, *People's War* (London, 1986), 202; McLaine, *Ministry of Morale,* 208.

36. MO File Reports 1623, 1492; MO, Politics, 1938-56, File 4, Box A; Tom Harrisson, "Public Opinion about Russia," *Political Quarterly,* November-December 1941.

37. PRO, INF 1/292, HI Weekly Report, No. 114.

38. George Orwell, *The War Commentaries* (London, 1987), 22.

39. Philip M. H. Bell, "Censorship, Propaganda and Public Opinion: The Case of the Katyn Graves," *Transactions of the Royal Historical Society,* 5th series, 39 (1989), 69-70.

40. Hadley Cantril, ed., *Public Opinion 1935-1946* (Princeton, N.J., 1951), 367.

41. Isaiah Berlin, "Meetings with Russian Authors in 1945 and 1956," *Zvesda,* No. 2, 1990, 129 (in Russian).

42. Ralph B. Levering, *American Opinion and the Russian Alliance, 1939-1945* (Chapel Hill, 1976), 57.

43. Hadley Cantril, *Gauging Public Opinion* (Princeton, 1944), 228.

44. *Christian Science Monitor*, 13 September 1941.

45. George C. Herring, *Aid to Russia 1941-1946: Strategy, Diplomacy, the Origins of the Cold War* (New York, 1973), 22.

46. Vladimir V. Poznyakov, "American Public Opinion and the Problem of Soviet-U.S. Cooperation, June-December 1941," *Annual Studies of America, 1988* (Moscow, 1988), 117-26 (in Russian).

47. See *The Road to Smolensk: American Authors and Journalists on the Great Patriotic War of the Soviet People 1941-1945* (Moscow, 1985) (in Russian).

48. V. V. Poznyakov, "Soviet-American Relations and the Public Opinion of the United States (December 1941-October 1943)," *Annual Studies of America, 1989* (Moscow, 1990), 12-13, 27 (in Russian).

49. Harold F. Fisher, ed., *American Research on Russia* (Bloomington, Ind, 1959), 6-7, 21.

50. Cantril, ed., *Public Opinion, 1935-1946*, 372, 1063.

51. PRO, FO 371/34167, copy of Office of War Information. Weekly Media Report No. 44. 5 December 1942, 9-10; see also Warren F. Kimball, "Stalingrad und das Dilemma der amerikanisch-sowejetischen Beziehungen," in *Stalingrad. Ereignis, Wirkung, Symbol*, im Auftrag des Militärgeschichtlichen Forschungsamtes, ed. Jürgen Förster (München & Zürich, 1992), pp. 327-49.

52. PRO, FO 371/37005. British Information Services, Survey by A. McKenzie, "American Attitude to Russia," May 1943. The changes in *The Battle of Russia* were reported in the *New York Times*, 15 November 1943, 23, as cited in Kimball, "Stalingrad," 328-29.

53. David M. Glantz, "American Perceptions about the Operations on the Eastern Front during the Second World War," *Problems of History* 8 (1987), 33 (in Russian).

54. *Time*, 4 January 1943: cover and 21-24; Charles C. Alexander, "'Uncle Joe': Stalin's Image at the Height of the Anti-Hitler Coalition," *Annual Studies of America, 1989* 32-41 (in Russian); *idem.*, "The US and the USSR: Views from America 1933-1942," in *Soviet-US Relations 1933-1942*, G. N. Sevost'ianov and W. F. Kimball, eds. (Moscow, 1989), 24-25.

55. See public opinion polls, 1942-45 in Cantril, ed., *Public Opinion 1935-1946*, 370.

56. Levering, *American Opinion*, 127, 203.

57. Cantril, ed., *Public Opinion 1935-1946*, 371.

58. Thomas E. Hachey, ed., *Confidential Dispatches: Analysis of America by the British Ambassador, 1939-1945* (Evanston, Ill, 1974), 302.

59. Herbert G. Nicholas, *The United States and Britain* (Chicago, 1975), 86.

60. MO File Reports 1569, 2548.

61. PRO, INF 1/292, HI Weekly Report 64, 24 December 1941, appendix: "Public Attitude towards the USA."

62. MO File Reports 2548, 1569.

63. PRO, INF 1/292, HI Weekly Report 112.

64. See Hachey, ed., *Confidential Dispatches,* and Herbert G. Nicholas, ed., *Washington Dispatches: Weekly Political Reports from the British Embassy* (Chicago, 1981).

65. Historical Record, British Army Staff, Washington, WO 202/917 (PRO).

66. See Allan M. Winkler, *The Politics of Propaganda: The Office of War Information, 1942-1945* (New Haven, Conn., 1978); John M. Blum, *V Was for Victory: Politics and American Culture during World War II* (New York, 1976); Clayton R. Koppes and Gregory D. Black, *Hollywood Goes to War* (New York, 1987); and Holly D. Shulman, *The Voice of America: Propaganda and Democracy, 1941-1945* (Madison, Wis., 1990).

67. See Norman Longmate, *The G.I.s: The Americans in Britain, 1942-1945* (London, 1975); Graham Smith, *When Jim Crow Met John Bull: Black American Soldiers in World War II Britain* (London, 1987); and two articles by David Reynolds: "GI and Tommy in Wartime Britain: The Army 'Interattachment' Scheme of 1943-44," *Journal of Strategic Studies* 7 (1984), and "The Churchill Government and the Black American Troops in Britain during World War II," *Transactions of the Royal Historical Society,* 5th series, 35 (1985).

68. David Dimbleby and David Reynolds, *An Ocean Apart: The Relationship between Britain and America in the Twentieth Century* (London, 1988), 150.

69. McLaine, *Ministry of Morale,* 268.

70. MO File Report 1569, 22 January 1943.

71. According to MO data, in 1941, 45 percent of British respondents expressed a positive attitude toward Americans; 47 percent in 1942; 34 percent in 1943; 45 percent in 1944 and 58 percent in 1945 (MO file reports, 2454, 1669).

72. MO File Report 2454.

73. PRO, INF1/293, HI Special Reports.

74. MO, file reports 1569 ("Report of Feeling about America") 2222 (MO Panel on the Americans, February 1945).

75. David Reynolds, *The Creation of the Anglo-American Alliance, 1937-1941: A Study in Competitive Co-operation* (London, 1981), 23; Manfred Jonas, *Isolation in America, 1935-1941* (Ithaca, N.Y., 1966), 194-95, 202.

76. Reynolds, *Creation,* 23.

77. Dhangir G. Nadzhafov, *US Neutrality, 1935-1941* (Moscow, 1990), 134 (in Russian).

78. Bradley Smith, *War's Long Shadow*, 123.

79. Cantril, ed., *Public Opinion*, 976, 1162.

80. *Economist*, 19 November 1942, 360-61.

81. Lydia V. Pozdeeva, *Anglo-American Relations in World War II, 1941-1945* (Moscow, 1969), 263, 272-73. (in Russian).

82. PRO, PREM 4/26/8. Halifax to FO, 30 October 1943.

83. Cantril, ed., *Public Opinion*, 1065.

84. PRO, FO 371/34121, Ronald Campbell to FO, 20 Oct. 1943.

85. R. Butler and M. E. Pelly, eds, *Documents on British Policy Overseas*, ser. 1, vol. III (London, 1986), 10, 13-15.

Part IV ■ Foreign Policy

13

Great Britain: Imperial Diplomacy

David Reynolds

In 1940 the United Kingdom of Great Britain and Northern Ireland comprised 48.2 million people. By contrast, the population of the Soviet Union was about 195 million and that of the United States 132.1 million.[1] This discrepancy in size is fundamental to an understanding of British diplomacy. The United States and the USSR were vast continental powers, to a large degree economically self-sufficient; Britain was a small offshore European island, highly dependent on trade with the non-European world. Yet, to an extent that seems remarkable today, much of that non-European world was under British control and influence. In 1933 the British Empire encompassed 502 million people, nearly one-quarter of the world's population, including the Indian subcontinent, Australasia, and much of southern Africa.[2] In terms of international power, it was the empire that made Britain great. Back in 1903 Lord Curzon, the British viceroy of India, pontificated: "As long as we rule India we are the greatest power in the world. If we lose it we shall drop straight away to a third rate power."[3]

Britain, then, was an island state and also a global power. That is the first and fundamental introductory point to be made because it determined most of British war-time diplomacy. Also important is the contrast between Britain's policy-making structures and those of its war-time allies. Britain was unusual among the major powers in having a deeply entrenched career civil service, reaching up to the highest levels of policy-making, whose tenure persisted regardless of the ebb and flow of political ministries.[4] In the United States changes of administration entailed substantial shakeouts of most senior policy-making positions, which were held by political appointees, while in the USSR the Foreign Ministry was overshadowed by Stalin himself. Thus, in Britain the Foreign Office, with its various regional departments, had a peculiar influence over government policy and helped shape the thinking of the two war-time foreign secretaries, Lord Halifax (1938-40) and Anthony Eden (1940-45). This is not to deny the role of the prime ministers of the era, Neville Chamberlain and, from May 1940, Winston Churchill—both of whom had firm convictions about foreign affairs and were ready to act upon them. But it is to say that, to a greater extent than in Roosevelt's America and Stalin's Russia, British diplomacy resulted from the interplay of prime minister and Foreign Office.

A third distinctive feature of the British milieu was its pattern of adversarial party politics. Under Stalin, the Soviet Union did not have an effective independent legislature, while in the United States, which did have one, the two rival parties, Democratic and Republican, did not enjoy the same tight party discipline as the Conservative (or "Tory") and Labour parties in Great Britain. In the United States, the president and the Congress are elected independently—often one party will control the White House and the other Capitol Hill. In Britain it is the party with a working majority in the elected House of Commons whose leader becomes prime minister. Nor did American parties, even in the confrontational days of Roosevelt's New Deal, have the clear ideological differences of their British counterparts. The Tories were rooted in business and the landed interest, while Labour rested on the support of the trades unions. Nominally, Chamberlain's ministry from 1937-40, like those of Ramsay MacDonald and Stanley Baldwin before him, was a national government, but in fact it was largely Tory in composition and Chamberlain was hated by the Labour party, for his acerbic manner as well as his policies. From May 1940 a genuine coalition was formed with Churchill taking charge of the conduct of the war, while Labour politicians under Clement Attlee were given almost a free hand to promote their agenda of domestic reform. But Attlee and his colleagues also had strong views on aspects of foreign affairs and their importance in Churchill's coalition gave them considerable leverage, as we shall see, over Germany and India.

A final introductory point should be made about Britain's experience of the period. Talking of the "Second World War" may disguise the fact that each of the three allies experienced the conflict in fundamentally different ways. For the British the distinctive facts were, first, their involvement in hostilities against Germany right from September 1939; second, the collapse of their main ally, France, in June 1940, leaving Britain facing invasion or the possibility of a negotiated peace; and, third, the predicament of fighting on, virtually alone, for a year thereafter until the war-time alliance was gradually forged in the second half of 1941. The crisis of 1940 and the coalition of 1941 shaped British war-time diplomacy.

In what follows I shall explore four themes which, together, gather up many of the main threads of that diplomacy. They are policy towards Germany both in the immediate- and longer-term; ideas about a concert of great powers to win the war and safeguard the peace; attitudes to alliances with the countries of continental Europe, particularly France; and the advancement of Britain's global interests in its formal and informal empire.

For the British, the fundamental issue over which the war was fought was the place of Germany in Europe. They entered the war in September 1939 with two potentially conflicting approaches. The first was their long-standing conviction, apparent since the end of the First World War, that a strong and prosperous Germany was essential to the peace and stability of Europe. Unlike the French, they did not regard Germany as intrinsically a threat to their interests, and British diplomacy for much of the inter-war period was directed to restraining French revanchism. In 1932 Alexander Cadogan, a senior Foreign Office official, described the aim of British policy as being "to bring to an end the 'post war period'" and to "allow Germany to resume her place and rights as a great power on equal footing with the others."[5] On the other hand, it had gradually been apparent from 1933 that Germany under the leadership of Adolf Hitler was a malevolent force. Initially Chamberlain and his entourage believed that Nazi ambitions lay mainly in Eastern Europe. They took no action when Hitler annexed Austria in March 1938 and the crisis over the Sudeten parts of Czechoslovakia was resolved on essentially Hitler's terms. But the pogrom against the Jews in November 1938, the persistent war scares of early 1939 and, finally, the Nazi entry into Prague in March convinced them that the whole balance of power in Europe was in danger. More than that, they now believed that Britain was in fact Hitler's primary target. In the words of Cadogan, by then permanent under-secretary at the Foreign Office: "I believe that what he would like best, if he could do it, would be to smash the British Empire."[6] The result was a series of panicky guarantees of Eastern European countries, which took the decision for peace or war out of British hands. Hitler's invasion of one of these, Poland, was the immediate casus belli in September and the future of Poland also became a major issue in war-time diplomacy.

The British government therefore entered the war belatedly, convinced that Hitler was incorrigible but still sure that a strong Germany was both inevitable and desirable. Thus Chamberlain wrote a week after war began: "The difficulty is with Hitler himself. Until he disappears and his system collapses there can be no peace. But what I hope for is not a military victory—I very much doubt the feasibility of that—but a collapse of the German home front."[7] This helps explain the passivity of British policy during the so-called phoney war of the winter of 1939-40 and the persistence of Whitehall contacts with elements of the German opposition. Britain saw little hope of destroying Germany; nor did this seem desirable. A strong, but peaceful, non-Nazi Germany was the objective.

During the disastrous summer of 1940, the issue of negotiation with Hitler's regime was briefly broached. In the early days of the Dunkirk evacuation, when it seemed that only 50,000 troops could be saved, Halifax, the foreign secretary, raised in the War Cabinet the idea of using Mussolini to discover Hitler's peace terms. He argued that if these did not impugn Britain's independence and integrity, then they should be given serious consideration. Churchill did not dispute that principle, commenting "that he would be thankful to get out of our present difficulties on such terms, provided we retained the essentials and the elements of our vital strength, even at the cost of some territory."[8] He even mentioned Malta, Gibraltar, and some African colonies as expendable. Where Churchill differed with Halifax was on the matter of practicality. He believed that such generous terms were "most unlikely" and that Britain "would get no worse terms if we went on fighting, even if we were beaten, than were open to us now."[9] And, by fighting the battle of Britain, they might inflict sufficiently heavy losses on Germany to extract more generous terms. This was the basis on which Britain fought on that summer and Churchill dealt firmly with Halifax and his parliamentary under-secretary, R. A. Butler, when they told the Swedish envoy in London in June, for German consumption, that "common sense and not bravado" would dictate future British policy.[10]

For the next three years there was little meaningful debate about Germany. Until the military situation was far more favourable, planning for peace seemed irrelevant. Within the FO, faith in the German resistance faded, while the idea of Goering as an acceptable alternative leader, entertained in 1939-40, lost its attractions after his *Luftwaffe*'s Blitz on London in 1940-41. FO attitudes towards Germany had hardened by 1942, and this made the fait accompli of Roosevelt's public proclamation of "Unconditional Surrender" in January 1943 easier to accept.[11] But the British goal remained, in Churchill's phrase, a Germany that was "fat but impotent"—an engine of prosperity for Europe, not a war machine menacing its neighbours.[12]

Serious planning for the future of Germany began in the summer of 1943. With Churchill pre-occupied by grand strategy, Attlee was given chairmanship of the two key committees on Armistice Terms and the Post-War Settlement (later fused in 1944). Attlee used this to promote the case for tough treatment of Germany, backed by other Labour Cabinet members such as Ernest Bevin and Hugh Dalton. They advocated the destruction of a central German government and the dismemberment of the country. Bevin spoke of a return to pre-Bismarck days—a patchwork confederation—while Attlee favoured three or four successor states. Equally important in their view was internal reform: the eradication of the "Prussian virus" of a militaristic caste and the break-up of the big industrial combinations.[13]

The Foreign Office did not share such an approach. It opposed dismemberment, believing that this was unnatural in view of German nationalism and unenforceable except by a degree of repression that could not long be sustained in peace-time conditions. Nor did the FO endorse deindustrialization, of the sort proposed in the Morgenthau Plan, arguing in line with the "fat but impotent" principle that Britain needed a wealthy Germany as a trading partner and as a motor for European recovery. The FO placed its hopes for a peaceful Germany in effective external supervision via an Allied "protectorate," which could "control" the government of Germany through the deterrent prospect of prompt military action if Germany misbehaved. This assumed the maintenance of an Allied coalition after the war.[14]

This latter premise was challenged most radically by the Chiefs of Staff and their advisers on the Post-Hostilities Planning Committee. They favoured the dismemberment of Germany, not merely to stop a future German revival but also to prevent the use of German resources by the Soviet Union. And if the USSR "were eventually to develop hostile intentions towards us . . . we should require all the help we could get from any source open to us, including Germany."[15] Such ideas were anathema in the FO. Convinced that the military were obsessive anti-Bolshevists, it warned that by focusing on a possible distant danger from the USSR Britain "might fail to guard against the immediate danger, which was the resurgence of Germany." Moreover, it feared a self-fulfilling prophecy. If such talk became widespread, the Russians might hear of it and be prompted to create the very conditions the Chiefs of Staff feared.[16]

Churchill's own views lay between those of the Foreign Office and the Chiefs of Staff. He favoured some dismemberment of Germany, particularly what he called "the isolation of Prussia,"[17] and in September 1944, under pressure from the Americans at the Quebec conference, he flirted with the idea of deindustrialization. But, like the FO, his thinking took shape in the context of alliance diplomacy, in relation to that of Roosevelt and Stalin. Ultimately Churchill and the Foreign Office, for all their differences, agreed that the German question could only be solved if Britain addressed it as part of a Grand Alliance with the United States and the Soviet Union.

Since the beginning of the century, many British policymakers had seen a close Anglo-American relationship as crucial for protecting Britain's overextended interests. The war-time association of 1917-18 promised much, but thereafter American unwillingness to accept political entanglements in Europe was a recurrent source of irritation in London. Summing up the accumulated wisdom of a generation Chamberlain wrote in 1937: "It is always best and safest to count on nothing from the Americans except words"[18]—an axiom apparently justified by the U.S. Neutrality Acts from 1935, which banned the provision of arms and credits to belligerent countries. The inter-war period also saw considerable friction over parity between the two navies and over commercial rivalry in various parts of the world. Britain's Imperial Preference and embryonic Sterling Area—both protectionist responses to the depression—were a particular grievance in Washington. Despite some improvement once war began, in 1939-40 Anglo-American relations remained aloof and suspicious. "Heaven knows," wrote Chamberlain in January 1940, "I don't want the Americans to fight for us—we should have to pay too dearly for that if they had a right to be in on the peace terms. . . . "[19]

All this changed with the fall of France. Bereft of continental allies and facing the prospect of imminent invasion, Britain had no choice but to hope for prompt and munificent aid from the United States. Even Chamberlain, deeply cynical about the Americans, recognized this, but the change of policy was reinforced by the accession of the half-American Winston Churchill to the premiership on 10 May. Churchill made the creation of a war-time alliance his prime objective in 1940-41, and he cultivated his contacts with Roosevelt assiduously. First fruits of the new relationship was the "Destroyers-for-Bases" Deal of September 1940, by which Britain eventually obtained 50 old U.S. destroyers. By March 1941 Roosevelt had responded to Britain's looming shortage of dollars with the Lend-Lease Act, and during the following months he gradually extended U.S. naval patrolling across much of the Atlantic. But, although a state of something close to "undeclared naval war" existed by December 1941, it took the surprise Japanese attack on Pearl Harbor to pitchfork America into the war.[20]

What Churchill called "the natural Anglo-American special relationship"[21] was fundamental to his planning for war and peace. His conception of it was highly personal—"my whole system is based upon partnership with Roosevelt," he told Eden in November 1942[22]—and the president's sudden death in April 1945 was undoubtedly a grievous blow for Churchill politically as well as personally. Nevertheless, his conception of the relationship also developed a clear institutional form. Churchill referred repeatedly to the need for maintaining the Combined Chiefs of Staff and for shared use of military bases, along the lines of the 1940 Destroyers Deal. As he wrote in February 1944: "It is my deepest conviction that unless Britain and the United States are joined together in a special relationship, including Combined Staff organization and a wide measure of reciprocity in the use of bases—all within the ambit of a world organization—another disastrous war will come to pass."[23]

British policy towards the Soviet Union developed very differently.[24] If relations with America in the inter-war years had been cool, those with Moscow had been positively frigid. Historic rivalry over the borders of India had been overlain since 1917 by fears of Bolshevik revolution. Britain did not establish diplomatic relations with the USSR until 1924 and they were severed by the Tories between 1927-29 over accusations of Soviet espionage. In the late 1930s, following Stalin's purges, the British had little faith in the Red Army and no intention of making firm commitments in Eastern Europe. In the summer of 1939 Chamberlain's government was ready for a loose political pact with Moscow, in the hope that this would help deter Hitler, but not for a close military alliance. Awareness of this encouraged Stalin to sign his pact with Hitler in August 1939, followed by a wide-ranging trade agreement the following February. During the winter of 1939-40 the British were even contemplating bombing Soviet oil installations to stop the flow of supplies to Nazi Germany. The fall of France did little to improve the situation and attempts by the British ambassador Sir Stafford Cripps to secure a trade agreement that might pull Moscow out of Hitler's economic orbit proved unavailing in 1940-41.[25]

The Nazi invasion of Russia in June 1941 did signal a change in relations, however. As with Anglo-American relations after the fall of France, mutual need dictated closer co-operation. Churchill had been a longstanding critic of what he called in 1919 "the foul baboonery of Bolshevism,"[26] but in June 1941 he made clear that the destruction of Nazism was his top priority: "If Hitler invaded Hell, I should at least make a favourable reference to the Devil in the House of Commons."[27] The Soviet government needed more than kind words, however—particularly supplies and a Second Front—neither of which the British were able to provide in the form Stalin wanted. During 1941-42 London debated whether to buy goodwill by conceding Stalin's demand for recognition of his 1940 conquest of the Baltic states. Eden and senior FO officials with the exception of Cadogan were willing to do so, as was Lord Beaverbrook, who eventually resigned from the Cabinet over the issue. But Churchill, Attlee, and many MPs were strongly against these concessions, reinforced by warnings from Roosevelt. Only a change of tack by Stalin and Molotov enabled the Anglo-Soviet treaty of alliance to be signed in May 1942.

By this time the broad pattern of British diplomacy towards the Soviet Union had been set. Although Soviet policy seemed unpredictable and moods in London oscillated, the Foreign Office was generally willing to go further than Churchill in conciliating the USSR. In particular, the FO was convinced that, "to facilitate and encourage Soviet co-operation in the post-war settlement . . . it is essential that His Majesty's Government should on all possible occasions treat the Soviet Government as partners, and make a habit of discussing plans and views with them as a matter of course. Only in this way will it be possible to break through the crust of suspicion which results from the previous relations between the two countries and our widely differing institutions."[28] There was a feeling in some quarters of the FO that Churchill regarded FDR as "much more of a buddy than Joe" and that, whatever the premier said about Big Three collaboration, his practice was one of "consulting the Americans" and then "informing the Russians."[29] This was regarded as unwise, not least because many in the FO, mindful of Anglo-American relations after 1918, feared that after the war was won the United States would "swing back to . . . an expansionist isolationism of a highly inconvenient character."[30] In particular, it was assumed, not least from various statements by the president himself, that U.S. troops would not remain in Europe for more than two years after victory.[31] This meant that Britain would be heavily reliant on Soviet help for the post-war containment of Germany.

The differences of approach between Churchill and the Foreign Office were real, but they should not be exaggerated when it came to concrete policy.[32] Although Churchill's bias lay towards the United States, he had no doubt that a good working relationship between the Big Three was vital for the future. Counterbalancing his fears of communism was his belief in his own capacity for personal diplomacy. After each of his meetings with Stalin, with the partial exception of Tehran, Churchill returned impressed with the Soviet leader and hopeful that a good personal relationship was being forged. Back from Moscow in August 1942, for instance, Churchill told his Cabinet that he "had formed the highest opinion of his [Stalin's] sagacity."[33] Moreover, Churchill's fears for the future ebbed and flowed. In January 1944 he told Eden that his feelings had changed towards recognition of Stalin's conquest of the Baltic states since the issue had first been raised more than two years before. "The tremendous victories of the Russian armies, the deep-seated changes which have taken place in the character of the Russian State and Government, the new confidence which has grown in our hearts towards Stalin—they have all had their effect. Most of all is the fact that the Russians may very soon be in physical possession [again] of these territories, and it is absolutely certain that we should never attempt to turn them out."[34]

This mixture of preference and pragmatism explains the search by Churchill and Eden for a modus vivendi with the Soviet Union. In October 1943 Eden had tried and failed at Moscow to obtain a "self-denying ordinance" from the Soviets about spheres of influence in Europe. In 1944-45, faced with the impending reality of a Soviet sphere as the victorious Red Army spread out over Eastern and southeastern Europe, the British tried to ameliorate it as best they could. In May 1944, Eden and Soviet ambassador Feodor Gusev evolved a loose understanding that the Soviets would take the lead in getting Romania out of the war, while the British would play the same role in Greece. This constituted the basis for the notorious "percentages agreement" fleshed out by Churchill with Stalin in Moscow in October. Greece would be 90 per cent under British influence, 10 per cent Soviet; the reverse would be the case in Romania; while Bulgaria would be 75 per cent Soviet and there would be a 50-50 division in Yugoslavia and Hungary. Although Roosevelt acquiesced, the place of the United States in these agreements and the precise meaning of percentages of influence were left vague. But Churchill's basic intention was clear—a spheres of influence agreement for the Balkans, centring in this case on Romania and Greece.[35]

It was with essentially the same objective that Churchill went to Yalta in February 1945. The issue of the Polish borders had long since been settled de facto—thanks to the intransigence of the London Poles and the Soviet military victories. What Churchill wanted was a Polish government friendly to the USSR and its security concerns, while not dominated by communists or openly violating the principles of the Atlantic Charter. It is important to remember that Poland had been the immediate issue on which Britain had gone to war in 1939 and Churchill was conscious of strong backbench concern in the Commons. The agreements on Polish elections and the Declaration on Liberated Europe seemed for the moment to satisfy his needs and, with his customary optimism in the afterglow of a summit meeting, he made the remarkable statement to a meeting of British ministers: "Poor Nevil[l]e Chamberlain believed he could trust Hitler. He was wrong. But I don't think I'm wrong about Stalin."[36] The Yalta agreements meant very different things to Churchill and Stalin and, once the Soviets failed to observe the British understanding of democratic processes, the line taken by Churchill and the Foreign Office hardened perceptibly. Poland became for them a test-case of Soviet post-war intentions and from early March Churchill kept up a barrage of cables to Washington, urging the Americans to take a tough line on Soviet noncompliance. On 12 May 1945 he told Truman that "an iron curtain is drawn down upon their front" and asked: "Surely it is vital now to come to an understanding with Russia, or see where we are with her, before we weaken our armies mortally?"[37] Even here, his point was negotiation from a position of strength—to hold the USSR to his understanding of the agreements they had reached for a Soviet sphere of influence in Eastern Europe but not a closed Stalinist bloc.

In all but his darkest moments, therefore, Churchill clung to the hope of a Big Three Concert. And he and the FO considered it essential to locate this within the framework of a new international organization, to replace the discredited League of Nations. But, again, there were significant differences of approach between them on this issue.[38] In 1942 Eden and the FO had been anxious to have some detailed proposals on the table, to prevent Roosevelt springing further surprises like the Atlantic Charter of 1941. Churchill, though always ready to air his own views, dismissed bureaucratic analyses as irrelevant until victory was much closer. He told Eden in October 1942 that the FO should "not overlook Mrs. Glass's Cookery Book recipe for Jugged Hare—'First catch your hare.'"[39] Furthermore, Churchill saw the new organization mainly as a vehicle for great-power control, whereas the FO wanted a fully fledged international body. And they were also at odds over Churchill's idea for regional councils—in Europe, the American hemisphere, and the Pacific—through which the great powers would exercise their local predominance. For the FO, sensitive to State Department concerns, this smacked too much of naked power politics. By mid-1944, the combined opposition of the FO, the United States, and the British Dominions had eliminated Churchill's regional dimension. But his ideas for a "Council of Europe" and, eventually arising out of it, "a United States of Europe,"[40] hinted at another aspect of British diplomacy on which he and the FO did not see eye to eye—namely Britain's relationship with the continent of Europe.

Like the United States, Great Britain had a historic aversion to entangling alliances in Europe—and for much the same reason. In an era of sea power, the island country's security did not depend as much on the continental balance of power as that, say, of France. Although the "splendid isolation" of the Victorian era has been exaggerated,[41] Britain did hold itself aloof from the Continent for much of the nineteenth century and the ententes it concluded with France and Russia in the decade before 1914 were not fully fledged alliances. The war changed all that, but only temporarily, for after 1918 the British again avoided commitments to French security. It was only in the winter following Munich, as perceptions of Hitler changed, that the British entered into staff talks and then a wartime alliance with France.

Thereafter, policy moved apace. By early 1940 senior FO officials, chastened by the disastrous failure of Britain's inter-war policy, were convinced that only a permanent Anglo-French post-war alliance could provide a basis for European peace and stability. Sir Orme Sargent, the deputy under-secretary, wrote a minute calling for "such a system of close and permanent co-operation between France and Great Britain—political, military, and economic—as will for all international purposes make of the two countries a single unit in post-war Europe." This, he believed, would be "perhaps the only effective counter-weight to the unit of 80 million Germans in the middle of Europe . . . ."[42] Sargent's views were endorsed by Halifax, the foreign secretary, and Chamberlain, the prime minister, but such radical thinking was completely overturned by the fall of France. In the wake of that international revolution, Halifax judged in July 1940 that henceforth "the possibility of some sort of special association with the U.S.A. . . . ought, I think, to replace the idea of Anglo-French Union among the various plans which we may make for the future."[43]

It is hard to overestimate the significance of the events of May-June 1940 for British attitudes towards the Continent. Having been forced reluctantly in 1939 to conclude that their isolationism had helped to cause the war, they were now left angry and contemptuous at the failure of France and the low countries to resist Hitler. Henceforth, survival, let alone victory, over the Axis would depend on the resources of Britain and the Empire, coupled increasingly from 1941 with those of its new allies, America and Russia. And, as we have seen, British leaders deemed continued great-power co-operation essential for post-war peace. Only that could keep Germany in its place.

This was Churchill's attitude in his dealings with the French during the war. France had been far from being the centrepiece of British diplomacy in 1939-40, and had, by 1942, slipped to the status of second-class citizens in the new international polity, as far as London was concerned. Part of the problem was the Free French leader General Charles de Gaulle. Churchill had done much to promote him in the dark days of 1940 when de Gaulle unilaterally took command of the exiled French forces who did not accept German domination and the Vichy regime. But privately Churchill, like most of the British, found de Gaulle's arrogance hard to bear. "He is animated by dictatorial instincts and consumed by personal ambition . . . he shows many of the symptoms of a budding Fuhrer" and is "thoroughly anti-British," Churchill wrote in July 1943.[44]

The Foreign Office was somewhat less allergic to de Gaulle, but the fundamental source of its tension with Churchill lay in policy not personalities. In principle, Churchill insisted that "my unchanging goal is a strong France friendly to Great Britain and the U.S.A."[45] But, where these two poles of policy conflicted, as Churchill told de Gaulle in a bitter exchange on the eve of D-Day, "each time I have to choose between you and Roosevelt, I shall always choose Roosevelt."[46] The FO, by contrast, less hopeful than Churchill about America, was more interested in trying to build up a separate framework of European co-operation in which France would play a major role.

This difference was apparent in the summer of 1943, when London and Washington were arguing about whether to recognize the Free French as the future government of France and its empire. Churchill, sensitive to and sharing Roosevelt's aversion to de Gaulle, opposed the idea, but Eden justified recognition in the following terms:

> Our main problem after the war will be to contain Germany. Our treaty with the Soviet Union . . . for this purpose . . . needs to be balanced by an understanding with a powerful France in the west . . . . In dealing with European problems of the future we are likely to have to work more closely with France even than with the United States, and while we should naturally concert our French policy so far as we can with Washington, there are limits beyond which we ought not to allow our policy to be governed by theirs.[47]

The problem surfaced again in the autumn of 1944, as Whitehall debated the idea of a Western European bloc. The Chiefs of Staff favoured this, as a device to contain Germany and a longer-term insurance against Russia. They commented: "We consider the inclusion of a strong France is of paramount importance."[48] The FO agreed but, as we have seen, it emphasized the German threat and deprecated any reference to Russia as a possible future enemy. On France, however, they were at one with the Chiefs of Staff. Eden told Churchill: "It has always seemed to me that the lesson of the disasters of 1940 is precisely the need to build up a common defence association in Western Europe. . . . The best way of building up such an association would obviously be to build up France. . . ."[49] Churchill, however, was sceptical of the whole idea. The sense of continental betrayal in 1940 still rankled. "Until a really strong French Army is in being, which may well be more than five years away, there is nothing in these countries but hopeless weakness. . . . That England should undertake to defend these countries . . . before the French have the second Army in Europe, seems to me contrary to all wisdom and even common prudence." Churchill was adamant on this point. And, like the Chiefs, he aired his periodic fears of the USSR, calling it "the only other Power which after the extirpation of German military strength can threaten Western Europe."[50]

But it would be wrong to leave this as Churchill's last word. More representative of his hopes and aims were these comments on a gloomy memo about Anglo-Soviet relations from the British ambassador in Moscow and on related FO comments about a Western bloc. Reading them at Yalta in February 1945, he summarized their apparent moral as follows: "1. The only bond of the victors is their Common Hate. 2. To make Britain safe she must be responsible for the safety of a cluster of feeble states." He then added: "We ought to think of something better than these." That "something better" in his view was still the UN as a vehicle for maintaining the Grand Alliance. He ticked approvingly a sentence in the ambassador's memo: "The Russians think of the future world order in terms of a concert of the three major allies."[51] And in a critique of the Western bloc idea five weeks earlier, he insisted that "the first thing is to set up the World Organization, on which all depends."[52]

Although much of the diplomatic discussion between Churchill, Eden, and the FO dealt with Europe, their perspective was global in scope. For all these men, products of the late Victorian era, the existence of Britain's empire was axiomatic. The so-called white Dominions—Canada, Australia, Ireland, New Zealand, and South Africa—were self-governing by the 1930s. Although Ireland declared its neutrality in 1939, the others assisted Britain considerably in the war, and Australasia in particular was still heavily reliant on Britain for its defence, particularly by sea against Japan. Much of the empire in Asia and Africa, however, remained Crown Colonies—ruled by a British governor in consultation with local elites and without meaningful democratic participation. The most sensitive case was India—a major source of military manpower—which by 1939 enjoyed some representative government on the provincial level but which was still ruled by a British viceroy. His unilateral declaration of war in 1939 provoked a campaign of opposition from the main Indian political grouping, the Congress party.

British diplomacy was dedicated to maintaining this global empire, while also promoting its evolution towards greater local autonomy. Not only would the latter be a response to growing nationalist pressures, it would also relieve the burden of formal rule on the British exchequer. Ideally, the British wanted the privileges of empire—especially access to bases and raw materials—without the costs of running the country. In the phrase of one historian, empire would be conducted "informally if possible, formally if necessary."[53] The development of global war, however, made both elements of this policy problematic. In the face of Italian and Japanese expansion, informal rule became harder to sustain, yet formal rule was often more than an over-stretched Britain could afford.

In 1940 foreign policy narrowed virtually to the issue of national survival. With Italy entering the war and threatening Britain's position in the Mediterranean, the Royal Navy had no ships to spare for the Pacific. At the end of June, the Australian and New Zealand governments were informed that in the immediate future they should look to their own resources in the event of trouble with Japan.[54] In 1940-41, despite periodic war scares, Japan remained outside the conflict, and by late 1941 Britain had a token fleet of two capital ships in place off Singapore. But Pearl Harbor saw the onset of a wide-ranging Japanese campaign against Western power which not only eliminated those ships in a couple of hours but also entailed the loss of Malaya, Singapore, Hong Kong, and much of Burma. By the spring of 1942 both Australia and India seemed in danger. With no military resources to spare for the Pacific, Britain was forced back on diplomacy in an effort to preserve what remained of its Far Eastern empire.

The crucial battleground was India. Churchill was a die-hard supporter of the British Raj, but the desperate military situation made it essential to maximize Indian support for the war. This was also Roosevelt's line. His frequent advice on the matter and the activities of U.S. representatives in India were becoming a major headache for Churchill. At home, the disasters in Asia had obliged him to reconstruct his Cabinet, giving Labour members a greater say. They had long advocated a forward policy on India, involving the concession of Dominion status, and early in 1942 Attlee pressed the issue insistently. He told Churchill: "Now is the time for an act of statesmanship. To mark time is to lose India."[55] In March Sir Stafford Cripps, one of Labour's leading spokesmen on India, was despatched to Delhi with an offer of participation in the war-time government and some form of independence when the war was over. Caught between Churchill, the Hindu Congress party, and its rivals in the emerging Muslim League, Cripps's mission foundered, but not before Britain had committed itself in principle to a rapid post-war transfer of power. What Churchill saw as Roosevelt's meddling finally elicited a veiled threat of resignation from the prime minister.[56]

One of the benchmarks for the new diplomacy of empire was the Atlantic Charter of August 1941. Drafted at the prompting of the Americans, it had been accepted by Churchill as a way of associating Roosevelt more closely with the Allied cause at a time when the United States remained neutral. Its clauses about self-determination were mainly directed to occupied Europe, but they were quickly appropriated by the Roosevelt administration as part of its attack on colonialism in general. And, as over India, Labour politicians and reform-minded bureaucrats in the Colonial Office provided complementary domestic pressure. In 1942-43 Britain therefore defined its imperial policy more clearly, particularly through the July 1943 Declaration on the Colonies and the creation of several regional consultative councils, through which the United States could have some loose involvement in colonial reform. The Foreign and Colonial offices also sponsored a more vigorous development and welfare program in blighted areas such as the Caribbean, prising £120 million ($500 million) out of the Treasury in 1945.[57]

During the war the British also faced a renewed challenge to their informal empire of trade and finance. Despite the Anglo-American alliance, the U.S. State Department had not abandoned its campaign against the Sterling Area and Imperial Preference. In 1941-42 it tried to make their elimination the quid pro quo for Lend-Lease, but the British Cabinet managed to avoid any compromising commitments. The issue recurred in the discussions about the post-war international economic system. To parts of the Tory party and some in the Treasury and Bank of England, the network of war-time commercial and financial controls seemed a viable policy for post-war Britain. But a majority of British policymakers were willing to relax them, particularly in financial matters, and move back towards multilateral international trade, if the Americans made complementary moves. The eventual agreements reached at Bretton Woods in 1944 reflected American preferences more than British, but, from London's point of view, the United States was beginning to recognize its responsibility, as the world's leading creditor and second-largest importer, for international liquidity.[58]

In 1942 the threat to Britain's Asian empire had seemed acute. There had also been intense American pressure to dismantle informal imperialism.

By the autumn of 1945, however, it could be proudly claimed that "no British colonies had been permanently lost as a direct result of foreign conquest."[59] The sudden Japanese surrender in August 1945 had enabled small British forces to move in quickly, rather than having to wait for the Americans to reconquer Britain's lost territories and then impose their own anti-imperialist agenda. Moreover, the American challenge to Imperial Preference and the Sterling Area had been checked if not negated.

Despite these successes, however, British global power was never the same again. India was now politicized and increasingly unmanageable. Amid mounting communal violence, the British abandoned the effort to hold on in 1947. Elsewhere, the critique of formal empire, from the Americans and at home, gathered force and Attlee's post-war Labour government was receptive to this view. Yet the war should not be seen simply as loosening the ties of empire. The growth of informal imperialism—in the sense of developing colonial resources behind the protection of trade and financial agreements—was enhanced. The 1945 Development Act was the harbinger of a vigorous and unprecedented post-war effort to exploit colonial raw materials. Malayan rubber, West African cocoa, and Rhodesian tobacco were all fostered for their dollar-earning potential within the sterling area. Thus, the war-time diplomacy of imperialism—devolving formal empire yet exploiting informal empire—pointed clearly on to the period after 1945.[60]

British policymakers ended the war acutely conscious that their world had been irrevocably changed. Formal empire had been undermined, and the United States and the Soviet Union were now the major international powers. As Churchill observed after Yalta, "a small lion was walking between a huge Russian bear and a great American elephant."[61] Moreover, the British lion had lost much of its muscle, having expended 28 per cent of its total assets during the conflict.[62] Yet that did not mean that Britain ended the war as an international irrelevance. Its continental rivals, particularly France and Germany, had all been far more severely damaged by the war, and Britain was unquestionably the strongest European power in the post-war decade. Furthermore, the British had evolved diplomatic strategies to maximize their advantages. Globally, they were ready to loosen the ties of empire where these were burdensome, while tightening them where that seemed advantageous. They hoped that a close relationship with Washington would enable Britain, in the words of one FO memorandum, "to make use of American power for purposes which we regard as good."[63] And it was intended that co-operation with the USSR should be maintained as far as possible to contain German resurgence.

There were differences of emphasis, of course. Eden and the Foreign Office were less ready than Churchill to dismember Germany. They were also keener on close co-operation with France and her neighbours. Churchill, for his part, placed greater faith in the Anglo-American "special relationship" and, like the Chiefs of Staff, was more fearful of the Soviet Union. But the basic British diplomatic objective was clear. In the record of Churchill's words to senior American policymakers in Washington in May 1943: "The first preoccupation must be to prevent further aggression in the future by Germany or Japan. To this end he contemplated an association of the United States, Great Britain and Russia . . . . On these powers would rest the real responsibility for peace."[64] How, why, and with what consequences that association crumbled into a state of Cold War is explored in the last chapter of this volume.

NOTES

1. Statistics from Carlo M. Cipolla, *The Fontana History of Europe*, vol. 5, *The Twentieth Century*, part I (Brighton, England, 1977), 22; Philip S. Bagwell and G. E. Mingay, *Britain and America, 1850-1950: A Study of Economic Change* (London, 1970), 1.

2. D. K. Fieldhouse, *The Colonial Empires: A Comparative Survey from the Eighteenth Century* (London, 1982), 242.

3. David Dilks, *Curzon in India*, vol. I (London, 1969), 113.

4. See Zara S. Steiner, "Decision-making in American and British Foreign Policy: An Open and Shut Case," *Review of International Studies* 13 (1987), 1-18.

5. Memo of May 1932, quoted in Uri Bialer, *The Shadow of the Bomber: The Fear of Air Attack and British Politics, 1932-1939* (London, 1980), 10.

6. David Dilks, ed., *The Diaries of Sir Alexander Cadogan, O.M., 1938-1945* (London, 1971), 152. See generally the magisterial study by Donald Cameron Watt, *How War Came: The Immediate Origins of the Second World War, 1938-1939* (London, 1989).

7. Neville Chamberlain to Ida Chamberlain, 10 September 1939, Neville Chamberlain papers, NC 18/1/1116 (Birmingham University Library).

8. CAB 65/13, pp. 179-80, 27 May 1940 (Public Record Office, London—henceforth PRO). Also see David Reynolds, "Churchill and the British 'Decision' to Fight on in 1940: Right Policy, Wrong Reasons," in Richard Langhorne, ed., *Diplomacy and Intelligence during the Second World War* (Cambridge, 1985), 147-67.

9. CAB 65/13, folios 180 (27 May) and 187 (28 May).

10. See Thomas Munch-Petersen, " 'Common Sense not Bravado': The Butler-Prytz Interview of 17 June 1940," *Scandia* 52 (1986), 73-114.

11. See also Victor Rothwell, *Britain and the Cold War, 1941-1947* (London, 1982), 26-28.

12. Hugh Dalton diaries, vol. 25, 26 August 1941 (British Library of Political and Economic Sciences, LSE, London).

13. See T. D. Burridge, *British Labour and Hitler's War* (London, 1976), esp. 94-95, 168-69; Burridge, "Great Britain and the Dismemberment of Germany at the End of the Second World War," *International History Review* 3 (1981), 565-79.

14. Rothwell, *Britain and the Cold War*, esp. 33 ff. On Eden's equivocations about partition see Keith Sainsbury, "British Policy and German Unity at the End of the Second World War," *English Historical Review* 94 (1979), 791-92 ff.

15 Chiefs of Staff memo of 9 September 1944, quoted in Anne Deighton, *The Impossible Peace: Britain, the Division of Germany and the Origins of the Cold War* (Oxford, 1990), 19.

16. Minutes of FO/COS meeting, 4 October 1944, in FO [Foreign Office] 954/22A, Pwp/44/29, PRO.

17. Churchill annotation, 26 January 1944, on Attlee to Churchill, 25 January 1944, PREM 3/197/2, PRO.

18. Neville Chamberlain to Hilda Chamberlain, 17 December 1937, Chamberlain papers, NC 18/1/1032.

19. Neville Chamberlain to Ida Chamberlain, 27 January 1940, Chamberlain papers, NC 18/1/1140.

20. For an overview, see David Reynolds, "Roosevelt, Churchill, and the Wartime Anglo-American Alliance, 1939-1945: Towards a New Synthesis," in Wm. Roger Louis and Hedley Bull, eds., *The "Special Relationship": Anglo-American Relations since 1945* (Oxford, 1986), 17-41. Essential on the personal relationship is Warren F. Kimball, ed., *Churchill & Roosevelt: The Complete Correspondence* (3 vols.; Princeton, 1984).

21. Churchill to Attlee and Eden, tel., 14 September 1943, FO 954/22A.

22. Churchill to Eden, 5 November 1942, PREM 4/27/1.

23. Churchill to Richard Law, 16 February 1944, PREM 4/27/10. Despite his purple prose, Churchill's view of the relationship was not sentimental. This is clearly evident in his policy about the atomic bomb. See ch. 8 in this volume for a discussion of Anglo-American concord and dispute on this matter.

24. For background see F. S. Northedge and Audrey Wells, *Britain and Soviet Communism: The Impact of a Revolution* (London, 1982). Anderson to Churchill, 30 July 1942, PREM 3/139/8A.

25. Basic studies for this period are Gabriel Gorodetsky, *Stafford Cripps' Mission to Moscow, 1940-1942* (Cambridge, 1984) and Steven M. Miner, *Between Churchill and Stalin: The Soviet Union, Great Britain, and the Origins of the Grand Alliance* (Chapel Hill, N.C., 1988).

26. Quoted in Martin Gilbert, *Winston S. Churchill*, vol. IV (London, 1975), 257.

27. John Colville's essay in Sir John Wheeler-Bennett, ed., *Action This Day: Working With Churchill* (London, 1968), 89.

28. Eden to Sir Archibald Clark Kerr, 4 February 1943, quoted in Graham Ross, ed., *The Foreign Office and the Kremlin: British Documents on Anglo-Soviet Relations, 1941-45* (Cambridge, 1984), 121. The long introduction to that volume, also Martin Kitchen, *British Policy towards the Soviet Union during the Second World War* (London, 1986) and P. M. H. Bell, *John Bull and the Bear: British Public Opinion, Foreign Policy and the Soviet Union, 1941-1945* (London, 1990) are basic studies of the war-time alliance.

29. Geoffrey Wilson to Clark Kerr, 8 August 1943, in Ross, ed., *The Foreign Office and the Kremlin*, 134-35.

30. Richard Law, January 1945, quoted in Christopher Thorne, *Allies of a Kind: The United States, Britain and the War against Japan, 1941-1945* (London, 1978), 502.

31. For example, this comment by the permanent under secretary at the FO: "President Roosevelt is determined . . . not to get 'entangled' in Europe—which means leaving all the 'headaches' to us, with the President securely and comfortably ensconced in his pulpit." Cadogan, minute, 22 January 1945, FO 371/44595, AN 154/32/45.

32. See the perceptive discussion in Elisabeth Barker, *Churchill and Eden at War* (London, 1978), ch. 16 and ff.

33. Quoted in Martin Kitchen, "Winston Churchill and the Soviet Union during the Second World War," *Historical Journal* 30 (1987), 424—a useful survey article.

34. Churchill to Eden, l6 January 1944, PREM 3/399/6.

35. See esp. the minutes of his meeting with Stalin at the Kremlin on 9 October 1944, PREM 3/434/2. On the meetings, see Albert Resis, "The Churchill-Stalin Secret Percentages Agreement on the Balkans, Moscow, October 1944," *American Historical Review* 83 (1978), 368-87; Joseph M. Siracusa, "The Meaning of TOLSTOY: Churchill, Stalin, and the Balkans, Moscow, October 1944," *Diplomatic History* 3 (1979), 443-63.

36. Hugh Dalton, diaries, vol. 32, 23 February 1945.

37. Winston S. Churchill, *The Second World War* (6 vols., London, 1948-54), 6: 498-99.

38. E. J. Hughes, "Winston Churchill and the Formation of the United Nations Organization," *Journal of Contemporary History* 9 (1974), 177-94; also Sir Llewellyn Woodward, *British Foreign Policy in the Second World War* (5 vols., London, 1970-6), esp. ch. LXI. These volumes, often closely paraphrasing official FO records, remain a basic guide to British war-time diplomacy.

39. Churchill to Eden, 18 October 1942, PREM 4/100/7.

40. Churchill, "The Post-War World Settlement," 8 May 1944, CAB 99/28, PMM (44), 5.

41. David Reynolds, *Britannia Overruled: British Policy and World Power in the Twentieth Century* (London, 1991), 19-20.

42. Sargent, minute, 28 February 1940, FO 371/24298, C4444/9/17.

43. Halifax to Hankey, 15 July 1940, FO 371/25206, W8602/8602/49. For fuller discussion, see David Reynolds, "1940: Fulcrum of the Twentieth Century?" *International Affairs* 66 (1990), 329-33.

44. Churchill, draft memo for Cabinet, "United States Policy towards France," 13 July 1943, PREM 3/181/8. See generally François Kersaudy, *Churchill and de Gaulle* (London, 1983).

45. Churchill to Duff Cooper, 14 October 1943, PREM 3/273/1.

46. Charles de Gaulle, *War Memoirs: Unity, 1942-1944*, tr. Richard Howard (London, 1956), 227.

47. FO draft memo for Cabinet, "US Policy towards France," enclosed with Eden to Churchill, 13 July 1943, PREM 3/181/8.

48. Chiefs of Staff Committee, "Policy towards Western Europe," COS (44) 955 (0), 8 November 1944, FO 371/40725, U8652/180/70.

49. Eden to Churchill, 29 November 1944, PREM 4/30/8.

50. Churchill to Eden, 25 November 1944, PREM 4/30/8.

51. Clark Kerr to Eden, 19 November 1944; Churchill, minute, 8 February 1945, FO 371/40725, U8736/180/70.

52. Churchill to Eden, 31 December 1944, PREM 4/30/8.

53. John Gallagher, *The Decline, Revival and Fall of the British Empire,* ed. Anil Seal (London, 1982), 99.

54. David Day, *The Great Betrayal: Britain, Australia and the Onset of the Pacific War, 1939-1942* (London, 1988), esp. ch. 4.

55. R. J. Moore, *Churchill, Cripps, and India, 1939-1945* (Oxford, 1979), 56.

56. See esp. draft tel. to Roosevelt, l2 April 1942, communicated orally to FDR's emissary, Harry Hopkins; Kimball, *Churchill & Roosevelt,* I, 447-48 (C-68, draft A). For discussion, see Thorne, *Allies,* ch. 8.

57. The standard study is Wm. Roger Louis, *Imperialism at Bay, 1941-1945: The United States and the Decolonization of the British Empire* (Oxford, 1977). See also Kimball, *The Juggler,* (Princeton, 1991), ch. 7.

58. The basic texts are Richard N. Gardner, *Sterling-Dollar Diplomacy in Current Perspective* (3rd ed., New York, 1980); Alan P. Dobson, *US Wartime Aid to Britain, 1940-1946* (London, 1986); Randall Bennett Woods, *A Changing of the Guard: Anglo-American Relations, 1941-1946* (London, 1990).

59. John Darwin, *Britain and Decolonisation: The Retreat from Empire in the Post-War World* (London, 1988), 43.

60. See Reynolds, *Britannia Overruled,* 185-92.

61. Gilbert, *Churchill 7,* 1233.

62. R. C. O. Matthews, C. H. Feinstein and J. C. Odling-Smee, *British Economic Growth, 1856-1973* (London, 1982), 129-30.

63. FO American Dept. memo, "The Essentials of an American Policy," 21 March 1944, FO 371/38523, AN1538/16/45.

64. Record of conversation at British Embassy, Washington, 22 May 1943, CAB 66/43, WP (43) 233.

■ ■ ■

The Soviet Union: Territorial Diplomacy

Lydia V. Pozdeeva

In August 1939 the Soviet Union, skeptical that Britain and France, after their history of appeasement, would do anything to contain Nazism, signed a nonaggression pact with Germany to buy time. Its secret additional protocol, the original of which has now been found in the Russian archives, allowed the USSR to recover former Tsarist territory in the Baltic states, eastern Poland, and Romania that had been lost after the First World War. These also served as buffers against possible German attack. But in June 1941 Hitler broke that pact and threw his armies in a brutal assault on the Soviet Union. Thereafter Stalin sought to build an alliance with the Western capitalist states whom he had so much distrusted. For him the vital needs were military and logistic support against Germany—a Second Front and the successive supply protocols. But maintenance of the USSR's new borders and their extension into Eastern Europe—both as a buffer against future German aggression and as proof of imperial might—remained abiding goals. Wartime Soviet foreign policy was focused on security through territorial enlargement. For Stalin, inter-allied diplomacy was a tool of that policy.

Before 22 June 1941 Soviet-British relations were "exceedingly cool and hostile," according to the ambassador of the USSR in the United Kingdom, Ivan Maisky. Then came a sharp change.[1] Anthony Eden received Maisky at noon on that day. He promised on behalf of his government all possible assistance and reaffirmed its readiness to send military and economic missions immediately to the USSR.[2] On the same day in Moscow, Deputy Foreign Commissar Andrei Vyshinsky met with the British chargé d'affaires in the USSR, H. L. Baggalay, who raised the issue of establishing cooperation with the USSR and spoke about the possibility of sending supplies via Vladivostok or the Persian Gulf. He also suggested that British officers who had experience in combat against German tanks should be sent to the USSR. In reply Vyshinsky simply promised to inform his government about their conversation.[3]

In a radio address on 22 June at 9:00 , the British prime minister proclaimed his intention "to give whatever help we can to Russia. . . . The Russian danger is therefore our danger and the danger of the United States." However, Churchill left no doubts about his anticommunist views and insisted that "this is no class war."[4] The United States took in many respects a similar stand. The Department of State issued a statement that denounced Nazi aggression against the USSR, which was read out by Sumner Welles, the under-secretary of state, on 23 June. The concluding sentence was written by Roosevelt: "Hitler's armies are today the chief dangers of the Americas." In his address of 24 June the president promised all possible assistance to Russia in its fight against Germany, noting, however, that priority would be given to the task of ensuring supplies for the United Kingdom.[5]

The British and U.S. leaders specified neither the volume, nature, nor terms of future assistance. No matter how indefinite, however, these official statements were of great political importance. The Nazi gamble on forging a united anti-Soviet front of capitalist states had proved unrealistic and a real prospect opened up of Soviet cooperation with the countries opposed to the aggression of Nazi Germany and its allies.

However, there were numerous obstacles to the unification of the anti-Hitler forces because of mutual prejudice and open hostility. Plans for assistance to the USSR, proclaimed by Roosevelt, came under severe attack in America from prominent right-wing leaders. Most Americans viewed with distrust the Soviet totalitarian regime. Both before and after 22 June 1941 British military and diplomatic leaders showed no interest in extensive cooperation with the USSR, being especially opposed to alliance in the military sphere.[6] Thus the proposed cooperation with the USSR was strictly limited in the United States and the United Kingdom.

The Kremlin's attitude to cooperation was no less cautious. The steady distrust of the Western democracies felt by Soviet leaders was reinforced in May 1941, when Rudolf Hess landed suddenly in Scotland. The fears about a possible peace treaty to be signed between Germany and Britain were reflected in the conversations Soviet diplomats had in Moscow, London, and Washington in the initial period of the war. Molotov's first reaction to the statements about assistance made by Churchill and Roosevelt was quite typical: He confined himself to informing Maisky briefly that the government had no objections to the arrival of the British military mission and economic experts (both missions reached Moscow on 27 June). In his talk with Sir Stafford Cripps, the British ambassador, after he introduced members of the missions, Molotov first of all asked him for news about "the Hess affair." Even prior to that, while discussing the subject of Hess's arrival in the British Isles, Maisky tried to prevail on Churchill (via Eden) to confirm that "Britain is firm in its determination to fight to the end in that war."[7]

Stalin's reluctance to believe in Britain's determination to fight, his desire to determine the volume and nature of arms deliveries to the USSR, and his intention to involve the British Navy in the operations off Petsamo and Murmansk and in rendering other kinds of assistance are all quite revealing of the Soviet stance. Molotov spoke about the need to provide a political foundation for Soviet-British cooperation in his talk with the British ambassador as early as 27 June.[8] This was to be a major theme in the future.

Nevertheless, Stalin had no option but to overcome his personal aversion toward Western powers. In his radio address on 3 July 1941 he described the conflict (for the first time) as a war of liberation, and called Churchill's address "historic." He also spoke about the U.S. government's declaration of readiness to render assistance to the USSR. Another unusual step was taken. Stalin received Cripps on 8 July 1941 (he had not met the ambassador for nearly a year). The Soviet leader proposed in categorical terms that Britain sign an agreement with the USSR promising mutual assistance against Germany and no separate peace.[9]

British diplomats would have preferred a general declaration, but eventually the War Cabinet in London decided to accept Stalin's offer, concluding that it was of a general nature. On 12 July 1941 Molotov and Cripps signed in Moscow an agreement between the USSR and the United Kingdom on joint action in the war against Germany. The two sides undertook, first, to render assistance and all kinds of support to each other and, second, not to hold peace talks with Germany without prior mutual agreement.[10] Just as before, the volume and contents of mutual assistance were not specified. The agreement of 12 July was the first intergovernmental document that laid the foundation of an anti-Hitler coalition with Soviet participation.

Initially the USSR largely held talks on supplies and economic assistance with the United States, which still formally maintained its neutral status.[11] Decisions on military and economic assistance to the USSR were adopted owing to Roosevelt's energetic intervention and the efforts of certain American diplomats and politicians who sincerely wished to cooperate with the Soviet Union. The contribution made by Harry Hopkins, a firm advocate of close cooperation with the USSR, could hardly be overestimated in this regard. His visit to Moscow as Roosevelt's personal envoy, including talks in the Kremlin on 30-31 July 1941, led Stalin to conclude that a united Soviet-American-British bloc could become a reality.[12]

Nevertheless the Soviet leadership was not completely satisfied. On 9 August Vyshinsky pointed out to Cripps that America was dragging its feet, although he expressed hope that, after Hopkins's visit to Moscow, the necessary steps would be taken by the United States more rapidly and effectively.[13]

This and some other reproaches by the Soviet side were warranted. But the initial sharply negative Soviet reaction to the Atlantic Charter, promulgated by Roosevelt and Churchill on 14 August 1941 when they met near Newfoundland, was hardly justified. Although the document was of a general nature, it proclaimed principles that appealed to the popular struggle against Nazism and to the demand for democratic war aims. However, Eden's proposal that the USSR should adopt the declaration at an Allied conference to be held in London irritated Deputy Soviet Foreign Commissar Lozovsky. "The British and Americans," he wrote in a report to Molotov dated 23 August, "would like to reduce us to the status of governments in exile in London and dominions of the United Kingdom."[14]

Molotov's instructions, sent to Maisky on 24 August, were obviously written in the light of Lozovsky's opinion. The Soviet ambassador was instructed to inform the British government that the USSR had no objections to the Atlantic Charter's principles, but wished to include in it more resolute demands of Germany. Furthermore, the Soviet Union ruled out the possibility of signing the declaration, for it had not been informed or consulted in advance and also because "our comrades are very much irritated that plans are afoot to rivet the USSR to the chariot of other countries." In his talk with Eden on 26 August, Maisky couched his criticism in the form of friendly advice.[15]

If the Soviet government's official statement in support of the Atlantic Charter had been made immediately after its publication, this might have defused the tense atmosphere generated on some occasions in the course of Soviet talks with the West. Stalin, whose moods and opinions were echoed by Molotov and Lozovsky, often spoke in negative terms about British policy. "The British," Stalin said in his cable to Maisky dated 30 August, "seem to desire our weakening. If this supposition is correct, we must show caution in our relations with Britain."[16] Curiously enough, Cripps wrote in much the same vein in his diary on 21 October 1941:

"One should be darned cautious in dealing with the Russians, since old suspicions are very much alive and are manifest."[17]

The Inter-Allied conference opened in London on 24 September 1941. It was attended by representatives of the USSR, the United Kingdom, and governments in exile of occupied European countries. In a declaration, read out by Maisky, the Soviet government stated its acceptance of the Charter's main principles. The Soviet government proclaimed that final victory over Nazism was the most important goal of the states that were fighting against Germany and its satellites.[18] The joint statement in support of the Atlantic Charter, as well as the successful completion of the Harriman-Beaverbrook mission and the extension by the Roosevelt administration of Lend-Lease to the USSR, all testified to the growing strength of the forces arrayed against Hitler.

Apart from the issues of military cooperation and supply, since the autumn of 1941 Soviet diplomacy had stressed the need to formalize the Soviet-British alliance. At the Moscow conference on 30 September 1941, Stalin raised the issue of turning the Soviet-British agreement of 12 July into a treaty of alliance for wartime and afterwards.[19] In his message to Churchill on 8 November, couched in blunt language, he stressed the following two factors: "First, no definite agreement has been reached between our countries on war goals and plans for a peace settlement in the postwar period; second, no treaty of mutual assistance in Europe against Hitler has been signed between the USSR and the United Kingdom."[20]

London was in no hurry to undertake any specific obligations toward Moscow in the political sphere. Referring to strong opposition from MPs and Conservative circles at home as well as the Roosevelt administration, Churchill, and other ministers, as before, argued out that "political changes produced during the war ought not to be recognized de jure pending a general peace settlement."[21] The British government, as Maisky warned, preferred not to be too precise about its postwar plans because it wanted to retain its freedom of action till the moment of signing the peace.[22]

Soviet-British relations were certainly complicated due to the lack of military assistance to the USSR and to a number of political problems including Britain's delay in declaring war on Romania, Hungary, and Finland. However, German troops had besieged Leningrad and were on the edge of Moscow. It was, therefore, hardly the right moment for the USSR to raise such major issues that bore on the postwar settlement. An attempt to exert pressure on the British government ended in failure, having evoked only Churchill's anger. True, there was no open row. Replying to Stalin's message of 8 November Churchill expressed readiness to send

Foreign Secretary Eden to the USSR in order to discuss all military issues, although he made it clear that postwar settlement could be discussed only "at the conference table of victory."[23] That determined the limited nature of the British foreign secretary's mission.

In their talks with Eden (16-18 December 1941), Stalin and Molotov insisted on the need to recognize the USSR's 1941 borders with Finland, the Baltic states, and Romania. Immediate recognition of the Soviet-Polish border was not demanded on that occasion, in the hope of settling it later in talks with Britain and Poland. Since no agreement had been reached on the issue of the Soviet western borders, Stalin declared that there was no question of signing a Soviet-British treaty, and Eden agreed.[24]

However, the delay in signing the treaty, Cripps warned Molotov on 19 December, might encourage elements hostile to the Soviet-British rapprochement. Molotov, for his part, reiterated that without an agreement on the Soviet western borders, no treaty could be signed. "Comrade Stalin said openly that neither he nor the government would dare to convey such an answer to the people."[25] Naturally, neither Stalin nor his associates had any intention of telling the people about their confidential talks. It is clear that Stalin and his entourage sought to reach an agreement with the United Kingdom on those changes of the borders which the USSR had made in 1939-40.

Irrespective of the difference in views on many issues, by the close of 1941, the leading states of the anti-Hitler coalition had succeeded in solving a number of problems. Several official agreements were signed on cooperation between the Soviet Union, the United States, and the United Kingdom; joint Soviet-British action was taken in Iran; progress had been made in cooperation between the two navies; ways had been found to deliver supplies to the USSR; the First Moscow Supply Protocol was signed, and an official basis for deliveries thereby established, which made it possible to promote trilateral military and economic Allied contacts.

The successful counteroffensive at Moscow in the winter of 1941-42 and the entry of the United States into the war definitely accelerated the consolidation of the anti-Hitler coalition. The Declaration by the "United Nations" served as its founding document. The issue of agreement on the war's goals then became of major importance. The Roosevelt administration set about drafting a statement taking into account the Soviet-British agreement of 12 July 1941.[26] The Soviet government approved in principle the American draft, although introducing a number of amendments. In particular, it objected to wording that might make it binding on the USSR to join in the war against Japan at a time when almost all its forces were concentrated on the Soviet-German front.[27]

The U.S. president and some advisers treated with understanding the Soviet stand on the issue of the USSR joining the war against Japan. The British embassy reported from Washington: "It was recognized that having borne the brunt of German attack, she might not feel able at the moment to undertake a war on the second front."[28] On the morning of 30 December, Roosevelt scribbled "OK" on the text of the Joint Declaration which included all Soviet amendments. Next day he proposed entitling it "Declaration by the United Nations." The term "alliance" was not used, for it might have produced constitutional difficulties for the president.[29]

On 1 January 1942, Roosevelt, Churchill, Litvinov, and the Chinese representative, Sung Ziwen, were the first to sign the Declaration by the United Nations in Washington. Later it was signed in alphabetical order by representatives of 22 other states (hence its title—the Declaration by 26 States or the Washington Declaration), among them the British Dominions, Poland and other countries occupied by Germany, and some Latin American states that had declared war on the Axis powers. In Point One each of the 26 governments pledged itself "to employ its full resources, military or economic, against those members of the Tripartite Pact and its adherents with which such government is at war." In Point Two each government promised "to cooperate with the Governments signatory hereto and not to make a separate armistice or peace with the enemies." In conclusion, it was stated that "the foregoing declaration may be adhered to by other nations or authorities which are, or which may be, rendering material assistance and contributions in the struggle for victory over Hitlerism." By 1 May 1945, 21 additional states had signed the Declaration.[30]

However, that victory was yet to be won. The Nazi Reich redeployed its forces and launched a new offensive on the eastern front in the spring of 1942. A Second Front in the West was of vital importance for the Soviet Union. Stalin readily accepted Roosevelt's invitation and sent Molotov to America for an exchange of views on that issue.[31] It was agreed that before going to Washington Molotov should pay a visit to London.

As soon as the talks between Molotov and British leaders opened in London on 21 May, it became clear that the two issues—of the Soviet-British treaties (military and political) and of the Second Front—were closely interwoven. The urgency of the latter problem, and its political significance were strongly stressed by Molotov. The desperate position of the Soviet troops in their battles at Kharkov, in defensive operations to hold Sebastopol, and at other sections of the Soviet-German front was quite evident. Churchill, in his talks with the People's Commissar, avoided giving any promises of landing on the Continent in 1942, but mentioned that the British government planned such an operation for 1943.[32]

Discussion of the draft treaties was also not fruitful. At the morning session on 21 May, Churchill stressed the need for Britain to be in step with the United States and its unwillingness to violate the Atlantic Charter. He also referred to difficulties involved in the approval of the Soviet draft treaties by parliamentary circles. Molotov defended the "minimum terms" that were set forth in those drafts. These implied recovering the territory violated by Hitler plus additional "minimal" guarantees of Soviet security, primarily to the northwest and southwest of its borders. Without these guarantees, Molotov stated, "public opinion in the USSR would not understand and not approve the Treaty."[33] Until the very moment of opening the talks in London the Soviet government had excluded any thought of signing the treaties if they did not provide for acceptance of 1941 western borders of the USSR. "Without a Protocol [containing such a pledge] we shall not make a concession," reiterated Molotov to Maisky.[34]

On 23 May, however, Eden offered an alternative: to sign a single treaty, instead of two, for a term of 20 years, that would define the two countries' obligations in wartime and afterward. The border issue in this case had not been included in the proposed text of the treaty. Molotov sent to Stalin the new British proposition and noted the following points: the prime minister preferred this last version, and, according to Churchill and Eden, the American government and Roosevelt also approved the new project and did not want a treaty between Britain and the USSR containing controversial points. Molotov added that the American ambassador in London, John G. Winant, confirmed that this was indeed Roosevelt's opinion and asked for instructions to open discussion of that issue and to sign the treaty.[35]

The next day, on 24 May, Stalin answered Molotov that the British draft was not seen in Moscow as a mere declaration, but as an important document. It did not deal with the problem of border security, but this was, perhaps, not too bad, because "we" retain the freedom of action. The problem of borders, or rather, of guaranteeing Soviet borders, would be settled by force. Thus, a sharp turn took place in Stalin's attitude. He ordered Molotov to withdraw all previous Soviet proposals and to take the new British projects as a basis for the talks. Molotov informed Eden of his readiness to discuss new points and articles of the treaty on 25 May.[36] The Soviet government practically withdrew for the time being its demand on the borders issue.

There is every reason to suppose that the Kremlin had made such a switch in the hope of influencing the American government on the Second Front issue. After he had read Roosevelt's message of 12 April 1942,

Stalin knew about the president's desire to take concrete steps that summer to help the critical position of the Soviet troops. And Winant told Molotov on 24 May that the Second Front counted more for Roosevelt than treaties.[37] Thus, Moscow, as rightly noted by the British historian Michael Balfour, was encouraged to desist from mentioning the border's issue in the text of the treaty "by a promise from Roosevelt of a Second Front that very year."[38]

On 26 May 1942 Molotov and Eden signed in London a Soviet-British Treaty of alliance in the war against Nazi Germany and its satellites in Europe which also entailed cooperation and mutual assistance in the postwar period. Both sides undertook to render reciprocal military and other assistance in the hostilities against Germany (Part 1, Article 1); not to enter into any talks with Hitler's government, except by mutual agreement (Article 2); neither to enter into any alliance nor to take part in any coalitions aimed against the other signatory (Article 7); and to render each other every economic assistance in the postwar period (Article 6). Part 2 (Articles 3-8) dealt with cooperation in the postwar period. The treaty was to last for the next 20 years.[39]

It was pointed out in a memorandum of the Soviet Foreign Ministry that the treaty went much further than the Soviet-British agreement of 12 July 1941, signed by the two governments, because the treaty was concluded on a state level, and in the case of the United Kingdom, the Dominions' accession to any such document was implied.[40] This enthusiasm over the treaty may seem somewhat exaggerated, for in the ensuing Cold War it was terminated much earlier than planned. However, coming after a long spell of hostility in Soviet-British relations from 1917, it really looked like "an important historical landmark," as Maisky put it in his embassy's report of 15 June 1942, covering the period from January 1941 to May 1942. However, Maisky acknowledged: "The future will show in what direction this cooperation and friendship will develop."[41]

The decision not to include the border issue in the treaty enabled Molotov during his visit to Washington (29 May-4 June 1942) to secure a definite assurance from the American government on the main point under discussion. The Soviet-American communiqué published on 12 June 1942, stated that "a full agreement was reached on the issues of urgent tasks connected with the establishment of the Second Front in Europe in 1942."[42]

In his talk with Molotov on 1 June, Roosevelt said that he had handed a draft Lend-Lease agreement to the Soviet ambassador, and on 11 June, Maxim Litvinov and Cordell Hull signed in Washington a Soviet-U.S.

intergovernmental agreement on the principles of mutual assistance in the hostilities against the aggressor.[43] The Soviet-British Treaty and the Soviet-U.S. Agreement, both concluded in mid-1942, crowned the efforts by the leading countries of the anti-Hitler coalition to formalize their relations. Given their suspicions and hostility of the 1920s and 1930s, the change in relations was both substantial and striking.

However, the Second Front was not opened by the Allies as planned, and this, as well as the delay in supplies to the Soviet Union strained relations between the USSR and its new allies, the United States and the United Kingdom. At the talks held between Stalin and Churchill in August 1942 in Moscow (where Churchill had arrived to explain the delays) Stalin expressed his discontent in a peremptory tone, but, calming down, he later admitted that differences were "only natural, for allies may differ on some points."[44] At that time the Nazis had broken through the front to embark on an offensive in the Northern Caucasus and in the direction of Stalingrad and Voronezh, so open rupture with the British government was, naturally, highly undesirable for the USSR. Churchill himself warned the Soviet side that any quarrels between the Allies could only do a great deal of harm to the common cause.

In Moscow, Stalin informed the British prime minister of the grave situation at the Soviet-German front, and the latter confirmed for himself that the Russians were firmly determined to continue fighting. "There was never at any time the slightest suggestion of their not fighting on . . . ," Churchill stated in a message to Roosevelt.[45] That was an important conclusion, if one takes into account the fact that the Soviet side implied that the Soviet government and the Red Army might cease resistance, if the Second Front were not opened and if the USSR were unable to continue fighting. This was hinted, for example, by Vyshinsky on 16 July to the new British ambassador, Archibald Clark Kerr.[46]

The Soviet victories at Stalingrad, Kursk, and Orel in 1943 immeasurably raised Soviet military and international prestige. The Soviet armed forces held the strategic initiative firmly thereafter. The Western allies' final operations in Northern Africa and their campaign in the Mediterranean basin and Southern Italy also helped to undermine the Nazi bloc's military might. Thus, prerequisites were created for adoption of a number of important trilateral decisions on the issues of war and peace, although the process of thrashing them out, at conferences in Moscow and Tehran in late 1943, was laborious. The issues of postwar policy, particularly the Soviet Union's borders, could be ignored no longer. Face-to-face meetings of the Big Three had become essential.

Early in 1943, the Soviet Union's relations with the United States and the United Kingdom were extremely complicated. Just as before, the absence of the Second Front and incomplete fulfillment of obligations under the Protocols on Supplies largely accounted for the friction. Moscow's irritation was also attributable to the statement of U.S. Ambassador William Standley at a press conference, held on 8 March 1943, in which he expressed discontent about biased Soviet information on American aid to the USSR. New complications arose after the public had learned the truth about mass shootings by the Soviets of Polish officers in the Katyn forest and about the consequent rupture of diplomatic relations between the USSR and the Polish government in exile.

Concerned about the state of the Soviet-American relations, Roosevelt sought ways to improve them. In his message to Stalin, dated 5 May 1943, which was handed to Stalin personally in the Kremlin by the former U.S. ambassador in the USSR, Joseph Davies, Roosevelt offered to hold confidential unofficial talks in summer (a "meeting of minds," without Churchill).[47] In Moscow Davies was also received by Voroshilov, Molotov, Umansky, and Vyshinsky. According to Umansky's records of the conversation (on 21 May), the president's personal envoy stated that "he believed that the necessary atmosphere of mutual trust and close personal contacts between the governments had not yet been created in Soviet-American relations. . . ."[48] Hence Roosevelt's invitation to meet *à deux*.

Stalin's reply to the president sent via Davies was, however, restrained. He attached primary importance to the situation at the Soviet-German front. The future major Nazi offensive, Stalin pointed out, prevented him from accepting the invitation.[49] Once more he missed the chance to establish a personal contact—as with Roosevelt, so with Churchill (the latter offered Big Three talks at Scapa Flow, Scotland).

Nevertheless, some decisions by Stalin were interpreted by the Western leaders as evidence of his desire to promote mutual understanding. In the period of Davies' stay in Moscow a resolution was published from the Presidium of the Executive Committee of the Comintern with a recommendation to close down that organization.[50] Official American circles reacted favorably to this news. Hull declared at a press conference, held on 24 May, that "the elimination of that organization from international life and the cessation of the type of activity in which that organization has in the past engaged are certain to promote a greater degree of trust among the United Nations and to contribute very greatly to the wholehearted cooperation for the winning of the war and for successful post-war undertakings." The resolution by the Comintern Executive was also assessed positively by a London *Times* editorial (24 May) and by some British and U.S. diplomats. Likewise, Stalin's written answers to questions put by Harold King, a Reuters correspondent.[51] Stalin stressed that the dissolution of the Comintern was a timely measure in part because it should facilitate joint action by freedom-loving peoples against Hitlerism and the organization of international cooperation in the future.[52]

However, some Western politicians assessed the closing down of Comintern as an attempt to strengthen the position of the USSR at the future peace conference. Much skepticism was shown, for instance, by Walter Citrine, president of the British Trade Union Congress. He was of the opinion that Moscow would, as before, offer money to the foreign communists and that Comintern would not in fact cease to exist. His suspicions were not groundless: As is now clear, Comintern's activities continued, though in different ways and forms.[53]

Soviet relations with the Western allies did not improve much in the summer 1943. Soviet diplomacy continued to insist on a Second Front in France. Stalin's personal and confidential message to Roosevelt, dated 11 June 1943 (copied to Churchill), contained the most severe criticism of the decision, adopted in Washington, to postpone the Allied invasion in Western Europe until the spring of 1944.[54]

In their joint reply to Stalin, sent on 19 August 1943 by Roosevelt and Churchill while conferring in Quebec, they again turned to the idea of a summit meeting of the Big Three, this time in Fairbanks, Alaska. As an alternative they offered to hold talks of diplomatic representatives of the Big Three. Stalin approved only the latter idea.[55] Exchanges of messages by the Big Three (19-24 August) made possible agreement on a foreign ministers' conference.

The period of its preparation coincided with Italy's withdrawal from the war and the fascist bloc. Stalin believed that he had been cheated by the British and American side in their talks on capitulation with the post-Mussolini Badoglio government, and he said so, pointing out that he did not wish to play the role of "a third, passive observer." Stalin suggested to Roosevelt and Churchill that a military-political commission be set up comprising representatives of the three states, "to discuss the issue of talks with various governments breaking away from Germany." At the same time, Stalin supported the Western powers' principle of Italy's unconditional surrender. After the Soviet government had been informed of the terms of cease-fire with Italy, it gave powers to General Eisenhower to sign it on its behalf.[56] First "Short" and later "Long" terms of capitulation were signed on behalf of the governments of the three countries on 3 and 29 September

1943. Even prior to that, the three sides agreed to set up a military-political commission to include American, Soviet, and British representatives and those of the French Committee of National Liberation. At the Moscow conference this body was named the Advisory Council for Italy.

Soviet diplomats exerted great pressure on their Western counterparts at the talks on Italy's withdrawal from the fascist Axis, and Britain and America agreed to hold consultations with the USSR on peace terms with Italy. But despite such concessions, the western powers, nevertheless, preserved their control of Italian affairs.[57]

On the eve of the Moscow meeting of Soviet, American, and British foreign ministers in October 1943, the three sides manifested a desire for agreed international actions. Apart from signing the terms of Italy's surrender, such actions included the Declaration of heads of the three governments (dated 13 October 1943) on recognition of Italy as a co-belligerent, the agreement on recognition of the French Committee of National Liberation (irrespective of divergent wording of that recognition) that was formalized by correspondence 25-26 August 1943, and the approval of the Third Protocol on Supplies.[58]

At the session in Moscow on 19 October, the Soviet government suggested that discussion of measures aimed at the earliest termination of the war against Nazi Germany and its allies in Europe should be placed at the top of the agenda. Centrally, this meant the Second Front. That issue was finally agreed only later, in Tehran.

The problem next in importance was the postwar peace settlement and security. In Moscow on 30 October 1943 Molotov, Hull, Eden, and the ambassador of the People's Republic of China in the USSR, Fu Bingchang, signed the Four-Power Declaration on General Security, which established the principle of an unconditional surrender of the Axis powers and proclaimed (Point 4) "the need of the earliest establishment of a general international body for promoting peace and security" based on the sovereign equality of all peace-loving states, big and small.[59] Publication of this document (2 November 1943) and formation, on the Soviet initiative, of a trilateral commission for joint preliminary discussion of the associated problems brought closer the date of foundation of the Organization of the United Nations.

The first Soviet-American-British meeting of foreign ministers adopted a number of other documents: the Declaration on Italy, the Declaration on Austria, and the Declaration on the Nazis' responsibility for their atrocities. A European Advisory Commission was set up in London with the three powers represented on it. Its task was to discuss European problems associated with the termination of hostilities and work out joint recommendations.

The adoption in Moscow of decisions that were to a considerable degree agreed made it possible to smooth out differences in relations between the USSR and the Western powers. A broad propaganda campaign was launched in the USSR in connection with the tenth anniversary of the establishment of Soviet-U.S. diplomatic relations. On 17 November 1943 the new American ambassador Averell Harriman expressed satisfaction to Deputy Soviet Foreign Minister Dekanozov with the publication of friendly editorials devoted to the occasion.[60]

Thus, a more favorable climate was generated for the meeting—the very first—of the Big Three. It was held in Tehran between 28 November and 1 December 1943. The most important result of the talks was the decision taken on the last day of the conference fixing the precise date of operation OVERLORD (see above, part one). It reflected both the enhanced Soviet authority in the anti-Hitler coalition and also the dwindling military-economic influence of the United Kingdom in the U.S.-British alliance.[61]

At that time Western diplomacy attached great importance to involving the USSR in the hostilities against Japan. According to official records, since late 1943 the United States had pinned its hopes of defeating Japanese ground forces in the Asian theater of hostilities largely on the Soviet Union rather than on China or the United Kingdom. The United States estimated the future Soviet contribution as probably the greatest of these three.[62]

The USSR, whose attention at this time was entirely concentrated on the war against Germany, was simply unable to conduct offensive operations both in the West and the East. Even prior to that, at a dinner arranged in the Kremlin on 30 October 1943 as part of the Moscow conference, Stalin instructed Valentin Berezhkov to translate the following confidential statement for Cordell Hull: "The Soviet government has discussed the issue of the situation in the Far East and adopted a decision to attack Japan immediately after the end of hostilities in Europe, after the Allies have defeated Nazi Germany. Let Mr. Hull tell President Roosevelt about it as our official position. However, for the present, we'd like to keep it a secret." At the first sitting of the Tehran conference on 28 November, Stalin declared that the Soviet Union's entry into the war against Japan was possible after Germany's capitulation.[63] No matter that this promise was not included in the official decisions of the conference, it affected, with other factors, the decision adopted by the American leadership on the fixed date of launching operation OVERLORD.

No specific decisions were adopted at Teheran on the postwar peace settlement. The exchange of opinion there revealed both specific aspects of each leader's stand and their overriding desire to make the future peace settlement suit their own tastes and interests. Roosevelt's main political goal at the Tehran conference was to ensure Stalin's consent to the setting up of an international security organization.[64] In that situation Stalin largely preferred to let his interlocutors expound their plans. Having approved Roosevelt's structure of the United Nations (the Assembly, the Executive Committee of ten or eleven countries, and the "Four-Policemen" Committee) he pointed out that, apart from those bodies, it would be necessary to occupy the essential strategic points in Europe and the Far East in order to prevent aggression in future. Roosevelt replied that he agreed with Marshal Stalin "one hundred percent." The Three Power Declaration, signed on 1 December 1943 by Roosevelt, Stalin, and Churchill, reaffirmed only in general terms their determination "to work jointly both in wartime and in peacetime."[65]

Discussion of the future destinies of Germany and Poland and the issue of postwar borders was also of a preliminary nature. It was decided that the German issue should be discussed later in more detail by the European Advisory Commission. Stalin outlined in general some spheres of interest to the USSR as well as security zones in Eastern Europe and Asia, and those points were further developed in the Soviet government's subsequent plans and at its international negotiations. Soviet demands, as presented at the Tehran conference, were as follows: elimination of the vestiges of militarism in Germany and prevention of renewed aggression in future by different means, including establishment of Allied supervision over the main strategic points; recognition of the incorporation of the Baltic republics in the USSR; and restoration of the 1939 Soviet-Polish border. Moreover, the USSR insisted that the Baltic ports should operate in all seasons and that a corresponding part of East Prussian territory be transferred to it. If Britain accepted the Soviet demand with respect to the Baltic lands, Stalin said, the Soviet Union would accept Churchill's formula for the Polish borders (along the Curzon Line and the Oder River).[66]

Both Western leaders expressed their readiness in Tehran to take into account Soviet desires. For instance, on 30 November, Churchill recognized, in Roosevelt's presence, as self-evident "the fact that Russia should have access to warm seas." While discussing the issue of the Soviet postwar borders with Poland and Germany at the luncheon of the Big Three, held on 1 December, the British premier also supported the need to guarantee the security of the Soviet western borders.[67]

The decisions of the Tehran conference, primarily in the military sphere, contributed to the implementation of the main goal—the enemy's defeat at the earliest date. It also sketched out plans for the postwar era. The Tehran conference was a great success for the coalition against Hitler.

Energetic prosecution of Soviet diplomacy at the Moscow and Tehran conferences, publication of the agreed decisions, and, last but not least, the constant powerful westward offensive by the Soviet armed forces (by May 1944 the Red Army had advanced to the Soviet state frontier) further consolidated the Soviet Union's positions on the world scene. In the period prior to and immediately after operation OVERLORD, the prevailing trend in relations between the USSR and the Western allies was for broader military and political cooperation (see chapter 4).

Leading American politicians, who were the main advocates of an international body responsible for world security, had a stake in smoothing over contradictions with the USSR, namely on the issue of Poland. Roosevelt urged Stalin to avoid, for the sake of international cooperation, "any action that might prove an obstacle on the way to the Allies' main goal." When Harriman stopped over in London on his way back to Moscow, he remarked in a conversation with the Soviet ambassador Feodor Gousev on 26 May 1944 that Soviet-American relations were "developing under the sign of expanding and consolidating cooperation." There were some difficulties in those relations, Harriman admitted, but he believed they could be overcome.[68]

There are indications that while he was taking a stiff line on Polish issues (postwar borders, the government in exile, and the Warsaw uprising), Stalin at the same time intended to support U.S. efforts to establish an international body responsible for security. On 9 July 1944 the Soviet government announced its readiness to take part in the three-power talks on setting up an international organization. The Roosevelt administration received this move positively and reminded the Soviet side that it regarded the procedure of peaceful settlement of disputes as the main purpose of the future organization. It was decided that in August preliminary trilateral unofficial talks would be held in Washington.[69] In the course of preparations for the talks each of the three Great Powers drafted its preliminary proposals. In part one of its memorandum on the World Security Organization, dated 12 August 1944, the Soviet government mentioned, among the main goals of the organization, the following: "maintenance of world peace and security and the adoption, with that aim in view, of collective measures to prevent aggression and to organize suppression of real aggression." This wording went further than the version offered by the

British government, which did not provide for collective measures in order to suppress aggression. Taking into account the preliminary American proposals (handed over on 18 July), the Soviet side also stipulated among the organization's goals "settlement and elimination by peaceful means of international conflicts which may lead to the violation of peace."[70]

Soviet proposals on the rights and functions of the General Assembly were also closer to the American position. As distinct from the British proposals on the issue of voting in the Council (rejecting the principle of unanimity), the Soviet government stated its position as follows: "Decisions referring to prevention or suppression of aggression are to be adopted by a majority of votes given the agreement by all permanent representatives on the Council."[71]

The order of voting in the Security Council (like that of the founding membership of the future organization) provoked the main disputes at the conference at Dumbarton Oaks in Washington (21 August to 28 September 1944). The representatives of the three powers confirmed the principle of Great Power unanimity in the Security Council. But they disagreed upon the use of the veto in cases where the permanent members of the Council were interested parties. The Soviet delegation did not concur in the position of the British and American delegations who protested against voting by Great Powers immediately involved in a conflict. The matter was resolved when Roosevelt proposed to Stalin on 5 December 1944 a formula whereby unanimity among permanent members would be required on procedural issues; parties to a dispute would not vote on Security Council decisions concerning all other issues.[72]

Despite some exceptions, the Soviet Union, the United States and the United Kingdom reached agreement on a great number of points at Dumbarton Oaks. On 9-10 October 1944 communiqués were published in Moscow, Washington, and London, that summed up the results of the conference, together with the text of the adopted document ("Proposals on the Establishment of the World Security Organization").[73]

In general, 1944 saw the consolidation of the anti-Hitler coalition. This was due first of all to coordinated military campaigns of the coalition's members in the East and in the West of Europe. Operation OVERLORD and its support by the powerful offensive of the Red Army strengthened the political authority of Big Three. The United Nations were reinforced after Germany's allies—Finland, Romania, Bulgaria—were eliminated from the war and joined the coalition against Hitler.

Shortly before the Yalta meeting of the Big Three, the Soviet government reaffirmed both its desire to cooperate with the Western powers and the importance of the decisions adopted at Dumbarton Oaks. It also stated that "alliance of the USSR, the United Kingdom and the USA is based on vitally important factors." This declaration was received with satisfaction by the Roosevelt administration.[74] The president, moderate American politicians, and the U.S. military all believed that further cooperation with the USSR was necessary in order to bring to a successful end the hostilities against Germany and Japan and to ensure a peaceful postwar settlement.[75]

In late 1944 tension in Soviet-British relations eased. True, talks held between Churchill, Eden and the Soviet leaders in Moscow on 9-18 October 1944, did not produce any solutions to the issues of the Soviet-Polish border or the composition of the Polish government. The issue of Germany's future had also not been settled. However, the talks, according to Stalin, were held "in a friendly atmosphere and in a spirit of complete unanimity." Churchill's reference to the atmosphere of goodwill at the Moscow talks was not an overstatement either, according to Robin Edmonds.[76] One could almost speak of an identity of views then, especially in view of the confidential exchange of opinion on the division of the spheres of responsibility in the Balkans (at the first meeting in the Kremlin on 9 October, Churchill presented his "percentage" proposal). It was clear that the two leaders were prepared to divide spheres of influence in Eastern Europe. They spoke as if matters in that region were theirs and only theirs to decide.[77]

The Crimean (Yalta) summit conference of the USSR, the United States, and the United Kingdom, held on 4-11 February 1945, marks the apogee of trilateral cooperation between the leading countries of the coalition against Hitler. By now the Red Army was only 60 kilometers from Berlin. In Yalta the heads of government and their advisers coordinated Allied military plans for the final defeat of Germany and fixed the precise dates and scale of powerful blows to be dealt at the enemy in Europe. On 11 February Stalin and Roosevelt agreed, with the subsequent approval of Churchill, that, in some two or three months after Germany's capitulation and the end of hostilities in Europe, the Soviet Union would join forces with the Allies in the war against Japan. On Stalin's insistence, Soviet terms for the USSR's participation in the war against Japan were embodied in the document. Among these were transfer of the Kuril Islands to the Soviet Union, and restoration of the rights possessed by Russia and violated in the Russo-Japanese war of 1904-5, including return of the southern part of Sakhalin Island and of all adjacent islands.[78]

Apart from that, political and economic aspects of European postwar settlement were discussed at Yalta. Central was a joint policy on

Germany's democratization, demilitarization, and denazification. The Allied powers reached agreement on the terms, worked out by their representatives on the European Advisory Commission, for Germany's unconditional surrender, principles for occupation zones, the administration of Greater Berlin, and the mechanism of supervision. In their statement, published on 13 February 1945, Churchill, Roosevelt, and Stalin declared that their firm goal was "elimination of German militarism and Nazism and provision of guarantees that Germany should never again be in a position to violate world peace." Nevertheless, they added, "It is not our purpose to destroy the people of Germany. . . ."[79]

The issue of Germany's division was also discussed at the conference. Nothing was decided except the setting up of a commission to study procedure for this division, with the three powers to be represented on it. The members of that commission—Eden (the Chairman), Gousev, and Winant—stated at their first meeting in London on 7 March 1945 only that the problem of Germany's dismemberment was being studied. Soon a draft directive for the commission, written by Gousev, was sent to Moscow for approval. Nevertheless, Gousev had not received any clear instructions on the problem of dividing Germany and his draft was viewed as unsatisfactory by Molotov. On 24 March the latter told Gousev to offer the commission the following clarification: "The Soviet Government views the decision of the Crimea conference on Germany's division not as an obligatory plan for dismemberment of Germany, but as a possible option to put pressure on Germany, with the aim of security against it, should other means prove insufficient." On 26 March Gousev gave Eden a letter containing that clarification.[80]

At the second meeting of the commission on 11 April Eden indicated that all its members were in agreement with a British draft of the directive and with the Soviet interpretation of the Yalta decision. No further meetings were held. Stalin declared in his address to the Soviet people on 9 May 1945 that the Soviet Union "is not going either to dismember or destroy Germany."[81]

What lay behind the Soviet leaders' decision, which in fact struck the issue of Germany's division off the diplomatic agenda? It is difficult to give a full answer without proper access to Stalin's archives (still closed). We can guess, however, that one motive for changing the Soviet position (at Yalta Stalin had approved the decision on that issue "in principle") was disinclination to take the initiative by proposing any Soviet plans for the division. In his telegram to Gousev on 24 March Molotov informed him "for orientation" that the British and Americans, who were the first to put up the question of division, now wanted to lay the whole responsibility upon the USSR.[82]

The irritable tone of this telegram appears to square with the strong Soviet démarche on coincident conversations between American and British representatives and SS General Wolff in Bern, as exemplified by Molotov's letters to Harriman of 16 and 22 March and Stalin's message to Roosevelt on 29 March.[83]

Reverting to Yalta: talks there about the establishment of the United Nations Organization were very fruitful. First, they dealt with the procedure for voting in the Security Council. The Soviet delegation endorsed the "Proposals" worked out at Dumbarton Oaks, together with the amendments in Roosevelt's formula of December 1944. Thus, one cardinal issue, that of the unanimity of the council's permanent members, was settled. Second, on the initiative of the Soviet side, they discussed the problem of participation by two or three Soviet Union republics (at this stage) in the World Security Organization. The British and U.S. delegates undertook to support at the inaugural conference of the United Nations Organization the proposal to admit the Ukrainian SSR and the Byelorussian SSR among the founding members of the organization. An agreement also was reached on the date and venue of the inaugural conference (25 April 1945 in San Francisco) and on its participants.[84]

The longest discussion at Yalta was devoted to Polish issues. The Soviet leadership took great pains to push through its version of the Soviet-Polish border. So, according to the decision adopted by the conference, Poland's eastern border was "to run along the Curzon Line, with deviations from five to eight kilometers in Poland's favor from it in some regions." The decision on Poland's eastern borders was among the most important of those adopted at the Crimean conference in the framework of postwar settlement.[85] As to Poland's western border, the final decision was postponed until the peace conference.

After heated debate on the issue of the Polish government, it was decided that the provisional Polish government (created in Lublin by Polish communists from Moscow and recognized in January 1945 by the USSR, but not by America and Britain) should be "reorganized on a broader democratic basis, with inclusion in it of democratic leaders from Poland and Polish emigrés." The new government would then be called the Polish Provisional Government of National Unity.[86] However the different interpretation of the Yalta agreement by the Soviet Union and by the Western allies soon led to new contradictions. They also interpreted differently the Declaration on Liberated Europe, which was adopted at Yalta and provided for the establishment of a rule-of-law international order and democratic institutions, set up in accordance with each people's free choice. The Soviet government transgressed the limits of the agreements reached in Yalta: Stalin set himself the task of introducing the Soviet model of socialism in Eastern European countries and including them in its orbit. The U.S. and British leaders regarded as inevitable the provision of spheres of influence in Eastern and Central Europe for the Soviet Union in the postwar period, but they did not wish to permit the creation of communist regimes in the countries of that region.

Churchill was ready to prevent establishment of a "Russian version" of democracy in Poland. Roosevelt tried until his last days to minimize the differences with Moscow, but he too, in a message which Stalin received on 1 April, stated that any decision meaning a somewhat disguised prolongation of the now-existing Warsaw regime would be intolerable to the United States. The Polish issue became a test case for future relations of the three powers. Poland is now "a symbol of our ability to solve problems with the Soviet Union," Hopkins told Stalin on 27 May.[87]

Both the Soviets, as well as the British and the Americans (especially after the death of Roosevelt), were responsible for sharpening the controversies. It was hardly fortunate, for instance, that Stalin initially decided not to send Molotov to the conference at San Francisco—the Soviet delegation was to have been led by a figure of lesser stature. This aroused doubts in the West as to the sincerity of Soviet support for an international organization. But Ambassador Clark Kerr observed in a talk with Vyshinsky on 29 March that the Soviet government was making "a great error." The deputy people's commissar reacted strongly: "It would be better not to speak about errors, but to try not to make errors yourself." Harriman informed Maisky on 5 April about negative reaction of the Americans to the composition of the Soviet delegation and their concern over the state of the Polish issue and the events in Romania.[88] Stalin soon changed his mind and Molotov went to San Francisco. Nevertheless, according to an eye witness, his actions were not so friendly and the conference was at first "in a fever" because the Soviet delegates refused to elect Stettinius as its chairman.[89]

Disagreements over Poland and over other issues led to a crisis in the Soviet-American relations. The rift was widened by the American side after Acting Secretary of State Joseph Grew sent a note to the Soviet embassy on 12 May, which meant in practice that Lend-Lease supplies to the Soviet Union would be cut off on termination of the war in Europe (exception was made only for supplies needed for the Far Eastern operations). The Soviet chargé in Washington, Nikolai Novikov, considered the American decision repressive. He told Moscow that, according to General John York (acting chairman of the Soviet Supply Committee), the sudden cancellation of supplies was directly connected with the latest Truman-Stalin correspondence on the Polish issue.[90]

The Soviet official response stated that the stoppage of supplies was quite unexpected. The Americans soon resumed the shipments, but the whole story needlessly provoked the Soviet leaders. Stalin showed his displeasure and so did Mikoyan.[91] The cancellation of Lend-Lease, and attempts to use it for political leverage upon the USSR, were errors on the American side.[92]

The new Truman administration sent Hopkins to Moscow for discussion of the complex diplomatic agenda, above all the Polish issue. Stalin had six meetings with Hopkins between 26 May and 6 June 1945. It was possible to ease the tension aroused by the Lend-Lease affair. Hopkins secured Stalin's agreement to the inclusion of seven "non-Lublin" Poles in the Polish government (though three of them refused). German and Far Eastern problems were discussed, too. The approximate date and place of the Stalin-Truman-Churchill meeting were settled (mid-July 1945, in the environs of Berlin). Truman and Harriman were pleased with the Moscow talks. Clark Kerr even told Maisky on 13 June that he wished Hopkins were an Englishman.[93]

Not all the controversies could, of course, be solved through diplomatic channels. The victorious end of the war with Nazi Germany strengthened the Soviet regime and Stalin's bid for supremacy in the Eastern Europe. At the same time hard-liners became more active in the Western democracies. Nevertheless, the tendency to curtail the Allied ties did not yet prevail in the summer of 1945. The Soviet Union had suffered too much to risk another war, and Stalin hoped to secure his immediate objectives within a framework of collaboration with America and Britain.[94] The three powers came to an agreement on such important documents signed in Berlin as the act of military surrender of Germany (8 May 1945), and the declaration on the defeat of Germany and the adoption by the Allies of supreme power in Germany (5 June 1945).[95]

Soviet diplomacy played on the whole a constructive role in the formation of the World Security Organization. At the conference in San Francisco, which approved the Charter of UNO on 26 June 1945, the Soviet representatives extolled the great contribution of the coalition to the defeat of Nazi Germany.[96] Before departing for the Potsdam conference Stalin sent a message to Truman acknowledging the positive role of Lend-Lease.[97]

The Truman administration tried by demonstration of force to strengthen its position in the talks with Stalin, but it did not want to rupture the alliance with the USSR. Similarly, the British Foreign Office did not exclude the policy of collaboration with the Soviet Union, though it viewed Moscow as a difficult partner. So the conference of the three powers did not open in an atmosphere of direct confrontation.[98]

At Potsdam (17 July-2 August 1945) the German problem dominated the discussions. The Allies agreed relatively easily on political principles governing the relations with Germany in the initial control period. The USSR, the United States, and the United Kingdom (France joined soon) also pledged to exterminate German militarism and Nazism, to prevent forever their rebirth, and to take all necessary measures to ensure "that Germany never more poses a threat to her neighbors or to the maintenance of world peace."[99]

The USSR and the Western allies had coordinated the tasks of the Control Council—the supreme body of the Four Powers for Germany comprising their Commanders-in-Chief. The Soviet representative in the Control Council was Marshal G. K. Zhukov. In the period of its work (30 July 1945-March 1948) the Control Council had 85 meetings. Half the problems that the Allies had to solve were discussed before July 1946, during which time laws on curtailment and liquidation of Nazi organization were signed, as well as on punishment of the war criminals, and on the demobilization and disbandment of German armed forces.[100]

Much time at Potsdam was spent on the problem of reparations. The USSR refused to fix a definite sum for Germany's payments, as it had been insisting at Yalta. According to the agreement reached, the Soviet reparation claims should be met by withdrawals from the Soviet zone of occupation, from the corresponding German foreign investment, and also by receiving 25 percent of industrial equipment from the Western zones. The USSR promised to satisfy the reparations claims of Poland from its own quota.[101]

Only after it had assured agreement on German reparations, did the American delegation consent to the proposal of the USSR on the western border of Poland. In accordance with the Potsdam decision, that border was established along the line of the rivers Oder and Western Neisse. A part of Eastern Prussia was included in Poland, and also the city of Danzig (Gdansk). The American and British delegations confirmed their Tehran agreement on transferring to the USSR the city Königsberg (Kaliningrad, from 1946) with the adjacent region.[102]

Far Eastern issues were not officially included on the agenda of Potsdam negotiations. However, when he had first met Truman on 17

July, before the opening session of the conference, Stalin on his own initiative began to talk about the war against Japan. After the president noted that the United States was awaiting Soviet entry, Stalin assured him that the USSR would be ready to act by the middle of August and that it would keep its word.[103] Some American leaders, especially after the successful test of the atomic bomb at Alamogordo, were inclined toward ending the war in the Far East without the help of the Soviet ally. Truman himself did not now see an urgent need for the USSR to enter the war. But at this stage, America could not avert Soviet military participation.[104] Nor were Western politicians in a position to exclude the USSR from the decisions connected with political settlement in that region.

On 5 April 1945 the Soviet government denounced the Soviet-Japanese Neutrality Treaty of 1941. In his talk with Byrnes on 27 July Molotov showed his displeasure with the fact that the Potsdam Declaration on Japan by America, Britain, and China had been published (the day before) without the knowledge of the USSR. On 28 July Stalin himself reproached both heads of the governments, complaining that "we are not informed properly when any document is prepared concerning Japan."[105] Taking into account, however that the Potsdam Declaration aimed at the speediest attainment of peace, the Soviet government officially approved this document on 8 August and announced that the USSR would be in a state of war with Japan beginning 9 August 1945. With the Act of Capitulation of Japan, signed on 2 September 1945 by representatives of the United States, the USSR, the United Kingdom, and other states, the Second World War came to an end.

Soviet influence on international affairs was substantial at the very beginning of the postwar period. This was due principally to tremendous military victories of the USSR. The international activity of the Soviet government also contributed much to the rise of Soviet authority (all the shadowy sides of foreign policy-making were unknown to the public). Propaganda about antifascism, campaigns for the opening of the Second Front, and other diplomatic actions aimed at shortening the war and drawing the Soviet Union into the process of peace settlement—all these elicited support from public opinion in different countries and corresponded to the national aspirations and patriotic feelings of most of the Soviet populace.

Soviet foreign policy was under the direct guidance of a single figure—Stalin. There is no doubt that he succeeded politically in exploiting the fact of participation of the USSR in the war and in the coalition as well as meetings with Western leaders in the interests of glorifying his personality.

It is difficult to ignore, at the same time, the harm caused by the "bloc," imperial mentality of the Stalinist leadership. This contributed to the division of the world after 1945 and the emergence of opposite military groupings. Stalin and his aides not only trampled underfoot the rights of their own peoples, but tried to impose their diktat on neighboring countries. As early as 1941 they had insisted on extending the Soviet Union's borders, on grounds born of history and security, and these territorial demands grew as the war progressed. Whatever was said publicly about the UN and the Atlantic Charter, for Stalin and his colleagues, what ultimately mattered was territorial security and the maximum possible influence. They did not see the necessity to find new principles of international behavior with the beginning of a new, nuclear era. Like the political leaderships of the West, they took the path toward aggravation of the international situation and toward the Cold War.

However, a critical assessment of Stalin's foreign policy should not lead to an underestimation of the positive aspects of the program which was worked out in the war years with the active help of the USSR. The members of the Grand Alliance were inspired by the slogans of antifascist struggle that were embodied in the decisions of the Moscow, Tehran, Yalta, San Francisco, and Potsdam conferences. The principles of interstate relations elaborated at those international conferences were consonant with the universal human values of freedom, justice, and a stable peace.

NOTES

1. Foreign Policy Archive of the Russian Federation (FPA RF). Fund 69, schedule 26, box 78, file 49, p. 7-8 (in Russian).

2. *Soviet-British Relations in the Years of the Great Patriotic War 1941-1945: Documents and Materials* (2 vols.; Moscow, 1983), I, 45-47, 513 (in Russian)—hereafter Soviet-British Relations.

3. FPA RF. Fund 6, schedule 3, box 3, file 29, p. 60.

4. Winston S. Churchill, *The Second World War* (6 vols.; London, 1948-1954), 3, 332-33.

5. *FRUS, 1941,* 1, 767-68; *New York Times,* 25 June 1941.

6. Gabriel Gorodetsky, *Stafford Cripps' Mission to Moscow, 1940-1942* (Cambridge, 1984), 177; Sheila Lawlor, "Britain and the Russian Entry into the War," in Richard Langhorne, ed., *Diplomacy and Intelligence during the Second World War.* (London, 1985), 182-83; Stephen M. Miner, *Between Churchill and Stalin: The Soviet Union, Great Britain and the Origins of the Grand Alliance* (Chapel Hill, 1986), 169.

7. *Soviet-British Relations,* 1, 46-48 (in Russian).

8. *Ibid.,* 48-52.

9. *Ibid.,* 62-63, 69-70.

10. *Foreign Policy of the Soviet Union in the Period of Patriotic War: Documents and Materials* (3 vols.; Moscow, 1946-47), 1, 131-32 (in Russian).

11. *Soviet-American Relations in the Years of the Great Patriotic War 1941-1945: Documents and Materials* (2 vols.; Moscow, 1984), 1, 46, 58-59, 71, 81 (in Russian)—hereafter *Soviet-American Relations.*

12. Robert Sherwood, *Roosevelt and Hopkins. An Intimate History* (2 vols.; Moscow, 1958), 1, 547, (in Russian); Warren F. Kimball, *The Juggler: Franklin Roosevelt as Wartime Statesman* (Princeton, 1991), 21-41.

13. FPA RF. Fund 69, schedule 25, box 70, file 4, p. 72.

14. FPA RF. Fund 6, schedule 3, box 21, file 281, p. 57-58.

15. *Soviet -British Relations,* 1, 104-9.

16. *Ibid.,* 109.

17. "From the Diary and Letters of the Ambassador of the United Kingdom in the USSR, S. Cripps in 1941-1942," *Modern and Contemporary History* 3 (1991), 134 (in Russian).

18. *Soviet-British Relations,* 1, 128-30.

19. *Ibid.*, 138.

20. *Correspondence of the Chairman of the USSR Council of Ministers with USA Presidents and Prime Ministers of the United Kingdom in the Years of the Great Patriotic War, 1941-1945* (2 vols.; Moscow, 1989), 1, 42 (in Russian)—hereafter *Correspondence.*

21. Martin Gilbert, *Road to Victory: Winston S. Churchill, 1941-1945* (London, 1986), 112; Miner, *Between Churchill and Stalin,* 173-74.

22. FPA RF. Fund 48 "Z," schedule 11j, box 64, file 1, pp. 20-21.

23. *Correspondence,* 1, 43-44.

24. *Soviet-British Relations,* 1, 188-98.

25. FPA RF. Fund 6, schedule 3, box 8, file 82, p. 77.

26. *FRUS,* 1942, 1, 1.

27. *FRUS: The Conferences at Washington, 1941-1942, and Casablanca, 1943* (Washington, 1968), 368; *FRUS, 1942,* 1, 22.

28. Herbert G. Nicholas, ed., *Washington Despatches, 1941-1945: Weekly Political Reports from the British Embassy* (Washington, 1981), 5.

29. *FRUS, 1942,* 1, 22.

30. *FRUS: Washington and Casablanca, 377*; *FRUS, 1942,* 1, 38.

31. *Soviet-American Relations,* 1, 160, 164.

32. *Soviet-British Relations,* 1, 221-22, 227.

33. *Ibid.*, 222; Miner, *Between Churchill and Stalin,* 238-39.

34. FPA RF. Fund 48 "Z," schedule 11j, box 64, file 1, p. 38.

35. *Soviet-British Relations,* 1, 232; Graham Ross, ed., *The Foreign Office and the Kremlin. British Documents on Anglo-Soviet Relations, 1941-45* (Cambridge, 1984), 105-6.

36. On Stalin, see the discussion in "The Origins of the Cold War," *International Affairs* (Moscow) 10 (1990), 132 (in Russian); Llewellyn Woodward, *British Foreign Policy in the Second World War* (5 vols.; London, 1970-6), 2: 251; I. M. Maisky, *Recollections of a Soviet Ambassador. The War, 1939-1943* (Moscow, 1965), 247 (in Russian); *Soviet-British Relations,* 1: 519, 532.

37. *Soviet-American Relations,* 1, 158, 160; *Soviet-British Relations,* I, 519.

38. Michael Balfour, *The Adversaries: America, Russia and the Open World 1941-62* (London, 1981), 8.

39. *The Foreign Policy of the Soviet Union in the Period of Patriotic War,* 1, 270-73.

40. FPA RF. Fund 6, schedule 3, box 8, file 88, p. 8.

41. FPA RF. Fund 69, schedule 26, box 78, file 49, p. 12.

42. *Soviet-American Relations,* 1, 203.

43. *Ibid.,* 188, 198-202.

44. *Soviet-British Relations.* 1, 279.

45. *Churchill & Roosevelt: The Complete Correspondence,* ed. with commentary by Warren F. Kimball (3 vols.; Princeton, N.J., 1984), 1, 566.

46. Ross, ed., *The Foreign Office and the Kremlin,* 111-12.

47. *Soviet-American Relations,* 1, 315-317. On Davies's Mission to the USSR (19-29 May, 1943) see V. L. Malkov, *Franklin Roosevelt. Problems of Domestic Policy and Diplomacy* (Moscow, 1988), 251-56 (in Russian); Elizabeth K. MacLean. "Joseph Davies and Soviet-American Relations, 1941-43," *Diplomatic History* 4 (1980), 73-93

48. FPA RF. Fund 129, schedule 27, box 148, file 3, p. 108.

49. *Soviet-American Relations,* 1, 323.

50. *Pravda,* 22 May 1943.

51. *FRUS, 1943,* 3, 532-34, 536-37; *Soviet-American Relations,* 1,323, 326.

52. *Foreign Policy of the Soviet Union in the Period of Patriotic War,* 1, 104-5.

53. Russian Center for the Conservation and Study of Documents on Contemporary History (RCCSDCH). Fund 495, schedule 73, file 173, p. 61, 64-65; N. S. Lebedeva, "The Shadow of the Comintern," in A. N. Bazhenov and O. A. Rzheshevsky, *Yalta, 1945: Problems of War and Peace* (Moscow, 1992), 73 (both in Russian).

54. *Soviet-American Relations,* 1, 330-31; *Soviet-British Relations,* 1, 393-94.

55. *Correspondence,* 1, 174-76.

56. *Ibid.,* 175-76; *Soviet-British Relations,* 1, 441-42, 448-49.

57. Robin Edmonds, *The Big Three: Churchill, Roosevelt and Stalin in Peace and War* (London, 1991), 338.

58. *Soviet-British Relations,* 1, 425-26, 440; *Soviet-American Relations,* 1, 364-65.

59. *The Moscow Meeting of the Ministers of Foreign Affairs of the USSR, the United States and the United Kingdom (19-30 October 1943),* (Moscow, 1978), 346-48 (in Russian).

60. FPA RF. Fund 129, schedule 27, box 148, file 3, p. 51.

61. Warren F. Kimball, ed., *Churchill & Roosevelt,* 1, 609; Keith Sainsbury, *The Turning Point: Roosevelt, Stalin, Churchill and Chiang Kai-Shek, 1943* (Oxford, 1986), 1; L. V.

Pozdeeva, "American-British Relations (The Fall of 1943-the beginning of 1944," *Annual Studies of America, 1990* (Moscow, 1991), 61-63.

62. R. W. Coakley and R. M. Leighton, *Global Logistics and Strategy, 1943-1945* (Washington, 1968), 688.

63. V. M. Berezhkov, *The Birth of a Coalition* (Moscow, 1975), 125-27 (in Russian); *The Teheran Conference of the Leaders of the Three Allied Powers—the USSR, the USA and the United Kingdom. 28 November-1 December, 1943* (Moscow, 1978), 95 (in Russian).

64. W. Averell Harriman and Elie Abel, *Special Envoy to Churchill and Stalin, 1941-1946* (New York, 1975), 279.

65. *The Teheran Conference,* 116-18, 169, 175.

66. *Ibid.,* 144, 165, 167-69.

67. *Ibid.,* 142, 164.

68. *Correspondence,* 1, 124; FPA RF. Fund 169, schedule 28, box 86, file 10, p. 161.

69. *Soviet-American Relations,* 2, 156-57, 167-69.

70. *The Conference of the Representatives of the USSR, the USA and the United Kingdom at Dumbarton Oaks, 21 August-28 September 1944* (Moscow, 1978), 102-3 (in Russian); FPA RF. Fund 129, schedule 28, box 160, file 47, p. 98.

71. FPA RF. Fund 129, schedule 28, box 160, file 47, pp. 100-101; *The Conference . . . at Dumbarton Oaks,* 105.

72. *The Conference . . . at Dumbarton Oaks,* 128, 178-79, 181; V. G. Trukhanovsky, *The Foreign Policy of England in the Period of the Second World War (1939-1945)* (Moscow, 1965), 557 (in Russian); *Correspondence,* 2, 181-83.

73. *The Conference . . . at Dumbarton Oaks,* 228-41.

74. *Soviet-American Relations,* 2, 252, 256.

75. *The Yalta Conference 1945: Lessons of History* (Moscow, 1985), 102-3 (in Russian).

76. *Soviet-British Relations,* 2, 229; Edmonds, *Big Three,* 389.

77. Warren F. Kimball, "Naked Reverse Right: Roosevelt, Churchill and Stalin: Eastern Europe from TOLSTOY to Yalta—and a Little Beyond," *Diplomatic History* 9 (Winter 1985), 1-6; Kimball, ed., *Churchill & Roosevelt,* 3, 349.

78. *The Crimean Conference of the Leaders of the Three Allied Powers—The USSR, the USA and the United Kingdom, 4-11 February 1945* (Moscow, 1979), 273 (in Russian); *FRUS: The Conferences at Malta and Yalta,* 970-71.

79. *Crimean Conference,* 266.

80. FPA RF. Fund 48 "Z," schedule 11j, box 64, file 2, pp. 52-54, 56-57.

81. *Ibid.*, 58-59; *Foreign Policy of the Soviet Union in the Period of Patriotic War*, 3, 45.

82. FPA RF. Fund 48 "Z," schedule 11j, box 64, file 2, 56-57.

83. *Correspondence*, 2, 212-14, 314-15.

84. *Crimean Conference*, 120-21, 267, 274.

85. *Ibid.*, 270; A. A. Roshchin, *Postwar Settlement in Europe* (Moscow, 1984) (in Russian).

86. *Crimean Conference*, 269.

87. *Correspondence*, 2, 215; Gilbert, *Churchill, 1941-5*, 1198; Sherwood, *Roosevelt and Hopkins*, 2: 628 (in Russian).

88. FPA RF. Fund 69, schedule 29, box 94, file 6, p. 23; Fund 129, schedule 29, box 166, file 4, p. 15.

89. A. A. Roshchin, "The United Nations Organization and the Cold War," *Modern and Contemporary History* 5 (1991), 76 (in Russian).

90. *Soviet-American Relations*, 2, 388-89.

91. *Ibid.*, 392; Sherwood, *Roosevelt and Hopkins*, 2, 622-26 (in Russian); *FRUS, 1945*, 5, 1021.

92. George C. Herring, *Aid to Russia 1941-1946: Strategy, Diplomacy, the Origins of the Cold War* (New York, 1973), 206-11.

93. Robin Edmonds, *Setting the Mould: The United States and Britain 1945-1950* (Oxford, 1986), 47; *FRUS: The Conference of Berlin (The Potsdam Conference) 1945* (2 vols.; Washington, 1960), I, 61; FPA RF. Fund 129, schedule 29, box 116, file 4, p. 41.

94. David Reynolds, "The Big Three and the Division of Europe, 1945-48: An Overview," *Diplomacy and Statecraft* 2 (1990), 115.

95. N. S. Lebedeva, *The Unconditional Surrender of the Aggressors* (Moscow, 1989), 257-87 (in Russian).

96. *The Conference of the United Nations in San Francisco, 25 April-26 June 1945* (Moscow, 1980), 123-24 (in Russian); V. L. Israeljan, *Diplomacy in the Years of War (1941-1945)* (Moscow, 1985), 325-66 (in Russian).

97. *Soviet-American Relations*, 2, 437.

98. Graham Ross, *The Great Powers and the Decline of the European State System, 1914-1945* (London, 1983), 145.

99. *The Berlin (the Potsdam) Conference of the Leaders of the Three Allied Powers—the USSR, the USA and the United Kingdom, 17 July-2 August 1945* (Moscow, 1980), 484 (in Russian).

100. FPA RF. Fund 48 "Z," schedule 11j, box 70, file 15, p. 22.

101. *The Berlin (the Potsdam) Conference,* 250, 411-412, 489-90, $2,675.8 million (U.S.) was the total sum of all the withdrawals for the period from 2 August 1945 to 1 January 1948. 239,300 tons of equipment, taken from 40 factories in the Western zones of Germany and valued at 81.7 million German Marks, was sent to the USSR and Poland. The equipment from 17 factories (valued at 10.3 million Marks) out of 40 was given by the USSR to Poland. See FPA RF, Fund 48 "Z," schedule 11j, box 70, file 16, pp. 273-76.

102. *The Berlin (the Potsdam) Conference,* 331-32, 417, 473, 494, 471, 491-92. The inviolability of European borders and the territorial integrity of all the states of Europe were confirmed much later in a series of treaties, including the Moscow Treaty signed by the USSR and the Federal Republic of Germany on 12 August 1970. The postwar political and territorial status quo was acknowledged also in the Helsinki Final Act signed on 1 August 1975 by 33 European states and by the United States and Canada.

103. *Ibid.,* 43.

104. Charles L. Mee, Jr., *Meeting at Potsdam* (New York, 1975), 93.

105. *The Berlin (the Potsdam) Conference,* 218, 222.

THE UNITED STATES: DEMOCRATIC DIPLOMACY

Lloyd C. Gardner and *Warren F. Kimball*

The development of the foreign policy of any nation is complex. Even in dictatorships domestic events and pressures produce foreign policy reactions, and vice versa. That interaction is even more immediate in democracies. United States foreign policy is patched together by a diverse and disparate array of influences, formal and informal. By tradition, precedent, and a few ambiguous court cases, the right of the president to make foreign policy appears clear. But that power is, in reality, circumscribed by practical considerations. Obviously, presidents do not want to jeopardize their electoral future. Yet, upon occasion, they do what they think right and suffer the consequences—Woodrow Wilson's stubborn support for the Treaty of Versailles, and Lyndon Johnson's obstinate commitment to the Vietnam War are but two examples. At the same time, the U.S. Congress has always demanded a role. Using both the power of the purse and legislation, the Congress has influenced foreign policy. Laws like Lend-Lease or the Marshall Plan for European Recovery after World War II required massive amounts of money. The president could propose, but Congress disposed. All the while, other influences ranging from the media to business interests to farmers and everything in between work to shape American foreign policy, and when one or more of these interest groups join forces, the electoral/ public pressure on the president can become irresistible. It is a system that confuses and bewilders other societies. What more structured European nations deride as "no foreign policy" is, in fact, a foreign policy that reflects public, bureaucratic, and interest-group pressures. That makes for shifts of position (contradictions?), public arguments, and a heavy infusion of domestic politics—but that is the price of being a democracy. Presidents try, with varying success, to impose their views on the process. The story of American foreign policy during the era of the Second World War is, to a large degree, the story of Franklin Roosevelt's attempts to shape policy—once he determined what that policy should be.

To summarize the foreign policy of the United States in the World War II era would take volumes. But it can be comprehended, perhaps, by looking at five topics that illustrate the complex and interconnected ways in which that foreign policy developed. The "triumphant nationalism" of the years between the First and Second World Wars gave way to the strategy of "Germany-first," an approach that insured creation of a clean slate in Europe. That led to dreams of a postwar continuation of the Grand Alliance, even if that raised the specter of spheres of influence, a concept that Americans associated with flawed European power politics and war. The extension of the wartime alliance was further complicated and perhaps made impossible by the "colonial problematic" and "atomic portents." Whatever the Cold War was, its nature and intensity was shaped by forces that the Big Three could not solve.

From the end of the Paris Peace Conference that followed the First World War, to the Japanese attack on the United States at Pearl Harbor in December 1941, the major stated objective of Americans, leaders and general public, was to avoid entanglement in another "European War." The bases for the belief that the United States could and should stay out of such a conflict were simple, and simplistic: (1) the Atlantic Ocean, the original geographic determinant of American beliefs, made independence from Europe (so-called isolationism) possible; (2) the high degree of American economic self-sufficiency made go-it-alone policies practical; and, (3) public disillusionment at Europe's rejection of President Woodrow Wilson's crusade at the end of the First World War to make the world "safe for democracy" prompted Americans to leave Europe to its own devices.

That is not to say that the United States was absent from the international scene. American diplomats actively pursued consultative arrangements in the Pacific Ocean region, suggesting that the Atlantic Ocean was as much a psychological as a geographical barrier. Naval disarmament, a favorite theme of liberal reformers as well as a major element in the strategic balance in the Pacific, became the principal thrust of United States foreign policy.[1] Yet even that leadership role in the Pacific was circumscribed by a reluctance, particularly on the part of the public and Congress, to get involved in cooperative efforts with the other major Pacific powers—which were, except for Japan, also the major European powers.

At the same time, the United States played an active, if somewhat contradictory role in the world economy, becoming a major capital exporter in the 1920s, while at the same time continuing to raise its protective tariffs to higher and higher levels. A net debtor to Europe in the era before the First World War, the United States emerged as a huge creditor nation. Yet, at the same time, agricultural interests exerted a political force against lower tariffs, even as the numbers of farmers declined. Moreover, a combination of partisan politics and American anger at what was considered European ingratitude worked to prevent any reasonable settlement of the war debts owed the United States by Britain and France—an issue that became emotional and intractable as time went on. The American political structure—the democracy—based as it was on a combination of geography and interests, made it difficult, both in the prosperous times of the 1920s and in the Great Depression years that followed, for the nation to adopt a clear-cut foreign economic policy.

The challenges to the status quo posed by an expansionist Japan, fascist Italy, and Hitler's Germany, coming in the 1930s after the onset of the Great Depression, only reinforced the American inclination to seek national rather than cooperative solutions to international tensions. Japanese military actions in Manchuria, German rearmament, Italy's invasion of Ethiopia, outside intervention in the Spanish Civil War—all made Americans increasingly inclined to avoid war by minimizing their nation's involvement in world politics. That went hand in glove with another curious inconsistency of those depression years—the economic determinist/conspiracy thesis of the origins of the First World War. This argument attributed the American decision to go to war to manipulation by special interests with investments to protect. That assumption prompted the United States to seek protection in itself, passing neutrality legislation (1936) designed to prevent the nation from being drawn into another European war by bankers and munitions makers as congressional "isolationists" (nationalists) claimed had happened in 1917. But such laws were actually an admission that Europe's quarrels could not be kept from America's shores. All the United States could hope for was to confront those crises on its own terms.

Relations with an expansionist Japan had also steadily worsened throughout the 1930s. Tokyo's occupation of Manchuria in 1931 had led Washington to promulgate the Stimson Doctrine of nonrecognition of "states" established by military force. Then, in 1937, Japan attacked China. Traditional American sympathies for China set the tone for American protests. In July 1939, the State Department announced that the 1911 Commercial Treaty with Japan would be allowed to lapse. Secretary of State Cordell Hull emphasized that the action meant no immediate change, only a desire to gain flexibility, but his meaning was clear—henceforth the United States would use economic coercion to back up its diplomatic representations to Tokyo. "It is a curious fact," mused a State Department aide, "that the United States, which bolts like a frightened rabbit from every remote contact with Europe, will enthusiastically take a step which might well be a material day's march on the road to a Far Eastern War."[2]

Hull, with general support from Roosevelt, ardently advanced the cause of economic "liberalism"—his version of British nineteenth-century free trade principles—and attempted to steer both foreign nations and New Dealers in that direction. Even after the outbreak of the European war in September 1939, the secretary tried to convince the Japanese of the error of their ways—with a promise that the postwar era would see a golden age for international trade. The Japanese special ambassador, Admiral Nomura, correctly observed that Hull had little interest in the specifics of Japanese actions in China: "He is thinking about readjusting the economic situation of the world after the conclusion of this war. . . ." As the secretary had put it:

> Now all along I've fought against the preferential system of the British Empire, . . . and now we are talking it over with England. I don't want you to tell anybody about this, but don't you know only lately Great Britain is coming around to my point of view.

One result of the war, concluded Hull, would be a German and British return to the gold standard, and an "all-encompassing" trade multilateralism. It was an odd "confidence" to share with a potential enemy on the verge of war, but it accurately caught the shift in Washington's thinking as the nation moved from the illusion of neutrality to the reality of intervention, and looked ahead to visions of the future.[3]

Although Roosevelt congratulated Prime Minister Neville Chamberlain on the outcome of the Munich conference in 1938, saving peace for Europe at the expense of Czechoslovakia, neither he nor other American leaders were very happy about it, nor did they believe the peace would last. The major European opposition to Hitler—France, Great Britain, and the Soviet Union—had all floundered in their attempts to quarantine German expansion. Fear of both military conquest and social discontent at home and throughout Europe drove Britain and France to appease Germany. Then in August 1939, the Soviet Union practiced its own form of appeasement, signing an agreement with Hitler. The war in Europe began within a few days.

In late spring 1939, the U.S. Congress, still fearful of public opposition to involvement in Europe's wars, had refused to change the neutrality laws to permit the cash-and-carry sale of war matériel to belligerents. But the Anglo-French declaration of war on Germany changed that, as Americans began what would be a two year-long attempt to prevent a German victory without having to join the war. In November 1939, the neutrality laws were modified to give the president more discretion, permitting American business to sell non-war materials to belligerents on a (pay) cash-and-carry (in your ships) basis. Profit and a degree of political influence were gained while maintaining the fiction of neutrality—a classic example of democratic diplomacy.

At the same time, Roosevelt worked to protect his flank by mending fences with the Latin American nations. He had earlier launched his Good Neighbor Policy, renouncing the right of the United States to intervene with force in the internal affairs of others in the Western Hemisphere. As war clouds gathered over Europe, fears of Italo-German subversion (a so-called Fifth Column) prompted the president to instruct his envoys to settle long-standing arguments. Most striking was that with Mexico over nationalization of U.S. property (largely mining, livestock, and oil interests). By the time war broke out, U.S.-Latin American relations had improved substantially, although Washington continued to worry about German influence in Brazil, Chile, and Argentina.

When Hitler invaded the low countries and France, American leaders (like the Soviets) thought history would repeat itself in a reincarnation of World War I-style trench warfare, leaving them ample time to respond to whatever developed. But the June 1940 collapse of French resistance and evacuation from the Continent of British troops shattered those assumptions. Roosevelt's reaction was painfully slow for a Britain awaiting an expected German invasion before winter; and far too quick for most Americans. The president took steps to increase war production and to insure that Britain could buy what it could pay for. But that was not enough. British Prime Minister Winston Churchill pushed for a gesture that would help both the military and morale. Churchill knew that, with the Nazi-Soviet Pact still in effect, only the United States offered Britain any realistic hope for survival. His pleas finally met with some success when, in mid summer 1940, Roosevelt authorized the transfer of a number of warships (destroyers of World War I vintage) while, in an obvious but unofficial arrangement, Britain leased a number of military sites in the

Western Hemisphere to the Americans. The ships played little role in the crucial and cruel war against German submarines in the Atlantic, but the image of mutual support heartened Britons and pushed the Americans closer into what one Roosevelt speechwriter called a "common-law alliance."

Even so, despite the picture of Axis solidarity suggested by the September 1940 Tripartite Pact between Germany, Italy, and Japan, President Roosevelt still paid obeisance to "isolationism" with a promise during his reelection campaign that "American boys are not going to be sent into any foreign wars." The commitment helped him win his third term in office, but also reflected his hope that American participation could be limited to ships and aircraft.

In December 1940, with Churchill warning that Britain's financial resources were about to run out and with the election campaign behind him, Roosevelt took the initiative and announced the Lend-Lease program, a move he said would make the United States the "arsenal of democracy." War goods, paid for by the United States, would be sent to nations designated by the president. The act, which Congress approved by a wide margin, allowed Roosevelt to dodge a direct confrontation over entry into the war since its stated purpose was "to promote the defense of the United States."[4] The concept also avoided the troublesome war debts problem by allowing the president full authority to determine what, if any, repayment terms.

Lend-Lease constituted a declaration of economic warfare against Germany, but it was not enough to insure even the containment of Hitler. What could Lend-Lease accomplish if German submarines continued to wreak havoc on transatlantic shipping? Even with British access to the German military codes (the ULTRA decrypts), merchant ship losses were staggering. Thus, in the summer of 1941, the United States, slowly but surely, became more and more involved in the actual fighting. U.S. warships began to escort convoys of merchant ships, American forces took over the defense of Iceland and Greenland (pushing the Western Hemisphere a good ways to the east), and the government froze German and Italian assets.

The decision of Japan to join the Axis Tripartite Pact, despite Washington's "signals," had completed the political lineup. The Axis Pact increased the threat of war, but it helped justify opposition to Japan's ambitions in Southeast Asia. Whatever the limits of Japanese ambitions, its decision to ally with Hitler was crucial both to the forging of a American national consensus and to an identification of the struggle as one of liberal or democratic politics and economics versus the now worldwide "fascist" bloc. With the definition of "liberalism" undergoing serious modification in New Deal America, as it would in postwar Europe later, both pro- and anti-New Deal figures believed that the *degree* of state intervention in the international and intra-national economic orders of the future would be determined largely by the outcome of the struggle with the autarchic forces, i.e., Germany, Japan, and Italy.[5]

Thus, when the United States tried "negotiations" with Japan, beginning in April 1941, Cordell Hull required pledges that Tokyo would not continue its forward movement into Southeast Asia, would accept the economic and political principles of the "Open Door" (America's traditional policy of equal access for all foreign nations in China), and would repudiate any obligation to support Germany and Italy in case America became involved in the European War. After Germany attacked the Soviet Union in June 1941, Washington also wanted a pledge that Japan would not strike north against the Soviet Far East.[6]

By mid-1941, the United States had applied an array of economic sanctions against Japan, but the addition in July of oil to the list forced Tokyo to make hard decisions. The outbreak of the Nazi-Soviet war on 22 June offered the opportunity to seize territory in eastern Siberia, but the natural resources needed by Japan's military lay in Southeast Asia, controlled by the European colonial powers. Moreover, it was the United States, not the Soviet Union, that threatened to block Japanese aspirations in China. Thus Japanese leaders decided to move south, toward Indochina and the East Indies.

The United States would not accept a Japanese dominated East Asia. Japan would not accept anything less. For both nations the confrontation had become a dangerous combination of interests and emotions; empire and nationalism. No third party could intervene, so without dramatic changes in position, war had become inevitable. Only the place and time were left to decide.

In fact, the place and even the approximate date were determined by September 1941. By then the Japanese had adopted a plan that called for an attack on the U.S. Pacific fleet, then based at Pearl Harbor. The Japanese, aware of America's size and potential strength, hoped to repeat what had happened 40 years earlier in their war against Russia. If the American fleet were destroyed, and Japanese military objectives in the Southwest Pacific were achieved, then the United States might conclude that defeating Japan was too costly and negotiate on Japan's terms, particularly given American concern about events in Europe.

That logic led to the Japanese air attack on Pearl Harbor in the Hawaiian Islands on 7 December 1941. In a daring raid executed across over 3,800 miles (6,200 kilometers)* with superb precision and blessed by good luck, especially cloud cover during transit, Japanese aircraft devastated the American battle fleet. Eight battleships and large numbers of other warships were sunk or damaged, and over 2,400 Americans killed. American intelligence had earlier broken the Japanese diplomatic code, but that disclosed only the collapse of negotiations. U.S. leaders, fearing a Japanese move into Southeast Asia or even an attack on their Philippine Island colony, were caught unawares.[7]

But the gratuitous German declaration of war against the United States on 11 December 1941, gave Roosevelt complete freedom of action to respond to Pearl Harbor by choosing to go after Hitler first.[8] Whatever his reasons, the president preserved Anglo-American alliance and made possible a Soviet-Anglo-American coalition against Germany and Italy when he assured Churchill, who had rushed over to Washington, that Germany-first was still the U.S. policy.

The Anglo-American reaction to the German attack on the Soviet Union on 22 June 1941—operation BARBAROSSA—had combined skepticism with prayerful hope. Military advisers told Churchill and Roosevelt that the Soviets could not withstand the onslaught, that Moscow would fall before winter, and that sending aid would be a waste of resources. But the chance that the Soviet Union could survive or at least inflict heavy losses on the Germans prompted both leaders to pledge support. After all, said Churchill, "Hitler is the foe we have to beat." Stalin responded with requests for military supplies and the establishment of a Second Front capable of diverting large numbers of German troops away from the east. Churchill, his rhetoric tempered by distrust of Bolshevism, pessimism about Soviet chances, and Britain's own precarious situation, dismissed any likelihood of an early cross-Channel invasion and procrastinated on dispatching military aid.

Roosevelt, using his closest aide, Harry Hopkins, as fact-finder in both London and Moscow, moved to implement his promise. He and Churchill agreed, at the Atlantic conference in August, to send a supply mission to Moscow, and in November 1941 the president extended Lend-Lease to the Soviet Union. The aid-to-Russia program also had, for Roosevelt, the political purpose of promoting good relations with the Soviet Union, and it performed that task well. But the Second Front issue would bedevil

*That distance is equivalent to London–Washington, D.C., or Moscow–Mys Dezhneva (East Cape) at the easternmost tip of Siberia.

Allied relations for the remainder of the war—and the historiography of war for decades after.[9]

With both the United States and the USSR finally in the war, tripartite diplomacy dominated the scene in 1942. Developing (or trying to develop) grand strategy dominated the attention of policymakers. But American diplomacy retained its own national objectives. The danger of a Russian collapse before Hitler's *Blitzkrieg* had both London and Washington deeply concerned about the threat of a separate Soviet peace with Germany which would not only prolong the war, but also deny the United States a complete (unconditional) victory and the opportunity to achieve its broad war objectives. Mere "containment" of Germany was just not good enough to rebuild the world on liberal democratic foundations.

Roosevelt knew very well that his vague offers of a full partnership in the postwar world order he envisioned would not satisfy Joseph Stalin. Russian diplomats always responded to such promises with a not unexpected countermove: failure to launch a Second Front in 1942, they warned, might end up with the West bearing the brunt of Hitler's armies. They did not say Russia would leave the war, but by implying the possibility of a collapse on the eastern front, they all but forced the desired response. Roosevelt did not hesitate. Were developments "clear enough," he asked General George Marshall when Soviet Commisar for Foreign Affairs V. M. Molotov came to Washington in May 1942, "so that we could say to Mr. Stalin that we are preparing a second front?" "Yes," came the reply. "The President then authorized Mr. Molotov to inform Mr. Stalin that we expect the formation of a second front this year."[10]

Marshall at once attempted to qualify the president's commitment, pointing out that there remained serious problems of transportation to overcome. He failed. FDR's language even shifted from a commitment to "preparing" a Second Front to "formation . . . this year."[11] And Molotov nailed down the pledge at a subsequent session the next day. After Roosevelt observed that an early Second Front might mean curtailing Lend-Lease convoys to Russia, Molotov retorted that the Second Front would be stronger if the shipments continued, and "with what seemed deliberate sarcasm," asked what would happen if the Russians agreed to curtailed shipments and then there was no Second Front. Becoming still more insistent, he asked, "What is the President's answer with respect to the second front?" Confronted in this fashion, Roosevelt replied, "We expected to establish a second front."[12]

Whether or not Molotov and Stalin believed FDR is beside the point—Roosevelt could not have his cake and eat it too. He could not ease Soviet suspicions and simultaneously maintain complete control of the peace process. Roosevelt's reaction to Soviet diplomacy revealed his desire to postpone long-term decisions unless they worked in favor of his vision of the postwar world. Stalin wanted Anglo-American acceptance of the Soviet frontier agreed upon in his pact with the Germans. The British were willing to discuss the issues, but Roosevelt firmly opposed making territorial arrangements in the midst of war—in part because such arrangements had caused Wilson such trouble; but primarily because FDR hoped to mold the peace structure to his broad conceptions. Yet it was too early, in 1942, to know how to translate those ideals into practical reality.

However cutely Roosevelt avoided a specific promise to launch the attack in 1942. Molotov had the freedom to assume that the president meant that year. But it was not to be until June 1944, and the dispute over broken pledges haunted the diplomacy of the war—and the historiography as well. Some American policymakers, who suspected British motives as much as did the Soviets, were quick to put the blame on Churchill for the failure to launch the Second Front in 1942, but truth was neither British nor American forces were ready for such an operation that year.

The major significance of the Roosevelt-Molotov conversations, then, was to add to the legacy of inter-Allied suspicion when, a few months later, the Americans seemed to accept the "British peripheral strategy" for defeating Hitler by first securing the "empire" with an invasion of North Africa.[13] Roosevelt also had to be concerned about those within the inner circle of his political and military advisers who chafed at the apparent inability of the president to free himself from Churchill's strategic designs, even to the point of toying with a Pacific-first strategy. It was not until 1943 that American planners extracted a firm commitment for a Second Front in Europe.

That commitment—in the form of a date for the invasion of western France—came at the so-called TRIDENT conference, held in Washington in May 1943. Whatever the strategic significance of that agreement, it served to announce a shift in the balance of power within the Anglo-American alliance. No longer would Churchill and his military be able to sell their idea of a war of attrition against Germany. American economic and military strength was coming to dominate, and that meant fighting on American terms.

As with guns, so with politics. Churchill's trip to Washington was on American terms—his third, with no return visit from Roosevelt. The meetings centered on military matters, but politics lay at the root of all the major discussions. British pleas for an intensified Italian campaign not only ran afoul of American desires for an invasion of western France, but threatened to involve the United States where Roosevelt did not want to go in the postwar world—the Mediterranean. Germany-first remained Roosevelt's priority. Only British arguments that pulling back on the Italian campaign would mean no active Anglo-American military support for the USSR for nearly a year salvaged some modicum of support for a follow-up to the expected capture of Sicily.

The Normandy invasion in June 1944 provided the backdrop for United States policy after mid-1944. The Americans had returned to continental Europe, giving them both real and psychological political leverage. Yet Franklin Roosevelt never stopped warning his wartime partners that the United States military presence in Europe would not last longer than two years after war's end—and probably much less.[14] Like many Americans (as well as Britons and Russians) of his generation, he disliked and distrusted the Germans. There was no doubt that Germany had to be tamed—the question was how? The answer came when Treasury Secretary Henry Morgenthau angrily intervened with FDR after learning of U.S. Army plans to reconstruct Germany so as to reduce the costs and difficulties of postwar occupation—plans that fit into State Department schemes for reintegrating Germany into the European economy. Denazification, disarmament, and dismemberment were part of most every plan, but Morgenthau's call for deindustrialization was a program to effect a long-term reform of the "Prussianized" German character by returning them to a pastoral, agrarian life. As absurd as that goal was, there were practical aspects. A harmless Germany would permit the quick withdrawal of U.S. troops, thus avoiding any involvement in the postwar political quagmire Roosevelt predicted for France. The elimination of German industry would offer new markets for Britain—an argument that helped persuade Churchill to accept the plan during the Quebec conference in September 1944. Turning Germany into a nation of small farmers would also avoid the kind of reparations controversy that followed the First World War. Most of all, it was a chance for the kind of social engineering that fascinated Roosevelt's New Dealers. Stalin also bought into the scheme, but protests within and without Roosevelt's administration prompted the president to back away from pastoralization.[15]

The Yalta conference in February 1945 brought the original Big Three together for the last time, and Roosevelt worked to create an atmosphere of agreement over German questions—but without success, as the big questions of reparations and postwar boundaries were put off once again. At the Potsdam conference in July, after many days of discussion, the

Allies agreed they were to take the major share of their reparations from their occupation zones, with special arrangements for other interzone shipments. Within months that agreement had fallen apart, with both sides blaming the other. Soviet demands for reparations forced Truman to choose between firm control of a western zone in Germany and joint control over all Germany. He chose the former—foreshadowing the division of Europe into the exclusive spheres of influence that Roosevelt had tried to elude. At the same time, the Americans concluded that dismembering Germany would destabilize Europe, leaving the Stalin with the prospect of a unified anti-Soviet German state. Moscow's response was predictable, if crude. Disagreements over the governments in liberated Eastern Europe were the first open signs that the Grand Alliance had failed, but the heart of the early Cold War was the failure to resolve the German question. Germany-first was the Allied military strategy, but Germany-postponed became the political reality.

The Grand Alliance, as Churchill labelled the wartime coalition, had its beginnings in Anglo-American agreement that Hitler had to be stopped, grew likely once the Germans invaded the Soviet Union, and became a reality with the combination of a Soviet victory in the battle of Moscow and the entry of the United States into the war after the Pearl Harbor attack. But most of all, it had its roots in the wistful hope that wartime cooperation could evolve into peacetime accord. Each of the Big Three spoke in such terms at one time or another; yet each set conditions for cooperation that enhanced their own state's interests. Churchill maneuvered to preserve Britain's empire so as to insure a role as a great power; Stalin pursued territory for his state and security for his regime; Roosevelt assumed the superiority of American institutions and worked to insure that doors were open to the spread of that system. As different as those approaches were, the Big Three made remarkable, if unsuccessful, progress toward the continuation of wartime cooperation into the postwar world. At the heart of those successes was Franklin Roosevelt's conviction that only Great Power satisfaction could avoid world war.

Hopes for cooperation in and after the war began as early as August 1941, when Churchill and Roosevelt held their first wartime meeting. Held aboard warships anchored in Placentia Bay, Newfoundland—off the east coast of Canada—it proved an extraordinary meeting. Roosevelt and Churchill hit it off, establishing a personal relationship that played a crucial role in wartime grand strategy. They both demanded that their military chiefs work together, thus minimizing the kinds of tensions that came to characterize some aspects of their relations with the Soviet Union.

According to Churchill, Roosevelt promised (hinted is more likely) to seek an excuse to go to war against Germany.[16]

The most publicized result of the meeting was the Atlantic Charter. Whatever it meant to Churchill, for FDR it was a statement of how the war would serve the cause of reform. He had promised that "if war comes we will make it a New Deal war," and the Charter was a step in that direction.[17] The provisions were deceptively vague, but they constituted a set of war and peace aims that would restructure the postwar world. Self-determination would replace colonialism. All nations would have equal access to trade and raw materials (the "open door"), and work together to secure "improved labor standards, economic advancement, and social security." Lastly, they would establish a "permanent system of general security" with the renunciation of force and disarmament as key provisions.[18] "Complete economic and commercial and boundary liberty," was how Roosevelt put it, though he warned that "America and England will have to maintain peace." Roosevelt never abandoned those designs, whatever short-term compromises and long-range adjustments he found necessary.[19]

Thus when Soviet Foreign Minister Molotov came to Washington in May 1942 Roosevelt made his first serious effort to engage the Soviets in formulating the postwar order. He had it in mind, he told Molotov, that the Soviet Union should join with Britain and the United States in a big-power consortium of sorts, not only to manage the central business of dealing with the defeated Axis powers, but with it understood as well that each would have specific regional obligations. These latter responsibilities were to include the problem of strategic areas to be put under some kind of international trusteeship.

No American policymaker had ever spoken in such terms to a representative of the Soviet Union. Yet Molotov was not terribly responsive to this overture. He had traveled to Washington with a very different object in mind. Roosevelt's formulas were all algebra, Stalin believed; he wanted his representative to talk about mathematics, specifically the number of divisions that the United States and Britain would commit to Europe in 1942 to open a Second Front.

Stalin may not have believed Allied, especially British, protests about the difficulty of establishing a Second Front, but he certainly played upon fears of a separate peace in the East to demand recognition of Russian postwar desiderata in Eastern Europe. As early as December 1941 Stalin sought to engage his allies in the broad outlines of a diplomatic settlement of postwar Europe. The Russian leader was far more precise at this stage about his notions of how postwar Europe should be organized than

Roosevelt ever was about resolving colonial issues. Given the nature of the war and the Grand Alliance, it could hardly have been otherwise. Russia's immediate obsession was Germany, today and tomorrow, and the frontiers needed for defense; Roosevelt's concern was with the trickier task of reconciling American dreams of a liberal democratic world with the realities of a cooperative world in which not everyone accepted that American vision.

Churchill and Roosevelt backed away from Stalin's initial efforts to create a "spheres of influence" arrangement. Stalin then attempted to put the question as an "either . . . or" proposition—either the Western allies agree to launch a Second Front in 1942, or they acquiesce in a treaty underwriting the proposed spheres of influence. The list of nations subject to such an arrangement began with the Baltic States, but as preliminary Anglo-Russian negotiations revealed, Stalin desired a free hand to establish Polish boundaries.[20]

Whether or not the Soviet leader understood British inability to mount a cross-Channel operation, he seems to have concluded he could at least gain diplomatic advantage. However that may be, the Anglo-Russian discussions had come to the attention of American policymakers, who did not like anything about them. Aside from the fate of specific countries to consider, there was the precedent being set: once established in a formal Anglo-Russian treaty, spheres of influence would no doubt dominate all postwar discussions, and the world would be plunged again into the chaos of the prewar decade. The dominant feeling in Washington was, "if we make a single commitment regarding the peace we have lost the chance of being free agents; . . . the acid test of our good faith in Russia is whether we deliver the supplies we promise. . . . Meanwhile Stalin . . . [has] tried to hurry matters by throwing out the possibility of a treaty with Germany."[21]

It was against this troubled background that Roosevelt had issued his invitation to Molotov, urging him to interrupt his London negotiations on the proposed Anglo-Russian treaty of alliance with its obnoxious political clauses and come to Washington—to hear an alternative proposal for military action. British policymakers welcomed the intervention, though they were less happy about the results of Molotov's dealings in the American capital.

The Churchill-Roosevelt talks of January 1943, held in the exotic atmosphere of Casablanca on Morocco's Atlantic coast, focused on military decisions, but politics was never absent when any of the Big Three met each other. Stalin had refused an invitation to attend, losing an opportunity to plead for a Second Front in 1943, and helping to establish an appearance of Anglo-American condominium. But that illusion could not last, as American policy moved in its own direction. Roosevelt surprised Churchill by announcing publicly what they had agreed upon privately—to seek the unconditional surrender of the Axis, a Roosevelt initiative designed to placate liberals at home and calm Stalin's fears of a separate peace in the West. More important, the policy would postpone decisions on the specifics of postwar settlements until the end of the war, when U.S. economic and military influence had reached their full potential.[22]

But it was the question of postwar relations with the Soviet Union that generated the most heat, though not much light. The USSR's military strength became increasingly clear—a victory at Moscow followed by the winter 1942-43 offensive that drove the Germans out of the Caucasus and Stalingrad, and the stabilizing of the front. All lay ready for the crushing victory at Kursk later that summer that would open the hard but sure path to Berlin. Sensing the changes, Roosevelt redoubled his efforts to convince Stalin that they could work together in both the wartime and the postwar world. He tried to avoid British plans to act as broker between the U.S. and the USSR by proposing a private meeting with Stalin, later lying awkwardly to Churchill that the idea had come from Moscow.

In the spring of 1943, when British foreign secretary Anthony Eden visited Washington, Roosevelt sketched out his vision for the postwar world. The Great Powers—the Big Four (China was then included)—would "police" the world. That required answers to two questions: How would they perform those duties, and who would watch the watchers? Roosevelt's answers revealed the tightrope he was trying to walk. Somehow, the Big Four had to be responsible for specific areas without that degenerating into old-style exclusive spheres of influence. In addition, the Great Powers, particularly the Soviets, had to be assured that their security and vital interests were protected. Policing would be regional; self-interested cooperation would prevail. The "family circle" Roosevelt called it later on, where they "would not only work in close cooperation for the prosecution of the war but would also remain in close touch for the generations to come."[23]

In the autumn, the president sent Cordell Hull to Moscow for a meeting of the foreign ministers of the three Allies. Whatever Hull's differences with Roosevelt, the secretary effectively defended FDR's conception of the postwar world structure against British attempts either to recreate a *cordon sanitaire* or to involve the U.S. in the details and intricacies of political settlements in Eastern Europe. It was a perfect run-up to Roosevelt's major effort at creating a reformed postwar international system—the first

Big Three conference, held in late November through early December in Iran's capital, Tehran.

The Tehran talks, and their prologue and epilogue—the two meetings at Cairo that featured Roosevelt, Churchill, and Chinese leader Chiang Kai-shek—provided Roosevelt with his most tempting opportunity to shape the world. Trying to persuade Churchill and Stalin to adopt ideas that Roosevelt himself had not thought out was no easy task. The fundamental was the idea of the "Four Policemen," but creating that sense of cooperation and security meant solving issues that would have frustrated Solomon. Whatever Soviet ambitions, a non-threatening Poland seemed indispensable to any postwar peace. Moreover, there remained the overall issue of Soviet frontiers.

The president firmly believed that only Great Power cooperation could avoid the problems that beset Woodrow Wilson's League of Nations. Yet FDR and his advisers repeatedly declared their opposition to spheres of influence, and they meant it—even if Churchill thought American objections were mere semantics, warning Stalin to avoid using the phrase lest the Americans "be shocked."[24]

Establishment of a cooperative international monetary system was the purpose of the 1944 Bretton Woods meetings, held in New Hampshire to escape the July heat of Washington. The idea was to get away from currency controls and bilateral exchange agreements that restricted currency exchanges and thus hampered the liberalizing of trade. A United Nations Bank for Reconstruction and Development would operate a "stabilization" fund that would dampen extreme swings in currency values. British economist John Maynard Keynes presented a brilliant, if unorthodox, alternative scheme, but the Americans insisted on their plan—a plan that made the U.S. dollar the international currency for 25 years. As Roosevelt revealingly told the conferees: "Commerce is the lifeblood of a free society. We must see to it that the arteries are not clogged again."[25] Positing commerce as a prerequisite to a *free* society displayed both Roosevelt's liberal convictions and the means he thought necessary to implement those convictions.

There remained the task of fleshing out the vague commitments to an international organization made in the Atlantic Charter and periodically thereafter. The venue—the lovely Dumbarton Oaks mansion in the Georgetown section of Washington, comfortable even in heat of August and September—again marked both America's commitment and its leverage. As at Bretton Woods, the Big Three left the details to subordinates, although conferees soon ran up against disputes that only their leaders could decide. Perhaps arguments over the veto (could it be used to prevent even discussion of an issue in which one of the Great Powers was involved?), the "X" issue (membership for additional Soviet republics), or regionalism could have been resolved right then and there, without letting them fester and create tensions. Instead, solutions had to await the Big Three meeting at Yalta. Moreover, Roosevelt's conception was as imperfectly understood by his representatives as it was imperfectly articulated by him.

The president's scheme called for a United Nations Organization that would accept the leadership of the Great Powers. He had effectively marshaled domestic support for American membership in an international organization, now the trick was to get the rest of the world to go along. Their disarmament would lessen tensions, while the UNO would provide a forum for them to blow off steam, as he put it. But the UNO was only a small part of Roosevelt's grand concept, for the Great Powers were to be in charge. The problem was that Great Power rule could degenerate into *exclusive* spheres of influence; precisely what Churchill had in mind when he proposed locating a regional council for Europe in London, and obviously what Stalin sought in Eastern Europe. As Anglo-American negotiations over postwar civil aviation agreements made clear, trade and commerce were not to become the closed, private operation that spheres of influence permitted. The same was true for ideas and information.[26]

To answer predictions that Great Power leadership would result in exclusivity, Roosevelt pointed to his Good Neighbor Policy toward the nations of the Western Hemisphere. In that region, by Roosevelt's reckoning, United States leadership made the use of force unnecessary. Most of those nations were becoming democratic and acting responsibly; prosperity would follow as they liberalized their trade and integrated their economies. Roosevelt claimed to have conducted a seminar for Stalin on the Good Neighbor Policy during the Tehran Conference.[27] It never dawned on him that U.S. relations with Latin America were hardly analogous to British and Soviet relations with Europe. Nor did he confront the challenge nationalism in Latin America posed even for the most benevolent *patrón*.

There were several Soviet-American difficulties that defied solution and threatened cooperation. From its inception, the Lend-Lease program for Russia had two objectives: to keep that nation in the war, and to lay the foundations for a new relationship with the Soviet Union after the war. No one had been more closely associated with the decision to send large-scale aid to Russia than Averell Harriman. He had come back from an initial visit to the Soviet Union in 1941 convinced that both goals were achievable. "I left feeling that he [Stalin] had been frank with us and if we came through as had been promised and if personal relations were retained with Stalin, the suspicion that had existed between the Soviet Government and our two governments might well be eradicated."[28]

Harriman was pleased, then, when Roosevelt named him ambassador to the Soviet Union in late 1943. His first assignment was to inform Stalin of the president's interest in finding ways to aid Russia in the postwar period. Talking on the record to British and American correspondents on 4 November 1943, the new ambassador to the Soviet Union declared that a matter that "deserves the greatest possible consideration" was assistance to Russia after the war. "We will have the plans to produce machinery and equipment needed by the Soviet Union and in so doing we will help our own people to convert from war to peace production."[29]

Yet through all those months from the Moscow conference of 1943 to midsummer 1944, nothing was accomplished to bring speculations—either positive or negative—about Russian-American economic relations down to earth. In part this was because of a developing argument over where the substantive negotiations should be held, Washington or Moscow; in part it was because of reluctance to ask Congress for approval of a large credit to the Soviet Union; and, in large part, it was because Roosevelt failed, for whatever reasons, to follow up on his early determination to cut through all the red tape by using "personal relations" as Harriman had insisted had to be done from 1941 on. On 13 March 1944 the ambassador had pled yet one more time for consideration about the larger issues at stake. "I am impressed with the consideration that economic assistance is one of the most effective weapons at our disposal to influence European political events in the direction we desire and to avoid the development of a sphere of influence of the Soviet Union over Eastern Europe and the Balkans."[30]

The Russian-American negotiations in Washington over Lend-Lease arrangements for the future broke down in mid-September, 1944. Harriman's own accounts of Soviet attitudes during this period showed that he believed there was less and less inclination to accord much attention to U.S. wishes. By the time the issue of economic aid came up again in early 1945, Harriman's own attitude had hardened. Then, perhaps the greatest irony of all, in the immediate aftermath of Roosevelt's death in 1945, Harriman became one of the original hard-liners advising Harry Truman to get tough with the Soviets.

Roosevelt's reaction to the Moscow (TOLSTOY) talks between Churchill and Stalin in October 1944 had revealed the widening gap between expectation and reality. Churchill and Stalin were determined to discuss their respective policies in Eastern Europe, and where the dividing line should be, thus implying the composition of postwar governments in those areas. Roosevelt protested in a message sent through Ambassador Harriman that America could not recognize those arrangements as anything but temporary, pending another meeting of the Big Three. Yet, when the two Europeans finished their discussions—most of which were reported back to Washington by Harriman—the president seemed to accept the spheres of influence (percentages) arrangement that resulted. How could he reconcile such a division of Eastern Europe with his idea of cooperative, regional, and Great Power leadership?

In part the answer was that he had no interest in the specifics of any Eastern European settlement. What did it profit world peace to have agreements that made Poles or Estonians happy if that drove the Soviet Union away from postwar collaboration? In larger part the answer was that Roosevelt viewed spheres of influence in two discrete pieces. Great Power cooperation depended on those nations feeling secure—and that meant their ability to exercise political control over nearby regions. But that political domination was not to be accompanied by locked doors and high fences. The world was to be left open to commerce of all kinds—goods, people, ideas, and information. Democracy and liberalism went hand in glove in the Western Hemisphere. But in Eastern Europe that pairing would have to wait. Roosevelt sought cosmetic gestures that would give the American public the impression of democracy, but even when those failed to materialize, he stuck to his policy of avoiding a political confrontation—either with the Soviets in Eastern Europe, or with the British over Greece where Churchill had sent in troops to prevent a leftist takeover and reinstall the monarchy. It was a strategy he repeated a few months later at Yalta, one that brought the much-reviled Declaration on Liberated Europe with its ambiguous promise of self-determination and democracy. Roosevelt's promises of a liberal, democratic world created public expectations that could not be fulfilled, and created domestic pressures that his successor deflected by accusing the Soviet Union of violating the Yalta agreements.[31]

Harry Truman came to the presidency with little or no experience in foreign affairs. Roosevelt—first busy at Yalta, then tired and ill—had no chance to tutor his vice president, even had he chosen to. Like John Adams after Washington and Lyndon Johnson after Kennedy, Truman had succeeded a legend—hence his promise that he would merely continue FDR's policies. Truman seems to have thought himself a practical

Wilsonian, but his was the internationalism of a nationalist—do it our way or we will go it alone. Certainly that was what he heard from the men he sought out for guidance in the immediate aftermath of Roosevelt's death. Occasionally Truman's own impulsiveness took over. To the regret of Averell Harriman, one of those key advisers, the new president angrily lectured Molotov about Soviet policies in Eastern Europe, claiming the Russians had not kept their promises.[32] Similarly, Truman abruptly cut off Lend-Lease shipments to the Soviet Union with the German surrender in May, claiming that the law gave him no choice since the Russians were not at war with Japan.[33] But the key shift was one of attitude. The time had come to get tough—to draw lines in the sand. No longer did American policy focus on convincing Stalin that the Americans could be trusted and that his regime was not threatened by Western intrigue. Now it was Truman and his coterie who felt threatened, as the Soviets crudely imposed their conditions on the sphere of influence that Churchill had negotiated. The complex subtlety of Roosevelt's combination of political security with open doors, practical or not, was either lost or dismissed both by the new policymakers in Washington and their constituents, who soon began to wonder how the United States could have "won" the war and yet once again, as in 1919, find itself unable to "win" the peace.

Truman remarked to an aide at the Potsdam conference, "Jimmy, do you realize that we have been here seventeen whole days? Why, in seventeen days you can decide anything!"[34] The Potsdam Big Three of July 1945 ended in a series of "decisions" that came unraveled almost at once. Debates over the composition of governments in the liberated countries of Eastern Europe, and what they would have to do to be recognized by the United States; disputes over a Truman plan for internationalizing the waterways of that area; dissension about the mechanism for writing the peace treaties; these and other issues divided the victors.

Truman, uncertain of his ability to handle international affairs and awed by the company he was keeping, was more than happy to get away from Potsdam.

Roosevelt received much advice during the war about what to do in the face European "backwardness" on the colonial question. He usually answered in the same evasive way. As he wrote one Cabinet official: "You are right about India, but it would be playing with fire if the British Empire were to tell me to mind my own business."[35] Was this a case of Roosevelt hemmed in by the American public's antagonism to European empires, or a case of the president using that attitude to foster his own policies? In democratic diplomacy, that is often a distinction without a difference.

Roosevelt believed as firmly as any other American that European rule in Asia and Africa was on its way out, that the war had greatly speeded up an inevitable process. His self-imposed restraint in the name of Allied wartime unity did not prevent him from "thinking out loud" upon occasion. French colonial failings were his special target, especially their behavior in Indochina—stemming partly from disgust at the way the Vichy French government[36] had virtually handed over the colony to Japan in 1941, though he condemned British colonial rule in West Africa in equally contemptuous terms.

But first things first. Prime Minister Churchill had been asked if the Atlantic Charter, with its pledges of self-determination, referred to the British Empire. He replied that it did not, that the progressive development of self-government within the empire was an internal question, quite separate from the Charter. But Roosevelt could not answer that way. On Washington's Birthday 1942, he declared that "the Atlantic Charter applies not only to the parts of the world that border the Atlantic but to the whole world."[37] Even though, a month earlier, at the signing of the Declaration of the United Nations during his conference with Churchill in January, American diplomats had pressured the British to allow India to sign for itself, Roosevelt always pulled back when he felt (or Churchill told him) he had pushed too far in pressing London to accede to Indian nationalist demands. The Grand Alliance, during and after the war, took precedence.

Instead of confronting the prime minister about the fate of the colonial empires, FDR regularly broached ideas on internationally accountable trusteeships, as a transition stage to independence, often in a breezy off-the-cuff manner that belied his intensity. In early August 1942, for example, Roosevelt told British chargé d'affaires Sir Ronald Campbell that there were places in the world such as Korea, Malaya, and the Dutch East Indies, where the people "were simply not ready to manage their own affairs." The trustees for Korea should be the United States and Russia and China; China, the United States, and Great Britain for Malaya; the Netherlands would have to be included, he supposed, for the East Indies. And so on.[38]

When Campbell sought to discover the details of the trusteeship machinery Roosevelt had in mind, he "waved my question aside." The president's vagueness was understandable in 1942, but as the war went on, despite a steady stream of critical comments about colonialism, Roosevelt became increasingly hesitant about forcing a resolution of what he knew would become a perilous confrontation between the metropolitan countries and the soon-to-be-called Third World of former colonies and protectorates. The problem was that his vision of postwar Great Power cooperation, built on the wartime alliance, required full British cooperation—and that cooperation seemed conditional on a restoration of European empires.

The Casablanca conference in January 1943 offered Roosevelt an opportunity to enlarge on his proposals for decolonization. He spoke of international control of strategic "strongpoints" (like Dakar on the western bulge of West Africa). In mildly rebuking his diplomatic representative in the North African area, Robert Murphy, for making promises that the French empire would be restored intact, Roosevelt indicated, instead, he was planning "extensive reductions" in that empire.[39]

Churchill could hardly eat a meal in peace at the conference it seemed without hearing Roosevelt use the occasion, as he did with the Sultan of the French protectorate of Morocco, to express sympathy for the aspirations of colonial peoples for independence, and to suggest pointedly that he hoped to expand economic relations with all areas of the world.[40] In Roosevelt's mind, these notions, along with Roosevelt's conviction that French politics were a hopeless morass, merged into a grand scheme for a United Nations. Returning to Washington after the Casablanca conference, the president outlined a postwar security organization to the British ambassador that would consist of three bodies: a general assembly, an executive committee (the Big Four—not to include France), and an advisory council, which would meet from time to time to provide counsel to the Big Four. The executive committee would have the key responsibility for "all the more important decisions and wield police powers of the United Nations." The general assembly would meet once a year to let "the smaller powers . . . blow off steam."[41]

At the same time, whatever the president's conviction that colonialism posed a threat to stability, he could not afford to alienate the British—nor would that hasten the decolonization process. And the British consistently sought the restoration of France as a major European (and colonial) power.

As for China, his man in Chungking was a thin reed on which to lean. Not only was Chiang reluctant to fight the Japanese, but at the meeting in Cairo preceding the Tehran conclave, he had been distant and reluctant to accept Roosevelt's leadership, ignoring Roosevelt's urgings to work out some sort of coalition with the Chinese communists.[42]

Washington had hoped that somehow, some way, the outcome of the war in the Far East would see China emerge as the major stabilizing power in Asia, replacing Japan. The alternatives of Russian ascendancy, or, on the other hand, a scramble for power among various successor states, were equally distressing to contemplate. Roosevelt wanted his allies to support him in this endeavor. The State Department, as usual more pessimistic about Russia than the White House, had watched Soviet moves in the Far East with a rising suspicion that the Kremlin expected to interject itself into the affairs of China and its neighbors. One Asian expert had voiced deep suspicions that Russia's support for a "Free Korea" movement was a method of expanding Soviet influence.[43]

Skeptical in prewar years about the possibilities of resolving China's difficulties in his lifetime, FDR threw himself into the task once the war had begun. He would, at various times, suggest to British policymakers, including Foreign Secretary Anthony Eden, that the expensive *beau geste* of returning Hong Kong to Chinese rule would go far toward establishing a better atmosphere in postwar Asia. The Chinese would, Roosevelt predicted, allow the Union Jack to continue to fly over Hong Kong, and would honor it each day with a proper 21-gun salute. Eden punctured one of these reveries with the pointed comment that he did not see Roosevelt suggesting a similar gesture for such U.S. territories as the Panama Canal Zone.[44]

Nevertheless, Roosevelt and his advisers were serious about promoting China's fortunes, and that meant bringing Chiang Kai-shek inside the tent. As Secretary of State Cordell Hull explained at the Moscow Foreign Ministers' conference, the United States view was very simple: It was too dangerous for the security of the postwar world to have China outside the big power consortium. As the war went on, fear of a Chinese collapse caused Roosevelt the same anxiety, producing a tendency to make rash promises, including a declaration promising the return of all of China's territories "lost" to Japan during the war, the sort of opening gambit he had used with Russia in 1942. Churchill could not prevent Roosevelt from boosting Chiang as an equal partner, though he both distrusted China's worthiness and feared its localized ambitions, but he could and did block plans for military ventures aimed at supporting Chiang—using the Tehran conference's overriding commitment to the Second Front in 1944 as his reason.[45]

As Roosevelt's hopes for a Chinese "renaissance" evaporated, so did his plans for China as a member of the Four Policemen. Moreover, American military plans no longer called for an invasion of Japan from China, eliminating the chance that an American military presence there could control events at war's end, forcing Roosevelt to be mediator instead of arbitrator. Thus, later in 1944, he actively explored his earlier suggestion of an accommodation with Chiang Kai-shek's bitter rival, Mao Tse-tung, leader of the Chinese Communist movement. That "Dixie Mission," as it was called, aimed at avoiding civil war in China by working with both sides. How could the United States support two governments in China? Well, he told journalist Edgar Snow, he had been working with two governments already, and "I intend to go on doing so until we can get them together."[46] The Pacific region would remain one of Roosevelt's four regions, but its Chinese "policeman" would require some tutelage, from the United States of course, before taking over the job.[47]

Returning home from the Yalta conference in February 1945, Roosevelt shocked newsmen with a wistful statement that the Atlantic Charter was hardly more than a "beautiful idea." Apparently hoping to lower public expectations, he professed not even to know the exact whereabouts of the document or if it actually bore the signatures of Roosevelt and Churchill. He went on to talk about Indochina. The French talked about recapturing the colony, he said, but they lacked the shipping to get there. The best idea remained a trusteeship, but the British would object. "Better to keep quiet just now."[48]

Churchill's strategy for dealing with Roosevelt's ideas was precisely the same: keep quiet and wait for developments to decide the issue. He was convinced that eventually the United States would come to its senses about empires and such, and provide the necessary aid and official approval for the return of the colonies to their rightful owners. Facing the dilemma of reconciling decolonization with the need for British (and French, for the British insisted on bring them into the picture) cooperation in the postwar system, Roosevelt did nothing. If the Europeans would not listen to his warnings, what else could he do? Roosevelt believed, or hoped, that his plans for internationally accountable trusteeships—where politically developed nations tutored the colonies in the art of governance—would prevent the inevitable transition from being violent and anti-Western, but postponement is often the same as defeat. Nor had the president laid out his schemes, even privately to his advisers. Thus, after 12 April 1945, when Franklin Roosevelt died of a cerebral hemorrhage, his successor, Harry Truman, could claim that he was following FDR's lead no matter what he did.

The ambiguities quickly surfaced. During the San Francisco conference in April and May 1945 the United States lined up with the colonial powers to oppose efforts by Egypt to give the General Assembly a voice in determining when areas put under UN trusteeship should be declared ready for self-government, and to make them so. These were more than straws in the wind. Puzzled by this turn of events, local American representatives wished to be informed of what was going on in Washington.

"Could I . . . be informed as to what our policy toward Indochina now is?," queried a diplomat in Kunming, China, near the border. "Whether the late President froze it into mañana status or whether the living are doing something about it?"[49] By the fall of 1945, American policy toward Indochina had become one of "neutrality," while British troops landed to restore the French in Saigon.

As it developed, the demands of subject peoples more than American insistence prompted the British to divest themselves of Empire, the Dutch required considerable urging from the United States, and the French successfully pleaded Cold War needs to ward off American pressure—until Washington itself became convinced of the need to support them.

One of the poisons that may have made a cooperative world harder, if not impossible, was brewed during talks between Churchill and Roosevelt in September 1944 at Roosevelt's home on the Hudson River in Hyde Park, New York.

When America initiated its Manhattan Project to construct an atomic bomb, the Soviet Union and Germany were still operating under the aegis of their 1939 treaty. But even after the U.S. and the USSR became allies, Anglo-American efforts to build a bomb were kept secret from the Russians. Secretary of War Henry L. Stimson was particularly anxious that an Anglo-Russian agreement in late 1942 to share information on new weapons might include atomic bomb research, and Roosevelt agreed "that it would be very bad policy."[50]

They need not have worried about the British, however, for Churchill was just as fully determined—if not more so—to keep atomic energy, both for military and postwar economic purposes, an Anglo-American monopoly. When the Danish scientist, Niels Bohr, who had escaped from the Nazis, argued for multinational control of atomic energy, he was firmly rebuffed by both Churchill and Roosevelt. They agreed that Bohr should be put under close observation and "steps taken" to insure that he would leak no secrets to the Russians, then went on to sign an agreement on 19 September 1944 to exchange nuclear information between them after the war.[51]

Since Soviet intelligence had some knowledge of the Manhattan Project, Stalin knew, no later than midwar, that the Anglo-Americans were engaged in creating a new weapon. Yet, despite their partnership, neither of his allies said a word. The suspicion and distrust that lay beneath withholding the secret of the bomb guaranteed suspicion and distrust when the common enemy disappeared.

In what remains a shadowy episode, President Truman attempted at Potsdam to inform Stalin of the weapon's existence in terms that would not reveal any details, nor yet cause him to be criticized later for "holding back." But holding back was exactly what he wanted to do. From Stalin's expressionless response, Truman could not tell if the Soviet leader understood.

Potsdam marked the end of wartime diplomacy, and, for United States leaders and their public, the beginning of faith in a world they could control and thus shape in their own liberal democratic image. At the midpoint of the conference, General George C. Marshall left Truman for an afternoon to visit Generals Maxwell Taylor and George Patton, who awaited him at the former Nazi hideaway, Berchtesgaden. Sitting with them and watching American soldiers compete in a track meet on the local sports field, Marshall told them about the atomic bomb test. His terse comment drove home the potential of the weapon—for war and for peace: "Gentlemen, on the first moonlight night in August, we will drop one of these bombs on the Japanese. I don't think we will need more than two."[52] In August 1945 President Truman turned away Charles de Gaulle's requests for a Franco-American alliance with the comment that the world needed no more special relationships or secret treaties because of the discovery of the atomic bomb.[53] The new world had at last, it seemed, triumphed over the old.

NOTES

1. Witness the Washington Naval Conference in 1924 and its less successful successors in Geneva (1927) and London (1930). See Roger Dingman, *Power in the Pacific: The Origins of Naval Arms Limitations* (Chicago, 1976).

2. Adolf Berle, quoted in William L. Langer and S. Everett Gleason, *The Challenge to Isolation* (New York, 1952), 158.

3. Nomura to Tokyo, 18 November 1941, reprinted in U.S. Congress Joint Committee on the Investigation of the Pearl Harbor Attack, *Hearings*, 79th Congress, lst sess., 39 parts (Washington, 1948), 12, 148-50.

4. The legislation is titled "An Act Further to promote the defense of the United States, and for other purposes"; Public Law 11-77th Congress, 1st Session, Chapter 11 (1941).

5. "Liberal" became a dirty word in American domestic politics during the Ronald Reagan years, but "democracy" and George Bush's "new world order" meant what Franklin Roosevelt referred to when he spoke of a liberal world—freer trade, protection of property, and elective governments.

6. See Paul Schroeder, *The Axis Alliance and Japanese-American Relations, 1941* (Ithaca, N.Y., 1958) and Jonathan Utley, *Going to War with Japan, 1937-1941* (Knoxville, Tenn. 1985).

7. The long, angry debate over whether or not American leaders did know or should have known in advance about the Japanese attack is well summarized in David Kahn, "The Intelligence Failure of Pearl Harbor," *Foreign Affairs* 70 (1991), 138-52.

8. The reasons for Hitler's declaration of war remain obscured by the combination of zealotry, bravado, and cunning that characterized his thinking. He did assume that the United States would, in anger, focus its efforts on the war against Japan, permitting Germany to declare war with impunity. See *Führer Conferences on Matters Dealing with the German Navy* (tr. and mimeographed by the Office of Naval Intelligence; Washington, 1947) 1941, II, 79.

9. See Theodore A. Wilson, "In Aid of America's Interests: The Provision of Lend-Lease to the Soviet Union, 1941-1942," in *Soviet-U.S. Relations, 1933-1942,* G. N. Sevost'ianov and W. F. Kimball, eds. (Moscow, 1989), 121-39, and Warren F. Kimball, *The Juggler: Franklin Roosevelt as Wartime Statesman* (Princeton, 1991), ch. 2.

10. Memorandum of Conference, 30 May 1942, United States, Department of State, *Foreign Relations of the United States* [*FRUS*] (Washington, 1862-), 1942, III, 575-78.

11. Harry L. Hopkins papers, Sherwood Collection, Franklin D. Roosevelt Library (Hyde Park, N.Y.).

12. "Memorandum of Conference, June 1, 1942," *FRUS,* 1942, III, 578-83.

13. Although, as shown in ch. 3, Roosevelt's reasons for insisting on the North African invasion were political—partly to offset cries for taking the offensive in the Pacific, partly to reassure the Soviets in the light the delay in launching the Second Front.

14. See, for example, *FRUS, Tehran,* 256; and Warren F. Kimball, ed., *Churchill & Roosevelt: The Complete Correspondence* (3 vols.; Princeton, 1984), II, R-483/1.

15. See Warren F. Kimball, *Swords Or Ploughshares? The Morgenthau Plan for Defeated Nazi Germany* (Philadelphia, 1976).

16. See Kimball, *Churchill & Roosevelt,* I, 229-30.

17. Kimball, *The Juggler,* 3.

18. See Theodore A. Wilson, *The First Summit: Roosevelt and Churchill at Placentia Bay, 1941* (rev. ed.; Lawrence, Kans. 1991), ch. 9. See also *The Atlantic Charter,* D. Brinkley and D. Facey-Crowther, eds. (New York, 1993).

19. "Unfinished Notes" [Aug. 1941], Belle Willard Roosevelt papers, Library of Congress, Washington, D.C. (courtesy of Theodore Wilson). FDR's comment came during casual dinner conversation with various British and American dignitaries.

20. See, for example, Anthony Eden to Clark Kerr, 1 May 1942, Foreign Office (FO) 371/32880, (N2336/86/G), Public Record Office (PRO), Kew, England.

21. Diary Entries, 2, 3, 4 March 1942, J. Pierrepont Moffat papers, Houghton Library, Harvard University, Cambridge, Massachusetts.

22. It appears that Roosevelt did not foresee that, given a chance to develop, the Soviet Union's leverage would likewise be very great. See Kimball, *The Juggler,* ch. IV.

23. *FRUS, Tehran,* 487.

24. FO 800-302/7505 (PRO), 4.

25. As quoted in James MacGregor Burns, *Roosevelt: The Soldier of Freedom* (New York and London, 1970), 514.

26. See Alan P. Dobson, *Peaceful Air Warfare: The United States, Britain and the Politics of International Aviation* (Oxford, 1991); Kimball, *The Juggler,* 102-82.

27. Forrest Davis, "What Really Happened at Teheran," *Saturday Evening Post,* 116 (13 and 20 May 1944). See also Kimball, *The Juggler,* 110-11.

28. Quoted in Lloyd C. Gardner, *Architects of Illusion: Men and Ideas in American Foreign Policy, 1941-1949* (Chicago, 1970), 29.

29. *FRUS, 1943,* III, 586-89.

30. *FRUS, 1944,* IV, 951.

31. Lloyd C. Gardner, *Spheres of Influence: The Great Powers Partition Europe, from Munich to Yalta* (Chicago, 1993), is a comprehensive examination of the title subject.

32. James Byrnes, Dean Acheson, and Clark Clifford were the other of Truman's guiding lights. Harriman's apprehension is mentioned in W. Averell Harriman and Elie Abel, *Special Envoy to Churchill and Stalin, 1941-1946* (New York, 1975), 453-54.

33. Truman also cut off Lend-Lease to Britain once Japan surrendered. But the British soon obtained other aid while the USSR did not.

34. Robert Murphy, *Diplomat Among Warriors* (Garden City, N.Y., 1964), 278-79.

35. Ickes to Roosevelt, 10 August 1942 and Roosevelt to Ickes, 12 August 1942, Franklin D. Roosevelt Papers, PPF 3650. For a general treatment of Roosevelt's "colonial policy," see Warren F. Kimball and Fred E. Pollock, "'In Search of Monsters to Destroy': Roosevelt and Colonialism," in Kimball, *The Juggler*, 127-58.

36. When French military resistance collapsed in June 1940, the government signed an armistice with Hitler and relocated to the city of Vichy in central France while the Germans occupied the northern part of the country. When the Anglo-American forces invaded North Africa, the Germans dispensed with the fiction of French independence and occupied the entire country. However, the same French colonial authorities remained in power in Indochina until early in 1945 when the Japanese finally took complete control. See Stein Tønnesson, *The Vietnamese Revolution of 1945* (Oslo, 1991).

37. Robert Sherwood, *Roosevelt and Hopkins* (New York, 1950), 507.

38. Lloyd C. Gardner, *Approaching Vietnam: From World War II through Dienbienphu* (New York, 1988), 30-31.

39. Murphy, *Diplomat Among Warrior*, 192.

40. *FRUS, Casablanca Conference*, 701-4; Kimball, *The Juggler*, 70-71.

41. Lord Halifax to the Foreign Office, 28 March 1943, FO 371/35366, U 1430/G (PRO).

42. Edgar Snow, "Fragments from F.D.R.—Part II," *Monthly Review* 8 (March 1957), 396.

43. "The USSR in the Far East," 18 August 1943, Charles Bohlen papers, National Archives, Washington, D.C.

44. The story is told in several places, but see, Anthony Eden, *The Memoirs of Lord Avon: The Reckoning* (Boston, 1965), 433.

45. For Anglo-American disputes over China policy, see Christopher Thorne, *Allies of a Kind: The United States, Britain, and the War Against Japan, 1941-1945* (New York, 1978).

46. Edgar Snow, *Journey to the Beginning* (New York, 1958), 347-48.

47. The president toyed having Australia purchase certain nearby European colonies like Portuguese Timor; Roosevelt to Churchill, 21 June 1943, *Churchill & Roosevelt*, II, R-292. See also David Day, *The Reluctant Nation* (South Melbourne, Australia, 1992), 137.

48. Gardner, *Approaching Vietnam*, 50-51.

49. William Langdon to Ellis O. Briggs, 18 May 1945, Record Group 84, National Archives, Washington, D.C.

50. Diary Entry, 27 December 1942, Henry L. Stimson papers, Sterling Library, Yale University, New Haven, Conn.

51. Dan Kurzman, *Day of the Bomb: Countdown to Hiroshima* (New York, 1986), 218-19.

52. Maxwell D. Taylor, *The Uncertain Trumpet* (New York, 1959), 3.

53. Note by Henri Bonnet of conversations between de Gaulle and Truman, 22 August 1945, in Charles de Gaulle, *War Memoirs: Salvation, 1944-1946, Documents* (London, 1959), 286. Similarly see Fletcher Knebel and Charles W. Bailey II, *No High Ground* (New York, 1960), 2-3.

16

Legacies: Allies, Enemies, and Posterity

David Reynolds, et al.

The legacies of the war experience for America, Britain, and Russia are multitudinous. Some are noted in the essays on strategy, the economy, and the home front. Consideration of others would take us deep into the political histories of the three countries, such as the way in which victory reaffirmed existing institutions that had been under strain during the 1930s or the war—American democratic capitalism, Stalinist bureaucratic communism, and British parliamentary liberalism. In all three countries, in fact, the war strengthened executive power—in the United States, for instance, it is often taken as marking the origins of the modern "imperial presidency."[1] The main focus of this essay, however, is on the war's significance for diplomacy and foreign policy. This will be examined by reference to time-period, for much depends on whether we are talking about the shorter or longer term. But, in the process of this discussion, some threads from other essays will be woven in, to offer a broader tapestry of the allies at war.

For students of diplomatic history, World War Two marks the beginning of our modern age of summit diplomacy. National leaders had met before, of course. The "raft at Tilsit" that Roosevelt mentioned in a message to Churchill in 1942 referred to the meeting in 1807 between Alexander I of Russia and Napoleon Bonaparte of France which (briefly) divided Europe between them.[2] A little over a century later, the "Big Three" of World War One—Woodrow Wilson, Georges Clemenceau, and David Lloyd George—dominated the peace-making that followed the "Great War." Two particular developments, however, combined to make 1939-45 novel in international history. First, the war was truly global in its extent and ramifications, unlike its predecessor in 1914-18. Second, it was the first world war of the air age, which set it apart from the earlier "Great War" waged by the European states against France from 1792 to 1815.

The victorious Fourth Coalition against Napoleon in 1813-15 had required sustained personal contact between its principals: Alexander I left Russia with his armies in January 1813 and did not return until August 1814, while Lord Castlereagh, the British prime minister, "lived on the continent for the greater part of eighteen months after January 1814. . . ."[3] No twentieth century democratic leader could afford to be absent from his country for several months, as Wilson found to his cost in 1919 when trying to sell the League of Nations to the U.S. Senate. Air travel, however, made possible a completely new pattern of diplomatic intercourse. In 1941-45 this crystallized around the conferences between Churchill, Roosevelt, Stalin, and their aides.

The early history of that tripartite relationship was, however, neither easy nor smooth. "Munich" and British "appeasement" helped push Stalin into his ill-fated pact with Hitler. That pact, in turn, soured British and American attitudes towards the Soviet Union in 1939-41, while the contemporaneous doubts in both London and Moscow about American commitment to the war fed on the legacy of interwar U.S. isolationism. Nor did mutual suspicions abate as the war progressed. At times each leader feared that his new allies might desert him; at other times he played on the others' doubts about him. In May and June 1940, for instance, Churchill hinted to Roosevelt that, without speedy American help, Britain might have to sue for peace with Nazi Germany. The still mysterious flight by Rudolf Hess, Hitler's deputy, to Britain in May 1941 left Stalin convinced that an Anglo-German deal against him was in the offing. He told his ambassador in London three months later that "the English Government helps the Hitlerites by its passive, temporizing policies. . . . Do the English understand this? I think they do understand. What do they want? They want, it appears to me, our weakening."[4] In mid-1942 the Americans toyed with the same card. Desperately pressing for a Second Front in France that year, General George C. Marshall, the U.S. army chief of staff, combined with his naval colleagues to threaten wholesale diversion of American resources to the war against Japan if their European strategy was rebuffed.[5]

For the Soviets, the delay in the Second Front until 1944 was the greatest reason for distrust of their Anglo-American allies, though it was reinforced in the summer of 1942 by suspension of the hazardous Arctic supply convoys. Stalin's telegrams reek of his suspicious resentment at such "improper . . . puzzling and inexplicable" actions.[6] Churchill and

Roosevelt, for their part, constantly feared that Stalin would conclude another pact with Hitler. Russo-German contacts in Stockholm after Stalingrad, although always rejected by Hitler, aroused considerable alarm in London and Washington as the details seeped out.[7] As for the post-war world, the State Department viewed with distaste anything that smacked of an overt Anglo-Russian agreement on "spheres of influence," such as the negotiations over the Baltic states in 1941-42 and the notorious "percentages" agreement of October 1944. Similarly, in the second half of the war Churchill was acutely suspicious of Russo-American deals struck over his head and at the expense of the British Empire.

Thus, this ménage à trois was no happy family. In fact, as Theodore A. Wilson has pointed out in chapter four, it was scarcely a full alliance until the last year of fighting. Britain struggled on alone for a year after France fell until June 1941 and only in December 1941 did the United States fully and formally enter the war. Only from June 1944 did America and Britain join the Soviet Union as an equal partner in the war against Hitler's Fortress Europe. And only in the summer of 1945 was the Soviet Union ready to join in America's "real war" against Japan. That roughly symmetrical alliance, involving concerted planning and operations, was short-lived.

In foreign policy, however, the three leaders sought mutual understandings from an early stage, and here the new instrument of air-age diplomacy played a crucial, though by no means unequivocally beneficial, role. There were two encounters between the "Big Three"—Tehran at the end of November 1943 and Yalta, in the Crimea in early February 1945. In addition, Churchill, Stalin and Roosevelt's successor, Harry S. Truman, met at Potsdam in July 1945. Churchill and Roosevelt met seven times as a twosome between August 1941 and February 1945, as well as conferences at Cairo before and after Tehran and at Malta prior to Yalta. Churchill visited Stalin twice in Moscow, in August 1942 and October 1944, but Roosevelt, to his chagrin, was never able to confer with the Soviet leader *à deux*. Of the three Churchill was the most peripatetic, constituting, to quote historian Robin Edmonds, "the pivot of the Big Three's relationship" in 1941-42 as he shuttled between the other two. Stalin (the ex-seminarian) joked in 1944 that if the Big Three were the Holy Trinity then "Churchill must be the Holy Ghost. He flies around so much."[8] Roosevelt, of course, was physically handicapped by the crippling legacy of polio, and Stalin, for his part, was initially preoccupied by the life-or-death struggle on the Soviet western front, though he also had a morbid fear of airplanes and of travel abroad, outside secret police chief Lavrenti

Beria's security net. His journey to Tehran in November 1943 was his first trip outside the USSR after the Revolution.[9] Connecting these visits was a steady correspondence: 1,161 messages from Churchill to Roosevelt and 788 in reply; 504 communications exchanged between Churchill and Stalin and 290 between Roosevelt and Stalin.[10] Linking visits and messages between the Big Three was the spider's web of journeys by trusted lieutenants, such as Harry Hopkins and Averell Harriman from the American side, Max Beaverbrook and Anthony Eden for Churchill, and Foreign Minister Vyacheslav Molotov on behalf of Stalin. In particular, the conference of Foreign Ministers at Moscow in October 1943 not merely cleared the way for Tehran but also made basic decisions about the future of Europe.

On the personal level, the Roosevelt-Churchill relationship was much the closest, but it had its own distinct morphology. It was very much a product of war time. Before the war, the two had only been briefly introduced, in 1918, and Churchill, in particular, had a somewhat chequered reputation in Washington for instability and insobriety. But necessity brought them together and in the global crisis of 1941-42 they forged a genuinely personal bond. After Churchill's lengthy visit to the White House over Christmas and New Year 1941-42, Roosevelt bade him farewell with the pledge: "Trust me to the bitter end."[11] For FDR, however, unlike Churchill, the relationship was never an exclusive affair. By 1943 the president's personal fascination with Churchill, so evident in 1941, had abated, while the Soviet victories at Stalingrad and Kursk intensified his desire for a direct encounter with Stalin, now emerging as *the* force to be reckoned with in the post-war order. On the face of it, Roosevelt simply wanted to do what Churchill had already done—meet Stalin alone—but he also wished to disabuse Stalin of fears of an Anglo-American axis and to undermine Churchill's bid to make Britain the intermediary between the emerging Big Two. Such was Churchill's sensitivity on the matter that the president "flatly lied" to the prime minister in June 1943 by claiming that the idea of a Roosevelt-Stalin meeting emanated from "Uncle Joe."[12]

Tehran confirmed some of Churchill's fears of becoming the short side of the new international triangle, and thereafter the Russo-American connection became ever more important, despite his continued visits to Washington and Moscow. Roosevelt's journeys to Persia and the Crimea, at considerable physical cost, show, literally, just how far he would go to reach a meeting of minds with the Soviet leader. The intensity of the Anglo-American relationship, particularly in planning the invasions of

Europe in 1944, and the difficulties of working with Stalin, particularly as post-war issues overtook military concerns, combined to ensure that FDR's contacts with Churchill would be maintained. Nevertheless, in the last months of the war, feelings were cooler on the president's side. Moreover, as his health declined, many of his messages after Yalta were largely the work of his aides, whereas for Churchill it remained a truly personal correspondence.

Stalin, for his part, seemed anxious in 1943-45 to achieve his ends within the framework of Great Power co-operation. Tehran and Yalta saw direct speaking but also warm tributes that were not merely hyperbole. For Stalin, the credibility of the relationship depended above all on America and Britain honouring the commitment to a Second Front. When it became clear in the autumn of 1943 that they were in earnest, his mood changed dramatically. Veteran Foreign Office Russianists, for instance, considered the after-dinner badinage at the end of the Moscow Foreign Ministers' conference to be "really remarkable," with Stalin teasing Molotov in front of his guests and proposing toasts to the American, British, and Soviet forces meeting in Berlin.[13] At Tehran Stalin toasted the British Conservative party and Churchill drank to "the Proletarian masses." What Stalin really made of his Western counterparts is hard to assess. His famous quip that, although both needed watching, Roosevelt would take nothing less than ruble out of your pocket whereas Churchill would snatch even a kopek, suggests greater respect for the president. Certainly it was Roosevelt's objective, in all their meetings, to convince Stalin of his friendliness and good faith. Yet Stalin's observation that "we like a downright enemy to a pretending friend" suggests that he knew where he was with Churchill and that FDR's bonhomie did not alter basic ideological realities.[14] All the same, the transition from the emollient Roosevelt to the abrasive Truman did nothing to ease Soviet suspicions. The latter's handling of the end of Lend-Lease and of the news of the bomb caused enduring bitterness in Moscow.

If this was the pattern of Big Three diplomacy, what were its achievements? One legacy was a series of political statements of lasting significance. When Roosevelt and Churchill had their first war-time meeting at Placentia Bay, off Newfoundland, in August 1941, its main result was a declaration of common aims that was quickly dubbed "the Atlantic Charter." This included Article 2, which ruled out "territorial changes that do not accord with the freely expressed wishes of the peoples concerned" and article three which spoke of "the right of all peoples to choose the form of government under which they will live." The reference in Article 8 to "a wider and more permanent system of general security" was a first intimation of the United Nations Organization.[15] British and Soviet adherence to the charter was somewhat grudging. Churchill viewed the charter as a poor substitute for a U.S. declaration of war, while in London Soviet Ambassador Maisky observed that it sounded "as if England and the USA fancied themselves as Almighty God, with a mission to judge the remainder of the sinful world, including my own country."[16] Both Britain and the USSR sought to qualify its provisions where their own commercial and territorial interests might be affected. But in the long run it was the principles and not the qualifications that were remembered. For instance, the Declaration on Liberated Europe, signed by the Big Three at Yalta in 1945, specifically referred to the Atlantic Charter and developed its provisions with regard to free elections in the countries of the former Nazi Reich. The Charter became a moral benchmark for the post-war settlement, both in Europe and the colonies.[17]

The war-time conferences also stimulated the creation of international institutions that are still with us today. In January 1942, while Churchill was visiting Washington, the Declaration of the United Nations was signed by the United States, Great Britain, the Soviet Union, and 23 other countries. In subsequent years the three leaders spent a good deal of their time thrashing out the details of the new institutions, as chapter 14 in particular reminds us. Despite haggling over use of the veto and the number of seats, however, they emerged in 1945 with a working organization of 51 countries and with themselves as three of the five permanent members of the Security Council. Also significant for the future were the International Monetary Fund (IMF) and the International Bank for Reconstruction and Development (World Bank), born at Bretton Woods, New Hampshire, in July 1944. Again America and Britain were the principal architects, but the USSR was also a founding member. At the end of the conference the principal Soviet delegate, M. S. Stepanov, presciently declared:

> The stabilization of the currencies of the various countries, the expansion of world trade, the balancing of international payments, long-term capital investments intended for the reconstruction and development of the democratic nations and especially for the restoration of economy [sic] of those countries who suffered severely from enemy occupation and hostilities—all these aspirations will have exceptional importance for the postwar organization of the World and for the maintenance and strengthening of peace and security.18

Statements such as the Atlantic Charter and the Declaration on Liberated Europe, institutions like the UN and the IMF—these were lasting legacies of war-time diplomacy. But they were also flawed legacies—statements that were honoured in the breach not the observance, institutions that became arenas for conflict not instruments of reconciliation. In the end, the Soviets did not ratify the Bretton Woods agreement or join the IMF and the World Bank. Even more seriously, divergent interpretations of the Declaration on Liberated Europe lay at the heart of the Cold War in 1945, while Soviet-American rivalry soon reduced the UN Security Council to deadlock. Any attempt to address the diplomatic legacies of the war-time alliance must acknowledge both its achievements and its failings—victory in World War and disintegration into Cold War. These are the themes of the next two sections of this essay. Only after considering them can we move finally to the legacy of the alliance for our own day.

The fundamental point about the war-time coalition between America, Britain, and the Soviet Union is its victory. Had the Axis won and the Allies lost, the second half of the twentieth century—as it was, no edifying spectacle—would have been very different and, surely, much, much worse. The ideologies of war-time Germany and Japan offered little but death and destruction. For Hitler, conflict was the natural state of things, peace a temporary aberration: "One being drinks the blood of another. By dying, the one furnishes food for the other. We should not blather about humanity."[19] His "New Order" based on Aryan supremacy meant the loss of countless lives, especially the extermination of most of European Jewry and millions of Slavs. In Asia, Japan's victories permanently eroded the mystique of the white peoples and accelerated the growth of nationalist movements. But Tokyo's own propaganda about an Asian "New Order" on the principle of *Hakko Ichiu*—"all nations in one family, each enjoying its own proper place within it"—was soon exposed as a sham. Japan's brutal exploitation of the "liberated" peoples led much of Southeast Asia to regard its talk of "waging a sacred war on behalf of all Asians as a cynical deception."[20]

Not that the Allies were above reproach. As this volume has shown, each waged war to a large extent for its own interests. Stalin's conduct in Eastern Europe was brutal; the British often treated their imperial subjects with cynical indifference; while America's use of the atomic bomb on Japan, an act motivated in part by racial hatred, will always be a matter of moral controversy. Nevertheless, the Allies were fighting for more than victory. Documents such as the Atlantic Charter and the UN Declaration, even when hedged by reservations, were offering something to replace not only the Axis "New Order" but also the old order that had preceded it.

Yet the Allied victory was by no means a foregone conclusion. In the 1930s the Axis appeared to be the dynamic global force. "International fascism" was seen as a unified and powerful entity, characterized by right-wing militarism, contempt for parliamentary democracy, and virulent hatred of communism. The Anti-Comintern Pact between Germany and Japan in November 1936 was strengthened by the adherence of Italy a year later. May 1939 saw the "Pact of Steel" between Hitler and Mussolini and September 1940 the Tripartite Pact between the three powers, aimed particularly at deterring the United States. In December 1941 they signed a no-separate-peace agreement, days before the Japanese attack on Pearl Harbor.

During these years, by contrast, their opponents circled uneasily around each other. Relations between America and Britain remained wary, well into 1941, while the latter half of that year saw only the beginnings of suspicious contact with Stalin. Ideologically, the Axis seemed far more united than their enemies, and no one knew for sure what secret military agreements lay behind the rhetoric. Germany and Japan were certainly better prepared for war by the late 1930s than tentative Britain, disarmed America, or the purged Red Army. Germany's drive east in mid-1941 and Japan's dramatic victories that winter left the Axis apparently poised for a new division of the world.

These devastating reverses, however, shocked the Americans, British, and Russians into working more closely together. "The living closed the eyes of the dead. The dead opened the eyes of the living."[21] It is instructive to compare briefly the co-operation between the Allies in 1941-45, documented in earlier chapters, with the increasing isolation of the three Axis powers. In signals intelligence, for instance, the Allies improved rapidly after 1941. The growing penetration by the British and Americans of Axis codes, through the ENIGMA and MAGIC decrypts, gave them increasingly assured knowledge of enemy dispositions—what Churchill called his "golden eggs." By 1943 the British, for instance, were reading some 3,000 German signals a day, while "to Germany, Italy, and Japan the Allied ciphers were by then virtually invulnerable." Equally important was the fact that "the geese who laid the golden eggs . . . never cackled."[22] In contrast with the appalling British and American security lapses of the late 1930s, the breaking of the German and Japanese codes remained a well-kept secret. Despite Italian warnings, Berlin and Tokyo were not shaken "in their conviction that their own systems remained impregnable."[23] As in most areas, British and American collaboration remained the most extensive, but the Soviets were provided with much information gleaned from ENIGMA material, especially when the German onslaught was at its fiercest in 1941-42, though this sometimes duplicated material from Moscow's own "Lucy Ring" in Switzerland. In 1944 the three intelligence services cooperated fully in a tripartite campaign of deception, code-named BODYGUARD, to help mislead the Germans as to the time and place of the D-Day landings.[24]

The economic links between America, Britain, and the USSR also proved much more substantial and important than those between their adversaries. During 1941-45 America and Britain each diverted to the other about 4.75 per cent of its national income. Although this suggests a rough equivalence of mutual aid, American support was particularly important for the British economy, with U.S. credit covering about 54 per cent of the country's payments deficit over the whole course of the war.[25] As for Anglo-American aid to Russia, it proved too small and too slow in 1941-42 to play much material part in halting the Nazi tide, but it became valuable after Stalingrad. In 1943 and 1944, according to recent recalculations, that aid amounted to nearly one-fifth of Soviet net national product and it particularly enhanced the mobility of the advancing Red Army through the supply of trucks, jeeps, and armoured vehicles.[26]

Against this, the Axis had nothing to compare. Japan's basic economic ties before 1939 were with America and Britain, and the various Axis pacts did not produce any marked change. The British blockade of Germany cut off most maritime German-Japanese trade in 1939-40 and then BARBAROSSA severed the overland route via Russia which had existed during the era of the Nazi-Soviet Pact.[27] If Japan was of negligible economic value to Germany, Italy was a positive liability. Because it was so deficient in key raw materials, many German planners in 1939-40 actually desired Italy's continued neutrality. In the event Hitler's vast territorial conquests in 1940 made it easier to sustain Mussolini's belligerency in the short term but from 1942 the Italian economy disintegrated, despite German aid. By 1945, Italy's GDP, at less than 60 per cent of 1938 values, had reverted to levels characteristic of the era before World War One.[28] Allied economic co-operation may have been limited and unequal, but in comparison with that of the Axis it was both genuinely impressive and also an important contribution to eventual victory.

The Grand Alliance also manifested a level of human contact not apparent among the Axis. Hitler and Mussolini, geographical neighbours, did meet frequently and the Nazi leader seems to have felt a loyalty to Mussolini for his early support, sustaining him, at cost, when the Italian war effort fell apart. But Hitler never met the Japanese leadership—indeed he kept Japan at arms length until 1943. Nor did the Axis stage anything to match the great Allied war-time conferences whose centrepieces were Tehran, Yalta, and Potsdam. These symbolized for all the world to see an Allied unity that the Axis never matched. Not only did the leaders confer and correspond, there was also extensive interaction among the military staffs and civilian officials, particularly on the Anglo-American side. Many of these ties were of great importance in the post-war world, as demonstrated by the careers of George Marshall, Dwight Eisenhower, Dean Acheson, Anthony Eden, Harold Macmillan, or Hastings Ismay (Churchill's military secretary who became the first Secretary-General of NATO). On the Soviet side the experience of the West gained during the war by Vyacheslav Molotov, Andrei Gromyko, and others was invaluable for their practice of post-war diplomacy. On a popular level, the presence of American troops in Britain, peaking at some 1.7 million prior to D-Day, gave depth to the relationship, while enthusiasm and sympathy for the Soviet people and their heroic efforts became a feature of British and American public opinion from 1941. Nothing on the Axis side resembled this.

The personal relationships were made possible by and, in turn, facilitated an underlying strategic consensus, or at least compromise. On the face of it, the Axis also had a combined strategy. Their answer to the Roosevelt-Churchill conference in Washington in late December 1941 and British foreign secretary Anthony Eden's concurrent visit to Stalin in Moscow was a German-Italian-Japanese military convention signed in Berlin on 18 January 1942. This divided the world between them, at longitude 70 degrees east (running roughly through Omsk, Kabul, and Bombay) with Germany and Italy operating west of there round to the Atlantic coast of the America, while to the east, Japan dealt with Southeast Asia and the Pacific. The convention provided for assistance from the Japanese if the British and Americans concentrated their fleets in the Atlantic and for comparable German-Italian support for Japan should the Allies converge on the Pacific.[29] The three Axis powers also committed themselves to combined trade and economic warfare. Despite the high-flown rhetoric, however, nothing came of these promises of co-operation. Hitler chose to bail out Mussolini, but, crucially, there was no strategic convergence between Germany and Japan. Tokyo had about two weeks' intimation of BARBAROSSA; German Foreign Minister Ribbentrop learned of Pearl Harbor from a British radio broadcast.[30]

On 2 July 1941, in a fateful decision, the Imperial Conference in Tokyo decided not to join Germany against the USSR but to take the opportunity to push south, at risk of war with America and Britain.[31] Thereafter Japan did its best to keep the Soviet Union neutral while Stalin, fighting for his life in the west, had no desire to add to his list of enemies while

Germany remained a threat. In the winter of 1941 the German and Japanese navies talked of combined operations against the British Empire, converging on its exposed position in the Middle East from the Mediterranean and Indian Ocean respectively, but these were minority opinions, running against the grain of grand strategy in Berlin and Tokyo. Hitler's preoccupation from 1941 was Russia in Europe; for Tojo and his colleagues the enemy became the United States in the Pacific. Admittedly, the three Allies retained their own divergent strategic priorities—Germany in the case of Russia, and Japan (at the emotional level) for Americans, while Churchill always kept one beady eye on the Mediterranean. But the Big Three did make common cause, and, in the last year of the war, they had a common strategy. On the other side, Hitler and Tojo simply fought separate wars, while after 1941 Italy was not an ally but a weak appendage of Nazi Germany.

Reinforcing these differing geopolitical interests was a fundamental ideological rift. Despite their common international image as the "dictatorships" or "totalitarians," Germany and Japan were divided by racism far more virulent than anything on the Allied side. Hitler's obsession with Russia was racially motivated: He wanted to destroy what he saw as the Slavic *Untermenschen* and their Jew-ridden, Bolshevik leadership. He flatly rejected Japanese offers of mediation.[32] Moreover, Hitler (unlike Foreign Minister Ribbentrop) wanted no involvement by the "yellow Japanese" in the Aryan race's epic struggle. Apart from one heady moment in July 1941, it was not until after defeat at Stalingrad, in January 1943, that the German leader personally called on Japan to enter the war against the Soviet Union. By then, with Japan also pushed back on to the defensive, his words fell on deaf ears. Hitler's world view had its counterpart in Tokyo. Despite the alliance with Germany, Japanese propaganda frequently presented the war in racial and cultural terms. The Japanese were portrayed as the world's leading race (*shido minzoku*) who were purifying Asia of corrupt Western influences. A typical magazine cartoon in July 1942 depicted Japan as a huge roller-type blotter removing the dirty splodges of Western presence from the map.[33] Such propaganda, feeding on entrenched Japanese concepts of uniqueness and purity, left little room for a European ally in the reordering of Asia.

Ideological differences undoubtedly also complicated inter-Allied relations. Neither the Anglo-American arguments over imperialism nor the mutual suspicion between capitalists and communists can be glossed over. Yet the Allies overcame them. Roosevelt's gratuitous advice about the handling of India and his threats of imperial trusteeships were never allowed to imperil his relationship with Churchill. For his part, Stalin did not permit Marxism-Leninism to impede pragmatic co-operation.

Of course, the ultimate success of the war-time alliance owed much quite simply to superior economic strength. In 1943 the Allies accounted for at least twice the manufacturing output of the Axis and three times its national income. Their armaments production was triple that of their enemies while the balance of aircraft output that year was 151,000 for the Allies and 43,000 for the Axis. By 1944 the USSR alone was producing 60 per cent more tanks than the Germans.[34] But raw economic potential by itself is a *necessary* yet not a *sufficient* condition of victory. Potential has to be realized and effectively applied. In the spring of 1942 the Axis controlled 13 per cent of the world's land area, 35 per cent of its population, and about one-third of its mineral resources.[35] That was a formidable position, yet it was squandered—to a significant extent because the Axis never concerted their enhanced resources. Anglo-American naval supremacy played an important role in foiling this, but the Axis also failed themselves. Their limited intelligence co-operation, the lack of economic links and sustained personal contacts, the underlying differences of strategic priorities and ideological aspirations—all these prevented the Axis from becoming a true alliance. By contrast, America, Britain, and the Soviet Union made a better job of concerting their separate war-making power. A far from perfect job, admittedly, as this book has amply shown. But good enough in a world in which all is relative and imperfect. If victory goes to the big battalions, it is also won by those who make the least mistakes.

The sweet taste of victory soon turned sour, however: World War was followed by Cold War. In fact, the one grew out of the other. To say that is not to ignore deep, underlying tensions—especially the basic rift between capitalism and communism and the long-standing expectation that America and Russia were the coming world powers. Nor is it to deny that in many ways the Cold War stemmed from the imposition of the Stalinist system on Eastern Europe, and that it ended when that system collapsed, both in Eastern Europe and in the USSR. Nevertheless, just as it takes two sides to make a hot war, so it takes two to make a cold war. The origins and the extent of bipolar animosity after 1945 owe much to the flaws in the war-time coalition.

That coalition was a remarkable attempt to concert policies, but it failed to reach diplomatic agreement on key issues. Stalin, Roosevelt, and Churchill differed fatefully, for instance, in their interpretations of the Yalta agreements about Poland. That became clear within weeks of the agreements being signed. More fundamental still, they were not of one mind on the treatment of Germany. The issues of reparations, dismemberment, and a post-Nazi administration remained unresolved in May 1945, and the German question lay at the heart of the emerging Cold War. In large measure these arguments reflected a basic difference of interest between the three Allies. The Soviet Union had lost 27-28 million dead in the war against Hitler—over 14 per cent of the 1939 population—compared with 350,000 British dead (0.75 per cent) and 300,000 Americans (0.25 per cent).[36] The casualties in the besieged city of Leningrad alone exceeded those in the United States, Great Britain, and the British Empire put together. Security against Germany was literally a life or death issue for the USSR in a way not true for America or even Britain.

Divergent interests notwithstanding, it must be acknowledged that the Allies failed to take diplomacy with sufficient seriousness. It is striking how little attention the Big Three devoted at Tehran and Yalta to a careful discussion of the cardinal issue, the future of Germany. "Decisions" were often made on the basis of brief exchanges or, as with the short-lived Morgenthau Plan, in unconsidered response to inventive ideas. For all three powers, albeit in different ways, security lay less in diplomacy than in territory. Stalin's case is the most obvious. Throughout the war he had sought a buffer zone in much of Eastern Europe as security against a resurgent Germany. In 1941-45 this policy was advanced in tandem with his attempts to secure an overall Great Power consensus, but as relations deteriorated in 1945-46 it assumed priority over diplomatic collaboration. In retrospect, his famous speech in the Bolshoi Theatre on 9 February 1946, which achieved such notoriety in the United States, may perhaps be seen as marking the public shift from the still-official Communist party policy of "security in cooperation" to a stance of "security in one country."[37] Yet Stalin was only the most aggressive practitioner of security through territory. For Churchill, as chapter 13 shows, the security of Britain was inextricably linked to the perpetuation of the British Empire. Although the war accelerated the decline of the formal empire, it did not destroy it, and the informal empire of commerce and finance was strengthened in the short term by the war. In different ways, British imperialism was anathema to both the Americans and the Russians. Molotov observed, for instance, in September 1945, that the British were left "holding a monopoly in the Mediterranean." Could they not "at least find a corner" for the Russians?—who, after all, had a more proximate interest in access through that sea than the British.[38] Even the Americans, despite public aspersions on spheres of influence in Europe, had contrived an informal sphere of their own for decades in the Caribbean and South

America. When Roosevelt advocated international trusteeships, he ran into fierce opposition in 1944-45 as the Joint Chiefs of Staff urged unequivocal American political control of Japanese islands in the mid-Pacific for post-war naval and air bases.[39]

The policy of security through territory was itself the manifestation of a propensity among all three Allies to neglect the rights of smaller nations. Managing a global war effort was a heady experience. A select triumvirate was both more agreeable and more manageable than an international zoo. Churchill resented Roosevelt's efforts to include China; the president, for his part, was reluctant to accept France at the top table. More generally, the policy of security through territory implied that small states were the pawns of the great powers. That, self-evidently, was the philosophy of empire. It was widely assumed in war-time London that certain small colonies, such as Aden, Gibraltar, or British Honduras, would never be capable of independence.[40] The United States, less overtly, had similar inclinations—as small neighbours such as Cuba have repeatedly discovered—and Roosevelt himself frequently spoke of the great powers as "tutors" of the colonies, educating them into full independence. As for Stalin, he officially dissolved the Comintern in May 1943, but its role in managing communist parties abroad in the interests of Moscow was partly assumed by the International Information Department of the Central Committee.[41] In short, each of the triumvirate looked down on the rest. At Yalta Churchill urged Stalin to allow lesser states their freedom: "The eagle should permit the small birds to sing and care not wherefor they sang."[42] But he, no less than Roosevelt and Stalin, always assumed that the small birds would flutter and sing within a cage designed by the Big Three.

This brings us to the most basic flaw in the alliance. The neglect of diplomacy, the assertion of security through territory, the undervaluing of small powers—all these testify to the exaggerated reliance of all the Big Three on military power. The British Empire rested, ultimately, on force or at least the threat of force. That was why the fall of Singapore in 1942 and, later, the Suez fiasco of 1956 were such damaging blows to the credibility of British imperialism. Even more overtly, Stalinist rule in Eastern Europe rested on the ultimate authority of the Red Army: 1956 in Hungary or 1968 in Czechoslovakia were reminders of that. When the threat of military intervention was removed, in 1989, reform was free to swell into revolution. Most of all, U.S. policy after 1945 aimed at a "preponderance of power,"[43] resting on America's economic strength, expressed in a "national security state," and culminating in the Vietnam

War. Experience of victory in war left a generation of American leaders with a conviction of their own power and rightness, with what British historian Denis Brogan called in 1952 "the illusion of omnipotence."[44]

At the heart of each state's power was nuclear weaponry. Post-war America, as the world's first nuclear power, rejected international atomic co-operation. The British, as war-time junior partners in the Manhattan Project, were excluded from further co-operation in 1946, and proceeded to build and test their own bomb in 1952. The Soviets were always officially kept outside the circle, even during the war. Suspicions about what this portended, particularly since the Kremlin had extensive intelligence about the U.S. atomic bomb from 1942 onwards, intensified Stalin's determination to develop the USSR's own atomic program, with comparable lack of sharing with the West. The first Soviet test occurred in 1949. For each of the Big Three, then, its own manufacture and possession of the world's most appalling weapon became essential as an instrument of power and a symbol of status.

That the United States, the Soviet Union, and Great Britain placed great emphasis on military power was perhaps understandable. They had just come through a major war in which their armed forces had proved decisive where those of small states had dismally failed. And their moral rightness seemed confirmed by victory over brutal, racist ideologies. However, their war-time predominance was to prove somewhat artificial—as each would discover, with varying degrees of anguish.

The erosion of empires was the most striking transformation, especially for Britain and Russia. It is a matter of debate how far the United States actively undermined the British Empire or, more probably, contributed to a decline that had deeper, internal and international, roots.[45] But the Atlantic Charter of 1941 served as a criterion against which all imperialism would be judged. That acid began to eat away at the status of Britain's empire almost immediately, prompting questions about India and the West Indies. Apart from South Asia in 1947, rapid decolonization did not occur until the 1960s, after the French pull-out from most of Africa, but then it became an avalanche. Twenty-seven British colonies gained independence between 1960 and 1968.[46]

The demise of Russian imperialism took longer but its end was more dramatic. The Romanov empire, built up over three centuries, was taken over by the Bolsheviks and survived, in truncated form, the bloody civil war of 1918-21. Under the repressive rule of Stalin and his successors ethnic differences and rivalry between the republics were held in check, and Soviet influence was extended over much of Eastern Europe. But in the more open Gorbachev era the empire finally fell apart, first in Eastern Europe in 1989 and then in the Soviet Union itself two years later. Its demise marked the end of the last great European empire and the dénouement of the debate set in motion by Woodrow Wilson three-quarters of a century before.

Of the Big Three, in fact, it was America whose foreign policy was at first the most successful in the post-war period. Its informal empire of investment, trade, and military bases, backed by an economy that generated half the world's manufactured goods in 1945, provided a framework of political and economic order for much of the developed world. Recovery was assisted by major aid programs, notably the Marshall Plan for Europe. The Wilsonian aims of a more open world economy were gradually realized in the 1950s. This created the setting for Germany and Japan to revive and to gain the commercial position denied them between the wars by colonial and protectionist blocs. Moreover, they were able to flourish under an American security arch that assumed most of the weight of their defence. The extension of America's informal empire to the "Third World" was less clearly beneficial. The United States tried to keep its distance from the colonial powers, as the Suez crisis of 1956 demonstrated, but in practice anti-colonialism usually took second place to anti-communism. Nationalism was a threat to stability; instability benefited the extension of Soviet influence; hence nationalism was a threat to U.S. interests. This syllogism became familiar, from Guatemala to the Lebanon, from Indochina to Chile: "because of the possible coincidence of Soviet and 'radical' objectives, the United States was led to a defense of the conservative status quo."[47] In an irony of history, albeit self-inflicted, America, the great scourge of empires, became stigmatized by the 1970s as the world's leading imperialist power.

The end of empire was itself the result of self-assertion by small states and embryonic nations. The international oligarchy of World War Two—America, Britain, and Russia as "world policemen"—was soon shown to be artificial. Whatever Roosevelt might have hoped, China would not be America's proxy; while France, especially under de Gaulle, took particular delight in frustrating Britain and America. The end of empire also meant a rapid increase in the membership of the United Nations. At its foundation in 1945 the UN had 51 members, of which 15 were European and 20 from Latin America. By 1970 there were 127 members, 42 of them African and 30 Asian. The result was a General Assembly less susceptible to management by the United States. In 1945 about 40 member states could be considered to be U.S. allies or clients; a quarter-century later most were hostile to America or its ally, Israel.[48] The disenchantment of American administrations with the UN in the 1970s and 1980s owed much to the fact that it was no longer an instrument of decisive U.S. influence. By the 1990s, in fact, with the end of the Cold War and the collapse of the USSR, the assembly was the tool of none of the great powers. Of its 175 members (in March 1992), some two-thirds were developing states who questioned the international dominance of those variously described as "the West" or "the North."

For America, Britain, and Russia the last half-century has demonstrated the limits of the military power they wielded with such success in 1941-45. By 1952 all three possessed nuclear weapons; all three envisaged those weapons as the heart of a defence policy aimed at keeping the peace by deterring attack. Whatever the utility of nuclear weapons in preventing war between the superpowers, the concomitant arms race proved ultimately detrimental to the basic aim of maintaining national power. The British were the first to bow out, unable by 1960 to maintain a nuclear deterrent except with American assistance. The Soviets kept in the nuclear "game" only through a command economy that diverted perhaps 15 or 20 per cent of GDP to the military-industrial sector, at fatal cost to technological advance, consumer production, and environmental health. The judgments of Mikhail Gorbachev and Boris Yeltsin that this burden was economically and political unsustainable began a process of reform that finally undermined the whole Stalinist system.

Again, the United States has proved ostensibly the most successful—its "preponderance of power" seemed even more impressive with the collapse of the USSR. But the limits of that power were apparent in the disaster of Vietnam. By 1967 the Johnson administration had dropped a larger tonnage of bombs on that country than the United States had used in all theatres in World War Two; the tonnage dropped on Indochina during the Nixon era exceeded that of the Johnson years.[49] The spectacular pyrotechnics of operation DESERT STORM in 1991 to some extent dispelled the "Vietnam syndrome," but American military might nevertheless rested on shaky foundations by the early 1990s. The economic growth of Germany, Japan, and Pacific Rim countries undercut America's relative economic strength and the vast Reagan defence build-up of the 1980s—which made possible DESERT STORM—was financed on global credit through a vast budget deficit that neither president nor Congress appeared able or even inclined to control.

In the 1990s we live in a world that Churchill, Roosevelt, and Stalin would each have found difficult to imagine. A world in which empires have collapsed and new states have proliferated, a world in which the Soviet Union has crumbled and Marxism-Leninism is discredited, a world in which nuclear weapons and arms races have stimulated new philosophies of war and peace. It is not necessarily a much safer world. The end of the Cold War thawed out historic national enmities and warmed up endemic regional conflicts. It exposed the true scope and gravity of other problems such as nuclear proliferation, environmental pollution, and economic dependence. But it also offered a chance for the Big Three's more positive legacies to take effect, having been frozen in the era of Cold War. Above all, it made diplomacy possible again.

That was what the Big Three tried, however haltingly and imperfectly, to do in 1941-45. Unlike the Axis, who fought in isolation, they sought to concert not merely their war-time strategies but also their post-war aims. To do so they created institutions, notably the United Nations and the IMF, which, frozen or marginalized in the Cold War, assumed greater utility in its aftermath. A simple indication of the changed role of the United Nations is the number of its peace-keeping missions—only possible when some degree of international consensus is forthcoming. Eleven operations were established between January 1988 and March 1992, ranging from Cambodia to Yugoslavia, and including, most notably Iraq and Kuwait in 1991. This compares with only 13 in the previous 40 years of the UN's history.[50] Thinking back to Franklin Roosevelt's "world policemen," we must acknowledge that the policemen have changed and that those to be policed are very different. But in the 1990s the institutions of international policing that he and his colleagues created at last had some chance to come into their own.

What, then, are the diplomatic legacies of the Big Three and their war-time coalition? As we have seen, much depends on the time-period in question.

Most of all, they succeeded in defeating states and ideologies that, if successful, would, in Churchill's words, have plunged the whole world "into the abyss of a new Dark Age, made more sinister, and perhaps more protracted, by the lights of perverted science."[51] To do so, they gradually developed a coalition that was not only more powerful but also more co-ordinated than their opponents. That co-ordination was centred on the efforts of all three heads of government to reach a meeting of minds, aided by the novel instrument of air-age shuttle diplomacy.

In the medium-term, however, the legacy was flawed and tragic. Among the costs of victory was the shoring up of the Stalinist system in the USSR and its extension to Eastern Europe. This was a central issue in the Cold War, but that confrontation, to some extent, grew out of the failings of the wartime alliance itself—inadequate diplomacy, security through territory not co-operation, neglect of the rights of small powers, an exaggerated emphasis on military power.

The baleful consequences of the Cold War took nearly a half-century to play themselves out. The end of the Cold War era and the collapse of communism in Russia in one sense marked the triumph of Woodrow Wilson's vision of a world made "safe for democracy." But, to end the analysis there would encourage an excessive note of American triumphalism. For American power, on the scale of the Cold War era, was also on the wane. The radical and unprecedented arms control agreements concluded between both superpowers from 1988 onwards, notably the START treaty ratified in 1992, were not only significant steps towards a safer world but also reflected a very different concept of security from the philosophy of preponderance developed during the Cold War. Moreover, democracy, 1990s-style, was different from and more complex than what Wilson had envisaged in 1917. As Vietnam had shown, America's attempts to impose its own blueprint for "democracy" could lead to oppression and tragedy. More apt was John F. Kennedy's call in June 1963, a few months before his death, for a "world safe for diversity."[52] Kennedy was, of course, an apostle of American democracy, but his gloss on Wilsonianism was appropriate for a diverse international community. And diplomacy is the mediator of diversity.

The last word on this should, however, be reserved for our three great protagonists. On 30 November 1943 Churchill, Roosevelt, and Stalin dined together at Tehran to celebrate the prime minister's 69th birthday. At the end Roosevelt took up the theme of co-operation between countries of differing political complexions:

> I like to think of this in terms of the rainbow. In our country the rainbow is a symbol of good fortune and of hope. It has many varying colors, each individualistic, but blending into one glorious whole.
>
> Thus with our nations. We have differing customs and philosophies and ways of life. Each of us works out our own scheme of things according to the desires and ideas of our own peoples.
>
> But we have proved here at Tehran that the varying ideals of our nations can come together in a harmonious whole, moving unitedly for the common good of ourselves and of the world.
>
> So, as we leave this historic gathering, we can see in the sky, for the first time, that traditional symbol of hope, the rainbow.[53]

Conference dinners, in diplomacy as in academe, are noted for hyperbole. As Roosevelt well knew, this was a flawed alliance. But in a flawed world it was both more effective and more creative than the opposition. In this post-Cold War era, Roosevelt's vision of the rainbow may now seem merely premature and not totally preposterous. Certainly, it remains the abiding goal.

NOTES

1. Arthur M. Schlesinger, Jr., *The Imperial Presidency* (New York, 1974), ch. 5; Walter LaFeber, "American Empire, American Raj," in Warren F. Kimball, ed., *America Unbound: World War II and the Making of a Superpower* (New York, 1992), 55-72.

2. Warren F. Kimball, ed., *Churchill & Roosevelt: The Complete Correspondence* (3 vols.; Princeton, 1984), 2, 55.

3. Roy Bridge, "Allied Diplomacy in Peacetime: The Failure of the Congress 'System,' 1815-23," in Alan Sked, ed., *Europe's Balance of Power, 1815-1848* (London, 1979), 34.

4. Kimball, ed., *Churchill & Roosevelt*, 1, 40, 49-50; USSR, Ministry of Foreign Affairs, *Sovetsko-angliiskie otnosheniia vo vremia velikoi otechestvennoi voiny, 1941-1945* (2 vols.; Moscow, 1983), 1, 109.

5. Larry I. Bland, with Sharon R. Stevens, eds., *The Papers of George Catlett Marshall* (3 vols to date; Baltimore, 1981-91), 3, 269-80.

6. Quotations from Stalin to Churchill, 23 July 1942, in USSR, Ministry of Foreign Affairs, *Correspondence between the Chairman of the Council of Ministers of the USSR and the Presidents of the USA and the Prime Ministers of Great Britain during the Great Patriotic War of 1941-1945* (Moscow, 1957), 1, 56.

7. Bernd Martin, "Deutsch-sowjetische Sondierungen über einen separaten Friedensschluss im Zweiten Weltkrieg," in Inge Auerbach, *et al.*, eds., *Felder und Vorfelder Russischer Geschichte* (Freiburg, 1985), 284-87; Vojtech Mastny, *Russia's Road to the Cold War* (New York, 1979), 73-84.

8. Robin Edmonds, *The Big Three: Churchill, Roosevelt and Stalin in Peace and War* (London, 1991), 298; W. Averell Harriman and Elie Abel, *Special Envoy to Churchill and Stalin, 1941-1946* (New York, 1975), 362.

9. Alan Bullock, *Hitler and Stalin: Parallel Lives* (London, 1991), 44; Dmitri Volkogonov, *Stalin: Triumph and Tragedy* (London, 1991), 488.

10. Kimball, ed., *Churchill & Roosevelt*, 1, 3; Stalin, *Correspondence*, 1, 373, 2, 214. Note also 12 messages between Stalin and Attlee, and 94 between Stalin and Truman.

11. War Cabinet minutes, WM 8 (42) 1, 17 January 1942, CAB 65/25 (Churchill quoting FDR).

12. Kimball, ed., *Churchill & Roosevelt*, 2, 283.

13. John Balfour, draft letter to Christopher Warner, 1 November 1943, and Warner to Clark Kerr, 11 November 1943 (quotation), FO 800/301, pp. 235-36, 248.

14. Edmonds, *Big Three*, 455; Robert H. McNeal, *Stalin: Man and Ruler* (London, 1988), 254-55.

15. U.S. Department of State, *Foreign Relations of the United States* (Washington, 1862-), 1941, 1, 368.

16. Maisky to Narkomindel, 27 August 1941, *Sovetsko-angliiskie otnosheniia,* 1, 108.

17. See Douglas Brinkley and David Facey-Crowther, eds., *The Atlantic Charter: Then and Now* (New York, 1993).

18. Armand Van Dormael, *Bretton Woods: Birth of a Monetary System* (London, 1978), 220-21.

19. Joachim C. Fest, *Hitler,* tr. by Richard and Clara Winston (New York, 1975), 209.

20. Quoting from Christopher Thorne, *The Far Eastern War: States and Societies, 1941-45* (London, 1986), 145, 160.

21. Oleg Rzheshevsky, *Europe 1939: Was War Inevitable?* tr. by Stepan Apresian (Moscow, 1989), 178.

22. F. H. Hinsley, "British Intelligence in the Second World War," in Christopher Andrew and Jeremy Noakes, eds., *Intelligence and International Relations, 1900-1945* (Exeter, 1987), 210; Martin Gilbert, *Finest Hour: Winston S. Churchill, 1939-41* (London, 1983), 612.

23. John W. M. Chapman, "Japan, Germany and the International Political Economy of Intelligence," in Josef Kreiner and Regine Mathias, eds., *Deutschland-Japan in der Zwischenkriegszeit* (Bonn, 1990), 60.

24. Bradley F. Smith, *The Ultra-Magic Deals: And the Most Secret Special Relationship, 1940-1946* (Novato, Calif., 1992). See also above, ch. 4.

25. R. S. Sayers, *Financial Policy, 1939-1945* (London, 1956), 498, 522, 543.

26. John Barber and Mark Harrison, *The Soviet Home Front, 1941-1945* (London, 1991), 189-93, 221.

27. Erich Pauer, "Die wirtschaftlichen Beziehungen zwischen Japan und Deutschland, 1900-1945," in Josef Kreiner, ed., *Deutschland-Japan: Historische Kontakte* (Bonn, 1984), 161-210.

28. Alan Milward, *War, Economy and Society, 1939-1945* (Berkeley, 1977), 97.

29. The convention is printed in full in Bernd Martin, *Deutschland und Japan im Zweiten Weltkrieg: Vom Angriff auf Pearl Harbor bis zur deutschen Kapitulation* (Göttingen, 1969), pp. 232-34. This paragraph and the next follow Martin's analysis, esp. chs. 3 and 5.

30. Gerhard Krebs, "Japan und der deutsch-sowjetische Krieg, 1941," in Bernd Wagner, ed., *Zwei Wege nach Moskau: Vom Hitler-Stalin Pakt bis zum "Unternehmen Barbarossa"* (Munich, 1991), 569-70; Martin, *Deutschland und Japan,* 43.

31. Robert J. C. Butow, *Tojo and the Coming of the War* (Stanford, 1961), ch. 8.

32. Martin, *Deutschland und Japan,* 284.

33. John W. Dower, *War without Mercy: Race and Power in the Pacific War* (London, 1986), 229.

34. Paul Kennedy, *The Rise and Fall of the Great Powers: Economic Change and Military Conflict, 1500-2000* (London, 1988), 352-56.

35. Alfred E. Eckes, Jr., *The United States and the Global Struggle for Minerals* (Austin, Tex., 1979), 84.

36. Barber and Harrison, *Soviet Home Front,* 40-41 (27-28 million). Cf., on USA and UK, R. A. C. Parker, *Struggle for Survival: The History of the Second World War* (Oxford, 1989), 131, 281, 285. The Russian figures keep being revised upward. One estimate by Boris Sokolov in April 1991 puts the total war-time deaths "including continued Stalinist terror" at 37-38 million people. Cited by Nikolai Rudensky, "War as a Factor of Ethnic Conflict and Stability in the U.S.S.R," in G. Ausenda, ed., *Effects of War on Society* (San Marino, 1992), 187-88.

37. A. O. Chubarian, ed., *Wars and Peace in the 20th Century* (Moscow, 1990), 6-7.

38. Graham Ross, ed., *The Foreign Office and the Kremlin: British Documents on Anglo-Soviet Relations, 1941-45* (London, 1984), 240.

39. Wm. Roger Louis, *Imperialism at Bay: The United States and the Decolonization of the British Empire, 1941-1945* (Oxford, 1977), esp. chs. 16, 22-23, 30-32.

40. Lord Moyne [Colonial Secretary] to Leopold Amery, 26 August 1941, CO 323/1858, file 9057/4.

41. Natalya S. Lebedeva, "The Shadow of the Comintern (1943-1945)," in A. Bazhenov and O. Rzheshevsky, eds., *Yalta, 1945: Problems of War and Peace* (Moscow, 1992), 73-9 (in Russian).

42. *FRUS, Conferences at Malta and Yalta,* 590.

43. Melvyn P. Leffler, *A Preponderance of Power: National Security, the Truman Administration, and the Cold War* (Stanford, Calif, 1992).

44. D. W. Brogan, *American Aspects* (London, 1964), ch. 2.

45. See the exchange between Max Beloff and Roger Louis in Wm. Roger Louis and Hedley Bull, eds., *The "Special Relationship": Anglo-American Relations since 1945* (Oxford, 1986), chs. 15-16.

46. Bernard Porter, *The Lion's Share: A Short History of British Imperialism, 1850-1983* (London, 1984), 335.

47. William Stivers, "Eisenhower and the Middle East," in Richard A. Melanson and David Mayers, eds., *Reevaluating Eisenhower: American Foreign Policy in the Fifties* (Chicago, 1987), 194.

48. David Armstrong, *The Rise of the International Organisation: A Short History* (London, 1982), 60-61.

49. George Herring, *America's Longest War: The United States and Vietnam, 1950-1975* (New York, 1986), 145, 256.

50. Access Security Information Service, Washington, "Resource Brief," vol. 6, no. 1 (March 1992).

51. Winston S. Churchill, *The Second World War* (6 vols.; London, 1948-54), 2, 198.

52. *Public Papers of the Presidents of the United States: John F. Kennedy, 1963* (Washington, 1964), 462.

53. *FRUS, Conferences at Cairo and Tehran, 1943*, 585.

NOTES ON THE CONTRIBUTORS

Charles C. Alexander is Distinguished Professor of History at Ohio University. In addition to books on the Ku Klux Klan and one about the U.S. space program, he has written extensively on American intellectual and cultural history during the World War II era. These works include *Nationalism in American Thought, 1930-1945* (1969) and *Here the Country Lies: Nationalism and the Arts in Twentieth-Century America* (1980). He is author of *Holding the Line: The Eisenhower Era, 1952-1961* (1975), and two biographies, *Ty Cobb* (1984) and *John McGraw* (1988), plus *Our Game: An American Baseball History* (1991).

Alexander O. Chubarian, a scholar in the field of nineteenth- and twentieth-century European history, heads the Department of Twentieth Century International History and is Director of the Institute of World History of the Academy of Sciences in Moscow. He is also Deputy-Chair of the Russian National Committee of Historians, Vice-President of the International Association for Contemporary European History, Vice-President of the International Commission of the History of International Relations, and a member of the Bureau of the International Committee for the Historical Sciences. He has published over 150 pieces of research, including *The Brest Peace* (1964), *Europe in the 20th Century: Problems of Peace and Security* (coauthor and editor in chief, 1985), and *The European Idea in History: Problems of War and Peace* (1987).

Alex Danchev is Professor of International Relations at Keele University in the U.K. He was born in 1955 and educated at the universities of Oxford, Cambridge, and London. He served for a number of years in the British Army, lecturing at the Royal Military Academy, Sandhurst, and elsewhere. He has held fellowships in the Department of War Studies at Kings College, London; the Woodrow Wilson Center in Washington, D.C.; and St Antony's College, Oxford. He is author or editor of two books on Anglo-American relations in the Second World War, collections of new works on recent conflicts in the Falklands and the Gulf, and a study of the philosopher-statesman Oliver Franks.

Lloyd C. Gardner is Charles and Mary Beard Professor of American History at Rutgers University. He has written extensively on the history of American foreign policy, beginning with *Economic Aspects of New Deal Diplomacy* (1964) and including *Architects of Illusion: Men and Ideas in American Foreign Policy, 1941-1949* (1970), *Safe for Democracy: The Anglo-American Response to Revolution, 1913-1923* (1984), *Approaching Vietnam: From World War II through Dienbienphu* (1988), and *Spheres of Influence: The Great Powers Partition Europe* (1993).

Jose Harris is a reader in Modern History at the University of Oxford and a fellow of St. Catherine's College. She is author of a biography of William Beveridge, founder of the British welfare state, and of numerous articles on the social history of the Second World War. Her Social History of Britain, 1870-1914 was published by Oxford University Press and Penguin Books in 1992. She is currently working on an intellectual history of modern social welfare, and on the thought of the German sociologist Ferdinand Tonnies.

Warren F. Kimball is Robert Treat Professor of History at Rutgers University, the State University of New Jersey. Twice a senior Fulbright lecturer, he was Pitt Professor of American History at Cambridge University for 1988-89. He has published extensively on the subject of Franklin Roosevelt's foreign policy, most recently *Churchill & Roosevelt: The Complete Correspondence* (3 vols., 1984), *The Juggler: Franklin Roosevelt as Wartime Statesman* (1991). He edited a collection of essays titled *America Unbound: World War II and the Making of a Superpower* (1992) in the Roosevelt Institute series on Diplomatic and Economic History.

Mikhail N. Narinsky is a Doctor of Science (History) and has been with the Institute of World History in Moscow since 1968, where he is currently Deputy Director and Head of the Department of Contemporary History of Western Europe. A specialist in international relations and twentieth-century Europe, he has written two books, *Great Britain and France in Postwar Europe, 1945-1949* (1972) and *Classes and Parties in France, 1945-1958* (1983), as well as contributing to a number of collections including *The Second World War: A Short History* (Moscow, 1984) and *The Resistance Movement in Western Europe, 1939-1945* (Moscow, 1990).

Richard J. Overy is Professor of Modern History at King's College, London. His books include The Air War, 1939-1945, *Goering: the "Iron Man"*, and *The Road to War*. He is currently completing a history of World War II and a history of the Nazi economy.

Lydia V. Pozdeeva is Professor of History, a senior research fellow in the Institute of World History of the Russian Academy of Sciences, and a specialist in the history and diplomacy of World War II. Her published works include *England and the Remilitarization of Germany, 1933-1936* (1956), *Anglo-American Relations during the Second World War* (2 vols. 1964, 1969), and essays in a number of books including *The Second World War: a Short History* (1984), and *1939: The Lessons of History* (1990).

David Reynolds is a Fellow of Christ's College, Cambridge University. His publications include *The Creation of the Anglo-American Alliance, 1937-1941: A Study in Competitive Co-operation* (1981), which was awarded the Bernath Prize in 1982; *An Ocean Apart: The Relationship between Britain and America in the Twentieth Century* (1988), which accompanied the BBC/PBS TV series for which he was principal historical adviser; and *Britannia Overruled: British Policy and World Power in the Twentieth Century* (1991).

Oleg A. Rzheshevsky is Professor of History and a specialist on the history of the Second World War. Since 1979 he has headed the Department of the History of War in the Institute of World History of the Russian Academy of Sciences in Moscow. He is Vice-President of the International Committee for the History of the Second World War. Among his published works are *War and History* (1976, 1984), *Myths and Realities of the Second World War* (1984), and *Europe 1939: Was War Inevitable?* (1989)

Mark A. Stoler is Professor of History at the University of Vermont, where he has taught since 1970. He is the author of *The Politics of the Second Front: American Military Planning and Diplomacy in Coalition Warfare, 1941-1943* (1977); *George C. Marshall: Soldier-Statesman of the American Century* (1989); and numerous articles on U.S. strategy and diplomacy in World War II. He has been a visiting professor at the U.S. Naval War College, and a Fulbright lecturer at the University of Haifa.

Theodore A. Wilson is Professor of History at the University of Kansas. His first book, *The First Summit: Roosevelt and Churchill at Placentia Bay, 1941* (1969, rev. ed., 1991) won the Francis Parkman Prize. He is author or editor of four other works—*WW2: Critical Issues* (1974), *Makers of American Diplomacy* (1974), *Three Generations in Twentieth Century America* (1976), *The Marshall Plan, 1947-1951* (1977)—and a number of articles. He is currently completing a study about the selection and training of U.S. ground combat forces in World War II.

INDEX

A

ABC-1 talks, 59, 82, 91
  establish US/UK strategy, 83-84
ABDA Command, 87
Acheson, Dean
  and Lend-Lease Master Agreement, 214
Advertising Council (US)
  and wartime propaganda, 303
aid to Russia (see *also* United States; Soviet Union)
  aviation Lend-Lease, 163
  discussed, 160-65
  evaluated, 425
  statistics concerning, 163-64
Alamein
  battle of, xi
  Churchill's reaction to, 4
Aldridge, James
  and USSR, 315
Amalgamated Engineering Union report (UK) (quoted), 137
American-Russian Chamber of Commerce
  disbanded, 203
Anderson, Sir John
  Lord President of the Council, 118
Anglo-American alliance
  and Soviet Union, 94-95
Anglo-American cooperation
  1940-41, 82
Anglo-Soviet Alliance
  negotiations for, 359-63
Antipenko, Gen. G. (quoted), 45
ANVIL
  agreed to, 69
  renamed DRAGOON, 71
Arapiyev, H.
  quoted on deportations, 276
ARCADIA Conference (Dec.-Jan. 1941-42), 16, 62, 89
  and Anglo-American staff cooperation, 86
  Anglo-American strategic planning at, 61
Ardennes, battle of the (Bulge)
  and Soviet military action, 47
  and U.S. mobilization, 194-95
armaments production
  statistics of, 428
Arnhem, battle of, 71, 99
Arnold, Gen. Henry H.
  appointed head of U.S. Army Air Force, 62
  quoted, 206
Atlantic Charter, 341, 379
  and colonialism, 407, 431
  and decolonization, 347
  and U.S. policy, 399
  British references to, 362
  FDR comments on, 410
  provisions of, 421-22
  Soviet reaction to, 358-59
Atlantic Conference (Aug. 1941), 398-99
  and military cooperation, 84
atomic bomb, 73, 351
  and Allied relations, 378, 411-12, 431
  industry developed for, 189
  joint US/UK project established, 220
  kept secret from USSR, 97
  MAUD Committee established (UK), 220
  Quebec agreement concerning, 220
  Soviet research on, 155, 220
Attlee, Clement
  heads peace settlement committees, 336-37
  influence on Churchill, 334
  on Indian nationalism, 346
Auchinleck, Field Marshal Sir Claude, 4
Axis powers
  mutual aid among, 425
  strategy of, 426

B

Babington, Air Marshal Sir John
  quoted on Soviet transport capabilities, 151
Baggalay, H. L., 355
BAGRATION, 98
Baidukov, Georgy
  quoted on American customs, 309
Baldwin, Stanley, 334
Balfour, John, 314
Baltic states
  and Anglo-American policy, 340
  and Nazi-Soviet Pact, 355
  and Soviet policy, 369, 400
  Churchill's attitude regarding, 341
  Soviet occupation of, 319
Bandera, S., 275
BARBAROSSA, xv, 3, 206, 207, 425
  German losses in, 39
  German plans for, 30-31
  launched, 35
  military plan described, 36
  Soviet preparedness for, 31-36
  U.S. reaction to, 394
Barnett, Correlli
  The Audit of War, 237
Bartlett, Jean, 289
Beaverbrook, Lord, 420
  aid mission to Soviet Union, 207

and "tank week," 161
as Minister of Aircraft Production, 117-118
resigns from Cabinet, 340
Beaverbrook-Harriman Mission (1941)
Beaverbrook-Harriman, 86
Bedny, Demyan
quoted on the Second Front, 311
Belgium
and financial aid to Britain, 121
Berggolts Olga (poet) (quoted), 269
Berle, Adolf
quoted on economic cooperation, 225
Berlin
drive for, 99
Beveridge Report, 193, 234, 244, 246
and social change, 249
issued, 241-42
Beveridge Social Insurance committee, 252
Beveridge, Sir William
and work force investigation, 131
characterizes Beveridge Plan, 234
Bevin, Ernest, 132
and harsh treatment for Germany, 337
and labor disputes, 135-36
appointed Minister of Labour, 238
as chairman of the Production Executive, 118
as Minister of Labor and National Service, 131
heads Production Executive, 117
on British Cabinet, 6
quoted on Britain's command economy, 134
quoted on social change, 234
Big Three
as military leaders, xxi
Blum, Leon (French Premier)
and Soviet Union, 28
Blumentritt, Gen. G. (quoted), 31
BODYGUARD, 102
Bohr, Niels
and atomic bomb, 411
BOLERO
adopted, 91
approved by FDR, 63
Bowen, Elizabeth
The Heat of the Day, 251
Bretton Woods Conference (1944), 222, 402, 422
agreements at, 347
British Army
doubts concerning, 3
British Purchasing Commission (US)
activities of, 82
British Supply Council
and combined production, 215
British Supply Mission, 90
Brogan, Dennis
quoted on U.S. omnipotence, 431
Brooke, Gen. Sir Alan, 4, 9
and Second Front, 18, 20
on American generals, 5
opposes TORCH, 17
Bullock, Alan (quoted), 35
Butcher, CPT Harry C. (quoted), 103
Butler, R.A.
and German peace terms, 336

C

Cadogan, Alexander
on role of Germany (1932), 335
Cairo Conferences, 402, 408
and military strategy, 69
Canada
and financial aid to Britain, 121
Munitions Assignment Committee, 90
Price Control Law, 180
Cannadine, David (quoted), 236
Canol Project (U.S.), 177
Capra, Frank
Why We Fight series, 300, 319
Casablanca Conference (1943)
and Allied relations, 400
and strategic plans, 65
decolonization discussed at, 408
military plans at, 94
Cassidy, Henry
Moscow Diary, 318
casualties
comparison of, xvi
Central Scientific Office (US/UK)
established , 219-20
Chamberlain, Neville, 334
congratulated by FDR, 390
on Anglo-American relations, 338
quoted on Hitler (1939), 335
total war policies of, 238
Chamberlin, William (quoted), 317
Chandler, Alfred D.
quoted on Eisenhower, 88
Chaney, Gen. James
supports unified command structure, 88
Chiang Kai-shek, 402
and FDR, 408
China
as Great Power, 408-09
diverts U.S. resources, 67
war effort in 1944, 72
Christiansen, Gen. James
quoted on importance of Red Army, 95

Chrysler Corporation
and industrial production, 189
Churchill, Winston S.
American strategy of, 81
and Atlantic Charter, 407
and atomic bomb policy, 351 n.23
and British strategy, 1, 8, 10, 14-15, 83, 92, 96
and businessmen in politics, 135
and China, 409
and conquest of Berlin, 48
and continuation of the Grand Alliance, 345
and decolonization, xxi, 410
and Foreign Office, 340
and France, 343-44
and German attack on USSR, 339, 356, 394
and "iron curtain," 326, 342
and Morgenthau Plan for Germany, 337
and "percentages agreement," 341, 372
and Polish question after Yalta, 375
and relationship with FDR, 340
and Second Front (1942), 361
and social reform, 244
and Soviet-American relations, 420-21
appeals to FDR for aid, 121, 204-05
as phrasemaker, 2
becomes Prime Minister, 238
concern about Communism (1941), 315
food supplies a priority for, 123
on Britain between U.S. and USSR, 348
on British economic problems, 138
on de Gaulle, 344
on German peace terms (1940), 336
on "Mrs. Glass's Cookery Book. . . ," 342
on repayment of Lend-Lease, 222
on social reforms, 138
on Stalin after Yalta, 342
on the Red Army, 4
postwar views of, 342, 349, 430
promises aid to the USSR (1941), 356
quoted, 2, 81
restructures government for mobilization, 117
sketch of, xix
speeches broadcast in USSR, 310
Churchill-Roosevelt relationship, 2, 338-39, 398
significance of, 81-82, 420
Churchill-Roosevelt-Stalin
correspondence between, 420
Chuyev, Felix
quoted on Molotov's suspiciousness, 313
Citrine, Walter
and the Comintern, 366
Clausewitz, Carl von, 8
quoted, 2
Clayton, William
quoted on economic reform, 221-22
coalition (UK, US, USSR)
and military cooperation (1944-45), 86-88, 100
and Soviet cooperativeness, 96-97, 360
assessment of, xii-xxiii, 101, 103-04, 423-24
and "theaters" of military operations, 87, 93
economic cooperation within, 90, 208, 224, 226, 425
effect of BARBAROSSA on, 85
meetings (see specific conferences)
institutions of, 79-81, 89
postwar continuation of, 398
tensions within, 94-96, 428-30
Cold War
reasons for, 428-30
colonialism
and WWII, 431
Combined Boards (US/UK), 118
establishment of, 216-17
Roosevelt supports establishment of , 86
Combined Chiefs of Staff (UK/US)
created, 9, 61, 83, 86
Soviets excluded from, 87
combined production (US/UK), 215
Soviet Union excluded from, 219
Comintern, 28
disbanding of, 365-66
Committee for Economic Development (U.S.), 194
Corwin, Norman, 299
and wartime propaganda (US), 302
Cozzens, James G. (quoted), 3
Cripps, Sir Stafford, 357, 360
and Anglo-Soviet relations, 339
mission to India, 346-47
Crowley, Leo
heads Foreign Economic Administration, 206
Cunningham, Admiral Sir Andrew
and Churchill, 7
Curzon, Lord
on Indian Empire, 333
ultimatum to Soviet Union, 308

D

Dale, Sir Henry, 315
Dallin, Alexander
quoted on Ukrainian resistance, 275
Dalton, Hugh
and harsh treatment for Germany, 337
Minister of Economic Warfare, 117
Danilova, M.
quoted on labor unrest in Moscow, 267

Darlan, Admiral Jean
British criticism of U.S. support for, 322
Davies, Joseph E.
Mission to Moscow (motion picture), 298, 309
visit to Moscow (1943), 365
Davis, Kenneth
quoted on Stalin, 298
Days and Nights
quoted on Second Front, 311
Deane, Gen. John R., viii
and Soviet assumptions about Second Front, 95
Declaration by the United Nations (1942)
negotiations for, 360-61
Declaration on Liberated Europe, 341, 374, 405
DeWitt, Gen. John
and Japanese-Americans, 293
Dill, Field Marshal Sir John, 5, 8-9
"Dixie Mission" (1944), 409-10
DOWNFALL operation (invasion of Japan), 100
Dreiser, Theodore, 318
Drum, Barbara Holmes, 290
Dumbarton Oaks Conference (1944), 371, 402-03
Duncan, Sir Andrew
as Steel Controller (UK), 135
Durbin, Evan, 241
Dykes, Brigadier Vivian, 9

E

Eastern Europe
Soviet expansion into, 430
Eaton, Evora Bonet
and "furlough nightgowns," 290
Eden, Anthony, 4, 420
and Foreign Office, 334
and settlement in Eastern Europe, 341
Eden, 355
quoted on social change, 234
visit to Moscow (1941), 360
visit to Washington (1943), 401
Ehrenburg, Ilya, 272
calls for Second Front, 310-11
quoted on British character, 309
Eisenhower, Gen. Dwight D., 4, 99
and drive for Berlin, 99
become commander of U.S. European Theater, 88
proposes cross-channel invasion, 63
supports invasion of Italy, 12
Eisenstein, Sergei (quoted), 309
Emergency Powers Act (UK)
and civil liberties, 237
Emmons-Strong Mission (1940), 82
European Advisory Commission, 367, 369
Evansville, Indiana (U.S.)
as typical boom-town, 191

F

Fair Employment Practices Commission (US), 294-95
Ford, Henry
Willow Run plant constructed by, 189
Ford, John
and wartime motion pictures, 300
FORTITUDE, 102
Four-Policemen concept, 369, 434
proposed by FDR, 401
Four-Power Declaration on General Security, 367
FRANTIC, 97
French Committee of National Liberation
recognition of, 367

G

Garfield, John, 300
Gaulle, Gen. Charles de
and Churchill, 343-44
General Maximum Price Regulation (U.S.), 179
geography of Allies
comparison of, xiii
Germany
at Potsdam Conference, 377, 397-98
at Yalta, 373, 397
capitulation of, 49
declares war on the U.S., 394
economic resources in 1940, 145
final campaigns against (1944-45), 72-73
losses in Russia (1942), 41
military strategy in 1943 assessed, 46
Morgenthau Plan for, 397
plans for conquest of the USSR, 147
postwar goals in USSR, 36
postwar policy concerning, 429
submarine warfare by, 91, 93, 201, 392
Glushnev, V. (quoted), 266
Golikov, Gen. F. I., 85
Gorbachev, Mikhail, 433
Gorbatov, Boris, 273
Gould, Morton, 297
Gousev, Feodor, 370
Grand Alliance (see coalition)
Great Britain (*see also* Churchill, Winston S.)
and alliance with U.S., 338-39
and appeasement, 418
and collectivist sentiment, 241
and consumption restrictions, 127
and German role in Europe, 335-38
and Hitler's peace terms (1940), 336
and immigrants, 253

and Imperial Preference , 347
and imports, 119-21
and industrial mobilization, 114-19, 128-30, 132-34
and labor disputes, 135-38
and official propaganda in U.S., 322
and recognition of "Free French," 344
and recognition of Soviet boundaries, 359-62
and role in postwar Europe, 342-45
and Trade Unions, 126, 131
and USSR, 313-17, 339-42
and work force, 130-31
attitudes toward USSR, 313-17
capitalists and wartime policies, 134-35
centralization of government structure, 118-19, 242
class structure in, 243-44
crime in, 245
damage from aerial bombing, 239
declares war on Germany, 335
dependent on trade, 113-15
distribution of income in, 243
"Dunkirk spirit" in, 233, 251
economic effect of submarine war on, 123
effect of war on economy of, 139
election of 1945 in, 242, 247
Empire and war (see *also* India), 345-48
evacuation in, 239, 246
finances of, 115, 120-21, 124-26, 134
foreign policy structure, 333-34
geographic position of, 333
impact of American culture on, 253
Import Executive, 117-18
institutional changes in, 237-44
long-term effects of war on, 253-54
Lord President's Committee, 117
losses, 429
Mediterranean strategy of, 65
military missions to the U.S., 89
Ministry of Production established, 118
Ministry of War Transport established, 123
monarchy in, 242
Production Executive, 117
rationing in, 121, 239-40
reaction to U.S. military racism, 322
religious practices in, 251-52
social consensus in, 250-51
society, transformation of , 233
wages, prices and consumption (table), 137
wartime consensus in, 244-47
weapons output (table), 133
welfare state in, 247-29
women in work force, 132
Great Britain, public opinion (see *also* Mass Observation)
distrust of USSR, reasons for, 317, 327
view of U.S. postwar role, 321-24, 340
Greece
British forces sent to, 405
Greenfield, Kent Roberts (quoted), 95
Greenwood, Arthur
as Minister of Reconstruction, 241
Griffiss, Lt. Col. Townsend
death of, 86
Gromyko, Andrei
and aid to USSR, 207
on FDR, 312
Grossman, V., 272
Guadalcanal, battle of, xi
Gusev, Feodor, 341

H

Hahn, Dellie, 290
Halifax, Lord
and cooperation with France and U.S., 343
and Foreign Office, 334
and German peace terms, 336
Harriman Mission (1941), 202
Harriman, W. Averell, 420
aid mission to Soviet Union, 202, 207
and aid to the USSR, 403-04
on cooperation with the USSR, 207, 370
Harriman-Beaverbrook Mission, 359
Harris, Roy, 297
Harrisson, Tom, 316
interviews by, 236
Hart, Sir Basil Liddel, 8
Hawley-Smoot Tariff (1930), 202
Helsinki Act (1975), 386
Henderson, Leon, 176
Herring, George
quoted on aid to Russia, 161
Hess, Rudolf
flight of, 356-57, 418
Hinsley, Sir F. H. (quoted), 101-02
Hitler, Adolf
obsessions of, 427
Hogg, Quintin, 241
Hong Kong
FDR suggests return to China of, 409
Hopkins, Harry L., 420
and aid to the USSR, 160, 358
and combatting inflation, 184
and Lend-Lease program, 205
visit to Moscow (1941), 85, 394
visit to Moscow (1945), 376
Hottelet, Richard C., 301
Howard, Sir Michael (quoted), 102
Hull, Cordell

and international economic reform, 202, 205
Japanese policy of, 390
visit to Moscow (1943), 401
HUSKY (invasion of Sicily), 65-66, 94

I

Ickes, Harold L.
and mobilization of energy resources, 184-85
Imperial Chemical Industries (UK), 129
Imperial Preference (U.K.-Ottawa Agreement, 1932), 202
India
signs Declaration of the United Nations, 407
U.S. policy regarding, 346
intelligence
Allied cooperation in, 424-25
and Axis codes, 394, 424
and battle of Midway, 65
and Battle of the Atlantic, 66
role of, 100-103
Ironside, Gen. Sir Edmund, 7
Italian campaign, 12-13, 66, 70-71
Italian surrender, 366
Iwo Jima, battle of, 72

J

Japan
capitulation of, 50
final campaigns against (1944-45), 73
prewar relations with U.S., 388-93
Jehovah's Witnesses
imprisonment of, 292
Jessup, John E.
quoted on Soviet mobilization preparations, 147
Johnson Act (1934, U.S.), 202
Johnson, Lyndon, 387
Johnston, Eric (American Chamber of Commerce)
quoted on reception in USSR, 312
Jowitt, Sir William
as Minister of Reconstruction, 241
JUPITER
rejected, 10

K

Kaganovich, L. M.
removed as head of Council of Evacuation (USSR), 150
Kaiser, Henry J., 189
Kapitsa, Academician Peter
quoted on scientific research in USSR, 155
Kasserine Pass, battle of the, 19, 66
Katyn Forest executions
and Soviet-Western relations, 365
and British public opinion, 317
Katyusha rocket launchers
first used, 152
production delayed, 146
Keegan, Frank, 285
Kennedy. John F., 435
Kent, Rockwell, 318
Kerr, Sir Archibald Clark
quoted on Soviet recovery (1942), 153
Kershner, Marguerite, 288
Keynes, John Maynard, 241
and end of Lend-Lease, 225
and Lend-Lease Master Agreement, 214
as Treasury official, 238
at Bretton Woods, 402
quoted on finances, 124
Keynesianism
promoted by WWII, 234
Kharlamov, Adm. Nikolai, 85
tours Normandy beaches, 99
Kimball, Warren F.
quoted, 94
King, Adm. Ernest J.
appointed head of U.S. Navy, 62
supports Pacific-first strategy, 92
Knox, Frank
appointed U.S. Secretary of the Navy, 59
Komarov, Acad. Vladimir, 315
Korneichuk, Alexander, 273
Kourchatov, I. V.
and Soviet atomic research, 155, 220
Kursk, battle of, 44-46, 95
Kuznetsov, Admiral Nikolai (quoted), 34

L

Lamont, Corliss, 318
Layton, William (quoted), 121-22
Lend-Lease, xx, 85, 90, 94, 325, 338
and postwar aid to USSR, 404
assessment of , 206
British White Paper concerning (1941), 213
cancellation of, 165, 224, 375-76, 406
cost to Gt. Britain of, 123
established, 59-60, 122, 205-06, 392
extended to the Soviet Union, 206, 208-09, 359
in Soviet propaganda, 310
Master Agreement, negotiation of, 214
repayment of, 222-23
reverse, 165, 211
Stage II, 223
statistics on [209-12, 122, 163, 208-12
Lenin, Vladimir
body removed to Siberia, 266
Leningrad (St. Petersburg), battle of, 44-46, 151

and home front, 268-69
Levering, Ralph (quoted), 320
Leviathan (Thomas Hobbes) (quoted), 173
Lewis, John L., 180, 185
Liberty Ship program, 189, 289
Litvinov, Maxim, 298
Ljubljana gap
Churchill proposes attack through, 71
Low, Ivy, 298
Lubin, Isador
and combatting inflation , 184
Luce, Henry R.
praises Stalin, 320
Lyttelton, Oliver
made Minister of Production, 118
supply mission to U.S., 138, 218

M

MacArthur, Gen. Douglas
and Pacific strategies, 68
ignores ABDA Command, 87
praises Soviet military, 50
MacDonald, Ramsay, 334
Mahan, Alfred Thayer
influence of, 58, 83
Maisky, Ivan
on Anglo-Soviet relations , 355
Manhattan Project (see atomic bomb)
Mao Tse-tung, 409
and Chinese civil war, 74
Marshall, Gen. George C., 194
and FDR, xx
appointed U.S. Army Chief of Staff, 58
Mason-Macfarlane, Gen. N.
heads British military mission in Moscow, 85
Mass Observation surveys, 236, 243, 246, 250, 251, 252
and British views of Communism, 315-16
British attitudes toward USSR, 313-14
on British opinion of U.S., 321
Mel'nyk, A., 275
merchant shipping
difficulties of, 122-24, 212, 218
Meretskov, Gen. Kirill
quoted, 34
Mitchell, Col. William "Billy"
and airpower, 58
Molotov, V. M., 420
and aid to the USSR, 207
and Hess episode, 356-57
and U.S., 313
quoted, 261
visit to London & Washington (1942), 91, 363-64, 395, 399, 400
Molson, Hugh, 241
Monnet, Jean
and coordinated allocations, 85
Montgomery, Field Marshal Sir Gen. Sir Bernard, 4, 21, 99, 100
commands grounds forces for OVERLORD, 70
Morgenthau, Henry, Jr., 224
and end of Lend-Lease, 225
Morocco, Sultan of, 408
Moscow (TOLSTOY) Conference (1944), 372
FDR's reaction to, 404-05
Moscow Foreign Ministers Conference (1943), 367-68
Moscow Treaty (1970), 385
Moscow, battle of
and home front, 266-68, 266
assessment of, 40
begins, 39
effect on British public opinion, 314
evacuation during, 151
Munich Conference (1938), 390
Murphy, Robert
promises restoration of French Empire, 408
Murrow, Edward R.
broadcasts from London, 301
quoted on British government expansion, 238
mutual aid programs (US/UK/USSR)
described and evaluated, 208-22
(see *also* Lend-Lease and specific countries)

N

National Defense Research Council (U.S.), 190
NATO, 104
Nazi-Soviet Non-Aggression Pact (1939), 355
and British foreign policy, 339
and economic relations, 203
Soviet motives, 29
Nelson, Donald, 177
and War Production Board, 192
Neutrality Act (U.S.); changes in, 203
Newall, Air chief Marshal Sir Cyril, 7
Nimitz, Adm. Chester
and Pacific strategies, 68
Nomura, Adm. K.
and talks with U.S., 390
Norden bombsight
monopoly of, 194
Normandy, invasion of
and German forces on Eastern Front, 47
and Soviet supporting offensive, 47
North Africa invasion (TORCH), 11-21, 46, 60-66, 93, 101, 209, 396
The North Star (motion picture)
shown in USSR, 309
Nuffield College Social Reconstruction survey, 244

O

O'Connor, Gen. Sir Richard
victory against Italians, 8
Office of Economic Stabilization (U.S.)
established, 180
Office of Price Administration
established, 176
Office of Production Management (U.S.)
established, 175
Office of War Information (US)
and motion pictures, 299
Okinawa, battle of, 72
Organization of Ukrainian Nationalists, 275
Organization of Young American Writers
calls for international cooperation , 307-08
Orwell, George
on popularity of USSR, 316
OVERLORD (Normandy invasion), 18, 70
as "tyrant," 21
coalition cooperation concerning, 98

P

Pacific War
campaigns described, 64-65, 71-72
effect on logistics, 218
1943 campaigns summarized, 68
strategic disputes (Pacific-first), 62-63, 71, 92
Passos, John Dos
on home front conditions, 291
Paton, Evgeni
quoted on women workers in USSR, 277
Patterson, Robert P.
quoted on manpower problems, 182
Pershing, Gen. John, 84
Petroleum Administration for War (U.S.), 185
"Plan Dog," 82
POINTBLANK (1943), 66, 97
Polish question
after Yalta, 375-76
at Teheran conference, 369
at Yalta, 341, 374-75
discussed at Potsdam, 377
"pooling"
supported by the UK, 82
Popular Front (US), 297
Portal, Air Chief Marshal Sir Charles, 7
postwar economic reform
U.S. policy and, 221-24
postwar international relations, 432-36
postwar settlement
economic aspects of, 422
Potsdam Conference (1945), 377-78, 411-12
Priestley, J.B.
and USSR, 315
quoted on social change, 234
Prokofiev, Sergei, 297

Q

Quebec Conference (1943), 69, 366
Quintus Fabius Maximus (quoted), 16

R

Rainbow 5, 82
reparations
discussed at Potsdam, 377
statistics on (n. 101), 385
Robbins, Lionel, 244
Robeson, Paul, 318
Roosevelt, Franklin D.
administrative style of, 184-85
and aid to Britain (1941), 204-06
and aid to USSR, 207, 212-13, 356
and colonialism, 406-08
and Great Power leadership, 403
and Indochina, 410
and interservice rivalry, 58
and merchant shipping, 123
and postwar cooperation with USSR, 395-96, 398-405
and primacy of Grand Alliance, 407
and relations with the USSR, 365
and role of small nations, 430
and Stalin, 420
and Second Front (see Second Front), 363, 395
and trusteeships, 407, 430
and United Nations Organization, 369, 371, 403, 408
and Yalta agreements, 405
approves North African invasion, 63-64
as "Dr. Win the War," 192
death of, 312, 410
image in USSR, 312
Latin American policy of, 391, 403
message to Stalin quoted, 40
on the Munich Agreement, 390
opposes territorial agreements, 396
popularity of in Britain, 323
postwar vision of, 399, 435-36
quoted on wartime economics, 216
reaction to German attack on USSR, 394
sketch of, xviii, xix
speeches broadcast in USSR, 310
strategic views of, 56, 61
suggests meeting with Stalin, 365
ROUNDUP, 17, 91
described, 63
Royal Ordnance Factories, expansion of, 129

S

Salerno landings (AVALANCHE), 66
Salter, Sir Arthur
  and shipping mission to the U.S., 123
San Francisco Conference (1945), 376
  and trusteeships, 410-11
Sargent, Sir Orme
  and cooperation with France, 343
Sayers, R.S.
  quoted, 234
Schumak, Frank, 292
Second Front
  alternatives, 10
  and British strategy, 17
  and inter-Allied relations, 310-11, 365-66, 400-01, 421
  and supplies to the USSR, 90
  and U.S. foreign policy, 394-95
  for 1942, 18, 41, 91-93, 364
  for 1943, 18
  information to USSR concerning, 98
  planning for, 69-70
  proposed by Eisenhower, 63
  Soviet Union requests, 361-64, 395-96
Selective Service Act (U.S.), 182
Semenov, G.
  quoted on rationing in USSR, 279
Sergius, Metropolitan
  appeals to patriotism, 272
Sevareid, Eric, 301
Shakhurin, A. I.
  quoted on aircraft production in USSR, 160
  quoted on relocation of Soviet industry, 152
Shakhurin, A. I. (Aviation Industry Commissar)
  quoted, 150
Shcherbakov, A.
  quoted on battle for Moscow, 267
Shinwell, Emanuel
  quoted on social change, 234
Sholokhov, Mikhail, 273
Shostakovich, Dimitri, 297
  seventh symphony of, 273
Shvernik, N. M.
  heads industrial relocation, 150
Simonov, Konstantin, 272
  describes aid to USSR, 310
SLEDGEHAMMER, 91
  British withdraw support for, 63-65
Smith, Brig. Gen. Walter Bedell, 9
Solid Fuels Administration (U.S.), 185
Somervell, Gen. Brehon B.
  and military supply priorities, 178
  heads Army Service Forces, 177
Soviet Academy of Sciences
  wartime publication projects, 314
Soviet Purchasing Commission; created (1942), 90
Soviet Union
  agricultural production in, 157, 269-70, 279-80
  aid to, 160-65, 206-10, 358
  aircraft production, 146, 160
  and "winter war" (Finland), 29, 32
  and Berne peace talks, 48
  and collective security in 1930s, 28
  and declaration of war on Japan, 49, 96, 100, 368, 372, 378
  and economic effect of German attack (1941), 148-49
  and information controls, 264
  and invasion of North Africa, 46
  and Japan (1942), 42
  and Lend-Lease (see *also* Lend-Lease), 209
  and mutual assistance agreement with Great Britain, 357
  and negotiations with Germany, 419
  and Orthodox Church, 272
  and recognition of 1941 borders, 359-62
  and Turkey (1942), 42
  and war finance, 270-71
  arms production, 1941-1942 (table), 154
  as totalitarian society, 273
  attitude toward the U.S., 312
  collaboration with Germans in, 275
  collectivization in, 262
  demographic effects of war in, 276-78
  deportations during wartime, 275-76
  distrust of Western Allies, 308, 356-57
  economic development statistics, 1941-45 (table), 157
  economic situation in 1941, 145
  effect of totalitarianism on, 145
  emergency production facilities (1941), 149-50
  GULAG network in, 274
  housing in, 280
  industrialization of, 261-62
  losses, 52, 429
  Manchurian campaign (1945), 49-50
  military production statistics, 153-56, 159
  military strategy assessed, 50-52
  military strength (1941), 32
  military operations, 40, 46-47, 401
  mobilization in, 262-63, 274
  mobilization plans (1941), 147-48
  munitions and military production, 158-60
  partisan movement in , 39, 274
  postwar influence of, 378
  prewar talks with U.S., 52-53

propaganda in, 308-10, 378
public morale in, 280-81
rationing in, 263-64
reconstruction during war in , 278
relocation of industry in, 150, 153, 265-66
scientific research, 155
State Defence Committee created, 38, 148
strategic options, 27
supports UNO, 376
violates Yalta agreements, 375
women workers in, 277
(see *also* BARBAROSSA; Stalin, Josef)
Spender, Stephen, 244
and privacy, 249
spheres of influence, 369, 403
and Nazi-Soviet Pact, 29
proposed by Stalin, 400
U.S. rejection of, 419
Stalin, Josef, xviii, 267
accepts postponement of boundary agreements, 362
addresses troops, 268
American image of, 298, 320
and "no retreat" orders, 42
and concession in East Asia, 372
and dismemberment of Germany, 373
and Italian surrender, 366-67
and prewar preparations, 146
and shipping difficulties, 212-13
apotheosis of, 273
appeals to Russian patriotism, 271-74
assessment of, 378-79
authority of, 148
dissatisfied with aid to Russia (1942), 162
fear of flying, 419
foreign policy goals of, 355
on Churchill, 421
on FDR, 421
outlines Soviet spheres of influence, 369
pledges not to negotiate with Germany (1942), 364
pledges to declare war on Japan, 96
purges by, 27
quoted on production, 202
quoted on the Big Three, 419
quoted on the Normandy invasion, 311
reaction to U.S. postwar proposals, 399-400
speech of 9 Feb. 1946, 429
suspicious of Allies, 207, 224
3 July 1941 statement of, 263, 308
to be evacuated from Moscow, 266
Stalingrad, battle of, xii, 90, 93, 310
and British public opinion, 316
and U.S. public opinion, 319
described, 42-44
losses, 43-44
significance of, 193
Standley, Adm. William
criticizes Soviet Union, 94, 365
Stark, Adm. Harold E.
appointed U.S. Navy Chief of Staff, 58
Stettinius, Edward R., Jr.
and postwar cooperation with the USSR, 224
heads Lend-Lease Administration, 206
quoted on economic reform, 222
Stimson, Henry L.
appointed U.S. Secretary of War, 59
quoted, 67, 194
strategic bombing campaign
evaluated, 66
submarine warfare
effect on British economy, 123
(see *also* Germany)
summit diplomacy
in World War II, 417, 419-20

T

T-34 tank (USSR), 146
Tawney, R.H., 241
Taylor, Robert, 300
technological and scientific cooperation (US/UK/US), 219-21
Teheran Conference (1943), 368-70, 421
and postwar settlement, 369
and postwar structure, 402
and Second Front, 69, 96
British position at, 21
Titmuss, Richard
and *Problems of Social Policy*, 234-36
quoted, 247
thesis of, 248, 249
Tizard, Sir Henry
and UK scientific collaboration with US, 219
mission to Moscow of, 97
Tobruk
British defeated at, 3, 90
Tolstoy, Alexei, 273
TORCH (see North Africa invasion)
Trades Union congress (UK)
consults with wartime government, 135
Trans-Iranian railway, 162
TRIDENT Conf. (May 1943), 69
Tripartite Pact (1941), 392
Truman Committee, 190
investigates mismanagement, 177
investigates U.S. national defense program (1941), 175
Truman, Harry S, 155
and atomic bomb, 411-12

and defense contracts in Kansas City, 201
and Germany, 398
and policy toward USSR, 406
and relations with USSR, 376-78
British reaction to, 323
ends Lend-Lease, 225
inexperience of, 405-06
Trusteeships (see Roosevelt, Franklin D.)
Tucker, Robert C. (quoted), 272
Tvardovsky, Alexander (poet), 273

U

ULTRA (signals intelligence), 95, 101
given priority, 6
Umansky, Konstantin (Soviet Ambassador in U.S.)
presents Soviet aid requests, 207
unconditional surrender
agreed to by Allies, 367
announced, 336, 401
proclaimed, 297
supported by Stalin, 366
United Nations Organization
Allied discussions concerning, 370-71
discussed at Yalta, 374
founded, 432
Soviet support for, 370
United States (see *also* Roosevelt, Franklin D.)
agricultural production, problems of, 187-88
and "full employment" programs, 194
and boom-town economies, 190-91
and British commercial policy, 213
and command economy, 178
and destroyer-bases deal, 338, 391
and economic effect of war production, 174-75
and full-employment policies, 193
and Hearst press attacks on USSR, 317
and inflation, 178
and international economic reform, 225-26
and Japan First pressures, 67
and Pacific-first arguments, 418
and postwar aid to USSR, 404
and prewar aid to Britain, 391-92
and rationing, 179
and the Great Depression, 174
and war financing, 180-82, 189, 291
and WWII as a "good war," 174
assessment of Red Army in 1941, 85
business failures in, 190
censorship in, 303
China policy of, 72, 74, 408-10
civilian war-support activities in, 291
civilian work force, 183
conscientious objectors in, 292
cooperation with Britain (1940-41), 59-60
dislike of Communism in, 297
distrust of British goals, 60-61
economic liberalism of, 173, 390
economic power of, 225, 389
economy as Leviathan, 196
economy, contraction of, 192
effect of radio in, 301-02
employment increased by war, 286
ends Commercial Treaty with Japan, 390
foreign policy after WWI, 388-93
foreign policy-making structure, 387
German-Americans in, 292
government reorganization for mobilization, 176-77
grand strategy of, 56-57
growth of military in WWII, 55
housing in, 290-91
image of Soviet Union in, 297-99
importance of bureaucratic advocacy, 184
industrial mobilization, shortcoming of, 188
interservice rivalry, 58, 60, 67-68
isolationism in, 388, 389, 397
Italian-Americans in, 292
Japan, prewar relations with, 388-93
Japanese shelling of, 286
Japanese-Americans, relocation of, 293-94
Joint Chiefs of Staff, 62, 83
labor disputes in, 183, 185-85
labor force, statistics on (1940-45), 183
liberalism in, 393
losses in WWII, 56, 73, 429
manpower problems, 182-84
matériel production in WWII, 56
military policy, change in, 60
military reorganized (1942), 62-63
motion pictures in, 300
national unity in, 296-97
Neutrality legislation, 389, 391
90-division mobilization plan, 70
Pacific War diverts resources, 65, 69, 297
Pearl Harbor attack, reaction to, 285-86
Plan "Dog" (1940-41), 59
popular culture in, 302-03
postwar economy of, 195-96
promises aid to USSR (1941), 356
public attitudes toward USSR, 317-20
public opinion about Gt. Britain, 324-26
racial unrest in, 294-96, 299-300
RAINBOW plans, 57-60
rationing in, 287
reaction to end of war, 304
reaction to European War (1939), 391
relations with Mexico, 391

spectator sports in, 300-01
standard of living in, 287-89
strategy of, 61, 65-66, 70-71, 73-75
Victory Program (1941), 182, 216
wage controls in, 180
wartime production, statistics on, 186-87
wartime status of blacks in, 294-96
withholding-tax instituted, 291
work force changes in, 186
working women in, 288-90
United States Congress
and foreign policy, 387
United States, public opinion
and Anglo-American alliance, 326
and colonialism, 325
distrust of USSR, reasons for, 327

V

Vandenberg, Sen. Arthur
quoted on Lend-Lease, 215
Vasilevskaya, Vanda, 273
Vasilevsky, Marshal Alexander
quoted, 43
Vatter, Harold G.
quoted on wartime finance, 180
Vietnam War, 433
Volga Germans
deported, 275
Voznesensky, N. A.
and shift of Soviet industry (1941), 148
Vyshinsky, Andrei, 355, 358

W

Wagner, Alice R., 288
Wallace, Henry
addresses Congress of Soviet-American Friendship, 297
and "economic imperialists," 192
and Board of Economic Warfare (BEW), 177
War Manpower Commission (U.S.)
established, 176
War Production Board (U.S.)
established, 177
War Relocation Authority (WRA)
activities of, 293-94
Warsaw uprising, 99
Washington (TRIDENT) Conference (1943)
and Second Front date, 396
Washington Conference, 1941-42 (ARCADIA), 3
Wavell, Gen. Sir Archibald
heads ABDA, 87
Wayne, John, 300
Welles, Sumner
and German attack on USSR, 356
Wells, H.G
and USSR, 315
Wells, Lillis, 289
Wemyss, LTG Sir Colville
and intelligence, 89
Werth, Alexander
"Russian Commentary," popularity of, 315
quoted on Stalin, 273
Willkie, Wendell
on Stalin's image, 320
ONE WORLD, 299
Willow Run plant, 189
Wilson (motion picture), 299
Wilson, Woodrow, 387, 418, 435
and FDR's policies, 402
foreign policy of, 388
Winant, John G., 362
on British administrative efficiency, 119
winter war (see Soviet Union)
Wood, Kingsley
appointed Chancellor of the Exchequer, 238
Woolton, Lord
Minister of Food, 117
WWI ("American and British Strategy" paper), 16

Y

Yalta Conference (1945), 372-75
and military coordination, 100
British policy at, 341
Yamamoto, George, 294
Yeltsin, Boris, 433
Yezhov, Nilolai, xviii

Z

Zhukov, Marshal G. K.
quoted on Soviet production, 147
"zoot suit" riots (US), 296